Anthony Bruce Wilkinson
106 Dubois Hall
Morehouse College
Atlanta, Ga. 30314

# RELIGION
# AND
# MODERN MAN

## *A Study of the Religious Meaning of Being Human*

## JOHN B. MAGEE
### UNIVERSITY OF PUGET SOUND

## HARPER & ROW
### PUBLISHERS
*New York, Evanston, and London*

RELIGION AND MODERN MAN:
A Study of the Religious Meaning of Being Human

LIBRARY OF CONGRESS CATALOG CARD NUMBER: 67–15791

FOR

*John, Gregory, Mary, and Kathryn*

LIVELY CITIZENS OF THE GENERATION

FOR WHICH THIS LABOR WAS

UNDERTAKEN

# Contents

vii

## PART FIVE
## *Social and Psychological Dimensions of Religion*

## PART SIX
## *Logic, Science, and God*

## PART SEVEN
## *The Religious Meaning of Being Human*

# *Preface*

I am convinced that a clarification of the issues that are associated with religion is one of the most important things that can occur in the process of education. This no doubt looks like a natural bias in favor of one's specialty. If it were only that, it could be easily discounted. But religion, as I shall maintain, is life orientation, a man's mode of getting his bearings in the world. And reflections on such issues are no man's specialty; they are entailed in the fact of being human.

This book, then, is an introduction to an encounter with those modes of life orientation that are live options to students in the Western world. Unfortunately, there are many barriers to this confrontation. For one thing, on many university campuses religion is a "non-okay word." Several times during the writing of this book, for instance, it was suggested that the title not contain the word religion.

Another obstacle to the student's serious occupation with this study is that religion has been associated with doctrines and practices which many intelligent people look upon with contempt or even horror. They may quite understandably say, "Include me out!" This rejection, I believe, is the fruit of a misunderstanding of the meaning of religion. If men cannot live without some kind of ultimate orientation and are inevitably religious, then the sensible thing is not to reject religious claims wholesale, but to examine them critically and even sympathetically. Fortunately, a new climate of seriousness about these matters is appearing in collegiate life. The time may be auspicious for a fresh inquiry.

During the writing of the book the thought occurred many times that a textbook in religion is an impossible project. "Textbook" stands for objectivity and impartial treatment of all related matters. "Religion" stands for commitment to a given life orientation. Impartial objectivity calls for a language that is detached and devoid of evaluation. Commitent calls for a language rich in personal overtones. Is there a satisfactory middle ground? The fact that the work is finished implies that I believed a workable compromise was possible. The reader himself will have to judge how successful the enterprise has been. It is comforting to note that a similar problem plagues the writers of textbooks in such field as art, ethics, political science, and indeed in all those areas of study where the human stakes are high. The problem is aggravated in religion because it is by definition the realm where men have the highest stakes of all.

These remarks suggest that the reader has a right to know what I consider those stakes to be, so that he can protect himself against the natural biases that religious discussions entail. Let me briefly make two points: First, since it is impossible to avoid having some life orientation, let me confess what will be plainly evident, that mine is Judaeo-Christian theism. I am not unaware of the lure of other views. In fact, I owe a great debt to many writers and teachers who stand for other ways of life. Many of my teachers were naturalistic humanists, and I have found myself in substantial agreement with much of what they taught. My own awakening to serious religious thought can be traced to the influence of Oriental religion, mediated at first through Western writers, and then confronting me directly in the basic texts of the Far East. One of the heroes of my student days was Mahatma Gandhi, whose shining goodness remains undimmed by death. And the figure of the Buddha looms up from the ancient past as one of the greatest teachers of mankind.

As a teacher of philosophy I cannot divest myself of the perennial relevance of the pagan Socrates, from whose teaching—seen also in the example of such contemporary non-Christians as Bertrand Russell or that endlessly fruitful Jew, the late Martin Buber—I have learned to trust the process of dialogue. In fact, and this is my second point, I am certain that nothing is lost in the dialogue of good will among men who may differ in their faiths. St. Paul is correct: ". . . we cannot do anything against the truth, but only for the truth" (II Cor. 13:8).

By my own training and orientation I am required to maintain an open and hospitable view of alternative ways of thought. I am optimistic that this perspective is generous enough to permit the student ample room to engage in the dialogue for himself. My purpose has not been to make a case, but to witness as intelligently as possible to one man's point of view as he tries to do justice to the alternatives that the modern world of learning has made available. My hope is that the student will do likewise, emulating not the content but the spirit of the inquiry. He will be responsible for his own conclusions, as I must be responsible for mine.

Looking at the table of contents and the length of the book, the student may ask why religion has to be so complicated. The answer is that if he had not already become so well-versed in science, history, and other academic fields, he would not need to think so deeply about faith. He is asking for a simplicity that cannot be granted to him. He has already forced the option by becoming sophisticated in the subjects of higher learning. If he were willing to remain simple in the whole range of his life, accepting without question his inherited faith, then he would not need the help of critical thought in his religion. But he can hardly go on in collegiate life to sophistication in every other area and leave his religion in the kindergarten.

For better or worse, the modern student has perplexities in faith that cannot be dismissed without honest and painfully complex reflection. In the last analysis, of course, the spirit of faith is simple. In fact, the goal of the spiritual life is a simplification of the inner life which goes with maturity and integrity. But simplification by amputation is not the same thing as simplification by maturation. Men such as Whitehead, Einstein, or Schweitzer, with all their immense learning and brilliant accomplishments, exhibit a simplicity and directness of nature that matches the essential spirit of early faith.

Sometimes the objection to a critical and dialectical approach takes a different form: The student wants quick and final answers. In the end, of course, he has a right to some firmness in his belief, but not from a text, and not without asking the right questions first. When he works his way through the maze, with the will to grasp the essence of things, he will win the right to answers, and he will know that certainty is a matter of degree. There is enough certainty to live by—but he need not have the cosmos by the tail, so to speak, in order to live well. In fact, what he will discover, I believe, is that as he explores religion in good faith, the Real will grasp him, Reality will disclose itself—and he will do what he has to do.

This book is an introduction to, not a summary of religion—a beginning, not a conclusion. It is an attempt to confront the student with the big questions that are often avoided in academic life: Does the universe make sense? Does my life have a meaning? Are there any values which hold for all men? What may I believe? What may I hope? How should I live?

Introductory university courses in religion most often take one of two forms: either a study of world religions or an examination of the literature of the Bible. I believe that the approach of this book is logically and psychologically prior to both of these. I have become skeptical about the usefulness of pouring religious information into students prior to taking their questions seriously. This book is built on the questions that students have asked about religion in my more than twenty years of university teaching. I mean such questions as these: Are science and religion compatible? What do the major terms of religious creeds mean? How do I know that religion is true or false? How can I judge one religion to be better than another? The questions are so far-ranging that the attempt to supply background for any reasonable answer to them has forced me to range outside the traditional boundaries of comparative or biblical studies. This very fact is, of course, a threat. It involves such a range of topics that the danger of amateurism is inescapable. At every stage it points to the specialist for a fuller answer. No doubt too, despite my efforts and the vigilance of many readers, the text contains mistakes, perhaps serious ones. But a worse danger, I believe, is to fail to supply the means for a study in which the student can begin the formulation of general answers and develop a guide to inquiry into the things that concern him most.

The text begins with general religious questions, such as the definition of religion and a short history of the religious quest. After a brief look at Asian religion it plunges directly into the heritage of the West—the Judaeo-Christian biblical literature. Turning from this to more recent epochs, it then attempts to give a reasonable account of how our modern consciousness, with all its perplexities, arose, and to describe the place of faith in that period. The rest of the book deals with special problems: first, the problems of a personal and social nature; then the more logical questions raised by science and philosophy, concluding with a brief account of religious knowledge. The final section of the book is a summary of what it means to exist as a human being under the guidance of faith.

The Epilogue is short, but important. It calls attention to the fact that, in the final analysis, each man must do his deciding for himself.

My indebtedness to numerous teachers and authors not mentioned appears on nearly every page. I am personally grateful for the American system of higher education that exposed me to their influence. I also owe an incalculable debt to my many mentors in the realm of faith, who will overlook not being mentioned since they have other, more important, rewards.

Without the dialogue with students over more than two decades my thinking on these matters would be unrecognizably different. I wish it were possible to thank them personally. I could wish the same for those scholars who took time from their own labors to read the manuscript either wholly or in part: Gordon Allport, Hadley Cantril, Alburey Castell, Nils Ferre, Hideo Hashimoto, John Hutchison, Linden Mander, Harold Minor, Randolph Sasnett, Douglas Straton, Horace Weaver, and especially my colleagues at the University of Puget Sound, Robert Albertson, Arthur Frederick, and John Phillips.

A project of this kind also depends upon the tedious work of manuscript preparation. I wish to thank the several typists, Mrs. Lucy Hill, Mrs. Irene Lawrence, and Mrs. Doris Anderson; also Mrs. Ava Gordon, who printed the book in its preliminary form for trial use by students at the University of Puget Sound. I am also grateful for the University of Puget Sound summer study grant that enabled me to thoroughly revise the manuscript after its trial use in classes.

JOHN B. MAGEE

*January, 1967*

# *Acknowledgments*

The author expresses his gratitude to the following authors and publishers for use of material from their works.

ANANDA-ASHRAMA: for selections from *Bhagavad Gita*, trans. Swami Paramanda, Vedanta Centre.

ANDERSON-HOUSE: for a selection from *Key Largo*, by Maxwell Anderson. Copyright 1939 by Maxwell Anderson. Copyright renewed 1967 by Gilda Anderson, Alan Anderson, Terence Anderson, Quentin Anderson, and Hesper A. Levenstein. All rights reserved. Reprinted by permission of Anderson-House.

APPLETON-CENTURY-CROFTS: for a selection from *The Study of Man*, by Ralph Linton, pp. 326–327. Copyright 1936 by D. Appleton Century Company, Inc. Reprinted by permission of Appleton-Century-Crofts.

ROBERT A. BAKER: for a selection from "The Twenty-Third Psalm—Modern Version" in *A Stress Analysis of a Strapless Evening Gown*, by Alan Simpson, R. A. Baker, and Lester del Rey, ed. R. A. Baker, Prentice-Hall, Inc., 1963.

THOMAS Y. CROWELL COMPANY: for a selection from *The Persian Poets*, eds. Nathan Haskell Dole and Belle M. Walker, Thomas Y. Crowell Company, 1901, pp. 208–209.

THE JOHN DAY COMPANY, INC.: for selections from *The Way of Life: According to Laotzu*, by Witter Bynner, pp. 34, 37, 39, 41, 42, 73. Copyright © 1944 by Witter Bynner. Reprinted from *The Way of Life: According to Laotzu* by Witter Bynner by permission of The John Day Company, Inc., publisher.

E. P. DUTTON & CO., INC.: for a selection from the Koran, trans. J. M. Rodwell, Everyman's Library, Sura 90. Reprinted by permission of E. P. Dutton & Co., Inc. and J. M. Dent & Sons Ltd.

HARCOURT, BRACE & WORLD, INC.: for selections from *Four Quartets*, by T. S. Eliot, Harcourt, Brace & World, Inc., pp. 17, 27.

HARPER & ROW, PUBLISHERS: for a selection from *The Bible: A New Translation*, by James Moffat. Copyright 1935 by James Moffat. Reprinted by permission of Harper & Row, Publishers.

HARVARD UNIVERSITY PRESS: for a selection from *Buddha's Teachings*, by Robert, Lord Chalmers. Reprinted by permission of the publishers from Robert, Lord Chalmers, *Buddha's Teachings*, Cambridge, Mass.: Harvard University Press.

HOLT, RINEHART AND WINSTON: for a selection from "The Road Not Taken" from *Complete Poems of Robert Frost*. Copyright 1916 by Holt, Rinehart and Winston, Inc. Copyright 1944 by Robert Frost. Reprinted by permission of Holt, Rinehart and Winston, Inc.

HOUGHTON MIFFLIN COMPANY: for selections from "Epistle to Be Left in the Earth" in *The Collected Poems of Archibald MacLeish*, by Archibald MacLeish, Houghton Mifflin Company, 1963, p. 71; *J. B.*, by Archibald MacLeish, Houghton Mifflin Company, 1958, pp. 11, 12, 13, 153.

DIVISION OF CHRISTIAN EDUCATION OF THE NATIONAL COUNCIL OF THE CHURCHES OF CHRIST: Unless otherwise noted, the Scripture quotations in this publication are from the *Revised Standard Version* of the *Bible*. Copyrighted 1946, 1952 by the Division of Christian Education of the National Council of Churches, and used by permission.

THE NEW AMERICAN LIBRARY, INC.: for selections from *The Way of Life: Lao Tzu*, trans. R. B. Blakney, The New American Library, Inc.; *The Teachings of the Compassionate Buddha*, ed. E. A. Burtt, The New American Library, Inc., 1955, pp. 46–47.

SWAMI NIKHILANANDA: for a selection from *The Gospel of Sri Ramakrishna*, ed. and trans. Swami Nikhilananda, Ramakrishna-Vivekananda Center, 1942.

OXFORD UNIVERSITY PRESS, INC.: for a selection from "Discordants" in *Collected Poems*, by Conrad Aiken, Oxford University Press, Inc., 1953, p. 18.

RANDOM HOUSE, INC.: for selections from *Tao Tê Ching* in *The Wisdom of China and India*, ed. and trans. Lin Yutang, pp. 583, 587, 592, 594, 595, 601, 607, 609, 610, 615, 617, 618, 624. Copyright 1942 by Random House, Inc.; *Brother to Dragons*, by Robert Penn Warren, p. 41. Copyright 1953 by Random House, Inc.; "Christmas Oratorio" in *The Collected Poetry of W. H. Auden*, by W. H. Auden. Copyright 1945 by Random House, Inc.

CHARLES SCRIBNER'S SONS: for a selection from "Sonnets at Christmas" and "More Sonnets at Christmas" in *A Little Treasury of Modern Poetry*, by Allen Tate, ed. Oscar Williams, pp. 391, 392. Copyright 1952 by Charles Scribner's Sons.

THE VIKING PRESS: for selections from *Portrait of the Artist as a Young Man*, by James Joyce. Copyright 1916 by B. W. Huebsch, Inc., 1944 by Nora Joyce. Reprinted by permission of The Viking Press, Inc.; *Letters of James Joyce*, ed. Stuart Gilbert. Copyright © 1957 by The Viking Press, Inc. Reprinted by permission of The Viking Press, Inc.

## PART ONE

# GENERAL CHARACTERISTICS OF RELIGION

# 1

# An Introduction to the Study of Religion

❖❮❖❮❖❮❖❮❖❮❖❮❖❮❖❮❖❮❖❮❖❮❖❮❖❮❖❮❖❮❖❮❖❮❖❮❖❮❖❮❖❮❖❮❖❮❖❮❖

This book investigates a subject with which most people no doubt feel very familiar—religion. The reader has seen it about him all his life. It is statistically probable that he has affirmed some of its major tenets or joined a church. No doubt he feels that he knows enough about it, quite possibly more than he cares to know. He may ask why teaching about religion should be a part of the curriculum of a university. Such a question deserves attention, but to answer it properly requires that we take a further look at popular attitudes toward religion.

## STUDENT ATTITUDES TOWARD RELIGION

In a poll of more than 5000 students in 11 American universities (1960),[1] both public and private, 80 percent answered Yes to the question, "Do you personally feel you need to believe in some sort of religious faith or philosophy?" Seventy-five percent subscribed to one or the other of the following statements: "I believe in a Divine God, Creator of the Universe, Who knows my innermost thoughts and feelings, and to Whom one day I shall be accountable"; "I believe in a power greater than myself which some people call God and some people call Nature." Only one student said, "I am an atheist."[2]

3

But these same students showed over and over again that they thought of religion chiefly as a means of personal adjustment or private happiness. They had little if any concern for applying religious standards and beliefs to social, economic, or political matters or to the reform or upbuilding of religious institutions. The poll showed that students are rarely committed to religion in a decisive way, but take a highly relativistic and individual approach to religious beliefs. They shy away from any absolute positions (even from atheism) and from "orthodoxy." They consequently dislike too much religious enthusiasm or decisiveness. They are inclined, as the study points out, to "play it cool."[3]

Most students, then, proved to have an interest in religion, but few held it in a place of high or absorbing importance. Only 4 percent named religion as of first importance when asked, "What three things or activities in your life do you expect to give you the most satisfaction?" On this question, family, career, and friends, in that order, came off best.[4]

Professor Philip Jacob's study (1957)[5] of the values of college students comes to much the same conclusion. He says that the dominant characteristics of the current generation are that they are "gloriously contented" with themselves, "unabashedly self-centered" in that they aspire for material gratifications for themselves and their families.[6] "They intend to look out for themselves first and expect others to do likewise."[7]

But this individualism is consistent with a cheerful expectation to "conform to the economic status quo and to receive ample rewards for dutiful and productive effort."[8] Here are Jacob's summarizing words: "Students normally express a need for religion as a part of their lives and make time on most weekends for an hour in church. But . . . their religion does not carry over to guide and govern important decisions in the secular world. Students expect these to be socially determined. God has little to do with the behavior of men in society. . . . His place is in church and perhaps in the home, not in business or club or community. He is worshiped, dutifully and with propriety, but the campus is not permeated by a live sense of His presence."[9] There is ample evidence that these attitudes are but a faithful reflection of the attitudes of the American people as a whole.[10]

The poet W. H. Auden parodies this kind of religion in his Christmas Oratorio "For the Time Being": "O God, put away justice and truth for we cannot understand them and do not want them. Eternity would bore us dreadfully. Leave Thy heavens and come down to our earth of waterclocks and hedges. Become our uncle. Look after Baby, amuse Grandfather, escort Madam to the Opera, help Willy with his home-work, introduce Muriel to a handsome naval officer. Be interesting and weak like us, and we will love you as we love ourselves."[11]

These observations need to be qualified somewhat. Since Professor Jacob's study, there are signs that the attitudes of American students may be changing. There is unrest and protest, though no one seems sure just what the protests are about. Employers complain that it is less easy to recruit college graduates for positions in industry merely with promises of fringe benefits and high salaries. Some applicants have said that they are now more interested in social significance than affluence.

Quiet student bodies have become aroused by the idealism of such programs as the Peace Corps, the cause of civil rights, an enlightened foreign policy. The so-called Twisted Age may become an age of social causes, not, to be sure, the radical ideological causes of the 1930s, but causes that may help alleviate some of the inequities of social life in the less privileged parts of the modern world.

However, there is not much evidence of any connection between religious faith and this new dissatisfaction with things as they are. The latter seems rather to reflect mute gropings for some kind of meaning for life in a society which does not seem to need them very much. While a great majority of students still profess a belief in God, most of them claim that their experiences in college make them question their faith, especially its relevance to living issues, and apparently the doubts increase as the students grow older.

## WHY STUDY RELIGION IN A UNIVERSITY?

In the light of the attitudes revealed by these studies, we come back to our earlier question. Why should teaching about religion be an integral part of the curriculum of higher education? The first answer to this question arises out of the facts we have just considered, namely, that students show a basic misunderstanding of the meaning of religion, even when they regard themselves as believers.

In what way? An adequate answer to this anticipates my later definition of religion. However, here it is sufficient to say that what the student identifies as religion is really not religion—it is pseudo religion, a social convention. A man's religion is what he really takes to heart as most reliably real and most convincingly valuable; it is the standard by which he judges everything else. Another way of saying this is that a man's faith is the ground upon which the rest of his life stands; it is an estimate of what is ultimately trustworthy and dependable. Students in the above studies were clearly not referring to this dimension of depth when they talked about their "religion." Religion to them was just one of the many interests (and a minor one at that) that they shared with the great majority of fellow students. It was an interest which they expected to support more important concerns, such as vocation, family, or personal status—but there was no hint that religion might call these other interests into question by judging them according to some higher standard. In short, religion, as they conceive it, is a useful convention for respectable people.

This view has nothing in common with the character of religious faith in its great seedtimes nor with the religious consciousness of the authentic spiritual leaders of mankind. It does have a great deal in common with the pseudo religion that authentic religion has always attacked, often with the utmost vehemence. A quick perusal of the Old Testament prophets, the Gospels, or the works of the Catholic mystics or Protestant reformers will support these contentions. The same protest (though in different form) can be found in the sacred texts of other faiths.

In short, nothing more clearly indicates the necessity for religious study in depth than the present student concept of what religion is and does. Now let us turn to another claim, namely, that education without religion is incomplete.

## EDUCATION IS INCOMPLETE WITHOUT THE STUDY OF RELIGION

Education, as distinguished from training, aims at the emancipation of a human being. It achieves this by making available to him the knowledge whereby he may attain a genuinely human existence. Education invites the student to join the human race, to be human in more than a biological or mechanical sense. It calls him to participation in human life in depth. To achieve these goals the student must be given access to the major meanings and values of civilization. He must become conversant with the recurring problems in the major areas of humanistic and scientific studies and with the historic attempts to solve them. Since existence goes on both during work and after the whistle blows, education seeks to humanize a student's total relationships—to persons, to institutions, to himself, and to the inclusive whole that we shall call reality, which means to grasp the significance and meaning of human life and destiny.

Everyone knows the pressing competition for time during school years. The growth of skills and information is occurring at a frightful pace. The factual information available to man has doubled since 1950 and will no doubt double every 20 years thereafter. This seems to favor allotting more time for training. But this must not blind us to the fact that the learning of information and skills, as important as it is, is no substitute for grasping fundamental concepts and values. Otherwise, with the flood of new techniques and information, one's formal education is outmoded soon after graduation. But principles, concepts, and values—and all the dimensions of a true education— endure long after information has become stale and skills have been superseded.

If this account of education is anywhere near the mark, we may then ask how religion fits into the picture. First of all, religion belongs in an educational program for the same reason that any other humanistic study does. It is a human interest as profound and enduring as science, art, or literature.

As President Nathan Pusey of Harvard University has said: "It is still uncertain what formal education can do to help us toward a religious life. Yet despite many difficulties, there is a growing recognition that an education that ignores this large, central, perennial and life-giving area of human experience [religion] is a kind of play education, and finally a shallow thing."[12] Nearly all the universities and colleges in America acknowledge this in part by including at least some courses in which religion is a major topic of concern, and the number and range of such courses has increased decisively in recent days.

Beyond this, as I have said, religion is the realm of the ultimately real and ultimately valuable. It is a universal human fact, because everyone is incurably concerned in one way or another with what is really real and what is genuinely of worth. Contrary to popular belief, religion is not the prerogative of professionals or of those who by temperament happen to enjoy sermons or hymn singing. It is not for the few, the esoteric, or the scholarly, or for those with some special elevation of feeling and sensibility; it is one study that is for everybody, for it rests on the base of our fundamental human need for meaning and a reliable measure of reality. Nothing touches everyone so intimately or so ultimately as this concern.

Of course there are those who are so unaware of their own religiousness that they will deny it—usually by giving it another name (if they name it at all), such as "the pursuit of happiness," "dedication to scientific truth," "humanity," "patriotism," "anticommunism," or one of a thousand names in which human religiousness mirrors itself. But the fact is that in these various ways the religious impulse seeks to fulfill itself. This fact alone would justify giving time for the study of religion.

A second reason for the study of religion is that our own culture is not comprehensible to us without grasping the religious elements that have gone into it. Judaeo-Christian religion, since the beginnings of Western culture, has been inextricably bound up with our major institutions—government, economy, family. It has likewise been inseparable from our thought systems— ethics, philosophy, art, science. In short, to understand what it means to be a member of our society requires some comprehension of religious faith.

To an age which is rapidly moving toward a global culture, it must be further pointed out that every great culture is bound up with its religion in just the way the West has been bound up with Judaeo-Christian thought forms. As religious illiterates we cannot possibly understand these other cultures, and it will be a tragedy if we enter the coming world dialogue of cultures without our homework done.

But more fundamental than understanding culture is the issue of becoming authentically human. This is a third reason for our study. It is hard to be a human being; there is nothing automatic about it. It involves a sense of fundamental values as a guide to responsible decision. It means finding some ground for personal existence in depth and for authentic relationships to other persons that go beyond mere externals and manipulation. And, lastly, if the Judaeo-Christian faith is right, it involves the ultimate relationship—to God himself. If this is right, nothing is more important; if it is wrong, few things can rival the significance of having worked one's way clear of it.

The study of religion, then, opens up the vision of a depth in existence that awakens man to awe and reverence. He for whom these emotions are absent can scarcely call himself a man, even if he functions efficiently in a technical and conformist society.

A fourth value of the study is that it cultivates standards by which the ultimates that men worship can be criticized and evaluated. False worship—idolatry—is more common than the lack of worship, and for this reason more devastating. It is generally not faith that men lack, but faith in the right thing. The sentimental view that it is belief that matters, not what you believe, has become popular, no doubt out of a false sense of democratic tolerance. Men of the mid-twentieth century are in a position to know better after the hideous spectacles of torture and wanton destructiveness that have been perpetrated in loyalty to false ideals. An unexamined faith is not worth having. It is important to discover what is truly worth trusting and worshiping.

To relate this to education again, we may say that the central task of education could be interpreted as finding for each person a true center of reverence that can function as the root and nourisher of every other good, leading to a great commonwealth of human sharing and fellowship.

All this is especially relevant to the period of life during which students are in college. Late adolescence is an age during which the formation of a value scale often becomes final, and many of the difficulties of this period can be plausibly traced to the fact that the norms and values of our society remain too uncertain or superficial to commend themselves to students with genuine conviction.

These observations are not made primarily to raise courses in religion high above the rest of the curriculum. The function of religious awareness in college is to enable a person to discover the dimension of depth in the whole range of the curriculum.

Below the technical and factual surface of each discipline lie the fundamental presuppositions of truth and value from which the discipline springs. In this sense every study presupposes religious study, and the specific investigation of religion as such should point to an enrichment of the entire educational process, not simply to sophistication in one compartment of the curriculum.

In spite of these considerations, the invitation to study religion is often rebuffed with the accusation that religious teaching breeds narrowness and fanaticism, that it is partisan and parochial, and that it is consequently opposed to the free exercise of intelligence, inquiry, and the openness of search for truth which properly characterize the enterprise of higher education. " 'I believe' and 'I have discovered,' " writes Conrad Moehlman, "are not commensurate."[13]

No doubt a great deal of teaching about religion is contrary to the spirit of true education. But such teaching is surely a caricature of true teaching and it should be avoided in every subject, including religion. Religion as it will be understood in this work makes an entirely different requirement of both student and teacher. It instills a fundamental humility that requires further growth in knowledge. Authentic religion teaches that the really ultimate cannot be grasped in neat formulations. It continually undermines all human pretensions to finality. It demands the serving of God with the whole mind as well as body, will, and emotions. In its highest expression it unites men, because it fosters faith in a divine charity at the heart of all true human goodness.

Genuine religious study is a disciplined dialogue concerning ultimates. It recognizes the variety of traditions and the gravity of the difficulties. It urges each person to first understand his own personal faith and then go on to appreciate the faith of others.

This ideal of study is drawn from two sources. The first is a concept of religion that turns its back on narrowness and dogmatism as contradictions of its true spirit. The second is the tradition of fair play and inquiry that has been codified by nearly a thousand years of university life in Western society that harkens back to the academies of the Greeks, who prized dialogue above everything else. This tradition makes a clear distinction between indoctrination and investigation. It is the latter that regulates the spirit of this work.

## OURS IS AN AUSPICIOUS TIME FOR THE STUDY OF RELIGION

Present conditions in both the world of affairs and the world of scholarship make this an auspicious time for a serious collegiate study of religion. There is first of all a world-wide revival of interest in religion. The religious spirit has once again refuted the claims of those who would bury it, proclaiming with Nietzsche that "God is dead." It has exhibited a perennial power of resurrection that plagues all the predictors of its demise—all the successors of Auguste Comte (1798–1857), who prophesied that religion, the childhood of man, would give way to philosophy, which in turn would ripen into the maturity of an all-embracing science.

The traditional world faiths—Buddhism, Hinduism, Islam, Judaism, and Christianity—are stirring with astonishing new vitality. Even "atheistic" Russia, according to *Pravda*, is plagued by religion's stubborn refusal to die out in accordance with Marxian theory. Widespread "superstition" and the practice of illicit religious rites are reported even among party members. The late leader of the Communist party in Italy, Toghliatti, proposed in his will that the party cease fighting religion and join forces with religious liberals in a struggle for social justice.

Where the traditional faiths have been supplanted by other beliefs, these turn out to be quasi-religious in their own way. Communism, fascism, nationalism, even science and humanism, take the shape of religion in their claim to be all-embracing life orientations to their followers.

Many explanations have been advanced for this revival of religion in the mid-twentieth century, but none has been completely satisfying. One plausible suggestion is that it is a by-product of the emotional shock that the disasters of the twentieth century have inflicted on a humanity ill-prepared for them by its diet of nineteenth-century optimism. Never higher than in our time were the vital advantages, yet never has the threat to human existence towered so menacingly over humanity. This paradox has forced thoughtful men to realize that human existence needs more adequate guidance than a simple faith in inevitable progress and the inherent goodness of man.

Even in the United States, where the majority of men have been protected from the major disasters of the age, there is a hidden anxiety that all is not well, that the destructive forces may break out again and topple the fragile edifice of peace and prosperity. And this has occurred at the very moment in history when the non-Western peoples, many of them the new entrants onto the scene of civilized history, are surging on a flood tide of expectations: the smaller nations looking toward liberty and self-determination, the races demanding equal dignity, the poor impatiently insisting on an end to their poverty through industrial development, and humanity—East and West— longing for peace.

Over against these hopes are the stubborn refusal of history to fall into reasonable order and man's seemingly incurable cruelty to his fellow man. This ambiguity is further evident in the imposing fact that just as science claims to be able to solve our technical problems, some fault in the human plastic has permitted their multiplication: rising populations outstripping economic growth; human communication faltering amidst the mushrooming of information, due to the pathetic misuse of our miraculous means of communication; and, lastly, the ever-present possibility of nuclear war.

How is all this relevant to the study of religion? Religion everywhere claims that there are deeper significances to life, that human reality is a much more complex affair than appears to secular observers, and that the universe itself is a well of mysterious forces and meanings which it is fatal to ignore.

This realization has led to a revival of theological thought in the West of such proportions that it is not unreasonable to say that we are living in an age of creative theological reflection. Western Christendom has enjoyed the presence of giants of theological thought whose work has contributed significantly to the contemporary revolution in culture.

The second reason for regarding this as an auspicious time for the study of religion is that there have never been more sources of reliable information available. Nearly 200 years of Western scholarship have produced an encyclopedic knowledge of world religions, their sacred texts in dependable translation, and social-psychological studies disclosing their functions in society and personality. If we take the studies of Christian origins, for instance, it is a fair statement that we know more about the New Testament and its background than did any previous generation, with the single exception of the age in which it was written. And such important issues as the relationship between science and religion have been given an unprecedented thoroughness of treatment and clarity of analysis. This is not to say that all the major problems have been solved—only that the major outlines are clearer than ever before and the fundamental issues better defined. Certainly, if we are to remain ignorant it will be by our own choice.

## THE SPIRIT OF THIS STUDY

This work is a broad survey of the data and issues in religion as seen from the point of view of a person living in Western Christendom. It was guided by the recurring questions that students have asked the author about religion during the past 20 years. It is in no sense an attempt at final answers or infallibility. It is based upon the faith that there is great value in critical knowledge, that from the vantage point of such knowledge a human being is better able to make the decisions about his own faith that will lead him into a deeper encounter with reality and into a more complete human existence.

It is based upon a further presupposition: that a deep religious faith is the clue to human existence in the twentieth century. Faith, incorruptibility, creativity, openness, compassion, and humility are rare—but they are the salt, seed, light, and hope of any age. These qualities may be harder to attain in our time amidst the welter of claims and counterclaims, the surfeit of information and distracting interests. But this is to say only that education in depth is desperately needed if men are to find the clue somewhere in this maze. The author believes this. The reader need not believe it in advance (nor at the conclusion), but he is invited to examine it for himself.

## HOW TO STUDY RELIGION

Every subject matter has peculiarities that determine the best way to approach it. Religion is no exception. Here are some suggestions on how to study it profitably.

### Clarify Present Beliefs

Begin where you are, with your present fund of information, beliefs, convictions, and commitments. The proposal of Descartes (1596–1650) to begin by discarding everything in the search for undoubted premises and then building a system upon them has proved philosophically bankrupt. The philosopher Socrates (?470–399 B.C.) is a better guide: Begin in the middle with whatever claims to knowledge you possess and then proceed outward from this center—backward toward the concepts that these beliefs ultimately presuppose to be true, and forward toward the experiences and consequences that they reasonably suggest.

Honest inquiry does not require that you despise what you have received. Above all, it does not mean that exotic material is preferable. Such materials must be examined in time, but they need not be preferred at the start, and they will probably be genuinely understood only after the familiar has been carefully examined.

This clarification of present beliefs moves along several interrelated lines: (1) *Analysis of the language of religion:* Define your major concepts as well as you are able—such concepts as "God," "salvation," "atheist," and "agnostic." Relate these major concepts to experience—your own preferably, but also to the experiences of the religious community from which they arose. (2) *Correlation:* Discover, if you can, the basic questions about the meaning of life which the major religious concepts are intended to answer. It is doubtful that a religion can be understood in the abstract. Its meanings to any given generation, when it is functioning vitally, are to supply to life's questions answers that cannot be secured from any other source. To take an example from Hinduism: Belief in karma (the moral law that "what you sow, you reap") and reincarnation answers for millions of people the question, "Why was I born into this particular life situation?" (3) *Consistency:* Tie together the whole body of concepts and experiences in such a way that they make a coherent body of thought.

### Consider the Critics

Learn from the honest critics; they have much to tell us. If we are to escape from mere credulity into an examined faith, they will be indispensable. More often than not they attack religion at the point where it has degenerated into mere superstition or meaninglessness. For instance, Sigmund Freud (1856–1939), the founder of psychoanalysis, attacked religion as a mere projection or fantasy based upon an infantile and neurotic need for a friendly power in the sky. Is there any reason to suppose that he was wrong about a vast amount of immature religion? Such criticism can force the believer to examine his own motives more realistically.

It is not necessary to swallow a critic's view whole, but at this stage in our inquiry it is more important to learn from a critic than to refute him. If we try to refute him too soon, we may fail to learn the lesson he has for us. He forces us to reexamine meanings, to look more closely at experience, and to overhaul the logic by which our beliefs are held together. There is always the possibility, of course, that he may persuade us to seek another faith.

### Expand the Fund of Knowledge

A third stage in our inquiry calls for an expansion of factual knowledge. At hand for this purpose is the rich fund of knowledge in the storehouse of modern scholarship. For more than two centuries scientific methods have been applied to various aspects of religion, with extraordinary results. Fiercely resisted in the name of piety during much of that time, these methods have come at last to be generally recognized as one legitimate way of obtaining publicly verifiable facts, even in religion.

With these methods, scholars from all varieties of religious and nonreligious backgrounds have been able to work on common problems and agree to common solutions. To take a recent case: Jews, Arabs, and Christians— Roman Catholic, Protestant, and Eastern Orthodox—have worked together in collecting, dating, deciphering, and interpreting the now famous scrolls discovered (1947) in the caves above the Dead Sea.

Gradually, over many decades at incalculable cost, workers in hundreds of fields ranging from linguistic studies to archaeology and radio chemistry have amassed a treasure of objective information about religions, from the most ancient and primitive types to the latest manifestations in sect and cult. They have used the techniques of historians, social scientists, psychologists, linguists, literary critics, biologists, and psychotherapists.

The sciences of religion as such fall into three main groupings: (1) the history of religion, (2) the sociology of religion, and (3) the psychology of religion. Each of these is a complex of several fields of investigation.

*The History of Religion.*   Investigators in this field attempt to set down in as objective a manner as possible the record of man's religious past. As historians they appeal to *anthropology* for a knowledge of preliterate cultures. They turn to *archaeology* for unearthing the past and interpreting the long-buried ruins of ancient cultures. The science of *documentary criticism* is a whole set of skills for decoding, dating, and interpreting ancient literatures, most of which are rich in religious significance. *Comparative religion* studies the similarities and differences in experience, organization, belief, conduct, and worship of the religions of mankind.

*The Sociology of Religion.*   This second field is also a complex of inter-related investigations, all seeking to clarify the interaction between man's religious institutions and the rest of his social and cultural life. R. H. Tawney, for example, in his *Religion and the Rise of Capitalism,* traces the relation-ships between the early forms of modern economic organization and the religious convictions about business activity prevailing at the same time. The sociologists can help us discover to what degree religious practices and beliefs are reflections of culture, and to what degree they are creators or critics of culture.

*The Psychology of Religion.*   The tools of psychology, social psychology, and the many theories of psychotherapy are being used to clarify the nature of religious experience and its relationship to other dimensions of human nature. The psychologist of religion studies such subjects as conversion, guilt, the search for meaning, anxiety, religious growth, prayer, types of belief, and the elements of religion in the abnormal experiences of the mentally ill.

The ideal of these sciences of religion is to set forth facts and theories in such a way that any scholar, no matter what his religious convictions, will be able to join objectively in the investigations. That such an ideal guides these studies is important even where it is not fully attained. Familiarity with the work in these fields will show, moreover, how often it has been approached, and how valuable such studies are to the serious student. In the better histories of religion, for example, it is very difficult indeed to detect the faith of the scholar or to see sectarian bias at work in his descriptions of the wide variety of religious phenomena.

With all its merits, however, it would be too much to claim that in science we now have the best or only method for a study of religion. It too has serious limitations. Science studies its material by incorporating it totally into an objective scheme of explanation unaffected by any human evaluation. It is ideally what the Germans call *wert-frei* (value-free). This, of course, is its great strength. But the essential strength of science proves to be a limitation in the study of religion.

If religion is the realm of what is most important, then to treat it as though one could stand off and view it with utter detachment is a contradiction in terms. If religion deals with the totality of reality that includes the thinker himself as well as his problems, then objectification is a distortion or an impossibility, something like trying to see one's own eye directly. Religion as a living fact always includes men who believe and live according to their beliefs. It is, in short, a subject matter that includes living responses to the content of faith. This human responsiveness, the existential element in religion, is the heart of any real understanding of the subject, and yet it is excluded by the very objectivity that is the heart of a scientific study. This naturally leads to our next point.

### Expand the Boundaries of Sympathetic Appreciation

A distinction needs to be made between an accurate description of public facts about religion—dates, personages, events, and so on—and the understanding of the meaning of these religious facts to the people involved with them. Such understanding requires something more than scientific skill. It demands a kind of imaginative sympathy, even a personal identification with the problems of existence to which the religious material answers in the experience of those undergoing the described events. Joachim Wach, a celebrated sociologist-historian of religion, calls this "integral understanding."[14] Professor Wilfred Cantfield Smith of Harvard University describes the changes in scholarship required by this kind of understanding in the following way: "The traditional forms of western scholarship in the study of other men's religion was that of an impersonal presentation of an 'it.' The first great innovation in recent times has been the personalization of the faiths observed, so that one finds a discussion of 'they.' Presently the observer becomes personally involved, so that the situation is one of 'we' talking about a 'they.' The next step is dialogue, where 'we' talk to 'you.' If there is listening and mutuality, this may become that 'we' talk *with* 'you.' The culmination of this progress is when 'we all' are talking *with* each other about 'us.' "[15]

Thus the expansion of factual knowledge—mere information—without sympathetic penetration is barren. It is important to understand why people embrace faiths so different from one's own. The mature student learns to unlock this secret insofar as it is open to an outsider. What he lacks in commitment to the subject of his study he must make up in a leap of imagination and human sympathy.

Sometimes we freeze up when approaching another faith, because we feel that loyalty to our own religion precludes deep appreciation for an alien religion. That this is far from true can be seen from the deep faithfulness of many Christian scholars who have become so expert in the faiths of other peoples that they can restate these faiths more expertly and convincingly than most of the adherents of those religions. Upon reading the chapter on Islam in a modern text on world religions, a Moslem student said, "I have never read so understanding and convincing an account of my own faith." And the best study of Rabbinic Judaism is probably still the work of a Christian scholar, George Foot Moore (1851–1931).[16]

### Integrate New Materials into Your Own Faith

We cannot study broadly beyond the ranges of our own religion without finding materials that come alive, won't stay inert. There is danger if we bring these new materials in by mere addition. This is syncretism—the poorest possible substitute for authentic religion. The syncretist compromises his own religion without gaining the strength of another. His fate is a hobby-shop mind—many things lying about without any principle of unity, without a center that could give coherence to the rest.

This is a genuine danger for the student of religion his powers of expansion may exceed his powers of integration, and he may wind up worshiping the study of religion rather than the substance of any. The remedy for this is for him to strengthen the center of his faith as he extends its perimeter. Considerable help for this can be had from the next suggestion.

### Practice What You Now Believe

E. A. Burtt suggests that there are two different ways of studying religion: one, to make ourselves more religious; the other, to achieve an accurate understanding of religion.[17] But it is doubtful that these two can be as logically separated as he assumes. Certainly in a study of art or music, becoming more aesthetically sensitive is a requirement for growth of understanding. This principle applies with even greater force to the comprehension of religion.

In religion we are involved with the data of our own study—what we are and how we think determines the data that will be open to us and the powers we will need to penetrate the essence of spiritual matters.

The verification of religion cannot take place without experiment, and there is no experiment so relevant as one's own experience. The experiment involves nothing less than the attempt to live by our faith so far as we understand it. We have to conduct this experiment with our own lives. This will finally determine what we will come to know by actual acquaintance, not merely by description. Unless we do this we cannot expect to move on to deeper levels of insight and understanding. We cannot receive insight above the levels of our present growth. To wait until we have received full knowledge before we move forward is fatuous. Following this policy we will receive less and less. Unless we are willing to test in life what we already believe to be true, our growing knowledge and widened sympathies may induce in us a feeling of drift and indecision. We are then threatened by the possibility of spiritual alienation and orphaning—what the historian Arnold Toynbee called "spiritual promiscuity."

Some people postpone decision and practice because they hope that someday reason will decide for them among the welter of claims which they encounter in the varieties of religion. But reason, as Kierkegaard (1813–1855) has said, is like the judge who hears all the evidence but is missing from the bench when the decision is called for. The fact is that reason itself takes on various meanings in the light of ultimate commitments. This is due to the fact that the concept of reason itself is based upon what one believes about the ultimate nature of reality. A materialist thinks of reason as the ordering of materials, much as in a computer. A mystic thinks of reason as the power to plunge into the depths of existence and discover new dimensions of meaning. Thus reason itself is subject to the rule we have already laid down, that the thinker always operates from within his own ultimate perspectives and commitments. What is reasonable proof for a Roman Catholic is not for a logical positivist or a Buddhist.

These remarks may seem to leave us with skepticism. This is not so. The skeptic himself works within his own perspective—that at the heart of existence there is nothing much of worth. Every great religion says he is wrong, and he is not right just because he says so. The skeptic's view of reason is therefore not a standard that we can use to adjudicate religious claims. More will be said on this later, but this will suffice to make our point that only a living experimentation can facilitate religious inquiry in depth.

### Continue the Inquiry

I have suggested the major elements in a sound method for studying religion. I have only to add that the investigation never ends. We repeat each stage of the inquiry over and over. At each turn of the spiral of self-examination, criticism, extension of knowledge and sympathies, and reintegration of belief, new and higher levels of investigation open up new issues, new comprehension, and new levels of personal and social being. Conceived in this way, religious study is continuous re-creation and growth.

This has been written as if the study of religion were a solitary one. But we are not alone. There are many pilgrims on this road. Some are way ahead of us, some far behind, but others are beset with the same problems and share the same enthusiasms. For this reason the normal setting for such a pursuit is a congenial group of fellow pilgrims from which the individual draws many strengths. The group gives balance, keeps up spirits when they flag, supplies perspectives that might be overlooked, and sorts out genuine discoveries from the eccentricities of excessive individualism.

If these remarks are anywhere near the truth, it is not hard to see that the study of religion is unrivaled as a personal adventure. We can now turn to one of the first great issues—the question of what religion really is.

## SUGGESTIONS FOR FURTHER READING

For a popular yet critical treatment of the various "gods" which presently attract the "worship" of undergraduates, see Chad Walsh's *Campus Gods on Trial* (Macmillan, 1953). Another study of student attitudes, including the place of religion in the hierarchy of student beliefs and attitudes, is *What College Students Think* (Van Nostrand, 1960) by Rose K. Goldsen and others.

There are a number of good books on the relationship of religion to education. Hoxie N. Fairchild has edited a collection of essays by outstanding scholars on the relationship of religion to the various subjects in the university curriculum, in *Religious Perspectives in College Teaching* (Ronald, 1952). Clyde A. Holbrook's *Religion, a Humanistic Field* (Prentice-Hall, 1963) is the most thorough study of religion as a field of academic study at the university level. *Religion* (Prentice-Hall, 1963), Paul Ramsey, ed., is a good summary of the present state of scholarship in various areas of religious studies. A well-known teacher of educational philosophy, Philip Henry Phenix, discusses the stake that present education has in religion, in *Religious Concerns of Contemporary Education* (Teachers College, Columbia University, 1959). Alfred North Whitehead's *The Aims of Education* (New American Library, 1949) is a statement of the over-all meaning of a balanced education by a famous philosopher.

## NOTES

1. Rose K. Goldsen and others, *What College Students Think* (Van Nostrand, 1960).
2. *Ibid.*, p. 154.
3. *Ibid.*, p. xxiii.
4. *Ibid.*, p. 24.
5. Philip E. Jacob, *Changing Values in College* (Harper & Row, 1957).
6. *Ibid.*, p. 1.
7. *Ibid.*
8. *Ibid.*, p. 2.
9. *Ibid.*

10. *Ibid.*, p. 4.
11. W. H. Auden, *Collected Poems* (Random House, 1945), p. 457.
12. Quoted by permission from an unpublished address by Nathan Pusey, President, Harvard University.
13. C. H. Moehlman, *School and Church: The American Way* (Harper & Row, 1944), p. 97.
14. See Wilfred Cantwell Smith, "Comparative Religion: Whither-and-Why?" in Mircea Eliade and Joseph M. Kitagawa, eds., *The History of Religions* (University of Chicago Press, 1959), p. 34.
15. *Ibid.*, p. 49.
16. George Foot Moore, *Judaism in the First Centuries of the Christian Era,* 3 vols. (Harvard University Press, 1927–1930).
17. E. A. Burtt, *Types of Religious Philosophy* (rev. ed.; Harper & Row, 1951), p. 3.

# 2

# What Religion Is

Religions in their full historical concreteness confront the investigator with the profusion of a tropical jungle. It is therefore not surprising that definitions of religion show wide disagreement, even among competent scholars. Religion, wrote the eminent historian Salomon Reinach (1858–1932), is "a sum of scruples which impedes the free exercise of our faculties."[1] Contrast this statement with the opinion of another eminent naturalist, John Dewey (1859–1952), who, though he also had no great love for institutional religion, nonetheless held that religion is "whatever introduces genuine perspective."[2]

Christian scholars do not seem to agree any better than the humanists. Friedrich Schleiermacher (1768–1834), often called the father of liberal theology, wrote that "the common element in all expressions of religion . . . is that we are conscious . . . of being in relation with God."[3] In direct contrast, one of the most celebrated twentieth-century Protestant theologians, Karl Barth, insists that religion is the action of men "who have fallen out of their relationship with God." For this reason, he says, "Religion must die. . . . In God we are rid of it."[4]

The skeptical psychologist James Leuba quoted 47 classic definitions of religion in the appendix to A Psychological Study of Religion (1912).[5] These reveal conflicts of the same order. Can a single definition do justice to such divergences of opinion? This chapter is an attempt to frame one that will.

## DEFINITIONS PERFORM WORK

It helps to understand the variety of definitions if we realize that they are tools designed for specific tasks. Reinach's definition, for example, reflects his contempt for religion and his desire to find ways and means of discrediting it, and thus neutralizing its influence. In this way a scholar often defines religion in such a way that it fits into and supports the main body of his own thought. Thus Ludwig Feuerbach (1804–1872), a cocreator of early Marxism, defined religion in such a way as to place it in the context of social revolution: "Man," he wrote, "is the beginning of religion, man is the center of religion, man is the end of religion."[6] Again, he claimed that religion is "the dream of the human spirit"—essentially an earthly dream.[7] Immanuel Kant (1724–1804), whose intense interest in moral philosophy strongly affected his view of religion, defined it as "the recognition of all duties as divine commands."[8]

Thus, if we ascertain what task a given definition performs for a thinker we can often understand the rationale underlying his definition. The task we will assign to our definition of religion is to guide this study, giving it at once broad scope and significant depth.

A truly useful definition will no doubt seem to prejudge the relative value of certain types of religious faith by bringing in at the start evaluations that should properly come at the conclusion of the study. But there is no escape from this. Unless the definition puts us on the trail of significant meaning to start with, we shall not be able to make much progress in our inquiry. We can perhaps offset the dangers of prejudgment by remembering that the definitions in this chapter are intended as hypotheses that can only be certified much later on. This admonition can serve to keep our definitions open to refinement and revision.

*I can summarize my remarks to this point by saying that any good definition of religion will have at least five characteristics: It will first of all be comprehensive, covering the whole range of religious phenomena. It will be coherent and self-consistent. It will be illuminating enough to give some insight into the depths of religious thought and experience while remaining tentative and open to revision in the light of new concepts and new data. And, finally, it will be useful as a guide to the study of religion.

## FOUR KINDS OF DEFINITION

Let us distinguish at the outset four types of definition: descriptive, normative, essential, and functional.

A good descriptive definition would specify the nature of religion in such a way that nothing would be omitted that any group or person chose to call faith. This would have to include such diverse elements as the hunting rites of the Hottentots and the high mass of the Roman Catholics. It would embrace both the passionate devotion of the saints and the indifference of the conventional churchgoer.

Unfortunately, years of effort to formulate a neutral descriptive definition have not been fruitful. The product of this is something like the following: *Religion is any belief, practice, or attitude which anyone or any group chooses to call its religion.* This is so broad as to be practically useless. It is a hypothesis without any risks, but equally without any promise of results. It is, ironically, not broad enough, for it does not include religious attitudes and beliefs that are concealed from its own practitioners, that hidden dimension of religion which we shall see is often more important than the overt and conscious dimensions. Finally, it is doubtful that it could be properly called a definition at all.

A normative, in contrast to a descriptive, definition doesn't aim at inclusiveness or impartiality. Its goal is to define not what religion *is*, but what it *ought to be.* Each of the great religions and every serious person's faith presupposes such a definition. The fact that no one of them succeeds in laying claim to the allegiance of all intelligent men of good will, or even a substantial majority of them, constitutes one of the fascinating difficulties in the study of religion.

A normative definition of religion from the Christian point of view, though by no means agreed to by all Christians, might go somewhat as follows: Religion is the life of joyful obedience to the God of sovereign, creative, holy love, as revealed in the Old and New Testaments, and more especially in the life, teachings, death, and resurrection of the Lord Jesus Christ, with all that this has meant to those of his followers through the ages who have been faithful to that revelation. Obviously a normative definition from a Jewish, Hindu, Moslem, or Buddhist point of view would be quite different. For this reason, though this definition may be very important, it is not one to which we can limit this study.

An essential definition stands somewhere between the empty descriptive definition and the exclusive normative one. Despite the risks, we must attempt some account of what religion essentially is, not how it merely appears, if we are to come to any genuine understanding. Such a definition can not be so narrow as to apply to only one religion or to one group of religions, nor so broad as to include absolutely everything that men call religious. I shall attempt, however, so to conceive this essential definition that nearly everything that men call religious appears in at least a marginal way in the account. This can be accomplished, however, only at the risk of making some categories more fundamental to religion than others. In short, we must attempt to strike at the essence of the religious spirit.

A functional definition, as the name implies, defines religion by the functions that it performs either in society or personality.

## AN ESSENTIAL DEFINITION OF RELIGION

Having already given examples of the first two kinds of definition, let us now consider in some detail the elements of an essential definition of religion.

### Religion as Ultimate Concern

The eminent American theologian Paul Tillich, in a statement that has been widely accepted in current thought, defined religion as a state of being grasped by an ultimate concern.[9] According to this view, whenever a human being speaks of the ultimate meaning of his existence, considers his absolute obligations, or relates himself by commitment or devotion to what he thinks is ultimately real—whenever he does any of these things, he is acting religiously, whether he realizes it or not.

A question naturally arises: When is concern ultimate concern? We will need criteria for making the distinction. First, ultimate concern is directed toward what is of final value, the supreme value that has top priority[10] in the hierarchy of life interests. It is the one thing for which a man would properly sacrifice any or all of his other interests. It is the standard by which he judges every other value and places them in the scheme of things, his key to the map of his own life orientation.

Such a key value at the real center of life is not always easy to discover either in others or in oneself. But since it is always presupposed in everything else human, pervading all that is said or done, it can be found out by a careful analysis of a society or person's attitudes, symbols, thought systems and, above all, actions. It becomes especially evident in times of difficult decisions or in affairs of such moment that the ultimate issues of life hang in the balance.

Value is thus the objective counterpart of concern. It is the element in religion that led the Danish philosopher Harald Höffding (1843–1931) to write in his *Philosophy of Religion* (1901) that the clue to religion was the "axiom of the conservation of values."[11] A generation later, Edward Scribner Ames improved on this by identifying the fundamental element as the "conservation of the *highest* values."[12]

A second characteristic of ultimate concern is that it is directed not only toward value, but toward what is believed to be the final truth about the nature of things, toward the ultimately real.

To be sure, these terms are not strictly equivalents, since religions differ greatly in their views of what reality ultimately is. Nevertheless, they universally agree that something is more real than all the rest and that this something stands fast in the tides of human affairs.

Whitehead's words, in a celebrated passage, eloquently express this view: "Religion is the vision of something which stands beyond, behind, and within, the passing flux of immediate things; something which is real, and yet waiting to be realized; something which is a remote possibility, and yet the greatest of present facts; something that gives meaning to all that passes, and yet eludes apprehension; something whose possession is the final good, and yet is beyond all reach; something which is the ultimate ideal, and the hopeless quest. . . . Apart from it, human life is a flash of occasional enjoyments lighting up a mass of pain and misery, a bagatelle of transient experience."[13]

Even naturalists—at the religious level—look to nature as a whole, or perhaps to some ineradicable tendency in nature, as the ground of their confidence in the future and as their hope for the endless flow of value into human life. Professor Julian Huxley proposes such a view in his *Religion Without Revelation* (1957).

## Pseudo Religion and Crypto-Religion

It should be obvious that by this definition much that passes for religion is not religion, whereas much that goes by another name, such as politics or business, is religion. A scientist, for example, who is confident that science has the answers to the ultimate nature of things and can alone save man from the problems that plague him, has taken a religious attitude toward science—it is his ultimate concern. Even if he regards himself as without religion, he has one—his science. Sigmund Freud was such a man.

On the other hand, a person who faithfully fulfills the conventional requirements of his church while discovering the meaning of his life according to other standards is not religious in the sense in which he believes himself to be.

We can call the first example an instance of *crypto-religion* (hidden religion), hidden because the man does not know the true sense in which he is religious. In our second example, the person's churchgoing activities represent a kind of *pseudo religion*. Pseudo religion appears to be religion, but actually is not, because it is unrelated to ultimate concern.

This definition restructures the study of religion by directing our attention toward what men actually feel or presuppose to be ultimate rather than to the conventional patterns of traditional religion.

Most Americans, for example, would be shocked much more by a military commander who committed an act of national desecration, such as tearing down a flag or otherwise treating it with disrespect, then by an out-and-out statement of atheism, or even by such an act as desecrating a chapel altar. Strong feelings often indicate where ultimate values lie. In this case, we may suspect, Americanism is more nearly the religion of most Americans than Christianity.

To sum up: Crypto-religion is ultimate concern cloaked in secular dress; pseudo religion is secular activity cloaked in religious dress. The word "secular" is here used to indicate human behavior that is not directly related to ultimate values. The secular is simply the nonreligious; it is a term of pure description, not intended to express any value judgment.

This discussion should make plain why we cannot begin by defining religion in terms of supernatural beings, such as God or gods. If we did so, the phenomenon of crypto-religion would be left completely unclarified. There also would be other difficulties. The Indian religion of Jainism is atheistic, as is the Sankhya system, one of the six orthodox Hindu schools.[14] Some scholars believe that this may also be true of primitive Buddhism. It would be a strange definition of religion that excluded all of these.

## The Category of the Sacred

Just as we experience the deliverances of conscience as "duty," or the contemplation of art as "beauty," just so religion as ultimate concern has its own typical experience, the experience of the "sacred." We are here in the realm of what Rudolf Otto has called the "numinous."[15] The "numinous," says Otto, is "perfectly *sui generis*," that is, "irreducible" to any other kind of experience.[16] It is, he goes on to say, an experience of "awful majesty" and "absolute unapproachability."[17] The numinous, then, is the feeling tone which envelops man in the presence of the fascinating yet awesome mystery of what is ultimate in or above the cosmos. At such a moment he cannot fail to humble himself in awe and adoring reverence.

Albert Einstein has defined religion in similar terms. Though he seems to differ from Otto in asserting the final rationality of ultimate reality, he nevertheless confesses that this rationality is infinitely removed from the poor powers of human intelligence and is therefore "numinous" in Otto's sense.

Here is Einstein's definition: "The most beautiful thing that we can experience is the mysterious. It is the source of all true art and science. He to whom this emotion is a stranger, who can no longer pause to wonder and stand, wrapped in awe, is as good as dead; his mind and his eyes are closed. The insight into the mystery of life, coupled though it be with fear, has also given rise to religion. To know that what is impenetrable to us really exists, manifesting itself as the highest wisdom and the most radiant beauty which our dull faculties can comprehend only in their most primitive form—this knowledge, this feeling, is at the center of true religiousness. In this sense I belong in the ranks of devoutly religious men."[18]

The late novelist Albert Camus wrote in the same vein: "The sacred is just the presence felt in the silence during the moment of genuine awareness."[19] The humanist is most apt to sense this moment of sacredness in connection with the nobility of man. "Religion . . .," wrote Joseph Needham, the English biologist, "[is] no more and no less than the reaction of the human spirit to the facts of human destiny and the forces by which it is influenced; and natural piety, or a divination of sacredness in heroic goodness becomes the primary religious activity."[20]

In religious history the realm of the sacred has taken many institutional forms. One is *taboo*. Émile Durkeim (1858–1917) in his now classic study of the *Elementary Forms of Religious Life*[21] wrote that the sacred is the realm of things set apart from the secular. It is the class of objects or actions that require special treatment in order that they not be profaned; it is the realm of the forbidden. This is, no doubt, the source of the popular saying that "religion is what you must not do." The ancient Jew, for example, did not presume to enter the Holy of Holies in the Temple. Only the high priest went into this place, and then but once a year. In an early Hebrew story, Uzzah put out his hand to steady the sacred ark of the covenant when the bearers stumbled. When he realized that he had touched the forbidden object, he suddenly collapsed and died.[22]

A couple of contemporary illustrations, which I would call crypto-religious, illustrate this same attitude. The body of Lenin, embalmed in the mausoleum in the Red Square of Moscow, is sacred to the pilgrims who file past the coffin in an attitude of veneration similar to that which the Russian masses formerly showed for Orthodox saints and relics. Any attempt to desecrate the shrine by an inappropriate act would be regarded with horror and would be severely punished.

Turning nearer home, the original document of the American Constitution is displayed for patriotic Americans in a crypt protected by bulletproof glass and capable of being lowered quickly into a steel vault upon the approach of danger. No doubt neither Americans nor Russians are consciously aware of performing anything like religious rites when they visit these relics of their sacred history, but their behavior can be best understood in religious terms.

Sacredness, we can see from these examples, may attach to places and things, to words (e.g., the Lord's Prayer), to writings (e.g., the Bible or Koran), to rites and rituals (e.g., the Mass or Baptism), and to persons (e.g., priests). Every fully developed religion has all of them. And because of the unique character of the sacred, religion characteristically develops a whole vocabulary of symbolic materials peculiar to itself: sacred languages and actions (such as prayers and liturgies) especially reserved for the religious sphere.

To summarize our remarks thus far we may say that the nuclear meaning of religion is ultimate concern and that the sacred is its primary category. Before we go further perhaps we should consider objections that have been raised against this way of defining religion.

### Some Criticism of the Concept of Ultimate Concern

Some critics have objected that Tillich's notion of ultimate concern is too subjective. Religion, I have said, claims to be the truth about existence, but it should be obvious that the mere fact of being gripped by an ultimate concern does not in itself establish that this concern is directed toward what is really ultimate. In other words, ultimate concern is not equivalent to concern for the ultimate. The object of concern may in this case be a mere personal illusion or an ideology that a person has uncritically accepted through his social inheritance.

Another peculiarity of religion that has led to a criticism of the concept of ultimate concern is that some human beings apparently respond simultaneously or successively to several ultimates. In religious terms this is polytheism —the worship of many gods. We know that polytheism is practiced not only in primitive religion, but that it continues to the present day. A person, for example, may worship the Judaeo-Christian God in church and commit himself unreservedly to his country in a patriotic celebration. A faithful concern for only one god—one ultimate—is no doubt rare among human beings in any age. A more common state of affairs can be illustrated by the so-called three religions of China. The Chinese, observers say, are Taoists at the birth of a child, Confucianists at weddings, and Buddhists at funerals. And under present conditions they no doubt manage to combine all this in some way with the required total allegiance to the omnipresent Marxist state.

A third criticism of the concept of ultimate concern comes from critics who complain that Tillich does not take their rejection of religion seriously. By insisting that everyone, without exception, must have something ultimate in his life even violent critics of religion are lumped together with devout believers. Critics and believers alike complain that this obscures some very important distinctions among human beings.

More adequate answers to these objections will appear as our study proceeds. Only a partial answer can be given here. The main point is that ultimate concern has a logic of its own, and as that logic is unfolded these criticisms lose their major force. Take first the criticism that ultimate concern is too subjective. Since religious reality, as I shall show later, cannot be grasped by objective method, it is normal that all religious knowledge should be rooted in the deeply subjective. It is only as a person is completely taken up in devotion to the object of his concern that he is able to grasp the nature of religious reality. However, as religion becomes conscious of itself and self-critical by its own standards, the question naturally arises as to whether this concern is directed toward the truly ultimate or not; that is, whether it is worthy of worship or not. By a dialectical development of evaluation lesser concerns are sorted out, and inadequate ultimates are exposed for what they are. For instance, upon careful reflection, it becomes clear that the nation state cannot serve as an ultimate for the simple reason that the nation state is conditioned on all sides by other nations, by historical development, and by nature itself. It falls, moreover, under the judgment of values that emerge among civilized men in the course of their thought! This same kind of development takes place for all ultimate concerns, changing and deepening or rejecting them as awareness broadens and becomes more sophisticated.

As we shall see in the next chapter, polytheism gradually gave way to a religious criticism that forced men to acknowledge some God or Power beyond the various gods. To put the point briefly: Ultimate concern tends toward some kind of single highest good or reality. In the competition for control over human attitudes and wills there appears to be a movement toward the single heart and mind, the one highest and clearly chosen loyalty. In actual history this logic appears as a kind of tension—like the lure of truth in science, for example—not as an actual achievement, except among the greatest saints and prophets. This, in substance, is the answer to the objection that men have several ultimates.

The criticism that the concept of ultimate concern lumps together believers and skeptics can be answered in this way. There seems to be no doubt that many so-called secular—even antireligious—philosophies have all the marks of religion. I have given some instances above. Perhaps communism is the clearest example. On the other hand, it must be admitted that it seems a strange use of language to call an atheist "religious." However, in a study of religion that is not to be superficial, the religious characteristics of such movements cannot be ignored. Perhaps we would protect ourselves against the charge of misusing language if we employed a term used by Tillich in his later works, the term "quasi religion" to stand for such phenomena as communism, nationalism, or scientism whenever they are characterized by a kind of ultimacy of devotion and serve as a life-orienting world view.

Perhaps we can clarify this point if we ask ourselves what would be the characteristics of a man who had absolutely no religion. I am not sure that such persons exist, for behind their passionate denials I suspect strong intimations of the religious spirit. However, as a logical exercise I would suggest that the completely irreligious person would be one for whom nothing is sacred save his own immediate selfhood, for whom there are no depths of significance and meaning beyond his own immediate experiences, no reliable truth or power beyond his own immediate capacity to live and be, and for whom the whole natural and social world reveals itself as fundamentally empty, nauseating, or destructive, as "sound and fury, signifying nothing." A person who appears to satisfy this description is the French playwright and novelist Jean Genêt who has been celebrated by the noted existentialist and atheist Jean-Paul Sartre in his critical work *Saint Genêt*.[23]

In searching for other examples of the absence of religion, I should say that they are very rare indeed (even Sartre doesn't seem to qualify), and when one finds them, a strong suspicion arises that there is more than meets the eye. They are more often rebelling against some aspect of religiousness than embracing complete irreligion. Bertrand Russell, for all his announced atheism, shows himself in his essay on "A Free Man's Worship" and in his courageous struggles on behalf of social justice to be a religious man in the larger sense in which we have been defining the term.

We must return now to our essential definition of religion. What follows is a treatment of some of the major characteristics that emerge in the course of religious development as the logic of ultimate concern unfolds. These characteristics need to be noted if we are to complete the definition, because it is only in the developed faiths that the nature of religion becomes clear.

## The Development of Ultimate Concern in the Higher Religions

*The Holy.* One of the emergent facts of developing religion is that the sacred becomes fused with the holy. The relationship between the sacred and the holy has vexed men throughout religious history. Holiness conveys a strong ethical and moral quality, whereas much that men have held to be sacred lacks moral content. In the higher religions (granting some important exceptions) these two qualities tend to become nearly synonymous. This did not come about without struggle. The message of the Hebrew prophets was largely a rebuke to people whose sense of the sacred had become divorced from the moral laws of God. They were performing their religious rituals, but neglecting the weightier matters of social justice. These words of Amos (*c.* 740 B.C.) are a typical denunciation of the religious shrines at Bethel and Gilgal:

> *Go to Bethel, go on with your sins!*
> *pile sin on sin at Gilgal!*
> *ay, sacrifice in the morning,*
> *and every third day pay your tithes,*
> *burn your dough as a thank-offering,*
> *announce your freewill gifts—*
> *ah, make them public,*
> *for you love that, you Israelites!*
>
> *Your sacred festivals? I hate them, scorn them;*
> *your sacrifices? I will not smell their smoke;*
> *you offer me your gifts? I will not take them;*
> *you offer fatted cattle? I will not look at them.*
> *No more of your hymns for me!*
> *I will not listen to your lutes.*
> *No, let justice well up like fresh water,*
> *let honesty roll in full tide.*[24]

When the sacred and the holy appear as one, religious experience takes the form of repentance in the presence of the highest goodness. The prophet Isaiah (*ca.* 640 B.C.) during an exalted moment of vision in the Temple at Jerusalem, cried out, "Woe is me . . . for I am a man of unclean lips . . . for my eyes have seen the King. . . ."[25] In this new vision of the sacred he confessed shame at what he was over against what he ought to be, for the God of the Hebrews had enjoined men to be holy because God is himself holy.

In developed religion, the ideal judges the actual, whether this ideal is the Confucian ideal of "man-at-his-best," or the Buddhist ideal of the bodhisattva or the Christian ideal of a "man-in-Christ."

*Religion as Wholeness.* I have said that religion is a category distinct from other categories. This is true, but it does not mean that it is separated from the rest of life, or that the religious life is a compartmentalized affair. Only pseudo religion is compartmentalized. Mature religion as an awed sense of depth in existence, as ultimate concern for what is ultimately real and important, necessarily includes the whole of life in a special way, much as a building is related to its foundation, or the conclusion of a valid argument is related to its premises. As the philosopher John Hutchison says, it becomes "fully deployed."[26]

In his Gifford Lectures, *The Modern Predicament* (1955), H. J. Paton writes: "Religion is concerned, not with some special aspect or manifestation of life, but with the whole of life or with life as a whole. For religion is always a case of all or nothing. . . . If the finite individual is to become whole, he cannot do so either by himself or even in his relation to other finite beings: He must somehow in some sense become one with the Whole—the ultimate whole beyond which there is nothing else. . . . Such seems to be the minimum claim of developed religion."[27]

Many approaches to religion regard its essential nature as springing primarily either out of the mind, will, or feelings. James Leuba, for instance, classifies all 47 of his definitions as either intellectual, voluntaristic, or affective. In my opinion, there is a unity of the human spirit lying at a more fundamental level of human nature than these three, the level from which these divergences of thought, will, and feeling arise. And it is this more fundamental level that is the breeding place of faith.

The Judaeo-Christian faith, for example, makes plain this totality: The first and greatest commandment, to love God with one's whole heart, soul, mind, and strength, means that everything is gathered up into a whole so that nothing is unaffected by this supreme loyalty. To be sure, this ideal of perfect unity is rarely if ever achieved in actuality, since men easily forget themselves in their segmented activities. Nevertheless, as an ideal, nothing can escape the implicit valuation and reality estimate that religion presupposes as the deep root of existence.

It should be observed that the encompassing unity of the religious spirit is not a matter of mere breadth. Its inclusiveness proceeds through depth. Religious faith includes the whole of life through what Tillich calls the "ground" of existence. The unity that religion seeks includes all the rich unconscious elements that lie in the unfathomed depths of experience.

*Religion as a Sense of Kinship.* A special form of the drive toward wholeness in religion is its claim that man has a special if hidden kinship both to his fellow men and to ultimate reality.

Religions produce rules to govern human relations. In their narrower forms—which, unfortunately, are more common than universal forms—religions teach a unity limited to human beings within a designated group (nation, race, or church). However, in the higher religions (and this term "higher" is indispensable if we are to make sense of religious experience) they teach a direct relationship of man to man, undistorted by cultural, racial, or personal biases. When a scribe, seeking a rule of exclusiveness, asked Jesus, "Who is my neighbor?" Jesus replied that a neighbor is anyone in need.[28]

In Mahayana Buddhism the sense of kinship is summed up in the vow of a monk seeking Buddhahood: "I strive not merely for my own redemption. I must lead all these living beings . . . out of the flood of transmigration. I must take upon myself the whole mass of sufferings of all beings . . . in all parts of the universe."[29] In China, one of the distinguishing marks of the Confucian "man-at-his-best" is "man-to-manness" (jen), the ability to relate properly to his fellows.

What makes these beliefs in human kinship distinctly religious is that they derive not from empirical observations of men as they are, but from the more fundamental belief that man is essentially related to the Being that embraces the whole of reality. As Thomas Carlyle has said, "The thing a man does practically lay to heart and know for certain concerning his vital relationships to this mysterious universe and his duty and destiny there . . . creatively determines all the rest."[30]

This kinship with the social world is paralleled by a sense of kinship with the nonhuman environment. The Hindu is taught that his own soul (atman) is identical with the soul of the universe (Brahman), and the Jew or Christian is taught that the world was created as a stage for the drama of human salvation; in the words of St. Paul, "in everything God works for good with those who love him . . ."[31]

*Religion as Faith in the Unseen.* The basic premises of religion are never "seen" directly. They are rather the light in which everything else is seen. They are like the presuppositions of logic that determine the logic itself, or the nonmathematical assumptions that control mathematical thinking. ". . . the things which are seen are temporal," writes the Apostle Paul, "but the things which are not seen are eternal."[32] This is not to deny that men experience a religious dimension, but only to make clear that such experience is always a depth experience, a confrontation with ultimates which cannot be explained by less ultimate realities. In this sense, "God," "Brahman," "Allah," or "Tao" are nonempirical realities.

Even humanistic religions think of basic reality as in some sense hidden from casual observation, and refer, for example, to the "forces making for progress" or the "dialectical processes of history." Immediate forces are thus not conceded to have the final word in human affairs. The all too evident victories of destructive powers are not accepted as final. Religious faith sees something more ultimate operating in and through them.

Immediate values, likewise, are not held to be the most important, but are graded in the light of ultimate values. Immediate sensory qualities are believed to conceal the ultimate sacredness or hidden providential meaning of things. The apparent separateness of the many factual and value aspects of the world is regarded as an illusion hiding the secret kinship and unity which they have at some deeper level. Separate and conflicting partial values or truths are perceived as refractions of a Truth and a Good which are fragmented by the special senses and by the fraility of human thought and perception.

Some of the most striking examples of this characteristic of religious apprehension are in theories about the nature of selfhood. From the most primitive levels upward men have believed themselves to possess a kind of selfhood that is distinct from, yet related to, the everyday self. This is the reason for such special terms as "soul" or "atman."

The goals of selfhood in religious vision surpass all empirical possibilities. It is held that men are not yet what they really are; that they can scarcely imagine what they yet may be.

The same can be said of the social order. The whole human order is envisaged by religious faith as a community ready to be transformed into an unearthly beauty and order. Toward the end of Plato's *Republic*, for example, Socrates is challenged with the remark that his ideal republic "exists nowhere on earth." Agreeing with this observation, he replies, ". . . in heaven, perhaps, a pattern of it is indeed laid up, for him that has eyes to see, and seeing to settle himself therein. It matters nothing whether it exists anywhere, or shall exist; for he would practice the principles of this city only, no other."[33]

*Religion as a Special Knowledge of Reality.* Against all agnosticism and doubt, against all feelings of unreality, religion claims that man is in some authentic way in touch with final reality. As the American philosopher William Ernest Hocking says, ". . . religion has never as yet been able to take itself [merely] as a matter of feeling."[34]

In Western religions (Judaism, Christianity, Islam) this special form of knowledge is characteristically *relevation*. These religions claim that God has revealed himself in special ways to man. In the Far Eastern tradition (Hinduism, Buddhism, Taoism), this knowledge is held to be available through special states of consciousness which grow out of the various methods of mystical training. The point that is important for our definition is that religion claims to know, to be in touch, to have a true word.

*Religion as Both Social and Personal.* Personal and social dimensions are equally important in religious thought. A scholar like John MacMurray defines religion as what a person does with his social relations, whereas Alfred North Whitehead says that religion is what the individual does with his own solitariness.

These definitions are not as contradictory as they seem. They are, in fact, essential to one another. The context of Whitehead's statement makes this clear: "Religion is what the individual does with his solitariness . . . if you are never solitary you are never religious. Collective enthusiasms, revivals, institutions, churches, rituals, bibles, codes of behaviour, are the trappings of religion, its passing forms. . . . But the end of religion is beyond all this. Accordingly, what should emerge from religion is individual worth of character."[35] In another passage Whitehead contrasts intellectual learning in such a field as mathematics with religion by saying: "You *use* arithmetic, but you *are* religious. Religion . . . enters into your nature."[36]

In this statement, Whitehead is not denying that religion has social dimensions—certainly "character" would be meaningless except in human relations—what he is insisting on is the inner integrity of the genuinely religious experience, an integrity that stands against all outward show or prudent social agreement. He is urging that "ultimate concern" really be one's own authentic personal concern, not merely the verbal ritual of a social group to which one belongs. This latter, to use a term we have already introduced, is merely pseudo religion.

We can now summarize our essential definition of religion somewhat as follows: Religion is a state of being grasped by an ultimate concern. As this concern evolves toward its natural maturity it supplies to men a sense of kinship with one another and a wholeness of life. It grants in its own way an assurance of some trustworthy and significant truth below the surfaces of existence.

So much for our essential definition. Let us turn now to a definition of religion in functional terms. This new angle should sharpen our focus on the meaning of religion.

## A FUNCTIONAL DEFINITION OF RELIGION

Functional definitions are derived by answering the question, What special work does religion do in human life? If, as we have said, religion is a unique category, these functions will be unique in the sense that only religion can perform them—or, conversely, anything that claims to perform them is, by definition, religion. Let us being by distinguishing the social from the individual functions of religion. On the social side, Gerhard Lensky and his associates, in a recent sociological study defined religion functionally as a "system of beliefs about the nature of force(s) ultimately shaping man's destiny, and the practices associated therewith, shared by the members of a group."[37] Milton Yinger, another sociologist, gives us a similar definition: Religion is a "system of beliefs and practices by means of which a group of people struggles with [the] . . . ultimate problems of human life."[38] By ultimate problems he means such facts as suffering and death, the events "that press in on us, endangering our livelihood, our health, the survival and smooth operation of the groups in which we live—forces that our empirical knowledge is inadequate to handle."[39]

Since we shall be dealing with the role of religion in society at length in another chapter, let us here concern ourselves chiefly with the unique function that religion performs in the lives of individuals. Human beings experience a special class of needs which arise because of man's peculiarity as man, needs which he does not share with prehuman forms of life. Let us call them noetic needs to distinguish them from physiological, or sociocultural needs. As we shall see, there is some overlapping in our classification, but my meaning should become clear with further discussion.

Briefly, man's peculiarity as man lies in his reflective consciousness, his ability to think, his awareness of events (even of his own thinking processes) from a standpoint transcending the events themselves. He asks questions that are meaningless except from a human perspective. The philosopher Immanuel Kant formulated the basic human questions this way: What can I know? What must I do? What may I hope? What is man?[40] Conscious knowledge, moral obligation, a sense of destiny—these and others like them are specifically noetic dimensions. Man cannot help asking questions about his knowledge, his obligation, his destiny, and his own nature. So far as we know, no other beings ask such questions, because they are not capable of that reflexive turn of consciousness which we call thought.

Out of this fact emerge certain needs that can give us a clue to the nature of religion. "Religion is to be understood," writes Hocking, "as a product and manifesto of human desire; and that of no secondary and acquired desire, such as curiosity, but of deep-going desire, deep as the will-to-live itself."[41] But before we turn to a brief treatment of some of these questions, it is important to avoid a misunderstanding. Not all human needs are religious needs; yet since religion permeates human existence, it is common for these nonreligious needs to become mixed up with religious experience and distort it. Needs for food, security, and affection, for example, are sometimes so demanding due to the lack of means to satisfy them that religion is dragged in to substitute for the proper technical means. This has led men to rely upon religion to increase crops, defend them against enemies, or to supply them with a Friend in the absence of satisfying human associations. When this happens, religion is usually distorted into magic or wishful thinking, and provides the chief target for the skeptical critique of religion.

The critic, unfortunately, does not distinguish this false use of religion from its proper one and thus condemns religion as a whole. Recalling Freud's account of religion as a parent substitute for adults who refuse to grow up, we could very well agree that such a substitution is unfortunate. But we need not condemn religion in its proper sphere on this account. It is not surprising that having made this mistake Freud should have regarded all religion as an "illusion."

In order to make this clearer let us consider briefly the kinds of human questioning that lead to the religious consciousness proper.

There are, first of all, the needs of man that arise from his awareness of his precariousness. Man is the being who knows that he will die and that nothing he can do will prevent this eventuality. "Death," writes Karl Barth, "is the meaning of religion; for when we are pressed to the boundary of religion, death pronounces the inner calm of simple and harmless relativity to be at an end."[42] Against the vastness and permanence of nature man knows himself to be finite and frail. The reflex of this awareness gives rise to religious thought and behavior. He wants life, yet he is faced with death and disruption. He wants to preserve the things that matter most to him, yet he is powerless against the cosmos.

This sense of precariousness, to be sure, can lead to a false religious response, a willingness to believe anything that will allay human fear. But the search for security in a craven sense is not what lies at the heart of religion at its best. What does lie at its heart is man's longing for something that is reliable and permanent, something not subject to the fate he knows he must suffer.

Then, second, there are the needs that arise from the human experience of separation, alienation, and loneliness. Man suffers alienation at three levels—from himself, from his fellows, and from the ultimate power or powers that underlie all existing things.

He is alien from himself in the sense that he is not what he knows he ought to be; he is not his own true self. He seeks an identity with that self, but it eludes him continually. This self, he realizes in his best moments, is more than he is or can intend to be, yet it is his real self.

He also feels a tragic separation from his fellows. He exists in competition with them even when he loves them. He feels in his deepest moments that somehow he is made for a richer and more authentic communion with his fellow men, but he and they frustrate this communion. Understanding fails to come to fruition; love perishes; unity is eroded away by irrelevancies or by outright denials. How can he find his way to a higher fellowship, a true communion, a genuine human community? This is a religious need, the longing in man which gives rise to the forms of faith.

Man also feels alienated from nature and from the power or powers which sustain nature. In certain clear moments he feels himself a part of nature; then he is flung back into his own separateness. He even feels his body (which is a part of nature) as alien to him. His sexuality, for example, along with the other powers of his body, puzzles and distracts him. How can he overcome this "unnatural" condition and "return" to being a true child of the nature from which he has sprung?

Religion offers a saving answer to each of these questions, reminding man that he is more than he presently is; that he is in the deepest sense one with his fellows, and that these truths can be felt, genuinely if fugitively, in the mystical moments of the common ritual; that he is likewise fundamentally one with the powers of nature, or the power that stands under or behind nature, and that therefore he need not fear.

It should be evident that the species of alienation which here concerns us can have no "objective" scientific answers. The whole realm of physical facts in space and time, no matter how rearranged, cannot still the uneasiness that is at the bottom of man's feeling about himself.

It is true, of course, that some men have turned their backs upon faith as a solution and preferred to live with the problems unsolved, bearing them, so to speak, in their most painful forms. Though such men are rare, we shall have to consider them before we are through with our inquiry; but for the present it is enough to point out that the classical religious answers have more or less well satisfied millions of their practitioners. And it is a simple matter of history that this is an important element in defining the nature of religion.

I must also point out that the various religions have proposed different paths to the solution of man's sense of alienation—different "paths" to salvation. These arise from a difference in diagnosing the source of man's alienation. The major religions of the West have defined the problem as *sin*, whereas the religions of the East have defined it as a species of *ignorance*. The conquest of sin requires a different strategy than the conquest of ignorance, and many of the contrasts between East and West lie in the ways they propose to do spiritual battle with man's foes.

One might be tempted to think that modern man, with all his technical resources, could forgo religion, and find salvation in his superior knowledge and technical ability. Some scholars claim this to be true and they propose a humanistic religion of science. This claim will have to be examined later; for the present, however, it must suffice to point out that students of modern life are in remarkable agreement that the difficulties to which religion speaks have grown worse rather than better with the rise of modern civilization. The growth of outer culture and civilization has left man inwardly impoverished and distracted.

A third typically human need can be called the demand for meaning. Life without ultimate significance is not only flat and stale, it leads finally to the negation of life itself. Men lose heart even in the midst of success and physical well-being when they are convinced that their existence is meaningless. A man with a fine car but no place to go can hardly be happy. Similarly, a human being with all the means of life but no point to it as a whole will find himself in ever deepening frustration. Particular values, such as pleasure, health, wealth, reputation, social status, satisfy only up to a point. Beyond that these values demand a deeper sanction.

Two universal human experiences seem in a special way to demand explanation: the experience of unmerited suffering and the experience of unmerited good.

Religion invariably arises around such boundary situations as disease, old age, and death. In the story of the religious conversion of the founder of Buddhism, we are told that the young prince Siddhartha (later, the Gautama Buddha) escaped from the sheltered world of his father's palace and encountered the three "signs"—a sick man, an old man, and a corpse. Returning from the sight of these "three woes," the young prince, says an ancient text, "passed by the palaces of the nobility, and Kisa Gotomi, a young princess and niece of the king, saw Siddhartha in his manliness and beauty and, observing his countenance, said, 'Happy the father that begot thee, happy the mother that nursed thee, happy the wife that calls husband this lord so glorious.'" The prince upon hearing this greeting replied in a most unexpected way for one so favored, "Happy are they that have found deliverance."[43]

The religious response to these elemental events is an act of faith that they portend some profound and hidden significance for man. Moreover, such faith often claims that this meaning can be discerned most strikingly in those very features of life that are empirically the most puzzling—the vagaries of fortune and the unaccountability of destiny. Thus, for example, Christians look to a man on a cross.

The nonreligious perception of existence, by contrast, is illustrated in the view of Bertrand Russell that the cosmos is an idiotic accident. All this biological and physical order, according to him, is a fortuitous circumstance, a momentary collocation of atoms that will dissolve into pure chaos.

What has been said of suffering can likewise be said of unmerited good. The uncontrollable vitalities that erupt into existence from beyond the human realm, bringing with them unearned increments of goodness also cry out for explanation. Some of these are the powers of procreation, growth, good fortune (such as a bumper crop), creative inspiration, moral experience and love, or the mysterious fascination of beauty and truth. The religious person comes to feel that these arise from the unsounded depths and that they bear on the significance of life as a whole.

We can sum up these remarks about the search for meaning by saying that human life needs a sense of direction, an answer to the questions of whence and whither—in short, a way of life.

A fourth need closely related to what has gone before, but needing special notice, is man's need for a deep sense of well-being, an experience of joy, happiness, even ecstasy, that will not crumble under the attrition of life.

If we turn to the testimonies of the early religious communities in Buddhism, for example, the *Songs of the Sisters* or the *Songs of the Brethren*, we discover a deep contentment running through their experiences of liberation. The same joyful quality can be seen in the revival music of the American frontier, in the Protestant music of Bach, or in the songs used in the Hindu institution of *Kirtan* (religious dance), a sample of which can be seen in the following stanza:

> Lord, thus hast lifted all my sorrow
> with the vision of Thy face,
> And the magic of Thy beauty
> has bewitched my mind.[44]

## SUMMARY

At this stage of our investigation we must admit the possibility that the religious response to existence is not directed toward reality at all; that it is, in short, a pure illusion, and that therefore some other response would be more to the point. This objection must be dealt with later. For the present we must content ourselves with the fact that this is one way to understand what we mean by religion.

These remarks on a functional definition of religion can be summed up in Henry Nelson Weiman's analysis of the traditional claims made by the great historical religions: First, the predicament of man is so serious individually and collectively that he cannot escape from it by his own power. Second, there is a power which is able to deliver him, and which will do so if man meets the required conditions. Third, these conditions are variously specified, but they seem always to include the most complete self-giving of the individual to this power to be transformed by it. And, finally, the good to be attained by the transformation is the greatest good that can ever come to humankind.[45]

## RELIGION, ART, SCIENCE, AND PHILOSOPHY DISTINGUISHED

We can now complete our definition of religion by commenting briefly about the way in which it is distinguished from some other basic human concerns, such as art, science, and philosophy. This task is made difficult by the way in which these other concerns are interwoven with religion. However, unless we can focus the central meaning of each of these disciplines in its purity, it is difficult to make much sense of their interrelationships. All four attempt in their own way to make some kind of sense out of the confrontation of a thinking human being with the concrete world.

Art deals with the values that men experience by embodying them symbolically in such media as sound, plastic, or paint; that is to say, in concrete artifacts. Works of art focus values for human contemplation and enjoyment. Thus, through art man often finds his experience heightened and clarified.

Science has only a minor interest in values. Its chief purpose is to describe the connections between events (facts) in the empirical world. It seeks a scheme of causal relationships in which each element in experience is assigned specific antecedent causes and specific subsequent effects. It wants prediction and control. Whenever it handles values it deals with them as facts in this scheme of causal description.

Philosophy in its classical meaning[46] is the attempt to see life critically and whole. Its goal is to relate the various fields of human knowledge and experience as closely as possible to a single coherent perspective. This book, for example, is philosophical inasmuch as it attempts to understand the nature of religion in all its manifold expressions and interconnections.

It should be apparent that religion has interests that overlap each of these three fields. Like art it is concerned with values; like science it longs for the truth about the structures of existence; like philosophy it seeks a coherent perspective.

Religion, however, is unlike art in that it is not satisfied with the mere contemplation of value; it seeks a union of life with the value contemplated. It is unlike science and philosophy in that it seeks understanding in order to relate existentially to reality. "The religious consciousness seeks being," writes Leuba, "the philosophic consciousness seeks knowledge."[47] Science, to be sure, appears to do the same thing, but whereas science seeks relationship with life through control, religion seeks a new quality of being through obedience to the ultimate order of things.

Magic, which is often confused with religion, is essentially an occult science that seeks to control existence by well-defined techniques. It is not religion. Fundamentally, religion has no more to do with the occult than with natural science. Perhaps much less.

Religion is thus different at the center from these other areas of human concern, while at the same time overlapping them. Since, however, art, science, and philosophy also converge on ultimate human concerns, there is a sense in which they contain religious elements. Or to put it another way, religious experience may arise in connection with any and all human experiences whenever they "touch ground," whenever they unveil, if even for a moment, the awesome depths of human existence. But in all of these cases experience does not become fully religious until it stakes claims over the whole of life and demands that existence conform to the vision that has been granted. For religion is more than a vision of ultimate mystery and beauty; it is a lifetime effort to become one with them in the entire range of thought, feeling, and action.

In order for us to understand this fact more fully, we must now turn to the concrete world of the historic religions.

## SUGGESTIONS FOR FURTHER READING

Paul Tillich's *Dynamics of Faith* (Harper Torchbooks, Harper & Row, 1958) is an easy introduction to the concept of ultimate concern that looms so large in my definition of religion. Rudolf Otto's *The Idea of the Holy* (Oxford University Press, 1943) is a classic description of the category of the "holy." From a sociological point of view, Émile Durkheim's *Elementary Forms of Religious Life* (G. Allen, 1915) does the same thing for the category of the "sacred." Mircea Eliade combines both approaches in *The Sacred and the Profane* (Harper Torchbooks, Harper & Row, 1961), in it he elucidates the nature of the sacred in such a universal way that it could serve as an introduction to comparative religion. G. van der Leeuw's *Religion in Essence and Manifestation*, 2 vols. (Harper Torchbooks, Harper & Row, 1963) has been regarded, since its appearance in German in 1925, as the most complete description of the religious dimension of human experience. Winston L. King's *Introduction to Religion* (Harper & Row, 1954) is a more recent descriptive study that defines religion by describing its major historic functions and defining its most characteristic concepts. Another excellent work in the same vein is Wilfred Cantwell Smith's *The Meaning and End of Religion* (New American Library, 1963).

William James' *Varieties of Religious Experience* (New American Library, 1958), a brilliant work of a famous philosopher-psychologist, has, since its appearance in 1902, excited generations of students and scholars. One of his critics,

James Leuba, wrote *A Psychological Study of Religion* (Macmillan, 1912), partly in refutation of James. This book contains an appendix with 47 classic definitions of religion.

For a single popular account of what I have called pseudo religion, see Peter Berger, *The Noise of Solemn Assemblies* (Doubleday, 1961).

## NOTES

1. Salomon Reinach, *Orpheus, A History of Religions* (Liveright, 1935), p. 3.
2. E. S. Brightman, *A Philosophy of Religion* (Prentice-Hall, 1950), p. 16.
3. *Ibid.*
4. Karl Barth, *The Epistle to the Romans* (Oxford University Press, 1933), pp. 246, 248.
5. James Leuba, *A Psychological Study of Religion* (Macmillan, 1912), pp. 339–361.
6. Brightman, *loc. cit.*
7. In Dagobert D. Runes, *Dictionary of Philosophy* (Littlefield, Adams, 1955), p. 108.
8. Immanuel Kant, *Religion Within the Limits of Reason Alone* (Open Court, 1960), p. 142.
9. Paul Tillich, *The Protestant Era* (University of Chicago Press, 1948), p. 59.
10. John Hutchison, *Language and Faith* (Westminster Press, 1963), pp. 114–116.
11. Harald Höffding, *Philosophy of Religion* (Macmillan, 1906), p. 215.
12. Edward Scribner Ames, "Religious Values," *International Journal of Ethics*, 38 (1928), 299.
13. Alfred North Whitehead, *Science and the Modern World* (New American Library, 1948), pp. 191–192.
14. See any standard work on the history of religions. A good one is John B. Noss, *Man's Religions*, 3rd ed. (Macmillan, 1956), pp. 158 ff.
15. Rudolf Otto, *The Idea of the Holy* (Oxford University Press, 1943).
16. *Ibid.*, p. 20.
17. *Ibid.*
18. In Louis Untermeyer, *Makers of the Modern World* (Simon and Schuster, 1955), pp. 540–541.
19. I cannot find the source of this remark, which was quoted in a letter to the editors of *The Christian Century* (Chicago).
20. Joseph Needham, *Time: That Refreshing River* (Hillary House, 1948), p. 57.
21. Émile Durkheim, *Elementary Forms of Religious Life* (G. Allen, 1915).
22. II Samuel 6:6–7.
23. Jean-Paul Sartre, *Saint Genêt* (Braziller, 1962).
24. Amos 4:4–5; 5:21–25 (Moffatt trans.).
25. Isaiah 6:5.
26. Hutchison, *op. cit.*, p. 115.
27. H. J. Paton, *The Modern Predicament* (Macmillan, 1955), pp. 62, 65.
28. In the parable of the Good Samaritan, Luke 10:29–37.
29. In Albert Schweitzer, *Indian Thought and Its Development*

(Holt, Rinehart and Winston, 1936), p. 128.

30. In C. E. M. Joad, *God and Evil* (Harper & Row, 1943), p. 3.

31. Romans 8:28.

32. II Corinthians 4:18 (KJV).

33. Concluding passage of Book IX, W. H. D. Rouse, trans.

34. William Ernest Hocking, *The Meaning of God in Human Experience* (Yale University Press, 1912), p. 57.

35. Alfred North Whitehead, *Religion in the Making* (Macmillan, 1927), p. 4.

36. *Ibid.*, p. 15.

37. Gerhard Lenski and others, *The Religious Factor* (Doubleday, 1961), p. 298.

38. Milton Yinger, *Religion, Society and the Individual* (Macmillan, 1957), p. 9.

39. *Ibid.*

40. In *Handbook* to his lectures on logic. For a discussion of these questions, see Martin Buber, *Between Man and Man* (Beacon Press, 1955), pp. 119 ff.

41. Hocking, *op. cit.*, p. 49.

42. Barth, *op. cit.*, p. 253.

43. Paul Carus, *The Gospel of Buddha* (Open Court, 1915), p. 16.

44. Swami Nikhilananda, trans. and ed., *The Gospel of Sri Ramakrishna* (Ramakrishna-Vivekananda Center, 1942), p. 736.

45. Henry Nelson Weiman in an unpublished lecture at the University of Puget Sound, 1948.

46. As against its currently narrower definition by philosophical analysts.

47. Leuba, *op. cit.*, p. 31.

# 3

# Religions in Space and Time

∻((∻((∻((∻((∻((∻((∻((∻((∻((∻((∻((∻((∻((∻((∻((∻((∻((∻((∻((∻((∻((∻((∻((∻((∻((∻((∻

Religions are institutions which everywhere and always arise; they possess both ubiquity and permanence. Search the dimmest human past or the most hidden corner of the earth and you will find this constant companion of man. This holds as well for the other basic human institutions: the family, government, language, art, and technology. Together with religion they form the complex constellation of human culture.

## PREHISTORY

At the dawn of time as man emerged still wet from the primordial sea of his infrahuman origins, there stirred in his newly equipped brain intimations of a mysterious portent that had never troubled his prehuman ancestors. The beginnings of religion, like the origin of the race, are lost in the mists of the most ancient past. Modern estimates suggest the high probability that man is at least a million years old, though the cultural remains of our antique cousins do not allow us to asertain what his culture might have been. Nonetheless we can hazard a safe guess that if he possessed the power of thought (and with his high brain case there is little doubt that he did), he must have felt in dim outline the existential questions that lie at the root of religious consciousness. Alone with his little family group, pitted against the mysterious forces that

41

lurk in the depths of nature, awed by the cycles of life both within and without, or grieved by the sight of his dead, he must have made those gestures of mind and body that we associate with religion. But it is not until we come to Neanderthal man, who flourished in Europe 100,000 to 25,000 years ago, that our evidence of religion becomes concrete. He left abundant witness to his faith. His graves give evidence of the dead buried ceremonially with implements and food offerings. His caves still betray the remnants of sacred bear skulls arranged on primitive stone altars that must have been the focus for group ritual.

In the next historical stratum, 25,000 years ago, Cro-Magnon man bequeathed the clearest evidence of his religiousness in paintings still so fresh and aesthetically rich that we stare today in astonishment at the achievements of those unknown priest-craftsmen. In the cave paintings of Trois Freres, Lascaux, Niaux, and Montespan we can still see the ancient priest in his mimic hunting dance guaranteeing success in the chase, and know the magical kinship which men felt with the animal world upon which they depended for food and life.

With neolithic man 10,000 to 3000 years before Christ, whose culture just precedes the great civilizations, the abundance and complexity of religious evidences increases geometrically. The scientific press reports nearly every week some new archaeological find: a votive figure such as the 6000-year-old mother goddess of Catal Huyuk (Turkey) or yoga figurines from an even earlier time in the valley of the Indus. Sometimes the evidence from prehistory comes to us as a vestigial survival. The historian of religion A. C. Bouquet recalls observing a deer-hunting dance performed by three Tibetans, which he recognized immediately as similar to dances he had seen in Scandinavia and in England; in the latter case, the antlers used in the dance were kept between times in the village church. Upon further reflection, Bouquet remembered seeing these dance patterns in the Pyrenees cave paintings, which date from 12,000 to 20,000 years ago. From these and similar data he concludes: "The truth is that even in the old Paleolithic a huge culture area extended from the Thames to the Cape, from the Atlantic to the Indies—nearly half the world . . . ."[1]

Such is the extent in space and time of man's prehistoric religion.

## FOSSIL RELIGIONS

Outside the centers of advanced civilization small groups of human beings practice what we today call primitive religions. Primitive is perhaps not the most appropriate word, because in their present state they show the complexity of long development. However, they lack certain characteristics that belong to the high religions of later times and have all the appearance of fossils out of the periods of prehistory that we have just described.

Though they are everywhere challenged by mortal enemies in encroaching modern civilizations, they still count their practitioners in the millions. In the middle of the twentieth century Africa leads the world in size of primitive populations with 75 million, Asia comes next with 45 million. South American Indians number about one million, North American about 50,000, and Australian aborigines about twice that number. The total comes to more than 121 million, spread, as we have seen, over all the continents except Europe.

In addition to possessing the qualities which in the previous chapter I indicated belong to religion as such, these fossil religions have certain other characteristics: The societies in which they appear all lack a written language, a fact which has led to their being called "preliterate" religions. This lack has profound consequences, one of the chief of which is the absence of any historical sense. They have no clear records of their antecedents. The past is embedded in the myths and rituals of the present, and these in turn are almost completely integrated into the customs and practices of the tribe. This supports a monolithic traditionalism that stands as an insuperable barrier to religious innovation. To be sure, there has been development over the thousands of years, but it has been the change effected by water dripping on stone.

In his celebrated descriptive work *Religion in Essence and Manifestation*,[2] the Dutch scholar G. van der Leeuw has given a fine account of the major features of religion, most of them already present at the primitive level of life and practice.

Primitive man, says van der Leeuw, feels himself confronted by the primordial power or powers underlying and producing all things and events. This confrontation awakens in him a sense of awe—the experience of the sacred. Already in primitive societies the formal embodiment of this sacred experience is well advanced. Religion thus takes the form of rituals, myths, formulas and prayers, and sacred social organization.

Elaborate rituals punctuate nearly every aspect of primitive life. Sacrifices, sacraments, and ceremonial dances are commonplace. Most of them are associated with two features of primitive society: the cycles of human development and the necessities of life. The former are the so-called *rites de passage*, rites connected with the critical moments of human existence: birth, puberty, marriage, death. The latter, associated with the demands of survival, center around the warding off of enemies and the guaranteeing of success in hunting, fishing, or planting. It is not surprising that these rituals take magical forms.

Myths are primitive man's creed and philosophy. They are sacred stories that satisfy his need for explanation and action at the same time. Telling a sacred story not only enlightens the mind, it also enhances and promotes action.

Sacred words, formulas, spells, and prayers are also common. They punctuate human activities, giving them their potency and hedging men against interference by dark powers.

Formalized religious functions give rise to sacred specialists, such as the medicine man and priest. It is the function of these persons to regulate and control the religious life of the community, thus guarding and promoting the welfare of the group.

All these aspects of religion are integrated into a social system in which each member of the tribe has his designated role, while the myths are harmonized into a kind of primitive metaphysic justifying the system itself.

Certain other primitive beliefs, though not all equally present in every society, are worth noting. Primitive man often believes in an impersonal nonnatural power to which anthropologists have given the name mana. He is also an animist; that is, he believes that things possess spirits which may aid or harm him. Both the spirits and mana may be influenced through religious rites or fetishes, artifacts presumed to have magical power and worn or owned by nearly all tribal members. One of the most important species of spirits comprises the souls of the dead. Primitive man's attitude toward them is ambivalent. Most often he makes sure through magical rites that they cannot return to the abode of the living, where they might do untold harm. Occasionally ancestors are worshipped as benign spirits and welcomed into the centers of habitation. One further belief, possibly a descendant from the religion of the cave painters, is totemism. According to this view, the members of a tribe are blood relatives or descendants of a species of animal or bird. Religious rites and taboos frequently celebrate the importance of this kinship.

## HISTORIC CULTURE-RELIGIONS

With the rise of the great cultures in the third and fourth millennia before Christ, religion also changed from primitive to a civilized form. In this early stage it remained identified with the cultural unit, just as primitive religion had been identified with the tribal unit. These religions arose with the civilization itself and, in turn, declined when the civilization perished, unless a transmutation occurred that gave rise to another species of religion. Such transmutations will be discussed later.

Because of their close identification with the cultures from which they arose, there was a strong tendency for religious and civic duties to coincide. The ancient Athenian, for example, did not distinguish between his loyalty to Athens and to Athena, and when Alcibiades, one of Socrates' more erratic pupils, committed sacrilege during a military expedition, he was capitally condemned for treason. Socrates' own condemnation and death (399 B.C.) was based on an indistinguishable mixture of religious and state charges.

### Dead Culture-Religions

To understand the dispersement of religions in space and time it is useful to distinguish culture-religions that have died through being displaced by a different species of religion from those that are still living in a form not too unlike that of their ancient existence.

The chief religions in the first class, roughly in order of their appearance, are the national religions of Egypt, Mesopotamia, Greece, and Rome.

Civilization developed first along the Fertile Crescent, an arc of land with Egypt at one end and Mesopotamia at the other. Egyptian religion very early developed out of the primitive stage of animism into an organized polytheism and a national code of ethics. The tendency for civilized life to gather together many tribes into a confederation is reflected in the amalgamation of one set of gods with another, resulting in a loosely organized pantheon. The chief gods of the Egyptian complex were Isis, Osiris, and Amon-Ra. Isis and Osiris were descendants of the fertility gods of the dim past. Amon-Ra was a sun god who was later transmuted into the god Aton whose worship inspired the finest hour of Egyptian religion: the monotheism of the pharaoh Ikhnaton, which in turn no doubt influenced Hebrew religious thought.

The newly discovered art of writing manifested itself in one of the earliest religious documents, the Book of the Dead. Egyptian religion, in fact, was all but wholly centered in a concern for the conquest of death, and the great monuments of that religion, which still impress the modern traveler, are the tombs of the great pharaohs.

Mesopotamian records are older than Egypt, and the religions of that area, at least in early antiquity, are not as clearly different from the primitive level. The Sumero-Akkadian pantheon, it is said, contained nearly 4000 deities, but with the passage of time the great Ishtar, a goddess of fertility, emerged into a prominent position, absorbing many lesser deities into her own person. Her maternal form can be seen in other cultures of the Near East under other names: Aphrodite in Greece, Venus in Rome, Anahita among the Zoroastrians, Kali in India, and Astarte among the Canaanites and Jews, whom the Hebrew prophets denounced for their apostasy.

The consort and rival to Ishtar was Marduk, the prototype of the male king of the gods, who also appears in other cultures as Zeus, Jove, and Varuna. Such unifications reflect the cultural fusions that went on for hundreds of years in the ancient kingdoms.

Greek religion is best known through the stories of the poet Homer, though his descriptions belong to a late stage of Greek polytheism when most of the gods had lost their power to arouse religious feeling, at least among the educated members of society.

Roman religion developed in its early stages (800 B.C.–200 B.C.) independently of Greece, but with the Roman conquest of Greek civilization the two religions merged into an indistinguishable amalgam.

The important thing is to grasp the characteristics of this stage in the history of religions. The culture-religions were, as I have said, identified with the needs of the societies in which they grew. They were extensions and amalgamations of the primitive religions which were on the ground when the civilized states arose. For this reason many primitive features still remained.

These can be summarized under three heads: They were conservative and traditional in that the innovating cultural forces, politics and economics, were largely nonreligious. Second, they were magical, largely preoccupied with such practices as astrological forecasts or with rites propitiating the gods of the various natural forces, such as the weather or fertility, or with ceremonies assuring protection from enemies. And, third, they were pluralistic in spite of the relative unifications of the pantheons.

### Surviving Culture-Religions

The religions we have been discussing have perished, but some culture-religions have survived into the present day. The chief representatives of this group are certain sects of Hinduism and Japanese Shinto. Shinto is the better example because Hinduism has been somewhat purified of its culture-religion characteristics by later reform movements. Except where Shinto has amalgamated with Buddhism it still represents a religion identified with a national culture, and its rites and rituals are all focused on national tradition and the local ethnic group.

### The Revival of Culture-Religions

One of the features of modern religion is the tension between universal faiths and the natural human desire for a more comfortable local religion, one that achieves personal and social peace by cutting the nerve of conflict between loyalty to local cultural groups (like national states) and loyalty to universal religious obligations, in favor of the former. This conflict appears in each of the world religions as it struggles to emerge from the cocoon of local culture into a wider consciousness. The intense national rivalries of the modern period favor a retreat from the global claims of such religions as Christianity, Buddhism, or Islam in favor of a national cult that interprets these faiths in local categories. This fact will concern us again in later chapters.

### THE AXIAL AGE

As we move into an account of the next era of religious history we can begin to see some patterns emerging from the data. Modern scholarship justifies dividing the history of man's religions into the following epochs:

Prehistory (up to 4000 B.C.)
The age of ancient Culture-Religions (4000 B.C.–A.D. 300)
The Axial Age (1000 B.C. to A.D. 100)
The Period of Incubation (up to about A.D. 1900)
The Global Age (1900 A.D. to the present time)

The first two epochs have been discussed. The axial age, a name given the third epoch by the philosopher Karl Jaspers because it is an axis upon which turns a major change in human religious consciousness, broke into history during the first millennium before Christ. During this period the great universal religions, Buddhism and Christianity, emerged.

The period of incubation represents the period of time during which the great religious traditions remained in relative isolation from one another, developing their own unique characteristics. This age lasted until the end of the nineteenth century, when the first tender shoots of a global consciousness began to show above the surface of history; its breakup was foreshadowed in the sixteenth-century voyages of exploration.

The present century, the global age, is the flowering of the great outward movements that began in the sixteenth century and that forced all the great religious traditions, formerly in relative isolation, into increasing contact and dialogue with one another. We have yet to see the fruit of this flowering.

The axial age now deserves to be described in some detail. During the first millennium before Christ, simultaneously, and as if by spontaneous combustion, in a half-dozen widely separated cultures stretching from Hellas to the Yellow Sea, a major shift in human religious consciousness occurred. This change first showed itself in individuals who stood outside the prevailing pattern of life and questioned whether it was really the best. As their new consciousness of a standard no longer derived from the traditions of an unquestioned past spread to their followers, the great religious faiths arose, which even today, nearly 3000 years later, show no signs of being surpassed by newcomers on the stage of history.

The major differences between axial religion and preaxial religion are briefly these: Preaxial religion was culture-religion whereas axial religion generally made appeals to transcultural truths rooted in a universal ontology or theory of being. Preaxial religion, moreover, was heavily infused with magic and was correspondingly ritualistic, whereas axial religion emphasized the primacy of ethics and universal human obligations. Preaxial religion included as its members only the ethnic group; axial religion was in principle universal, transcending social groupings of all kinds. Preaxial religion regarded the ultimate mystery as pluralistic, worshiping many gods and powers; axial religion tended toward either monotheism or monism in some form or other, unifying the sacred powers and significances of the world. Preaxial religion was heavily larded with sacred taboo; axial religion tended to break down the distinctions of sacred and nonsacred by universalizing the sacred. In this way traditional priesthoods and geographically restricted worship were challenged in a totally unexpected way. Another major feature of preaxial religion was propitiatory sacrifice to many deities; axial religion displaced this by making inner attitudes and moral self-sacrifice primary.

Only an extensive history of the period could detail all these changes, but a brief account can suggest something of the breath-taking character of the changes that this period initiated.

*Greece.* The axial age in Hellas is associated chiefly with the person of

Socrates (d. 399 B.C.), who believed himself called by the Delphic Oracle to examine freely the religious beliefs and practices of his day with the newly evolved tool of philosophic reasoning. "The classical axial age for Europe," writes A. C. Bouquet, "still remains the age of Socrates [and his disciples], Plato, Aristotle, and the Stoics. Their pioneer work has indeed shaped the thought of educated Europe ever since, and has even inspired, by its freedom and independence, and by insistence upon observed fact, the later work of empirical scientists."[3]

*Israel.* In the middle of the eighth century B.C. Amos, a herdsman, appeared as a prophet of God at the sacred shrine of Bethel in southern Israel to announce the theme of divine justice. He was followed by a remarkable series of great individuals whom we call the Hebrew prophets. The greatest among this select band were Hosea, Micah, Isaiah, Deutero-Isaiah, and Jeremiah. These men denounced the preaxial religion practiced in their day, often appealing to Moses (*ca.* 1250 B.C.) a lawgiver of the more distant past who had first announced the themes of this new faith. Scholars are also wont to trace some of these new ideas to a time even earlier than Moses, to unsuccessful reforms that took place in Egypt under the religious pharaoh Ikhnaton. His monotheistic "Hymn to the Sun" is echoed in the Hebrew Psalms.

*Iran.* Contemporaneously with the Hebrew prophets, in the seventh century B.C., Iran produced Zoroaster (later called Zarathustra). He taught a dualistic moral religion of light in struggle with darkness. He called his people to a rigorous ethic of honest labor and social justice. This prophet, whose religion was named after him, is still revered by the modern Parsees of India.

*India.* The axial age produced four major groups of leaders in India. The greatest was unquestionably Gautama, known as the Buddha, meaning "the Enlightened One." In the middle of the fifth century B.C., about the time of the birth of Socrates and the unknown prophet of the Hebrew exile, he broke from the religion of his fathers and taught what he called the Middle Way of high ethical endeavor and disciplined interior contemplation.

Somewhat earlier than Gautama, the sages of the Indian forests had protested the Brahmanical religion of rites and rituals by teaching a religion of discriminating contemplation that would lead to release through inner illumination. The writings of these unknown sages constitute one of the sublimest collections in religious literature, the Upanishads.

Almost contemporary with Gautama Buddha, another Indian, Mahavira, also protested the religion of his culture and founded the religion known as Jainism.

The high-caste Brahmans had lost in each of these reforms, because they were the chief bearers of the traditional religion of India. When the spirit of reform threatened to sweep their faith away, they responded with the religion of the Bhagavad-Gita. This best-loved and most widely known classic of Indian piety moved traditional Brahmanical religion into the column of axial religions.

*China.* The axial age appears in China during the sixth century B.C. in the person of Confucius and in the rival philosophy of Taoism with which the legendary name of Lao-tzu (*ca.* 640–531 B.C.) is associated. Scholars debate the place of Confucius in this axial history on the ground that he taught a feudal traditionalism. But at the base of his teaching was an appeal to a moral order which transcended time and place and was rooted in the nature of things. In this sense he was at one with the Taoists who rejected what they believed to be the undue formalism of Confucius' teaching in favor of a more "natural" life based upon the universal Tao. Both of these philosophies taught a universal ethic for "man-at-his-best" and sought the reform of both religion and the state.

## Later Phases of the Axial Age

Christianity emerged from Judaism during the first century of our era. It carried forward themes already announced in prophetic Judaism and proclaimed a religion of universal salvation through Jesus Christ. Its major literary record, the New Testament, was completed by about A.D. 100, a date that corresponds to the codification of Judaism by the Council of Jamnia, a move that prepared the Jews for a life outside their homeland.

Mahayana Buddhism, an important development from early Theravada Buddhism, emerged at about the same time, and mounted a religious enthusiasm that eventually carried missionaries into Tibet, China, and on to Japan. Zen Buddhism, a later (twelfth century A.D.) Japanese variant, sprang up as a by-product of this movement when it found a happy marriage with Chinese Taoism, which had reached the pinnacle of its development in the great teacher Chuang-tzu (? fourth century B.C.).

Vedantic Hinduism also emerged late under the great reformers Shankara (ninth century A.D.) and Ramanuja (twelfth century A.D.). This movement established a universal form of Hinduism which is today bidding for adherents in the West.

The last of the great religions to emerge was Islam. Due no doubt to the backward state of Arabian culture, this child of the axial age, born as it were out of season, appeared in the eighth century of our era.

## Postaxial Development

After an initial period of consolidation and expansion, each of these great religions settled into its own geographical region and became associated with the culture of that area. This period of incubation lasted in most cases for more than a thousand years. The specific characteristics of each religion became more and more clearly defined and expressed in the institutions of their respective cultures, so that today we can speak meaningfully of Islamic, Buddhist, or Christian culture.

## THE RISE OF THE GLOBAL AGE

Beginning with the European explorations of the sixteenth century, the cocoons of culture began to break open. For many reasons, political, economic, and ideological as well as religious, the world slowly began to become a single sphere of human action. We live today in the midst of the most strenuous movements of men and events toward some kind of global civilization in which, we may hope, the great religions will find the happiest expression of their true natures.

This brief history raises many questions, but one of the most significant is, Why did these religions emerge? What made the axial age?

## WHY THE AXIAL AGE?

No doubt in the intellectual climate of our day some kind of sociocultural explanation will seem the most plausible account of the rise of the axial age. Just as the earlier consolidation of gods into unified pantheons occurred under the political and social unification of kingdoms, so the new religions of the axial age may be regarded from one point of view as reflections of sociocultural developments that required a new social consciousness. This is plausible. However, it has a fatal flaw: The new religious consciousness is largely critical of social conditions and appeals beyond culture to transcultural norms whose significance can be fully appreciated only now in a global age.

Culture no doubt gave a stimulus to deeper reflection, but the truths which the great seers and prophets propounded were not confined to the situations in which they lived. Amos was a herdsman in a small Middle Eastern kingdom, yet he announced a vision of world justice. The same can be said of Zoroaster. The Buddha lived in a small kingdom of northern India, but his faith became the inspiration for societies as far away as Japan. The religion of Jesus, formulated in an unimportant backwater of the Roman Empire, now finds adherents in every country in the world.

The universal theme of these religions, despite the fact that they bear the marks of their cultural origins, is an appeal above culture to a reality which it is claimed can be the only basis of true culture.

If sociocultural explanations seem inadequate, then what? The answer must be drawn from some source other than history. It depends upon one's own metaphysical perspective. From a Judaeo-Christian point of view this epoch has all the appearance of a supernatural work: God initiating the changes in human consciousness necessary to his own mysterious, if not wholly inscrutable, purposes.

## THE PRESENT GEOGRAPHICAL
## DISTRIBUTION OF RELIGIONS

In the middle of the twentieth century, on the eve of the greatest dialogue between religions that the world has ever known, the living religions are deployed geographically as follows:[4]

The Christian faith, with nearly a billion adherents, has spread to every continent. Though still concentrated in the western hemisphere and Europe (800 million), there are 50 million in Asia, 305 million in Africa, and 11 million in Australasia. Of these 550 million are Roman Catholic, 217 million Protestant, 137 million Eastern Orthodox.

Since the monstrous genocide of Jews during the Nazi nightmare, their greatest concentration is in North America (6 million), with nearly 4 million in Europe, and 2.5 million scattered through Asia, Africa, and Australasia.

The Moslem faith flourishes in a broad band running from the Atlantic coast of North Africa across that continent, through the Near East and the Tigris and Euphrates valley to northern India. Farther east there are Moslem cultures in Indonesia and other islands off the southern coast of Asia, reaching to the Philippines and other islands of the South Seas. Their major concentrations are in Asia (331 million) and Africa (89 million), with Europe coming next with nearly 13 million. About half a million are scattered throughout the other continents.

Buddhism fanned out east from India, the land of its birth (where it has few adherents at present), reaching Tibet in the north, Ceylon and Malaya in the south, and Japan in the east. Its major concentration is thus in Asia, where all but a few thousand of its 153 million adherents live.

Confucianism still flourishes mainly in China, the land of its birth, and in Japan, where it fused with Buddhism and Shinto. Its adherents are numbered at 300 million. Hinduism also has remained chiefly in its homeland, India (335 million), with nearly two thirds of a million in Africa and half that many in South America.

There are still more than 120 million human beings in primitive societies where the religion can be classified chiefly as animistic. These, as I have said, are spread over the world but mainly concentrated in Africa, South America, and Asia.

At the latest estimate, about 500 million human beings remain after the count of those adhering to the major religions; some of these are adherents of no faith, but most of them are members of small groups that are not separately counted.

Such is the number and distribution of the living religions in the latter half of the twentieth century.

## HOW MAY WE CLASSIFY RELIGIONS?

Sound systems of classification help to reduce the great mass of historical data to manageable terms. But care must be exercised in the choice of categories, because every structuring of the data is to some extent a distortion, focusing on some features of the religions and making others obscure.

The tale just told, the history of religions from paleolithic times to the present, is itself an essay in classification, using historical criteria.

The most popular category for the classification of religion employing the concept of evolutionary development emerged in the nineteenth century. Considering the popularity of evolution as a hypothesis both in biology and social thought, this is understandable. However, recent sober second thoughts have led to the conclusion that evolution conceived as a straight-line development unduly distorts the subject matter of religion. One source of doubt has been the discovery of the most exalted religious ideas among primitive peoples, ideas that on this theory ought to appear only at the end of a long development.

An instance of this is the curious phenomenon of the primitive "high gods." Nearly all primitive groups, it seems, have a belief in one god whose status is radically different from that of all other deities. Their myths refer to this god as the originator, directly or indirectly, of everything that exists. However, popular religion does not traffic with this god except in unusual cases of disaster or extreme tribal need. As Mircea Eliade says, "This god has isolated himself from men, is indifferent to the affairs of the world."[5] He writes this of the god Puluga of the Andaman Islanders, but it applies to the gods of other primitive cultures as well. "Everywhere," he says, "the celestial supreme appears to have lost religious currency."[6]

But when disaster strikes, the lesser deities prove to be inadequate. To quote Eliade again, "Their worshippers . . . had the feeling that all these great goddesses and all these vegetation gods were unable to save them . . . in really critical moments."[7] The history of the Hebrews is an instructive example. "Each time that the ancient Hebrews experienced a period of peace and prosperity," Eliade says, "they abandoned Yahweh for the Baals and Astartes of their neighbors. Only historical catastrophes forced them to turn to Yahweh."[8]

Another fact that puts a simple evolutionary method of classification in doubt is that the great thinkers of the axial period often harkened back to themes that had been announced much earlier. The Hebrew prophets referred to Moses, and St. Paul goes back nearly 2000 years, to Abraham, to find a pure example of faith. Confucius claimed to be only an editor and purifier of an ancient tradition, and the Buddha's teaching likewise depends heavily upon more ancient Indian lore. Thus each line we draw must be qualified by many important exceptions.

I have postulated two major transformations in the history of religions: the shift from primitive to civilized religion and the leap from civilized to axial religion. We now must accept the fact that even the second period had important primitive antecedents.

One of the mistaken moves in evolutionary theory was to overintellectualize religion, to think of it chiefly in terms of its conceptual content. From this perspective there is no question but that Jeremiah, say, who flourished in the sixth century B.C., was much more advanced than Abraham, who lived a thousand years earlier. Abraham, we may suppose, had no knowledge of Jeremiah's theological conceptions of a God who was the Creator of heaven and earth and the Lord of universal history. But Abraham was a "friend of God" and an obedient servant of His will. What he knew existentially was no doubt fundamentally at one with what Jeremiah knew. In short, we can say that the idea of God evolved, but it is not quite correct to say that the experience of God evolved. Of course, experiences did change, but evolution is probably not the best word for that change, and certainly it is false to think that as in science the latest religious theory is likely to be the best. There is no reason to suppose, for example, that Buddhism will ever supersede Gautama or that Christianity will ever surpass Jesus or St. Paul.

Better than the idea of development seems to be the concept of the key experience or symbolic event, such as the enlightenment of Gautama or the crucifixion and resurrection of Jesus. After these occur, the maturation of a religion seems to be a working out of the significance implicit in the key event itself.

There is, furthermore, no evidence that any postaxial religion is in any significant sense of a higher order than the original religions of the axial age. Refinements, applications, and clarifications, yes, but no greater depth, no higher purity of spirit, and no greater power of expression or appeal.

With these provisos in mind, it is interesting to consider the historian A. C. Bouquet's rough outline of the main development of the human conceptions of what he calls the "Self-Existent" through human history: *Stage One:* Animatism: Belief in "a vague, potent, terrifying, inscrutable force which manifests itself in varying degrees with unequal potency in all types of phenomena, meteorites, bull-roarers, rocks, trees, water-falls, lightning, wild beasts, blood, eclipses, old women, women in certain conditions of sexual life, epileptics and so on."[9] *Stage Two:* Pluralistic personalism: A vast number of tricky and capricious spirits emerge from the impersonal background of impersonal mana. *Stage Three:* Polytheism: The supernatural forces have become unified into gods and goddesses with specialized functions usually within a hierarchy of some sort. *Stage Four:* Unification: The Self-Existent is conceived as One in terms of some kind of pantheism, theism, or deism.

If one is prepared to accept the qualification that this development is not simply in a straight line, something like this seems to have occurred in the history of man's religions.

From a somewhat different point of view, the historian Arnold Toynbee[10] suggests that mankind's religious quest has been for an Ultimate Being worthy of worship; that is, for an ultimate concern which would be truly ultimate. He traces religious worship through five stages (not necessarily chronological, since "earlier," less advanced stages often supervene "later," more advanced stages): (1) The worship of nature in various forms. (2) The worship of communities, the local group or culture. (3) The worship of "ecumenical communities"—the vast superstates that emerge in the late periods of civilization. The Roman Empire was such an ecumenical community. (4) The worship of man in the form of a universal humanism. (5) The worship of a Self-Existent beyond man, culture, and nature. This last form of worship emerged with the epiphany of the higher religions during the axial period, but it has still not become broadly acceptable to mankind which still remains largely at one of the earlier stages of religious development. What Toynbee regards as "idolatry," the worship of something less than the truly ultimate, is a recurring phenomenon in human history, the latest being the "idolization of the invincible technician."

Two other classificatory systems are worth mentioning.[11] The first is based upon the interplay of divine transcendence and immanence. John Hutchison suggests that the Supreme may be located (1) within the common world of nature and culture, (2) above and beyond that world, or (3) dialectically within and above.[12]

In the first type, the gods or god are found within the common world, either as projections of nature or humanity, or of both. Modern humanism is an example of this type, as are the ancient nature-religions. Vedantic Hinduism and Buddhism are cases of the second type, where the supreme is located "beyond" the common world of nature and culture. Christianity, with its doctrines of a supreme and exalted Creator, a historically incarnated Son, and a continuously present Spirit, is an example of the third type.

The last system of classification I shall mention is that used by Charles Morris in his *Paths of Life*.[13] He suggests that we may examine religions by comparing their conceptions of the ideal human being; for example, the Hebrew ideal of the righteous man, the Shinto-Buddhist ideal of the disciplined warrior, or the Hindu ideal of the detached ascetic. Properly used, this method can be very illuminating.

We have looked at the dispersement of religions in space and time. The survey has been admittedly sketchy. It has left out many of the details that make up the concrete life of the religions and without which it is often hard to see how they make sense. But my purpose has not been to survey the world's religions—this has been admirably done by others—but to establish a historical framework for the rest of this study.

In the next section the account of Asian religion is expanded by introducing three great classics of Eastern piety. All three are so brief as to be read easily in an evening, yet each one contains wisdom enough for a lifetime's contemplation: from Hinduism, the Bhagavad-Gita; from Buddhism, the Dhammapada; and from Chinese Taoism, the Tao Tê Ching.

A reading of these short works will enable us to encompass the essence of three great religious traditions without extensive historical surveys, and will supply a contrasting background for the rest of the book, which concentrates chiefly on the religious concerns of the West. Such contrasts help to deepen one's understanding of the faiths that are nearer and more familiar as well to broaden a man's sympathies, enabling him to enter the dialogue of faiths which is one of the major characteristics of the emerging world civilization.

## SUGGESTIONS FOR FURTHER READING

*Man's Religions*, 3rd ed. (Macmillan 1963), by John B. Noss, is one of the best standard histories of religions. Three philosophically oriented studies are A. E. Burtt, *Man Seeks the Divine* (Harper & Row, 1957); Frederic Spiegelberg, *Living Religions of the World* (Prentice-Hall, 1956); and Huston Smith, *The Religions of Man* (Harper & Row, 1958; New American Library, 1963). The last-named book is probably the one that would appeal most to the beginner in this field. Spiegelberg's work is neo-Oriental in outlook.

Two good books that emphasize the comparative approach to the world's religions are A. C. Bouquet, *Comparative Religion*, rev. ed. (Penguin, 1950), and Mircea Eliade, *Patterns in Comparative Religion* (Meridian, World Publishing, 1963).

Three inexpensive collections of the sacred writings of the world's religions are A. C. Bouquet's companion to his comparative study, *Sacred Books of the World* (Penguin, 1954); Robert O. Ballou, *World Bible* (Viking, 1944); and Lin Yutang, ed., *The Wisdom of China and India* (Random House, 1942; Modern Library, 1955).

## NOTES

1. A. C. Bouquet, *Comparative Religion*, 3rd and rev. ed. (Penguin, 1950), p. 31.
2. G. van der Leeuw, *Religion in Essence and Manifestation*, 2 vols. (Harper & Row, 1963).
3. A. C. Bouquet, *op. cit.*, p. 87.
4. According to *The World Almanac*, 1964. A later estimate by a German Protestant research office in Hamburg, Germany, places the world population of Christians at 877 million, which is 29.23 percent of the world population; 500 million of these are Roman Catholics; 256 million, Protestants; 98 million, Eastern Orthodox; 24 million, other confessions. Other statistics (in millions) are as follows: 13 Jews, 427 Muslims, 300 Confucianists, 190 Buddhists, 30 Taoists, 150 primitive religion, and

591 either belonging to other classifications or having no religion (*Die Welt,* October 27, 1965).

5. Mircea Eliade, *The Sacred and the Profane* (Harper & Row, 1961), p. 123.

6. *Ibid.,* p. 125.

7. *Ibid.,* p. 127.

8. *Ibid.,* p. 126.

9. Bouquet, *op. cit.,* pp. 46–47.

10. Arnold Toynbee, *An Historian's Approach to Religion* (Oxford University Press, 1956).

11. Van der Leeuw also has a valuable classification of religions in *op. cit.,* pp. 597–647.

12. John A. Hutchison, *Language and Faith* (Westminster, 1963), p. 252.

13. Charles Morris, *Paths of Life* (Braziller, 1956).

## PART TWO

# THREE CLASSICS
# OF ASIAN RELIGION

# 4

# *Hinduism*
# *and the Bhagavad-Gita*

"There is no more absorbing story," writes Mircea Eliade, "than that of the discovery and interpretation of India by Western consciousness."[1] When the first Indian documents came into the hands of Western scholars they were received with boundless enthusiasm. Max Müller (1823–1900), one of the greatest of the Indologists, expressed the common mood: "If I were asked under what sky the human mind . . . has most deeply pondered over the greatest problems of life, and has found solutions of some of them which well deserve the attention even of those who have studied Plato and Kant—I should point to India."[2] Arnold Toynbee has even predicted that in the hegemony of the twenty-first century it is possible that "India the conquered will conquer its conquerors."[3]

Hinduism is a good place for the student who is unfamiliar with religions other than his own to begin, for its Oriental flavor is in such striking contrast to the Semitic quality common to those religions that originated at the eastern end of the Mediterranean—Christianity, Islam, and Judaism. An encounter with a religion of such qualitative differences can broaden sympathies and sharpen critical powers. It enables us to see that there are other venerable and profound faiths than those which permeate our own culture.

## HINDUISM AND THE WEST

Hinduism's contact with the West began with the advent of Western missionaries and colonial powers in India. Contrary to the prevailing view, the

59

latter were hostile to the introduction of Western religion into the field of their exploitations and made life miserable for the emissaries of the Christian faith.

The first reaction of Indian pundits to Christianity was one of acceptance. They embraced Christianity as a superior faith. Hinduism at the time was in a moribund state in which the authentic wisdom of India was completely concealed in degenerate customs. Swami Ranganathanadna says of this period: "Hindu religion itself had fallen on evil days. The pure religion of the Upanishads and the Gita had degenerated into meaningless formalism; superstition was rampant."[4]

The second phase of the Indian reaction came with the uncovering of those treasures. To their surprise they discovered that India has a tradition of wisdom that deserved the attention of the world. In time they became convinced that they had a religion equal in antiquity and profundity to that of the missionaries. This phase also proved to be transitional, leading to the present-day claim that Hinduism is superior to Western religion. From this stance Christianity and its Semitic counterparts, Judaism and Islam, appear to be inferior forms of spirituality. It is not difficult to find Western scholars who share this view.[5] A suspicion that this may be true has even showed itself in the consciousness of many Western Christians. The world reputation of the late Mahatma Gandhi no doubt contributed very substantially to this opinion, though it is doubtful that he should be regarded as the product of pure Hinduism. He is better viewed as a child of the encounter between Hinduism and Christianity, not belonging exclusively to either.

## A SHORT HISTORY OF HINDUISM THROUGH ITS SACRED LITERATURE[6]

The history of Hinduism can be traced in the successive layers of religious documents that now comprise the sacred scriptures of that faith. The dates, though approximations, are good enough for our purposes.

*The Rig-Veda* (1500–900 B.C.). The native Dravidian religion of India prior to 1500 B.C. is still unclear to us. Hinduism as a historical religious phenomenon begins with the great texts of its earliest scriptures, the Rig-Veda, a collection of more than a thousand lyrics formally similar in some ways to the Hebrew Psalms. These boisterous and life-affirming devotional songs disclose the religion of the so-called Aryan invaders who swept into India during the second millennium before Christ.

*The Brahmanas* (1000–800 B.C.). After the domestication of the invaders, a change occurred in the religious mood. The more prosaic Brahmanas justify the status of a priestly class which had risen to power and which has stayed at the pinnacle of the Hindu caste system to the present day, the longest-lived class structure in the history of mankind. These documents are chiefly instructions for the highly formalized rituals that characterized the religion of this period.

*The Upanishads* (800–600 B.C.).   The Upanishads represent a rebellion against the priestly monopoly of the preceding period, a kind of Protestant reformation directed against the ecclesiastical rigidity of the Brahmans. These profound philosophical poems were the work of forest sages who proposed an alternative to salvation through rites and rituals. In substance they proposed that salvation comes to the man who realizes inwardly who he really is. They taught that reality is essentially an all-embracing Oneness which has been fragmented into the illusion of multiplicity by the ignorance of the human mind. Through careful analysis and meditation this ignorance can be abated. The message of the Upanishads can be summarized as follows: Whoever knows "I am Brahman" becomes one with this All.[7]

*The Laws of Manu* (about 250 B.C.).   The rebellion of the Upanishads was eventually absorbed into the structure of Hindu thought and the entire social system was codified in the celebrated Laws of Manu. A biblical parallel can be found in the codification of the Law of Moses in Israel. Manu defined the caste system, which we will discuss later, and gave definitive form to the four *asramas*, or stages of life, which synthesized the life of ritual and the life of meditation. The first stage is that of the youthful student who is introduced to both the sacred and secular lore of his culture. This is followed by the stage of the householder who earns his living and rears his family to maturity. During this stage he faithfully follows the ritual formalities of Brahmanism. In the third stage he becomes a student again as a retired hermit. Here he learns to meditate upon the deeper wisdom of his religion, and if he succeeds in penetrating its esoteric depths he emerges into the fourth stage as a wandering ascetic who has broken all ties with the world. As Albert Schweitzer has pointed out, this arrangement goes beyond the view of the Upanishads and makes heavy concessions to the value of life in the world, legitimizing family life and work in the householder stage. But its final goal is nevertheless a rejection of the world for a deeper wisdom that lies beyond in a state of unconditioned freedom.

*Devotional Hinduism—the Bhagavad-Gita, the Epics, and the Puranas* (200 B.C. to A.D. 250).   Popular religious needs were not satisfied by either ritualistic Brahmanism or the philosophic religion of the Upanishads. The gods of popular religion come now to the fore in the sacred literature, the greatest example of which is the Bhagavad-Gita which we shall discuss below in some detail. Religious writings (*Puranas*) proliferated innumerable stories of the gods, and religious devotion took the form of worship of these gods, many of whom assumed the forms of animals and men. This phase produced the veritable jungle of gods, beliefs, rites, and rituals which all observers of Hindu spirituality have described for us.

In our quest for an understanding of Hindu spirituality we can do no better than to examine the Bhagavad-Gita in some detail. It is not only the most compact statement of the basic concepts of Hindu religion; it is likewise the most popular among both Indians and Westerners. Gandhi revered it as the greatest document of faith, and nearly every Indian sect appeals to it as authority for its own creed. "The Bhagavad-Gita," writes Eliade, "represents . . . the highest point of all Indian spirituality."[8]

Albert Schweitzer says that its early appeal to European thinkers is due to the fact that it is the first life-affirming mysticism to stand in opposition to the tradition of world-denying medieval mysticism with which alone Europe was familiar at the time.[9] Another characteristic of the Bhagavad-Gita also appealed to the European consciousness: The central character of the work is the God-man, Krishna, thus echoing the incarnational theme of the Christian Gospels.

### The Battlefield of Kurukshetra

The Bhagavad-Gita opens on a battlefield with the armies of the Pandavas arrayed against the Kurus. This crisis was the culmination of a long struggle between the two royal houses of Pandu and Dhritarashtra. The Bhagavad-Gita is the sixth canto of India's favorite epic, the Mahabharata, in which the story of this struggle is recounted.

Arjuna, the champion of the Pandavas, rides out in his chariot, driven by Krishna, his friends and charioteer, to survey the battlefield. When he sees the assembled enemy, "grandfathers, fathers-in-law, uncles, brothers and cousins, his own sons and their sons, and grandsons, comrades, teachers, and friends" (1:26),* he confesses to Krishna that he has lost his will to fight. ". . . I do not wish to kill," he says, "even though I am killed by them . . ." (1:35). "Alas!" he complains, "what a great sin we resolved to incur, being prepared to slay our kinsmen, actuated by greed of kingdom and pleasure." (1:45). As Arjuna sinks to the floor of the chariot, overwhelmed by sorrow, Krishna, the charioteer, who has by now revealed himself as an incarnation of God himself, begins to instruct him, and not him alone, but any man who will harken to his words. Arjuna's paralysis of indecision is a common human condition that can be remedied only by the wisdom which reveals the ultimate meaning of the human situation and gives each man's life a valid orientation. Krishna's words to Arjuna on the meaning of human life and action lay bare the heart of the Hindu faith.

### The Meaning of Caste and Duty (Dharma)

Krishna explains that it is Arjuna's duty as a member of the warrior caste to wage war. Krishna is himself the author of the caste system with its fourfold scheme of *Brahman* (priest), *Kshatriya* (warrior), *Vaisya* (merchant-artisan),

---

* Numbers in parentheses refer to chapter and verse of the Bhagavad-Gita, translated by Swami Paramananda, in Lin Yutang, ed., *The Wisdom of China and India*, pp. 57–114.

and *Sudra* (unskilled worker). The whole social system is summed up in this sacred hereditary scheme. "The fourfold caste," he says, "was created by Me . . ." (4:13).

What is caste? So intricately is it woven into the texture of the Hindu scheme of values that some writers have gone so far as to say, "Hinduism is caste." Blunt writes of caste: "From the cradle to the grave caste custom regulates . . . every action, almost every movement. It governs [a man's] relations alike to God and man and gives shape to his environment, whether social or religious."[10] It has three characteristics: (1) heredity: everyone stays in the caste into which he is born; (2) endogamy: there is no marriage out of caste; (3) restrictions on commensality: very rigid rules are prescribed concerning the people with whom a given caste member may eat.

The original four hereditary castes have given birth in the course of history to many other kinds of caste: functional castes based upon occupation; tribal or racial castes; sectarian castes and castes of people united by some common beliefs; hill castes; outlaw castes; and, finally, the outcastes, or pariahs, who have fallen to the lowest level through violation of caste regulations. Each of the great religious divergences from basic Hinduism—Jainism, Sikhism, Christianity, Islam—have in turn become special castes within the Hindu social system.

It was to this system that Krishna pointed in reminding Arjuna of his duty as a member of the warrior caste. According to its regulations, a man's duty is identified with the tasks and responsibilities of the caste into which he is born, duties which, as Krishna says, are "born of their nature" (18:43). The Hindu word for this is *dharma*.

The first stage of Krishna's advice, then, is to remind Arjuna of the sacred social system to which he belongs and his specific class role in it. Western thinkers find difficulties in this solution. They complain that it is incurably traditional and incapable of fitting into the highly mobile social structure of modern society. Another difficulty is that its ethical system seems exclusively social in its sanctions, not firmly related to ultimate principles. It is to this problem that Krishna now addresses himself: What appeal beyond society can be offered as a sanction for conduct?

To answer this question it is necessary to look at the whole scheme of Hindu faith. No one part of a religion makes much sense out of context. Our problem, then, becomes one of examining the major concepts—what Eliade calls the "kinetic ideas"—of Hinduism.[11]

### The Nature of the True Self

Having reminded Arjuna of his caste duty, Krishna turns now to the nature of human selfhood. The true Self, he says, is not the visible body; it is the "dweller in the body," and this dweller is "ever indestructible" (2:30). "These bodies," he says, pointing to the assembled armies, "are perishable; but the dwellers in these bodies are eternal, indestructible and impenetrable"

(2:18). From this the Lord concludes: "Therefore . . . arise and be resolved to fight" (2:37). Death is nothing, the Real cannot be destroyed.

The reason for the eternal character of the Self is that it is one with the eternal principle of Reality itself, namely, Brahman, or as we would say in Semitic religion, God. This is the great principle of the Upanishads re-affirmed: ". . . all creatures are unmanifested in the beginning, manifested in their middle state, unmanifested again in the end" (2:28). Krishna will return later to the nature of the ultimate Brahman that lies at the root of all true selfhood. For the present, he is content to remind Arjuna of his own nature as an eternal Self appearing and reappearing in time as an incarnate self. He tells Arjuna: "As a man casts off worn-out garments and puts on others which are new, similarly the embodied soul, casting off worn-out bodies, enters into others which are new" (2:22). This is the classical Indian doctrine of reincarnation.

## REINCARNATION AND KARMA

This doctrine was firmly established very early in Hindu thought and is a key concept in the system. It is related to a companion concept, *karma*. Karma is the doctrine that the universe keeps books; there is a law of cause and effect: Every action leads to an equal reaction. In a secondary sense, one's karma is the accumulated causality that has yet to expend itself in some form of existence. Every deed accumulates karma that requires to be discharged. This discharge may take place in the present life, but much of it is left over and remains to be expended in a future embodiment.

There is good karma—the result of good deeds—and bad karma—the result of evil deeds. Karma is related to the social system in the following way: If a man fulfills his dharma (his caste obligations) faithfully, he will be rewarded by a better life next time; evil deeds are requited in the opposite way. Thus the caste system receives its justification. The higher castes are made up of those who have earned a good embodiment; the lower castes likewise deserve their less fortunate fate.

Hindu spirituality regards this wheel of rebirth as something to be ulti-mately surpassed. A high birth is not the summit of spiritual achievement; the summit lies outside the system of births in an entirely different dimension. To escape rebirth is the goal of those who know the truth about life.

### The Goal: Self-Realization and Release (Moksha)

Self-realization is rare. The Lord Krishna says, "Among thousands of human beings, scarcely one strives for perfection; and among (the thousands of) faithful strivers after perfection, scarcely one knows Me in truth" (7:3). But the effect of this is softened by the fact that each person has innumerable lives—perhaps millions of them—in which to come to this high state. When the "great-souled ones" have reached the goal they "do not come to re-birth, the ever-changing abode of misery," says Krishna, "for they have attained the highest perfection" (8:15). Those who have arrived at this state are somehow fused, or joined, to the "Unmanifested, which is eternally existent . . ." (8:20).

This is the state of release, *moksha*. It is not a new existence in heaven or some other determinative state. It is beyond existence. This state, we are reminded over and over again by Indian commentators, is not one about which we can either affirm anything or deny anything; it is beyond all our concepts and all our words. "That which has been described as Unmanifested and Imperishable is called the Highest Goal . . ." (8:21).

## Ignorance (Avidya) and Knowledge (Jnana)

If we ask what it is that keeps humanity from the attainment of self-realization, the answer is "ignorance." This ignorance is not an unawareness of a body of facts, but an inner veil that keeps men in a state of hypnotic illusion, or semimadness. We imagine that we are separate, struggling, suffering agents, and this conviction is the source of our difficulty. When ignorance (*avidya*) is supplanted by "knowledge" (*jnana*), then we pass beyond the human condition. Such knowledge, in turn, is not a knowledge of facts or theories. It is an inner or intuitive realization of the true state of affairs, a grasping of the essential truth that "I am That"; that the action of my life is not my own; that, in fact, the whole range of "I—me—mine" conceptions is a false set of notions. There is only That!

Krishna tells Arjuna how to recognize the truly enlightened man: "O Partha, when a man is satisfied in the Self by Self alone and has completely cast out all desires from the mind, then he is said to be of steady wisdom. He whose mind is not agitated in calamities and who has no longing for pleasure, free from attachment, fear and anger, he indeed is said to be a saint of steady wisdom" (2:55–56). Conversely, the unenlightened man is plagued by sense attachments. He is filled with desire and this leads to anger, lust, and greed. "Lust, anger and greed," says the Lord, "these three are the soul-destroying gates of hell" (16:21).

## Illusion (Maya) and the "Play" of God (Lila)

The reason why these emotions debase the soul is that they bewilder it with attachments to the world. To understand this we must consider another basic Hindu concept: *maya*. This has been variously translated, but most often as "illusion." The example of a magic show is often used to illustrate the meaning of the word. The magician bemuses us with an unreal situation that appears real. If we saw through the magic, we would see the true situation. By analogy, this world and this self are illusions, distortions of reality, and spiritual insight leads to release from these distortions and emergence into an entirely different dimension to which our worldly and egoistic concepts simply do not apply.

From another point of view, this world is the play (*lila*) of Brahman, or God. It can be likened to an artist painting for the sheer pleasure of painting, or a child blowing bubbles and bursting them with a cry of joy. No purposes inhere in such a world. It is a "show" to be watched in complete detachment. If one identifies himself with the show, involves himself in the play, he suffers. It is from this that true knowledge releases him.

These concepts are in sharp contrast with a Semitic understanding of reality. The biblical concepts of "creation" and serious "history" yield a different view of the world and reality than maya and lila. In Semitic religion God created the world as the stage upon which his purposes could be historically enacted. There is nothing illusory or playful about them. Salvation does not consist in seeing through them, but in coming under the rule of the Divine Will in and through them.

## THE SEVERAL PATHS

Having made these principles clear to Arjuna, Krishna turns to the practical problem of what a man who has had a glimpse of the true human situation should do. He carefully marks out the "paths" which the wise man can tread, leading on to enlightenment and self-realization.

There are many paths to the final goal of man's existence. In fact, no one can help following some path, either consciously or unconsciously. The Lord Krishna says: "In whatever way men worship Me, in the same way I fulfill their desires. . . . in every way men follow My path" (4:11). Even "those who long for success in this world worship the gods . . ." (4:12). But such a path is not a very wise one for it leads to many incarnations and much suffering before it emerges into a different dimension and comes to wisdom. As Krishna says, "Even those devotees who worship other gods with faith, they too worship Me, but contrary to the law. . . . but they do not know Me in truth, hence they return (fall into re-birth)" (9:23–24).

This doctrine of the many paths, all of which eventually lead to the same goal, is the basis of the widely proclaimed doctrine of Hindu tolerance. Hinduism has exhibited a great capacity to incorporate other religions freely into its own structure. Islam, Sikhism, and Christianity, each in turn has found a place within the system, and the "gods" of these religions have been incorporated into the Hindu pantheon. As the yogi Ramakrishna (1834–1886) says, "It is one and the same Avatar [incarnation of deity] that, having plunged into the ocean of life, rises up in one place and is known as Krishna, and diving down again rises in another place and is known as Christ."[12] Whether they are indeed all as much the same as the Hindu doctrine claims is something that remains to be examined with more care in another place. The point is that this doctrine is the basis for Hindu tolerance and explains much of the character of Hindu spirituality.

But, as the Bhagavad-Gita points out, though all paths may lead to God, they are not all equally efficacious. The nonorthodox paths take more time. It is as though a person were to set out from Chicago for New York, traveling west. He would eventually arrive, to be sure, but only after the most senseless and painful detours. For this reason Krishna instructs Arjuna in the paths that lead more directly to the goal.

## Karma-marga (the Path of Works)

Karma here acquires some new meanings beyond those already given. It can mean the "works" of ritual: praying, offering sacrifices, and so on. It can also mean, in a larger sense, the work of carrying out one's caste duty, such as fighting, buying and selling, or menial service. Krishna says that the person who knows what the goal really is can perform these "works" in such a way that they will lead directly to self-realization and final salvation.

Of the karma of performing sacrifices (the normal work of high-caste Brahmans), Krishna says that if he performs these actions with the "consciousness of Brahman, he reaches Brahman alone" (4:24). In this way sacrifice is transmuted from an outward act to an inward and knowing act. "Wisdom-sacrifice" (that is, sacrifices performed in a knowing detachment), he says, "is far superior to the sacrifice performed with material objects" (4:33). This spiritualization of the religious rites recalls a comparable Hebrew teaching: "The sacrifices of God are . . . a broken and a contrite heart" (Psalms 51:17, KJ version). The whole ritual system is spiritualized, made a matter of true inwardness and intention rather than outward performance.

But when we recall that Arjuna, like most of mankind, is not a priest, we can see that his problem is different. How can he live and work as a layman in such a way that he too may come to self-realization? To this Krishna says that all work can be undertaken as a spiritualized sacrifice. The rule is: "That man attains peace who, abandoning all desires, moves about without attachment and longing, without the sense of 'I' and 'mine'" (2:71). ". . . Therefore, being unattached, perform thy duties unceasingly; for through the performance of action, unattached, man attains the highest" (3:19). In a practical sense this means that the warrior must fight without thought of victory or defeat, the businessman must work without thought of profit or loss, and the servant must perform his service without hope of any reward or fear of any punishment. It is unnecessary to point out what a revolution in human motivation is involved in this advice. But, according to Krishna, the alternative is to remain bound to the world in an indefinite round of existences which involve suffering.

Krishna's teachings on this subject of work are of the utmost importance to modern Hinduism. It is the one orthodox way in which the demands of a going society can be joined to the demands of traditional Hindu values. Whether a modern industrial society can operate on such a motivation remains to be seen, but the great minds of India have committed themselves to this solution of the problem. If we were to seek a parallel in the West we would have to ask: Would it be possible to sustain a modern industrial civilization on the Judaeo-Christian demand to love God with one's whole being and one's neighbor as one's self? This rule would likewise involve a suspension of the many material motives that presently operate to keep the wheels of Western society turning.

### Bhakti-marga, the Path of Devotion to God

This way of putting the matter leads to another of Krishna's paths of salvation, *bhakti-marga*. Following this path, the wise man can find salvation by devoting his entire life's work to the Lord. The word bhakti means love or devotion. "He who performs all actions, surrendering them to Brahman and abandoning all attachment, is not polluted by sin, as lotus-leaf [is not moistened] by water" (5:10). Since Brahman is the invisible, unmanifested form of Reality, some devotees might find it difficult to focus their devotion on so intangible a being. Krishna therefore offers an alternative—devotion to Krishna himself as the human form of Brahman. He says, ". . . those who, surrendering all actions to Me and regarding Me as the Supreme Goal, worship Me with singlehearted devotion . . . for them . . . I become ere long the Saviour from the ocean of mortal Samsara . . ." (12:6–7). He goes further and claims that this is the best way of all: "Those who, fixing their minds on Me, worship Me with perpetual devotion, endowed with supreme faith, to My mind are the best knowers of Yoga" (12:2).

This text at one stroke reconciles the great monistic tradition of the Upanishads and the popular worship of the sectarians who center their devotion upon one or another of the many Hindu gods. But it does so by insisting that the worship be done with a proper intuitive knowledge; namely, that Krishna is the human form of the Unmanifested One who is the ultimate Reality. This awareness is absolutely essential. The Hindu term for such knowledge is jnana, which is the next path.

### Jnana-marga, the Path of Knowledge

Intuitive knowledge (jnana-marga) is the key to all the paths. If this knowledge is present, then, whether one meditates on scripture or performs rituals or works in the world or worships a god, the results are all the same: release from the cycles of rebirth, the attainment of self-realization, and unity with the ultimate Reality.

Students of the Bhagavad-Gita have complained that its teaching is not entirely consistent at this point, and that different concepts of religion are placed side by side without a genuine reconciliation. Thus, in Book 13, four great texts, each representing a traditional idea of salvation, appear as though they were synonymous:

*Indivisible, yet It exists as if divided in beings* . . . (13:16). This teaches the monistic doctrine of the Upanishads: All the multiplicity of things which we experience in the world are illusory forms of the One Being, Brahman.

*Know thou both Prakriti (Nature) and Purusha (Soul) to be without beginning* (13:19). This teaches that both nature and the separate soul of each individual have existed from eternity.

*The Supreme Lord [Isvara] abides in all beings equally; (He is) undying in the dying; He who sees [thus] sees truly* (13:27). Here the teaching is that the personal God, Isvara, is real and that salvation is a mystical union with Him.

*My devotee* . . . *becomes fitted to enter into My Being (oneness with Me)* (13:18). This text teaches that it is union with Krishna, the visible avatar of the invisible Brahman, that leads to salvation.

We will have to leave it to other commentators on the Bhagavad-Gita to determine whether these are merely apparent or real contradictions. If they are unified in theory, which one is more primary than the others? We are not told.

A Christian could find in the concept of mystical union with God or with his incarnate Son, Jesus, parallels that are congenial to his own training. But the other two alternatives would remain alien. The question that remains is this: Is the goal mystical union with God or is it a kind of reabsorption into the Unmanifested One? Perhaps we are asking a question that cannot be answered without a great deal more experience; perhaps only the saints can illuminate our doubts on this matter. We do know that in the West the saints have rarely spoken of reabsorption, though they have often spoken of mystical union. It may be that they have sometimes meant the same thing, though this appears doubtful.

Suffice it to say at this point that the Bhagavad-Gita gives the stamp of orthodoxy to each of these views, and they have remained side by side in Hindu spirituality to this day.

We have one more important concept to explain before we leave the subject of the paths of salvation, namely, yoga.

## Yoga

Yoga is a familiar term to most Westerners, though it is doubtful that it is properly understood. From the earliest times India developed a special set of physical and psychological exercises that were believed to have unusual efficacy in spiritual matters. The Bhagavad-Gita gives high prominence to this tradition. Yoga practices are recommended for all those who would follow any path at all. Here is a typical passage: "A Yogi [one who is practicing yoga] should constantly practice concentration of the heart, remaining in seclusion alone, subduing his body and mind and being free from longing and possession (sense of ownership). . . . Being seated . . . making the mind one-pointed and subduing the activities of mind and senses . . . let him hold his body, head and neck erect and motionless, fixing his gaze on the tip of his nose. . . . Being serene-hearted and fearless, ever-steadfast in the vow of Brahmacharya [sexual continence] and controlling the mind, let him sit steadfastly absorbed in thoughts of Me, regarding Me as his supreme goal" (6:10–14).

The Bhagavad-Gita thus approves this venerable tradition and places it in great prominence. The sense of the teaching is that whatever form of religious life one chooses to embrace, he should undergird it with yoga practices. Such practices focus the mind and spirit and make possible the detachment and devotion that look with scorn upon worldly achievements and allow the soul to pass beyond all attachments to earthly existence in preparation for full self-realization.

### The Vision of Brahman

As Krishna comes to the close of his instruction, Arjuna becomes very intent. He longs for something beyond instruction. He asks for a vision of Reality itself. "O Lord," he pleads, ". . . if Thou thinkest me able (worthy) . . . show me Thine Infinite Self" (11:4). What follows is one of the greatest passages in all religious literature, an attempt to describe the greatness of God as he is in himself. Kenneth Saunders says that it is like wending one's way through the labyrinth of a Hindu temple and at last coming upon the central shrine, where the god himself reigns in awesome splendor.

Krishna grants Arjuna his wish. "Behold . . .," he says, "My various celestial Forms, of different colors and shapes, by hundreds and by thousands" (11:5). Then he shows to Arjuna his "supreme Godly Form . . . with many faces and eyes, with many wondrous sights, with many celestial ornaments and with many celestial weapons uplifted . . . the all-wonderful Deity, infinite, facing the universe everywhere. If the effulgence of a thousand suns were to shine at once in the sky, that might resemble the splendor of that great Being" (11:9–12).

As Arjuna watched, "overpowered with wonder, and his hair standing on end" (11:14), he saw "the entire universe resting together . . . in the body of the God of gods" (11:13). He saw all the things of the world coming into existence and passing out of existence by the power of this supreme Being. He saw all living things coming to birth, sustained, and passing into death "as the many torrents of rivers rush toward the ocean . . ." (11:28). He saw God's "fierce, radiant rays, filling the whole universe" (11:30).

As this terrifying vision faded at last and Krishna returned to his familiar human form, Arjuna "spoke to Krishna in a choked voice, bowing down, overwhelmed with fear [awe]" (11:35). "Salutations to Thee before," he cried, "salutations to Thee behind, salutations to Thee on all sides! O All, infinite in power, and immeasurable in valor, Thou pervadest all, therefore Thou art All" (11:40).

Such, in brief, is the message of Hindu spirituality as it is taught in its greatest scripture. Even from the standpoint of an outsider it is impossible to deny its sublime character and power. To be sure, it has about the same remote relationship to average Hindu religious practice as the Gospel according to St. John (with which it has often been compared) has to Christian practice in the West, but neither religion can be understood without recourse to their great fountainheads of inspiration.

If we would understand Hinduism more fully, we could do no better than to study intimately the lives of such great twentieth-century Indians as Gandhi, Sri Aurobindo, Radhakrishnan, or the nineteenth-century saint who is held by many to be the incarnation of Hindu spirituality at its purest and best, Sri Ramakrishna. The serious student will withhold his judgment until he has exposed himself to the minds of these great exemplars of a spirituality so different from our own.

As we turn to the Buddhism of the Dhammapada in the next chapter we will have yet another opportunity to see the depth of Asian religious inspiration.

## SUGGESTIONS FOR FURTHER READING

There are three books that will help the beginner get a feel for Hindu religion. *The Hindu View of Life* (Macmillan, 1927), by S. Radhakrishnan, is a simple statement of his own faith by an articulate Hindu philosopher trained in both the East and West. He has served as both Vice President and President of India. *Ramakrishna, The Prophet of New India* (Harper & Row, 1948), by Swami Nikhilananda, is a journal account of one of the major figures in the nineteenth-century revival of Hinduism. William James would have had to write another book on religious experience had he known this material. The third book is Louis Fischer's *Gandhi, His Life and Message for the World* (New American Library, 1954).

A. C. Bouquet's *Hinduism* (Hutchison's University Library, Preface dated 1948) is a brief history of India from the perspective of its religion. Albert Schweitzer's *Indian Thought and Its Development* (Holt, Rinehart and Winston, 1936) is a critical approach to Hinduism by a famous Western thinker. By contrast, Heinrich Zimmer's *Philosophies of India* (Pantheon, 1951) is a sympathetic study of the philosophic bases of Hindu thought. An older book, now regarded as a classic of sociological writing, is Max Weber's *The Religion of India, The Sociology of Hinduism and Buddhism*, Hans H. Gerth and Don Martindale, trans. (Free Press, 1958).

The following texts of the Bhagavad-Gita can be consulted for comparative translations: Swami Paramananda, "The Blessed Lord's Song" in Lin Yutang, ed., *The Wisdom of China and India* (Random House, 1942; Modern Library, 1955);

Swami Prabhavananda and Christopher Isherwood, *The Song of God: Bhagavad-Gita* (New American Library, 1951); and Sarvepalli Radhakrishnan, *The Bhagavad-Gita* (Harper & Row, 1948), which contains both text and full devotional commentary.

Students interested in comparative literature will enjoy Kenneth Saunders' *The Gospel for Asia* (Macmillan, 1928), which is a study of three religious masterpieces: the Gita, the Buddhist Lotus Sutra, and the Gospel according to St. John. Another comparative study is Rudolf Otto's *Mysticism East and West* (Meridian, World Publishing, 1957), which shows both the striking similarities and fundamental differences between the great Western mystic Meister Eckhart and the great Hindu mystic Sankara. In connection with Hindu mystical practice, a good work to consult is Mircea Eliade's *Yoga: Immortality and Freedom* (Pantheon, 1957).

## *NOTES*

1. Mircea Eliade, *Yoga: Immortality and Freedom* (Pantheon, 1957), p. xiii.

2. Huston Smith, *The Religions of Man* (New American Library, 1958), p. 23.

3. Quoted in *ibid.*, p. 25.

4. In his pamphlet entitled *Religion in India Today*, p. 6.

5. For instance, such men as Aldous Huxley, Alan W. Watts, E. A. Burtt, and Sir John Woodroffe.

6. The classic study of this literature is M. Winternitz' *A History of Indian Literature*, 2 vols. (University of Calcutta, 1927). A briefer, but sound treatment is

J. N. Farquhar's *The Religious Quest of India: An Outline of the Religious Literature of India* (Oxford University Press, 1920).

7. R. E. Hume, *The World's Living Religions* (Scribner, 1946), p. 25.

8. Eliade, *op. cit.*, p. 153.

9. In his *Indian Thought and Its Development*.

10. E. A. H. Blunt, *The Caste System of Northern India* (Oxford University Press, 1931), p.253.

11. Eliade, *op. cit.*, p. 3.

12. Quoted in Robert O. Ballou, ed., *World Bible* (Viking, 1944), p. 82.

# 5

# *Buddhism and the Dhammapada*

❖❖❖❖❖❖❖❖❖❖❖❖❖❖❖❖❖❖❖❖❖❖❖❖❖❖❖❖❖❖❖❖❖❖❖❖

Buddhism was born and nourished in the bosom of Hinduism. Though it arose as a protest against the mother faith, it nonetheless shared many of the parent religion's basic concepts. It flourished in India for about a thousand years and then disappeared from the country of its birth. Before its demise in India, however, it had spread to the adjacent lands of the south and east and has remained a powerful force to this day. Many reasons have been suggested for its withering in India, but the most plausible seems to be that it died in a fraternal embrace. With the reformation of Hinduism on the pattern of the Bhagavad-Gita and the evolution of Buddhism, which greatly enlarged its original precepts and practices, the two faiths converged toward a point at which they were almost indistinguishable. However, one decisive difference remained: Gautama the Buddha.

## GAUTAMA AND THE BEGINNINGS OF BUDDHISM

Buddhism is fortunate in having in Gautama one of the world's winsomest and greatest of men. His towering figure still dominates the imaginations of millions. His career began in a small and obscure kingdom of northern India, where he was born to the royal house. Sacred legend holds that at his birth it

73

was prophesied that Siddartha was to become either a world ruler or a world saviour.

Though his royal father, like many a modern parent, favored a political career for his son, the prince very early showed signs of religious unrest. According to the oldest scriptures this unrest was aroused by the sight of three things: A sick man, an old man, and a corpse.[1] Meditating upon these three "signs," Gautama longed for an answer to the human condition symbolized by them. Soon afterward, it is said, he saw a holy man, and this nourished in him a resolve to leave the pleasures of the palace, his beautiful young wife and infant son, and begin in earnest the search for salvation. "In all the beauty of my early prime," an early passage runs, "with a wealth of coal-black hair untouched by grey—despite the wishes of my parents, who wept and lamented—I cut off my hair and beard, donned the yellow robes [of a monk] and went forth from home to homelessness."[2]

His first experiments with religion took the form of extreme asceticism, denying himself human companionship, food, drink, and even the most elementary physical comforts. After six years of strenuous self-denial he was no nearer his goal than at the first, and in a gesture of despair he broke his ascetic vows by eating solid nourishment and settled himself under a fig tree to meditate, resolving not to leave the place until the meaning of existence became clear to him.

### The Enlightenment

Under the Bo tree Gautama experienced a burst of contemplative insight that changed his whole life and became the central symbol of the Buddhist faith—the Enlightenment.

A long period of joyful rapture followed, but it was in due time marred by temptation. The temptation was to remain aloof with his secret and enjoy salvation for himself. In a gesture of even greater self-renunciation than that which attended his early renunciation of the world, Gautama resolved to return to the habitations of men and preach the new wisdom that had come to him. Soon he gathered about himself several disciples who together with him formed the original Sangha, or Order, and the religion of Buddhism was formally established.

### THE DHAMMAPADA

The Dhammapada, which we shall explore briefly as a clue to basic Buddhist wisdom, is a part of the sacred scriptures of the Theravada, or Southern School of Buddhism, in contrast to its great rival, the Mahayana school. The difference between these two traditions will be discussed later.

Dhammapada, literally translated, means "religious sentences," and it stands in approximately the same relationship to Buddhism as the Sermon on the Mount does to Christianity. While scholars disagree on whether these are the Buddha's own words, the thoughts no doubt represent correctly the Buddha's own teachings. I believe that the Chinese philosopher Lin Yutang is right in his estimate of the book's importance: "The Dhammapada is a great spiritual testimony, one of the very few religious masterpieces in the world, combining genius of spiritual passion with a happy gift of literary expression. . . . The Dhammapada . . . belongs to the world and to all time."[3] It contains a message that is especially appropriate to men of the present age. To quote Lin Yutang again: It is "a clear call to rouse oneself from the life of sloth, indolence and thoughtlessness of the common man, to achieve the greatest of all conquests, the conquest of self, to escape from the snares of evil passions, lust, hatred and anger, and to attain the highest human freedom, the moral freedom of one who has overcome himself."[4]

### The Message of the Dhammapada[5]

*The Importance of Mental Self-Possession.* It's opening sentences announce the major theme of the Dhammapada: "All that we are is the result of what we have thought: it is founded on our thoughts, it is made up of our thoughts. If a man speaks or acts with an evil thought, pain follows him, as the wheel follows the foot of the ox that draws the carriage. . . . If a man speaks or acts with a pure thought, happiness follows him, like a shadow that never leaves him" (1).*

The thoughtless man is lost before he begins: "Death carries off a man who is gathering flowers, and whose mind is distracted, as a flood carries off a sleeping village" (4). The prime Buddhist virtue is to possess one's thoughts, to be mindful and aware, to be awake. The Buddha is said once to have called himself "the one who is awake." As the Dhammapada says, "Even the gods envy those who are awakened and not forgetful . . ." (14). Or again: "As a fletcher makes straight his arrow, a wise man makes straight his trembling and unsteady thought . . ." (3).

This mental wakefulness has both a negative and positive aspect. The negative aspect is an alertness to the threats to a liberated human existence. The positive aspect is an awareness of the meaning of the self and its true goal.

*The Self.* The wise man is aware of the nature of the self: "Self is the lord of the self, who else could be the lord? With self well subdued, a man finds a lord such as few can find" (12). Theravada Buddhism does not say much about the true self, assuming that only the man who knows from experience would understand the explanation. The Mahayana doctrine is somewhat less reticent on this matter; it tends to revert to the teaching of the Upanishads and Bhagavad-Gita, and to identify the true self with the ultimate nature of things.

---

* The numbers in parentheses following the quotations refer to the chapters of the Dhammapada. The quotations are from a translation made by Max Müller in 1870.

*Nirvana.* Another positive aspect of mindfulness is a clear realization that the goal is nirvana. Again Theravada teaching is reticent; it refers to nirvana simply as a blowing out of the flame of self and desire. Mahayana teachings more boldly assert that nirvana is a positive condition which, to be sure, we cannot literally describe in any terms drawn from experience, but which is a state of being so gloriously full that the loss of the finite and limited self is a minute loss in exchange for it. This state lies beyond all concrete states of existence, beyond the cycle of rebirths. The Dhammapada quotes the Buddha: "Looking for the maker of this tabernacle [the body and mind of a man], I have run through a course of many births, not finding him; and painful is birth again and again. But now, maker of this tabernacle, thou hast been seen; though thou shalt not make up this tabernacle again. All thy rafters are broken, thy ridge-pole [roof beam] is sundered; the mind approaching the Eternal (. . . nirvana), has attained to the extinction of all desires" (11).

*Wrong Thoughts and Actions.* The negative aspect of continuous mindfulness is an awareness of those attitudes and actions that destroy the possibility of release into the bliss of nirvana. The chief of these are possessiveness, anger, hatred, and lust. "There is no fire like passion, there is no shark like hatred, there is no snare like folly, there is no torrent like greed" (18). The reason for their evil effect is that they tend to nourish the illusion that the finite ego is real and important. So long as this ego-sense remains, nirvana is far away.

Greedy actions and the multiplication of possessions are fatal. " 'These sons belong to me, this wealth belongs to me,' with such thoughts a fool is tormented. He himself does not belong to himself; how much less sons and wealth" (5)? If you seek release from such attitudes, you are advised to "look upon the world as you would on a bubble, look upon it as you would on a mirage" (13).

Anger, resentment, and the holding of grudges serve also to strangulate life into its ego form. " 'He abused me, he beat me, he defeated me, he robbed me'—in those who harbor such thoughts hatred will never cease. . . . Hatred does not cease by hatred at any time" (1). "Let a man leave anger, let him forsake pride, let him overcome all bondage! No suffering befalls the man who is not attached to name and form, and who calls nothing his own" (17).

Passion similarly dooms the foolish man: "There is no fire like passion . . ." (18). "The thirst [desire] of a thoughtless man grows like a creeper; he runs from life to life, like a monkey seeking fruit in the forest" (24). Sexual passion only serves to perpetuate the illusion that one's own separate finite existence is real. So long as such passions burn in a man he cannot hope to attain the highest life.

*Right Thoughts and Actions.* The good life consists in subduing evil thoughts and attitudes and taking on the habits of detachment and compassion. "Cut down the whole forest of desires," advises the Dhammapada, "not a tree only" (20)! In this way a great calm settles over life and one is no longer worried about the multiplication of preservation of one's possessions. "We live happily indeed, free from greed among the greedy . . . we call nothing our own" (15). Even the attachments of affection are best left aside: "From affection comes grief, from affection comes fear; he who is free from affection knows neither grief nor fear" (16).

The evil of anger is overcome by compassion: "The disciples of Gautama (Buddha) are always well awake, and their mind day and night always delights in compassion" (21). ". . . hatred ceases by love—this is an old rule" (1) "We live happily indeed, not hating those who hate us . . ." (15)! No holy man, even "if attacked, should let himself fly at his aggressor" (26)! "Let a man overcome anger by love, let him overcome evil by good; let him overcome the greedy by liberality, the liar by truth" (17)!

*The Four Noble Truths.* A good summary of the Buddism of the Dhammapada is this text: "The best of ways is the eightfold; the best of truths the four words; the best of virtues passionlessness; the best of men he who has eyes to see. This is the way, there is no other that leads to the purifying of intelligence. Go on this path" (20)! The Eightfold Path, called by the Buddha the Middle Way, is set forth in his famous sermon at Benares as encompassing "right views; right aspirations; right speech; right behavior; right livelihood; right effort; right thoughts; right contemplation."[6]

These eight key phrases can be paraphrased in the following way: Begin with a clear understanding of the basic Buddhist doctrines which alone can be a faithful guide to salvation; set your aspiration and ideal firmly upon obtaining release from the false consciousness of self and release into nirvana; guard your speech so that it does not deflect your mind and actions into a wrong course; guard your actions so that you do not fall into violence or grasping and thus enlarge your false ego-consciousness; choose a way of earning your living which likewise does not tempt you to possessiveness or fear, but allows you to become progressively more detached from things and to practice the virtues of compassion; learn to focus your thoughts at all times, especially by the practice of disciplined meditation which will lead finally to the highest forms of contemplative awareness and at last to nirvana itself. As the Dhammapada says : "Without knowledge there is no meditation, without meditation there is no knowledge: he who has knowledge and meditation is near unto Nirvana" (25).

The Eightfold Path is the fourth of what the Buddha termed the Four Noble Truths. We have already encountered aspects of them, but the Sermon at Benares presents them in their classic form. They are these: the Noble Truth concerning suffering; the Noble Truth concerning the origin of suffering; the Noble Truth concerning the destruction of suffering; the Noble Truth of the Eightfold Path.

The Noble Truth concerning suffering is that the whole sentient world suffers. This is Buddha's analysis of the condition from which man must be saved: "Birth is attended with pain, decay is painful, disease is painful, death is painful. . . . In brief, bodily conditions which spring from attachment are painful."[7]

The Noble Truth concerning the origin of suffering is that its source lies in selfish desire (*tanha*; literally, thirst). This is Gautama Buddha's analysis of the chief barrier to man's release: "Verily, it is that craving which causes the renewal of existence, accompanied by sensual delight, seeking satisfaction now here, now there, the craving for the gratification of the passions, the craving for a future life, and the craving for happiness in this life."[8]

The Noble Truth concerning the destruction of suffering is that by cutting the nerve of selfish desire the false ego that feeds upon such desire will gradually fade away, and with it will fade life's painful experiences. This is the heart of the Buddha's proposal for man's salvation: "Verily, it is the destruction, in which no passion remains, of this very thirst; it is the laying aside of, the being free from, the dwelling no longer upon this thirst."[9]

Of the Noble Truth of the Eightfold Path, his practical proposal for human liberation, the Buddha says: "Right views will be the torch to light his way. Right aspirations will be his guide. Right speech will be his dwelling place on the road. His gait will be straight, for it is right behavior. His refreshments will be the right way of earning his livelihood. Right efforts will be his steps: right thoughts his breath; and right contemplation will give him the peace that follows in his footprints."[10]

### Summary of the Dhammapada

The following is a brief summary of the message of the Dhammapada:

Human life has gone wrong in some fundamental way, making existence miserable even for the most fortunate. The palliatives of pleasure, power, and fame do not assuage this grief. Men need a diagnosis of their condition sound enough to provide the basis for an authentic cure that will, in turn, yield a happiness unchallenged by the circumstances of existence. That diagnosis is at hand. It is not superficial, and the way out of the human condition that it proposes is not easy. But the rewards are very great indeed. The trouble with man is selfish desire, ignorant craving, which is rooted in a false notion of selfhood. Release can only come from cutting the nerve of that desire and dispersing the false notions of the self as a permanent and important entity. The only person who can perform the surgery of self-analysis and the cutting of the nerve of passion is each man himself. It is not necessary to settle speculative metaphysical matters; what counts is the practical business of reorganizing one's thoughts, attitudes, and practices. The whole of life should be focused on the cultivation of a deep detachment and universal compassion. This can be achieved through the skilled practice of meditation and the cultivation of a life in harmony with it. In time, with patient persistence, victory over self and every wanton desire will come, and at the summit, when the extinction of self and desire has been achieved, will loom the blessed consummation—nirvana, release, total freedom, eternal happiness.

## THEORETICAL AND PRACTICAL
## PRESUPPOSITIONS

The way of life proposed in the Dhammapada presupposes certain truths about life. Some of these presuppositions were inherited from the general Hindu culture in which the Buddha lived. Others were the results of his brilliant analytical mind. He never questioned, for instance, the Hindu teaching about karma and rebirth. In this he is at one with the teaching of the Bhagavad-Gita. Nor did he question that life as it appeared to unculti-vated human experience was what the Hindu called maya. The Buddhist word for the same idea is samsara, experience shot through with ignorance and false identifications. One of the chief of these is the identification of the present self with the true self. Another error is the identification of the things of the world as permanently real. With great dialectical skill the early Buddhists showed that all these supposed permanent entities were really artificial and temporary collections of elements and that they disappeared when their components were scattered. "All component things pass away" is a favorite early saying.

Another error of the ordinary man and the prevailing tradition, the Buddha taught, was a belief that the gods were real and helpful in matters of ultimate human concern. The gods, he said, were subject to the same laws as men, and would, like them, also pass away. For this reason, rites and rituals, prayers and sacrifices to them could be of no avail in man's salvation. Man must depend upon himself for salvation. According to one tradition, the Buddha's dying words to his disciples were: "Be ye lamps unto yourselves."

One aspect of the Hindu tradition that the Buddha rejected was the tendency to endless metaphysical speculation. Such knowledge, even if it were accurate, he taught, would be mere words, not personal experience—as the Dhammapada says, "like a cowherd counting the cows of others" (1). In a celebrated account, the monk Malunkyaputta determined to leave the Master unless he explained whether the soul and the world were eternal or not, and other questions of a similar kind. When he put the questions to the Teacher, Gautama admitted that his teaching did not contain answers to such ques-tions, because, he said, "this profits not, nor has to do with the fundamentals of religion, nor tends to aversion, absence of passion . . . and Nirvana; therefore have I not explained it?"[11]

The crucial thing, he explained, was a practical matter. Suppose, the same account relates, a man has been wounded by a poisoned arrow and refuses to have it removed until he has learned all about the caste of the doctor, the type of man who wounded him, the type of poison used, and so on. This foolish man would die. The same applies to man's present religious condition. If he waits for all the answers to speculative questions he will surely perish in the stream of samsara. The wise man will arrange to have the arrow immediately removed and leave speculative questions to a later time.

## THE RISE OF MAHAYANA BUDDHISM
## AND THE EMERGENCE OF A NEW IDEAL

Moving from the Dhammapada of Theravada Buddhism to the Mahayana scripture known as the Lotus of the True Law is almost like moving from one religion to another. Yet both of them owe their inspiration to the same source, however distant from one another they may seem since their courses diverged. In this they are not unlike the varying traditions of Christianity or Islam. Just as an account of Christianity would be incomplete without a survey of both Roman Catholic and Protestant ideals, so is the Buddhism of the Dhammapada incomplete without a brief consideration of the Mahayana ideal that emerged several centuries later. Like Protestantism, which claimed to return to the original sources of inspiration to produce a more faithful Christianity, in the same way the Mahayana thinkers believed that they were more faithful in their understanding of the Buddha's original message. We are not in a position to judge in this dispute, but we may get a more balanced account of classical Buddhism by looking briefly at the new teaching.

The Theravada looked upon the Buddha as the one who had set the pattern of release from existence through the disciplined practice of detachment. From his teaching and example they drew the ideal of the ahrat (monk) who had quenched his passions by withdrawing systematically from the burning world of tanha (desire), and had forged a pathway into liberation. It was up to each man to tread that path insofar as he was able, following the careful instruction laid down by the Teacher. The Dhammapada is the classical handbook of directions for achieving this goal.

The Mahayana teachers, on the other hand, agreed that Gautama had forged the great and new way to liberation, but they were more impressed by his refusal of the temptation to enjoy freedom for himself. They were fascinated by his gracious return from the nirvana of contemplation to the task of helping his fellow men on their own way out of the burning house of the world. In short, they were attracted by his compassion. Out of this they fashioned a new ideal, the ideal of the compassionate saviour, the bodhisattva, who lingers short of his own final liberation in order to wait with pity for the salvation of every living being. The bodhisattva vows to himself: "My endeavours do not merely aim at my own deliverance." Instead, he looks with pity upon the world of sentient beings and pledges: "I must rescue all these beings from the stream of Samsara. . . . I myself must grapple with the whole mass of suffering of all beings."[12]

In keeping with this new ideal, Mahayana taught that all men possess within themselves the true Buddha-nature, and that through a realization of this nature they could themselves become Buddhas. This represents a revival of the Hindu ideal of self-realization that we have seen in the Bhagavad-Gita, with the important difference that the new statement of the old goal is not left abstract but is now invested with a feature that Hinduism never had; namely, the towering personal character of the great teacher himself. And though theoretical Buddhism, unlike Christianity, could continue without the memory of its founder, it would be immeasurably impoverished if it were forced to do so.

This new state of selfless compassion carries with it a logic that required the Mahayana teachers to redefine the final goal of nirvana. For the Theravadin nirvana was defined as the state of ultimate detachment beyond all desire. But if this is true, the bodhisattva who most nearly emulates the Buddha himself would seem to have turned his back upon the true goal by remaining in the world to help others. The solution to this problem led to one of the most profound religious conceptions of human history; namely, that the state of compassionate oneness with all beings was itself nirvana, for it, unlike the selfish contemplation of the ahrat (monk), made no real distinction between self-salvation and the salvation of all beings. In this new sense nirvana includes samsara (the world), and the bodhisattva lives in the bliss of liberation while embracing the world itself. As A. E. Burtt puts it: "Paradoxically . . . the spiritual insight here is that to renounce Nirvana for oneself, in love for others, is to find oneself in Nirvana, in its real meaning."[13]

In the next chapter we shall see how this new ideal found a fertile ground in the Taoism of China and led to the establishment of Zen Buddhism. But that is to get ahead of our story. At this point we can pause to appreciate the towering genius who arose in India's axial age and taught a sublime ideal of self-understanding, coupled with compassionate concern for the welfare of others, and in so doing introduced into history one of its most winsome religious ideals.

### SUGGESTIONS FOR FURTHER READING

Aside from the excellent chapters on Buddhism in the general books recommended in Chapter 3, I would recommend three others: J. B. Pratt's *Pilgrimage of Buddhism* (Macmillan, 1928) is a fascinating account of a Western philosopher's trip through Buddha lands. Edward Conze's *Buddhism: Its Essence and Development* (Philosophical Library, 1955) is perhaps the most complete all-round account. Christmas Humphreys has been a leader of the Buddhist Society of England for a long time and his summaries of various aspects of Buddhist history and thought are very valuable, especially his attempt to show the unity of Buddhism as a religion. See his *Buddhism* (Penguin, 1951).

It is important to become acquainted with a religion through its primary sources. Fortunately, there are good documents for this purpose. Clarence H. Hamilton's *Buddhism: A Religion of Infinite Compassion* (Liberal Arts, Bobbs-Merrill, 1952) is a broad selection from Buddhist literature. E. A. Burtt's *The Teachings of the Compassionate Buddha* (New American Library, 1955) clarifies some of the theological development in Buddhism as it moved from Theravada to Mahayana. His commentaries are very illuminating. *The Gospel of Buddha* (Open Court, 1915), by Paul Carus, is organized around the documents which tell the story of the Buddha from birth to death. The favorite scripture of the Mahayana sect is now available in an inexpensive edition, *Saddharma Pundarika, or Lotus of the True Law*, translated by H. Kern (Dover, 1963).

For references on Zen, see the suggestions at the end of Chapter 6.

## NOTES

1. Paul Carus, *The Gospel of Buddha* (Open Court, 1915), pp. 14–19.
2. Quoted in John B. Noss, *Man's Religions* (Macmillan, 1963), p. 171.
3. Lin Yutang, ed., *The Wisdom of China and India* (Random House, 1942; Modern Library, 1955), p. 326.
4. *Ibid.*, p. 321.
5. The quotations from the *Dhammapada* are from a translation made by Max Müller in 1870, reprinted in Lin Yutang, ed., *ibid.*

6. From the Buddha's Sermon at Benares, quoted in Lin Yutang, ed., *ibid.*, p. 362.
7. *Ibid.*, p. 361.
8. *Ibid.*
9. *Ibid.*
10. *Ibid.*
11. Quoted by E. A. Burtt, ed., *The Teachings of the Compassionate Buddha* (New American Library, 1955), p. 36.
12. *Ibid.*, p. 133.
13. *Ibid.*, p. 162.

# 6

# *Taoism*
# *and the Tao Tê Ching*

❖❧❖❧❖❧❖❧❖❧❖❧❖❧❖❧❖❧❖❧❖❧❖❧❖❧❖❧❖❧❖❧❖❧❖❧❖❧❖❧❖❧❖❧❖❧

The Tao Tê Ching is the principal scripture of a religion which has so departed from its ancient inspiration that it is for all practical purposes a different religion. It is, because of this, doubly instructive: It not only contains profound wisdom, but the history of its transmission confronts us with the melancholy aspect of complete deterioration. Apart from its originator Lao-tzu and the elaborator of his teachings, the mystic Chuang-tzu, who lived decades or centuries later (depending on the dating of the book), it produced no persons of first-rate religious power. Perhaps as a result of this it descended gradually into magic and occultism. Its priests became brewers of love potions and elixirs of immortality. They busied themselves with amulets and incantations. The major figure in this descent into magic was Chang Tao-ling who built a powerful organization based upon an alleged revelation from Lao-tzu out of the spirit world. In time, they became entangled in the fatal embrace of imperial politics. The so-called "Yellow Emperor" is said to have made Taoism the official religion in the second century A.D. in order to secure his own power and the tranquility of the state, thus leading Taoism further from its original inspiration.

## THE TAO TÊ CHING

In spite of this, I have selected the Tao Tê Ching for study here for several reasons. It is, in the first place, one of the wisest and most appealing books in

83

all the sacred literature of mankind. And though its own official heirs seem impervious to its appeal, it expresses a view of life that has had great influence throughout the Far East, eventually joining up with Buddhism to produce that unique religion called Zen. Moreover, its unreserved naturalism is a fine complement to the ascetic flavoring of the Bhagavad-Gita and the Dhammapada. With its acceptance of the natural as a part of the ultimate wisdom of things it has nourished that love of nature that has been a saving grace of the Chinese even in the bleakest circumstances.

This last observation suggests that the Tao Tê Ching may offer a much needed corrective to Western attitudes toward nature. In both our religion and science, nature has been mistreated in the West. Religion has suspected her and science has stretched her on the rack to control or exploit her. In other ways, too, the teachings in this book might prove a corrective. It introduces some attitudes desperately needed by a culture overbalanced toward strenuous competitiveness and egocentric status-seeking, and unduly confident of the saving power of vigorous action. Many of the ills of the West spring from this imbalance. We could very profitably learn that we are an organic part of nature and cultivate the quiet eye that experiences joy in the beauty of simple things, either of art or nature. The fact that China herself may now neglect these things in her headlong rush toward industrialization suggests that perhaps the West may become a trustee of this portion of her ancient wisdom.[1]

One more reason for studying the Tao Tê Ching is that, like the other two Asian works we have studied, it underscores the mystical tradition—the quiet, passive, trustful, female component in religion—an aspect of faith that has been all but lost in the Western emphasis on struggle, aggressiveness, and collective institutional efficiency in religion. To be sure, both aspects are present in the full Western tradition and cannot be reduced or eliminated from any adequate account of Christianity. Nevertheless, it is probably true that the most essential part—faith, trust, love, waiting upon God—is nearer to Taoism than it is to many of the distortions of Christianity that have gathered strength from aggressive nationalism and religious partisanship. The mystical tradition that is very much alive in all three of these books has been all but forgotten in the orthodox churches of the West. And even though Christianity is not simply mysticism, it is not understandable apart from it. The excessive "muscular" Christianity of America, with its failure to understand anything but a competitive activism, needs the reminder of this quiet book from the axial age of China.

### Translations and Sources

Lin Yutang says that "if there is one book in the whole of Oriental literature which one should read above all others, it is, in my opinion, Lao Tzu's Book of Tao."[2] This is one book, he claims, which can "interpret for us the spirit of the Orient."³ Non-Chinese scholars would seem to agree, if we may judge by its many translations. It is the most translated of all Chinese books. There are more than a dozen of them in English alone, and new ones appear every decade.

For the American student of Taoism, two books are especially valuable: Holmes Welch's *The Parting of the Way,*⁴ for its history of Taoism as a religion, and Arthur Waley's *Three Ways of Thought in Ancient China,*⁵ for the cultural and philosophical significance of the *Tao* concept.

### The Setting of the Book

Though the documentary problems are so great—perhaps insoluble—that we cannot be sure, it is probable that the Tao Tê Ching was originally a series of open letters of instruction to the rulers of China in a time of feudal chaos. As is usual in such a time, the ruling powers were depending excessively upon weapons, strategic cunning, and large armies. The resulting conflicts led to a state of near-anarchy, in which the common people, as usual, bore the heaviest burdens. Men were sick of the costly failures of those who would restore civilization through force and cunning alone. Something much deeper was needed. This was the situation to which the book was directed. Confucius (*ca.* 551–479 B.C.), of whom unfortunately we can say little within the space of our study, was another Chinese sage who was likewise proposing a nonmilitary approach to the problems of the ruptured social fabric of his society.

In a time of similar social chaos in the West, Niccolò Machiavelli (1469–1527), the supreme strategic "realist" of the Italian Renaissance, blamed the disorders of his age on the Church for having discredited by its cynical worldliness the spiritual tradition of Christianity, leaving men no options but cunning and power. Ancient China had its own forms of Machiavellianism. It was against these views that the Book of Tao was directed. Considering the international anarchy of our own time, the study of this book might possibly suggest some live options to the arbitrament of force and deceit among the nations of the twentieth century.

## THE MESSAGE OF THE BOOK OF TAO

### The Tao

The Tao is the fundamental concept of the work; once this concept is grasped, the message is within reach. Because the Chinese language is composed of pictograms, not letters and words, translation into our alphabetized language is extraordinarily difficult. This accounts in part for the wide variations in the English versions of the book. The Chinese character for *tao* is a composite pictogram of a head and a man walking. It literally means "walking-man sign, head-walking, or headway, or mainroad," and is translated as "Way."[6]

Interpreters have suggested three levels of meaning for Tao, or Way. It is first of all the norm or standard for human behavior, the authentic Way of Life, the way which leads to life in its fullest sense. A second meaning of Tao is the Way of the universe or of nature. It is the natural flow of things in their own integrity.

The fundamental message of the Tao Tê Ching is that the nature of reality is such that if man will shed the artificial and egoistic accumulations of a false culture and return to living by the simplicities of nature he will discover his true life. In this personal discovery he will also uncover the best way to lead society into a genuinely humane habitation. The book is at once mystical and practical. It suggests a path to self-knowledge and social peace. Its meaning is richer than our contemporary notion of a natural physical law, for it carries with it the force of moral law as well. It is nearer to what medieval philosophers called "natural law." To understand it is to stand at the "gate to the root of the world" (1–B).*

A third meaning for Tao is that it is the way of ultimate reality; it is "like the fountain head of all things. . . . An image of what existed before God" (4–LIN). Blakney translates the same passage, "It is like a preface to God" (4–B).

The reason for putting these three meanings in this order is that one can reach the second and third only through the first. Taoism is not a speculative system; it is a practical *way*, and one can learn its meaning only by living it. In this it shows a kinship to the Buddha's refusal to consider speculative questions before the questioner has begun treading the path. If one is faithful in practice, he will come in due time into such harmony with the Tao that he will come to know in his very bones the true nature of things.

> *If you work by the Way,*
> *You will be of the Way. . . .*
>                           (23–B)

This is mysticism, but not the mysticism of withdrawal from the world. It is a positive mysticism that sees the ultimate shining in and through the world of nature and the conduct of good men. Thus, in ascending order,

> *Man conforms to the earth;*
> *The earth conforms to the sky;*
> *The sky conforms to the Way;*
> *The Way conforms to its own nature.*
>                           (25–B)

---

* Note 7, at the end of this chapter, explains the meaning of the numbers and letters following each quotation from the Tao Tê Ching.

### The Meaning of Tê

Tê, the second Chinese character in the title of the Tao Tê Ching,* has been translated both as "virtue" and "power." Arthur Waley, for instance, entitles his translation of the book *The Way and Its Power*. But power is not an adequate equivalent. Virtue is a word that at one stage in its usage combined just that fine balance of both power and goodness which the concept Tê carries with it. Virtue, before it acquired a moral significance, originally meant simply the power by which anything produces its proper effects. The word virility still conveys this significance. But in its transition from Roman to European usage the word virtue was transposed from meaning the generative virility of a man to signifying the sterile chastity of a woman.

Tê suffered a reverse decline in meaning at the hands of the official Taoists. They gradually dropped the moral component and kept only the concept of power, by which they then reinterpreted the book entirely in terms of magic and occult manipulation.

Tê, then, is the force of genuine goodness, a power great enough, according to the book, to transform men and societies, because it is in league with the actual nature of things.

### On Talking About the Tao

If these explanations of the fundamental concepts of the book of Tao seem somewhat opaque, we have already been warned in its opening stanza:

> The Tao that can be told of
> Is not the Absolute Tao. . . .
> (1–LIN)

And the final stanza repeats the warning:

> True words are not fine-sounding;
> Fine-sounding words are not true.
> (81–LIN)

This is not surprising, since the "Tao is the mysterious secret of the universe . . ." (62–LIN). It can be known, as I have said, only by living it well. We may be pardoned, I believe, if we note here that the whole book is a successful effort to express this inexpressible truth.

The Tao is not open to the clever man who succeeds in ordinary affairs, trafficking with the appearances of things. It is disclosed only to the simple man of insight who has discovered what the later Taoist sage Chuang-tzu called the "child's heart." In this he is at one with all the mystics of every great religion.

---

* Ching, the third Chinese character, simply means Book.

*Wu-wei.* This reticence in speaking is simply part of the whole plan of living by the Way itself, a plan that could simply be called humility if that word too had not lost much of its larger meaning in modern usage. Wu-wei is a kind of actionless action, a way of affecting changes by patiently allowing one's self to be transformed by the Tao itself. It has been called a "creative quietude," accomplishment by being rather than doing, a "visible simplicity of life, embracing unpretentious ways" (19–B).

This submission to Tao may seem like doing nothing, but it is the most powerful way of being and doing. A man who abides by this rule is like water, the "softest substance of the world," which "goes through the hardest" (43–LIN).

> *Nothing is weaker than water,*
> *But when it attacks something hard*
> *Or resistant, then nothing withstands it,*
> *And nothing will alter its way.*
>
> (78–B)

Wu-wei is thus the supreme activity and the supreme relaxation because it emulates nature's secret way. Such relaxed quietude leads first to insight:

> *The secret waits for insight*
> *Of eyes unclouded by longing.* . . .
>
> (1–B)

And like the warnings of the Bhagavad-Gita and the Dhammapada, false desire is the great distorter which keeps most men blind:

> *Those who are bound by desire*
> *See only the outward container.*
>
> (1–B)

Once the insight is gained the quality of life begins to change and to effect profound alterations in the environment. "One may move so well that a footprint never shows" (27–WB).

> *Accordingly, the Wise Man*
> *Knows without going,*
> *Sees without seeing,*
> *Does without doing.*
>
> (47–B)

This is so contrary to Western ways of thought and action that it is worth while to emphasize it. Consider it in application to learning:

> *The student learns by daily increment,*
> *The Way is gained by daily loss,*
> *Loss upon loss until*
> *At last comes rest.*
>
> (48–B)

The reward is a new effectiveness on a completely different level:

> *By letting go, it all gets done;*
> *The world is won by those who let it go!*
> *But when you try and try,*
> *The world is then beyond the winning.*
>
> (48–B)

It reminds one of the enigmatic words of Jesus' Beatitudes: "The meek shall inherit the earth."

The Tao Tê Ching is not advising a way of retreat from wordly affairs. It proposes the Way as a means of changing events and transforming the world. The first change, to be sure, is in one's personal existence: The man who follows the Tao will first discover his "Simple Self," embrace his "Original Nature" (19–LIN). In doing so he will discover a wholeness and sanity which the life of frantic self-effort cannot achieve:

> *The surest test if a man be sane*
> *Is if he accepts life whole, as it is. . . .*
>
> (21–WB)

He will likewise discover a kind of personal invulnerability:

> *The weapons of the soldier cannot avail against him.*
> *How is this so?*
> *Because he is beyond death.*
>
> (50–LIN)

The second change is in outward events, the man of Tao accomplishes things in the world—why? Because the Tao

> *. . . gives them birth and does not own them,*
> *Acts . . . and does not appropriate them,*
> *Is superior, and does not control them.*
>
> (51–LIN)

This point is made in another way by Blakney's translation of the same stanza:

> *The Way brings forth,*
> *Its Virtue fosters them,*
> *With matter they take shape,*
> *And circumstance perfects them all:*
> *That is why all things*
> *Do honor to the Way*
> *And venerate its power.*
>
> (51–B)

The whole philosophy of the book is simply that by becoming one with the Way, the whole power of the universe works through you to accomplish its own ends. The human problem is not to interfere.

*If you work with the Way,*
*You will be of the Way;*
*If you work through its virtue*
*You will be given the virtue*
*Abandon either one*
*And both abandon you.*

(23–B)

The paradoxical rule of Tao seems to be "Be still while you work" (3–B).

Since this book was probably written as advice to rulers, its principles can be illustrated by showing how the Way applies to government:

*A leader is best*
*When people barely know that he exists,*
*Not so good when people obey and acclaim him,*
*Worst when they despise him.*
*"Fail to honor people,*
*They fail to honor you;"*
*But of a good leader, who talks little*
*When his work is done, his aim fulfilled,*
*They will all say, "We did this ourselves."*

(17–WB)

The principle of good government thus lies not in the activity but in the quality of being of its leaders. If the leader is "good at keeping low," that is, practicing the art of obedience to the Tao, his country will abide in peace and the arts of prosperity will flourish.

*When the Mystic Virtue becomes clear, far-reaching,*
*And things revert back (to their source),*
*Then and then only emerges the Grand Harmony.*

(65–LIN)

## Yin-Yang

The polarity of all things is a very ancient Chinese axiom. Life is a complementary balance of seeming opposites, the *yin* and the *yang*: male-female, summer-winter, day-night, light-dark, action-rest, good-bad, and so on. The Tao is the full organic unity of these opposites. This is partly why it cannot be named. The names are always one side only of the paradoxical tension of things. The truth, as the Greek philosopher Heraclitus was saying at about the same time, lies in the tension between the bow and the lyre. The wise man accepts these opposites, knowing that each has its proper place and function. He is aware of his feminine as well as his masculine nature:

*"One who has a man's wings*
*And a woman's also*
*Is in himself a womb of the world."*

(28–WB)

He also keeps a balance of the heavenly and the earthly:

> *The Heaven and Earth join,*
> *And the sweet rain falls,*
> *Beyond the command of men,*
> *Yet evenly upon all.*
>
> (32–LIN)

The wise man also knows the futility of contention; he has learned to accept life in its mysterious richness:

> *To yield is to be preserved whole.*
> *To be bent is to become straight.*
>
> .    .    .
>
> *Therefore the Sage embraces the One,*
> *And becomes the model of the world.*
> *He does not reveal himself,*
> *And is therefore luminous.*
> *He does not justify himself*
> *And is therefore far-famed.*
> *He does not boast of himself,*
> *And therefore people give him credit.*
> *He does not pride himself,*
> *And is therefore the ruler among men.*
> *It is because he does not contend*
> *That no one in the world can contend against him.*
>
> (22–LIN)

## Degeneration

The subtle meaning of the Tao often escapes our efforts at positive definition. Perhaps we can understand its nature better by observing the way of the world when its essential principles are violated. Selfishness and ugliness make generosity and beauty more urgently desirable; the man of the world, thoughtless of the Tao, soon discovers his lack in many painful ways.

The egoist, pushing, overweening, pressing his luck, falls into trouble as a man "standing at tip toe loses balance" (24–WB).

> *Stretch (a bow) to the very full,*
> *And you will wish you had stopped in time.*
>
> (9–LIN)

The man who loses his natural openness and tender vulnerability becomes hard and rigid and is easily broken.

> *Man, born tender and yielding,*
> *Stiffens and hardens in death.*
> *All living growth is pliant,*
> *Until death transfixes it.*

*Thus men who have hardened are 'kin of death'*
*And men who stay gentle are 'kin of life.'*
*Thus a hard-hearted army is doomed to lose.*
*A tree hard-fleshed is cut down:*
*Down goes the tough and big,*
*Up comes the tender sprig.*

(76–WB)

The social effects of ignoring the Tao are equally disastrous:

*Try to conquer the world;*
*This tactic is like to recoil.*
*For where armies have marched,*
*There do briars spring up;*
*Where great hosts are impressed,*
*Years of hunger and evil ensue.*

(30–B)

*He who delights in slaughter*
*Will not succeed in his ambition to rule the world.*

(31–LIN)

The reason for this failure is simple: The world simply will not stand for such manipulation. Reality resists such desecrations.

*As for those who would take the whole world*
*To tinker with as they see fit,*
*I observe that they never succeed:*
*For the world is a sacred vessel*
*Not made to be altered by man.*
*The tinker will spoil it;*
*Usurpers will lose it.*

(29–B)

Degeneration often takes a form that seems to be an affirmation of the Tao. Knowledge degenerates into intellectualization, goodness into rigid moralizing, and religion into mere ceremony. This often turns men away from the Tao, for they believe that they are being invited to embrace a way of death rather than life. But these degenerate forms are not the Tao—they are merely its husk. To be sure, one can justify formal learning, moral regulations, or ritual religion as the husk that protects the vital seed of life, but without the kernel within they are less nourishing than straw.

*Truly, once the Way is lost,*
*There comes then virtue;*
*Virtue lost, comes then compassion;*
*After that morality;*
*And when that's lost, there's etiquette,*
*The husk of all good faith. . . .*

(38–B)

No wonder that the student, feeling that the life has gone from his classes, echoes the Book of Tao:

> *Be done with rote learning*
> *And its attendant vexations. . . .*
>
> (20–B)

And formal religion often arouses the feeling that the world would be better off if we were rid of those "righteous men too!" (19–B).

The same with politics: When fanatical patriotism supplants its genuine counterpart, then "official loyalty [becomes] the style" and brings with it "a great hypocrisy," with the inevitable consequence: "The fatherland [grows] dark, confused by strife" (18–B).

## SUMMARY

One stanza from the Tao Tê Ching can serve as a summary of its message:

> *I have Three Treasures;*
> *Guard them and keep them safe:*
> *The first is Love.*
> *The second is, Never too much.*
> *The Third is, Never be first in the world.*
>
> · · ·
>
> *For love is victorious in attack,*
> *And invulnerable in defense.*
> *Heaven arms with love*
> *Those it would not see destroyed.*
>
> (67–LIN)

Love, simplicity, humility—these three are the great virtues of the Way in practice. Love, or compassion, a sense of the oneness of all things, is the prime virtue. Simplicity, never too much, back to the natural, the uncarved block, the core, is the second. In this it resembles folly rather than sophistication, but it puts one close to the power of life. Humility, selflessness, nonegotism, is the third. With ambition and contention gone, life can mature naturally and silently like a growing plant.

## TAOISM AND ZEN

In the last chapter we left Buddhism where it had evolved to the stage of the Mahayana ideal of the compassionate bodhisattva who realizes that nirvana and samsara (the world) are the same. It was in this form that Buddhism came to China. Though its ascetic and monkish temper was out of harmony with the Chinese acceptance of the world, it nonetheless found in mystical

Taoism a native Chinese tradition compatible with its own message. Out of the marriage of these two came Ch'an, or Zen Buddhism.

### Spiritual Oxherding

There is not space to further extend this discussion of Asian spirituality, but it may prove instructive to show how these two traditions, Taoism and Zen, grew into an organic unity. This can be done briefly by looking at the famous Zen spiritual oxherding pictures of the Zen master of the Sung Dynasty known as Kaku-an Shi-en.[8] Many series of such paintings have been done, but the series of Kaku-an, with its accompanying commentary, is the most complete, and represents the tradition at its fullest and best. They are a graphic representation of the course of spiritual development, from the moment the student begins his quest until he arrives at his goal.

1   The pictures begin with the oxherd searching for his lost ox. He wanders through the countryside looking everywhere. The ox represents man's spiritual nature that has somehow been lost track of. According to Zen this spiritual nature has become lost or invisible only because the oxherd, who represents mankind, has "violated his inmost nature."[9]

2   In the second picture the oxherd comes upon traces of the animal deep among the mountains and forests. He is encouraged because he is now on the right track. To find traces means to become at least vaguely aware of one's true nature. This awareness is the result of faithful attention to the guidance of qualified teachers.

3   Following the tracks of the ox the oxherd at last catches a glimpse of the hindquarters of the animal disappearing in a thicket. He is getting closer to his true nature.

4   The fourth picture shows the oxherd with a rope secured tightly around the ox's neck. The animal is hard to control. The reason for this is that the distractions of the world prevent an easy mastery. His own nature keeps slipping out of his grasp, for "wild nature is still unruly."[10]

5   At last, in the fifth picture, we see the oxherd quietly leading the ox by the nose string. The animal is now sufficiently broken to discipline so that he follows meekly; the slack line is there only as a reminder. At this stage in spiritual discipline the student finds meditation easy. He need not work as hard as formerly; thoughts follow quickly and in order without distractions.

6   In time the nose string is no longer necessary. In the sixth picture the oxherd rides homeward on the ox's back piping a tune on his flute. The ox knows its own way without external guidance. Here spiritual discipline has become second nature. The illusions of the world no longer intrude to stir up unruly thoughts and passions. The student goes forward almost automatically toward enlightenment.

7   In the seventh picture the oxherd has reached his home and is sitting lost in meditation, contemplating the moon rising out of the clouds over the mountains. The ox is out of sight as at the beginning of the series, but this

is now because the oxherd's spiritual nature is integrated into his whole being. He no longer needs the disciplines of a beginner; "his whip and rope are idly lying."[11]

8   The eighth picture is surprisingly a blank circle. Nothing at all shows. This represents the individual in the moment of his highest achievement, the ahrat nirvana of personal liberation, the "forgetting one's self while sitting" of Taoist mysticism. Both the ox and man are gone out of sight; the flame of desire has flickered out. In many of the oft-painted spiritual oxherding pictures the series concludes at this stage. But in its highest tradition there are two more that represent a restatement of Mahayana and Taoist ideals in their unity.

9   Picture nine shows the return of samsara, the world. It is a lovely springtime of fresh growth. The new buds are opening on the branches of the trees. The man who has come close to the center (Tao or Buddha nature) discovers that things are transformed: They spring forth in all their naturalness—"the waters are blue, the mountains are green"—and the man, sitting alone, observes things undergoing their "maya-like transformations."[12]

10   The last picture is the culmination of the Zen-Taoist ideal. We see the oxherd completely transformed into a perfectly integrated natural man. With a gay smile on his face he enters the city "with bliss-bestowing hands."[13] Following the Mahayana ideal of compassion he is completely at home in the city with the world of men. "No glimpses of his inner life are to be caught; for he goes on his own way without following consciously the steps of the ancient sages. Carrying a gourd he goes into the market, leaning against a staff he comes home. He is found in the company with wine-bibbers and butchers, he and they are all converted into Buddhas."[14]

Here, at last, you might say, is the supremely natural and complete man. He is one with himself, his fellows, nature, and the ultimate nature of things: "He touches, and lo! the dead trees are in full bloom."[15] Such is the Taoist-Buddhist answer to man's essential question, the promise of salvation. This represents, in my opinion, the supreme vision of both Buddhism and Taoism in its most developed form.

The Western observer may ask himself whether he sees in this teaching a vision of Christ, or not: The complete man who lives with sinners, rejecting moral rigorism and ritual regulations, and makes these same sinners into saints. Perhaps there is here an intimation of the ideal of the Divine Logos (see the first chapter of the Gospel according to St. John) which becomes flesh and dwells among men, "full of grace and truth."

I suggest this in concluding this brief study of Asian spirituality because the Western student is going to have to make some reconciliation with these Eastern traditions. Just how he will do it is problematical. We will return to this theme in a later chapter. But before we can do that we must consider in greater depth the ideal of Western spirituality and the fate it has suffered in the modern world.

## SUGGESTIONS FOR FURTHER READING

Huston Smith and Frederic Spiegelberg are especially good on Taoism in the general books already recommended. For a general work on the religious background of China, see Arthur Waley's *Three Ways of Thought in Ancient China* (Anchor, Doubleday, 1956). Holmes Welch's *The Parting of the Way: Lao Tzu and the Taoist Movement* (Beacon, 1957) is the best book on the history of Taoism as a formal religion.

For the texts of Taoism, the most complete is the recent reprinting of James Legge's translation of *The Texts of Taoism (Sacred Books of the East)*, Max Müller, ed., 2 vols. (Oxford University Press, 1891; Dover, 1962). Volume I contains the Legge translation of the Tao Tê Ching and the writings of the other famous figure in Taoism, Chuang-tzu. *The Wisdom of China and India*, Lin Yutang, ed. (Random House, 1942; Modern Library, 1955) has Lin Yutang's own translations of the Tao Tê Ching as well as Chuang-tzu's writings.

Three other translations of the Tao Tê Ching are available in inexpensive editions: R. B. Blakney, *Lao Tzu, The Way of Life: Tao Tê Ching by Lao Tzu* (American Library, 1955); Witter Bynner, *The Way of Life According to Laotzu* (John Day, 1945); and a recent translation by D. C. Lau, *Lao Tzu—Tao Tê Ching* (Penguin, 1963).

The most famous writer on Zen is D. T. Suzuki. William Barrett has chosen representative material from Suzuki's voluminous works and published them under the title *Zen Buddhism, Selected Writings of D. T. Suzuki* (Anchor, Doubleday, 1956). Alan W. Watts has for years been an interpreter of Zen to the American public. His *Way of Zen* (Pantheon, 1957) makes this Oriental philosophy plausible to the Western student.

Since comparisons are bound to arise, a good book to consult is D. T. Suzuki's, *Mysticism Christian and Buddhist* (Harper & Row, 1957; Collier, 1962). It should be compared with Otto's book on *Mysticism East and West*, recommended in Chapter 4.

## NOTES

1.  A work by Dom Aelfred Graham, *Zen Catholicism* (Harcourt, Brace & World, 1963), is an interesting example of the attempt to embrace the substance of Zen within Roman Catholic thought and practice.

2.  In *ibid.*, p. 579.

3.  *Ibid.*

4.  Holmes Welch, *The Parting of the Way: Lao Tzu and the Taoist Movement* (Beacon Press, 1957).

5.  Arthur Waley, *Three Ways of Thought in Ancient China* (G. Allen, 1939; Anchor, Doubleday, 1956).

6. Frederic Spiegelberg, *Living Religions of the World* (Prentice-Hall, 1956), p. 299.

7. The numbers in parentheses stand for the stanza of the Tao Tê Ching quoted. The letters indicate the translations as follows: B–R. B. Blakney, *The Way of Life: Tao Tê Ching by Lao Tzu* (New American Library, 1955); LIN–Lin Yutang, ed. and trans., "The Book of Tao," in *The Wisdom of India and China* (Random House, 1942; Modern Library, 1955); WB–Witter Bynner, *The Way of Life According to Laotzu* (John Day, 1945).

8. These pictures and the stanzas describing them are reproduced in D. T. Suzuki, *Manual of Zen Buddhism* (John F. Rider, 1950), pp. 127–144.

9. *Ibid.*, p. 129.

10. *Ibid.*, p. 131.

11. *Ibid.*, p. 132.

12. *Ibid.*, p. 133.

13. *Ibid.*, p. 134.

14. *Ibid.*

15. *Ibid.*

✦◖◗◖◗◖◗◖◗◖◗◖◗◖◗◖◗◖◗◖◗◖◗✦

## PART THREE

# BIBLICAL RELIGION

*Parts 3&4 — (Mostly 4)*

# 7

# *Modern Scholarship and the Bible*

No body of literature in the history of the West can compare in importance to the Judaeo-Christian Bible. It is literally ploughed into the life and consciousness of our civilization. Even when questioned or rejected it constitutes a force that polarizes human thought and energy. Like a great mountain range it is simply there and must be taken into account in mapping our cultural terrain.

But despite, or perhaps because of, its importance the Bible has been viewed ambivalently. Even its admirers, like Jacob wrestling with the angel who blessed him only after a struggle, have had to employ their best intellectual powers to receive its benefits. With the coming of modern scientific scholarship, that struggle took a special turn. It is the province of this chapter to examine some features of biblical scholarship, the problems which were encountered, the means that evolved for dealing with them, and some of the solutions that were finally adopted.

## THE SCIENTIFIC APPROACH
## TO SCRIPTURE

Throughout most of Christian history the attitude toward the Bible was dogmatic rather than literary or scientific. Theologians quoted ceaselessly from it in their debates. A scriptural text, unless reinterpreted or countered by another text, was decisive evidence for a position. Interpretation became largely a matter of weighty tradition, and such tradition was often substituted for the Bible itself.

With the coming of the Reformation and the invention of printing, the Bible became a popular book. Protestants became known as "people of the Book," and printing reproduced it cheaply enough to permit wide ownership by the laity as well as the clergy. In the seventeenth and eighteenth centuries, immediately following the age of the Reformation, the rise of physical science and the age of the Enlightenment fostered a critical spirit that was to have a lasting effect upon Western attitudes toward the Scriptures.

This change can be briefly summarized as a shift away from the view that the Bible is verbally or literally inspired. In the light of scientific scrutiny, verbal inspiration or the divine dictation of the text became untenable. The choice became clear: either scientific studies or verbal inspiration, but not both.

The reason for this conclusion was that scientific scholarship revealed biblical fallibility on many matters of fact. Discrepancies were pointed out both in the Bible's own multiple reports of the same events, and by comparing biblical records with facts of the ancient world verified from other reliable sources. Martin Luther, well before the era of scientific historical criticism, had noted that, for example, First and Second Chronicles were more reliable history than First and Second Kings. And with the increasing knowledge of the history of the ancient Near East it became apparent that the biblical writers had faltered at other places. The duration of the Persian Empire, for example, was miscalculated by nearly two hundred years.

Such claims were naturally met with consternation by many who saw in the new scholarship the work of the Devil himself ranging out from his lair in German universities. More hardy souls undertook the studies for themselves, and gradually the new spirit of critical study, among those who were acquainted with its methods, became all but irresistible.

The two founders of modern biblical criticism are the Jewish philosopher Spinoza (1632–1677) and Richard Simon, a French Catholic theologian (1638–1712). Spinoza proposed to study the Scriptures "in a spirit of entire freedom without prejudice."[1] Simon, in his *Histoire Critique du Vieux Testament*, published in 1678, raised some of the basic questions regarding Old Testament sources that became the foundation for much later work.

Jean Astruc (1684–1766), French physician and biblical scholar, who is credited with the first clear formulation of critical method, distinguished two different sources for the five so-called Books of Moses (the Pentateuch), also known as the Law of Moses, with which the Old Testament opens. A century later the first full-fledged critical history of Israel was completed (1878) by the celebrated German Protestant theologian and Orientalist Julius Wellhausen (1844–1918). At the same time, G. R. Driver and Robertson Smith, among the Protestants, and Baron von Hügel and Pére Lagrange, among the Roman Catholics, were working in England and Scotland.

The year 1859 is a critical year in intellectual history. We associate it with the publication of Darwin's *On the Origin of Species*. Another, though lesser work, published just one year later, created in its own circle nearly as much dispute: *Essays and Reviews*, a symposium by Christian scholars who had accepted the scientific point of view. This book was denounced by clergy and laity alike, but one of the essayists, Frederick Temple (1821–1902), nevertheless went on to become the Archbishop of Canterbury. The progress of scientific scholarship could not be stopped. It was this gradual acceptance of science by thinking minds in every religious persuasion that led William Sanday (1843–1920), a distinguished British biblical scholar of the century's end, to say that by the year 1900 the premises of critical biblical research (so-called "higher criticism") had become international and interconfessional.

Acceptance did not come without a struggle. After all the field of higher criticism was highly specialized, and it threatened traditional modes of thought so ominously that only the passage of time and continual education at last brought the world of Christian scholarship to all but complete acceptance. At the present time this critical method is the approved procedure in nearly all the graduate seminaries of the Christian churches.[2]

What is this method? Perhaps one of the chief objections to it is that it begins by putting in brackets the theological claims concerning the Bible; it thus places the book in the context of human history where it may be examined as any other secular work of history or literature. This bracketing is not a denial of theological claims; it is merely a methodological postponement of their consideration until other matters, which can be settled by scientific scholarship, have been thoroughly considered.

What are these other matters? Briefly, they consist in answering such questions as the following: When was the book or passage written? Who wrote it? Why was it written?; that is, what were the circumstances that called forth this book? What was the author's message in these circumstances? The theological justification for pursuing these questions is the belief that God revealed himself to the men and women of the Bible through the total context of human life. Knowing the context should illuminate the message rather than obscure it. It was natural, however, that this new knowledge would require a reinterpretation of many hallowed passages and the abandonment of long-held views, and unfortunately, the human mind is not designed to accept such consequences without a struggle.

## The Results of the Scientific Approach

The chief result of more than 150 years of scholarship has been a breathtaking clarification of the background of the biblical writings. We know now the original languages in which the texts were written, the circumstances of the writing, significant information about many of the authors, the customs and practices of the times, and the fund of ideas upon which the writers drew in expressing their meaning. The result is a body of factual information so extensive that no reasonable biblical interpreter would dare now ignore it.

One of the most competent modern biblical scholars sums up the long history of research in this way: "Broadly speaking we may reasonably claim that the literary and historical problems of biblical research have been solved, at least in general outline, and that the results of the labors of scholars in the biblical sphere are just as secure as those of scholars in any other branch of scientific literature and historical inquiry."[3]

This statement needs to be balanced with the observation that in another sense biblical studies are at present in a ferment of reexamination concerning both method and content, but present debates do not in any sense call into question the genuine achievements of scientific scholarship nor do they suggest in the least a return to the prescientific era of biblical interpretation. The meaning of these remarks will become clearer as we examine more specific questions in later parts of this chapter.

### Some Examples of Scientific Inquiry: Old Testament

The character and significance of the results of critical biblical studies can best be appreciated by examining a few examples. Let us start with the problem with which the whole investigation began: the sources of the first five books of the Bible: Genesis, Exodus, Leviticus, Numbers, and Deuteronomy. The traditional view was that their author was Moses, even though they narrated events that occurred hundreds of years after his death and even contained an account of his death and burial.

Astruc had proposed at least two sources for these books. Later studies yielded evidence of yet other sources, and the present conclusion of scholars is that we must distinguish at least four. Since the authors are not known by name they are usually designated as "J," "E," "D," and "P."

Astruc had noted that in the writings the name for God alternated between "Jahweh" and "Elohim" and the documentary strands thus distinguished were named for the first letter of these names as J and E, sometimes referred to as the "Jahwist" and "Elohist." Later studies suggested that the former was a Judean and the latter an Ephriamite from the northern kingdom (Israel), so that the letters also distinguished the writers' homelands.

Following this clue, the separate strands of the literature were sorted out into their probable original form. In the process more became known of the characteristics of the two authors: their styles, theology, and historical points of view. The E literature is more sophisticated and refined than that of J, and contains a more spiritualized view of God. J, being the more primitive in theology and spirit, also possesses the greater dramatic and narrative force. And each of them favors his own region in the way the stories are slanted.

The reader can discover some of these differences for himself by examining the account of the escape of the children of Israel through the waters of the Red Sea. According to J's account, God providentially sent a strong east wind which blew back the shallow waters of the Sea of Reeds (a probable translation of the original Hebrew words) during the night and permitted the Israelites to cross over, the wind subsiding and the waters returning as the Egyptians tried to drive through the wet sand with their iron-wheeled chariots. E makes the whole story more miraculous. Moses raised his arm and the waters divided into walls on both sides, and when the Israelites had passed through he again raised his arm and the waters returned, drowning the pursuing Egyptians.

The story of this literary analysis is much too long to fairly summarize here, but the main conclusions can be indicated. The first five books of the Bible are the result of the progressive amalgamation and editing of at least four strands of tradition. J had been written by around 860 B.C. and E a century later. Around 650 B.C., still another century later, an editor combined them into one document (JE). The extraordinary skill of this documentary fusion assures us that this editor was no mere journalistic hack.

The next stage in the growth of the Pentateuch was the writing of another work known as the Deuteronomic Code (D), a summary of the development and application of Hebrew law from the time of Moses to around 621 B.C. This work was also later melded with the JE document, and some of the editor's emendations can be seen in the passages of J and E.

The completion of the Pentateuch came after the writing of yet another body of literature known as "P," since it represents the point of view of a newly established priestly class. This so-called Priestly Code was then fused with the former material to complete the Pentateuch as we now know it, the whole work reaching completion by about 430 B.C.

Consider how different a picture these books now present in the light of research. Instead of a single work composed by Moses in the thirteenth century B.C., we have a carefully edited anthology by a whole corps of writers from the tenth century B.C. to the fifth. Consider also the dramatic changes of interpretation required by this enormous shift of perspective. It should not take much imagination to grasp why this scholarly development was at first regarded by the faithful with the utmost suspicion. Now, ironically, it is the staple content of seminary courses for rabbis, priests, and ministers.

Another battle surged around the authorship of the Book of Isaiah. Using the same tools of literary analysis, scholars concluded that this is not the work of a single hand but, again, an anthology representing at the very least three authors writing many decades apart in different regions of the Near East.

The episode of the Dead Sea Scrolls, discovered in a cave above the Dead Sea in 1947, has, more than any other event, dramatized to the layman the methods and skills of scholars who work with biblical documents. When the scrolls first came to the attention of responsible scholars, their initial problem was to determine whether they were forgeries. This could best be determined by ascertaining their date of composition. This was achieved in the following way: First, by examining the style of the script that appeared in the scrolls the paleographers, who have classified scripts in the order of their appearances in history, were able to date the writings so accurately that later methods only served to confirm their judgment. Then the archaeologists compared the pottery jars in which the scrolls were found with their charts of ancient pottery styles. This evidence also pointed to the same general period—the century preceding the Christian era. Later studies by these same scholars of the ruins at Qumrân, a ruined settlement near the site of the find, confirmed the dates further by coins, other artifacts, and by earth faults from ancient earthquakes in the region.

Then the chemists had their turn, analyzing the ink in which the scrolls were written and the traces of radioactive substances in the materials used in wrapping them. Their estimate of probable dates converged toward the former estimates.

Last of all, since this involved a more time-consuming study of the content of the scrolls themselves, scholars in the fields of comparative history and literature began their analyses of literary styles, historical allusions, quotations from known material, and so on.

When all these experts had completed their work it became as certain as scientific scholarship can be that the scrolls were genuine, that they had come from a religious community that had lived on the shores of the Dead Sea in the century prior to the coming of Christ. Here was an instance in which all the tools of biblical research, developed over nearly two centuries of diligent toil, were simultaneously available for the examination of a newly discovered body of ancient literature, with the assured results that I had just summarized.

### Examples from New Testament Studies

The title of Albert Schweitzer's *Quest of the Historical Jesus*, which appeared shortly after the turn of the century, served to focus the first major New Testament problem that scientific scholarship undertook to solve. Though greatly modified, this problem is still in the foreground of New Testament research. The historical question early resolved into a discussion of the authorship, dating, and sources of the first three Gospels, Matthew, Mark, and Luke, and it became known as the "Synoptic Problem."

Within a few minutes of careful study even the uninitiated layman can grasp the outlines of the problem by looking at an edition of the Synoptic Gospels, in which similar stories and teachings from the first three books of the New Testament are printed side by side for comparison. When this is done, several things immediately stand out: (1) Most of the content of Mark is repeated in Matthew and Luke. Where this has occurred the passages are called the "Triple Tradition." (2) In many cases, Matthew and Luke have parallel passages that do not appear in Mark. This is called the "Double Tradition." The remaining material, appearing in either Luke or Matthew alone, is called the "Single Tradition." (3) Much of this paralleling is word for word, precluding the likelihood of independent observers reporting the same events. (4) The three Gospels do not agree in all cases on the order of events.

Several questions naturally arise in the light of such data: In what order were the Gospels written? Who wrote them? What were their sources?

One answer to these questions that has been widely accepted among scholars can be summarized in this way:[4] (1) Mark was the first Gospel and it was available, possibly in different versions, to the authors of Matthew and Luke. The source of Mark is probably the recollections of the Apostle Peter, then residing in the western part of the Roman Empire. It is for this reason quite Roman in spirit. (2) Matthew and Luke were composed at about the same time in different parts of the Empire; Luke in the Greek world and Matthew in the Palestinian. To account for the similarities between Luke and Matthew that are not traceable to Mark, scholars have postulated an early document, called "S" or "Q" (the German *Quelle* is translated Source), which circulated prior to both Gospels, and consisted mainly of the sayings of Jesus and a story of his death. (3) To account for the material of the "Single Tradition," material found in Luke or Matthew alone, it is proposed that the authors of these Gospels in their earliest editions had information which they had collected on their own. Luke prefaces his Gospel with a frank statement that he is undertaking a compilation. Both Matthew and Luke would have been in a position to possess such information, and their difference in perspective and natural opportunity would account for their divergences. This assumes that both these later Gospels were given their final form by editors (around A.D. 80 to 90) who incorporated later traditions that had become current by their time.

There is not space here to indicate the countless labors and researches that contributed to these conclusions, or to do justice to other alternatives that have been proposed. But the student can at least begin to grasp what a critical literary study of the Gospels involves.

## NEW PERSPECTIVES IN RECENT BIBLICAL RESEARCH

While contemporary scholars gratefully accept the monumental work of critical scholarship over the past two centuries, they nonetheless have been confronted by serious issues growing out of these studies. The new questions and their answers have changed the whole tenor of the three-cornered debate perpetually going on among the keepers of orthodox faith, biblical scholars, and the secular critics of religion. A comprehension of these new currents promises to enhance the understanding of the meaning of religion in general and biblical faith in particular.

## Demythologizing

This is the name of a program of New Testament studies proposed by the celebrated German scholar Rudolf Bultmann in his famous work *New Testament and Mythology* (1941). He contends that the message of the Bible, written as it was in an ancient culture, is embedded in a world-picture which has become unbelievable to modern man. The modern world-picture, based upon science, makes the whole Bible seem alien. To meet this problem Bultmann proposes to reinterpret the mythological material and thus recover the basic teaching shining through the antique forms. Only thus, he believes, can modern man appropriate the message of the Bible.

Bultmann's conviction was forged only in part by his sensitivity to secular thought. Ongoing biblical studies shaped the tools that made this analysis possible. One investigation that helped in this direction was a study of the way in which the New Testament literature arose. The study of early Christian literary creativity—*Formgeschichte*—as it is called, had established that the earliest literary impulse of the Church expressed itself not in documentary histories but in stories, teachings, creeds, prayers, and in other aids to worship. Central to all this literature was the kerygma—the proclamation of the events of salvation: the ministry, death, and resurrection of Jesus Christ. This kerygma was the chief motif of preaching in the early Church. Its primary purpose was to challenge hearers with what God had done for them in Jesus. It was not a biographical effort but a call to faith, a confrontation of those who would listen with a new kind of human existence.

All the New Testament books sprang from this kerygmatic setting. They were not intended as journalistic reports. The Acts of the Apostles, for instance, is an account of how the faith spread. The Epistles contained the doctrinal implications and ethical exhortations that were contained in the gospel itself. The Gospels, a new literary form, were created as a distinctive way of telling the sacred story. Its writers told the story not as reporters but as preachers calling men to a changed existence through acceptance of the proclaimed faith.

Bultmann took the conclusions of *Formgeschichte* scholarship, combined it with the modern secular analysis of the human condition set forth by existentialist philosophy, and the result was his program of demythologizing.[5] Simply stated, existentialism is thinking that is concerned with man as an existing and decisional being rather than as a theoretical thinker. It is concerned not with intellectual speculation but with the commitments required in the process of becoming a real man.

Bultmann holds that the New Testament confronts men with a choice between two radically distinct ways of existing. The first is a life outside of faith where a man lives by contriving ways and means of saving himself out of his own resources. The second is a life within faith. The first way, according to the New Testament, says Bultmann, leads inevitably either to despair—

because finite man cannot but fail in attempting to establish his own existence—or to idolatry, in which he gives over his life to frail finite supports that cannot bear the weight that he would place upon them.

A life within faith—the life to which the New Testament calls man—is one in which a man gives up all self-contrived efforts at establishing his existence and gives himself completely to God as revealed in Jesus. This means abandoning adherence to all visible tangible realities and opening one's self to the forgiving grace of God, thus finding release from one's own past and from all fear of the future. This is what Bultmann calls true existence.

What has Jesus to do with this? It is the coming of the Christ that makes all the difference. This event is a call to men to enter authentic existence through faith. It reminds man of his true state as a creaturely fallen sinner and therefore also of the fact that salvation is not something he can achieve for himself.

The essence of the New Testament kerygma, according to this view, is that Jesus' teaching and deeds, especially his death and resurrection, are a call to authentic existence in God and for one's neighbor.

Bultmann's critics have maintained that the Bible is already demythologized and that its writers had quite consciously rejected the mythologies of paganism and set forth a radically demythologized gospel.[6] Other critics, taking a different tack, point out that "myth" (in the sense of living symbol) is the very language of faith, and that to demythologize it in favor of literal statement is to distort out of recognition the very substance which Bultmann seeks to set forth with greater clarity.[7] Yet others have maintained that in his enthusiasm for existential philosophy Bultmann has underestimated the nonexistential historical elements that are important in the actual life of faith itself. We cannot take time here to adjudicate this debate. No doubt some of the criticisms are based upon misunderstandings, but the issues are important and they offer clues to some important directions in biblical interpretation.

## The New Hermeneutic

This will no doubt seem to the reader to be yet another barbarous word, but anyone who would enter into these debates must learn at least a few of the key terms, such as kerygma, demythologizing, and hermeneutic. This last word means simply the theory of interpretation. The so-called old hermeneutic focused on interpreting the biblical documents in such a way that one could get back to the original situation and meaning. The new hermeneutic, following Bultmann's lead, is more existential. It strives to interpret the documents in such a way that they speak relevantly to present-day man. The old hermeneutic was scientific, the new one asks how the ancient material answers man's perennial religious quest.

Using this as a key, what, for example, is the meaning of such biblical words as creation, providence, salvation, the Word of God? "Creation" says: You are not your own; you were brought into existence by the loving power of

God. "Providence" says: You cannot exist on your own power; even when you think that you do so, it is God's presence that makes your existence possible. "Salvation" is not a ticket to heaven. It means a state of existing in God and by his power, both here and forever. The "Word" is not a set of doctrines but the power of God to arouse man to an authentic existential response.

Thus, a careful reading of the Scriptures is not primarily in order to discern the meaning that the authors had in mind, but to discover *in life* the meaning of the words here and now. Biblical writings are not literature in the sense of a body of compositions to be enjoyed or studied scientifically, but a means of arousing faith—a meaningful response to existence. For the new hermeneutic the problem is, as James Robinson says, to retranslate the canonical writings so that they may "assert their authority in a situation to which they no longer directly speak."[8]

One way to understand what these thinkers are working at is to contrast the so-called objective approach to the meaning of biblical language with this more existential one. The objective method approached the literature from the outside, so to speak. It was concerned with the elimination of subjectivity as a source of prejudice. The new method, writes Robinson, is to realize that "subjectivity provides an access to the subject matter of the text that is indispensable . . . if it is really that subject matter, serious both then and now, that he is seeking to understand."[9] Far from introducing distortions, subjectivity—in this special sense—"insures that the phenomena with which the text was grappling—if it is a serious text—are not overloooked or distorted into (mere) curiosities."[10] The issue, stated quite clearly, is "whether the interpreter decides to understand his being the way the text understands existence."[11]

In the older, objective approach the subject matter was to make, as the philosopher Heidegger says, "everything . . . give account of itself, state its cause, to the investigating subject to which it is answerable."[12] The new way, says Robinson, asks, "Can we even conceive of a scholarly relation to reality that would instead consist in beings calling up their being to us, so that the scholar's role would be to answer responsibly with his own words this tolling of the being of beings as it comes to him?"[13]

Critics of this new approach, like Ernst Käsemann, have insisted that this goes too far in leaving the objective historical material behind and that some scholars must be left to "administer the estate left by the historians."[14] Certainly we can agree with the philosopher Karl Jaspers that the foundations of scientific history are a "corrective against groundless fantasies"[15] that might tempt interpreters who lacked them. But we have to oppose continually the sufficiency of "mere critical investigation that dispels every shred of reality."[16] For such is the effect of mere factual history which does not have the courage to risk interpreting human beings humanly.

Perhaps I may be permitted to comment that as new tools of investigation are forged it is not necessary or wise to discard the old ones that have served so long and so well; rather, we should extend our investigations in new directions without neglecting the old, like the scribe who, in Jesus' words, "brings forth from his treasures things both old and new."

## The New Quest of the Historical Jesus

Albert Schweitzer in his *Quest of the Historical Jesus* brought the old quest to a final stage that revealed many of its difficulties. For him and his predecessors the quest of the historical Jesus meant discovering what can be known of Jesus of Nazareth by means of the scientific methods of the historian. The way historians viewed this quest was determined largely by the standards of historical research formulated in the nineteenth century on standards derived from the Enlightenment of the eighteenth century.

Since it was clear that the books of the New Testament were written by believers, the quest could be stated simply as finding the "historical" Jesus behind the theological formulations of the authors. Schweitzer's conclusion was rather depressing. He pointed out that every attempt to describe this historical Jesus only produced biographies of him that reflected the bourgeois values of their modern authors. Schweitzer attempted to remedy this by recognizing the apocalyptic element in the gospel accounts and attempting to interpret Jesus radically in these terms. In this, however, he introduced no new methods—only a more rigorous application of the old ones. The Jesus of his account remains an enigmatic first-century figure who was deluded by the hope of an early end to history.

After the disastrous events of the twentieth century, beginning with World War I, a new approach to biblical faith was introduced by scholars who sought a way to answer the doubts about culture that these events had nourished. They proposed an entirely new approach to the New Testament faith—from the inside, so to speak, instead of from the outside, as their scientific predecessors had done. The chief figure in this theological revival was Karl Barth, and the major announcement of this position came in his great commentary on Paul's Epistle to the Romans. We must put off until later a discussion of this work, but what follows here presupposes this theological transformation.

The new quest of the historical Jesus, which is organically related to the two themes we have just discussed, accepts the impossibility of getting back behind the theological elements of the New Testament to a nontheological, historical figure.[17] The historian's Jesus—if we mean by this the person discovered by strict objective rationalistic methods—is clouded by two difficulties. The first is that almost nothing can be known of him. We simply don't have the records to write such a biography. The second defect is that he would not be of any interest to faith. No intelligible way can be charted from such a hypothetical figure and the community of faith which arose from his life and work. In this case he wouldn't even make sense sociologically.

The new quest, to be sure, recognizes two layers of tradition in the New Testament—but they are not the theological and the nontheological. They are, first, the layer of interpretation characteristic of the early Church and, second, the layer of Jesus' own interpretation of himself. Insofar as we can use historical methods to sort out these two layers, we have the new quest.

The point is that Jesus is not understandable even to himself except as a kerygmatic person. To be sure, he no doubt thought of himself in somewhat different terms from those of the early Church, but they are not the purely humanistic terms that the old quest presupposed.

This position is supported by a wholly new understanding of what it means to be human, which is quite distinct from the understanding of the Enlightenment. It contends that every man seeks to find the meaning of his existence in the world, and that this implies a religious dimension to all historical existence. Jesus' own understanding of himself, then, is reflected in that part of the New Testament that cannot be directly traced to the early Church.

It is not appropriate here to discuss in detail the principles by which this distinction is made, but the general conclusions are that Jesus himself understood his life kerygmatically and that the true historical Jesus is a faith figure from the very beginning. Several things point directly to this conclusion. His ministry began with a call to the new Kingdom of God just being inaugurated. His teachings were an account of the new life within that kingdom. Within this new era of the Kingdom he exercised the authority of a special emissary by forgiving sins, healing the sick, and teaching that in the final judgment men will be judged by their relationship to him.

The Church's position was that it saw Jesus from a time following his death and resurrection, and tended to read back into the earlier time meanings that became clear only in the light of these later events. But the new-questers hold that these meanings are not radically distinct from Jesus' self-understanding, and that therefore the "Jesus of history" is not essentially different from the "Christ of faith."

We may note in conclusion that these new themes of biblical study are related in many ways to the reinterpretation of history and existence that have arisen in many secular fields of scholarship. Some of these will become more evident as we proceed.

## HOW DID THE BIBLE BECOME A SACRED BOOK—A CANON?

Another matter that critical scholarship can help illuminate is the issue of how the Bible came to be looked upon as a sacred book, or canon. The earliest writers and prophets, and those who read or listened to them, had no idea that they were involved in creating a sacred book. A canon, the name given to any accepted body of sacred writings, takes a great deal of time to arrive on the scene of history. What Christians have named the Old Testament took more than a thousand years from the composition of its first materials to its final canonization in present form as the sacred book of the Jews. The New Testament waited nearly four hundred years before final acceptance by the Christian churches.

Let us consider the process of canonization in general. First, there must be a historical situation and a man in whom ultimate concern breaks forth in some vivid way. The Prophet Isaiah, for example, is caught up in a profound experience in the Temple and receives a message for the meaning of the time in which he is living (740 B.C.). Or Gautama experiences his "enlightenment" under the Bo tree. Such experiences pass into the stream of social life through word of mouth or written report. In time the group to which it comes perceives it as having ultimate import and treasures the account. If the significance of the experience proves to be lasting, the record of it becomes part of the history of the people, enters their sacred lore, and is incorporated into the ways in which they worship.

At this point an important shift takes place. Some serious crisis that threatens the group's existence compels its members to sift through their traditional materials in order to clarify the meaning of the times. This sifting often leads to a collection of definitive writings. The process continues until at last (often centuries later) a point is reached in which the most fundamental materials, those most persuasively defining the group's basic and ultimate meanings, are rounded out, and the process of addition to the collection stops. This marks the beginning of learned commentary (the work of scribes) as distinct from inspired primary composition (the work of prophets).

Now let us apply this pattern to the history of the Judaco-Christian canon. The experiences of the Jews from the time of Abraham (ca. 1900 B.C.) to King Josiah (621 B.C.) were recorded in writings of all kinds and were gradually edited, as we have briefly indicated, into the form which we call the Pentateuch. A portion of this work, the Book of Deuteronomy, was "discovered" in 621 B.C. during a renovation of the Temple at Jerusalem and was adopted by King Josiah as an official document of his reign with the full support and assistance of the religious leaders who had carefully preserved these traditions through less favorable regimes. This restatement of the noble theology and ethical religion of earlier times enabled the tradition to pass on into the active religion of the day.

With the destruction of Jerusalem in 586 B.C. and the transportation of its chief citizens into captivity in distant Babylon, Judaism experienced a soul-tormenting crisis. Thoughtful reflection on this event recalled and vindicated the warnings of the Prophets and led to new prophetic writings interpreting afresh the terrible times through which the Hebrew people were passing. With the return of the captives to Jerusalem a century later, it became imperative to standardize the people's heritage in order to give guidance and meaning to the national life. The great writings were thus collected and set forth authoritatively by the scribe Ezra around 440 B.C. Note that this is prior to the writing of many of the books now in the Old Testament.

By about 200 B.C. the sacred collection grew to include the so-called "Former Prophets" (Joshua, Judges, Samuel, and Kings) and the "Later Prophets" (Isaiah, Jeremiah, Ezekiel, and the Twelve). The process of experience and writing continued, but the conviction became general in the Jewish community that only writings composed before 444 B.C. should be looked upon as divinely authoritative.[18] From this time the question of what constituted a "sacred" book became entirely a historical matter; namely, whether the date of composition preceded 444 B.C. or not.

Since the Jewish scholars did not have the tools of modern research it is not surprising that when the last stage of the canonization took place at the Council in Jamnia around A.D. 100, many books written after the fifth century were inadvertently included in the authoritative collection. The final determination at Jamnia was due to the catastrophies that had befallen the Jewish community in the destruction of Jerusalem (A.D. 70) and their dispersement throughout the gentile world. If the Jewish faith was not to perish, it was imperative to establish an authoritative standard.

This story explains why many fine ancient books of the Jews, such as the Wisdom of Ben Sirach, remained outside the canon. They were known to have been composed too late. They took their place, however, in a secondary collection of books known as the Apocrypha. Later, when the Christian canon had been determined, the Roman Catholic Church included them in its Latin version of the Scriptures. No doubt this was because the early Church had a tradition of reverence for these writings, having received them in the Septuagint, the earliest Greek translation of the Hebrew scriptures that comprised what came to be called the "Old Testament."

The Christian canon took less time to write, but it took centuries to attain clear status as the authoritative body of sacred writings. The first stage was the acceptance of the Old Testament by Christians as their own Bible. This was due to the fact that the first Christians were devout Jews. But their own experiences surpassed the interpretations of life and faith contained in the Old Testament. They had known Jesus and the subsequent outpouring of life which had shaped the early Christian community. This led first to oral reporting and then to fragmentary collections of writings such as, perhaps, Q (S) and the letters of the Apostle Paul.

With the passage of time disputes arose over the proper meaning of the faith. Writings with apostolic authority became imperative to settle these matters. This led to a gradual collection of the most authoritative documents into regional collections. By early in the second century, roughly a hundred years after Jesus' death, these collections abounded in the various churches and were locally authoritative.

The so-called Muratorian Canon, a manuscript discovered in Milan about A.D. 800, lists the books that were sacred in Rome about A.D. 200. It contained some books not now in the canon (the Revelation of Peter and the Wisdom of Solomon), and was still uncertain as to some of the General Epistles. However, the Gospels and the main Epistles were already accepted without question. In about the year A.D. 192 some unknown author coined the title "New Testament" for this collection.

The first official Church statement that lists the books as we presently have them was issued by Athanasius, Bishop of Alexandria, in A.D. 367. There was still some dispute over some of the books, but his list practically settled the matter, and St. Jerome used it as the basis of his translation of the Greek New Testament (the Septuagint) into Latin, a version known as the Vulgate. The New Testament thus became the undisputed canon of the Christian Church.

When people ask whether new books could be added to the biblical canon, an understanding of this history can give them the answer. The books of a sacred canon have a very special relationship to the spiritual history of a people, and to be included in this list would require that the author be born in a previous age. If in the future scholars should discover another Gospel which had the marks of apostolic authority it is conceivable that the canon might be reopened to include it, but only such a work could possibly qualify.

We have explored thus far only the outermost edge of the vast continent of biblical scholarship, but this sampling should give a fair idea of its methods and spirit. In conclusion let me summarize the relationship between the spirit of unfettered research and the life of faith.

Our brief account of modern biblical scholarship shows that it began under a cloud of suspicion, but that it has now emerged as the standard instrument of biblical studies. The following principles are now generally recognized: The biblical scholar must be as free as any scientist to pursue his studies to their logical conclusion. If the conclusion is foregone, the research is precluded. Scholarship is not in the service of propaganda however holy; nor does it offer an apology for any tenet of faith however sacred. The scholar cannot be faithful to his method (or to his God) if he consciously biases his work to promote any preconceived position.

All this does not mean that the scholar is disloyal to his faith. It means that he has come to some conclusions about it that are consistent with his scholarly standards. This can be simply stated: If the God of his faith is indeed the truth about existence, nothing he will discover can in the slightest injure that truth. On the contrary, in the long run it can only serve to make it shine the brighter.

A second view of religious faith that reassures the scholar in his work is the knowledge that scientific scholarship with all its illuminating power is in itself helpless to unveil the inner substance of the Bible. That substance still remains to be examined after critical scholarship has done its work; all research is mere preface to the earnest personal probing of the Bible for the authentic Word which is spoken there. Biblical scholarship points beyond itself by showing that the biblical record is not mere history or literature in a secular sense, but salvation history and literature concerned with awakening man to the meaning of his relationship to God, the Self-Existent, the

Ultimate Being upon whom all life, history, and personality rest. Objectively, the Bible appears to the scholar as an ancient collection of books of great beauty and historical profundity. But to faith, the Book is vastly more. It is the record of God's actions, his salvation reaching out toward all men, his compassionate care encompassing all beings, his eternal Kingdom being born and reborn over again in the hearts of men. Just as science cannot discover such a truth, it can likewise not refute it. Just what means we have for dealing with it must be considered later when we ask more specifically about the logic that controls our knowledge of God.

We must recognize, however, that a certain tension exists between the tenets of the Judaeo-Christian faith and historical research. It is reported that Paul Tillich once commented that he grew tired of waking each morning wondering what historical research had done to his theology. But there is no way out of this tension for a faith that is historical in nature. Theology must accustom itself to living with the necessity for continuous revision. There is now no going back. Once having tasted of the fruit of scientific knowledge we must leave the garden of innocent ignorance and enter the toil and sweat of scientific work. Those who would go back invariably find the path guarded by angels with flaming swords.

After nearly 200 years of the most intense scrutiny the biblical faith still remains, I believe, stronger and clearer than ever. No other sacred literature has been subjected to such critical examination, though they all must eventually pass through this purifying fire. Out of the studies have come a new respect for the integrity of rational thought and a new concept of the authority of the Bible undistorted by misapprehensions of its character and purpose.

We should now be somewhat prepared to turn to the Bible itself to see what meaning and message it has for our time.

## SUGGESTIONS FOR FURTHER READING

Robert Pfeiffer's *Introduction to the Old Testament* (Harper & Row, 1941) contains a good account of the history of the scientific approach to the Scriptures. This is also worth consulting in order to examine the detailed reasoning behind the documentary analysis of the Pentateuch into J, E, P, and D, the similar documentary analysis of Isaiah, and the dating of Daniel. *The Philosophy of Spinoza*, Joseph Ratner, ed. (Modern Library, 1927), opens with this philosopher's arguments for a rational approach to the Scriptures, for which he was excommunicated from the Jewish community. Maurice Goguel in his *Jesus and the Origins of Christianity* (Harper Torchbooks, Harper & Row, 1960) gives the first chapter to a quite complete study of this critical history. Another good reference on the same point is Alan Richardson's splendid little book, *Preface to Bible Study* (Westminster, 1944).

For the question of the order in which the Gospels were composed (the synoptic problem), see B. H. Streeter's classic *The Four Gospels* (Macmillan, 1924). A more recent study by William R. Farmer, *The Synoptic Problem* (Macmillan, 1964), shows how scientific scholarship may shift its conclusions in the light of evidence. Farmer denies the priority of Mark, and rearranges the accepted chronology of Gospel writing.

For information about archaeology, see two fine paperbacks, *Biblical Archaeologist Reader* I and II (Anchor, Doubleday, 1961, 1966). The first volume is edited by G. Ernest Wright and David Noel Freedman, the second by Edward R. Campbell, Jr. and David Noel Freedman. William Barclay's *The Making of the Bible* (Lutterworth & Abingdon, 1961) gives a good brief account of the growth of the Old and New Testament canon.

Recent New Testament scholarship is well summarized by Reginald H. Fuller in *The New Testament in Current Study* (Scribner, 1962). James M. Robinson's *A New Quest of the Historical Jesus* (Student Christian Movement, 1959) is the best single account of this subject. He and John B. Cobb, Jr., have also edited a good account of the debate on biblical interpretation, *The New Hermeneutic* (Harper & Row, 1964). It might be interesting to contrast this new approach with an older classic by one of the great liberal scholars, Adolf Von Harnack, *The Origin of the New Testament* (Macmillan, 1925).

Hans Werner Bartsch has edited a very interesting debate on Bultmann's demythologizing, *Kerygma and Myth* (Society for the Promotion of Christian Knowledge, 1957). On the very interesting history of the Dead Sea Scrolls there are two books to note: Millar Burrows, *The Dead Sea Scrolls* (Viking, 1955) and Theodor H. Gaster's translation of the Dead Sea Scrolls with Introduction and notes, *The Dead Sea Scriptures*, rev. ed. (Anchor, Doubleday, 1958). For those who like their scholarship in fictional form, James A. Michener's *The Source* (Random House, 1965) is a fascinating account of an archaeological "dig" at a fictional excavation site, Tell Makor, based upon actual excavations at real sites. Michener reconstructs imaginatively the lives of long-vanished people as 14 archaeological layers are painstakingly uncovered. He maintains faithfulness to scholarly material without being limited to it.

## NOTES

1. Robert H. Pfeiffer, *Introduction to the Old Testament* (Harper & Row, 1941), p. 46.

2. Exceptions would be some Roman Catholic and Fundamentalist schools that are still suspicious of these studies.

3. Alan Richardson, *A Preface to Bible Study* (Westminster, 1944), p. 29.

4. The documentary hypothesis that I have followed here is best set forth in B. H. Streeter, *The Four Gospels: A Study of Origins* (St. Martins, 1924).

5. For Bultmann's program of demythologizing, see Rudolf Bultmann, *Jesus Christ and Mythology* (Scribner, 1958). For his combining of existentialism and New Testament theology, see a collection of his shorter writings entitled *Existence and Faith*, selected, translated, and introduced by Schubert M. Ogden (Meridian, World Publishing, 1960).

6. Alan Richardson, *The Bible in the Age of Science* (Westminster, 1961), chap. 6.

7. For instance, Martin Buber and Paul Tillich.

8. James M. Robinson and John B. Cobb, Jr., *The New Hermeneutic* (Harper & Row, 1964), p. 8.

9. *Ibid.*, p. 23.

10. *Ibid.*

11. *Ibid.*, p. 25.

12. *Ibid.*, p. 27.

13. *Ibid.*, p. 28.

14. *Ibid.*, p. 42.

15. Karl Jaspers, *The Great Philosophers*, Hannah Arendt, ed., Ralph Manheim, trans. (Harcourt, Brace & World, 1962), p. 9.

16. *Ibid.*, p. 74.

17. James M. Robinson describes the new point of view in *A New Quest of the Historical Jesus* (Student Christian Movement, 1959).

18. See Pfeiffer, *op. cit.*, for an explanation of this principle.

# 8

# *The Literature and Faith*
# *of the Old Testament*

❖❖❖❖❖❖❖❖❖❖❖❖❖❖❖❖❖❖❖❖❖❖❖❖❖❖❖❖❖❖❖

If we were to name the greatest benefactors of the living generation, we would be compelled, as Arnold Toynbee reminds us, to name the great prophets of Hebrew antiquity. Unfortunately, though the book which records their achievements is the most honored and widely owned in our literature, it is as politely ignored. This neglect may come to an end as modern society, plagued by its own shallowness, rouses itself from its complacent slumbers to search more deeply for desperately needed sources of wisdom. It is this wisdom to which we now turn.

## THE CONTENTS OF THE OLD TESTAMENT

The Old Testament is not a single book. It is a small library of 39 books, written as we have seen, over the space of a thousand years. It is the history of a people to whom faith in God was the central category of self-understanding both collectively and personally. It is this that gives to the 39 books the coherence and unity that allow us to consider it as a single work.

### The Key to the Old Testament

Biblical history, as Martin Buber has so eloquently explained,[1] is best conceived under the image of a living dialogue between a people and their

God. This primary dialogue entails a secondary dialogue of face-to-face meeting between human beings who exist under the shadow of the Self-Existent. The two great commandments, according to this view of biblical faith, are to love God with all one's heart, soul, mind, and strength, and one's neighbor as one's self. In a secondary sense, biblical history is also covenantal history, the story of a binding agreement between God and his people. Because God is also holy, the covenant is thoroughly ethical in its understanding of the relationships between men and societies.

Biblical history, then, has both a vertical and a horizontal dimension in dialogue and covenant. The literature of the Bible makes it crystal clear that the destiny of the Hebrews is understandable only in terms of their faithfulness to this essential meeting between God and man, and the progressive transformation of the human community in the light of that meeting.

The central event of Old Testament history is the sealing of the covenant at Mount Sinai around 1260 B.C., shortly after the miraculous deliverance of Israel from the Egyptians at the waters of the Red Sea.

Anchored thus to the rock of Sinai, Old Testament history reaches back in time to the Patriarch Abraham, at the beginning of the second millennium before Christ, and back behind Abraham to the legendary time of Noah, and beyond Noah to Adam, whose "fall" consisted in breaking the primeval covenant of Eden. It reaches forward in time from Sinai to a promised kingdom of universal righteousness, in which the acknowledgment of God's sovereignty will cover the earth "as the waters cover the sea."

### Old Testament History: Abraham and the Patriarchs

The story of the Jews begins with the tale of Abraham who left his home in the Tigris and Euphrates valley, traveling the arc of the Fertile Crescent into Palestine, where he received assurances from his God that this land would belong to his descendants, who would become as numerous as the sands of the sea. Abraham is the model of covenantal faithfulness. He did not withhold even his beloved son Isaac when God, testing him, asked for a living sacrifice. Isaac was also faithful and "dug again the wells of his father Abraham." Jacob (whose name God changed to Israel), son of Isaac, though less honorable, having won the birthright blessing from Isaac through deception, nonetheless became the father of twelve sons whose descendants were the twelve tribes of Israel.

Joseph, the eleventh and pampered son of Jacob's old age, became the envy of his brothers, who sold him into slavery in Egypt. Through the providence of God he won the favor of the Pharaoh, who made him his viceroy, second in power to himself, and administrator of the grain stores that, accumulated at his advice, saved Egypt from starvation during a long, terrible famine. The same famine forced the sons of Jacob (Israel) to seek grain in Egypt, where, without recognizing him, they were at last confronted by their long-lost brother. The tale of Joseph's magnanimity and the final reconciliation of the brothers is one of the great stories of all literature. At the meeting in which Joseph reveals his identity, he reassures his dismayed brothers: ". . . . do not be distressed, or angry with yourselves, because you sold me here; for God sent me before you to preserve life. . . . So it was not you who sent me here, but God" (Gen. 45:5, 8).*

Here is the theme of biblical history: The prime mover in all events is God, and He, not man, is the Lord of history. Man's duty is obedience to the gracious if inscrutable will of the Eternal.

Thus God saved Israel through his faithful instrument Joseph, and brought him and his family to Egypt where they and their descendants flourished in peace for four centuries. But time brought many changes; the tribes increased in number and a new pharaoh[2] "who knew not Joseph" came to power. The Hebrews were peremptorily deprived of their status as guests in the land and reduced to slavery.

## From Egypt to Sinai

The story of Israel's deliverance from Egypt is another of the great Hebrew epics. The major figure is Moses, who forsook the comforts of the Pharaoh's palace, where he was reared, to take the part of his enslaved countrymen. At the conclusion of a long exile, self-imposed to avoid punishment for having killed an Egyptian overseer, he heard the call of God to return to Egypt and lead his people out of slavery into their destiny as a free nation. This deliverance, especially the safe passage through the waters of the sea, became for the Hebrews the great mark of God's favor. "When Israel was a child, I loved him," wrote the prophet Hosea, "and out of Egypt I called my son" (Hosea 11:1).

Once in the desert, safe from the pursuing Egyptian army, Moses led the people to Mount Sinai, the site of his own earlier confrontation with God. Here he served as intermediary in sealing the covenant by which the Hebrews again recognized themselves as a special people, called by God for his own special purposes. This call, they were reminded, was due not to their own merits, but solely to God's arbitrary choice for his own inscrutable purposes.

A scholarly reconstruction of the covenant at Sinai reveals in ten brief sentences (commandments) the substance of a code of law which, in expanded form, inspired not only the later codes of Israel but has also influenced many modern legal structures as well. In their most primitive form they appeared as follows:

> God spoke all these words: I am Yaweh your God, who brought
> you forth out of the land of Egypt, out of the house of slaves.
>
> 1   You shall have no other gods before me.
> 2   You shall not make me any graven image or any likeness.

---

* Unless otherwise noted, all biblical quotations are from the Revised Standard Version of the Bible.

3   *You shall not invoke the Name of Yahweh your God in vain.*
4   *Remember the Sabbath day to keep it holy.*
5   *Honor your father and your mother.*
6   *You shall not commit murder.*
7   *You shall not commit adultery.*
8   *You shall not steal.*
9   *You shall not bear false witness against your neighbor.*
10  *You shall not covet your neighbor's house.*[3]

In the first four of these laws the requirements of a proper dialogue with God are set forth in great simplicity. The remaining six lay the foundations of a just social life: the security of persons, the sanctity of the family, the right to personal property, the integrity of the courts of justice, and a warning against the inner spirit of covetousness which can undermine the most secure social order.

The covenant was no sooner made than it was broken by the fickle Israelites, who revived their pagan worship while Moses was absent on the sacred mountain. Repentant again, they began a 40-year period of wandering, during which they were gradually welded into a social unit and learned through suffering the self-reliance of a free people.

### The Promised Land: Invasion and Victory

At the end of the 40 years, under a new leader, Joshua, the tribes were prepared to assault the cities west of the Jordan River, and to begin their long conquest of the land promised to them through their father Abraham a thousand years before.

The struggle was not entirely military. To the nomadic Israelites the cultural difficulties of urban life in a strange land were increased by the enticements of a strange religion—the culture-religion of the native Canaanites. The Israelites compromised the covenant repeatedly, only to be called back time and again by the spokesmen of God. The fluctuating military fortunes of this age of conquest were interpreted by the prophets as punishments or rewards for the fluctuating loyalties of the people.

Out of these experiences the earliest creed of the Hebrew people emerged as a summary of their national experience and faith: A wandering Aramean was my father; and he went down into Egypt and sojourned there, few in number; and there he became a nation, great, mighty, and populous. And the Egyptians treated us harshly, and afflicted us, and laid upon us hard bondage. Then we cried to the Lord the God of our fathers, and the Lord heard our voice, and saw our affliction, our toil, and our oppression; and the Lord brought us out of Egypt with a mighty hand and an outstretched arm, with great terror, with signs and wonders; and he brought us into this place and gave us this land, a land flowing with milk and honey. And behold, now I bring the first of the fruit of the ground, which thou, O Lord, hast given me (Deut. 26:5–9).

### Israel Imitates the Surrounding Nations and Becomes a Monarchy

One of the chief evidences of Israel's accommodation to alien ways was the installation of a new government in the style of an Oriental despotism. In theory the new kingship was subject to the priests and election by the tribes. In practice the kingdom gradually deteriorated into a tyranny. The first king was the noble warrior Saul. After his fall from priestly favor, David was secretly anointed in his place. Out of the bitter struggles of this period has come one of the great literary masterpieces of Davidic composition—his sad lament at the death of Saul and Jonathan in their final battle with the Philistines:

> "Thy glory, O Israel, is slain upon thy
>     high places!
>   How are the mighty fallen!
>
> "Saul and Jonathan, beloved and lovely!
>     In life and in death they were not divided;
> they were swifter than eagles,
>     they were stronger than lions.
>
> "How are the mighty fallen
>     in the midst of the battle!
> "Jonathan lies slain upon thy high places.
>     I am distressed for you,
>       my brother Jonathan;
> very pleasant have you been to me;
>     your love to me was wonderful,
>       passing the love of women.
> "How are the mighty fallen,
>     and the weapons of war perished!"
>           (II Samuel 1: 19, 23, 25–27)

David fluctuated between the exercise of arbitrary power and loyalty to the covenant. The representatives of the latter, the perennial conscience of Israel, were the Prophets. One of the earliest confrontations in all history of these two forces—political power and prophetic conscience—is the classic story of Nathan's reproof of David. David fell in love with Bathsheba, the wife of Uriah, a loyal officer of his armies. In order to possess her he sent Uriah to his death in battle and ensconced Bathsheba in his harem.

The biblical account continues: "And the Lord sent Nathan to David. He came to him, and said to him, 'There were two men in a certain city, the one rich and the other poor. The rich man had very many flocks and herds; but the poor man had nothing but one little ewe lamb, which he had bought. And he brought it up, and it grew up with him and with his children; it used to eat of his morsel, and drink from his cup, and lie in his bosom, and it was like a daughter to him. Now there came a traveler to the rich man, and he was unwilling to take one of his own flock or herd to prepare for the wayfarer who had come to him, but he took the poor man's lamb, and prepared it for the man who had come to him.' Then David's anger was greatly kindled against the man; and he said to Nathan, 'As the Lord lives, the man who has done this deserves to die; and he shall restore the lamb fourfold, because he did this thing, and because he had no pity.' Nathan said to David, 'You are the man . . .' " (II Samuel 12:1–7).

Despite a certain spottiness in his career, David was adjudged by the biblical commentators to have been a faithful king, interested in Israel's loyalty to its religious tradition. One of the marks of this faithfulness was the large treasure which he accumulated during his reign for the construction of the first great Temple in the capital city of Jerusalem.

The Temple was completed by his so-called wise son Solomon, who, ironically, also set the nation on the steep slope into paganism. The new Jerusalem with its splendid Temple, surrounded by the pagan chapels of Solomon's harem favorites, became a symbol of the divided soul of the nation.

It is not then surprising that the chroniclers of these events contended that subsequent events were God's judgment upon Israel. Solomon's successor Rehoboam refused an impassioned appeal to return to the way of the covenant, and the country, torn by civil war, was divided thenceforth into two nations: Israel in the north, and Judah in the south. The ensuing history of these two countries, related by both blood and faith, became one of almost continuous intrigue and war.

### The Northern Kingdom of Israel: Apostasy and Final Judgment

From the middle of the tenth century, Israel followed the example of her neighbors politically and culturally into despotism and paganism. The prophets continued to protest, but their voices were drowned in a sea of indifference.

The first great prophetic protest[4] arose with Elijah in the reign of King Ahab. Ahab and his queen, Jezebel, conceived a bitter hatred for the prophet who courageously and alone stood in their way, denouncing their arbitrary actions in the name of the Lord. One of the great stories of scripture is Elijah's singlehanded battle with this unprincipled political power (I Kings 21). One event reveals the character of this struggle. Naboth, a prominent citizen of Jezreel, owned a vineyard adjoining the royal estates. The king cast greedy eyes upon it, but dared not possess it when Naboth refused to sell his ancestral land. Jezebel, whose upbringing in Tyre had instilled in her no scruples in such matters, chided her husband for his weakness and contrived to have Naboth "legally" executed and his properties impounded for the crown.

When the king arrived with his bodyguard to take possession of the vineyard, Elijah appeared as the incarnate conscience of Israel and spokesman for the Lord. Ahab cried out in dismay, " '. . . Have you found me, O my enemy?' He answered, 'I have found you, because you have sold yourself to do what is evil in the sight of the Lord' " (I Kings 21:20). Then the prophet delivered the Lord's judgment: " 'Have you killed, and also taken possession? . . . In the place where dogs licked up the blood of Naboth shall dogs lick your own blood' " (I Kings 21:19).

Ahab, who still retained a superstitious reverence for the ancient religion, was terrified and, fearing to touch the person of Elijah, withdrew instead to fast and pray. This scene could not have taken place in any other nation of the Near East. Their literature is singularly devoid of any parallels. The power of the Israelite state was still tempered by an ineradicable awe for the God of the covenant. This story reveals one of the main historical sources for the Western democratic belief in a Law above the law, a moral order to which all rulers and peoples owe obedience.

It also reveals the character of the basic struggle between the demand for social righteousness of the Hebrew faith and the accepted social practices of the times. In the view of the biblical chroniclers, the final destruction that came to the northern kingdom in 722 B.C. was the judgment of God on a people who had fallen hopelessly into apostasy and unfaithfulness. The pitiless armies of Assyria poured out of Mesopotamia and swept the leading citizens of the northern kingdom into a captivity from which they never returned. This was a common strategy for guaranteeing the continued subservience of a vassal state that had shown resistance to Assyrian rule. The ten tribes of Israel disappeared into the mists of history. Speculations concerning their disappearance have been numerous, but the most probable answer is that, having lost the distinctiveness of their own faith, they were prepared for assimilation into their conqueror's culture.

Before leaving this period of biblical history, we must look briefly at two of the greatest prophets of the time immediately preceding the collapse of Israel —Amos and Hosea.

Amos' writings (750 B.C.) are the first book in the Bible to attain the form in which it has come down to us. While herding sheep in the semidesert of Tekoa he had been over-shadowed by an experience from which he could not turn away. When challenged by the high priest Amaziah at the royal chapel of Bethel, he appealed to this experience: . . . " 'I am no prophet, nor a prophet's son; but I am a herdsman, and a dresser of sycamore trees, and the Lord took me from following the flock, and the Lord said to me, "Go, prophesy to my people. . . ." ' " (Amos 7:14–15). The call was irresistible:

> "The lion has roared; who will not fear?
> The Lord God has spoken; who can but prophesy?"
>                                      (Amos 3:8)

This lonely farmer is the voice of the rural billions who throughout history have known the bitter oppression of urban commercialism and corrupt government. In him the suffering silence of multitudes finds expression:

" '. . . they sell the righteous for silver, and the needy for a pair of shoes—
they that trample the head of the poor into the dust of the earth, and turn
aside the way of the afflicted . . .' " (Amos 2:6–7).

The great covenant of Mosaic justice had long since been forgotten. For
the flourishing religion of the day, which consisted of elaborate rituals but
neglected simple human relationships, Amos had only scornful contempt.
One of his greatest speeches is a classic indictment of all such ingrown
religion:

> "I hate, I despise your feasts,
>     and I take no delight in your
>         solemn assemblies.
>
> Take away from me the noise of
>     your songs;
>         to the melody of your harps I
>         will not listen.
> But let justice roll down like waters,
>     and righteousness like an ever-
>         flowing stream."
>                 (Amos 5:21, 23–4; Author's
>                 roman)

He tried to make the people realize that they were contesting the sovereignty of God himself:

> He who made the Pleiades and Orion,
>     and turns deep darkness into the morning,
>     and darkens the day into night,
> who calls for the waters of the sea,
>     and pours them out upon the
>         surface of the earth,
> the Lord is his name. . . .
>                             (Amos 5:8)

But God is not merely the creator of nature, he is also the sovereign and holy
Lord of history who demands justice. To deny it is to pit oneself against
doom:

> ". . . on the day I punish Israel for
>     his transgressions. . . .
>
>                 .      .      .
>
> I will smite the winter house with
>     the summer house;
>         and the houses of ivory shall perish,
>     and the great houses shall come to an end. . . ."
>                             (Amos 3:14, 15)

The only hope is for the faithful remnant of those who remain true to the
covenant of righteousness: "Thus says the Lord: 'As the shepherd rescues

from the mouth of the lion two legs, or a piece of an ear, so shall the people of Israel who dwell in Samaria be rescued, with the corner of a couch and a part of a bed' " (Amos 3:12). This melancholy prophecy was to prove all too true.

Hosea, a younger contemporary of Amos, is more hopeful. He too inveighs against the gross decay of social righteousness, but he sees the covenant more in the light of a family relationship and the unfaithfulness as a family quarrel. God says to the people: "When Israel was a child, I loved him . . . it was I who taught Ephraim to walk . . . I led them with cords of compassion, with the bands of love . . ." (Hosea 11:1, 3, 4). He preaches a God of love: "How can I give you up, O Ephraim! . . . My heart recoils within me, my compassion grows warm and tender . . . for I am God and not man, the Holy One in your midst, and I will not come to destroy" (Hosea 11:8–9).

But Hosea does not sentimentalize: "Samaria shall bear her guilt, because she has rebelled against her God . . ." (Hosea 13:16). Hosea had tasted the bitterness of personal betrayal in his own domestic life and knew the high price that love must pay for renewal. But beyond all judgment he saw the eternal loving intention of God: "I will heal their faithlessness; I will love them freely . . . they shall return and dwell beneath my shadow, they shall flourish as a garden . . ." (Hosea 14:4, 7).

Here, in passages of unforgettable power and beauty, are the great themes of prophetic Judaism. Micah,[5] another prophet, this time from the southern kingdom, has summed it up in these words:

> He has showed you, O man, what is good;
> and what does the Lord require of you
> but to do justice, and to love kindness,
> and to walk humbly with your God?
> (Micah 6:8)

The great tragedy of Israel was that these promises and warnings of the prophets went unheeded. Is it not also the perennial tragedy of humanity in every age?

## The Southern Kingdom of Judah and Two of Its Prophets

While these things transpired in the north, the same bitter struggle between faith and culture raged in Judah in the south. At times the pagan elements were in complete ascendancy. We read that King Manasseh installed the shrines of Assyria in Jerusalem and even sacrificed his own son to Moloch. But the voices of prophecy were not silent. Either Isaiah or Jeremiah, greatest of those who were inspired to speak in the name of God, would have crowned with greatness so small a nation as Judah.

Isaiah. In the year 740 B.C., after the death of the leprous King Uzziah, Isaiah was transported by a vision while praying in the Temple. He ". . . saw the Lord sitting upon a throne, high and lifted up; and his train filled the temple." The retinue of angels[6] cried: " 'Holy, holy, holy is the Lord of hosts; the whole earth is full of his glory.' " The Temple shook and the prophet was overshadowed by darkness. Transfixed by this vision of holiness, he cried: " 'Woe is me! . . . for I am a man of unclean lips, and I dwell in the midst of a people of unclean lips; for my eyes have seen the King, the Lord of hosts!' " (Isaiah 6:1, 3, 5).

In this encounter, Isaiah, like the prophets before him, received his commission to serve as the conscience of his people and to recall them if possible to the covenant of Sinai. Isaiah is without question not only one of the greatest figures of Hebrew history but also of the history of mankind. His service to his nation over almost 40 years can be but briefly suggested here.

Isaiah's message can be summarized as follows: First, he denounced in clear and unmistakable terms the religious and social situation of his day. As a man in intimate contact with the governing powers, he was able to speak with greater authority than his predecessors. He shared Amos' detestation of a merely ritual religion that salved the consciences of men without changing social conditions. He saw, moreover, that the reason why such a religion did not result in justice was that it was focused on false gods, gods of men's imaginations that were, as we might say, mere projections of the wishes and desires of the oppressive social powers.

Second, such a situation was bound to be dangerous. God could not be mocked. In his sovereign holiness he stood above the kingdoms of men and controlled the destinies of nations. Isaiah saw in Assyria the instrument of God's judgment: "Assyria, the rod of my anger." And when Assyria seemed immune to judgment, Isaiah pointed out that when God was through with Assyria it too would be made accountable for its terrible deeds.

The third element in Isaiah's message was that the faith of the Hebrews must be ethical through and through. God was not only the universal power, but he loved righteousness and hated unrighteousness. His primary demand was faithful worship and this entailed holy obedience to his righteous will.

I will quote further from Isaiah only this final passage, which those who think prophecy is outmoded in a nuclear age would do well to contemplate:

> Behold, the Lord will lay waste the earth
>   and make it desolate,
> and he will twist its surface and
>   scatter its inhabitants.
> And it shall be, as with the people,
>   so with the priest;
> as with the slave, so with his master;
> as with the maid, so with her mistress;
> as with the buyer, so with the seller;
> as with the lender, so with the borrower;
> as with the creditor, so with the debtor.
> The earth shall be utterly laid waste
>   and utterly despoiled;

> for the Lord has spoken this word.
> The earth mourns and withers,
>   the world languishes and withers;
>   the heavens languish together
>     with the earth.
> The earth lies polluted
>   under its inhabitants;
> for they have transgressed the laws,
>   violated the statutes,
>   broken the everlasting covenant.
> Therefore a curse devours the earth.
>   and its inhabitants suffer for
>     their guilt;
> therefore, the inhabitants of the
>     earth are scorched,
>   and few men are left.
>
> (Isaiah 24:1–6)

Perhaps such warnings did not go entirely unheeded. Judah's semi-independence survived for over a hundred years, with intermittent periods of faithfulness and apostasy. With the coronation of Josiah a new spirit was briefly infused into the national life of Judah, and in 621 B.C. he decreed that Deuteronomy, newly "discovered" in the renovation of the Temple, was to be the law of the land. Unfortunately, with Josiah's tragic death in battle, this short-lived reform practically ceased.

With the approaching end of Judah there arose another great figure, second to none in the mighty fellowship of the prophets—Jeremiah.

*Jeremiah.* Jeremiah began his ministry as the shadow of these dire prophetic predictions began to fall across Judah's national life. He revived the great Mosaic tradition with an understanding that is not matched by any of his predecessors. He could not understand a people so foolish as his countrymen:

> Be appalled, O heavens, at this,
>   be shocked, be utterly desolate, says Yaweh,
> for my people have committed two evils:
>   they have forsaken me,
> the fountain of living waters,
>   and hewed out cisterns for themselves,
> broken cisterns,
>   that can hold no water.
>
> (Jeremiah 2:12–13)

From one high moment in Jeremiah's career we get an intimate glimpse of the actual composition of a portion of his book. Baruch reports the reading of a scroll to King Jehoiakim, who cut off pieces of it as it was read and contemptuously threw them into the fire. Afterwards the scroll was rewritten, and "many similar words were added" (Jeremiah 36:32).

The burden of Jeremiah's message was this: God's judgment was coming quickly upon a people who had forsaken their God. The situation was compounded by the blindness of the nation's spiritual leaders, which more than anything else infuriated the prophet: "Woe to the shepherds who destroy and scatter the sheep of my pasture! Both prophet and priest are ungodly; even in my house I have found their wickedness." These blind guides were saying to the people, "It shall be well with you . . . no evil shall come upon you." Jeremiah accused them, saying, " 'They have healed the wound of my people lightly, saying, "Peace, peace," when there is no peace' " (Jeremiah 6:14). Outraged by these accusations, his enemies sought the prophet's death, and he was saved only by the intervention of the princes.

He could see that everyone wanted to hear good news when the news was bad. He anticipated in this sense the discoveries of modern depth psychology:

> *The heart is deceitful above all things,*
> *and desperately corrupt;*
> *who can understand it?*
> (Jeremiah 17:9)

Instead of a world of peace, the truth was that the habitable earth was in danger of returning to the chaos that preceded creation:

> *I looked on the earth, and lo, it*
> *was waste and void;*
> *and to the heavens, and they had*
> *no light.*
> *I looked on the mountains, and lo,*
> *they were quaking,*
> *and all the hills moved to and fro.*
> *I looked, and lo, there was no man,*
> *and all the birds of the air had fled.*
> *I looked, and lo, the fruitful land*
> *was a desert,*
> *and all the cities were laid in ruins*
> *before the Lord, before his fierce anger.*
> (Jeremiah 4:23-26)

It is fashionable now to see in such critics of society an air of superiority, even a malevolent joy, in pronouncing judgment upon their fellows. The truth is, the prophets often complained of the burden of criticism that God laid upon them. They longed to become heralds of good news. But so long as the Judeans remained confirmed in their rebellion against the holy covenant the outlook was bound to be gloomy. Jeremiah, like his predecessors, suffered intensely under the burden of pronouncing judgment against his own people: "My anguish, my anguish!" he cried out. "I writhe in pain! Oh, the walls of my heart!" (Jeremiah 4:19).

During the final siege of Jerusalem, Jeremiah's position became completely intolerable. He was cast in the role of a traitor who urged the city to surrender to the enemy. He was imprisoned for undermining the morale of the people and the troops; only the king's superstitious awe of the prophet's spiritual integrity saved him. In the middle of the night he was called to an audience with the king, who asked desperately, "Is there any word from the Lord?" Unfortunately, the word was the same—doom, unless you change and follow new ways. And the doom finally fell—first in 597 and again in 586 B.C., the city succumbed to the same fate that had befallen the northern kingdom more than a century earlier. All the chief citizens and skilled artisans were carried into captivity by the Babylonians.

### Two Great Prophets of the Exile

The Exile was a bitter experience for the Judeans, but for them it had a different result than for the northern Israelites. In their adversity they were now ready to believe the prophets whom they had scorned. They revived the Mosaic covenant, thus reviving their identity as a people with a destiny in history. In the midst of their suffering they sang:

> By the waters of Babylon,
>     there we sat down and wept,
>     when we remembered Zion.
> On the willows there we hung up our lyres.
> For there our captors required of us songs,
> and our tormentors, mirth, saying,
>     "Sing us one of the songs of Zion!"
> How shall we sing the Lord's song
>     in a foreign land?

> .     .     .

(Psalms 137:1–4)

A great unknown prophet whose writings appear in the Book of Isaiah (chap. 40 and following), gave the exiles a new perspective from which they could sing the Lord's song in a foreign land. He taught them that God is not the God of Palestine alone but of the whole earth:

> Have you not known? Have you not heard?
> Has it not been told you from the beginning?
> Have you not understood from the foundations
>     of the earth?
> It is he who sits above the circle of the earth,
>     and its inhabitants are like grasshoppers;
> who stretches out the heavens like a curtain,
>     and spreads them like a tent to dwell in;
> who brings princes to nought,
>     and makes the rulers of the earth
>     as nothing.

(Isaiah 40:21–23)

This Unknown Prophet of the Exile, sometimes known as Deutero-Isaiah, carried the spiritual understanding of Judah beyond anything known until then. He told his people that though they had been punished for their sins, their very suffering had a meaning for all men. They had become, he said, the "suffering servant of the Lord," in whom the whole of mankind would be blessed.

> *Behold my servant, whom I uphold,*
>   *my chosen, in whom my soul delights. . . .*
>
>                 .        .        .
>
> *"I have given you as a covenant to the people,*
>   *a light to the nations,*
>   *to open the eyes that are blind,*
> *to bring out the prisoners from the dungeon. . . ."*
>
>                           (Isaiah 42:1, 6–7)

The message changed from judgment to promise:

> *Comfort, comfort my people,*
>   *says your God.*
>
> *Behold, the Lord God comes with might,*
>   *and his arm rules for him;*
>
>                 .        .        .
>
> *He will feed his flock like a shepherd,*
>   *he will gather the lambs in his arms,*
>   *he will carry them in his bosom,*
>     *and gently lead those that are with young.*
>
>                        (Isaiah 40:1, 10, 11)

Ezekiel was another prophet who persuaded his fellow exiles to be of good cheer. He has been credited with transforming Hebrew belief from a nationalistic religion to the religion of a holy people centered in their faith rather than in their politics. So long as Jerusalem still stood, Ezekiel preached doom to the city and its inhabitants, but when the Exile began, his message changed, and he foresaw a different destiny for his people. It was his vision more than any other that refocused the Jewish self-image into a community of faith rather than a nation in the usual sense. Thus the bitter experience of the Babylonian captivity was reinterpreted as part of the providence of God, and the apparently senseless suffering of his people acquired a new meaning.

### The New Exodus and the Renewal of the Covenant

Under the Persian dynasty that replaced the Assyrian empire the faithful Jews were permitted to return to Jerusalem under the leadership of Nehemiah and the scribe Ezra. The walls of the city were rebuilt, and the people heard the Torah solemnly read in its entirety in the city square. They subscribed afresh to its conditions. This reestablishment of the holy city of the Jews led unfortunately to a narrowing of the great visions of the Exile—a return to a view of Judaism as reserved to a racially pure and religiously circumspect people. Non-Jews were roughly sent packing from the city, even when it meant the breaking up of families.

### The Great Visionary Prophecies

The larger view of the great prophets remained only in the literature, and in the hearts of a few. It was these visions that were later to inspire Christianity in its universal dimensions. Here are a few of the great passages from the prophetic books of the Old Testament.

In a classic passage from Isaiah there shines the vision of a new era for the whole of humanity. He predicts that from the descendants of David a new leader will arise:

> And the Spirit of the Lord shall rest upon him,
>     the spirit of wisdom and understanding,
>     the spirit of counsel and might,
>     the spirit of knowledge and the fear of the Lord.
> And his delight shall be in the fear of the Lord.
>
> The wolf shall dwell with the lamb,
>     and the leopard shall lie down with the kid,
> and the calf and the lion and the fatling together,
>     and a little child shall lead them.
>
> They shall not hurt or destroy
>     in all my holy mountain;
> for the earth shall be full of the knowledge of the Lord
>     as the waters cover the sea.
>
> (Isaiah 11:2–3, 6, 9)

This same prophecy is echoed in the so-called new covenant of Jeremiah: "'Behold the days are coming, says the Lord, when I will make a new covenant with the house of Israel. . . . I will put my law within them, and I will write it upon their hearts; and I will be their God, and they shall be my people. And no longer shall each man teach his neighbor and each his brother, saying, "Know the Lord," for they shall all know me, from the least of them to the greatest, says the Lord; for I will forgive their iniquity, and I will remember their sin no more'" (Jeremiah 31:31, 33–4).

The great Unknown Prophet of the Exile proclaimed a final judgment on all parochial narrowness. He saw the return of Judah as a portent of great things to come for mankind as a whole:

> .   .   .
>
> "It is too light a thing that you
>     should be my servant
>     to raise up the tribes of Jacob
>     and to restore the preserved of Israel;
> I will give you as a light to the nations,
>     that my salvation may reach to the
>         end of the earth."
>
> (Isaiah 49:6)

Some of the nonprophetic writings of the Old Testament underline the same theme. The unknown author of the Book of Ruth rebukes the racial narrowness of the Jews in the story of a gentile whose faithfulness puts to shame the blood-heirs of the promise; and in due time she becomes the ancestor of David, their greatest king. The Book of Jonah pleads the same cause. Jonah is a racially minded prophet who refuses to preach to the populous foreign city of Nineveh. He wants God to destroy it. When under divine prodding he warns the city of the danger of ungodliness, their unexpected repentance spares them from the divine wrath. Instead of rejoicing in his successful mission, Jonah sulks at God's mercy toward non-Jews. The whole book is a protest against bloody-minded racism and religious bigotry—a message, incidentally, lost amid silly quarrels as to whether a man could live in the belly of a whale.

Ruth and Jonah are counterposed to Esther and Nehemiah: the universal versus the parochial perspective. The Old Testament literature closes with this tension between an ingrown parochialism and an outgoing universalism, a theme that is carried forward into Christianity, the offspring of Judaism.

## CYNICISM AND FAITH: THE FINAL LITERATURE

Another tension that emerges from this complex story of Hebrew history is between cynicism and faith. It is not to be expected that a sacred canon would include the literature of doubt, but there were some exceptions. Job is a great drama of doubt. Its author wonders, sometimes bitterly, at the suffering of the faithful. The final upshot of the drama is faith, but spiritual doubts have never been more passionately stated.

Ecclesiastes is more quietly and persistently cynical. The continued suffering of good men and the disappointments of history led the author to conclude that "All is vanity" (Ecclesiastes 1:2). Pious editors softened the message enough to allow its inclusion in the sacred canon, but the burden of the book is clear: "What has a man from all the toil and strain with which he toils beneath the sun? For all his days are full of pain, and his work is a vexation; even in the night his mind does not rest. This also is vanity" (Ecclesiastes 2:22–23). The author sees the perpetuation of injustice and the failure of every human strategy to guarantee happiness, and concludes that "The heart of the wise is in the house of mourning . . ." (Ecclesiastes 7:4. The mood of many modern thinkers is presaged in such estimates of human existence.

Faith, on the other hand, made two responses to these same human disappointments. The first was through eschatology (from *escaton*, the Greek word for "end"). As hope faded for any satisfactory conclusion to the catastrophes of history, Hebrew faith transferred expectations to a time beyond history, to the end of history, which God in his own time would bring to pass. The prime example of this eschatological literature is the Book of Daniel, written during the desperate time of oppression under the Syrian-Greek tyrant Epiphanes, who enforced a policy of cultural Hellenization among the Jews. Its author looks forward to God's catastrophic intervention, the end of history, and the establishment of the eternal reign of the faithful. This expectation was lively at the time of the birth of Christianity, as we can see in reading the Dead Sea Scrolls. It passed over into the new faith and is clearly reflected in the final book of the New Testament, the Revelation of St John the Divine (or the Apocalypse).

Eschatology also revived in a special form the earlier prophetic expectation of a Great King who would rule righteously from Mount Zion, and whose reign would extend over the whole of mankind. As this hope faded, it too was transferred to a time beyond the end of history, when God would send his heavenly ambassador, the Messiah, to rule for him. For the Old Testament community this hope was expressed most clearly in the Book of Daniel. Christians later appropriated this belief also and cast Jesus in the role of the expected Messiah, who would return again to judge the world and would become such a universal ruler. One of the major questions of New Testament scholarship, as we have seen, is to what extent this view was held by Jesus himself, and to what degree it was merely attributed to him by his followers.

A second reply by the Hebrews to the disappointments of history was in a life of quiet faithfulness and waiting. Here was a mixture of optimistic wisdom about the satisfactions of a truly good life joined to faith in God's undergirding mercies. The Book of Proverbs is our best guide to the former; the Psalms is a prayer book of the latter.

Let us take a sample from the wisdom of Proverbs on a single subject—the tongue: The tongue can hurt. Bearing tales, the tongue can curse: "The words of a talebearer are as a wound, and they go down into the innermost parts of the belly" (18:8, KJV). The tongue is small, yet "a soft tongue will break a bone" (25:15). But it also turns back upon its owner. As the New Testament book of James says, "It can poison the whole body; it can make the whole of life a blazing hell" (3:6, Phillips trans.).

There is wisdom also in silence: "A fool uttereth all his mind, but a wise man keepeth it in till afterwards" (29:11). Good advice is given about self-praise: "Let another man praise thee" (27:2). A social group that cannot control its language is hard to bear: "Better a dish of vegetables, with love, than the best beef served with hatred. . . . Better a morsel of dry bread and peace than a house full of banqueting and quarrels" (15:17; 17:1).

The tongue can also heal and help. ". . . the tongue of the wise brings healing" (12:18). "A gentle tongue is a tree of life . . ." (15:4). ". . . rash words are like sword thrusts, but the tongue of the wise brings healing" (12:18). "A word fitly spoken is like apples of gold in a setting of silver" (25:11). And "he that keepeth his mouth keepeth his life" (21:23, KJV). Echoing these wise sayings, the author of the New Testament General Epistle of James writes: "If anyone appears to be 'religious' but cannot control his tongue he deceives himself and we may be sure that his religion is useless" (1:26, Phillips trans.).

The Book of Psalms is the prayer book of the Bible and its greatest collection of poetry. Here the depths of both social and personal life are revealed in an incomparable way. The use of the Psalms in corporate worship reminded the faithful community of the great covenant and joined them to the history of their ancient past. The 106th Psalm illustrates this:

> *Praise the Lord!*
> *O give thanks to the Lord, for he is good;*
> *for his steadfast love endures for ever!*
> *Who can utter the mighty doings of the Lord,*
> *or show forth all his praise?*
> *Blessed are they who observe justice,*
> *who do righteousness at all times!*
>
> *Both we and our fathers have sinned;*
> *we have committed iniquity, we have done wickedly.*
> *Our fathers, when they were in Egypt,*
> *did not consider thy wonderful works;*
> *they did not remember the abundance of thy steadfast love . . .*
>
> *Yet he saved them for his name's sake,*
> *that he might make known his mighty power.*
> *He rebuked the Red Sea, and it became dry;*
> *and he led them through the deep as through a desert.*
>
> *But they soon forgot his works;*
> *they did not wait for his counsel.*
> *But they had a wanton craving in the wilderness,*
> *and put God to the test in the desert;*
> *he gave them what they asked,*
> *but sent a wasting disease among them.*
>
> *They made a calf in Horeb*
> *and worshiped a molten image.*
> *They exchanged the glory of God*
> *for the image of an ox that eats grass.*
>
> *. . . they mingled with the nations*
> *and learned to do as they did.*
> *They served their idols,*
> *which became a snare to them.*
> *They sacrificed their sons and their daughters to the demons;*
>
> .      .      .
>
> *and the land was polluted with blood.*
>
> *Many times he delivered them,*
> *but they were rebellious in their purposes,*

*and were brought low through their iniquity.*
*Nevertheless he regarded their distress,*
*when he heard their cry.*
*He remembered for their sake his covenant,*
*and relented according to the abundance*
*of his steadfast love.*

*Save us, O Lord our God,*
*and gather us from among the nations,*
*that we may give thanks to thy holy name*
*and glory in thy praise.*
*Blessed be the Lord, the God of Israel,*
*from everlasting to everlasting!*
*And let all the people say, "Amen!"*
*Praise the Lord!*

(Psalms 106:1–3, 6–7, 8–9
13–15, 19–20, 35–37, 38, 43–
45, 47–48)

Other Psalms are more personal and constitute a prayer book for the soul.
A soul in anguish cries:

*Out of the depths I cry to thee, O Lord!*
*Lord, hear my voice!*
*Let thy ears be attentive*
*to the voice of my supplications!*

*I wait for the Lord, my soul waits,*
*and in his word I hope;*
*my soul waits for the Lord*
*more than the watchmen for the morning. . . .*
(Psalms 130:1, 5–6)

Another Psalm realizes the power of God beyond all earthly threats, and
rejoices:

*God is our refuge and strength,*
*a very present help in trouble.*
*Therefore we will not fear though*
*the earth should change,*
*though the mountains shake in*
*the heart of the sea;*
*though its waters roar and foam,*
*though the mountains tremble*
*with its tumult.*

(46:1–3)

The prophetic message of inward purity and righteousness is reflected in
other Psalms.

> Have mercy on me, O God,
>    according to thy steadfast love;
> according to thy abundant mercy
>    blot out my transgressions.
> Wash me thoroughly from my iniquity,
>    and cleanse me from my sin!
>
> (51:1–2)

Above all, through the Psalms there is shouted the glory of God:

> Great is the Lord, and greatly to be praised,
>    and his greatness is unsearchable.

> The Lord is gracious and merciful,
>    slow to anger and abounding in steadfast love.
> The Lord is good to all,
>    and his compassion is over all
>       that he has made.

> Thy kingdom is an everlasting kingdom,
>    and thy dominion endures
>       throughout all generations.

> The Lord is near to all who call upon him,
> to all who call upon him in truth.
>
> (Psalms 145:3, 8–9, 13, 18)

## THE END OF THE OLD TESTAMENT: FINAL DISAPPOINTMENT

The Old Testament ends before the story is really finished. In the Maccabean rebellion of 164 B.C. the Jews made one last effort toward building an independent national life. They won their independence from the Syrian-Greek Empire and embarked once again on a national existence of their own. But the Hasmonean dynasty that stemmed from the Maccabeans proved bitterly disappointing, and the leading citizens were relieved when the Romans annexed their country in 63 B.C.

From this time forward the religious future of Judaism lay with the party known as the "Pious," or "Pharisees," as they are known in the New Testament. They become henceforth the chief bearers of the faith of Israel.

### The Jews After the Old Testament

Christianity grew out of the root of Israel and went its own way to a larger life among the gentiles. But the Jews who could not see in Jesus the fulfillment of their own faith still wait in faithfulness to this day, hoping to see the salvation that God has promised them. With the fall of Jerusalem in 70 A.D. and the dispersement of the population, the leaders of the Jewish community found a center of loyalty in their great sacred Book. Though the canon was now closed they continued to probe its deeper meanings and to record their thoughts in voluminous commentaries. The two great works that resulted from these age-long dialogues are the Mishnah and the Babylonian Talmud. These works, unknown to most Christians, possess the rich wisdom of a suffering and persecuted people who are religiously akin to them.[7] Aside from the sacred writings, the Jews maintained their synagogues and preserved their way of life through the rhythmic celebration of their ancient holy days, especially the Sabbath and the Passover. They remain to this day a people with the longest unbroken cultural heritage in history. The secret of their survival must be sought somehow in the sacred covenant sealed at Sinai.

## SUGGESTIONS FOR FURTHER READING

Julius Bewer's *The Literature of the Old Testament* (Columbia University Press, 1933) is still an excellent introduction to this literature.

A fine introduction to the history is Elmer W. K. Mould's *Essentials of Bible History* (Ronald, 1951). For a recent study of both history and literature, see Bernhard W. Anderson, *Understanding the Old Testament* (Prentice-Hall, 1957).

A famous Jewish philosopher's point of view on the covenant and on the dialogue that fostered it is found in Martin Buber's *Moses, The Revelation and the Covenant* (Harper Torchbooks; Harper & Row, 1958). Another Jewish scholar, Leo Trepp, has traced the Jewish people from their beginnings to the present time in *Eternal Faith, Eternal People* (Prentice-Hall, 1962). Judah Goldin has translated selections from the voluminous Talmudic literature in *The Living Talmud* (New American Library, 1957).

## NOTES

1. In many works, chiefly *I and Thou* (T. Clark, 1937; Scribner, 1958).
2. The pharaoh of the oppression was very likely Seti I, who was an Egyptian. The pharaoh of Joseph's time was a non-Egyptian Semite (one of the Hyksos), and therefore of the same racial stock as Joseph. The Hyksos were driven out by the Egyptians around 1580 B.C., and no Hebrew would dare remind an Egyptian pharaoh that his ances-

tors held places of authority when the Hyksos were the dynastic rulers of their land.
3. Bernhard W. Anderson, *Understanding the Old Testament* (Prentice-Hall, 1957), p. 56.
4. The unknown writer of the J document was no doubt the author of the first protest. Genesis (in chaps. 3 to 11) contains parabolic criticisms of the reign of Solomon with his refusal to abide by the Com-

mandments, and his building of a grand Temple (represented in Genesis by the Tower of Babel). I have chosen to emphasize Elijah because he is the first towering personality among the prophets.

5. I have displaced Micah in this chronology for purposes of summarizing the prophetic message. His work, done around 705–701 B.C., follows the work of Isaiah, with which he was familiar.

6. The Bible does not write about angels. The language of this pas-
sage is difficult to interpret, since the word translated cherub has various connotations. Ezekiel, for instance, portrays cherubs as pedestals upholding the throne of God. "Retinue of angels" is therefore not quite accurate, but, symbolically, the phrase suggests the scene as the passage portrays it.

7. For a good introduction to post-biblical Judaism, see Leo Trepp, *Eternal Faith, Eternal People* (Prentice-Hall, 1962).

# 9

# The Literature and Faith
# of the New Testament

❖❖❖❖❖❖❖❖❖❖❖❖❖❖❖❖❖❖❖❖❖❖❖❖❖❖❖❖❖❖❖❖❖

We have seen that the covenant at Sinai is the key to understanding the Old Testament. This holds true for the Jewish community, which, of course, considers it as complete in itself. For the Christian faith, however, the Old Testament is incomplete without the New, and when we take them together another center appears. The writers of the New Testament see Jesus Christ as the key to both Testaments. The Old Covenant looks forward to the New; the meaning of the Law and the expectations of the prophets find their fulfillment in Christ's coming. Thus the New Testament is about man's relationship to God as it is altered by the fact of Jesus Christ.

As we shall see, the authors of the 27 books in the New Testament do not agree in all matters concerning the meaning of Jesus' presence in history, but they all converge on one point: Man and history are decisively different because he appeared. As in the Old Testament, the primary thing is the dialogue between God and man, but in the New Testament that dialogue is given new form and significance by the coming of Jesus.

## THE CAREER OF JESUS

We must write of the "career" of Jesus, for it is no longer feasible in the light of modern scholarship to speak of a "life" or "biography" of Jesus. Gunther

Bornkamm, one of today's most eminent New Testament scholars, has written: "No one is any longer in the position to write a life of Jesus. This is the scarcely questioned and surprising result today of an enquiry which for almost two hundred years had devoted prodigious and by no means fruitless effort to regain and expound the life of the historical Jesus, freed from all embellishment by dogma and doctrine."[1] We have already seen in Chapter 7 why this is the case.

Because of the complexity of the critical problems it is necessarily a hazard to attempt, as I shall, to reconstruct the career of Jesus. At almost every point some scholars would give a different interpretation to the material. But it would be a mistake to fail to tell the story of Jesus just because we have such a large critical literature about it. And it would be too cumbersome to take all possible variations into account. Nonetheless, I have tried in what follows to keep mindful of the work of these scholars. The interested student can turn to the critical literature for alternative ways of telling the story.

## Background

Jesus was born into the late Hebrew world which we have described as it was at the end of the Old Testament. It was a world in which the political fortunes of the Jews were completely at the mercy of Roman power. Within that setting they survived as a religious people awaiting their deliverance at the hands of God. We can understand Jesus' career better if we are aware of the major parties and classes that divided the Jews during this time.

The Zealots were a party composed of fanatical Jews who longed for the military destruction of the occupying Roman power. They believed that if they cast themselves into war with Rome, a hopeless enterprise from the human point of view, God would send his Messiah with legions of angels to support his faithful warriors. This faith fomented frequent rebellions which were mercilessly crushed by the Roman legions. As a child, Jesus may have seen the 5000 crosses at Sepphoris where one such rebellion met its end. Two Zealots were later to join Jesus' intimate band of disciples, and one of them would betray him. At his trial the Zealot Barabbas was chosen by the people to be released in his stead.

The Sadducees were the priestly party, the remnants of the proud clan that had serviced the Temple for a thousand years. The New Testament image of them is of a proud and worldly caste willing to make weighty concessions to Rome for its support of their social prerogatives.

Another group, the Pharisees, were the descendants of the party of the "pious" who had formed the hard core of spiritual resistance to all cultural intrusions from Greece and Rome. They had become by the time of Jesus the chief bearers of the spiritual message of Judaism. Since they were, correspondingly, the chief opponents of the new message of Jesus they are cast in a rather bad light by the writers of the Gospels, but on the whole they were the most religiously enlightened and morally upright group in the Jewish community. Their long resistance to alien cultural intrusions had made them brittle and proud, but this is not entirely their fault. Some of the blame for this can be placed upon the social environment in which they and their ancestors had lived.

A third religious party, the Essenes, has emerged from the dimness of antiquity into a clearer light since the discovery of the Dead Sea Scrolls.[2] From this source we now get a more detailed picture of first-century Jewish sectarianism. The Essenes can be regarded as the more extreme branch of Pharisaism. They formed communities of the faithful, some of whom lived apart in the desert awaiting the Messiah, practicing meanwhile the austerities of personal purity in readiness for the final accounting.

In addition to the formal parties, there were the common people of the land, Am ha'aretz, as they were called. They were despised by the meticulous keepers of the law for their laxity, which was in part due to ignorance and grinding poverty. Little was left over after the combined taxes of the Roman and Jewish authorities. They developed, accordingly, a bitter hostility to both government and priest, and rallied quickly, if somewhat inconstantly, around prophetic leaders who stood out against their enemies. Jesus mingled freely with them and gained for this reason a popularity that was balanced by an equally bad reputation among the governing classes.

## Childhood

Jesus' birth date is put by scholars at around 6 to 4 B.C.[3] This discrepancy is due to the fact that the Julian calendar was not invented until many centuries later and was based upon a miscalculation.[4] Aside from the date itself, the remainder of the accounts of Jesus' birth and childhood must be considered as faith literature rather than scientific history.[5] This distinction must be made if we are to examine the biblical materials with scientific integrity. This does not mean that materials incapable of scientific verification are false. It means only that they are not subject to the public verification that is the measure of scientific knowledge.[6] The stories of the angelic visitation to Mary, the heavenly choir that sang to the shepherds, and the kings (magi) from the East who laid their gifts at the manger do not belong to verifiable history. If they did, there would be no difficulty in getting non-Christians to agree to their occurrence, as they do agree (when they are acquainted with the documentary studies) to a great part of the other gospel material. Christians accept these stories as integral parts of their understanding of Jesus, but they must not assume that this is done on scientific grounds. This would lead in the long run to intellectual and religious confusion.

Jesus was reared in Nazareth in the home of the carpenter Joseph and his wife, Mary. We are told that he had four brothers—James, Joses, Simon, and Jude—and at least two sisters.[7] At the age of twelve his devout parents took him with them on the considerable journey to the Temple at Jerusalem for his ritual initiation (Bar Mitzvah) into full Jewish manhood. After this, from the records, we know nothing of his life until he emerges as a grown man at the Jordan to hear the preaching of John the Baptist. Pious imagination has filled these "hidden years" with many romantic speculations, but the Gospels are silent on the entire period. We may reasonably presume that as the son of a carpenter he learned the trade and may have been the chief support of his family after the death of Joseph, who was not alive at the time of his ministry. From his own later teaching we may also gather that he received religious instruction at home and was trained, as were most youths of his day, in the synagogue school. The content of this training can be surmised from our knowledge of the Jewish educational system. It consisted chiefly of memorization of the Hebrew scriptures and hearing classical Rabbinic commentary. Beyond this he must have participated fully in the seasonal celebration of the holy feast days, having been instructed in their historic meaning. In short, his education was no doubt typical of a boy in a devout Jewish home.

## The Beginnings of the Ministry

When Jesus was about thirty years old, his cousin, John the Baptizer, appeared at the Jordan River preaching a message of repentance in preparation for the approaching last days. Jesus left Nazareth and went to hear John, who preached with the passion and authority of the great prophets of the past. He warned the people that the last days were at hand, that the "axe is laid to the root of the trees" (Matthew 3:10), and men should prepare themselves for the new age by a baptism of repentance and by faithful waiting for the showing of God's power.

Jesus went forward at John's invitation and was baptized in the river, an event of decisive significance. In the symbolic language of the Gospels, when he went up from the water "the heavens were opened and he saw the Spirit of God descending like a dove . . . and lo, a voice from heaven saying, 'This is my beloved Son; with whom I am well pleased' " (Matthew 3:16–17).

We may suppose that this experience was so overwhelming that Jesus felt compelled to leave the company of John and his friends and withdraw into the wilderness for meditation and prayer. We have a dramatic account of his experience in the wilderness that can only have come from Jesus himself (Matthew 4:1–11). The Gospels say he was "tempted by the devil." If we examine these temptations, we discover that their content involved the messianic expectations of the Jews of the time. The Messiah was expected to be a wonder-worker and a universal military ruler. In his solitary wrestling to discover God's true will as guidance in his career, Jesus came to view these expectations as demonic rather than divine. He rejected the traditional teachings and began to shape his own message of the Kingdom of God in radically different terms.

Many commentaries have been written on these temptations, but none more eloquent than Dostoevsky's "dream" of Ivan in *The Brothers Karamazov*. In this account Jesus' goal of a truly free spiritualized humanity is set over against the tempter's proposal of a slave humanity bound to a leader who would control them by bread, miracle, and political domination.[8] The melancholy fact is that humanity has perennially preferred the proposals of the desert demon to the Kingdom which Jesus preached. On this score, even the Church has been "hard of heart and slow to understand."

### The Galilean Ministry

Shortly after Jesus returned from the wilderness, John was arrested by Herod for his disturbing insistence that the king was living in adultery with his brother's wife. This dangerous political fact and some quarreling between his own followers and those of John led Jesus back north to Galilee.

His ministry consisted chiefly of healing and preaching. Perhaps the healing ministry came as a surprise, but he quickly incorporated it into the heart of his message. Matthew summarizes Jesus' preaching as follows: "Jesus began to preach, saying, 'Repent, for the kingdom of heaven is at hand' " (Matthew 4:17). This is so like the preaching of John that we must ask wherein it is different. The difference lies in the fact that for Jesus the Kingdom of God was not only about to come, but had in a sense already been inaugurated in his own healing and teaching ministry. He interpreted the healings as signs that the powers of darkness were already in flight and that the sovereign power of God was becoming manifest.[9] Moreover, he taught, if men would put their trust in the assurance of this divine presence among and within them, they would find rising in their midst incontestable evidence of the sovereign spirit of God. So confident was he of God's loving presence that he not only taught what the new life in the Kingdom would be like, but he lived out its attitudes and values in company with his disciples.

He was not satisfied to preach and heal. He gathered an intimate circle of twelve disciples about him for training in the new way of life. No doubt the number was symbolic of the twelve tribes of Israel. Much of his teaching took the form of such symbolic acts. When the Church later probed the meaning of his career, these actions became as important or even more important than the words he spoke. Thus St. Paul would summarize the whole gospel in terms of Jesus' death: ". . . we preach Christ crucified . . ." (I Corinthians 1:23).

Beyond this inner circle of disciples Jesus gathered a larger group called "the seventy," whom he sent on missions to the surrounding Galilean cities. There were other followers who at the height of his popularity must have numbered in the thousands. It was said that "the common people heard him gladly" (Mark 12:37, KJV).

Jesus' popularity with the common people aroused suspicions among the leaders of orthodoxy and government. The Roman power must have eyed the crowds that followed him with considerable apprehension. Between 67 and 37 B.C. no fewer than 100,000 men had perished in abortive rebellions, and a mere 40 years after the crucifixion (70 A.D.), Rome was forced into a total war with the exasperated Jews, who were ready at a moment's notice to spring at their oppressors' throats.

The nervousness of the religious leaders sprang from Jesus' unorthodox teaching and behavior. He habitually broke the ritual prescriptions of the Sabbath and did not rebuke his disciples when they followed his example (Luke 5:33–6:5).

So long as he was popular, however, it was strategically impossible to attack him. But with time it became apparent that Jesus was not going to fulfill the aspirations of the populace any more than the prescriptions of the orthodox, and his popular following began to melt away. John the Baptist sent messengers from prison to inquire whether he really was "he who is to come, or shall we look for another?" (Matthew 11:3). In the light of John's probable intention, Jesus' reply was ambiguous. John's conception of the kingdom was no doubt apocalyptic, and he waited eagerly in his prison for the marching feet of the army of the Lord. Jesus told John's messengers to go and tell John what they had seen and heard; ". . . the blind receive their sight, the lame walk, the lepers are cleansed, and the deaf hear, the dead are raised up, the poor have good news preached to them" (Luke 7:22–23).

With his popularity fading and the political authorities becoming more menacing (John had been executed by Herod), Jesus retired with his disciples into the north country of Tyre and Sidon. This may well have been for the purpose of reexamining his strategy. His appeal to the Galilean cities had failed. In his disappointment he cried out, "Woe to you, Chorazin! woe to you, Bethsaida! for if the mighty works done in you had been done in Tyre and Sidon, they would have repented long ago, sitting in sackcloth and ashes" (Luke 10:13). His most decisive failure was in his home town of Nazareth (Matthew 13:54–58). When he presumed to teach in the synagogue, proclaiming the advent of the new age prophesied by Isaiah, the Jewish religious leaders sought to kill him, and he barely escaped with his life. Jesus said to them, "A prophet is not without honor except in his own country, and among his own kin, and in his own house" (Mark 6:4)—a reply which suggests that even his own family had doubts about the propriety of his message.

His exile in the north country was brief, and he returned for another preaching tour that resulted in the same disappointments. This led to a second withdrawal, this time to the slopes of Mount Hermon in the region of Caesarea-Philippi. We have only a brief account of this retreat, but it is of decisive importance for our understanding of Jesus' ministry. He asked his disciples who they thought he was. The apostle Peter replied, "You are the Christ" (Mark 8:29). This was an outward and decisive confirmation of Jesus' growing awareness of his own vocation as the Messiah. (Christ is the Greek word for Messiah.) At no time had he spoken openly of his own views on this subject. The confession came from Peter unprompted.

In saying this I must point out that I am depending upon the Synoptic records—Matthew, Mark, and Luke. In contrast, the Gospel according to St. John begins with Jesus' open announcement of his role as the Christ. There is no way to reconcile these different accounts. Scholars solve the historical problem by assuming that John's account, written later than the Synoptic Gospels, was not intended as a report of the developing events of the ministry, but as a thoroughgoing interpretation of the meaning of the ministry. If John is taken as a guide, Peter's confession at Caesarea-Philippi is reduced to a mere echo of Jesus' continued proclamations of his own messiah-ship. But if the Synoptic order of events is to be trusted, this confession is a decisive turning point in the whole ministry.

### The Journey to Jerusalem

From now on Jesus turns his back on Galilee and sets his face toward Jerusalem. He foresees the dire end that is foreshadowed by his rejection in Galilee. He warns his disciples to expect the worst, but they cannot believe him. To them, as to the general populace, it is unthinkable that the Messiah could be crucified. In the enveloping gloom there is one bright moment—atop a "mountain" to which Jesus and his disciples had repaired for prayer. Peter reports this ecstatic experience as follows: ". . . he [Jesus] was trans-figured before them, and his garments became glistening, intensely white . . . And there appeared to them Elijah with Moses; and they were talking to Jesus. . . . And a cloud overshadowed them, and a voice came out of the cloud, 'This is my beloved Son; listen to him' " (Mark 9:2–3, 7). This is the second time that the Synoptics report the heavenly voice that earlier had spoken at Jesus' Baptism. But this time it is also heard by the disciples, not by Jesus alone.

The mood of the journey south lacks the bouyant optimism of the Galilean ministry where Jesus had appealed to the loving care of God revealed in the lilies of the field and the birds of the air. He now sees God's purpose burning in the dark fires of suffering. Like exiled Israel before him he seeks the divine meaning of tragedy. This mood has its effect on the way in which he con-fronts those who consult him.[10] He presents a sharp either/or alternative. The time is growing short, men must choose, discipleship is no longer a leisurely fellowship but a case of leaving everything, taking up the cross, and following Jesus even to death.

### The Last Days in Jerusalem

As Jesus approaches Jerusalem he provides one of those symbolic gestures which the prophets before him had used to impress the people. He enters the crowded city—it was the time of the Passover feast—in symbolic triumph, riding upon an ass, his followers waving palms and laying their garments in his path. The prophesies of Zechariah must have occurred to more than one person in that shouting crowd:

> Rejoice greatly, O daughter of Zion!
>
> .    .    .
>
> Lo, your king comes to you;
>
> .    .    .
>
> humble, and riding on an ass. . . .
> (Zechariah 9:9)

Once in the city, Jesus went directly to the Temple, where he drove out the money-changers and those who bought and sold the sacrificial birds and animals. Again the words of the prophet must have occurred to many: "The Lord . . . will suddenly come to his Temple . . ." (Malachi 3:1). The area of the Temple ground that had become so cluttered with commerce was called the Court of the Gentiles. This nonreligious use of the outer court had the effect of excluding the gentiles from prayer. Jesus reminded them of the words of Jeremiah: " 'My house shall be called a house of prayer,' but you," he said, "make it a den of robbers" (Matthew 21:13). In prophetic promise the Temple was to be a "house of prayer for all nations." Jesus took possession of it in the name of that prophecy and the God whose universal kingdom he preached.

Jesus entered Jerusalem on the first day of the week. In the evening he withdrew with his friends to Bethany, beyond the reach of his enemies. Each day thereafter he returned to the Temple during the day, surrounded by the Passover crowds who pressed about him to hear his words and so prevented the authorities from taking him. Each evening he retired again to his secret hideout. It was this fact that compelled the authorities to seek out a member of his own circle who would betray him.

### The Drama of Death

On Thursday night of the Passover week Jesus gathered with his disciples in Jerusalem to celebrate a final meal together. He knew that the end was drawing near, and on this sad, solemn occasion he turned the simple act of breaking bread and drinking wine into a sacrament of fellowship which they remembered ever afterward. From this simple beginning it evolved into the central act of solemn worship for the Christian community.

After the meal Jesus withdrew with three of his disciples to the Garden of Gethsemane for prayer. Judas had meanwhile carried out his unforgettable deed of betrayal, and the Temple police soon appeared. Jesus was taken first to the home of Caiaphas, the father of the high priest, for preliminary questioning. Then the Sanhedrin, the ruling presidium of the Jewish community, was summoned, even though it was the middle of the night.

The Gospel accounts of the trial do not agree in detail, but something like the following must have occurred:[11] False witnesses were called first, but their testimony failed to agree on Jesus' alleged threat to destroy the Temple. The charge was dropped. Than the high priest asked Jesus directly whether he claimed to be the Messiah. Jesus replied, "I am." At these words, the high priest cried out, "Why do we still need witnesses? You have heard his blasphemy. What is your decision?" (Mark 14:62, 63–64) The court quickly reached a verdict of guilty and called for the prisoner's death.

In its haste to secure conviction the Sanhedrin violated repeatedly procedures that had been prescribed to protect prisoners from such summary judgment. Since, under Rome, the Sanhedrin no longer had the legal power to carry out a capital sentence, Jesus was taken to the Roman procurator, Pontius Pilate. Pilate was ambivalent. He did not wish to please the Sanhedrin, nor could he appear indifferent in matters of public order. He tried twice to release Jesus. Once he had him scourged, thinking this would satisfy the crowd. Then he proposed that Jesus be released according to the custom of the Passover in which one condemned prisoner was set free. But when given a choice between Jesus and Barabbas, a revolutionary Zealot, the crowd chose Barabbas. When at last Pilate was told, "If you release this man you are not Caesar's friend," he yielded to the people's wishes and turned Jesus over to the executioners.

Throughout this whole terrible night Jesus revealed an unshakable dignity and composure. Though the account is simple and lacking invective against either Pilate or the Sanhedrin, the impression throughout is that the condemned man is master of the situation. He alone is sure of himself and confident of ultimate vindication. He had forecast what has now proved to be the case, that in the future he would appear as judge and they as the judged.

Around nine in the morning Jesus was taken with two malefactors and crucified on Golgotha Hill just outside the city. Within a few hours he was already dead, no doubt the result of both the scourging and the cruelties of the crucifixion itself. The legs of the other two victims were broken to hasten their deaths. In order to avoid profanation of the doubly holy day which would fall at sundown, the Sabbath and the Passover, the body of Jesus was removed from the cross by his friends and buried in a tomb lent for the purpose to the sad company by a rich member of the Sanhedrin, Joseph of Arimathea.

## The Resurrection

With the death of Jesus we come to the end of what can be called in any sense public history. But for the followers of Jesus, this is not the end, it is only the beginning. Whatever others chose to believe, the early Christian community was absolutely convinced that Jesus returned from the dead and appeared in their midst. Stories of his appearance spread quickly among the scattered disciples, who had hidden for fear of the authorities. The proposal that this faith was in fact a hoax imposed upon history by the disciples has received a stern rebuke from the great Jewish scholar Joseph Klausner, who wrote: "That is impossible; *deliberate imposture* is not the substance out of which the religion of millions of mankind is created . . . the nineteen hundred years' faith of millions is not founded on deception."[12]

The fact is that if Jesus was wrong, then we must find some explanation for the mistaken notion that he was still alive after the ordeal of death by crucifixion. But if he was right? If God is the Father of sovereign, creative, holy love then the resurrection is a natural if surprising conclusion to the story. Modern efforts to give a wholly natural explanation for this arise from the inability to accept the premises of Jesus' teaching. It must not be supposed, however, that the disciples themselves logically deduced the resurrection from his teaching, for they expressed stunned incredulity at news of the resurrection, and received a rebuke from Jesus himself for their lack of faith. The apocryphal Gospel of Peter reveals their state of mind when it reports Peter saying, "But I with my fellows were in grief, and we were wounded in our minds, and would have hid ourselves."[13] This matter cannot be settled in the historian's court, for the issues are more than matters of public historical fact.

To return to the historical records: A bare 20 years after the event, St. Paul wrote to the Corinthian Church that Jesus "was raised on the third day . . . he appeared to Cephas [Peter], then to the twelve. Then he appeared to more than five hundred brethren at one time, most of whom are still alive. . . . Then he appeared to James, then to all of the apostles (I Corinthians 15:4–7). But this was not all. After this recital of appearances, St. Paul writes, "Last of all, as to one untimely born, he appeared also to me" (I Corinthians 15:8). The New Testament is not a testimony merely to the resurrection—all of its books assume this as fact—it also testifies to the continued presence of Jesus Christ in the Church. The presence does not often take the form of a personal appearance as in Paul's case, but manifests itself as a Holy Spirit breathing life into the Church in the way in which Genesis says the first man Adam received his life from the breath of God. From this perspective the life of the Church is an inspired life, entirely dependent upon the resurrected Christ and the Spirit of God which witnesses to him. In this sense we might say that for the Christain the "career" of Jesus which began at the Jordan River with the baptism of John has never ended, and that he presides over the destinies of men until the end, when all shall be turned over to the Father who will then be, as St. Paul says, "everything to everyone" (I Corinthians 15:28).

It was this faith that produced the Church as the institutional expression of the life of the Spirit. This same Church, as we have seen, composed the New Testament, and gradually evolved those forms of Christian expression that are familiar to history.[14]

## THE TEACHING OF JESUS

*His Method.* Jesus taught concretely. In this he followed the tradition of his culture. His method, unlike the abstract rational methods of the Greek philosophers, remained close to the rich context of human living. His teachings were epigrammatic rather than expository: "Blessed are the pure in heart, for they shall see God" (Matthew 5:8). He told stories, interpreted events, or performed symbolic acts to awaken the spiritual understanding of his followers. The logic of his thought was poetic, moral, and existential rather than rational in the syllogistic or scientific sense.[15] He prepared his inner circle for deeper understanding by sharing his life and death with them.

Teaching of this kind loses a great deal of its inner meaning in being summarized. In spite of this difficulty, I shall attempt to map the major contours of the world view into which he so successfully initiated his followers.

## God

God is the central reality for Jesus. God is sovereign, creative, holy, love, and the first commandment is to love him with all one's heart, soul, mind, and strength. He is sovereign as the creator and controller of nature and history. Not even a sparrow falls without his notice. In the long run nothing can withstand his loving purpose. He is creative, inexhaustibly resourceful in the face of human rejection and the postponements of history. To men many things are impossible, but "with God all things are possible" (Matthew 19:26).

He is holy, the wellspring of all good impulses in man. He is the perfect measure of all fallible human goodness. But his holiness must be understood under the rubric of love. This is the significant New Testament word for God's true nature: Love, *agape*.[16] The agape of God is inexhaustible and impersonal-personal. It is poured out upon the good and the evil alike, none are excluded from his light. As agape he is also an available God, a God who reveals himself, makes himself known to those who turn to him. The God of the philosophers is available only to the talented contemplative, but this God of love is ready at hand for the simplest person who humbly waits upon him. God is involved in the human situation. As Paul Tournier says, "Jesus Christ is the dialogue re-established."[17]

Jesus taught that God is not content with the good men who are already "in the fold," but seeks out those who have lost their way. It is not the well who have need of a physician, but the sick. God dwells no longer in a sacred place such as the Holy of Holies in the Temple; he has come out into the common life; he lives among sufferers and sinners. He lives among them to inspire them to call him Father, and to enjoy the most intimate life of communion with him.

## The Kingdom of God

Jesus inherited the concept of the Kingdom of God and transformed it. In so doing he reinterpreted its meaning in terms of the prophetic tradition that had largely been forgotten. When he came into the synagogue at Nazareth he read from the sixty-first chapter of Isaiah:

> *The Spirit of the Lord is upon me,*
> *because he has anointed me to preach*
> *good news to the poor.*
> *He has sent me to proclaim release to the captives*

> and the recovering of sight to the blind,
> to set at liberty those who are oppressed,
> to proclaim the acceptable year of the Lord.
>
> (Luke 4:18–19)

He stopped in the middle of a verse; the words of Isaiah continue: "to proclaim . . . the day of vengeance of our God" (Isaiah 61:2). Jesus' message was clear: The new kingdom he was proclaiming was not the old notion of God providing final victory over the enemies of Israel, but the God who in his mercy reaches out to include all men in their many needs.

This kingdom was to be the heart of true prayer: "Thy kingdom come, thy will be done, on earth as it is in heaven." The Kingdom is simply the earthly fulfillment of God's heavenly will in the most total way. Jesus could see that this was already on its way. In his own life he was living it out, and the little community of friends was demonstrating the presence of God in their midst. In this sense the Kingdom had already come. It is "within you," Jesus said to those who gathered about him. Another translation of the same words reads "among you," and suggests the social significance of the presence of God's agape in the community of men (Luke 17:21).

But in another sense it was apparent that the Kingdom had not come. Many still refused God's invitation and lived by different values than the kingdom. Because of this, Jesus taught that the Kingdom was yet to come, that God in his own time would usher in a day of fullness such as the prophets had foretold. The Kingdom is thus both present and future.

### The Value of Life

All life was made by God out of his limitless agape. Thus life comes first—before all institutions and regulations, however sacred. Jesus healed on the Sabbath, thus breaking the Hebrew law against work on that day, but he justified his act: "The Sabbath was made for man, not man for the Sabbath . . ." (Mark 2:27). Racial and religious lines are not barriers for God, nor should they be for his people. He made a despised Samaritan the hero of a story of mercy, much to the consternation of a Pharisee who had hoped to trap him by the question, "Who is my neighbor?"[18] In the light of the story only one answer is possible: My neighbor is anyone who is in need, and the man who answers that need is obeying the will of God, even if he is a shunned, half-caste foreigner with an alien religion.

Jesus had great love for the common people, who were excluded from many religious benefits because of their ceremonial uncleanness. He continually transgressed these ancient boundaries and insisted that God was not concerned with the pettiness of ceremonial holiness. The central fact, he said, was the quality of human compassion, and he illustrated his point by a story of the Final Judgment, in which men were judged by God not on religious grounds but as to whether they had shown mercy to their fellows in need—the imprisoned, the hungry, the lonely, and the oppressed.

## Ethics

The ethics which Jesus taught were based upon the agape of God and the value of life. The highest duty, he taught, went far beyond the legalistic rule-obedience of the good men of his day. He claimed that in his teaching the Law of Moses found its fulfillment (Matthew 5:17). The law against murder was fulfilled by substituting love for anger. The law against adultery was fulfilled in the abolition of lust from the heart. The law against false swearing was fulfilled by the spirit of integrity, in which one's Yes meant Yes and one's No meant No. He taught an inner love and trust which dissolved hypocrisy and anxiety. The things that men need, he taught, God already knows. If they would seek His kingdom and His righteousness first, everything else would be theirs as well (Matthew 6:33).

## His Teaching About Himself

We are not certain what Jesus taught about himself. This is the purpose of the new quest which we discussed in Chapter 7. The records attribute to him sayings about himself that are clearly the faith about him that arose in the Church after the resurrection. But if the new questers are right, there is a logical continuity in what Jesus taught about himself and what the Church came to believe about him. In this sense, if one accepts the Christian faith, they are not false claims. However, they are nonetheless not his own claims about himself.

Some things have emerged from recent scholarship as fairly clear. Jesus understood that he was inaugurating the age of the Kingdom of God which John the Baptist had been the last to forecast. In this new era he understood himself to have a special vocation and authority. He forgave sins, preached the new way, and healed, all with an authority that struck his followers as divine. He did not hesitate to call men to leave all and follow him with faith. Moreover, he taught that at the end of the age, when God would finally bring his Kingdom fully to pass, he himself would have a special role and men would be judged by their relationship to him.

The details of this last role are uncertain to us. For instance, we cannot say for sure whether Jesus used the term "Son of Man" for himself or not, despite the fact that it occurs 81 times in the Gospels. And if he did, we cannot be sure that it had messianic significance. We do know that Jesus disappointed the popular interpretation of messianic expectations. In his interpretation of the meaning of the Messiah he turned away from the popular apocalypticism of his day, back to the late writings of the Prophet Isaiah, who had predicted a suffering servant of God who would save men through humbling rather than exalting himself.[19] Only in this light does Jesus' acceptance of the crucifixion make sense. And the Church later seized upon this explanation as the correct one.

Did Jesus think of himself as the Son of God? Again our evidence is oblique rather than direct. It is true that he must have reported the heavenly voice heard at his baptism to his disciples, and the same words, "This is my Beloved Son," are heard again on the Mount of Transfiguration in the setting that presumes that Jesus accepted this announcement as truth. Certainly he used the word Father for God in a way that rings with greater intimacy and assurance than any of the prophets before him.

It is useful to distinguish the sonship from Messiahship. The Messiah was not necessarily the Son of God in Jewish thought, and even today Jews who look for the Messiah deny that he will be the Son of God. It may help to think of sonship as a relationship of profound unity with God, whereas messiahship is a particular role to be played in the cosmic drama of history. In Jesus, Christians believe, the two are fused in a single person. It is likely that Jesus believed as much himself, though in saying this we must humbly confess uncertainty. With our modern interest in inner motives and psychological histories it is natural that we should burn with curiosity about these questions, but they were beyond the concern of the Synoptic authors.

## THE CHURCH'S TEACHING ABOUT JESUS

I have tried to sort out Jesus' own deeds and teaching from those which the Church later attributed to him. Most of the former material is in the earliest strata of the Synoptic Gospels. When we turn to the rest of the New Testament we are fully in the realm of faith's interpretation. But we must not exaggerate the differences between the Synoptics and the rest of the New Testament, since these books too were written backward, so to speak, from the time when Jesus was the acknowledged Lord of their faith.

The Christian Church often gives the impression that the New Testament interpretation of the significance of Jesus Christ is a single system of theology. This is far from the case. The New Testament contains many interpretations,[20] each writer seeking to do the greatest justice to the original faith and life that had come to him through Jesus. Christianity is not a theology but a faith—in God as seen in Jesus—and this faith is forever seeking, so to speak, an adequate formulation. The faith is given once for all; theologies have to be rethought every generation. In this process the New Testament clues are the seeds from which all viable later systems spring.

St. Paul also suggests a variety of interpretations in his own writings. So far as we can ascertain the chronology of events in his life, he gives evidence of changing as he grew older and struggled with the great meanings he was trying to clarify. His letter to the Roman Church appears to be his final and most definitive statement. The author of the letter to the Hebrews proposes another system based on a theology of the priesthood of Christ. The author of the Gospel according to St. John uses Hellenic concepts to express what Jesus meant to him. Each in his own way illuminates the meaning of Jesus.

But this diversity of the New Testament writers must not be exaggerated, for they all agree on one point: Jesus Christ is the focal point for an understanding of God and for his action in history on behalf of humanity. St. Paul says, "God was in Christ reconciling the world to himself . . ." (II Corinthians 5:19). St. John says that the eternal *Logos*, the principle of creation and rational order in the universe, became flesh in Jesus (John 1:1–18). The author of Hebrews says that in "many and various ways God spoke of old to our fathers by the prophets; but in these last days he has spoken to us by a Son . . ." (Hebrews 1:1). Beyond this agreement, these writers explore all the resources of symbol and imagination to find proper means for conveying their meaning. But none of them alone is fully adequate. The Church wisely perceived that they were all needed to express the faith of the Christian community.

It is a popular belief of the recent past that the Church took the simple faith of Jesus and turned it into the religion of Christ.[21] We have seen how contemporary scholarship has modified this view. The truth in that assertion rests upon an inescapable fact of the Christian faith: that the faith consists not only in what Jesus taught but in what he did and was, and, beyond this, in what God did through him for those who had faith in him. For this reason it became impossible to equate the Christian faith with, say, the ethical precepts of the Sermon on the Mount or the winsome teachings of the parables. Jesus was the best example of what the teachings meant; he embodied them. Moreover, his death and resurrection clarified them more than any other event in his life. Hence, an attempt to proclaim the Christian faith as the religion *of* Jesus without the faith *about* Jesus separates things which belong inherently together. The Jesus of the Sermon on the Mount and the Jesus of Golgotha and Easter morning are the same person.

St. Paul realized this more than most. He taught that the new ethical life of the Christian rose from a personal identification with Jesus in his death and resurrection. We die to the old life, he said, and are raised to a new life, one in which we are spiritually free to love our enemies and fulfill all the other high ethical demands that Jesus so clearly laid upon his followers.[22] But in St. Paul, as in many other New Testament writers, Jesus' own central emphasis on the Kingdom of God has all but completely faded. This is a warning against taking any one thinker as the final interpreter of Jesus. He has yet to find his definitive interpreter—unless it be the Holy Spirit of God which St. John says Jesus promised would come after his death and lead men "into all the truth" (John 16:13).

Albert Schweitzer's justly famous concluding words to his *Quest of the Historical Jesus* seem truer now than when he wrote them more than half a century ago: "He comes to us as One unknown, without a name, as of old, by the lakeside. He came to those men who knew Him not. He speaks to us the same word: 'Follow thou me!' and sets us to the tasks which He has to fulfill for our time. He commands, and to those who obey Him, whether they be wise or simple, He will reveal Himself in the toils, the conflicts, the sufferings which they shall pass through in His fellowship, and, as an ineffable mystery, they shall learn in their own experience Who He is."[23]

## SUGGESTIONS FOR FURTHER READING

For the various problems of interpreting the life of Jesus, see the suggested readings for Chapter 7. For a complete, though more traditional account of Jesus by a competent biblical scholar, see William Barclay's *The Mind of Jesus* (Harper & Row, 1961).

Rudolf Bultmann has given his version of the teachings of Jesus in *Jesus and the Word*, Louise P. Smith and E. H. Lantero, trans. (Scribner, 1959). A recent "life" of Jesus based upon the most critical modern scholarship is Gunther Bornkamm's *Jesus of Nazareth* (Harper & Row, 1960). Joseph Klausner's *Jesus of Nazareth* (Macmillan, 1926) is a famous Jewish life of Jesus. For those interested in the way in which the Christological pattern can be used in literature, Nikos Kazantzakis' *Greek Passion* (Simon and Schuster, 1959) will make fascinating reading. *The Picaresque Saint* (Lippincott, 1959) by R. W. B. Lewis, deals critically with a group of modern writers who are concerned with such "Christ figures" in their work.

For the thought of St. Paul from the modern point of view, two commentaries on his Epistle to the Romans are valuable: the famous commentary of Karl Barth, *The Epistle to the Romans*, E. C. Hoskyns, trans. (Oxford University Press, 1933) and C. H. Dodd, *The Epistle of Paul to the Romans* (Hodder, 1952; Fontana, 1959). Rudolf Bultmann's *Existence and Faith*, Schubert M. Ogden, trans. (Meridian, World Publishing, 1960) is a collection of his shorter writings on the relationship between the New Testament faith and existentialism. Paul looms large in this collection.

*Understanding the New Testament* (Prentice-Hall, 1957), by Howard Clark Kee and Franklin W. Young and *An Introduction to New Testament Thought* (Abingdon, 1950), by Frederick C. Grant, are two good basic references for the New Testament as a whole.

For the text of the New Testament I recommend the paraphrase by J. B. Phillips, *The New Testament in Modern English* (Macmillan, 1958). For students who can read German, French, or Spanish, the American Bible Society has inexpensive editions in those languages. The effort of translation often fosters a fresh understanding of a familiar text. Another useful way of examining the text is to read the Huck-Lietzmann *Gospel Parallels based on the Revised Standard Version*, with alternative readings from the ancient manuscripts and noncanonical parallels (Nelson, 1946).

## NOTES

1. Gunther Bornkamm, *Jesus of Nazareth* (Harper & Row, 1960), p. 13.

2. For a translated text of the Scrolls with a short introduction and notes, see Theodor H. Gaster, *The*

*Dead Sea Scriptures* (Doubleday, 1956).

3. For a discussion of this date, see D. M. Beck, *Through the Gospels to Jesus* (Harper & Row, 1954), pp. 339 ff., or Elmer W. K. Mould, *Essentials of Bible History*, rev. ed. (Ronald, 1951), pp. 488–489.

4. See also for this, Beck, *op. cit.*, and Mould, *op. cit.*

5. See Bornkamm, *op. cit.*

6. For a discussion of the standards of scientific verification and faith literature, see H. Richard Niebuhr, *The Meaning of Revelation* (Macmillan, 1941); Alan Richardson, *The Bible in the Age of Science* (Westminster, 1961), especially chapters 3, 6, and 8, and the works of Rudolf Bultmann, especially *New Testament and Mythology* (Scribner, 1941).

7. Matthew 13:55–56.

8. In Book V, chapter V, "The Grand Inquisitor."

9. This is the implication of nearly all the healings recorded in St. Mark's Gospel. See also healing in Matthew 12:22–28.

10. As in the story of the rich young man, Matthew 19:16–26.

11. For a detailed analysis of the legality of the trial of Jesus, see

12. William Barclay, *The Mind of Jesus* (Harper & Row, 1961), chap. 25.

12. Joseph Klausner, *Jesus of Nazareth* (Macmillan, 1926), pp. 357–359.

13. Quoted in Barclay, *op. cit.*, p. 304.

14. For a history of the Holy Spirit in the Christian Church, see Charles Williams, *The Descent of the Dove* (Meridian, World Publishing, 1956).

15. See the later chapters on science and language for a study of these questions.

16. For a study of this word, see Anders Nygren, *Agape and Eros* (Westminster, 1953).

17. Quoted in Barclay, *op. cit.*, p. 106.

18. In the parable of the Good Samaritan, Luke 10:30–37.

19. Isaiah 49, 53.

20. See Frederick C. Grant, *An Introduction to New Testament Thought* (Abingdon, 1950).

21. For a standard treatment of this theme, see Adolf Deissman, *The Religion of Jesus and the Faith of Paul* (Doubleday, 1923).

22. For a crucial passage, see II Corinthians 4.

23. Albert Schweitzer, *The Quest of the Historical Jesus* (Macmillan, 1911).

# 10

# The Authority and Significance of the Bible

❖❖❖❖❖❖❖❖❖❖❖❖❖❖❖❖❖❖❖❖❖❖❖❖❖❖❖❖❖

In an age that has accepted the critical study of sacred documents, what remains of the spiritual authority of the Bible? The Judaeo-Christian Bible is the source of faith for nearly a billion people now living. By what logic can it continue to exercise such authority over the minds of men? It is this question that we must examine here.

## WHAT THE BIBLE IS NOT

There are several misconceptions concerning the nature of the Bible that prevent a clear understanding of its claim to spiritual authority. These must be cleared away before we can undertake our main task.

First of all, the Bible is not a textbook of science. Wherever scientific statements appear in the Bible they are based on the outmoded "science" of the past age. It is a mistake to think that the authority of the Bible lies in its power to enunciate scientific principles without benefit of scientific method and that these dicta are guaranteed from error by the author of nature Himself. Science, properly understood, is an enterprise that has been left to human beings, and is neither the content of revelation nor the basis of biblical authority. The quarrel centering on the six days of creation as outlined in Genesis and the order of natural events as described by natural science is a tragically misconceived debate.

Nor does the authority of the Bible consist in its prevision into future events, either those that have come to pass or those yet in the future. The Bible is not an almanac of the future as some so-called interpreters of "prophecy" would have us believe. Those who spend their time painting a picture of the Bible as a book of forecasts have evidently not familiarized themselves with what modern research has made abundantly clear. The prophecies that they seek to interpret refer in most instances to events contemporary with their writers rather than to events of the twentieth or twenty-first centuries.

The Book of *Daniel*, for example, was written around 168 B.C., and the supernatural deliverance expected by the author was to have taken place within three and a half years. The deliverance came, but not in the form prophesied by the book. Judas Maccabaeus inflicted an improbable defeat upon the forces of the tyrant Ephiphanes and established a free Jewish state. The Temple was cleansed of the "abomination" that had been set up in the holy place. But there was no descent of the expected Son of Man with his legions of angels. The same kind of analysis holds for the Revelation (or Apocalypse) of St. John. Written toward the end of the first century, it promised quick deliverance for the persecuted Christian Church.[1]

The true meaning of prophecy is obscured by making it a mere forecast of events. This is a parody of the prophetic message. What the prophets announced was that if men are faithful to the righteousness of God they may depend upon his support and blessing in all they do; if not, they must prepare for personal and social ruin. The prophets, to be sure, did on occasion refer to specific events—and in some cases they were proved right, as in Jeremiah's forecast of the destruction of Jerusalem—but their chief role was as interpreters of the righteous will of God. And it is surely a dubious service to religious faith for later commentators to twist and turn the symbolic language of the prophets to fit the circumstances of subsequent generations for which it was not intended.

If God had intended to make the authority of scripture consist of supernatural foresight, he surely would have done better. The language of prophecy is often so obscure that misinterpretations are inevitable even for the faithful, and especially for readers of later generations who do not understand the circumstances in which they were first published. No doubt Daniel's contemporaries understood quite well what the highly poetic images of that book intended, but later generations have quarreled over the most fantastic and contradictory interpretations.

But even if the prophecies had been much clearer and without error, they still would fall short of true revelation. They would have become the basis of a mere occultism, which is a species of religion entirely different from the biblical faith. Mankind can't even make wise disposition of its knowledge of the past and present. Could it be trusted with a clear knowledge of the future? All men need know about the future is that it is in good hands, and that what is required here and now is an authentic response to life's challenges.

The Bible is, third, not a textbook of systematic theology containing answers to all important religious questions. This can be easily appreciated by a simple comparison of any work of theology with the Bible itself. In systematic theology, propositions are arranged in rational order supported by reasonable arguments. The Bible, on the other hand, contains practically no such reasoned discourse. Its materials are of a different character: songs, prayers, narratives, histories, epigrammatic teachings, letters. These supply the raw material for theologians but do not themselves constitute systematic theology. To be sure, there are some fragments of theological reasoning, as in the letters of St. Paul, but these hardly amount to a clear and consistent system. In fact, as I have already pointed out, the writers were searching for concepts, both rational and poetic, to convey the profound meanings about life which they had experienced through Jesus Christ. This experience, not a system of concepts, was their basic reference. Roman Catholics, along with Fundamentalists and other Protestants who balk at accepting the full results of critical scholarship, insist that the divine character of the Bible carries with it a guarantee that all its theological statements are consistent with one another, and thus constitute, at least implicitly, a system.

There are many difficulties with this view, especially when it is held to be the central significance of the Scripture. The chief problem lies in the fact that out of the Bible not one but many conflicting systems have been spun. Differences of opinion are notorious. The Roman Catholic Church holds that this diversity supports their contention that God has also ordained, in addition to a divine Book, a supernaturally inspired authority—namely, the Church—to interpret the Bible authoritatively. But even the Roman Catholic Church has been loath to give final status to any single theological system.

Sometimes the so-called plan of salvation is held to be the core of all theological systems. But this plan cannot be stated in a form acceptable to all Christians unless it is framed in the most general terms that still leave the systematic formulations in question. All Christians may, for example, agree with St. Paul and "God was in Christ reconciling the world to himself" (II Corinthians 5:19), but when this statement is expanded into a theology of the atonement or the incarnation, differences abound, even within Catholicism. This supports the view that the authority of the Bible lies elsewhere than in its systematic theology.

In concluding this point I should add that the Bible is not an abstract scheme at all, theological, scientific, or philosophical. Abstract schemes and rational interpretations of the biblical substance come and go, but the living heart of the Book, being other than this, beats on.

In saying these things, have we discarded the authority of the Bible? It is a common argument that if you begin questioning the Bible at any point you undermine its authority all along the line. It is my contention that instead of challenging the Bible's entire validity, such analysis has cleared the way for seeing the true nature of its authority over the lives of men.

## THE BIBLE AS REVELATION

We can understand the Bible's authority only if we understand it as revelation. To the objective historical scholar, the Bible is merely a library of ancient books of special sacredness to Jews and Christians, much as the Vedas are of special sacredness to Hindus. To the philosopher interested in studying the phenomena of religion, the Bible is more than this. It is a rich sourcebook of religious experience, the record of a people seeking for and sought by God. It is a thousand-year notebook of experimental faith. But for neither of these is the Bible the revelation of God, or the Word of God, as those under its spiritual authority hold it to be. We must examine this crucial conception. What do we mean by revelation?

Revelation involves two closely related elements. It is first of all an unveiling of what is ultimate. If it does not clarify ultimate concern, it is not revelation, no matter how informative or sublime the topics it unfolds. The ancient Jew, for example, saw in the Law of Moses the unveiling of a supreme claim which he could not evade and remain true to himself. Christians saw in the event of Christ the unveiling of what ultimately concerned them.

The second element in revelation is that it possesses an authority that changes the person or group to whom it has come. It is a contradiction in terms to say that a person has discovered his ultimate concern and that it makes no difference to his existence. The revelation of religious truth, as we have defined it, provokes and requires change. It is a power that remakes and reorients men. It restructures the inner self and resettles men in the human community in a startlingly new way. In this sense it is existential rather than theoretical in character.

Mere information, no matter how profound, does not do this. New scientific theories do not change men, but the unveiling of a new God does.

Take friendship as an analogy. We may construct a profile of a person by consulting the many files that modern organizations keep on their members. Such knowledge is theoretical and nonexistential. But suppose that one of these punchcard persons becomes a friend. This can occur only if he chooses to make himself present and known to us. If he reserves himself we are irrevocably cut off from his friendship. He must reveal himself, open his life to our view and invite our participation. What we cannot achieve by extended research can be ours by a simple gift from him. But this revelation, because it is an invitation to participation, effects a change in us. We experience new claims and new values which alter us. If we find these claims frightening, as many people do, we withdraw, refusing the proffered revelation. The relationship fails to ripen into friendship.

In an analogous, but of course much more exalted way the revelation of God involves a double self-revelation: God to us and we to him. Without response there is no revelation. What sense would it make to say, "I know God, but this knowledge makes no difference to me." It would be as reasonable to say, "I have found the most beautiful thing in the world, but I wouldn't give two cents for it."

Again, as in friendship, revelation occurs in the full context of life. It involves the continued dialogue of living beings. This is what the Bible says about human fellowship with God: "Do justice, love mercy, and walk humbly with thy God" (Micah 6:8, KJV). If the Bible is the Word of God it must be the basis for a living dialogue between humanity and that God. It cannot be the dead knowledge of an abstract system.

Another aspect of this analogue also applies to the concept of biblical revelation. A friend reveals himself in words, to be sure, but his words gain their assured meaning from his acts. The Bible reveals God in words, yes, but much more in events. For the Christian, the supreme revelation is not verbal propositions but the total event of Christ. The Christian finds God not only in what Jesus said but in what he was and what he did, especially in his death and resurrection. The revelation of God cannot come through Jesus except to the person who responds to the new claims and the new experiences opened to him by that unveiling.

Let us take another analogy, this time from art. What constitutes the "authority" of a painting or a musical composition? The authority of a painting or a musical composition comes from looking and listening. If after patient waiting the art does not speak to you, it does not possess any power over your feelings. It is possible, however, that you have in some way shut yourself off from its appeal. In the same way, we may say, if you contemplate the world of the Bible in full openness and it does not speak to you, it does not possess power over your life. Again, however, it is possible that in some way you have shut yourself off from its appeal.

Of course, in neither case will a single glance, or a single hearing, do. Often we are impelled to return to what we have failed to see or hear by the testimony of others whom we respect. Critics do this for us in art; the prophets and saints do it for faith. They point us to the source of the goodness we admire in them, until, hopefully, we see for ourselves. Revelation that cannot become our own understanding cannot be authentic revelation.

It should be clear that in following this procedure we need not fear a "sacrifice of intellectual integrity." The biblical claim, like the claim of sublime art, is simply that open waiting and responsive dialogue will bring any person to the place of natural dialogue for which he was created.

Let us consider the matter in yet another way. Biblical scholars have shared in the modern intellectual revolution which has rethought the meaning of history. In fact, this modern revolution is a turning away from the effort to reduce history to a form of natural science and a return to more biblical modes of thought. Men who write history are within history; they cannot objectify it without falsifying their subject matter. The events of the human past enter into the very constitution of the thinker who is recounting them. Because of this, history has to be continuously rewritten as men reshape their own understanding of themselves.

Biblical history is thus existential in the most profound sense. It is what biblical scholars call *heilsgeschichte*—the "history of salvation." By this they mean that an understanding of the events in the Bible is a form of self-understanding that leads to the transformation of human existence. Biblical history—to those who understand its inner meaning—is not simply a narrative of events that have occurred to other men; it is my history, or our history. To the Jew, Abraham is Father Abraham; to the Christian, Jesus is Our Lord. There is thus a world of difference between objective history—events in impersonal time—and existential history.

No one has made this clearer than H. Richard Niebuhr in his work *The Meaning of Revelation*.[2] He compares Lincoln's Gettysburg Address with a passage in the *Cambridge Modern History* as follows: Lincoln began his address with a reference to history: "Four-score and seven years ago our fathers brought forth upon this continent a new nation, conceived in liberty and dedicated to the proposition that all men are created free and equal." The *Cambridge Modern History* describes the same event as follows: "On July 4, 1776, Congress passed the resolution which made the colonies independent communities, issuing at the same time the well-known Declaration of Independence. If we regard the Declaration as the assertion of an abstract political theory, criticism and condemnation are easy. It sets out with a general proposition so vague as to be practically useless. The doctrine of the equality of men, unless it be qualified and conditioned by reference to special circumstance, is either a barren truism or a delusion."[3]

These accounts differ in fundamental ways. For our purposes the prime difference is that Lincoln was within the history to which he was referring, whereas the Cambridge historian was outside it. To Lincoln the founders were "our fathers," to the Englishman they were a foreign "Congress." To Lincoln the principles of the Declaration were a commitment and a focus of devotion; to the Englishman they were abstract philosophy. To men within that history the principles of the Declaration evoked a dedication of life, fortune, and sacred honor; to the historian they suggested a need for philosophic criticism.

Turning again to the Bible, we may say that the biographies and histories of scripture have authority over the man who is within that history, over the person to whom the saints and prophets are "our fathers" and to whom the religious teachings of these men are a call to the total dedication of life. To such a man the Bible is revelation, and to such a man alone.

A question naturally comes to mind. Who is right, Lincoln or the Cambridge historian? the Christian or his critic? How do we logically evaluate such claims? Considerations of this kind we must postpone until later chapters, when we will deal with the logic of religious knowledge. However, enough has been said to indicate that revelation is not a category of objective history but of existential history; it occurs within a given history to the participants who are immersed in it.

## THE LIFE-WORLD OF THE BIBLE

The Bible, as we have now seen, is not a theology or philosophy competing for the minds of men; it is a world view commending itself to man as a total life orientation. It offers a perspective from which to see the meaning of existence and the way to an authentic relationship to all life. Philosophies and theologies may be sired by this world view, but they never exhaust it.

The Bible introduces us into a life-world,[4] in contrast to a thing-world, or law-world, or abstract-world. The world of the Bible is peopled, it is alive. Whatever abstract principles appear, such as moral laws or generalizations about the movements of nature and history, are always rooted in the living will of God in dialogue with the living wills of men. Biblical teaching is in essence personal, historical, and dramatic. It places concrete men in total dialogue with the full concreteness of life. It resists all tendencies for the impersonal to slip into controlling position, whether it be legal, religious, or philosophical in nature. To the legalistic men of his day, Jesus said, "The Sabbath is made for man, not man for the Sabbath . . ." (Mark 2:27). The prophets taught that the state grows out of the dialogue of men with each other and with God—it is a covenantal affair. Morality is not an impersonal rule, it is the code regulating interpersonal dialogue. Impersonal institutions and concepts thus have no status apart from the life-world itself.

With the Greeks it was different. They sought to ground their thought in impersonal principles. Under the influence of scientific thought, modern men tend to find that way of thought congenial. Our generation seeks understanding in terms of natural laws, relationships of cause and effect. The tension between this abstract-world view and the life-world view of the Bible is no small source of difficulty for contemporary man's attempt to take the Bible seriously. Science has made the abstract-world view so congenial that it is hard to imagine a reasonable alternative. The reader feels that he is being hailed back to a kind of primitive animism in which everything is thought to be inhabited by spirits.

But science is not imperiled if one accepts the life-world of the Bible as primary. On the contrary, a case can be made for the view that only such a ground can supply a satisfactory foundation for science itself. Moreover, once we understand the difference between the perspectives of biblical and scientific modes of thought, they need not interfere with each other. Science can have its head because most of the old conflicts, based as they were on false understandings of both the Bible and science, would disappear.

Nonetheless, one must decide which has priority: the life world or the thing-world. If the thing-world is primary, the entire life of the spirit becomes problematical, and the meaning of human life (including scientific research) is called into question. These are problems that will be treated later at more length. Here we are concerned only to clarify the difference between the two world views. Then we can explore the question, whether the modern preference for exclusively impersonal categories may not be a philosophic mistake— perhaps even a social obsession: A mistake, because reality may not be merely an impersonal collection of public objects arranged according to abstract laws; and obsession, because reducing reality to a thing-world may be resorted to in order to avoid the responsible and concrete encounter with existence that life-world categories invoke.

Let us spell out more particularly the life-world view of the Bible.

### History

Nonbiblical views interpret history impersonally. Ancient philosophies often viewed it cyclically, as under the control of an impersonal fate. Classical Hinduism shares this view. Under the influence of natural science modern man tends to see history as an upward development, in the sense of movement toward greater complexity. History, according to this account, is determined by impersonal forces which social scientists will progressively clarify through their programs of research.

According to the Bible, on the other hand, history is inherently purposeful. It has a meaning that has been implanted at its center: the coming of Jesus Christ. This event is the watershed of history. God is the Lord of history, and he has revealed the basic plot. All history is read backward and forward from this event. History is the realm of a free dialogue between finite beings and the eternal God who brought the whole enterprise into existence for his own purposes.

### Man

As the crown of creation, man is an essential part of the eternal dialogue. Though he is of the earth, his very being depends upon the breath of God that first awakened him to existence as a living soul. His whole meaning is to be a son of God. As St. Paul says, "He destined us in love to be his sons . . ." (Ephesians 1:5).

Because man is free and responsible, his movement toward his destiny is not fixed by impersonal laws. As a matter of fact, in the exercise of his freedom he has chosen over and again to reject that destiny. This is the meaning of sin. Sin is not an impersonal force or a hereditary taint; it is the mysterious tendency of man, observed in all ages and among all classes, to turn away from his fellows and God toward himself. The only way he can recover from the painful effects of such choices is to return to the dialogue and discover the renewal of life that flows again into his veins by virtue of the fact that God is eternally ready to resume the dialogue. This is the meaning of the waiting father in Jesus' great parable of the prodigal son. When he returns to the existential communion of the life-world he realizes in the marrow of his being that he has found his true home. As St. John says, "We know we have passed out of death into life, because we love the brethren" (I John 3:14).

The impersonal view of man differs decisively from this. As an organism derived exclusively from nature which is self-enclosed, man's destiny is entirely natural. His basic motivation is to maintain his own existence. To this end, to be sure, he may learn to treat his fellows more or less humanely, but the orientation is inevitably—by natural laws—centered around his organic structures. These structures in turn are in principle fully explicable in impersonal scientific terms.

It is impossible to summarize the view of man that arises out of abstract scientific accounts, for they have varied so greatly. The view varies from optimistic to pessimistic, depending on the particular science—and the state of that science—that is in the foreground at the time. Early evolutionary theory, for example, supported an optimistic view of man, as growing forever upward. But this same theory was later used to support the doctrines of Social Darwinism, which taught that man as a survivor of a long struggle is wise to continue "red in tooth and claw."[5] But all these accounts have in common one thing: Man is a part of nature and is to be understood in terms of the abstract principles that determine nature's behavior.

## Nature

The Bible knows nothing of the modern conception of a self-enclosed, autonomous nature. Nature is creation, the realm of God's action, the stage of history. Its rational order is not rooted in a complex of independent laws, but is an expression of God's trustworthiness, his eternal Logos, or holy will. No doubt confidence in this fact, as some historians of science have declared, was a major element in the rise of science, since it gave an objective basis for the confidence that the investigation of nature would result in discovering coherent laws. But as scientific consciousness developed, the rationality of nature was gradually separated from its bondedness to the will of God and assumed an autonomy of its own. The stages in this development are a fundamental part of the intellectual history of the modern age. In its mature form, the modern conception of autonomous nature is a thing-world as distinct from the original biblical life-world, and it stands therefore in contrast to the biblical view.

## THE UNIQUE

One of the effects of thinking in terms of an object-world rather than a life-world is that uniqueness becomes a meaningless category. The life-world is filled with uniqueness; each life and each moment are different. Abstract thinking, as Sir Arthur Eddington (1882–1944) the astronomer-philosopher once said, is committed to sameness. It is quite possible that every particle in the physical universe is different from every other, but science pursues general laws derived from similarities. Alfred North Whitehead suggests that it is as though Procrustes, the legendary Greek highwayman who stretched or cut his overnight visitors to fit his iron bed, were to have published an essay on the uniform size of Attic travelers.

In the life-world of the Bible uniqueness abounds. Each man has his own vocation. Not only Moses and Christ but every man is unrepeatable. When history has not yet been reduced to abstract categories this is bound to be the case. Once Moses or Christ has appeared, what need is there of another? Each fulfills his particular purpose, and history is carried a step further.

Even in a scientific era, I might point out, all knowledge is the result of the work of unique individuals. What would physics be without Newton or Einstein, or biology without Darwin, or psychology without Freud? What would music be without Bach, or art without Van Gogh? It is only by ignoring the mysterious character of creativity that we can believe that science, art, and music move forward by impersonal forces alone.

Of course, once the original contribution has been made it becomes the possession of the multitudes and the basis for the work of others. But there is no way to abolish the individual or the unique circumstances of history that supported all these advances. Nothing is gained in understanding by reducing each great personage to the level of "just another man." Such reduction is mainly the work of personal envy rather than the necessities of thought. To be sure, I may never be Beethoven or Van Gogh—and certainly not Moses or Christ—but that does not preclude my own uniqueness in my own way and in my own time. But it is just this conclusion that impersonal and nonhistorical modes of thought make it difficult to understand.

### Miracles

Another element in scripture that troubles the modern reader is the presence of miracles. Ever since the enlightenment this has constituted a special difficulty for modern men. Again, the reason lies in the fact that with the rise of modern science nature has been increasingly described as the realm of impersonal law. Miracles, thought to be breaches of natural law, were therefore declared impossible and consequently unbelievable.

This point deserves special note because biblical miracles have been a stock in trade for some modern apologists who have used them to prove that Jesus was a divine being. Today it is easier to believe in Jesus than in his miracles. And yet as doubt increased on this score, it spread to the remaining claims of scripture and facilitated the victory of skepticism.

How shall we treat this problem? A full answer would require considering in detail material I have reserved for later treatment. Here we must limit ourselves to a few brief comments. We could emulate Locke or Kant, followed incidentally by many modern liberal theologians, and simply excise the miraculous elements, leaving a religion "within the bounds of reason alone."[6] But this move only hastens the death of biblical faith by leaving a religious residue that is not recognizably Christian. The life-world of the Bible seems to be inherently "miraculous" in character. Remove this and the heart is gone.

The writers of scripture, as we have said, had no conception of an autonomous "nature." Hence, events like the passage through the Red Sea, or the healing of a paralytic, were not regarded as suspensions of natural laws. They were, to be sure, wonderful in quality, but only in that they inspired wonder in the beholder and marked the special nearness of God, and not at all because they were thought to be a setting aside of nature's laws. In a sense, all natural events were thought by writers of scripture to be "miraculous" in that they were part of the living dialogue of God and his people. Miracles were, then, simply events in which God was more clearly revealing himself.

Another important point is that these wonders were reported by men who had no interest or training in what we would call scientific reporting. They had no scientific generalizations to suggest to them what should happen in a given situation. The unusual showing of God's presence was in this sense a perfectly "natural" event, not be suspected as more doubtful than a so-called nonmiraculous event. We need special evidence for what we would term a "miracle," but this is due to our strong belief in a natural order in terms of which such an event would not be expected to occur. And, if we reported such an event, we would want to bolster our account with precautions against credulity or misjudgment. As a consequence of this lack of scientific awareness, no doubt many biblical events were inaccurately reported. This fact grants the modern reader a right to suspend judgment about whether a given event actually occurred as reported. We may rightly question, for example, whether an ax-head floated on the waters of the Jordan, as reported in the Elisha cycle (II Kings 6:5–7), or whether the bears which the prophet called out of the woods to eat the children who mocked him were a sign of God's special providence (II Kings 2:23–24). But these doubts are not merely scientific, they are also moral and religious. We may lay the reports to exaggerations of the pious imagination writing many years after the events and still unclear about the meaning of God's presence in the world.

What I am saying is that we may still question whether given events really occurred, but we must not pass judgment in an a priori manner and stipulate just what kind of events cannot occur. Whether events actually occurred depends upon the reliability of the reports, not on whether we think they could or could not happen. A knowledge of the history of science, and a little less dogmatism about naturalistic metaphysics might make us less cocksure. Take a couple of instances. The president of the French Academy of Sciences toured the continent to persuade the scientific community that Edison's phonograph was a fraud and scientifically impossible. According to the laws of classical chemistry the radioactive substances found by the Curies were obviously "impossible," and there is always—in nature—the bee, whose wing and body structure make it "impossible" (by the laws of aerodynamics) for him to fly.

Modern commentators on science are aware of this fact and have tended to agree that, at best, scientific "laws" are not binding on nature, but are simply shorthand accounts of our experience of events to date. There is no reason to suppose that our present scientific rules are an exhaustive account.

Take, for example, the remarkable events reported at the Roman Catholic healing shrine at Lourdes. In 1936 a man suffering from tuberculosis of the lungs, spine, and kidneys, reportedly ready to die, was X-rayed at the Lourdes Hospital and the diagnosis confirmed.[7] He was carried to the shrine on Saturday, September 5, and on the following Wednesday he was ready to go home with all his lesions healed. Our evidence for this event is scientifically excellent. Subsequent X-rays clearly show the scars on the healed organs. There seems little reason to doubt that the healing occurred. However, there are no explanations available to present-day science. To the devout attendants at the shrine this event was simply one more sign of God's unusual presence among them. To the person who still finds the life-world of the Bible believable this event is not surprising; it is what might be expected if human beings were more attentive to the spiritual dimensions of existence.

Or, take the quarrels over extrasensory perception—ESP, as it is called. Since ESP is not explicable in terms of any laws of physics there are many who claim out of hand that the reports of the careful experimenters at Duke University are either conscious or unconscious frauds.[8] They "know" that such things cannot happen. But the question of whether they happen or not is not to be settled this way. Only patient observation can tell us what happens. Our understanding will come trundling along much later to supply some plausible explanation.

In concluding this brief discussion of a thorny question let me suggest the following principles: First, "miracles" are simply unusual events that are to be constantly expected in the life-world. Second, we would be wise to heed Hamlet's rebuke to Horatio and remember that there are more things in heaven and earth than are dreamed of in our philosophy and science. And, third, we would do well to seek more diligently to emulate the total life responses surrounding these so-called miraculous events to see if they might not occur much more frequently, even for us.

A final word is needed to correct a possible misunderstanding. For the men of the Bible, as for all sensible men, the firm order of events which we call "nature" is a greater testimony to God's faithfulness than rare and unusual occurrences. By patient research into this reliable order, modern medicine, for instance, has produced cures for most of the illnesses that beleaguered ancient societies. Faith in God does not require that we despise such knowledge. The biblical attitude would be to take this knowledge as one more mark of God's providential order.

The authority of the Bible, then, rests in its power to woo us into the life-world in which a living God continuously encounters concrete men in an open dialogue of the spirit. Whether this can happen to modern men remains to be seen. In order to examine this question we shall, in our next section, deal with the forces that have shaped the modern mind, and the religious reaction to these forces.

### SUGGESTIONS FOR FURTHER READING

On the general question of the authority of the Bible, C. H. Dodd's *The Authority of the Bible* (Harper & Row, 1929) is an accepted classic. Two of Alan Richardson's works deal with this question in one way or another: *The Bible in an Age of Science* (Westminster, 1961) and *A Preface to Bible Study* (Westminster, 1944). Richardson is a very fine biblical scholar and aware of the subtle currents of contemporary thought. He also has a good book on miracles: *The Miracle Stories of the Gospels* (Harper & Row, 1942). I have treated this subject in connection with God's response to prayer in *Reality and Prayer* (Harper & Row, 1957), especially the chapters on petition, intercession, and problem-solving prayer. This also enters into my chapter on prayer and science.

Since the authority of the Bible depends upon the truth and appeal of its message, I would recommend Harold De Wolf's little book *The Enduring Message of the Bible* (John Knox, 1965) and Millar Burrows' *An Outline of Biblical Theology* (Westminster, 1956). Two fine works on revelation are John Baillie's *The Idea of Revelation in Recent Thought* (Columbia University Press, 1956) and H. Richard Niebuhr's *The Meaning of Revelation* (Macmillan, 1941).

On the concept of the "life-world," see John Wild, *Existence and the World of Freedom* (Prentice-Hall, 1963) and almost any of the writings of Gabriel Marcel. Marcel's fullest statement appears in his two volumes of Gifford Lectures, *The Mystery of Being* (Gateway, Regnery, 1960).

### NOTES

1.  For a treatment of the New Testament literature of hope, see Howard Clark Kee and Franklin W. Young, *Understanding the New Testament* (Prentice-Hall, 1957), pp. 451 ff. For an interpretation of

the Book of Daniel, see Robert Pfeiffer, *Introduction to the Old Testament* (Harper & Row, 1941), pp. 748 ff.

2. H. Richard Niebuhr, *The Meaning of Revelation* (Macmillan, 1941).

3. *Ibid.*, pp. 60–61.

4. The term life-world is taken from John Wild, *Existence and the World of Freedom* (Prentice-Hall, 1963).

5. For the influence of Social Darwinism, see Richard Hofstadter, *Social Darwinism in American Thought* (Beacon Press), 1955.

6. Immanuel Kant, *Religion Within the Limits of Mere Reason* (1793). A good recent edition is translated and edited by Theodore M. Greene and Hoyt H. Hudson (Open Court, 1960).

7. For documentation, see Smiley Blanton, "An Analytical Study of a Cure at Lourdes," *The Psychoanalytic Quarterly*, 9 (1940), 348–362.

8. For this debate, see J. B. Rhine, *The Reach of the Mind* (Sloane, Morrow, 1947).

## PART FOUR

# RELIGION IN MODERN
# WESTERN CULTURE

# 11

# *The Mind of the Modern West*

◆◆◆◆◆◆◆◆◆◆◆◆◆◆◆◆◆◆◆◆◆◆◆◆◆◆◆◆◆◆◆◆◆◆◆◆◆◆

What we call the modern West is the culture that had its seedtime in the twelfth century and emerged into history in the sixteenth. Looking back from the vantage point of the twentieth century, it is possible to speak of the "mind of the modern West" as a form of consciousness quite distinct from the "medieval mind" which preceded it. The passage from one to the other was a troubled time—similar in many ways to our own. In fact, the analogy is quite exact, for in my judgment we are now emerging from modernity into a postmodern period which I predict will be as distinct from modern forms of consciousness as the modern was from the medieval.

The present chapter will undertake a description of the main features of the modern mind. The chapter following will recount the struggle of religious faith during the emergence and eventual supremacy of modern modes of thought. During that period, wherever religion was alive it endeavored to take serious account of modernity, to bring itself up to date, so to speak. Following this account there will be a couple of chapters analyzing the crisis of the modern mind and the way in which faith, purged by its passage through the modern era, reacted to the failure of modernity. Here we will see how Christianity found its authentic voice and was at last prepared to speak again from its own vital center, as it once spoke to the decaying classical civilization of ancient Rome.

It is debatable whether the Renaissance belongs to the medieval or the modern world, but a clear beginning of modernity can be discerned in the work of René Descartes (1596–1650), sometimes called the Father of Modern Philosophy.[1] As a soldier in the Catholic armies, observing the senseless destruction of the wars of religion that began in 1618, it was natural that he should be assailed by serious doubts about the conflicting claims of the contenders. How, he asked himself, could knowledge be reestablished upon true and undoubted principles to which all reasonable men would naturally consent? In answer to that question he formulated his celebrated "Rules of Method,"[2] which can be summarized in three propositions: First, accept nothing as true except clear and distinct ideas that cannot be doubted. Second, analyze all problems into their simplest components. Third, proceed in an orderly way from the simplest items to the most complex, making sure that every element has been included.

Following these rules Descartes found himself in doubt about everything except his own existence, a fact he could not doubt without affirming it: "I think, therefore I am."[3] On this foundation he proceeded to erect an indubitable system composed of elements clearly and distinctly true. Indubitable, that is, to Descartes, for his successors were far from agreeable to his conclusions. Descartes was a mathematician as well as a philosopher, and he unconsciously turned to geometry for the model that satisfactory inquiry must emulate.

An analysis of the assumptions underlying Descartes's celebrated method can begin our definition of what we mean by modern mind. The first assumption is the rejection of tradition: "I rejected as false all reasons formerly accepted by me as demonstrations."[4] The second is an unbounded confidence in the power of human reason to plumb all mysteries and the rejection of any help from other sources, such as tradition or revelation. The third assumption is belief in the power of analysis to resolve the difficulties of complex experiences, the assurance that complex matters are in fact merely compounds of simpler elements. This was to have a decidedly reductive effect on the accounts which could be given of complex matters, such as moral, aesthetic, or religious experience. Descartes's fourth assumption is individualism: Inquiry is the work of individual minds whose relationship to one another and the world is purely external. In theory the thinker would not need the community of either the past or present. All that is needed can be provided by the individual's own experience coupled with his powers of thought. And, finally, true knowledge is expressible in clear and distinct language modeled upon mathematics. Mystery is banished in principle as mere intellectual fogginess.

Descartes's celebrated scientific contemporary Galileo Galilei (1564–1642), who in 1632 ran into trouble with the Inquisitional authorities for his published defense of the Church-condemned Copernican system (showing that the earth moves about the sun), completed the complex of metaphysical notions which can be properly regarded as the seeds of modernity. Going beyond Descartes's mathematical rationalism, Galileo added experiment to clear and distinct reflection and laid the enduring foundations of modern science.[5]

The quarrel with the Church really lay in the fact that Galileo's insistence on the truth of the earth's dependent relationship to the sun was a complete challenge to the world-picture that had come to dominate the late-medieval world. Acceptance of this simple scientific fact, established by Copernicus in his great opus (printed 1543), meant much more than a mere alteration of the elements of astronomy; it meant that the entire scheme of traditional religion and the political and social institutions dependent upon it were called into question. Galileo, whose writings, published in the common language, could "subvert" the layman, was regarded as a subversive in the most alarming and radical sense of the word.[6] He had laid the ax to the root of the tree of medieval culture.

## THE MEDIEVAL MIND

The medieval mind[7] had its historic roots in the break-up of ancient Roman civilization. Christianity had begun inconspicuously with the crucifixion of its leader in A.D. 33. From this humble beginning it had spread into the religious vacuum of the Roman Empire, reaching Rome by the middle of the first century. While the Empire entered the prolonged throes of decline, the Christian faith girded itself for a future of which it could not have dreamed by forging three instruments for the survival of its distinctive witness: a book, a creed, and an organized church. By the second century it had composed the New Testament and started the 300-year long process of joining it to the Old as a sacred canon. At the same time, in order to meet the challenge of variant definitions, it defined authoritatively its essential beliefs in simple creeds. The Church itself gradually formed, out of the spontaneous fellowship described in the Book of Acts, into a hierarchical organization with bishops at the head. By the middle of the fourth century, the bishop of Rome, reigning in the venerated Eternal City, had become in effect the head of a universal church modeled on the pattern of the vanishing secular empire. Although his authority would be often disputed and later even rejected, he was early accorded the position of "first among equals" among the bishops of Christendom.

Thus, with its authoritative canon and creed, and a well-knit organizational structure, the Church was prepared to endure the tests of heresy within and persecution without. Finally, in the course of destiny, in the fourth century under the Christian emperor Constantine, it became the official religion of the empire that had first ignored it and then, for 200 years, frantically sought to stamp it out. The reasons why this faith was able to outbid the rival religions of the age and survive the systematic efforts of a powerful government to destroy it are unfortunately beyond the limits of our inquiry. For whatever reason—be it the will of God or the course of natural events—the

Christian faith became the determining factor in shaping the civilization that arose on the ruins of Rome.

When in A.D. 410, for the first time in eight centuries, enemy forces under Alaric, the Goth, pierced the defenses of the Eternal City, the shock to the Empire was profound. In faraway Bethlehem, in a monastery, the aging Christian scholar Jerome (340?–420) wept at the prospect of the end of civilized existence. Pagan thinkers blamed the Christians for the neglect of the gods who had kept the city invulnerable for nearly a millennium. But from his See in North Africa, Augustine, Bishop of Hippo (354–430), wrote a defense of the Christian faith which became the blueprint for the 1000-year rule of the Church which was to come. He envisioned a City of God[8] rising on the ruins of the city of man. He foresaw a society rooted and grounded in obedience to the holy will of God. Medieval Christendom was to embody this ideal, however imperfectly.

Civilizations, insofar as they are culturally integrated, tend to articulate some major premise throughout all their thought systems and institutions. The major premise of medieval society is nowhere so concisely stated as in the Nicene Creed formulated at the First Council of Nicea in the early fourth century (A.D. 325): "I believe in One God, the Father Almighty, Maker of heaven and earth, And of all things visible and invisible. And in one Lord, Jesus Christ, the only-begotten Son of God; Begotten of his Father before all worlds, God of God, Light of Light, Very God of Very God. . . . And I look for the resurrection of the dead. And the Life of the world to come. Amen."[9]

Medieval Christendom articulated this major premise, insofar as it was culturally integrated, throughout all its cultural compartments. Architecture and sculpture were the "Bible in stone." Its literature, painting, and music were almost exclusively religious. Its philosophy was a handmaid to theology, which was hailed as the queen of the sciences. The highest truth was the supersensual mystery of God revealed to the Church. Its ethics and laws were but elaborations of the Gospel teachings. Its political organizations, both ecclesiastical and secular, were theocratic. The family was consecrated in a sacrament that was regarded as beyond the power of man to break. Economic activity was regulated according to rules that were religiously inspired. And the final and highest goal of human life was union with God.

This magnificent concept of life and the world received its most eloquent poetic expression in Dante's *Divine Comedy* (*ca.* 1318), which envisioned an *inferno* descending into the earth in an encircled hollow, while *purgatory* rose in a mountain on the side of the earth. At its top lay an earthly paradise leading, through seven heavens, to God's throne. Its leading thinker was Thomas Aquinas (1225?–1274), "Prince of scholastics," whose great Summae were systematic accounts of the same view of existence.

Through the power of this vision the medieval Church preserved what remained of the culture of the ancient world, educated the barbarian races which flooded into the ruined empire, and at last achieved a synthesis of life that covered Europe with great cathedrals and magnificent works of art.

And it was this vision of life that was blasted by Copernicus with his theories of a heliocentric universe, by Galileo with his telescope, and by Descartes with his all-corroding doubt. From the beginning of the seventeenth century onward, the modern spirit—a spirit of increasing secularism—grew and prospered.

## THE MODERN MIND

If God and his invisible kingdom were the major premise of medieval culture, what is the major premise of modern culture? A beginning has already been made on this question in reporting the thought of Descartes. In general we can say that it was a secularizing movement: from God to man, from the supernatural to the natural, from the spirit to the senses. Whereas the medieval mind regarded God as the final truth and ultimate worth as a thing of the spirit, the modern mind finds truth and value in autonomous human reason and in the life of the senses. It is this principle that is articulated by the institutions of modern culture—its art and science, its political and economic institutions, its law and ethics, its philosophy, even its religion.

*The Making of the Modern Mind.* It is of course impossible to describe all the important factors that went into the making of the modern mind, but it will be worth recounting a few that had special bearing upon the fate of religion in the modern world. To make this brief account as clear as possible it will be necessary to separate interweaving influences, recognizing that we are dividing what our predecessors experienced as a living whole.

### Theoretical Developments: Science[10]

I put first what was probably the most important single factor—the revolution in human thought that we call natural science. It did not come all at once, and its ultimate effects are still hidden from view. This revolution can be described in five stages. the most dramatic episode of the five came first: the rise of modern physics.

The half-century from the publication of Galileo's *Dialogue on the Two World-Systems* (Ptolemaic and Copernican) in 1632 to Newton's *Principia* in 1687 saw the initiation and completion of the theoretical foundations of modern physics. Galileo had begun by laying the groundwork of a workable method and in demonstrating its power to explain natural events. He turned his back on the 1000-year question of *why* the world was organized as it was to the question of *how* it was organized. Medieval science, based upon Aristotle and bolstered by a religious understanding of nature, had asked why a rock fell to earth after being thrown into the air. Galileo was content to measure the rate of its fall and formulate his measurements into a constant law of falling bodies. His successor, Johannes Kepler (1571–1630), was surprised by the thought that the moon could be regarded as a falling body which moved swiftly enough to stay in orbit. Sir Isaac Newton (1642–1727) completed the scheme by formulating his celebrated laws of motion.

The upshot of this simple change of intellectual perspective completely shattered the closed and cosy world of medieval thought, and put in its place an infinite world of unbounded space in which the sun had become one of untold millions of stars (*ca.* 100,000 million in our galaxy alone) and the earth a minor planet trailing it through lonely wastes for endless eternities of time. Gone were the concentric circles of the surrounding heavens with purgatory and paradise not far above and inferno not far beneath. Gone also was the comfortable feeling that man was at the center of creation and that the very stars conspired toward his salvation. Gone too, of course, were the smoldering fires of hell at the center of the earth, to which those who rejected salvation would be eternally consigned at the Last Judgment. With the disappearance of this world-picture, the system of rewards and punishments— the meanings of life—that had integrated a great culture was cast irretrievably into doubt.

It is understandable why shortly after the publication of Galileo's *Dialogue*[11] the Church authorities forced him to his knees to deny what he knew. It is as though they had a shuddering intuition of the cultural subversion that he had encouraged with his little tube equipped with crystalline lenses.

The second wave of the scientific revolution was anticipated in geology and completed in biology. It turned the scientific method on living organisms and introduced the concept of change and development.

The "medieval world-view," as Alan Richardson says, "did not disintegrate in all its parts at equal speed."[12] The corollary of this is that the modern mind did not emerge full-grown in the seventeenth century. The Copernican revolution achieved by physics was only a beginning. When the second wave of science struck, it created more havoc than the first, for it suggested that change was essential to nature and that the sphere of scientific law applied not only to inanimate nature but to living things as well.

The beginnings of the second wave were discernible in the science of geology, when Sir Charles Lyell (1797–1875) and others first made plausible the notion that this apparently firm and substantial earth was itself in process of evolving and had a history. On the basis of such findings the notion of development became popular even before Darwin published his *Origin of Species* in 1859, but this event proved to be the battle date for the new concepts. An all-pervasive rule of change applicable to organisms—and even to man's own body—now became a scientific presumption. The fixed and rigid hierarchy of the world, dear to Aristotle and the medieval mind, was called into question in the most basic way possible.

The third wave of the scientific revolution came in the wake of biological theory, and resulted from it: the historical revolution. On the naturalistic assumption that the causes and motives for human events that operate in the present are uniform with those that applied in the past, scholars extended the scientific method to history as the biologists had extended it to living substances. David Hume, in a century still not very congenial to notions of change, had first undertaken a scientific history in his six-volume *History of England* (pub. 1754–1761). Edward Gibbon in his famous (or notorious, depending on your point of view) six-volume *History of the Decline and Fall of the Roman Empire* (pub. 1776–1788) gave purely naturalistic reasons for the spread and victory of Christianity in the ancient world. Hermann Reimarus (1694–1768), Gotthold Lessing (1729–1781), and Ferdinand Christian Baur (1792–1860) applied the canons of historical criticism to the life of Jesus. Baur's *Critical Investigations of the Canonical Gospels* (1847) reduced all the Gospel events to purely natural occurrences, and explained the miraculous elements away as misunderstandings or mythical additions. More of the medieval mind was chipped away by the sharp tool of science.

Another aspect of the historical revolution was the way in which it treated Christianity, not as a special revelation but simply as one specimen of a whole species of historical phenomena called "religions." The science of comparative religion was born.

The fourth wave of the scientific revolution grew out of scientific history and set men searching for invariant laws governing the structure of all societies and social change. The great name at this stage is Karl Marx (1818–1883), the father of "scientific socialism." The details of his theories do not concern us—the essential thing is that he proposed to describe the laws of social development in a scientific manner. History for him fell completely under the rubrics of scientific method. Later in the nineteenth century Herbert Spencer (1820–1903) in his massive sociological works labored by the same rules. By the end of the century, not only nature and life but also history and society had come under the purview of natural science. There remained only one region still within the province of theology—the human mind itself. The assault upon that province by psychology is the fifth wave of the scientific revolution.

The great names here are William James (1842–1910) and Sigmund Freud (1856–1939), especially the latter, since James remained too empirical to subscribe completely to the scientific dogmas.[13] In scientific psychology the human spirit itself is completely subject to natural laws, and with the discovery of depth psychology, even the most exalted "spiritual" motives can be marked down as mere subjective by-products of an individual's psychological past. Ivan Pavlov (1849–1936), the Russian physiologist, establishes the experimental branch of psychology with his celebrated study of salivating dogs.[14] Contemporary cybernetics, a science that studies the interrelationship of man and machine, has added impetus to these inquiries.

The narrative we have so briefly recounted, roughly three centuries in duration, is the progressive victory of reason and observation over every region of existence, reaching at last into the sacred inner citadel of man's own mind. This achievement constitutes the glory of the scientific revolution. And as we shall see, it constitutes a major element in the human predicament in the latter half of the twentieth century.

### Theoretical Developments: Philosophy

Philosophy developed apace with each advance of science. Descartes, as we have seen, clarified the assumptions of Galilean physics, and by the same token set down the major characteristic of the modern mind. We do not have space to consider his continental successors, Leibniz and Spinoza, who were mainly bemused by Descartes's hopes for a system of truth erected exclusively upon reason. The British empiricists are more to our purpose.

John Locke (1632–1704) wrote his *Essay Concerning Human Understanding* (1690) only three years after Newton's *Principia* had marked the rounding out of physical theory. Locke's concern, as the title of his essay indicates, was to provide a philosophical method that would clarify the ways in which man could understand the world. His method is an epitome of the modern mind: For each concept find the experience that corresponds to it. His celebrated successor George Berkeley (1685–1753) applied this method to the concept of matter. Matter, he said, must be meaningless unless and until perceived, because every idea which I can entertain is an idea in a mind. Matter, by definition, must exist outside of a mind and must be distinct from all ideas whatsoever. But such an entity is by definition also beyond all human experience—therefore it should be discarded as meaningless and without foundation.

Berkeley's thought was carried to its logical conclusion by David Hume (1711–1776).[15] True, he wrote, "matter" is not a meaningful concept because it lies outside of experience. But so, he added, does the concept of mind. Search as you will, you will not find a "mind" in your experience. All you will discover is a flow of experiences, bundles of sensations. With this conclusion, Berkeley's "mind" and his "God" (the eternal mind which he postulated as necessary for finite experiences) both went out the window. But matter, mind, and God were not the only concepts that Hume discovered were not empirically grounded. He turned his rapier mind on concepts dearer to the scientists: such concepts as "causality." Causality, he said, was completely beyond experience. All we can safely conclude from experience is that a certain order of events does persist; from this we can assume that our feeling of causal connection is the product of psychological association. Hume's true importance in our story can only be seen when we later consider the crisis of the modern mind.

The same can be said of Immanuel Kant (1724–1804), who, awakened from his dogmatic slumbers by Hume, produced a critical synthesis of the two streams of thought—rational and empirical. We must delay a review of his work until a more appropriate place. Suffice it here to say that already by the eighteenth century, well before the scientific revolution had come to completion, critical minds were raising serious doubts about its rational foundations. But these doubts have had little practical significance until the present day. For the most part, scientists and technologists have been comfortable in the confidence that science has at last given to men the key to the knowledge and mastery of existence.

## Practical Developments

*The Reformation.* It would be a mistake to believe that these developments in thought were taking place in a cultural vacuum; they fed upon and nourished social changes of great importance in the shaping of the modern consciousness.

The first change worth noting preceded the rise of modern philosophy and natural science by a century. It was the Protestant revolt from Rome. As the medieval world drew to its close its chief power—religion—became a source of deep dissatisfaction to many of its most devout adherents. Isolated reformers, such as John Huss and Savonarola, arose to protest the progressive deterioration of the Church, but they were successfully disposed of. Even efforts by highly placed churchmen failed to reform Rome. The spirit of worldliness was too much for the Italians, surrounded as they were by magnificent Renaissance monuments to the delights of the senses.

It was in Germany to the north, beyond the reach of the blandishments of Italian culture and as yet untouched by the softness brought about by wealth, that the reform—or, as it now became, the revolt—succeeded. Martin Luther supplied the basic religious rationale for questioning the edifice of medieval Christendom. This loosening was a salutary prelude to the release of other forces which would soon turn away from the charismatic power of the Roman See. It is of course wrong to assume that Luther and such fellow reformers as Calvin in France and Zwingli in Switzerland foresaw the ultimate effects of weakening the power of Rome. Nor could they foresee that some of their own favorite doctrines—such as the priesthood of all believers, individualism, and the appeal to personal experience—would later strengthen immeasurably the secular forces with which their successors would have to contend. But this is the way with history makers. We must postpone to another place an examination of the religious significance of the Reformation —its return to the Bible, its world missionary vision, and its creation of a third force in Christendom to match Eastern Orthodoxy and Rome—now we are concerned with its influence on the making of the modern mind.

*The Voyages of Discovery.* Everyone knows the date 1492. It marks the beginning of the end of European isolation. After Columbus' voyage Europe could never be the same.[16] The closed world of medievalism was already doomed.

*The Rise of National States.* The Holy Roman Empire was, as historians have said, neither holy nor Roman—but it represented an ideal, the medieval ideal of a unified society under the aegis of the Church. As a national consciousness arose in England and France this ideal was fatally challenged. In spite of the brief cosmopolitan interlude during the eighteenth-century Enlightenment, nationalism had become, by the end of the nineteenth century, the standard belief of the average citizen in the major European countries.

*The Rise of a Money Economy.* The medieval mind was formed in an agrarian environment in which exchange was largely in kind. With the gradual growth of a money economy—hastened, as scholars have claimed, by the new ethic of the Protestants[17]—many changes were inevitable. Money facilitated the growth of trade with the new world opened up by the voyages of discovery. This form of enterprise produced new sources of great wealth, which were naturally eyed with covetous delight by the leaders of the new national states. A new middle class, the bourgeoisie, emerged, later to become the dominant power in the world of the nineteenth century. It was men of this class who inspired the revolutions in America, France, and England, and who guided those countries to their pinnacles of wealth and power.

*The Industrial Revolution.* By the middle of the eighteenth century, science had reached a point of sufficient sophistication for its principles to become increasingly applicable to the solution of problems of economic significance. Machines harnessed power for the production of goods. The moneyed class naturally became the masters of this new industrial complex, for they alone possessed the capital necessary to finance it. The industrial revolution produced another class destined to play a significant role in the present age—the working class. This class was recruited from the agrarian workers who left the farms and became city dwellers, working with the tools owned by the middle class.

*Population Increase and the Rise of Urban Society.* With the increase of wealth and the progressive application of elementary sanitary precautions made available through science, the population of Europe tripled between 1800 and 1900. Increasing percentages of this larger population moved into the cities, until an entirely new face was put upon Western civilization—a new urbanized civilization. The effect of this and the growing technological money economy altered the former face-to-face society of medieval communities and required a complete revamping of man's conception of social relationships. Instead of organic communities living together on common ground which their ancestors had also inhabited, the new society was increasingly composed of individuals whose relationships with their fellows were in the nature of temporary quasi-legal contracts. This applied progressively to all the relationships of human existence: employer-employee, state-citizen, and, lately, even to marriage, which is no longer considered an indissoluble sacramental union.

*Changing Social Ideals.* With the rise of new classes, new modes of existence, and new modes of thought it was natural that the basic ideals of men should change. Class ideologies developed in both the middle and working classes. Bourgeois standards of life, based upon property and civilized comfort, became progressively widespread even among those who denounced the bourgeoisie. Working-class ideals, inclining in many places toward socialism, led to social legislation and the struggle for industrial democracy. Democracy as a social ideal went through many changes but retained a strong appeal for increasing numbers of the human race.

All these remarks are of course subject to many provisos, and the person who wants to understand modern civilization will not be content to accept them without such qualifications. However, this review should at least enable us to sense the general shape of the modern mind. It forms the setting in which we can understand the 300-year struggle of religious faith, accustomed as it had become to medieval ways of thought, to come to terms with modernity. This gradual taking account of modernity is the theme of our next chapter.

## SUGGESTIONS FOR FURTHER READING

For the concept of the "modern mind," its development, and its major characteristics, I would suggest Crane Brinton, *The Shaping of the Modern Mind* (New American Library, 1953), John Herman Randall, Jr., *Making of the Modern Mind*, rev. ed. (Houghton Mifflin, 1940); and P. A. Sorokin, *The Crisis of Our Age* (Dutton, 1945). For contrast, Henry Adams' *Mont-Saint-Michele and Chartres* (New American Library, 1961) gives a moving if somewhat idealized account of the mind of the late Middle Ages.

For the development of modern physics from the sixteenth century, see A. E. Burtt, *The Metaphysical Foundations of Modern Science* (Anchor, Doubleday, 1954), Alexandre Koyré, *From the Closed World to the Infinite Universe* (Harper Torchbooks, Harper & Row, 1958), and Alfred North Whitehead's celebrated *Science and the Modern World* (New American Library, 1948). For the effect of geology on modern thought, see C. C. Gillispie, *Genesis and Geology* (Harvard University Press, 1951). For the shock of the new biology see John C. Greene, *Darwin and the Modern World View* (New American Library, 1963), and Loren Eiseley, *Evolution and the Men Who Discovered It* (Anchor, Doubleday, 1958).

Any good history of modern philosophy from Descartes on will show the way in which philosophers interacted with the new forces of modernity.

## NOTES

1. See his *Meditations* (1951) and *Discourse on Method* (1965), both published with good Introductions by Liberal Arts, Bobbs-Merrill.

2. In the *Discourse on Method*.

3. The conclusion of his *Meditations*.
4. From his *Discourse on Method*.
5. In his *Dialogue Concerning the Two Great Systems of the World* (1632). .
6. For this approach to Galileo's influence, see Giorgio de Santillana, *The Crime of Galileo* (University of Chicago Press, 1955).
7. For a classic account of the medieval mind, see Henry Adams, *Mont-Saint-Michele and Chartres* (New American Library, 1961).
8. In his great work *The City of God* (*De Civitate Dai*, begun A.D. 413).
9. Selected from the Nicene Creed, *Book of Common Prayer*.
10. For a good account of the rise of modern science, see E. A. Burtt, *The Metaphysical Foundations of Modern Science* (Anchor, Doubleday, 1954).
11. See Santillana, *op. cit.*
12. Alan Richardson, *The Bible in the Age of Science* (Westminster), p. 41.

13. This is John Wild's interpretation of James in *Existence and the World of Freedom* (Prentice-Hall, 1963).
14. For Pavlov's role in psychology, see any history of psychology.
15. In *Enquiry into the Human Understanding* (1959), and *Enquiry Concerning the Principles of Morals* (1957), both published with good Introductions by Liberal Arts, Bobbs-Merrill.
16. Arnold Toynbee makes the point that this was the moment when the modern world began to emerge.
17. The classic work on this theme is Max Weber, *The Protestant Ethic and the Spirit of Capitalism*, Talcott Parsons, trans. (Scribner, 1930). A more recent treatment is R. H. Tawney, *Religion and the Rise of Capitalism* (Harcourt, Brace & World, 1926).

# 12

# Religion Takes
# Account of Modernity

❖❖❖❖❖❖❖❖❖❖❖❖❖❖❖❖❖❖❖❖❖❖❖❖❖❖❖❖❖❖❖

Religious faith could not ignore the new climate of thought which we have called the modern mind. In an overly simple formula, we may say that religious thinkers either rejected the new spirit or accommodated to it. This chapter is chiefly concerned with the latter tendency. We cannot discuss this topic without becoming involved again with the progressive waves of scientific advance and the social revolution that accompanied it. However, this chapter is not a history of the relationship of science and religion nor a proposal of the proper relationship between the two. The latter project we shall undertake at another time. Here, I am concerned with the changes that Christianity—chiefly Protestantism—was willing to suffer in its sacred tradition in order to remain current with the age. Before we examine this question, consider briefly the spirit of those who refused to take the advance of science seriously into account.

## THE REFUSAL TO ACCOMMODATE TO SCIENCE

Official Roman Catholicism and the Fundamentalist sects of Protestantism declined to participate in any basic accommodation to the new science. Fundamentalism is a late-nineteenth-century word, but its spirit—the spirit of biblical literalism—was present much earlier, especially in those sects that owed their inspiration to the famous work of John Calvin (1509–1564), *Institutes of the Christian Religion* (1536). Sticking by the total adequacy and inerrancy of the Scriptures for all basic knowledge, the fundamentalist mind rejected modernity—except, of course, in those practical areas where science was remaking the daily life of men.

Roman Catholic thought did, to be sure, divest itself of such indefensible features of the medieval world-picture as the earth-centered universe, surrounded by its concentric crystalline heavens; but even in its later-day efforts to integrate the findings of modern science into its philosophy it turned quite naturally to the Aristotelianism of Thomas Aquinas, who had produced in his two Summae the greatest intellectual synthesis of Catholic culture. One of the basic premises of his philosophical system (known now as Thomism) is that the truth of reason and the senses cannot conflict with the truth of Christian revelation, because God is the author of all truth and cannot contradict himself. Science that contradicts any doctrine of the Church becomes thereby pseudo science and has evidently made a mistake within its own sphere.

Catholic thinkers confess that church officials often acted hastily in the rejection of scientific discoveries, only to retract later. Galileo was forced to recant his Copernican views, and his predecessor Giordano Bruno was burned at the stake (1600). But Catholic thinkers were not long in accepting the Copernican revolution in astronomy as compatible with basic Christian doctrine.

Unlike Protestant Fundamentalists, who were compelled in principle to abide by the literal text of the Bible, Catholic thinkers, with their authority lodged in the Church, were able to adapt many scriptural statements to scientific facts by using flexible allegorical and metaphorical interpretations of many seemingly contradictory passages in the Bible. Protestants had rejected the Church's right of interpretation in the belief that plain and simple Scripture was adequate authority for every man. They could not easily introduce complex interpretations without contradicting their own assumptions, and were therefore often compelled to reject scientific theories that could not be squared with the letter of the text.

Leo XIII in his encyclical *Profidentissimus Deus* (1893) warned against the spirit of modernism, veering in some of his language close to a literalist interpretation of Scripture. However, he was in many ways a "modern" pope, aware of the currents of social and intellectual change. Under his auspices Désiré Joseph Cardinal Mercier (1851–1926), disciple of Thomas Aquinas, founded the *Institut Supérieur de Philosophie* at the University of Louvain. At the same time, Leo declared Thomism to be the official philosophy of the Roman Catholic Church. Since that time Roman Catholic thinkers have engaged in a massive attempt to integrate all scientific thought into Thomist categories. The impressive intellectual quality of this effort can be appreciated by a study of the great modern Thomist, Jacques Maritain, especially three of his works: *Integral Humanism* (a Catholic interpretation of society), *The Degrees of Knowledge*, and *The Range of Reason*.

No such synthesis has been forthcoming from Fundamentalist quarters, though at present a transformation is taking place in their thinking. The very word fundamentalist has been set aside in preference for the term conservative, and their leading thinkers are prepared at last to use nonliteral interpretations for such difficult passages as the creation story in Genesis. We have yet to see the fruits of this line of investigation.

In 1951, Pius XII issued his encyclical *Humani Generis* which showed a considerable liberalization of the Roman Catholic spirit. He announced that the Church does not forbid that "in conformity with the present state of science and theology, the doctrine of evolution should be examined by experts in both fields, insofar as it deals with research on the origin of the human body. . . ."[1] The document also recommends a spirit of tentative accommodation to science while requiring the inevitable "condition that they [all investigators] are ready to submit to the judgment of the Church, to which Christ has entrusted the office of interpreting authentically the Holy Scriptures and defending the dogmas of the faith."[2]

It is easy to be unsympathetic to the resistance that literalist Protestants and Roman Catholics showed toward the modern mind. We should not forget that there were great scientists in both camps. High Roman Catholic churchmen were among Galileo's staunchest defenders. Kepler was a devout Protestant, and even the incomparable Newton spent his last days number-hunting in the Book of the Revelation. Pascal, Pasteur, and Mendel were faithful sons of the Church. But we can appreciate this resistance better if we consider what they were defending rather than what they were rejecting.

They were holding fast to a truth which they believed was far more important than any knowledge that could be derived from a study of nature. As Cardinal Newman said, "Nature may reveal the glory of God, but there is no reason to suppose that it reveals his will." Only God's self-revelation could achieve that—and it is by far the more important truth. The literalists intuitively felt that accommodation to the spirit of the new age would obscure and eventually obliterate man's knowledge of the saving truth of God's will for man. Even the total rejection of science, they thought, would be preferable to that. And the present age is better able to appreciate the threat than those who lived in the heyday of social progress grounded in scientific knowledge.

But the question may be asked whether the posture of resistance did not obscure these truths even more than a reasonable accommodation to the inevitable triumph of science—at least in its own sphere. In the main, through perhaps the largest part of modern history, those who resisted presented an inglorious image of a retreating army defending an obscurantism that was doomed to defeat. It is a moot question, however, whether the road of accommodation is really any safer—but here we anticipate our story.

## ACCOMMODATION TO SCIENCE, CHIEFLY PROTESTANT

Protestant thinkers who were prepared to make increasing concessions to the modern spirit tested it and found it good. They believed that many things that had been identified with the Judaeo-Christian faith were accidental accretions that had gathered around the faith in its passage through many centuries of culture. They found in the modern spirit many values reminding them of basic values in their own faith that tradition had obscured.

Some of these values can be quickly set down: the wholeness, or integrity, of truth and of all minds seeking truth; a method of investigation that led to agreement of informed minds, in striking contrast to the poisonous disputes that had characterized the traditional debates over faith; the value of freedom in investigation and the integrity of conscience; a knowledge and appreciation of the created world that no previous Christian age had possessed; a growing proof, no longer needing to be accepted upon faith, that the universe was indeed a harmonious cosmos; and the addition of a new dimension to the dignity of man, who had been created to rule the world and who, thanks to science, now possessed unprecedented knowledge and power over it.

These men saw in their colleagues who rejected the modern mind a dangerous retreating into the worship of archaic and outmoded thought and institutions, and an increasing irrelevance to the new life around them. At first timidly, and then with glowing confidence, they themselves embraced the new knowledge in the belief that it would result in a reformed and enlightened religion, faithful in every important respect to the intentions of its Founder. The fact is that in their enthusiasm—coupled with a frequent failure to grasp the historical and theological issues—they often compromised beyond the point of no return, and all but indistinguishably merged the faith with the current culture. But their achievement was nonetheless glorious. It is also plain that had they not exposed religion to the attrition of new thought as it passed through the modern era, granting all the mistakes, religion would not now be equipped to emerge in our age with a new and more authentically Christian voice. But again I anticipate.

## ACCOMMODATION TO THE PHYSICAL SCIENCES

After the first shock of looking at the world through Galileo's telescope, many religious thinkers had second thoughts. The new world of mathematically perfect order had a sublimity that the Ptolemaic Aristotelianism could not match. It only remained to conceive this new world as the work of a benign First Cause to accommodate it in all essentials to religious faith. In this, they had aid and comfort from the scientists themselves. "Whence is it that Nature doth nothing in vain," wrote Newton, "and whence arises all that Order and Beauty which we see in the world? . . . Does it not appear from Phaenomena that there is a Being incorporeal, living, intelligent, omnipresent, who in infinite Space, as it were in his Sensory, sees the things themselves intimately, and thoroughly perceives them, and comprehends them wholly by their immediate presence to himself?"[3] The great physicist and chemist Robert Boyle (1627–1691) found that the scientific contemplation of nature lifted his mind continually toward God. Erasmus Darwin asked:

> Dull atheist, could a giddy dance
> Of atoms lawlessly hurl'd
> Construct so wonderful, so wise,
> So harmonized a world?[4]

Gillispie writes that in this pre-Darwinian period "most scientists mounted the lecture platform without the slightest reluctance. Seldom did a British Association [for the Advancement of Science] meeting go by without Buckland or Sedgwick or Murchison addressing a public gathering, usually an outdoor one, on the megatherium or the iguanodon or the origin of British coal deposits, and seldom did a lecture go by without the moral beneficent Providence being pointed out."[5] Lyceums were provided for this kind of activity.

The theological basis was provided in such works as Archdeacon Paley's standard textbook *View of the Evidences of Christianity*. The watchword was Design, providential Order. Darwin himself describes how, when an undergraduate at Cambridge, not questioning Paley's premises and taking these on trust, he was "charmed and convinced by the long line of argumentation."[6]

To be sure, there had been some trouble over the Noachic flood and the Mosaic dates of the age of the earth when the geologists began to reckon the processes by which the contours of the earthly terrain had been formed. But the loss of these sureties was a small price to pay for the exhilarating picture of universal order, all designed for good.

## Accommodation to the Biological Sciences

Darwinian biology disturbed the picture of a static world of perfect order and for a time introduced some dismay into the ranks of those who believed that they had achieved a synthesis of biblical and scientific truth. With scientists themselves divided over Darwin's evolutionary thesis, one wing of the Church engaged the new science in debate. The most celebrated episode occurred at the very outset. The eloquent Bishop Wilberforce challenged Thomas Henry Huxley, Darwin's protagonist, to a debate before the British Association for the Advancement of Science. The result was a rout of the anti-Darwin forces.

Other religious thinkers took a different view. In 1860, F. J. A. Hort wrote to his famous colleague in biblical studies, Bishop B. F. Westcott: "Have you read Darwin? . . . In spite of difficulties, I am inclined to think it is unanswerable."[7] One of the theological contributors to the famous volume *Lux Mundi* (1889) wrote: ". . . Darwinism appeared under the guise of a foe and did the work of a friend. . . . Either God is everywhere present in nature, or he is nowhere. . . . It seems as if in the providence of God the mission of modern science was to bring home . . . the great truth of the divine immanence in creation, which is not less essential to the Christian idea of God than to a philosophical view of nature."[8]

Darwin himself, at least at the time of writing his great book, thought that his work was consistent with religion. In the final chapter of his *Origin of Species,* he wrote: "I see no good reason why the views given in this volume should shock the religious feelings of anyone. . . . A celebrated author and divine has written to me that 'he has gradually learned to see that it is just as noble a conception of the Deity to believe that He created a few original forms capable of self-development in other and needful forms, as to believe that He required a fresh act of creation to supply the voids caused by the action of His laws.' "[9] And in his concluding sentence Darwin wrote: "There is a grandeur in this view of life, with its several powers, having been originally breathed by the Creator into a few forms or into one; and . . . from so simple a beginning endless forms most beautiful and wonderful have been, and are being evolved."[10]

But there was a snag. Several of Darwin's conceptions were not easy to fit into the picture of a beneficent Providence. His four fundamental ideas were (1) the struggle for survival, (2) the survival of the most adaptable forms, (3) the constancy of heredity, and (4) variation. Two things created difficulty: First, the theory provided a natural account of the progressive adaptation of organisms to their environment. Such detailed adaptation had been a favorite argument for the providence and wisdom of God. The second was the violence and wastage of the natural process. Newton's view of nature doing "nothing in vain," seemed no longer to hold. God, the perfect draftsman, appeared to have bungled.

Despite these difficulties, which are yet to be adequately integrated into Christian conceptions, theologians accepted the basic premise of evolution. Shailer Matthews, Dean of the Divinity School of the University of Chicago, only a year after the infamous Scopes trial, set the tone of the new views in his *Contributions of Science to Religion* (1924). His thesis was that religion can best be understood as a set of attitudes and activities whereby life adjusts itself to the environment. The question of which religion is best can be decided by asking which best fits man for survival. The contest between them can be understood as "the struggle between religions for the survival of the fittest."[11] "That religion," he wrote, "which best enables the religious impulse to express itself in its increasingly complex environment will survive all others."[12] In the light of these conceptions, Matthews subjected the organized inheritance of dogma, rituals, and organization to "investigation and inevitable revaluation."[13]

In *Darwin and the Modern World View* John Greene summarizes Matthew's conclusions: "The *Bible* was reduced to the status of an important historical document attesting to the upward progress of the religious impulse. . . . Science, not Scripture, justified a religious view of nature for science alone revealed nature's aim toward the development of personality. . . . *Sin* was a stubborn clinging to outmoded values, a refusal to leave one's animal past and move onward and upward toward higher personal values in accordance with the immanent law of progress. *Salvation* meant adjusting oneself to this immanent purpose, 'with consequent progress and happiness.' "[14]

Lyman Abbott, in his *Theology of an Evolutionist,* had anticipated many of these same views a quarter of a century earlier, viewing the Bible as "a collection of literature, containing in a preeminent measure the growth of the consciousness of God in the human soul, interpreted by the preeminent religious leaders of a preeminently religious people."[15] In this light, the moral and theological crudities of the Bible simply represent early phases of a gradual religious evolution.

## ACCOMMODATION TO THE MODERN THEORY OF KNOWLEDGE

Theology could not be content to accommodate to the findings of the sciences; it had to take account of the method as well. Could faith adapt itself to a knowledge derivable from reason and experience alone? This was the problem. The vastly increased knowledge of nature derived from scientific modes of investigation suggested the tempting possibility that religion might also profit from the same method. Galileo had said: ". . . wisdom should be sought in the whole book of God which is the world, where more wisdom always may be discovered. It is to this book and not to the little books of men that Scripture sends us."[16]

*Deism.* The first stage in accommodation to the limits placed upon knowledge by science was deism. Deism was the doctrine that God had created a world order so perfect that it could fulfill his purposes without any further interference from him. Nature would testify so eloquently to his existence and goodness that no further revelation would be necessary or could exceed it in clarity. Miracles would constitute an admission that nature had need of tinkering and would detract from the image of divine wisdom. It was this view that John Locke expressed in his work on *The Reasonableness of Christianity* (1695). John Toland (1670–1722), in a supposed rebuttal to Locke, wrote a work entitled *Christianity Not Mysterious* (1696) that simply restated the same premises. Another exponent of deism, Edward Herbert of Cherbury (1583–1648), enumerated articles of belief alleged to constitute the natural religion held by all mankind in primitive and unspoiled simplicity: God exists; He is to be worshipped; virtue is his true service; man must repent of wrongdoing; and there are rewards and punishments after death. Herbert believed that these tenets were evident to all reasonable men without any supernatural help.

In the age of deism the great crime was religious *enthusiasm. En* means "in", *thu* is from the root of *theos*, meaning "god"; hence, etymologically, "enthusiasm" means "God in." To the deistic mind, God was definitely "out"; that is, of his creation, and all claims to direct contact with him or of events purporting to be his direct act were anathema. It was John Wesley's (1703–1791) claim of a direct experimental knowledge of God through faith in Christ, the basis of the evangelical revival, that made him *persona non grata* in the churches of his day. Clergymen and educated laity alike looked with horror on the "wild" revival meetings in which conversions took place amidst ecstatic commotions of all sorts. What could be more unseemly in a world so pristinely ordered as the deists believed?

*Immanuel Kant.* The second stage of theological accommodation to the modern theory of knowledge came with the critical work of Immanuel Kant, who was heir to both the skepticism of Humean empiricism and the rationalism of Descartes and his Continental successors. The empiricists had begun with the confidence of Francis Bacon (1561–1626) in experience as the guide to knowledge. Bacon felt that he had initiated a new age of man with the "new instrument" (*Novum Organum*) of empirical research. But a mere century later Hume had reduced this tradition to utter skepticism.

Descartes had expressed the same confidence in unaided reason that the empiricists placed in experience. As we have seen, he had hoped to build an entire system of truth upon undoubted rational principles. By Kant's time, despite the eminence of such thinkers as Leibniz and Spinoza, this tradition also was in tatters.

It is the glory of Kant's achievement to have synthesized these two streams of thought in his critical philosophy—especially in his major work *The Critique of Pure Reason* (1781; rev. 1787). Kant accepts Hume's conclusion that many of our most significant concepts, such as "self," "matter," "world," "causality," cannot be derived from sense experience. Moreover, he was also convinced that reason alone, as the rationalists had hoped, could not provide a ground for belief in them either.

Pondering these questions, Kant concluded that we are not able to know through natural means alone what reality in itself is. Our knowledge is limited to possible human experience. However, he observed, experience itself was bound to take certain fixed forms. Objects, for example, are inconceivable except under the form of space and time. We can therefore safely predict that we will never experience an object except under these conditions. Materialists had thought that such conditions were provided by nature, but Berkeley and Hume had exploded their arguments. The order of nature therefore must be provided by the mind itself as a condition of all possible experience of natural objects. *The Critique of Pure Reason*, as the synthesis of the rational and empirical streams of thought, sets the stage for almost every question that assails the modern philosopher who would give a defensible account of human knowledge.

Kant's first *Critique* deals primarily with sensory knowledge. He wrote two others, one on moral knowledge and another on aesthetic judgment.[17] In his account of moral knowledge he seems to transgress the limits he laid down in the first *Critique*, and to claim a knowledge of God, freedom, and immortality beyond the limits of experience. But he qualifies this by insisting that these concepts are not knowledge—proper. They, and other concepts like them (the "self," for example), are ideals or presuppositions of reason, not a knowledge of things in themselves. Kant thus leaves us, E. A. Burtt says, with "reality as unpatterned, inaccessible and mysterious to us," in contradiction to the confident assumption of the founders of modern thought that nature is patterned and accessible to unaided human reason. And by the same conclusion he leaves the deistic world view without foundation. This seems to have been the net result of ruthlessly applying the rigorous simplicity of Occam's Razor* to cut away all knowledge claims that cannot stand up to sense or reason.

But what is to become of religion when all metaphysics, whether theological or philosophical, is thrust beyond the pale of certifiable knowledge? Kant's theological successors attempted to answer.

*Challengers of Kant.*   Kant himself had written a rather weak postscript to his own critical work in *Religion Within the Limits of Reason Alone*, but despite its many profound observations it succeeds only in keeping religion within the bounds of Kantian ethics—a pale and ineffectual counterpart of the rich pietistic faith in which Kant himself had been reared. Friedrich Schleiermacher (1768–1834) took up the challenge of establishing faith on a new basis. Using Kant's work as a beginning, he claimed that religion was a matter of experience, not speculation.[18] God, he said, never had been a metaphysical question, but an experiential one. Religion is the experience of absolute dependence, and this experience has the same claims to validity as any other. If to have orderly sense experience we must presuppose what is beyond experience—namely, space and time—then, by the same token, if we are to have religious experience we may presuppose what is necessary to it—namely, God.

Albrecht Ritschl (1822–1889),[19] the German Protestant theologian, accepted Schleiermacher's view that religion was not properly understood as abstract speculative knowledge, and rejected metaphysics as an aid to Christian truth. But he felt that Schleiermacher's account of religion was too individualistic and narrow. The essential thing in religion, he said, was the preservation of the highest values—and these, he added, were to be found in the practical revelation of Jesus Christ, and in the community which he founded.

Considering the hampering restrictions which these men accepted as conditions for their thought, they made notable contributions to our understanding of religion. However, the net result was to reduce religion to human

---

* William of Occam (1300–1349) proposed that in rational explanations theoretical entities should not be multiplied beyond necessity. This principle, known as Occam's Razor, set the stage for Francis Bacon's philosophy.

consciousness: "feelings of absolute dependence" or "loyalty to the highest ideals." "From being an absolute principle of religious knowledge," Burtt writes, "God becomes for theological method a factor in man's religious consciousness."[20]

The road of accommodation seems to have led to a complete subjectivism, with all the old realities of religious faith spirited away. The question we shall ask later is whether the experience of religion, including its ethical earnestness, can be retained on such a basis. But before we can turn to that problem we must briefly note how religion accommodated to the social and practical changes of modernity.

## Accommodation of Social and Practical Changes

*The New Economy.* Protestant churchmen at first shared the medieval view of the rising money economy and sharply criticized it for its worldliness. However, the left hand did not know what the right hand was doing, for the over-all effect of Protestant doctrine and practice was to give the new capitalism its greatest support. This was accomplished in several ways: First, by opposing monastic asceticism—since salvation was now a free gift of God's grace—men were urged to find their vocation in the world, where God would prosper them if he were well pleased. Second, by releasing secular institutions from the control of an overarching Church authority, business was given the freedom to pursue profits without hindrance. As a consequence of this support, a great number of Protestants rose into the new middle class, and theologians were not long in finding ample justification for the mounting prosperity and power of this group.

*Nationalism.* Due to an accident of history, Protestantism was especially beholden to local political authority. In its early stages, when the Roman Church was exerting all its power to bring the "heretics" to heel they found protection in the bosom of secular governments, who were only too glad to have a religious reason for breaking their own allegiances to Rome. Another factor also favored Protestant support for the rising nationalism. Lacking a central supranational authority, Protestant churches were bound to be more local in character and to identify with the societies in which they throve. The seventeenth-century wars of religion had concluded with an agreement that each community would follow the religion of its prince, and when princes were no longer the fashion, the long established practice of politico-religious identification continued.

This identification with local culture was not limited to Protestants. Irish and Spanish nationalists were as passionately attached to their homeland as their counterparts in any Protestant country.

*Democracy.* Democracy has both religious and secular roots. For this reason it is impossible to distinguish to what extent the bias of religious thought toward democracy was due to accommodation to modernism and to what degree it was a natural outgrowth of basic Protestant convictions about man and society. But two things seem reasonably clear: First, it was the most liberal branches of religious thought—those most inclined to accommodation—that made the most of democracy as a social ideal. Second, the marks of modernity were very clear in those theological defenses of democracy that were most popular. Two of these beliefs are worth brief notation: (1) The inherent goodness of man, his basic desire for a harmonious personality well integrated with the personalities of his fellows. The evil in man, which had been a favorite argument for nondemocratic forms of government, was marked down to a pathetic clinging to an outmoded past that progress would soon bring to an end. (2) Progress is inherent in nature and history. The evils in society are largely due to cultural lag. As progress continues, these lags will be overcome and man will go on to increasing prosperity, peace, and universal brotherhood.

Both these assumptions are in marked contrast to classical Christian accounts of man and nature. They must be set down as signs of accommodation to the modern mind.


## CONCLUSION

In the last two chapters we have traced the rise of the modern mind and the religious accommodation to it. At this stage in our story, religious faith was poised in an unstable state between its classical origins and a form of belief that seriously challenged it. Faith was increasingly becoming a matter of experience alone, with no possible referent beyond human ideals. Voicing this concept of religious faith, Sir Julian Huxley, one of the lecturers at the University of Chicago's Darwin Centennial in 1960 had this to say: "The emergent religion of the near future . . . will believe in *knowledge*. . . . It should be able, with our increased knowledge of mind, to define our sense of right and wrong more clearly so as to provide a better moral support; it should be able to *focus the feeling of sacredness onto fitter objects, instead of worshipping supernatural rules,* so as to provide truer spiritual support, to *sanctify the higher manifestations of human nature* in art and love, in intellectual comprehension and aspiring adoration, and to emphasize the fuller realization of life's possibilities as a sacred trust."[21] (Author's italics.)

Professor E. A. Burtt contends that the whole logic of liberal Protestantism really tended toward humanism, and that it cannot rest until it has come to that conclusion. "Religion," he says, "is man's eager unshackled quest for whatever goodness and fineness life makes possible."[22] Instead of looking to some transhuman power and goodness, we should realize, says Burtt, that "the term 'God' [has] always meant to religious people essentially that power in the world to which we gain right adjustment when achieving the greatest goods of which human nature is capable."[23] "May we not," he asks, "thus define God by applying the idea of evolutionary adaption to our analysis of religious experience?"[24]

We should recognize, Burtt insists, that the universe is an impersonal order "taking no account of ends that are desirable from the human standpoint."[25] To be sure, on this ground prayer is "no longer relevant."[26] Why, then, call it religion? "Because," writes Burtt, "it meets the same needs that religion at its best always met; even though it meets them by uniting men in devotion to dependable supports of human joy here on earth rather than turning their eyes to a supposed transcendent providence."[27]

Such is the prospect for the Judaeo-Christian faith when it loses touch with its ancient sources and accommmodates in all respects to the spirit of modernity.

But at this juncture in history we may ask whether enthusiastic humanism is not itself a transitional form of faith without substantial ground. Many elements in contemporary life suggest that once the ontological root of faith is cut there is no stopping until the entire tree of human idealism has withered into an ugly specter, and man is delivered over to the abyss of nihilism.

This is the theme of our next two chapters.


## SUGGESTIONS FOR FURTHER READING

The best books for this chapter are the works of Greene, Burtt, and Gillispie, suggested in the previous chapter. Another book of Burtt's is important, however, since it gives a detailed account of this same movement of thought, though from a different perspective: *Types of Religious Philosophy* (rev. ed.; Harper & Row, 1951). One other good account of the process of religious accommodation from a more orthodox Protestant point of view is John Dillenberger and Claude Welch, *Protestant Christianity* (Scribner, 1958). Kenneth Cauthen's, *The Impact of American Liberalism* (Harper & Row, 1962) covers some of the same ground from the perspective of contemporary postliberal theology.


## NOTES

1. John C. Greene, *Darwin and the Modern World View* (New American Library, 1963), p. 24.
2. *Ibid.*
3. E. A. Burtt, *Metaphysical Foundations of Modern Science* (Anchor, Doubleday, 1954), p. 287.
4. C. C. Gillispie, *Genesis and Geology* (Harvard University Press, 1951), p. 33.
5. *Ibid.*, pp. 198–199.
6. *Ibid.*, p. 219.
7. H. G. Wood, *Belief and Unbelief* (Cambridge University Press, 1955), p. 50.
8. Quoted in John Dillenberger and Claude Welch, *Protestant Christianity* (Scribner, 1958), p. 206.
9. Quoted in J. Calvin Keene and others, *The Western Heritage of*

*Faith and Reason* (Harper & Row, 1963), p. 611.

10. *Ibid.*, pp. 611–612.
11. Quoted in Greene, *op. cit.*, p. 47.
12. Quoted in *ibid.*
13. Quoted in *ibid.*, p. 48.
14. *Ibid.*, p. 49. Author's italics.
15. Quoted in *ibid.*, p. 30.
16. Quoted in John Dillenberger, *Protestant Thought and Natural Science* (Doubleday, 1960), p. 90.
17. Burtt treats Kant's whole philosophy of religion in *Types of Religious Philosophy* (rev. ed.; Harper & Row, 1951), pp. 238–276.
18. For a brief account of Schleiermacher's thought, see Dillenberger

and Welch, *op. cit.*, pp. 182–187, 198 ff.
19. For a brief account of Ritschl's thought, see *ibid.*, pp. 198–200.
20. Burtt, *Types*, pp. 291–292.
21. Quoted in Sol Tax and Charles Gallender, eds., *Evolution After Darwin* (University of Chicago Press, 1960), III, 260.
22. Burtt, *Types*, p. 334.
23. *Ibid.*, p. 330.
24. *Ibid.*
25. *Ibid.*, p. 339.
26. *Ibid.*, p. 343.
27. *Ibid.*, p. 345.

# 13

# Contemporary Literature:
# Mirror of Man in Crisis

❖❖❖❖❖❖❖❖❖❖❖❖❖❖❖❖❖❖❖❖❖❖❖❖❖

Our time is the late evening of the modern mind. Beset with contradictions and ambiguities, it gives to the most sensitive spirits of the age an impression of a culture whose basic assumptions have lost their productivity, a vein of the human spirit that has been played out—all this despite the fierce activism of modern society. Before we consider the possibility of new premises, of starting over again with fresh materials, we must examine these claims. In this chapter we will do so by holding up the mirror of contemporary literature to modern man. In the next, we will consider the case more prosaically and describe what might be called the postmodern stance of faith.

The reason for turning to art and literature at this point is to show how pervasive is the human quest for meaning. It is a quest that is not limited to the professionally religious—it is felt deeply by all segments of society. And the work of the writer and artist is more often than not a magic mirror in which the current image of man may be viewed.

## LITERATURE AND ART AS THE
## MIRROR OF AN AGE

An image of each of the cultural epochs discussed in the last two chapters can be seen mirrored in three famous paintings: the thirteenth-century Franciscan frescoes by Giotto in the Church of St. Francis at Assisi; Michelangelo's fourteenth-century "Creation of Adam" in the Sistine Chapel, and Seurat's "Sunday Afternoon on the Island of La Grand Jatte," painted in the late nineteenth century and now in Chicago's Art Institute.

Giotto lovingly portrays the life of the holiest of the medieval saints—St. Francis of Assisi. Michelangelo's Adam is the idealized man of the Renaissance separated from God by only the merest gap across which crackles the creative divine energy animating his prodigious spirit. "Sunday Afternoon on the Island of La Grand Jatte" displays the prosperous middle class enjoying the sun along the Seine. Even the technique of these paintings is revealing. Consider only the last. Georges Seurat painted with tiny dots of color that the eye composes into figures. This style parallels in a precise way the bundles of sensations into which David Hume's philosophy had resolved the solid world of objects and persons. Despite the atomistic separateness of the colors, the figures are not fragmented. They hang together, so to speak, by habit. But consider now a fourth painting.

During the tragic Spanish Civil War of the late 1930s Picasso painted his masterpiece "Guernica." It unfolds the agony of men and societies in the despair of dissolution symbolized by the dive-bombing of a helpless Spanish village. Picasso's tortured human figures are symbols of the postmodern world. The sensate bundles of Seurat's world, lacking any organic connection, are coming tragically apart.

In his philosophy of art Jacques Maritain has said that "Beauty is the radiance of all transcendentals united."[1] This remark is highly inappropriate to modern art and literature, which so often strike us as not only lacking in beauty but as being positively ugly. What sense can we make of it?

Maritain holds that great art is both truth and beauty—that it plumbs the depth of being and lets the supernatural radiance shine through the forms. But modernity has lost the sense of depth in being and the corresponding faith that there is any radiance to shine forth. The great ideal of modern art is not beauty but truth—truth in the sense of a faithful expression of life as the artist perceives it. Since life in this century is not grounded in depth, since it is tortured by alienations of all kinds, the artist can but faithfully convey the chaos of man in this condition. "This world is dense, opaque, and unintelligible," writes William Barrett, "that is the datum from which the modern artist always starts."[2] Albert Camus explains: "Every writer tries to give form to the passions of his time. Today, just as yesterday, art wants to save from death a living image of our passions and our sufferings."[3]

Sufferings! That is the key. Not radiance! The artist is not to blame—he is fulfilling his vocation as the mirror of his time, and, as Goethe said, "If a monkey looks in, no apostle will be found looking out."[4]

To be sure, there is some radiant art in our day, but, as Barrett rightly explains, it is not authentically "our art."[5] The mystical figures of Dali's "Sacrament of the Last Supper" are a nostalgic recollection of an age when the radiance of the eternal shone on man as naturally as the light of the sun. The fact that it was painted in our time is in some sense an anachronism. It may be "true" art, but its truth is hard for men to see who have passed through the attrition of the modern era into contemporary times, and have witnessed the destruction of all received and traditional values and forms. Modern art, as we have said, is focused on truth; beauty must wait for some deeper unity and meaning than our present truth can perceive. For us, depth reveals horror, as in the Cardinals by contemporary painter Francis Bacon. As Camus says, ". . . the essential passion of man [is] torn between his urge toward unity and the clear vision he may have of the walls inclosing him."[6] Most men rebel against this vision, but this, writes Camus, is because "man is concerned with hope . . . that is not his business; his business is to turn away from subterfuge."[7]

### The World Reflected in the Art of Albert Camus

The late Albert Camus was one of the greatest contemporary writers. He was acknowledged in his lifetime as a spokesman for the contemporary mind. With supreme sensitivity his writings reveal the world we live in. Let us begin with the central problem that he poses. Toward the end of Camus' novel *The Plague* (*La Peste*, 1947), Tarrou, who has been fighting the bubonic plague in Oran shoulder to shoulder with the physician Rieux, speaks to his friend in one of those rare moments of self-revelation: " 'It comes to this,' Tarrou said almost casually; 'what interests me is learning how to become a saint.' " Dr. Rieux replies in stunned surprise, " 'But you don't believe in God.' " " 'Exactly!' " says Tarrou. " 'Can one be a saint without God?—that's the problem, in fact the only problem I'm up against today.' "

After a short distraction Rieux says to his friend: " 'Heroism and sanctity don't really appeal to me, I imagine. What interests me is being a man.' " And to this Tarrou replies, " 'Yes, we're both after the same thing, but I'm less ambitious.' "[8]

Camus knows that Tarrou could have replied to Rieux's ambition to become a man with the same words: "But you don't believe in God." This is the central problem: How can one become a man in a world without God? It is the theme of his powerful philosophical essay, *The Myth of Sisyphus* (*Le Myth de Sisyphe*, 1942). He begins with these words: "There is but one truly serious philosophical problem, and that is suicide. Judging whether life is or is not worth living. . . ."[9] He confesses his natural human "appetite for the absolute and for unity and the impossibility of reducing this world to a rational and reasonable principle. . . ." He also "knows that I cannot reconcile them."[10] "This ridiculous reason," he says, "is what sets me in opposition to all creation."[11]

The absurd world, he believes, is lucidly expressed in the myth of Sisyphus, whom the gods condemned to roll a huge stone to the top of a hill only to have it roll down again. Again he bends to his task, but the fates force him to repeat endlessly his futile and hopeless labor. Can man surmount so crushing a fate? Camus replies, "One must imagine Sisyphus happy."[12] Why? Because there is "no fate that cannot be surmounted by scorn."[13]

But he knows that this is mere hypothesis. To test the idea, I will follow his example by examining these same themes in the novels of Dostoevsky.

## The Novels of Dostoevsky

Dostoevsky, before Camus, had been passionately concerned with what might become of man after the death of God. Living at the turn of the century in a Russia which was hanging uncertainly between the medieval and modern worlds, he was uniquely situated to probe this central problem of the modern consciousness. "If there's no everlasting God," says Smerdyakov to his brother Ivan, in *The Brothers Karamazov*, "there's no such thing as virtue and there's no need of it."[14]

Dostoevsky explores human possibilities under these conditions. Raskolnikov, in *Crime and Punishment*, plots a senseless murder, out of simple curiosity to see how the victim will react. He believes himself superior to all moral injunctions. But in the end he is consumed with guilt and abjectly confesses his crime to the police. In *The Brothers Karamazov*, the elder Karamazov experiments with a life of the grossest sensuality, even betraying his own sons in pursuit of his carnal pleasures, and at last dying at the hands of one of them.

Ivan, in the same novel, is the model of Western scientific consciousness. He is the one who teaches that since on scientific grounds God is dead, all is permitted. But he is horrified to discover that his half brother, acting on this nihilistic principle, has murdered their father.

Kirillov, in *The Possessed*, argues: "If God does not exist, I am God." All meaning is centered in his own person. But how shall he prove his deity and demonstrate his divine freedom? His answer is suicide. "I shall kill myself in order to assert my insubordination, my new and dreadful liberty."[15] Stavrogin, another of Dostoevsky's inventions (also in *The Possessed*), living on the same premises, turns first to sadism and then in futility also commits suicide. Another character, Verhovensky, first plans a utopian society and then turns to political assassinations and nihilistic destruction—a preview of modern totalitarianism.

Dostoevsky's verdict is gloomy. The man-god who emerges when faith in the God-man Jesus Christ has faded, is tragically doomed. Camus's verdict is more optimistic: "One must imagine Sisyphus happy."[16] This is the problem of the neo-modern consciousness: Can an authentic human life be lived in an absurd world devoid of meaning? As we turn to the image of modernity in other writers, Dostoevsky's verdict seems the more plausible, except perhaps for a few rare, gifted, and tortured spirits, such as Camus himself.

## The Bankruptcy of Modernity

In *Thus Spake Zarathustra*, Nietzsche oracularly announced the ultimate theme of modernity: "God is dead!" He saw in the whole tendency of modern thought a movement toward nothingness. "Nihilism," he wrote, "represents the ultimate logical conclusion of our great values and ideals. . . ."[17] This X of nothingness is the goal of the modern mind; "since Copernicus man is rolling from the center toward X."[18]

Like Dostoevsky, Tolstoy wrestled with this painful problem. In *Anna Karénina,* Levin becomes a symbol of modern man aware (at last) of the ultimate results of the logic of modern thought: "Ever since, by his beloved brother's deathbed, Levin had first glanced into the questions of life and death in the light of these new convictions, as he called them, which had during the period from the twentieth to his thirty-fourth year imperceptibly replaced his childish and youthful beliefs—he had been stricken with horror, not so much of death, as *of life, without any knowledge of when, and why, and how, and what it was.* The physical organization, its decay, the indestructibility of matter, the law of the conservation of energy, evolution, were the words which usurped the place of his old belief. There words and the ideas associated with them were very well for intellectual purposes. But for life they yielded nothing, and Levin felt suddenly like a man who has changed his warm fur cloak for a muslin garment, and going for the first time into the frost, is immediately convinced, not by reason, but by his whole nature that he is as good as naked, and that he must infallibly perish miserably."[19]

Tolstoy says, "The question was summed up for him thus: 'If I do not accept the answers Christianity gives to the problems of my life, what answers do I accept?' And in the whole arsenal of his convictions, so far from finding any satisfactory answers, he was utterly unable to find anything at all like an answer. He was in a position of a man seeking food in toy-shops and tool-shops."[20]

Descartes had initiated the modern era with his celebrated axiom "I think, therefore I am." Camus at the end of that era found it necessary to translate that formulation into terms of rebellion: "I proclaim that I believe in nothing and that everything is absurd, but I cannot doubt the validity of my proclamation and I must at least believe in my protest."[21]

Another sensitive modern writer, James Joyce, describes in his autobiographical *Portrait of the Artist as a Young Man* how he discovered that to arrive at his new consciousness he must journey *away* from home, nation, and church. He takes a Dantean journey through the hell and purgatory of his received culture toward a new "paradise" of totally liberated modern consciousness. The modern thinker finds it impossible to go back. He feels he must explore new dimensions.

Going back might be interpreted in two ways: Going back to premodern Christian conceptions, or going back to the forms of idealism characteristic of the Enlightenment of the eighteenth century. Why can't he go back to Christianity?

The reason is that the premises of modernity have made that answer unintelligible. Already in the late nineteenth century Matthew Arnold had heard the "Sea of Faith" in

> *Its melancholy long, withdrawing roar,*
> *Retreating, to the breath*
> *Of the night-wind, down the vast edges drear*
> *And naked shingles of the world.*[22]

Allen Tate, in *More Sonnets at Christmas,* carries the doubts further: Sitting before the fire on Christmas day, looking into the "ancient crackle of Christ's deep gaze," he concludes

> *there's not a ghost to fear*
> *this crucial day, whose decapitate joke*
> *Languidly winds into the inner ear.*[23]

> *Citizen, myself, or personal friend,*
> *Your ghosts are Plato's Christians in the cave.*
> *Unfix your necks, turn to the door . . .*[24]

The melancholy tone of Tate's conclusions resonates in these lines:

> *The day's at end and there's nowhere to go,*
> *Draw to the fire, even this fire is dying. . . .*[25]

If not to Christianity, then why not return to idealism in one form or another? Again, the reason seems to be that the premises for such idealism have been eroded away. The limitation of truth to the deliverances of the senses gradually betrays even ardent idealism into cynicism. Maxwell Anderson describes the erosion of idealism during the Spanish Civil War. King, the chief character in *Key Largo,* deserts a forward battle position, thus abandoning his comrades to defeat and death. He explains his choice as follows:

> *We should know*
> *by this time—we've looked at Europe long enough*
> *to know there's nothing to fight for here—*
> *that nothing you win means freedom or equality*
> *or justice—that all the formulas are false—*
> *and known to be false—democracy, communism,*
> *socialism, naziism—dead religions nobody*
> *believes in—or if he does believe*
> *he's quietly made use of by the boys*
> *who long ago learned better and believe in nothing but themselves.*
> *      Long ago*
> *men found the sky was empty; it follows that*
> *men are a silly accident, meaningless,*
> *here in the empty sky. . . .*[26]

Archibald MacLeish lends emotional substance to the image of an empty sky in his "Epistle to be Left in the Earth." He describes the chilling earth drifting among the stars.

*Each man believes in his heart he will die . . .*
*None of us know if this wandering earth will be found.*
*Also none among us has seen God . . .*
*It is very cold*
   *there are strange stars near Arcturus*
*Voices are crying an unknown name in the sky.*[27]

Where in this picture is a basis for the humane, ethical enthusiasms of the Enlightenment, when man seemed the very paragon of the world with his omnicompetent rationality? As André Gorz, a disciple of Jean-Paul Sartre, says in *The Traitor*, "Being has no meaning which is not gratuitous. . . ."[28]

### Reduction to the Absurd

Modern literature seems to be engaged in reducing the whole received tradition, humanist and Christian, to absurdity by rigorously pressing modern premises to their logical conclusions. Ernest Hemingway's short story "A Clean, Well-Lighted Place," in his book significantly titled *Winner Take Nothing*, portrays a waiter in a café mumbling to himself: "Our nada, who art in nada, nada be thy name, thy kingdom nada, thy will be nada, in nada as it is in nada. . . ."* The Christian faith has become mere emptiness.

H. G. Wells does the same service for the humanistic tradition, for which he had labored so long and hopefully, in his last book, *Mind at the End of Its Tether*, where he abandons the whole enterprise as a false ideal. *The Croquet Player*, written during the Nazi era, foreshadows this conclusion. A comfortable middle-class gentleman becomes involved in a plot that unveils the rising panic of his generation—a panic rising from the bones of man's prehistoric past, sweeping away the superficial culture of modernity.

But no writer has more passionately revealed the artificiality of bourgeois optimism and ideals based on the ordered world of science and humane institutions than has Jean-Paul Sartre. In his autobiographical novel, typically entitled *Nausea*, Roquentin, the chief character, exposes the Self-Taught Man (the middle class) to contempt. His humanism, Roquentin shows, is entirely vacuous and betrays his inherent bad faith. He loves men in general, but has nothing to do with them as living, suffering individuals. "They all hate each other: as individuals," he cries, "naturally not as men."[29] The humanist betrays himself, because he has never found being human difficult. He has never plumbed the depths of the human situation.

Roquentin watches the grey shimmerings of the city of Bouville and feels that he belongs to another species. "They come out of their offices after their day of work, they look at the houses and the squares with satisfaction, they think it is *their* city, a good, solid, bourgeois city. They aren't afraid, they feel at home. All they have ever seen is trained water running from taps, light which fills bulbs when you turn on the switch, half-breed, bastard trees held

---

* *Nada* is the Spanish word for "nothing."

up with crutches. They have proof, a hundred times a day, that everything happens mechanically, that the world obeys fixed, unchangeable laws. In a vacuum all bodies fall at the same rate of speed, the public park is closed at 4 P.M. in winter, at 6 P.M. in summer, lead melts at 335 degrees centigrade."[30]

All this order is purely conventional (as in Hume's philosophy), but the good citizens believe it to have ontological grounding. "What," Roquentin asks, "if something were to happen? What if something suddenly started throbbing? Then they would notice it was there and they'd think their hearts were going to burst. Then what good would their dykes, bulwarks, power houses, furnaces and pile drivers be to them? It can happen any time, perhaps right now; the omens are present."[31]

He then envisions the conventional order breaking up. "For example, the father of a family might go out for a walk, and, across the street he'll see something like a red rag, blown toward him by the wind. And when the rage has gotten close to him he'll see that it is a side of rotten meat, grimy with dust, dragging itself along by crawling, skipping, a piece of writhing flesh rolling in the gutter, spasmodically shooting out spurts of blood. Or a mother might look at her child's cheek and ask him: 'What's that—a pimple?' and see the flesh puff out a little, split, open, and at the bottom of the slit an eye, a laughing eye might appear. . . . And someone else might feel something scratching in his mouth. He goes to the mirror, opens his mouth: and his tongue is an enormous, live centipede, rubbing its legs together and scraping his palate."[32]

Here the intellectual doubt with which Descartes initiated modern philosophy has been radically transformed into visceral anxiety. The foundations have all been swept away, leaving man, as Sartre says, "a useless passion," a kind of "waste product of the universe."[33] This is what is meant by saying that this literature functions as a *reductio ad absurdum* for all the premises of modernity. This is the basis for Tillich's dictum: "Little is left in our present civilization which does not indicate to a sensitive mind the presence of [a] vacuum."[34]

Let this suffice to illustrate my main thesis, that the mirror of contemporary art and literature reflects a deep crisis in the form of mentality that I have called the modern mind. It remains to specify more precisely, even at the risk of repetition, some aspects of that crisis.

## The Crisis in Values

The modern mind has enormously extended the range of factual knowledge, but in corresponding degree has cast the basis for rational evaluation into deepest doubt. A common way of saying this is that modern thought has greatly increased the means of life and left the ends unilluminated; the ship of man's estate has grown enormously larger, but the tiller and compass have dropped into the sea. "The only gain of civilization for mankind is the greater variety of sensations," writes Dostoevsky, "and absolutely nothing more."[35]

Sartre, in his study of the literary works of Jean Genêt, carries Nietzsche's program of the transvaluation of all values to its end term. *Saint Genêt*, as he calls him in his critical study by that name, is the epitome of criminal degeneration, and yet Sartre holds him up as the model of human self-transcendence. His defense of Genêt is the study of an unconditionally bad will. In Genêt's play, *The Balcony*, three psychotic customers of a brothel masquerade as a Bishop, a General, and the Chief Magistrate. Their pose deceives the people as they tour a city which has been all but destroyed by wanton bombing. The point seems to be that every value is empty deception. As F. H. Heinemann says, the last consequence follows: "The Good is nothing but an illusion; the Evil is a Nothingness that creates itself on the ruins of the Good." It follows then that the "evil man is explained away as a myth or a projection of the dishonest impulses of the honest man."[36]

### The Crisis in Meaning

All the works we have discussed point to a crisis in meaning. Another author who poignantly felt both the need and the hopelessness of finding any viable significance for human existence was Franz Kafka. His novels and stories are case studies in almost every existential problem which harasses neo-modern man. In the short story "The Great Wall of China," he imagines the plans for the construction of the Great Wall. The wall, it seems, was constructed in pieces according to some master plan. In this way, Kafka writes, "great gaps were left . . . which is probably merely one of the many legends to which the building of the wall gave rise, and which cannot be verified, at least by any single man with his own eyes and judgment, on account of the extent of the structure."[37] The concept of a master plan thus becomes more and more doubtful. The wall seems planned, but no one can really say. The sections took about five years to construct, but at the end of that time "the supervisors were as a rule quite exhausted and had lost all faith in themselves, in the wall, in the world."[38] He likens it all to the legendary Tower of Babel.

Not that there weren't learned hypotheses about the wall, writes Kafka: "Almost every educated man of our time was a mason by profession and infallible in the matter of laying foundations."[39] But this is mere conjecture. "In the office of the command—where it was and who sat there no one whom I have asked knew then or knows now—in that office one may be certain that all human thoughts and desires were resolved, and counter to them all human aids and fulfillments."[40] He concludes that the world is enigmatic: "Try with all your might to comprehend the decrees of the high command, but only up to a point; then avoid further meditation."

He meditates upon Imperial Peking, the center of the Empire, where, surely, the plan had originated. He would like to consult someone who had talked to the Emperor, but of course the Emperor who conceived the idea of the wall is now dead. Yet, he writes, "it is the sole curiosity that fills us—we are always trying to get information on this subject. . . ."[41] Sadly he concludes: "One hears a great many things, but can gather nothing definite."[42]

He imagines a messenger being sent from the Emperor on his deathbed with the requisite information. The messenger turns to go, but the palace is so crowded he cannot make his way. If he succeeded in making good his escape, the multitudes of the imperial capital would lie before him, "the center of the world, crammed to bursting with its own refuse."[43] The whole enterprise ends in failure: "Nobody could fight his way through here even with a message from a dead man. But you sit at your window when evening falls and dream it to yourself."[44]

The same theme appears in Arthur Miller's reputedly autobiographical play *After the Fall*. Talking about his life, Quentin says, "Underlying it all, I see now, there was a presumption. That I was moving on an upward path toward some elevation, where God knows what—I would be justified, or even condemned—a verdict anyway. I think now that my disaster really began when I looked up one day—and the bench was empty."[45] It had all been a "pointless litigation before an empty bench."[46]

### The Crisis in Knowledge

This crisis of meaning is related, of course, to the crisis of knowledge—knowledge of values and of God—that the modern premises have made so difficult, if not impossible. But the crisis of theological knowledge is paralleled by a crisis in natural knowledge itself. Recall in this connection Sartre's objection to the smug notion that the world is an ordered place. But without some such order, science itself is imperiled.

## ALIENATION

Alienation is a term referring to the sense of separateness from the reality of one's self, other people, and the world. It expresses itself in several ways, some of which—meaninglessness and doubt—we have already discussed. Alienation results from a breakdown in communication, connectedness, and communion. The classic study of this condition is Camus's novel *The Stranger*, or, as the title was translated in England, *The Outsider*. The story opens with Meursault's words: "Mother died today. Or, maybe, yesterday; I can't be sure."[47] He travels to Marengo, some fifty miles from his "home" in Algiers, for the funeral. But instead of sorrow he feels only a profound indifference to the social ritual in which he is expected to be the chief celebrant. After the funeral he says, "It occurred to me that somehow I'd got through another Sunday, that Mother now was buried, and tomorrow I'd be going back to work as usual. Really, nothing in my life had changed."[48] In

the same indifferent way he carries on a love affair with a girl whom he met
right after the funeral, and soon becomes involved in a senseless murder.
When he is tried, the issue becomes not one of guilt or innocence but of his
shocking indifference to social ritual. He is unable to make the proper
responses. "I've always been far too absorbed in the present moment, or the
immediate future." Even during the trial he ignores the proceedings to muse
on the "warm smells of summer, my favorite streets, the sky at evening,
Marie's dresses and her laugh."[49]

Sartre says of him that he is like a person whom we watch through a glass,
completely separated from us and from everyone else. He lacks organic
connection with his world. The fault, of course, is not wholly his. His society
has offered him only the cheapest substitute for genuine human communion
—and he instinctively refuses. There is, to be sure, a kind of nobility in his
refusal, but nevertheless he remains to the end a complete "stranger,"
illustrating in his way Sartre's own conclusion in the play *No Exit:* "Hell is
other people."

Strangeness toward others is integrally connected with a strangeness toward
one's self. In Miller's play *After the Fall*, Quentin cries, "My name is on this
man! Why can't I say 'I'?"[50] Throughout the play he is searching for himself.

## DEHUMANIZATION

The loss of self-identity and integral connection with others leads to the
dehumanization of man. Kafka's famous short novel *The Metamorphosis*, is
of a young man, Gregor Samsa, who woke up one morning "from uneasy
dreams . . . [and] found himself transformed in his bed into a gigantic
insect."[51] The author makes clear that in Samsa's life as a traveling salesman
he had already become subhuman. Even in his dreadful plight his chief worry
is what his employer will think. Kafka sees humanity thus transformed into
vermin. It reminds us of the attitude that the antagonists in modern total war
take toward their enemies: They are something subhuman to be crushed and
stamped out like insects.

A little-known European novelist, Vercors (Jean Bruller 1902–    ), in
*You Shall Know Them*, struggles with the definition of humanity. A scientific
expedition in New Guinea discovers a tribe of creatures which appear to be
the long-sought Missing Link and which resist any final classification as either
men or apes. Many problems arise: Shall the Church strive to convert them?
Are they eligible to be made into beasts of burden, like animals? When one
of the females gives birth as a result of human insemination, Douglas
Templemore kills the offspring. The question then arises: Is this murder? If
the "baby" is human, yes; if it is not, no. The court searches desperately for a
definition of *what it means to be human,* and in the process throws everything into relativity.

## THE RADICAL EVIL IN MAN

The modern mind found no room for the concept of sin and guilt. On the premises of modernity bad actions must be considered as a kind of mistake, not as sin. Guilt is not a meaningful category But contemporary literature is full of the agonizing struggle with guilt and the presence of evil in man.

William Golding's *Lord of the Flies* portrays an apparently innocent group of children marooned on an island where the whole human drama of sin and wickedness comes to a hideous finale as they hunt down one of their most enlightened members to decapitate him and mount his head on a pointed stick. In another novel, *The Temple of the Golden Pavilion,* by the Japanese writer Mishima, the chief character, a young monk, becomes obsessively jealous of the beauty of the Golden Temple and finally destroys it by fire. He found his life meaningful only by committing himself wholly to evil.

Robert Penn Warren, in his poem "Brother to Dragons," brings back that great exponent of human rights Thomas Jefferson to debate his own doctrine of man.[52] Warren revives a cruel story of Jefferson's nephew, Lilburn, who hacked to death a slave in the meathouse of his estate. Jefferson states his historical doctrine of humane optimism in these words: "If we might take man's hand, strike shackle, lead him forth from his own monstrous nightmare, then his natural innocence would dance like sunlight over the delighted landscape."[53] But the "scream in the midnight meathouse" shatters Jefferson's "sweet lie . . . concocted out of nobleness" and forces him to a reassessment of man. He says,

> *I have long since come to the firm and considered conclusion*
> *That love, all love, all kinds, descriptions, and shapes,*
> *Is but a mask to hide the brute fact of fact,*
> *And that fact is the immitigable ferocity of self.*[54]

Arthur Miller faces the same reality: "To choose, one must know one's self, but no man knows himself who cannot face the murder in him, the sly and everlasting complicity with the forces of destruction. The apple cannot be stuck back on the Tree of Knowledge."[55] He has Quentin say, in *After the Fall,* "I am bewildered by the death of love, and my responsibility for it."[56] He confesses that he feels like an accomplice.

Kafka's novel *The Trial* is the classic account of modern man's sense of guilt. K. is arrested one morning for a crime of which he knows nothing. He spends weeks trying to find out what he is charged with, and becomes involved in a nightmare of strange hearings and interrogations. At the end, still without any clue to his guilt, he is executed in a horrible way. Martin Buber sums up Kafka's world view: "His unexpressed ever-present theme is the remoteness of the judge, the remoteness of the Lord of the castle, the hiddenness, the eclipse. The human world is given over to the meaningless government of a slovenly bureaucracy without possibility of appeal."[57]

## ANXIETY

In the mirror of contemporary literature we see man as a profoundly anxious being; anxious about his world, his fellows, and himself. This anxiety is not the same as fear. In fear there is some determinate threat, against which one can mount rational defenses. Anxiety is a generalized feeling of threat without such a discernible object. This anxiety, we are led to believe, comes from a deep disorder in existence itself—the same disorder from which spring all man's other problems. In *The Burrow*, Kafka's image for anxious man is an underground creature who spends his entire existence digging new tunnels and plotting new strategies against enemies he has never seen. He is worried by an unidentifiable whistling noise which he reassures himself is only the "small fry," but his reassurances are short-lived. He returns to his frantic digging and worrying. At last he realizes the hopelessness of his condition. He should reconstruct all his defenses, beginning at once "with the vigor of youth." But "it is now far too late in the day."[58] At last he abruptly realizes: "I cannot comprehend my former plan. I can find no slightest trace of reason in what had seemed so reasonable. . . . I let everything slide; I would be quite content if I could only still the conflict going on within me."[59]

## FAITH IN CONTEMPORARY LITERATURE

Are there no glimmers of hope in contemporary literature? Yes, in a sense there are. Much of the literature reveals the honesty of profound search, the seriousness about the human question, which Paul Tillich has wisely noted to be a mark of being grasped by ultimate concern. In his critical work *The Picaresque Saint*, R. W. B. Lewis claims that modern writing is characterized by an earnest search for true humanhood, even saintliness of a sort. The "figure of a saint: a very peculiar kind of saint," he says, "seems to be the representative figure of the contemporary novel."[60] This saint is peculiar, because he is not a transcendental figure who finds his spiritual home in another world. He is rather a man "who tries to hold in balance, by the very contradictions of his character, both the observed truths of contemporary experience and the vital aspiration to transcend them."[61] I have already mentioned Tarrou and Rieux in Camus's novel *The Plague*. Other figures also appear. Pietro Spina, the chief character in Silone's *Bread and Wine*, recalls a high-school essay in which he wrote: "If the prospect of being displayed on altars after one's death, and being prayed to and worshipped by a lot of unknown people, mostly ugly old ladies, were not very unpleasant, I should like to be a saint."[62] And Greene, in his *Power and the Glory*, writes of the nameless drunken priest as he is about to die: "It seemed to him at that moment that it would have been quite easy to have been a saint."[63]

Other characters from the work of other writers could be cited, but the critics have already made much of the search for "Christ figures" in this literature.[64] However specious some of these critical findings may be, they point to a modern longing for a true manhood. And one of the positive features of this quest is the refusal to falsify the nature of man as he is known in our experience. These "saints" are not figures of victory; they live, as the Italian novelist Moravia has said, "a poor life, full of uncertainty and error."[65] Yet, though they may not be dedicated to a supernatural god, they do seem profoundly committed, as Lewis says, "to what yet remains of the sacred in the ravaged human community."[66]

There are, of course, some works that go beyond this, some writers who come close to a more classical affirmation of the God-committed saint. I mean such a figure as the lonely Negro minister in Alan Paton's *Cry the Beloved Country*, or the concept of the incarnational life as it is described in the last poems of T. S. Eliot, the *Four Quartets*. But these are not yet typical of contemporary man. Depending on your point of view, they may seem to be either a throwback to an older faith or a forecast of a more mature, more seasoned faith that has endured the modern epoch and won out.

To many readers this account of contemporary literature will seem melodramatic, exaggerated, or even contrived. The author, it may be said, has selected his material to prove his case, leaving out of account the great body of positive and optimistic writing. The writers themselves must be sick or unbalanced.

My reply is that these are the works of some of the most gifted and profound writers of our century. Moreover, the works cited are those which address themselves to the basic problems of the age in which we live. Theirs is not entertainment or escape literature. As we read we discover that they are talking about us and our problems—dimensions in ourselves and our world that we have somehow ignored.

We must accept the fact that the artist is an especially sensitive person, sounding depths of which the average person is unaware. But what he senses in the depths will emerge one day into the terrible glare of daylight. It is merely a question of time before the doubts and anxieties that these artists have described become operational in everyday life. These symptomatic doubts and anxieties are a warning of illness before the patient falls into a raging fever.

In terms of our study of religion, these writers form the background which alone makes it possible to understand the mood of modern faith and the profound human questions to which it speaks. So long as the optimistic progressivism of modernism prevailed, faith's voice was unheard because its message was not needed. It is the bankruptcy of the modern mind that leads men to understand St. Paul's cry: "Wretched man that I am, who will deliver me . . . ?" But, as Alexander Miller reminds us, "These are biblical words."[67]

It is to the revival of these biblical forms of thought in modern faith that we now turn.


## SUGGESTIONS FOR FURTHER READING

Critical studies in the field of literature and religion have multiplied so rapidly in recent years that it is difficult to sort out books for recommendation. William Barrett's *Irrational Man* (Doubleday, 1958; Anchor, 1962) is a good start because it also gives the background in existentialism that is needed for this subject. For another good introduction to existentialism, containing selections of both philosophy and literature, see Walter Kaufmann, *Existentialism from Dostoevsky to Sartre* (Meridian, World Publishing, 1956).

Hazel Barnes gives a good account of the literature of atheistic existentialism in *The Literature of Possibility* (University of Nebraska Press, 1959). I have mentioned previously R. W. B. Lewis' *The Picaresque Saint* as a source for the concept of the "Christ image" in literature. Julian N. Hartt's *The Lost Image of Man* (Louisiana University Press, 1963) is concerned with the broken image of modern man and the search for a possible answer to that brokenness.

There are many other valuable critical works on modern literature and the spiritual condition of modern man: Stanley Hopper, ed., *Spiritual Problems in Contemporary Literature* (Harper Torchbooks, Harper & Row, 1952); Nathan A. Scott, Jr., ed., *The Climate of Faith in Modern Literature* (Seabury, 1964); Amos N. Wilder, *Theology and Modern Literature* (Harvard University Press, 1958); C. I. Glicksberg, *The Tragic Vision in Twentieth-Century Literature* (Southern Illinois University Press, 1963); W. R. Mueller, *The Prophetic Voice in Modern Fiction* (Association Press, 1959); and Roland Mushat Frye, *Perspective on Man, Literature and the Christian Tradition* (Westminster, 1961).

For a contrast between two types of modern literature, the one nihilistic and atheistic and the other existentially Christian see Jean-Paul Sartre, *Nausea*, Lloyd Alexander, trans. (New Directions, n.d.) and Alan Paton, *Cry the Beloved Country* (Scribner, 1958).


## NOTES

1. This philosophy of art is developed by Maritain in *Creative Intuition in Art and Poetry* (Pantheon, 1953).

2. William Barrett, *Irrational Man* (Doubleday, 1958; Anchor, Doubleday, 1962, p. 49).

3. In *Resistance, Rebellion and Death*, quoted in Hazel Barnes, *The Literature of Possibility* (University of Nebraska Press, 1959), p. 76.

4. Quoted in Finley Eversole, ed., *Christian Faith and the Contem-*

*porary Arts* (Abingdon, 1962), p. 12.

5. Barrett, *op. cit.*, p. 47.
6. Albert Camus, *The Myth of Sisyphus* (Vintage, Random House, 1959), p. 17.
7. *Ibid.*, p. 102.
8. Albert Camus, *The Plague* (Modern Library, 1948), pp. 230–231.
9. Camus, *Myth*, p. 3.
10. *Ibid.*, p. 38.
11. *Ibid.*
12. *Ibid.*, p. 91.
13. *Ibid.*, p. 90.
14. Dostoevski, *The Brothers Karamazov* (Modern Library, 1950), p. 768.
15. Quoted in Camus, *Myth*, p. 78.
16. *Ibid.*, p. 91.
17. Quoted in Charles I. Glicksberg, *The Tragic Vision in Twentieth-Century Literature* (Southern Illinois University Press, 1963), p. 110.
18. *Ibid.*
19. Leo Tolstoy, *Anna Karénina* (Random House, 1939), II, 932. Italics added.
20. *Ibid.*, p. 933.
21. Albert Camus, *The Rebel* (Vintage, Random House, 1956), p. 10.
22. From Arnold's poem "Dover Beach."
23. Allen Tate, "Sonnets at Christmas," and "More Sonnets at Christmas" in Oscar Williams, ed., *A Little Treasury of Modern Poetry* (Scribner, 1952), p. 391.
24. *Ibid.*, p. 392.
25. *Ibid.*, p. 391.
26. Maxwell Anderson, Prologue from "Key Largo," in *Eleven Verse Plays* (Harcourt, Brace & World, 1940), pp. 22–23.
27. Archibald MacLeish, "Epistle to Be Left in the Earth," in *Modern American Poetry*, Louis Untermeyer, ed. (Harcourt, Brace & World, 1936), pp. 505–506.
28. Quoted in Glicksberg, *op. cit.*, p. 44.
29. Jean-Paul Sartre, *Nausea* (New Directions, n.d.; French ed. first published 1938), p. 158.
30. *Ibid.*, p. 211.
31. *Ibid.*, p. 212.
32. *Ibid.*, pp. 212–213.
33. Jean-Paul Sartre, *Being and Nothingness* (Philosophical Library, 1956), p. 615.
34. Quoted in Eversole, ed., *op. cit.*, p. 53.
35. In his *Notes from Underground*, quoted in Walter Kaufmann, ed., *Existentialism, from Dostoevski to Sartre* (Meridian, World Publishing, 1956), p. 69.
36. F. II. Heinemann, *Existentialism and the Modern Predicament* (Harper Torchbooks, Harper & Row, 1958), pp. 209–210.
37. Franz Kafka, *Selected Short Stories of Franz Kafka*, Willa and Edwin Muir, trans. (Modern Library, 1952), pp. 129–130.
38. *Ibid.*, p. 132.
39. *Ibid.*, p. 135.
40. *Ibid.*, pp. 135–136.
41. *Ibid.*, p. 140.
42. *Ibid.*
43. *Ibid.*, p. 142.
44. *Ibid.*
45. In Arthur Miller, *After the Fall*, in *Saturday Evening Post*, February 1, 1964, p. 34.

46. *Ibid.*, p. 34.
47. Albert Camus, *The Stranger* (Knopf, 1958), p. 1.
48. *Ibid.*, p. 30.
49. *Ibid.*, p. 132.
50. Miller, *op. cit.*, p. 51.
51. Kafka, *op. cit.*, p. 19.
52. Discussed and quoted in Alexander Miller, *The Renewal of Man* (Doubleday, 1955), p. 34.
53. Robert Penn Warren, *Brother to Dragons* (Random House, 1953), p. 41.
54. *Ibid.*, p. 47.
55. Arthur Miller, *op. cit.*, p. 32.
56. *Ibid.*, p. 49.
57. Quoted in Camus, *Myth*, p. 95.
58. Kafka, *op. cit.*, p. 293.
59. *Ibid.*, p. 294.
60. R. W. B. Lewis, *The Picaresque Saint* (Lippincott, 1959), pp. 30–31.
61. *Ibid.*, p. 31.
62. *Ibid.*, pp. 31–32.
63. *Ibid.*, p. 32.
64. See Edwin Moseley's *Pseudonyms of Christ in the Modern Novel* (University of Pittsburgh Press, 1963), or Frederick Dillistone, *The Novelist and the Passion Story* (Sheed and Ward, 1961).
65. Quoted in Lewis, *op. cit.*, p. 56.
66. *Ibid.*
67. Alexander Miller, *The Renewal of Man* (Doubleday, 1955), p. 38.

# 14

# *Beyond Modernity:*
# *Faith Rediscovers Its Message*

❖❧❖❧❖❧❖❧❖❧❖❧❖❧❖❧❖❧❖❧❖❧❖❧❖❧❖❧❖❧❖❧❖❧❖❧❖❧❖

In the last three chapters I have traced the rise of the modern mind and the doubtful state to which it has come in our time. In the last chapter this theme was announced through the medium of selected modern literature. Here I want to restate the thesis less dramatically and indicate the way in which religious faith has responded to the turmoil of modern thought.

ᶦˡThe events of our century have stirred religious thought to a deeper examination of its own sources, reaching back over the liberal thought of recent history to such creative periods of Christian history as the Reformation and the age of the New Testament. This deeper examination has produced a theological revival in which faith now speaks with a clearer and more authentic voice than in any period of the recent past. The epoch in which the major concern of theology was to accommodate itself to evolving modern thought has come to an end.ˊˊ

In America this theological change emerged in the 1930s. The revolt against orthodoxy which began in the last part of the nineteenth century as an attempt to accommodate faith to culture, and which reached flood tide in the first quarter of the twentieth century, began to recede under the influence of new gravitational forces. With the growing suspicion that there was some grave malady at the heart of modernity, the relationship between faith and culture changed.

The keynote of change in America was sounded by the great liberal preacher Harry Emerson Fosdick, toward the end of his career. In a now celebrated sermon, delivered in 1935, he said: "The Church must go beyond modernism. We have been all things to all men long enough. We have adapted and adjusted and accommodated and conceded long enough. We have at times gotten so low-down that we talked as though the highest compliment that could be paid to Almighty God was that a few scientists believed in him."[1]

Fosdick did not, nor should we, repudiate the achievements of the liberal period. "If we are successfully to maintain the thesis that the church must go beyond modernism," Fosdick said in the same sermon, "we must start by seeing that the church had to go as far as modernism."[2] He believed that the battle of modernizing had been largely won, and felt a new watchword should be raised: "Not, Accommodate yourself to the prevailing culture! but, Stand out from it and challenge it!"[3] He sounded the note that was central in the new theological orientation; namely, that modernism had gone too far and had often found that in accommodating faith to the modern mind it had often been guilty of watering down the faith and adjusting it to a man-centered culture.

We must not think that theology could have attained this new stance without the long period of exchange between modernity and faith. That exchange was essential to the vital life of religion and no advance into the future can be made without carrying the gains of that period along with us. Those who think that this new theological position can be attained merely by the rejection of science or other elements of modernity are simply mistaken and will suffer the disappointments of being thought merely dogmatic and largely irrelevant. It is because of this honest period of liberal exchange that Christianity is better equipped, in my opinion, than any other faith to speak to the condition of modern man. To write off the liberal period as a simple-minded error or a species of apostasy is therefore grossly mistaken. The misjudgments of liberal theology were in some ways inevitable considering the available resources for thought on both the religious and secular sides.

Having said all that, we must nonetheless concede that faith was to some extent compromised during the liberal period and that the new movement allows the authentic note of Christian faith to be heard in greater independence and richness than at any time before in our age. This has been due to a revival which is the concern of this chapter. Before dealing specifically with this new message in religion, we must briefly set the background against which it finds its full meaning.

## FROM GALILEO TO HITLER (1632–1932)

The 300 years from the publication of Galileo's *Dialogue* in 1632 to Hitler's appointment as Chancellor of Germany in 1933 represent in round numbers the epoch I have called modernity. This last date is chosen somewhat arbitrarily as the end of the modern period, much as historians selected A.D. 476 to date the "fall of Rome," the year in which another German, the barbarian Odoacer, was proclaimed king of Italy, the title and office of Emperor being abolished.

Galileo was the first modern to formulate in clear and precise terms the basic premises that lay at the base of every advance of modern thought and life. Hitler, on the other hand, represents the violent and thoroughgoing repudiation of these premises by the leader of a Western nation which was in many ways the most advanced in modern thought, one which had contributed as much as any other to its development.

Hitler, like Odoacer, marks an end. His ascendancy was no "wave of the future"; it was merely a portent of the last days of modernity, the twilight of the modern gods. Our days are filled with the signs and portents of this deepening twilight. We must be content to indicate only three of the most striking.

### Social and Personal Disorganization

When a culture's basic concepts no longer enable it to solve the basic social and personal problems of its people, it is an omen of the end. The most dramatic indications of failure at the social level are war and totalitarianism. War is rational only as a means of defense or aggrandizement. But modern war can neither defend nor enrich. Both defense and offense have ceased to have a clear meaning, since the results are the same in both cases—universal annihilation. Nuclear and bacteriological weapons are so powerful that no nation can use them without inviting self-destruction.

Totalitarianism is understandable only as a reaction against the failures of modern culture to make society humanely habitable. The wild irrationalism of the fascist and communist collectives is the futile attempt to reconstruct human life on some basis apart from modern premises. Modern thought, in its most optimistic movement in the eighteenth century, arrived at the "belief," as the historian, Crane Brinton, writes, "that all human beings can attain here on earth a state of perfection hitherto in the West thought to be possible only for Christians in a state of grace, and for them only after death."[4]

Late in that century the builders of the Church of Saint Margaret at Gotha, in Germany, placed a message on the steeple knob for our enlightenment. Here are some passages from that inscription: "Our age occupies the happiest period of the eighteenth century. Emperors, kings, and princes humanely descend from their dreaded heights . . . become fathers, friends and confidants of their people. Religion rends its priestly garb and appears in its divine essence. Enlightenment makes great strides. . . . Sectarian hatred . . . [is] vanishing. Love of man and freedom of thought are gaining supremacy. The arts and sciences are flourishing and our gaze is penetrating deeply into the workshop of nature. Handicraftsmen as well as artists are reaching perfection, useful knowledge is growing among all classes. Here you have a faithful description of our times."

The inscription closes with this preachment: "Do the same for your descendants and be happy."[5]

What would the writers of that inscription think if they could have heard the speeches of Adolf Hitler and witnessed the thunderous acclaim he received? Or what would be their reaction if they could have visited the battlefields of modern war or the concentration camps administered by the heirs of their own enlightenment? We do not know. But our impression is that some dreadful miscalculation has been made, that some ineluctable elements in human nature have been omitted in their proud catalogues of nature and man.

Paralleling these social troubles are the signs of personal disorganization: the widespread sense of meaninglessness, unappeasable guilt, and deep anxiety; the increase of mental illness and crime; the deepening alienation of human beings from one another and from themselves; the wide conviction that history and society have no healing pattern into which a man may integrate his life and thought. I refer here not to those at the margins of modern culture, but to its most prosperous, gifted, and enlightened members.

These difficulties, I have claimed, lie at the roots of culture. They are not temporary maladjustments or "cultural lags." They spring from the inadequacy of the modern view of man and nature. This inadequacy shows itself with especial clarity in two further ways: as a crisis in knowledge, and as a crisis in values. Let us consider these in turn.

### The Crisis in Knowledge

A previous chapter outlines the premises of modernity laid down in the thought of the greatest modern thinkers. In summary, those premises were these: (1) Reality is sensory. (2) Reason is restricted to discovering patterns in sensory data. To be sure, the exact meaning of these premises was not understood at the beginning. It has been elaborated in the course of modern history. It was not apparent, either, at the beginning how much was assumed by scientists that did not follow strictly from these lean premises. In other words, practical workers in the sciences assumed other things as well—such things as the uniformity and rationality of nature and the value of scientific studies. The crisis of modernity followed when it became clear that these hidden but necessary assumptions cannot be deduced from the two primary premises. This leaves even science itself with too narrow a base from which to operate effectively.

The advance of modernity was thus ambivalent. On the one hand it gave us the astonishing structures of modern science and technology; on the other it made increasingly doubtful all our nonscientific knowledge claims—about values, ourselves, nature, and God. It both gave and took away, and we can hardly be chided for questioning the price it exacted for its gifts.

So long as powerful remnants of prescientific convictions about life and value remained active in modern culture, the gifts of the modern mind could be used to foster a more comfortable and humane existence. But when, with the further advance of modernity, these remnants were fatally weakened, the full crisis of our civilization became apparent.

A technically adequate treatment of this matter is beyond the boundaries of this work—though some aspects of it will be discussed in the later section on logic and language (Chapter 21). Such a discussion would point out the inadequacies of all the efforts of modern thinkers to develop a logic that adheres strictly to modern premises. This inadequacy shows up in two ways: It is first of all logically defective—that is, it turns out to be self-contradictory on its own premises—and, second, it is existentially defective—that is, it shows itself increasingly incapable of making sense of the matters that are of utmost importance to life itself: such matters as goodness and morality, creativity and truth, aesthetic experience and beauty, personal and social existence, and religion.

It is this existential defect that is becoming most obvious to thoughtful men of all persuasions. The logical issues are too technical to concern any but a small group of thinkers. But from what we have discovered about logic in laying the foundations of modern thought, we would be foolish indeed to despise the technical work to which small groups of thinkers devote their lives. The Descartes, Kants, and Whiteheads of this world may not be widely read and understood—but neither are the foundations of buildings generally noted and admired. Yet without these foundations the superstructures themselves would soon collapse.

The modern period began in a marriage of sense and reason, but as modernity evolved it finally divorced itself from reason and embraced a passionate nihilism. The stages are not well marked, but they can be briefly traced. The first stage began in a honeymoon of confidence that reason and sense together could grasp unaided the nature of reality. This period, as we have said, contained many implicit understandings that were hangovers from the previous religious culture of medievalism—belief in the ultimate reality of a rational world order and in the values of individuals and civilization.

The second stage began in questioning these metaphysical beliefs, these implicit understandings, since they did not appear valid to thinkers who adhered strictly to the premises of modernity. Beliefs in God, universal moral law, and ultimate values were questioned by Hume and his successors. Efforts to reconstitute them did not receive universal acceptance. These efforts themselves revealed, as Ernst Cassirer (1874–1945) has said, a shift in the intellectual center of gravity. Natural science, history, law, politics, and art gradually withdrew from the domination of metaphysics and theology. "They no longer look," wrote Cassirer, "to the concept of God for their justification and legitimation." Rather, the existence of God became a problem; it became dependent upon other sources of knowledge. To quote Cassirer again: "That which formerly had established other concepts, now moves into the position of that which is to be established. . . ."[6]

The third stage was a full acceptance of humanism minus all metaphysical and religious elements: a confidence in human reason and human activity, in what men could do for and with man. Human knowledge moved happily within the realm of human experience and reason alone.

The fourth stage appeared in our own century when the apparently solid ground of human experience began to shake in an unexpected lack of stability. Intellectual difficulties were paralleled by social catastrophes in which whole segments of Western civilization passionately embraced the wild extravagances of fascism and communism—in effect seceding from the whole tradition of classical and modern civilized life.

The final stage is represented by such nihilistic thinkers as Jean-Paul Sartre, who, so to speak, still hold on to modernity by their fingernails, having kicked away almost all the supports thought by our predecessors to be necessary for civilized existence.

Up through the second stage, religion could hope for much by accommodating to modern thought. But after humanism became the presumed result of such a process, obviously faith had either to commit suicide or discover another alternative.

## The Crisis in Values

The crisis in human knowledge led directly to a crisis in values. In noting this development, let us consult one of the greatest exponents of modernity in the twentieth century, Bertrand Russell. In his comments on Dewey's pragmatism he criticizes the (for us) inevitable tendency of modern thought to become totally enclosed in the circle of human subjectivity. Dewey had built his own views upon William James' famous assertion that " 'The true' . . . is only the expedient in the way of our thinking, just as 'the right' is only the expedient in the way of our behaving."[7]

Dewey's philosophy, writes Russell, is essentially a "power philosophy" and it is this that seems to him "to make the philosophy of instrumentalism attractive to those who are more impressed by our new control over natural forces than by the limitations to which that control is still subject. . . ." In further warning he says: "In all this I feel a grave danger, the danger of what might be called a cosmic impiety. The concept of 'truth' as something dependent upon facts largely outside human control has been one of the ways in which philosophy hitherto has inculcated the necessary element of humility. When this check upon pride is removed, a further step is taken on the road toward a certain kind of madness—the intoxication of power— . . . to which modern men, whether philosophers or not, are prone. I am persuaded that this intoxication is the greatest danger of our time."[8]

One of the sources for Dewey's philosophy was biological evolution. He conceived the human mind in terms of biological adjustment and survival. But this proves to be a very narrow base for human thought. Darwin himself had doubts about human intelligence on this score. In 1881, he shared these doubts in a letter to his friend William Graham: "With me the horrid doubt always arises whether the convictions of a man's mind, which has been developed from the mind of lower animals, are of any value or are at all trustworthy. Would anyone trust in the convictions of a monkey's mind, if there are any convictions in such a mind?"[9]

With the dissolving of confidence in the mind's grasp of truth, human evaluation begins to wander in a trackless waste. Values tend to become either those of personal pleasure or of social power. Standards of rightness and goodness become merely personal or at best sociocultural, shifting from person to person or from society to society.

All this has occurred just at the moment in human history when the shrinking globe has brought mankind face to face with an unprecedented need for reliable universal standards of thought and value. As the ancient Chinese sage Mo Ti said: "Whenever the standards differ there will be opposition. . . . But how can the standards in the world be unified?"[10] Russell sums up his criticism of a way of knowing that has lost all grasp of objective truth in the wild words of King Lear: "I will do such things—what they are yet I know not—but they shall be the terror of the earth."[11] This is what is meant by a crisis in values.

## The Recovery of Faith

It was in the context of the failure of modernity that the spokesman for faith began to reconsider their awkward position as dependents of modernity. To the degree that the liberal point of view in theology has led men to attempt to derive faith from reason and experience, they themselves were caught in the difficulties of knowing and evaluating that have been described.

*Karl Barth.* The first and most authoritative voice to announce a new point of view was Karl Barth, a Swiss Protestant Reformed theologian, whose *Commentary on St. Paul's Epistle to the Romans,* published in 1919 at the close of World War I, became the manifesto of Christian independence. Daniel Day Williams summarizes the new point of view. Since the publication of Barth's work, he writes, "there has been a deepening of consciousness that there is a radical settlement to be made between Christianity and the thought and values of the modern world. . . . This settlement cannot be one of simple accommodation. In the modern period of Christianity there was an emphasis on the question, 'How can the Christian faith be made intelligible within and in harmony with the highest idealism and scientific thought of our civilization?' Now the question is, 'What is there in the Christian faith which gives us such an understanding of ourselves that we must assert out of loyalty to the Holy God above all the splendid and yet corruptible values of our civilization.' "[12]

The event, Barth tells us, that led to his break with the liberal tradition was the discovery one day in August, 1914, that almost all his revered liberal Protestant teachers in the German universities had signed a declaration issued by 93 German intellectuals supporting the war policy of Kaiser Wilhelm.[13] If the "deliverances of the religious consciousness" led to such uncritical equating of patriotic men's distorted idealism with the will of God, then there must be something terribly wrong with the whole approach to religious truth. He recalled Schleiermacher's historic sermons in support of the Prussian resistance to Napoleon. And in the 1930s, two decades after his own revolt, he was again shocked by the ease with which the so-called German Christians came to terms with Naziism, and how others justified with little dissent the harsh methods of Soviet Communism. Barth came to distrust man's subjective feelings, no matter how ideal and exalted they might seem to those who experienced them, and began to declare a truth which came from beyond the corruptible conscience of human beings. This truth he discovered in the Bible.

Barth's message—the message, so he thought, of the Christian faith—was a resounding *No* to all culture. Man in his presumption tries to save himself through his own achievements; but these achievements, magnificent as they may be, turn out to be his destruction. What interpretation of human culture could be more plausible in the light of the crisis into which the most extensive and sophisticated culture of human history—the Western world's last 300 years—had blundered?

Barth thought that this No was the most important and most neglected item in the whole catalogue of Christian thought—at least at our juncture in history. He has thunderously reasserted it in many—and voluminous—ways.

The point is that God is above man, infinitely so, and that man must accept this fact as primary. On the positive side, man's hope lies entirely in reliance on God and on his action in Jesus Christ, who descends vertically into history with the eternal Word for man. Barth turned his back on all attempts to derive the Christian message or any part of it from human culture, either ancient or modern. It is God's word, and his alone. Man's word is always death! only God's word can save.

*Sören Kierkegaard.* Barth's revolt had historical antecedents in the work of a hitherto neglected Danish theologian, Sören Kierkegaard, who lived in the middle of the nineteenth century (1183–1855). Like Dostoevsky and Nietzsche, he had diagnosed the sickness of modernity at a time when few people were prepared to believe him. He rebelled against the easy identification of Christianity with Christendom, or with philosophical systems such as Hegel's idealism that claimed to absorb the entire Christian faith without remainder into a rational scheme. He saw the authentic Christian faith as an offense to both culture and reason, a demand for a sharp either/or existential decision on the part of individuals. From this point of view, Kierkegaard developed in his numerous works an analysis of man as a being who exists in freedom and responsibility, and who therefore suffers anxiety and guilt.

He directed men back to the original offense of the Gospel when it was neither fashionable nor reasonable to be a Christian. Faith, he insisted, was not a form of rational knowledge, but an existential leap, urged upward by the full passion of the soul for its salvation, a salvation that could not come from culture, nature, or reason, but from the transcendent God alone.

He distinguished three stages in life. The first is the aesthetic stage, in which man is an observer and enjoyer of life. The second is the ethical, in which a man becomes a responsible participant by his choices and is bound by a universal ethical law. The third and highest stage is that of faith. In faith, man responds as a unique individual to God and becomes bound by the sovereign Divine Will alone. It is not hard to see why this kind of thought was rejected by a generation which had found that a religious accommodation to culture was working quite well, and who had not yet experienced the disillusioning events that have wracked the twentieth century. With the new mood in theology, Kierkegaard has become a popular figure.

*Reinhold Niebuhr.* In America the major figure in the critical return of theology to its own origins was Reinhold Niebuhr. Like Barth, Niebuhr conceived his work as a disentangling of the central biblical insights from the cultural compromises that had obscured their true meaning in both medieval and modern times. In the fifteenth century it had been the Roman Catholic synthesis of faith and culture that Luther attacked. In the present it was both what was left of this medieval synthesis in Catholicism and the new cultural synthesis in Protestantism, both liberal and orthodox, that Niebuhr conceived as the center of his attack.

It is not necessary to spell out all of what is meant by "central biblical insights," because the foregoing chapters on biblical faith and literature were written with these in mind. However, a few of Niebuhr's major ideas are eminently worth restatement. First of all, he reminded his fellow citizens of the reality of sin in human life and the limits of human achievement at its best. Sin, he wrote, is "inevitable" but not "necessary."[14] It is not necessary because it is rooted in man's use of his freedom and he is therefore responsible for it. But it is historically inevitable. Its inevitability can be best understood when sin itself is defined. Sin is man's attempt to "transmute his partial and finite self and his partial and finite values into the infinite good."[15] Sin is pride, man's turning in upon himself, establishing his life upon his own achievements. Sin takes collective form when a culture pretentiously places itself above all ethical and moral judgment, and conceives itself as first in the world. In all its forms, sin is a rebellion against God, for it attempts to substitute man in his place.

Niebuhr's special fury was reserved for those who felt that man could become "perfect." "Perfectionism" was for him a word of scorn which he did not limit to his fellow religionists. He believed that perfectionism was also the sin of secular reformers who built their programs around the moral purity of their own movements and became correspondingly blind to their own defects. He himself was an indefatigable social reformer, but he believed that man should aim realistically at a precarious balance of forces in the world and try to maintain the limited justice that could result. He exposed all utopian programs of both left and right as essentially blind to the nature of human nature.

Another insight drawn by Niebuhr from biblical sources concerned the historical nature of man's existence, the fact that the human self can only be understood historically. In a brief autobiography published in 1956, he said: "Though I have meditated on these issues for some time, I have only recently come to realize why the dramatic-historical account of the Bible . . . should give a truer view of both the nobility and misery of man than all the wisdom of scientists and philosophers. The fact is that the human self can only be understood in a dramatic-historical environment."[16]

This passage hints at a test Niebuhr was willing to employ in validation of these concepts. Though he rejected all so-called proofs of Christian wisdom, he nevertheless did believe that there was a kind of negative validation. He explored the pragmatic worth of his biblical hypothesis (if it may be so called) about human nature and history by applying it incessantly to the analysis of social and personal problems. The range of his writings is truly remarkable. The result of these explorations he summarized: "Negatively, the Gospel must and can be validated when the truth of faith is correlated with all truths which may be known by scientific and philosophical disciplines and proves itself a resource for coordinating them into a deeper and wider system of coherence."[17] This wider coherence, one of his commentators, Claude Welch, points out, "does not simply appeal to rational understanding, but merges with the power of renewed life."[18]

A more difficult but important part of Niebuhr's thought was his insistence on paradox, or, as he termed it, dialectic. The whole range of Christian insights, he said, must be understood dialectically. In a celebrated passage he wrote: "Reformation insights must be related to the whole of experience . . . dialectically. The 'yes' and 'no' of its dialectical affirmation; that the Christian is 'both sinner and righteous'; that history fulfills and negates the Kingdom of God; that grace is continuous with, and in contradiction to, nature; that Christ is what we ought to be and also what we cannot be; that the power of God is in us and that the power of God is against us in judgment and mercy; that all these affirmations which are but varied forms of the once central paradox of the relation of the Gospel to history must be applied to the experiences of life from top to bottom. There is no area of life where 'grace' does not impinge. There are no complex relations of social justice to which the love of the Kingdom of God is not relevant. There are on the other hand no areas or experiences where historical insecurity and anxiety are completely transcended, except in principle."[19]

*Paul Tillich.*   Another great figure in this Christian revival of faith is Paul Tillich (1886–1965), German theologian and philosopher who spent the greater part of his life in America. Tillich believed that human culture is not merely negative, as Barth thought, but ambiguous—that is, it contains a muted witness to the transcendent in its very agonized efforts to find meaning and release. With Barth, Tillich agreed that the saving word is from God—though he would say that this comes from the "Ground of Being" vertically upward rather than from the transcendent vertically downward. The reason for the change of metaphor is that Tillich believed that all life is inevitably grounded in God, whether it consciously affirms God or not. He held that without God there would be nothing at all; therefore, even pathetic modern man has some tenuous contact with Ultimate Being.

In saying that man's existence is ambiguous Tillich further means that all human culture raises the question of life's meaning, a question that can be answered only by God himself. The raising of the question—the very struggle of man with the experiences of guilt, anxiety, and meaninglessness—is itself a witness to the divine ground in which man's life is set.

The Christian faith, then, is a clarification of God's word to man when man asks the questions of ultimacy, questions about the meaning of his life, about the way out of guilt, about a courage that can transcend anxiety. The situation of modern man is that he has progressively cut himself off from his own ultimate ground, and only faith can show him the way back into the ground of his own being. Jesus Christ is the prime instance of man's true being, which Tillich calls "The New Being," a true man in touch with the ground of his being—God.[20]

Man, then, is understood to be ground not in himself, or in the state, or in any elaboration of his own works, but in God alone. It is this understanding which alone can bring him out of the wilderness into which he has been led by the misunderstanding of himself derived from a shallow modernity. The result of such a transformation at the base of life is a new life of faith, a life of courageous affirmation in the midst of the disruptions of guilt, anxiety, and meaninglessness, a life that leads to a new purity, serenity, and purposefulness greater than all the powers that threaten him from within or without. To quote the words of St. Paul: ". . . I am sure that neither death nor life, nor angels, nor principalities, nor things present, nor things to come, nor powers, nor height, nor depth, nor anything else in all creation, will be able to separate us from the love of God in Jesus our Lord."[21]

*Nels Ferré and Anders Nygren.* Two other contemporary theologians who have worked at this problem from a slightly different perspective, Nels Ferré and Anders Nygren, are concerned with the uniquely Christian word for God, *Agape.*[22] Though this word is translated "Love" in English, it must be differentiated from many non-Christian meanings of the word. Agape, they say, is the revealed character of God and the authoritative rule for Christian life. God is love and man is bound by that love. Divine love, however, is qualitatively different from human varieties of love. It is, says Nygren, "the transvaluation of all ancient value."[23] It can be summarized in the following way: (1) Agape is spontaneous and "unmotivated." This means that we cannot explain God's love in terms of the character of man or nature. It arises from God, out of his own holy nature. (2) Agape is "indifferent to value."

This does not add a new idea, but it makes it clear that God's love does not fall on good men alone; he loves both the sinner and the righteous man—to the same, unlimited degree. (3) Agape is creative. Nygren writes that "God does not love that which is already in itself worthy of love, but on the contrary, that which in itself has no worth acquires worth just by becoming the object of God's love. . . . Agape is a value-creating principle."[24] (4) Agape is the initiator of fellowship with God. This fellowship does not spring from man's longing for God, or his mighty efforts to rise from his human state to a divine one, but from God's overflowing goodness. "Agape is God's way to man."[25]

Ferré, who follows Nygren in his understanding of agape, realizes that unless the essential nature of the Christian message is differentiated from the many formulations that have been put forth in the name of faith, modern man will be able to reply quite rightly that it has nothing new to offer, and that, in fact, humanistic culture at its best is quite superior to the claims of faith. Despite the difficulty in doing so, the Christian must distinguish the essential from the accidental elements in historic Christianity. Agape is such an essential. God, says Ferré, is sovereign, holy, creative love, who has expressed his nature in creation, in Jesus Christ, and in the continued presence of his Holy Spirit among men. This trinitarian formulation coincides with the classic creeds of Christendom, but it is not put forth for that reason. It is affirmed because, in the opinion of these thinkers, that is the nature of God as understood in the Christian faith at its best.

*Dietrich Bonhoeffer.* Another significant figure in the restatement of the Christian faith in the twentieth century is Dietrich Bonhoeffer, a German theologian who was executed for being implicated in the plot against Adolf Hitler. Because his mature life was lived out under the most strenuous political circumstances, we have his thought chiefly from fragments of his writings smuggled out of prison by friends.[26]

Many of his insights came under the crushing impact of Nazi cruelty. "Surely," he wrote from prison, "there has never been a generation in the course of human history with so little ground under its feet as our own."[27] Like Barth before him, he noted that this "appearance of evil in the guise of light, beneficence, and historical necessity is utterly bewildering to anyone nurtured in our traditional ethical systems."[28] But he comforted himself that from the biblical perspective it simply confirms the "radical evilness of evil." Like Niebuhr, he was impressed with the naive lack of realism in rationalistic systems and thinkers: "The rationalist imagines that a small dose of reason will be enough to put the world right. . . . Disappointed by the irrationality of the world, he realizes at last his futility, retires from the fray, and weakly surrenders to the winning side."[29]

Under the pressure of his own experiences, Bonhoeffer noted that "we must form our estimate of men less from their achievements and failures, and more from their sufferings."[30] It was in this crucible of suffering that he brought forth his own deep reaffirmations of the biblical faith: "I believe that God both can and will bring forth good out of evil. For that purpose he needs men who make the best use of everything. I believe God will give us all the power we need to resist in all times of distress."[31] He realized that it was "easier to suffer in obedience to a human command (as soldiers did in battle) than to accept suffering as free responsible men."[32] The greatness of faith is that it brings man into such a relation to God that such responsible freedom is possible.

Bonhoeffer is perhaps best known for his plea for a faith without religion. Religion was for him the realm of escapes into pious attitudes and ecclesiastical preserves. Faith, on the other hand, he believed, set man squarely in the center of human existence. The world, he said, had "come of age," and had no longer any need of the sentimental protections of religion. "Man has learned to cope with all questions of importance without recourse to God as a working hypothesis. . . . it is becoming evident that everything gets along without 'God,' and just as well as before."[33] For this reason there is no reason for Christians to tilt at the intellectual structures of modern culture in the usual way. What really counts is "Christ and the newly matured world —[not] clearing a space for religion in the world or against the world."[34]

This is not easy to understand or assess, but what it appears to mean is this: The God of the Bible does not call men to a special life of religious piety, but to life in the world; not to a religious preserve but to unreserved vitality in the midst of worldly predicaments: "It is not with the next world that we are concerned, but with this world as created and preserved and subject to law and atoned for and made new. What is above the world is in the Gospel, intended to exist *for* this world."[35]

In an oft-quoted passage Bonhoeffer stated his thesis quite clearly: "God is teaching us that we must live as men who can get along very well without him. The God who is with us is the God who forsakes us (Mark 15:34). The God who makes us live in this world without him as a working hypothesis is the God before whom we are ever standing."[36] To Bonhoeffer, the only way God can make himself truly felt in the world is through suffering. In this way he can be with us and help us. This is why he himself found so much insight in contemplating Christ in his weakness and suffering as the primary mark of God's presence in nature and history, the starting point for a true understanding of life in the world.

The older concern for salvation as a way to heaven oppressed him. The faith of the Bible, he said, was not a "religion of salvation" that conceived of some life hereafter which justified life here and now. On the contrary, he believed that "The Christian hope sends a man back to his life on earth in a wholly new way. . . ."[37]

In keeping with the German experience of dividing life into the public and private sphere, Bonhoeffer had seen "God . . . driven out of the world, and from the public side of human life," and the corresponding attempt "to retain him at least in the sphere of the 'personal,' the 'innerlife,' the private life."[38] But he came to realize that "the Bible does not recognize our distinction of inner and outer. Why should it? It was always concerned with . . . the whole man. . . ." He remarked that this was why he was so "anxious that God should not be relegated to some last secret place, but that we should frankly recognize that the world and men have come of age, that we should not speak ill of man in his worldliness, but confront him with God at his strongest point, that we should give up all our clerical subterfuges, and our regarding psychotherapy and existentialism as precursors of God."[39]

With these brief summaries of major thinkers in the critical renewal of faith it should now be clear that they are not in agreement with one another at every point, and that any attempt to make a system of their various contributions would end in failure. Contemporary theology is great because it is engaged in profound debates about every matter, from the nature of God and man to the significance of the Bible and culture. The student who seriously embarks on making some of these ideas his own will discover time and again that he is shaken to the depths of his thought and life. Theology is not a dead, dull study for bearded scholars; it is a living investigation for vigorous men who would understand their existence and learn to live well in a very ambiguous world.

## THE NEW THEOLOGICAL CLIMATE

Though no adequate summary of the new theology is possible, with all its dialectical counter themes, it is feasible to indicate several ways in which it marked a shift from the era that preceded it. The major shift was, as we have said, from the practice of harmonizing faith with modern thought to a search for what is distinctive and authentic in the Christian faith as it appears in the Bible, "to set it forth in its purity," as Kenneth Cauthen says, "against all other competing faiths both ancient and modern."[40] Here are some of the major themes: skepticism concerning moral progress or human perfectibility on any kind of automatic evolutionary scheme of things, biological or historical; a realization of life's irreducible discontinuities in nature, history, culture, and personality; an appreciation of the distinctiveness of revelation over against philosophical speculation and science; a conviction concerning the distinctiveness of the Church over against other cultural institutions, and the distinctiveness of Christian experience over against "religious experience" in general; a faith in the transcendence of God, his otherness, his judgment and his grace, over against his simple presence in nature and history, with a corresponding belief in the dependence of man, a denial of his self-sufficiency in personal, social, and intellectual matters; a denial of man's autonomy, and an insistence on his radical dependence on God and on God's sovereign initiative.

Such a summary gives only the most meager suggestion of the richness and range of the new theological thought, but it should point the way into many exciting possibilities for the reinterpretation of religion.

This account might suggest to a generation suspicious of religious transcendence that contemporary theology has returned to the narrow enclosure of traditional thought. The contrary is true. With the discovery of an independent and authentic faith which is no longer a mere echo of modernity, it has been possible to embark anew upon a profound dialogue between faith and culture—the arts, literature, language, ethics, and politics—with more tangible results than formerly. The salt has regained its savor.

And, far from being self-enclosed, this new theology has become interconfessional and international. Very few theologians today work within the limitations of denominationalism. The new theology is the basis for reconsidering the meaning of the unity of Christendom. Beyond that it has laid the foundation for a more realistic dialogue with the non-Christian religions and the secular philosophies that are moving the minds of men in both the East and the West.

The leading figures in this renewed affirmation of Christian faith have been Protestants, of whom we have named only a few among many. However, Roman Catholic thought has underscored the same message in its own modern revival. Leading Roman Catholic thinkers, like Karl Adam and Christopher Dawson, hold a thesis similar to the one now familiar to us. They say that since the Renaissance man has been afflicted by a shallow rationalism cut off from both God and man. Opposing modern liberalism, Adam writes that it "behaves as though Christianity is and must be a mere object of knowledge, a mere subject for scientific investigation as though the living of the Christian faith could be resolved into a series of ideas and notions which might be examined, considered, and classified according to their prevalence and according to their relation to a supposed primitive Christianity."[41]

Space does not permit a close examination of such leading figures of modern neo-Thomistic Catholic philosophy as Étienne Gilson, Jacques Maritain, and Frederick Copelston, or the work of such contemporary theologians as Hans Küng and Cardinal Bea. These men have shown the power of Roman Catholic thought to come to grips with the fundamental issues of modern thought and to offer an affirmation of the Christian faith in terms that are of value not only to Catholics but to all men. How thoroughly their thought will permeate the massive traditionalism of the Roman Catholic Church cannot be predicted with assurance at this time.

## Contemporary Theistic Existentialists

While these developments were taking place in theology, a parallel intellectual movement was developing in philosophy. Existentialism as a philosophy emerged in our century in response to the agonizing situation into which modern man had been drawn. Its primary concern was to clarify the idea of man as an *existing* being rather than as merely a *thinking* being. Prior to existentialism, philosophy had been chiefly concerned with man as a knower of objects. Existentialism reflects on man as a chooser, sufferer, and struggler after significant existence. This philosophy had precursors in the nineteenth century, chiefly Nietzsche and Kierkegaard, who were largely disregarded in their time.

Modern existentialism is divided into atheistic and theistic camps. The leaders of the atheistic camp have been Jean-Paul Sartre and the late Albert Camus, both of whom we have had occasion to quote in the previous chapter. Their thought is valuable for the clarity with which they have delineated the tragic character of human existence apart from God. God does not exist, they say, but they do not rejoice in this fact in the manner of their atheistic predecessors, the naturalists. Atheism is a regrettable fact, they confess, and man must accept it realistically and find an authentic human existence in spite of the universal emptiness that surrounds him.

Theistic existentialism, on the other hand, represented by such thinkers as Gabriel Marcel, Martin Buber, and Karl Jaspers, claims that a truly radical examination of man's existence reveals religious or transcendent elements in human experience which the atheistic school has tragically overlooked. They  have sought to go back behind the abstractions of modern philosophy to man's full human existence.

It is their contention that when this kind of investigation is carried on rigorously man may be viewed not as a tragically orphaned being in an alien universe, but as a being who knows in the depths of his most profound experiences a ground of hope, a connection with a reality that gives him the power to be truly human. Buber says that man is fundamentally a being who exists in dialogue with other spirits like himself and with the eternal Thou who initiates and rules the human dialogue. Jaspers points out that the world of objects is merely what is before the eyes and mind, but that reality encompasses both that world and the world of the thinker himself, and is not capable of being described as a collection of mere objects after the manner of the sciences.

Existential philosophy is, to be sure, elusive to follow, but there is no reason to suppose that reality is easy to think about. These philosophers contend that the modern effort to reduce knowledge to mere sensation in order to make it manageable is a colossal mistake. A large part of the future of philosophy, in my opinion, will be taken up with the kinds of investigations that these men have initiated.

The point is this: From their own perspective, without direct benefit of revelation, the theistic existentialists have laid the groundwork for the work of theology itself and have opened up the possibility for a new departure in thought which cannot but have issue in results starkly different from modern skepticism and nihilism. This is in part the reason why Paul Tillich once said that existentialism is the "good luck of modern theology."

## Process Philosophy

Another kind of thought which seeks to speak to the condition of modern man is process philosophy—a philosophic point of view that takes its departure from a critique of the static character of traditional metaphysics, and accepts the view that dynamic change is of the essence of existence. By far the greatest name in this field is that of the English thinker Alfred North Whitehead (1861–1947), who began his career as a mathematician and consummated it by building a speculative scheme based upon the notion of change.[42] One of his most distinguished followers is Charles Hartshorne, who has spent most of his mature life detailing the significance of Whitehead's philosophy for faith.[43] Some younger theologians are trying to unite this kind of philosophy with both the new theology and existentialism. They believe that it is an analytical tool, furnishing fundamental categories of thought that will be significant in the most comprehensive kind of philosophical effort. Their hope is to construct a scheme that will make some coherent sense of the enormously disparate characteristics of the human scene, and show the relationship of these characteristics to the events of nature and the character of God as well.

### The New Naturalism

Changes of the magnitude of those that we have been examining are not limited to a single group, but can be seen manifesting themselves in almost every circle. Our survey of the reactions to the crisis of modernity would be incomplete if we did not note briefly the way in which naturalism has taken account of the new situation. While many of the heirs of naturalistic thought may have become philosophic analysts (a view of philosophy which we will have reason to explore in Chapter 21 on language), others have begun the gradual enlargement of the concept of nature to permit a much more serious taking account of value, meaning, and personality.

John Herman Randall, Jr., of Columbia University, for instance, believes that he can restate in revised naturalistic terms all the major concepts in Paul Tillich's theology.[44] Julian Huxley, the noted British naturalist, writes of his own philosophy under the title *Religion Without Revelation*.[45] A lesser known but equally competent thinker, Melvin Rader, has written most penetratingly about the naturalistic meaning of religion.[46] And certainly in the work of Albert Camus one cannot complain that human values are not taken seriously.

Among those in the social sciences who follow the guidelines of naturalistic philosophy—such men as Erich Fromm and Abraham Maslow—many important contributions have been made toward the enlightenment of modern men in their search for a truly humane existence.

It is true that from the perspective of the new theology these points of view are insufficiently grounded and therefore subject to many critical questions. Nonetheless, some of the leaders of theology—among them Reinhold Niebuhr—have proposed that it is important for religious thinkers to recognize their allies among secular thinkers. For very often, particularly in the sphere of social ideals, the new theology is more in agreement with such naturalists than with its traditional coreligionists.

A zoologist has recently written[47] that what concerns him, as it concerned the late Albert Schweitzer, is the possibility of establishing a common front for the service of man. He acknowledges that his view of man's spiritual ideals as products of evolution, social discovery, or development may not fully accord with the Judaeo-Christian tradition. However, he sees a remarkable harmony between the ideals of religious men and altruistic naturalists at their best, and bemoans the prospect of losing the strength of an alliance between them for human welfare. Certainly such an appeal should not go unanswered. Whatever the reservations of each side, the stakes are too high to neglect any resource which might speak to man's deep need for viable ideals and supply a rationale and motivation for healing the deep wounds that modernity has inflicted on modern man. And what has been said here of naturalism might well be repeated for the new developments in the non-Christian religions.

## The Reaction to Modernity in the Non-Christian Religions

Modern civilization, far from being confined to the Western regions of the world, has had such a uniquely expansive character that the whole globe, with its many ancient cultures, has found itself in the grip of the crisis that afflicts modernity. In the mid-twentieth century there is no nation which has not found its own soul deeply penetrated by the Western ethos. The most powerful emissary for Western thought is scientific technology, a mode of thought and life which is indispensable for any nation which hopes to conquer ignorance, disease, and poverty, and rise to a significant place in the family of nations. It is in this light that one must regard the phenomenal appeal of communism in Asia.

In the early stages, when the difficulties of Western civilization were first becoming apparent, non-Western countries hoped to adopt Western techniques while retaining their own traditional cultures intact. This has proved increasingly difficult, because the techniques of the West are the product of a way of thought and life which is largely inconsistent with the values and modes of thought of non-Western cultures.

Oriental thinkers have more recently come forward with less simple solutions to the crisis of modernity, cast in their own religious and philosophical terms. The most striking examples of this ideological counterattack derive from Buddhaic-Hindu sources. Sir Sarvepalli Radhakrishnan, for example, is a noted philosopher, trained in both the East and the West; as President of India, he is deeply involved with these problems, both practically and intellectually. He has put forward the Hindu Vedanta, based upon ancient scriptural sources, as the philosophy most likely to give to modern man, both East and West, a workable faith.[48] We examined in Chapter 4 the major Hindu scriptures in which this philosophy is expressed. Radhakrishnan propounds this view with immense erudition, from both ancient and modern sources. He is, moreover, a man whose personal integrity gives high plausibility to his religious and philosophical contentions. A less known, but perhaps in India an even more influential figure, is Sri Aurobindo, who retired from public life to solve precisely the problems that have concerned us. His solution he calls "Integral Yoga," a way of life combining the deep inwardness of Hindu ascetic institutions with modern active participation in the world.

Zen Buddhism is best known in America and England through the voluminous writings of the learned and wise D. T. Suzuki.[49] He inherited in Zen a religion which already had a tradition of life affirmation coupled with meditative depth.

The plausibility of these expositions of Oriental versions of religion has impressed many able scholars in the West. Such thinkers as Gerald Heard, Aldous Huxley, Alan Watts, A. E. Burtt, and Frederick Spiegelberg, can be properly classified as neo-Oriental in outlook. And many other less well-known thinkers follow them in their attempt to exploit Eastern modes of thought to meet the crisis of the West.

This is not the place for a critical confrontation of the Christian and non-Christian faiths, important as such a confrontation is. Principles for such an encounter will be suggested in a later chapter. The point of calling attention to this revival of neo-Oriental thought at this juncture is to show how the crisis of modernity has evoked a religious response in both the West and East. Both groups agree that the modern apprehension of reality as merely sensory, and the thought of the world as a collection of objects obeying scientific laws, will not do as a basis for human existence. Together they reflect an upsurge of human reaction to the critical times in which we live, a cry of faith which has not been heard in such penetrating tones since before the coming of the modern world. They may be the birth cries of an emerging new age.

In concluding this section, a basic idea that has appeared throughout must be clarified. I have referred to the "end of modernity," and have even likened it to the end of the Roman Empire. This may have conjured up images associated with Oswald Spengler's famous phrase "the decline of the West."[50] My use of the concept is different from his.[51] I do not envisage the destruction of all the major institutions of the West and the death of its populations (unless, of course, there should come a nuclear war). I have prophesied a shift from one set of basic premises to another, such as took place in the sixteenth century from medievalism to modernity. This shift will no doubt be accompanied, as it has been during the past fifty years, by social and personal disturbances on a large scale. Ours is already the bloodiest century of the past twenty-five—both absolutely and comparatively—and our people have suffered deeply the loss of significant meaning and direction in their personal existence.

As the change proceeds, no doubt, certain institutions which are now prominent will recede in importance, and others will take their place. Knowledge will move in different directions, and human resources will be allocated to different tasks. Just how or how rapidly these changes will take place is unpredictable. But if the basic assumption is correct—that the premises of modernity are outworn and are being set aside from their primary place in favor of other presuppositions about reality and value—then these results may be expected to follow. The task of contemporary man is to anticipate changes and facilitate them so that the transition will be as swift and painless as possible.

## SUGGESTIONS FOR FURTHER READING

The readings suggested in the three preceding chapters are also relevant to this one. For the new theology, however, the following works are recommended. For an overview of the new theology, the best short book is Daniel Day Williams, *What Present-day Theologians Are Thinking* (Harper & Row, 1952). A work more oriented to the effect on the Church of a theology of accommodation is Martin E. Marty's *The New Shape of American Religion* (Harper & Row, 1959). An excellent question-raiser is the work of a famous English free churchman, Leslie D. Weatherhead, *The Christian Agnostic* (Abingdon, 1965).

For the seminal work of the major theologians, see especially Karl Barth's famous *The Epistle to the Romans*. Other works of importance are Dietrich Bonheoffer's *Letters and Papers from Prison*, Eberhard Bethge, ed.; R. H. Fuller trans. (Macmillan, 1962); H. Reinhold Niebuhr, *The Nature and Destiny of Man*, 2 vols. (Scribner, 1964), Nels F. S. Ferré, *The Christian Understanding of God* (Harper & Row, 1951); Paul Tillich's monumental *Systematic Theology*, 3 vols. (University of Chicago Press, 1951, 1957, 1963); also Tillich's *Courage to Be* (Yale University Press, 1963) and his less technical account of the same concepts in his three volumes of sermons: *The Shaking of the Foundations; The New Being;* and *The Eternal Now* (Scribner, 1948, 1955, 1965).

For a good introduction to Bultmann's interpretation of the New Testament, see his two volume *Theology of the New Testament*, Kendrick Grobel, trans. (Scribner, 1954).

For existentialism, I recommend *A Kierkegaard Anthology*, Robert Bretall, ed. (Modern Library, n.d.); Karl Jasper's *Way to Wisdom* (Yale University Press, 1960); Gabriel Marcel's *Man Against Mass Society* (Gateway, Regnery, 1952); and two good summaries of the relation of this thought to theology: John Macquarrie, *An Existential Theology* (Macmillan, 1955) and David Roberts, *Existentialism and Religious Belief* (Galaxy, Oxford University Press, 1959).

For theologians interested in process philosophy, see again Ferré's *Christian Understanding of God* and W. Norman Pittenger's *The Word Incarnate: A Study of the Doctrine of the Person of Christ* (Harper & Row, 1959). Charles Hartshorne's *The Divine Relativity* (Yale University Press, 1948) is a clear statement of the process doctrine of God by the leading exponent of Whitehead's metaphysics.

The Oriental material has already been suggested in earlier chapters, but for a good book on how a great Eastern mind reacts to the crisis of modernity, see S. Radhakrishnan, *The Recovery of Faith* (Harper & Row, 1955). For the humanist reaction, let me again suggest Julian Huxley's *Religion Without Revelation*, and Henry Nelson Wieman's *The Source of Human Good* (University of Chicago Press, 1946).

## NOTES

1. Harry Emerson Fosdick, "The Church Must Go Beyond Modernism," *The Christian Century*, December 4, 1935, p. 1552.
2. *Ibid.*, p. 1549.
3. *Ibid.*, p. 1552.
4. Crane Brinton, *The Shaping of the Modern Mind* (New American Library, 1953), p. 113.
5. John Herman Randall, Jr., *Making of the Modern Mind*, rev. ed. (Houghton Mifflin, 1940), p. 385.
6. Ernest Cassirer, *The Philosophy of the Enlightenment* (Beacon Press, 1955), p. 159.
7. William James, *Pragmatism* (Longmans, 1928), p. 222.
8. Bertrand Russell, *A History of Western Philosophy* (Simon and Schuster, 1945), pp. 827–828.
9. John C. Greene, *Darwin and the Modern World View* (New American Library, 1963), p. 89.
10. Lin Yutang, ed., *The Wisdom of China and India* (Random House, 1948; Modern Library, 1955), pp. 791–792.
11. J. H. Hallowell, *Main Currents in Modern Political Thought* (Holt, Rinehart and Winston, 1950), p. 554.
12. Daniel Day Williams, *What Present-day Theologians Are Thinking* (Harper & Row, 1952), p. 12.
13. Alan Richardson, *The Bible in the Age of Science* (Westminster, 1961), pp. 88–89.
14. H. Reinhold Niebuhr, *The Nature and Destiny of Man* (Scribner, 1943), I, 242. Chapters 7 to 9 in volume I detail the author's concept of sin.
15. *Ibid.*, p. 122.
16. Quoted in Paul Ramsey, ed., *Religion* (Prentice-Hall, 1965), p. 243.
17. *Ibid.*, p. 244.
18. *Ibid.*
19. Niebuhr, *op. cit.*, II, 204.
20. Paul Tillich, *Systematic Theology* (University of Chicago Press, 1957), II, 118 ff.
21. Romans 8:38–39.
22. See Anders Nygren, *Agape and Eros* (Westminster, 1953) and Nels F. S. Ferré, *The Christian Understanding of God* (Harper & Row, 1951).
23. Nygren, *op. cit.*, p. 30.
24. *Ibid.*, p. 78.
25. *Ibid.*, p. 81.
26. Dietrich Bonhoeffer, *Letters and Papers from Prison*, Eberhard Bethge, ed., R. H. Fuller, trans. (Fontana, Collins, 1959), p. 26.
27. *Ibid.*, p. 135.
28. *Ibid.*
29. *Ibid.*
30. *Ibid.*, p. 141.
31. *Ibid.*, p. 142.
32. *Ibid.*
33. *Ibid.*, pp. 106–107.
34. *Ibid.*, pp. 108–109.
35. *Ibid.*, p. 126.
36. *Ibid.*, p. 122.
37. *Ibid.*, p. 112.
38. *Ibid.*, p. 116.
39. *Ibid.*, p. 118.

40. Kenneth Cauthen, *The Impact of American Religious Liberalism* (Harper & Row, 1962), p. 229.

41. Quoted in E. A. Burtt, *Types of Religious Philosophy*, rev. ed. (Harper & Row, 1951), p. 292.

42. The most complete account of this system is in his *Process and Reality* (Macmillan, 1929). However, for the beginning student a better reference would be his *Adventures of Ideas* (Macmillan, 1937).

43. For a comprehensive historical treatment by Hartshorne, see Charles Hartshorne and William L. Reese, *Philosophers Speak of God* (University of Chicago Press, 1953). For a more systematic and simpler treatment, see Charles Hartshorne's *The Divine Relativity* (Yale University Press, 1948).

44. See his chapter, "Naturalistic Humanism," in F. Ernest Johnson, ed., *Patterns of Faith in America Today* (Harper & Row, 1957; Collier, Crowell-Collier, 1962).

45. Julian Huxley, *Religion Without Revelation* (New American Library, 1957).

46. See especially chapter XVI, "The Spirit of Community," in Melvin Rader, *Ethics and the Human Community* (Holt, Rinehart and Winston, 1964).

47. In a letter to the author concerning the trial edition of this text.

48. Sarvepalli Radhakrishnan, "The Religion of the Spirit and the World's Need," in Paul Arthur Schlipp, ed., *The Philosophy of Sarvepalli Radhakrishnan*, pp. 5 ff., and Sarvepalli Radhakrishnan, *Recovery of Faith* (Harper & Row, 1955).

49. For a fuller knowledge of Zen, see D. T. Suzuki, *An Introduction to Zen Buddhism* (Rider, 1948).

50. See *The Decline of the West* (Knopf, 1937).

51. My view was nourished by the works of P. A. Sorokin, whose major concepts are summed up in his *Crisis of Our Age* (Dutton, 1941).

## PART FIVE

# SOCIAL AND PSYCHOLOGICAL DIMENSIONS OF RELIGION

# 15

# *Religion and Society*

The student of religion cannot avoid encounter with the social sciences that are the latest fruit of the scientific spirit. A study of them can deepen one's understanding of the dimensions of social existence and, correspondingly, of the role of religion in human life. It is for this reason that this section has been allotted to their examination. This chapter will be concerned with the light that sociology can cast upon the social function of religion. The next will deal similarly with psychology.

In Chapters 17, 18, and 19, the factual findings of social scientists will be used as a foundation for yet a different type of study: personal and social ethics in the perspective of faith. We can never be content with the purely descriptive materials of the social sciences. Men live by choosing, and choosing always goes beyond what is and invokes some standard of what ought to be.

The final chapter of this section will combine both descriptive and normative methods to deal with the specific problem of the relationship of religious groups to one another. Let us turn now to the problem of the relationship between religion and society to see how these two factors interact and affect one another.

## THREE KINDS OF QUESTIONS
## ABOUT RELIGION

Three different kinds of questions about religion, often confused with one another, need to be distinguished: (1) The descriptive question: What functions does religion perform? (2) The normative question: How well does it perform these functions, and are the results good or bad? (3) The truth question: How true are the claims which religion makes?

The behavioral sciences are chiefly concerned with the descriptive, or functional, question. But as soon as we begin to apply the findings of these sciences to practical problems, we invariably want an answer to the normative question. The example of medicine will make this clear. Once chemistry and biology are applied to medical problems, we make a natural value assumption that health is better than disease. In the same way, when we are living in a society, we must make value judgments about how well its various parts function in terms of human welfare. The fact that there is lively dispute about what constitutes good religion or a good society does not diminish the fact that we cannot operate humanly without risking this kind of value assumption.

### Some Problems in Method

The three questions mentioned above are at once independent and related. They can be investigated separately, but they presuppose one another much more than many investigators are willing to acknowledge. Paul Tillich says that "Religion is the substance of culture and culture is the form of religion."[1] If this be true, it will lead us to some truths about religion and culture that many secular investigators have overlooked. I intend to use it as a guide in full knowledge that alternative assumptions could and have been used by other scholars in their behavioral studies of religion.

Karl Marx, for instance, undertook his studies of society and religion on the assumption that religion was a fraud perpetrated upon society by the ruling classes. Sigmund Freud thought that religion was a mark of immaturity. Both these assumptions are in part correct. Religion has been used as an opiate to dull the rebellious spirit of exploited peoples, and it is closely interwoven with the neurotic complexes of many human beings. My quarrel with these assumptions is that they are incomplete. Religion could function neither as a powerful social ideology nor as a factor in neurosis unless it was more deeply grounded in human nature than Marx and Freud imagined.

I regard Tillich's assumption as a better guide, because it will give us a more reasonable clue to both the positive and negative influences of religion in culture and personality. On the assumptions of Freud and Marx, the relationships between religion and society are purely accidental and, in principle, religion might even disappear—as both of these "objective" scientists prophesied. Tillich's assumption is that the relationship between religion and society is so substantial that it will remain as long as men are human. The student can decide for himself which view is most reasonable when he has examined the evidence.

## Assumptions and Evidence

The relationship between such basic assumptions and the evidence accumulated according to the rules of the behavioral sciences is complex. Assumptions guide the search for evidence and control its systematic organization, but they are not "proved" by the evidence. On the other hand, the evidence itself must conform to empirical rules. What do these statements mean?

Milton Yinger, to whose fine work on *Religion, Society and the Individual* I shall often refer, writes: "Sociology inevitably takes a naturalistic view of religion. This is a necessary assumption, not a demonstrated truth, from which all science proceeds."[2] He is saying that from the behavioral point of view the elements of religion must be presumed to arise from the natural context of man's existence. I believe that this is one, but not the only, assumption which may be useful. It certainly should be exploited to the full. In so doing, it seeks to keep sociology within the sphere of the natural sciences, and allows it to seek completeness on its own assumptions, without invoking "nonnatural" or metaphysical elements, such as the divine. Moreover, a thoroughgoing naturalistic point of view may ferret out religious pretensions that otherwise might go unnoticed. For example, many alleged religious activities are simply a mask for economic or social interests. The naturalist sees these quite clearly, whereas the investigator who is keen on his religious presuppositions may overlook them. Nonetheless, these naturalistic assumptions taken by themselves distort what I believe to be the true nature of religion as I have defined it in an earlier chapter. Purely sensory data simply will not encompass what religion really means for man.

Having said that, however, I want to insist that when we operate with the tools of the social sciences, we are bound by rules of public evidence and cannot use beliefs about religion to settle matters of empirical fact. When, for example, we describe religious institutions or the structures of societies, we must support what we say with evidence available to men of all shades of religious or nonreligious opinion. In the final organization of this material into a coherent body of knowledge the varying assumptions again play an important role.

Rollo May, a psychotherapist interested in religious phenomena, clarifies this point: "One may gather empirical data, let us say on religion . . . from now on till doomsday, and one will never get any closer to understanding these activities if, to start with, his presuppositions shut out what the religious person is dedicated to . . . naturalistic presuppositions may uncover many facts about religion, but, as in Freud's terms, religion will always turn out to be more or less a neurosis, and what the genuinely religious person is concerned with will never get into the picture at all."[3]

In the light of these observations the question arises, How, if not through scientific method, will we be able to distinguish a true account of religion from a false one? The answer to that question, I believe, is simply this: The truest account is the one that is the most coherent; that is, the one that makes the most total sense about man and his activities as a whole. And this is, of course, a philosophical standard, not a scientific one.

Let there be no mistake; I am saying that science is not able to give us a final judgment on religion. It is an unmatched tool for collecting data and for revealing facts that might otherwise be concealed, but since it inevitably depends, like all human thought, upon philosophic assumptions that it cannot certify with its own methods . . . we need not grant it final authority.[4] Any quarrel I might have with the social scientists, then, will not be with their factual statements, provided they are accurate; it will be with their nonscientific or philosophical and religious interpretations of the data. If, therefore, I occasionally invoke theological concepts in this study, it is because in my opinion they alone provide the means for understanding certain elements in human behavior and experience. With this understanding, let us now turn back now to an account of the relationship between religion and society.

## TWO LEVELS OF INTERACTION BETWEEN RELIGION AND SOCIETY

To understand the relationship between religion and society it is necessary to distinguish two levels of interaction. One mode of interaction between religion and society is between the religious institutions of a culture and its secular institutions—between its churches, on one side, and its government, economy, family, and so on, on the other.

A second mode of interaction is between the often unstated, and even unconscious, assumptions about reality and value that characterize a culture, on the one hand, and its typical institutions, on the other. This could be called the level of implicit ontology—the society's tacit estimate of the nature of reality, or, in the term we have used to define religion, its ultimate concern.

A brief analysis of the nature of a human society will enable us better to understand this rather complex second mode of interaction. Society is not merely a collection of unrelated parts; it is a complex system. It maintains itself as a system because of a fundamental consensus about values among the majority of its members. Behavior in society is coordinated by a system of norms, prescriptions (things to be done), and proscriptions (things not to be done). Without such norms there could be no society at all. As the great sociologist Émile Durkheim said: "[Society] really turns out to be a system of normative rules backed by sanctions. . . . The social milieu involves . . . a common system of ultimate-value attitudes."[5]

The relationship between this theory of culture and the earlier definition of religion should be plain: If religion is a matter of ultimate concern, and society is a "common system of ultimate-value attitudes," then it follows that

Tillich's view of religion as "the substance of culture, and culture [as] the form of religion" makes good sense. It makes even more sense when we realize that Durkheim's assertion about culture and ultimate-value attitudes is not an isolated opinion, but represents a widely held sociological judgment.[6] To quote one more social scientist, P. A. Sorokin: Each of the vast cultural systems is based upon some " 'major premise' . . . which the civilization articulates, develops, and realizes in all its main compartments, or parts, in the process of its life-career."[7]

An implicit ontology, then, is that tacit assumption about the nature of what is real and what is valuable that constitutes the major premise upon which social institutions are founded.

## The Function of Religion as Implicit Ontology

Let me now spell out more completely the function of religion at this level of implicit ontology. At this level, religion, as society's reality-value premise, provides the basic gound plan for the society as a whole. This ground plan is in no sense dictated by the religious institutions. They may or may not accept the premises. It is the unconsciously accepted way in which reality is perceived by the vast majority of the members of the society. In turn, this basic perception, or reality-value judgment, articulates itself throughout the major institutions. Let us see how.

*Government and Law.* In an integrated society government has a status which we call legitimate. That is, it is recognized by its members as possessing the right to be obeyed within its proper jurisdiction. The state, to be sure, possesses a monopoly of force, but it does not and cannot rest upon this power. As Tallyrand once said, "You can do everything with bayonets but sit on them." The power itself must coincide with rightful use in the judgment of the members of the state. Religion, as the implicit consensus about ultimate values, is the source of political legitimacy and hence of legal order. A usurper—whether a single individual or group—must very soon make a connection between his power and the convictions of the people, or his regime will be short-lived. Religion performs this function in an entirely "self-enforcing" way. It acts by virtue of its presence in the personality structures of the members of the state. As the social-psychologists say, the norms and values of a society are interiorized by the members of the group. They thus obey the state out of conviction, not merely out of fear. Without this ground plan of conviction, the state would not long exist.

*The Economic Order.* Economic systems are concerned with the production and distribution of scarce goods. This requires numerous agreed priorities in the allocation of wealth and effort. Serious disputes over these matters could quickly destroy any society. Where a society is a going concern, we can, by analysis, detect the underlying value consensus. It expresses itself in such matters as the value attached to property and work, and the rules controlling the proper distribution of goods.

*Mores and Morals.*   The customs and morals of a people are generally felt by them to be as permanent and real as the natural world about them. They accept these forms of behavior and judgment because they share the underlying implicit ontology. All the institutions of society swim in a sea of custom and traditional moral approbation. They are the implicit ontology made visible.

*Social Stratification.*   All societies are stratified in such a way that some members of the group have higher status and privileges than others. This is acceptable only because it concurs with the agreed values. The respect accorded members of a higher status group, Supreme Court Justices, for example, is derived from a deep sense of appropriateness. The Brahmin of India is accepted as possessing, by right, his preeminence in the Hindu social order because of the Hindu reality-value consensus.

*The Family.*   Human marriage is not merely a natural mating arrangement; it is always related to the most sacred values of the community. All societies have strict rules about mating that exemplify their ultimate concerns. It is for this reason that marriage is a public affair and is celebrated by appropriate announcements and rituals. Historical experiments that treat marriage casually, as in the early Russian Soviets, founder on the recurring human conviction that this fundamental institution must be grounded in the ultimate values of the community.

*The Arts.*   We have seen earlier that art is the mirror of man in a given society. No other institution so perfectly reflects the basic apprehension of reality current in a society than the arts of that culture. If custom is the implicit ontology made visible in human behavior, the arts are that ontology made visible in sensuous form. A history of art is a faithful reflection of the changing assumptions about existence which men in successive epochs have entertained.

*The Sciences.*   I am using the word sciences here for all the cognitive, or knowledge-getting, institutions of a culture. The lengthy treatment of modernity in Part IV of this book is an illustration of this point: that the presuppositions of the sciences, philosophies, and theologies of a society reflect the ontological premises that are current in that society at the time. The ontological premises of "modernity," as we have denoted them, made for strong natural sciences and weak theologies, because they were congenial to the former and all but contradictory to the latter.

### The Institutional Function of Religion

All the institutions of society—during a period of high cultural integration—express the basic ontological premises, or ultimate concern, of its members. They are the "form," as Tillich says, of the "substance" that is religion. This is, of course, religion at a level logically prior to its special institutionalization in a church. But religion itself always becomes institutionalized and takes its place alongside the other institutions of society. As a separate institution, it interacts with society in many ways, some of which are harmonious with the account we have just completed, some counter to it. It is this varied interaction that we must now consider.

Every historic religion is characterized by a creed, a cultus, a code, a church, and a culture. P. D. Devanandan, of India, writes: "These may be regarded as forming a series of concentric circles. Each one of them takes years to gather form and content, and together they constitute what we call 'the religion of a people.' "[8]

A religion's creed is a set of accepted beliefs that are standard for the group. Its cultus is a pattern of worship and prayer proper to the celebration of the religion's conception of ultimate concern. The code is a body of rules regulating conduct deemed proper and right. The church is a social organization with regulations that specify the meaning of membership, the proper function of its clergy, its rationale of social activity, and the numerous other features that a full-fledged social institution requires. The religious culture is the broad aura of life and action that gradually grows around these nuclear institutions and gradually becomes a full-fledged way of life, often merged indistinguishably with the historic secular culture in which it resides.

Social scientists have made many comparative studies of each of these phases of the concrete manifestation of religion in culture. We cannot examine them all. As an example of their work, let us look at the various forms that churches have taken within Western culture. Social scientists have specified five different types.[9]

*The Universal Church.* A universal church is one that corresponds in function almost completely to the implicit ontology described above; that is, its institutional expression is universal for the society in which it appears, so that all institutions share in the life of the church. In medieval times the economic, political, familial, artistic, and cognitive orders all found congenial expression through the institution of the Roman Catholic Church. In Western history this is perhaps the only moment when such a moving equilibrium between church and society was achieved.

*The Ecclesia.* This church is not as successful as the universal church in incorporating all the divergent religious interests of a complex society. As Yinger says, "It has become so well adjusted to the dominant elements [of the society] that the needs of many of its adherents, particularly from the lower classes, are frustrated."[10] Examples of such churches are the state churches in Scandinavia, which share the field with numerous small sects, popular among the lower classes.

*The Class Church or Denomination.* The denomination, like the above churches, parallels the existing social order, but only in a limited way—by class, race, or region. A denomination's relationship to the secular power structure is revealed in the distribution of its members in the class structure. In the United States 90 percent of a lower class group, like the Negro Protestants, for example, belong to strictly Negro denominations that have practically no connection with the community power structure. Their religious classification coincides with their class deprivation. By contrast, a quarter of all Episcopalians and Congregationalists belong to the upper class, where wealth and power lie. Only 8 percent of the Baptists are in this class. The Methodist Church represents a broad middle band with about half of its people in the lower class, 35 percent in the middle class, and 13 percent in the upper class.

It is worth noting that the number of college graduates within a denomination parallels the rank order of that particular group at nearly every point. This is all the more significant when we consider that a college degree is one of the chief tickets to status in the United States.

*The Sect.* The sect is smaller than any of the previously noted types. It originates in a protest movement away from a church or denomination. It has a sharper definition of membership and keeps closer watch over the beliefs and behavior of its members. If the sect persists for very long it either grows into a denomination (an example of this is the Church of God, which is now bidding for denominational status), or it becomes what is called an "established sect." An example of this is the Quakers who since the sixteenth century have remained small, and faithful to their original peace witness. The Pentecostal groups are at present best classified as sects.

*The Cult.* A cult, like the sect, is small, but its nature is in other ways different. It lacks organizational structure and inner discipline. It is usually dependent on the presence of a charismatic leader and tends to break up after his or her death. The members are usually motivated by a search for some inner mystical experience or secret knowledge. They may later become assimilated into larger groupings of religion—or they may already be nominal members of the larger groups while enjoying membership in the cult.

These five forms illustrate the variety of religious organization even within one culture. If we were to attempt a similar analysis of India, the forms would be quite different. Hinduism, to be sure, has expressed itself in social organization, and possesses its creeds, codes, and cults, like all others. But in a strict sense the word church hardly fits the facts of Hinduism at all, unless it be used to stand for the bare notion of social organization as such.

Let us turn now to the specific functions of institutional religion. For purposes of simplicity they can be divided into two: the priestly, or conservative, functions; and the prophetic, critical, or creative functions.

## The Priestly, Conservative, Functions of Religious Institutions

*Celebrator of Shared Values.* The first of the priestly functions is to provide public opportunities for the celebration by the community of its shared values. The great symbols and ceremonies of religion are the means for this celebration. They are used in collective worship to remind the community of its reality-value commitments. In this sense it functions to strengthen the cement of the social order and to maintain its existence. Since, in our time, the quasi religions of the state are the nearest thing to a universal church, we can perhaps best appreciate this function of worship by recalling patriotic celebrations, such as Memorial Day[11] or the Fourth of July. On such occasions, work is suspended, the flag is displayed, speeches are given, and fanfare, parades, and fireworks make vivid to the beholder the community's feeling for shared traditions and values.

*Culture Bearer and Transmitter.* With every generation fresh life pours like a river into a community. If the society is to persist, these new members must be brought into sympathy with the society's basic reality-value premises. The church helps perform this educational function. It does this partly through formal teaching, but more typically through the means just described. Early and late, the church surrounds the individual with ceremonies that give significance to the transitional moments of human existence: birth, puberty, marriage, death. The universal rites of religion focusing on these transitional moments have been called the *"rites de passage."* Through infant rites, the newborn infant is acknowledged as a member of the spiritual community; at puberty he is given status as a new adult; at marriage he becomes sanctified as a householder; and at death his decease is solemnized in such a way that his personal importance is noted and the living are heartened to return to the necessary business of ordinary life. In addition to these rites, there are the weekly, monthly, and seasonal rhythms of regular worship—all serving in their own way the same ends. It is interesting to note how the quasi religions of communism or statism have adopted these same methods to underscore the values typical of their own views of community life.

*Maintainer of Personal and Social Morale.* The personal existence of the members of society is threatened by events that religion alone can make bearable. Social training, for example, inevitably induces a considerable amount of personal guilt. Competition with one's fellows arouses antisocial hostilities. Suffering, in the form of sickness, frustration, and personal loss, is common to the human lot. In modern industrial societies, loneliness and meaninglessness are additional widespread forms of suffering. But the greatest of these threats is death, anticipated in the passing of relatives and friends, and intruding a dread prospect, universally accompanied by pain and questioning. In most societies, religion provides ways of assuaging these experiences of guilt, hostility, suffering, and existential doubt, thus maintaining the morale necessary for continued social cooperation.

Milton Yinger makes this point clear when he defines religion as "the system of beliefs and practices by means of which a group of people struggles with . . . [the] ultimate problems of human life."[12] In that definition he supports what I have been saying about the function of religion as a maintainer of social morale. Following the lead of the great anthropologist Bronislaw Malinowski, Yinger writes: "A society that did not furnish its members with beliefs and practices that sought to deal with these ultimate problems would struggle along with an enormous burden of tragedy unallayed and hostility unrestrained—if indeed it could survive at all."[13]

*Facilitator of Religious Experience.* Religious institutions facilitate and channel religious experience by providing structures for the individual's expression of his religious needs, giving him the means for expressing his sense of awe, unworthiness, aspiration, and devotion in ways that have been tested in the course of history, and that will support rather than destroy the community life. Man's religious needs, as I have implied throughout this study—and shall have reason to underscore again—are integral to his nature and will find expression in one way or another. If these needs are ignored, they may be expressed in wild and antisocial ways that could tear the society into pieces. If the religious institutions are healthy, both the persons and the society are served through cultural patterning.

*Social Control.* No society can exist without widespread obedience to the rules of the social order. Religious institutions, as celebrants of the prevailing social values, tend to give divine sanction to the sustaining morals and customs of the society. In this way they serve to mitigate the conflicts of interest, the hostilities, and the egocentric drives that inevitably occur in social life. Since, in its conservative role, religion tends to ally itself with the dominant class of the secular power structure, it tends to support the values and directives of that class, commanding obedience even among the lower classes whose real secular interests may lie in quite other directions.

Since this is a major issue in the sociology of religion, let us consider some important examples. During the late-nineteenth century, Protestantism in the United States became all but completely identified with the dominant middle class. Henry F. May writes that in "1876 Protestantism presented a massive, almost unbroken front in its defense of the social status quo."[14] The words of Liston Pope from another study can be applied with equal truth to this situation: "At no important point did they [the Protestant churches] stand in opposition to the prevailing economic arrangements or to drastic methods employed for their preservation."[15] Yet during the period between 1881 and 1894 there were 14,000 strikes and lockouts in the United States, involving four million workers.[16] The extent of the conflict suggests a class war of extensive dimensions, and the churches were clearly on the side of the middle class. The same story is told in Richard Hofstadter's excellently documented work *Social Darwinism in America.*

A second example is taken from contemporary America. Since the nineteenth century, Protestantism has come to share the field with Roman Catholicism, and in the process even the small minority represented by Judaism has achieved social acceptance. At the same time, religion has enjoyed, in the mid-twentieth century, a considerable popular revival. The American Institute of Public Opinion reports that 97 percent of Americans identify themselves with one or another of the major religious groups.[17] Will Herberg contends, in his *Protestant, Catholic, and Jew*, that this revival can be best understood as the search for cultural identity on the part of Americans. Since the cessation of the vast immigrations that marked the nineteenth century, America has been assimilating its diverse population. In this process, third-generation immigrants have turned back to the religious affiliations from which they loosened their ties during the period in which they were trying hard to establish themselves as Americans. Now that these minorities have achieved social acceptance they are seeking for more specific self-identification within the broad culture of America, and have correspondingly returned to their traditional religions. As Marcus Hansen has graphically said, "What the son wishes to forget, the grandson wishes to remember."[18]

In this return to religion the keynote has been tolerance. It has been accompanied by the maxim that all the traditional faiths are truly American. But this very tolerance, says Yinger, suggests that the key values are not religious, but cultural. As Herberg puts it: "It is the American Way of life that supplies American society with an 'over-arching sense of unity' amid conflict. It is the American Way of life about which Americans are admittedly and unashamedly 'intolerant!' It is the American Way of life that provides the framework in terms of which the crucial values of American existence are couched. By every realistic criterion the American Way of life is the operative faith of the American people."[19]

In these two examples we can see a problem for religious institutions. If they are to perform the function of social control, they must ally themselves with, and be prepared to underwrite, the dominant values of the culture which they serve. But in so doing they may very well lose their distinctive quality as independent spokesmen for the divine. If the prevailing social values are in harmony with the church's own values, this loss will not be apparent. However, even in this case, the blurring of the distinction between social approval and religious approval may make the prophetic work of religion (which we will discuss below) all but impossible.

Some critics of religion are prepared to say that this function of religion as social control relegates religion to a sanctimonious supporter of the prevailing secular powers. If we were to follow them, we would have to advise religious institutions to abandon this function altogether. This, however, would be to deny that religion can ever be responsible for a society, or supportive of its main institutions. It would relegate religion to its critical function only. Perhaps this would be a gain for the vitality of religion, but it would certainly amount to a serious curtailing of the functions it has performed throughout history in most of the major cultures of the world. It would mean that the major decisions in a society—those bearing on social and economic justice, peace, and general human welfare—would be made entirely outside the sphere of religion. Whether that would be a clear gain is questionable.

What is not questionable, however, is that a religion that has become completely identified with its priestly role as cultural conserver is at best a fragmentary and probably moribund faith.

## The Prophetic, Critical, and Creative Functions of Religion

The massive evidence of religion's identification with socially approved values in a variety of cultures has suggested to some scholars that religion never performs a significant creative role in culture, that it is always a follower of trends initiated by other cultural forces. I do not believe that this is the case. It seems clear that in the history of faith there have been moments when the initiative in social change has come from religious forces, and that even its function as cultural conserver depends on the respect it has gained in these epochs of prophetic faith.

I have already called attention to the so-called axial period in religion (Chapter 3), when the religious consciousness changed so decisively across the globe that it became thereafter a new species of faith. Most of the universal humane ideals that today are normative for modern man at his best—justice, freedom, peace, and the value of individuals—are derived from the faiths of that era. To be sure, these ideals are distorted, rationalized, and perverted to support institutions (such as irresponsible national power or racial segregation) that are at odds with those ideals, but they nonetheless continue to affect human history. And institutions at odds with them find it progressively harder to maintain themselves in the forum of world opinion.

Creative periods of faith—such as those of the eighth-century Hebrew prophets (Amos, Micah, Hosea), the first-century formation of the Christian Church, the Protestant and Catholic reformations of the sixteenth century, or the eighteenth-century evangelical revival in England[20]—have had such an enormous impact upon the political, economic, and social life of subsequent cultures that it would be fatuous to deny their initiatory power.

What often obscures this influence is that from the moment religious ideals become institutionalized, they become inevitably and inextricably involved in the multiform compromises and complexities of social life, with all its other interests. It is easy, then, to study them in their compromised institutional form, and to conclude that they are merely reflections of nonreligious social forces. But this kind of transformation can be observed in all areas where creativity takes place. For example, a scientific invention, which could not have come about without someone's creative work, can be treated as a more or less inevitable outcome of social forces already at work. The phenomenon of simultaneous invention seems to suggest this conclusion.

The same can be said of the history of art. In fact, art history written from the social point of view makes it appear that the fluctuating art styles are purely social products, as though all the works of art happened automatically. This must be set down as a distortion that occurs when the sociological method of investigation is taken as a complete account of man's life.

The fact is that religion performs a creative role. Sometimes, in periods of religious flowering, this role is predominant. But even in relatively conservative periods it cannot be denied that religion inspires men to elevate their ethical standards, and leavens their social life with the inspiration that springs from faith. It may be very difficult to sort out this factor as a distinct variable, but it is nonetheless there. To conclude otherwise would be to make nonsense of the entire creative dimension of human existence, both religious and secular.

Even with respect to such conservative religious groups as the Southern Baptists, for example, it would be an oversimplification to say that they merely support the prevailing social values of their region. A more accurate account would point out that they suffer a serious tension between certain universalist and humanitarian elements in their faith and their cultural commitments to social institutions that contradict them. On the point of race, for instance, their Convention debates reveal a continuing dialogue between the ardent missionary programs to the colored peoples of the world and the practice of religious segregation in their own American churches. The prophetic element may not prevail at many points, but it is there as a factor when decisions are made. And it can be predicted that as long as that universal prophetic element remains, the Southern Baptists cannot be at peace with their present social and cultural practices.

## A Pathology of Religion

Pure science has little or on place for judgments of values. Its primary function is description. However, the moment we begin to apply our scientific knowledge of practical affairs, we must appeal to standards. We have already used the example of medicine. What follows is a brief account of what, in my opinion, is a pathology of religion. The value standards assumed have already received some accounting and will be made clearer in Chapter 17 on ethics. I shall not defend them here. Suffice it to say that if the assumed value norms are not acceptable, the following catalogue would have to be changed accordingly. In general, we can say that religion becomes pathological when it fails to strike a balance between the priestly and the prophetic spirit—becoming either too identified with culture or too remote from life to promote human welfare.

The following are characteristic aspects of a religion that has failed in one way or another to perform the function proper to its own sphere.

*Arrested Development.* The history of religion reveals, as I have tried to show in Chapter 3, a dialectical development, and some religions never evolve into their promised fullness. In fact, a religion may degenerate. Such seems to be the case with Taoism in China and Zoroastrianism[1] (the modern Parsee religion) in India. From being prime examples of axial religion in the sixth century B.C., they have returned to earlier forms of culture-religion.

*Institutional Hardening.* A religious institution that once served the needs of a culture may become rigid and incapable of change. This usually results from the temptation to make an idol of it—as though the institution itself were the ultimate concern. When this situation prevails, freedom and creativity disappear. Novel ideas in either religion or the other departments of culture are perceived as threats to the sacred establishment. A dangerous policy of forced suppression, invoking, if possible, the powers of the state, is embarked upon. This usually increases the doubts about the religion already latent in the culture, and leads eventually to its overthrow. Russian Orthodoxy prior to the Revolution is an example of this state of affairs.

*Idolatrous Identification with a Social System.* When a religion becomes completely identified with the culture in which it lives, it, in effect, makes that society its ultimate concern. This I have called culture-religion. It can be justified as a natural stage in the development of religion, but unless outgrown it is fatal to both the society and the religion. Yet this cultural identification is perhaps the chief temptation of the higher religions, especially when they are surrounded by many of the fruits of their own early creativity.

*Irrelevance.* Religion can become narrowed to so small a segment of human life that it no longer has relevance to the ongoing life of a culture, or to the lives of its own adherents. It loses in this way its power to relate the whole of life to its proper ultimate concern, and so becomes merely a competing private interest among the other interests of life. In effect, it becomes a pseudo religion. Numerous small sects fall into this category.

*Ecclecticism and Spiritual Promiscuity.* At the far end of the scale from this irrelevance is the faith that has lost its own inner coherence in the process of adding bits and pieces from every source. As a mere collection of beliefs and practices, it offers no coherent meaning and life orientation. It leads its adherents into a kind of spiritual promiscuity that may be temporarily exciting, but is in the long run enervating. This is an ever-present danger to men in a global age where they are surrounded by the exotic fruits of so many alien cultures. At first this ecclecticism may even appear in the guise of a wise universalism. But it buys breadth at the expense of depth, and loses its own soul.

*Divisiveness.* In the sixteenth and seventeenth centuries, which ran red with the blood of religious partisans killing and torturing one another in the name of God, Western culture experienced the full horror of religiously induced conflict. If the great boon that religion brings to a culture when it is healthy is a strong sense of true community, the curse that it brings in its pathological state is bitter divisiveness. And there is no division so hard to heal as that created out of religiously inflamed consciences.

*Descent into the Occult and Magic.* When religion becomes obsessed with a desire for hidden knowledge—"secrets of the universe"—and the magical control that allegedly follows from this knowledge, it quickly degenerates, leaving behind all remnants of healthy faith. The magical is always near the surface of human consciousness, and pride coupled with fear readily invokes it unless checked by the realities of a healthy faith.

Back of this brief account of the pathology of religion is the assumption that religion at its best would promote a culture that was at once universal and particular—coexistensive with mankind and at the same time rooted in the particularities of local conditions. It would accomplish this by focusing on an ultimate concern that is truly Ultimate; that is, worthy of the complete devotion of mankind. It goes without saying that such an Ultimate could not be the possession of any one individual or any group—but would be the Reality that grasps men totally as, and when, it reveals itself.

Such, in brief, is an account of our subject from the standpoint of the sociology of religion. Of course, many important topics have been omitted and many subtleties avoided, but enough has been said to suggest how important and revealing a social approach to religion can be.

We turn for fresh clues now to another of the social sciences: the psychology of religion.


## SUGGESTIONS FOR FURTHER READING

The best single work of commentary and readings on the sociology of religion is J. M. Yinger, *Religion, Society and the Individual* (Macmillan, 1957). His small paperback on the same subject is *Sociology Looks at Religion* (Macmillan, 1963). For a theoretical account of sociology that makes place for religion, see the works of the noted sociologist Talcott Parsons. An older classic in this field is Joachim Wach, *The Sociology of Religion* (University of Chicago Press, 1944).

For Tillich's profound comments on culture, see his *Protestant Era* (University of Chicago Press, 1948). Two important books on this same theme by another great theologian are H. Richard Niebuhr, *The Social Sources of Denominationalism* (Holt, Rinehart and Winston, 1929) and *Christ and Culture* (Harper Torchbooks, Harper & Row, 1956). The more recent work of Will Herberg, *Protestant, Catholic, and Jew* (Anchor, Doubleday, 1956), will interest the beginning student.

R. H. Tawney's *Religion and the Rise of Capitalism* (New American Library, 1926) is a fine account of the interrelationship between economics and religion. A more general work is William Warren Sweet, *American Culture and Religion* (Southern Methodist University Press, 1951).


## NOTES

1. Paul Tillich, *Protestant Era* (University of Chicago Press, 1948), p. vii.

2. J. M. Yinger, *Religion, Society and the Individual* (Macmillan, 1957), p. 309.

3. Rollo May, ed., *Existential Psychology* (Random House, 1961), p. 33.

4. Classic statement of this point appears in Max Weber's famous essay "Science as a Vocation" in H. H. Gerth and C. Wright Mills, trans. and eds., *From Max Weber* (Oxford University Press, 1946), pp. 129 ff., esp. p. 143.

5. Émile Durkheim, *Elementary Forms of the Religious Life* (G. Allen, 1915), p. 709.

6. See, for example, the work of Talcott Parsons and Lloyd Warner, among others.

7. P. A. Sorokin, *Social Philosophies of an Age of Crisis* (Beacon Press, 1950), p. 277.

8. P. D. Devanandan, *Christian Concern in Hinduism* (Christian Institute for the Study of Religion and Society, Bangalore, India, 1961), p. 10.

9. Yinger, *op. cit.*, lists these types, pp. 144 ff.

10. *Ibid.*, p. 148.

11. See Lloyd Warner's treatment of Memorial Day as a religious celebration in *The Family of God* (Yale University Press, 1961), pp. 257 ff.

12. Yinger, *op. cit.*, p. 9.

13. *Ibid.*, p. 10.

14. Quoted in *ibid.*, p. 227.

15. Liston Pope, *Millhands and Preachers* (Yale University Press, 1942), pp. 330–331.

16. Yinger, *op. cit.*, p. 220.

17. *Ibid.*, p. 279. For various polls giving the religious spectrum of the American people, see Will Herberg, *Protestant, Catholic, and Jew* (Anchor, Doubleday, 1960), esp. pp. 46 ff., 72 ff., 76, 91 ff., 219 ff., and 225–229.

18. Quoted in Herberg, *op. cit.*, p. 30.

19. *Ibid.*, p. 75.

20. For a study of the impact of the evangelical revival on the English-speaking world, see J. Wesley Bready, *England Before and After Wesley* (Hodder & Stoughton, 1939).

21. See John B. Noss, *Man's Religions*, 3rd ed. (Macmillan, 1956) for documentation.

# 16

# *Religion and Personality*

Harvard psychologist Gordon Allport defines psychology of religion as the effort to portray "the place of subjective religion in the structure of personality whenever and wherever religion has such a place."[1] In 1934, Canon Streeter wrote of psychology that "for the student of religion it will soon, I believe, be recognized as the most important of the sciences."[2] That promise, for several understandable reasons, has been delayed. Aside from a few books such as William James' great *Varieties of Religious Experience* (1901) and J. B. Pratt's *Religious Consciousness* (1923), both written before Streeter's prophecy, no really important psychological studies of religion have appeared until quite recently. And these have come not as standard studies of religious experience as such, but obliquely from an interest in other subjects, chiefly psychotherapy and existentialism.

These latter have turned to the subject of religion through having to come to grips with the profound problems of human existence. At present it looks as though this approach is likely to elucidate the nature of faith more decisively than a strict analysis of so-called religious experience as such. It is not that the latter approach is unimportant, but that it receives its decisive importance from the more embracing context of the human venture.

Two reasons can perhaps largely account for the relative sterility of the older approach. Psychology, as a new discipline, was enthusiastically bent on establishing itself as a science, and correspondingly focused its investigations

257

upon those features of human experience that were the most amenable to the experimental techniques then available. These experiences were on the whole remote from the interests of religion. Hadley Cantril and Charles Bumstead say that even today academic psychology is inclined to leave so much of human experience out of account that "many books which deal with 'human nature' at the level of scientific conceptualization do not seem to ring true."[3]

The second reason for the sterility of psychological studies of religion is that religious leaders were not friendly to a scientific exploration of their sacred precincts. Where this attitude did not prevail, religion was so bent on modernizing itself that the distinctive elements in faith were concealed even from its practitioners.

Recent changes in both psychology and religion have made a renewed scientific exploration into the relationship between religion and personality an exciting possibility. A sampling of these studies is the concern of this chapter. But before we can begin such sampling it is important to make a distinction between two trends within psychology, one of which, in my opinion, bids fair to outstrip the other in illuminating the meaning of religion.

## TWO TRENDS IN PSYCHOLOGY

There are two diverse trends within psychology. The first emphasizes the study of those aspects of human beings that they share with nonhuman organisms. The second is concerned with those aspects of human beings that are typically and irreducibly human.

The first type of psychological investigation grew up around the assumptions and experimental techniques that are chiefly suitable for studying behavior that is clearly related to biological processes. Its assumptions are causal-deterministic: Every event must be explained by reference to stimuli that excite the human nervous system in a determinate way. This is sometimes referred to as stimulus-response psychology, S-R for short. Its advocates hold that since human behavior is merely animal behavior of a complex kind, and since the lower animals can be more conveniently studied experimentally, psychology should focus on this area. The findings of this research are then extended to apply to human beings.

We can summarize the characteristics of this psychology as follows: It favors reductionist explanations of human behavior in terms drawn from animal behavior. It seeks to make all its inquiries experimental in a laboratory sense of the word. And it holds up the standard of objectivity familiar to the physical scientist, who assumes that the best way to study behavior is from the outside. As B. F. Skinner, one of the major exponents of this approach, has written: Science is the "power to influence, change, mould—in a word control—human behavior."[4] Further explaining his view, Skinner writes: "Man's vaunted creative powers . . . his capacity to choose and our right to hold him responsible for his choice—none of these is conspicuous in this new self-portrait [provided by science] . . . only another name for behavior for which we have not found a cause."[5]

The second kind of psychology has grown up around the conviction that human behavior has a distinctness from its subhuman analogues that requires different assumptions and methods. Within the past quarter-century this kind of psychology has been developed by men who, like Gordon Allport, were interested in personality theory; by gestaltists like Kurt Lewin; by transactionalists like Hadley Cantril; and by those who, like Carl Rogers, were forced to work with whole human beings in psychotherapy.

This latter group, concerned as they were with human beings working their way back from neurotic or psychotic states into satisfactory humanness, evolved an entirely different model of human nature to guide their work. In doing so they drew upon the more theoretical and experimental work of the personalists and gestaltists. Causal-deterministic assumptions proved to be of little help, because they merely revealed the causes of the patient's condition, leaving all hopes for change dependent upon the environment that produced him. To explain a person's existence in this way merely worsens the feelings of helplessness and alienation that are aspects of the illness. Only an appeal to the individual as free and responsible, capable of turning to a more liberated existence, helps him in such situations. The causal assumption was thus replaced by an assumption of freedom and responsibility.

For the same reason, the stimulus-response mechanism was replaced by the person's grasp of the meaning of his whole situation. S-R explanations leave the person at the mercy of his stimuli. A grasp of meaning opens to the person a world of free and responsible action. Instead of remaining a re-actor, he realizes himself as an agent.

In this kind of psychology, investigative techniques changed: objective laboratory methods of the S-R type were exchanged for a participant-observer relationship, using therapist-patient interaction as a model. A therapist cannot be a mere observer. He must to some extent enter the whole situation of the patient and interact with him in his effort to become fully human again. As Rollo May states it, the fundamental unit is not the patient's "problem" but rather "two-persons-existing-in-a-world, the world at the moment being represented by the consulting room of the therapist."[6]

This type of psychology is, then, nonreductionist, taking human behavior as it is in its wholeness and totality. It is clinical rather than experimental, and it replaces laboratory objectivity with the stance of the participant-observer.

A full elaboration of this second kind of psychology leads to applications transcending the clinical situation in which it was first discovered. It lays the foundation for a psychological investigation of human experience in its typically human dimensions. In contrast to the experimentalist's emphasis upon infrahuman, animal behavior, the existential psychologist seeks an understanding of noetic behavior—behavior that is characteristic of human beings as human beings.

The distinction between these two psychologies, objective and existential, has a great bearing on the study of religion and personality. For religion is a typically human enterprise completely missing from infrahuman behavior. Its nature is obscured by attempting to grasp it in S-R terms. This remark applies not merely to religion. It applies to all the noetic dimensions of human experience: logical thought, creativity, love, personal growth, aesthetic appreciation, and the psychological dimensions of culture.

Representatives of this type of psychology, to name a few, are Freud, Jung, Horney, Fromm, Sullivan, Gordon Allport, Rogers, Maslow, May, Weatherhead, and Frankl.

These remarks are not intended to downgrade objective psychology. That would indeed be foolish, for, as Carl Rogers has said, "This whole trend has behind it the weight of current attitudes in American psychology."[7]

Perhaps the whole discussion could be put in a more neutral way if we were to consider these divergent tendencies in psychological theory as preferences for different theoretical models of human beings and perhaps for somewhat different theoretical models of what is expected of science itself. This leaves the matter more operational and allows us to pick and choose our models depending on our pruposes, without needlessly quarreling with those who prefer other models and other purposes. It also leaves open the possibility that my rather dim view of the present usefulness of the "objective" model for the study of religion might be later proved mistaken.

## CONCEPTS COMMON TO EXISTENTIAL PSYCHOLOGY AND RELIGION

To give a name to the kind of psychology that concerns itself with the noetic, distinctly human aspects of experience, I will call it "existential psychology" to emphasize that it seeks to elucidate the conditions of man's existence as man.

Existential psychology and religion intersect at crucial points where they have certain basic concepts in common. Some of these concepts are the following:

*The Self-Concept.* In the following remark, Gordon Allport summarizes the current situation in his discipline: "Many psychologists have commenced to embrace what two decades ago would have been considered a heresy. They have reintroduced a self and ego unashamedly and, as if to make up for lost time, have employed ancillary concepts such as self-image, self-actualization, self-affirmation, phenomenal ego, ego-involvement, ego-striving, and many other hyphenated elaborations which to experimental positivism still have a slight flavor of scientific obscenity."[8] They have turned to the self-concept with good reason. Human experience is a struggle toward some kind of centeredness. Even the distracting experiences of neurosis and psychosis cannot be grasped without assuming a self which suffers under fragmenting experiences. The important advances in existential psychology would be impossible without this assumption.

*The Concept of Identity.*   Closely related to the self-concept is the notion of identity. This concept was necessary to understand the human drive toward self-understanding and responsible participation. We shall see later how important it is.

*Personality as a Dynamic Value-Attitude System.*   The bent of a great deal of recent literature in the culture and personality field is toward a definition of personality as a dynamic value-attitude system. The "primary fact," writes Andras Angyal in *The Foundations for a Science of Personality*, "is a situation having positive or negative value for a person."[9] Particular values in a concrete situation are all related to the entire system of values that go to make up the person's self-identity. This system can be described, in Angyal's words, more completely as follows:

"Any sample of behavior may be regarded as the manifestation of an attitude. Attitudes may be traced back successively to more and more general ones. In so doing one arrives at a limited number of very general attitudes which are unquestionable, axiomatic for a given person. They have been called *axioms of behavior*. When such axioms are intellectually elaborated we may speak of *maxims of behavior*. The axioms of behavior form *a system of personal axioms*. The system of maxims may be called a philosophy of life."[10]

Another well-known psychologist, Gardner Murphy, supports this view when he writes that persons "set up complex personal systems of wants which are relatively enduring and are maintained even in the absence of external reminders; they carry around within themselves personal systems of value. Personality is in large measure this personal value system."[11]

It is not a far call from this view of personality to our definition of religion as ultimate concern—the peak of the hierarchy of personal values, the concern that grips a man absolutely. Combining this view of religion with the psychological definition of personality, it is not hard to see how important a man's religion may be to his existence as a person. His faith is his life orientation, the key to his value-attitude system, the way in which he structures his entire relationship to the world in which he lives. We should recall at this point that ultimate concern may not correspond to the official or public religion that a man espouses; it may be that his implicit faith lies in an entirely other region, giving rise to what we have called pseudo religion.[12]

*The Person as an Ambiguous Being.*   Personality as we know it empirically is not perfectly unified. It seeks centeredness and unity, but it manifests all sorts of contradictory features. These contradictions are felt inwardly as stress, producing the typically human experiences of guilt, anxiety, and hate. Life processes, both biological and psychological, tend, as Angyal says, "toward an increase of autonomy."[13] That is to say, in the words of Mowrer and Kluckhohn, "all living organisms tend to preserve a state of maximal integration, or internal consistency,"[14] But this tendency always appears in tension with counterforces that tend to destroy the unity of the organism and the self.

Paul Tillich deals with this problem more theologically.[15] Man, he says, is always striving and failing to actualize his essential nature in experience. In the depths of his life he knows the pull of a truer and more authentic being, a greater and more significant unity, but he knows this pull in the context of partial submission to the forces of disintegration. This is the meaning of saying that a person is an ambiguous being.

In more experimental terms, Abraham Maslow speaks of the "self-actualiz- ing" tendencies in persons when they are motivated by genuine inwardness. But this self-actualization is rare. Maslow estimates that about 2 percent of the population achieve something like success in it. He divides the motiva- tions of men into those that unify and heal and those that winnow and scatter personality by interjecting alien standards from the outside. These latter motivations are largely based upon deficiencies in personality. Maslow calls people who act mainly on such motives "deficiency-motivated," to distinguish them from "self-actualizing" persons.

Again, it is not hard to see how closely related these concepts are to what we have called religion. Religion is fundamentally the lure of the fullness of personal and social being. It functions more as a pull, which may or may not be responded to, than as a drive. It is the call to be fully human. It can be heeded only in freedom and it leads to behavior that is quite distinct from the "driven" kind of activity that springs from physiological needs or psycho- logical compulsions.

To quote Tillich again: "Value is man's essential being, put as an impera- tive against him. The moral imperatives are not arbitrary ordinances of a transcendent tyrant; neither are they determined by utilitarian calculations or group conventions. They are determined by what man essentially is. . . . If man were united with himself and his essential being there would be no command. But man is estranged from himself, and the values he experiences appear as laws, natural and positive laws, demanding, threatening, promis- ing."[16]

*The Person as a Perceiving and Symbolic Being.*   Human behavior is not a simple unmediated response to environmental stimuli. Human beings are conscious. They reflect on the world in which they live. The world influences them only as they come to structure and understand it. The means for such structuring are symbols. The prime example of symbols is, of course, language. But there are also nonlinguistic symbols—such as hand-shaking or religious rituals—which are equally, if not more, important.

As the human organism goes about in the world it selects and orders the material of its experience into a perception of that world. Human beings ask what things mean, and then respond to their estimates of meaning. They continuously perform what Suzanne Langer calls "symbolic transforma- tion."[17] To illustrate her point she retells the familiar story of Helen Keller's first experience of words as symbols. Helen Keller's governess began her in- struction of the deaf and blind child by spelling out words on her hand. At first these words were mere "signals" that, say, water was at hand, or cake was coming, and so on. They had not yet become "symbols" by means of which the child could think about water or cake. The breakthrough came when Helen suddenly realized that the word w-a-t-e-r, spelled out in her hand, meant and stood for the thing that she was feeling under the faucet of the pump. From that moment she became "human." She was able to structure the world symbolically instead of merely reacting to it like an animal. This occurs to most human beings so early and so naturally that they do not realize what a leap has been taken beyond mere animal responsiveness to the environing world.

It is because man is a conscious, symbol-making creature that he "transcends" the world in which he lives. He stands, so to speak, above it, reflecting about it, questioning what it means. To a human being, the world is not simply there as a set of objects; it is a complex symbolic transaction between a perceiver and what he perceives.[18]

It should be apparent from these considerations how important this psychological study is for an approach to religion. Religion is the quest for meaning, and as such it is inherently symbolic in its nature. The world is experienced humanly in, with, and under the symbolic process—and at the peak of the whole system of symbols are those that give order and significance to all the rest. These are religious symbols. In the light of this analysis, their function in human existence can be made clearer.

*The Problem of Motivation.* This notion has already been suggested in what has gone before, but it needs special notice. On the S-R model the whole issue of human motivation is short-circuited. Existential psychology tries to elucidate why human beings behave as human beings, not animal organisms. Under the impact of religious loyalties, for instance, human beings undertake the most incredible labors and frequently forgo for long periods the satisfaction of merely biological or social needs. And more commonly even the average person's struggle to identify and integrate himself toward some kind of genuine wholeness cannot be understood without reference to religious elements in his make-up.

## THREE IMPORTANT PSYCHOLOGICAL CONCEPTS AND RELIGION

Among the many concepts that might be selected to illustrate the ways in which existential psychology furthers an understanding of religion, let us briefly consider three: The concept of persistent life concerns; the concept of identity; and the concept of maturity.

### Persistent Life Concerns

The notion of persistent life concerns has been most adequately elaborated by Erik Erikson in his widely respected work *Childhood and Society* (1950). Erikson postulates eight persistent concerns (or eight ages) that human beings experience in the course of their lifelong development. Each of these concerns is initiated in a particular developmental period and continues to function and develop throughout the rest of a lifetime. The infant, for example, experiences primarily an implicit concern for security. The experiences of the first year of life provide an attitude of trust or mistrust toward oneself and toward society.

In the next stage the issue is one of organic freedom or autonomy. This stage can be blighted by inflicting on the growing child a sense of shame and self-doubt. Later, during adolescence, the major concern is one of self-identity, and in the period immediately following there emerges a concern for a self-respecting and warm intimacy. In middle age the problem is one of significant work, or creativity. And finally, at the crown of human maturity, the issue becomes a concern for the integration of all these life needs into an authentic integrity.

The following is a chart of the eight stages, with their respective psychological characteristics:

1  Basic trust versus mistrust
2  Autonomy versus shame and doubt
3  Initiative versus guilt
4  Industry versus inferiority
5  Identity versus role confusion
6  Intimacy versus isolation
7  Generativity versus stagnation
8  Integrity versus despair[19]

What have these stages to do with religion? The answer is that at every stage the individual is creatively forming his life values, selecting his characteristic modes of human relationship, and growing toward maturity by the cultivation of some kind of final wisdom about existence. Thus at every stage the religious element is important, but in some of them it seems more crucial than at others. At the beginning, faith promotes an atmosphere of loving acceptance in which the infant can learn to trust. "Trust born of care," writes Erikson, "is, in fact, the touchstone of the actuality of a given religion."[20] As a person grows, faith ideally provides a climate in which he can express his own individuality while relating significantly to other people. For an adolescent it illuminates the meaning of the thrust toward a significant identity as a person, and guards that impulse with reverence. In postadolescence, when a person has transcended his concern for identity and is ready for intimacy, religion illuminates the meaning of sexuality and relates this stage to the following one—the stage of concern for the next generation. In the final stage, faith offers resources of wisdom that make possible the full integration of personality that is rightly called maturity.

The richness and complexity of this scheme can only be hinted at here. It is endless in its implications for the role of religion in human development. A further discussion of two of these stages will illustrate what this means.

*The Concept of Identity.* The period of late high-school and college life is, according to Erikson, an age of crisis in identity. At this stage the human being is physically mature and is awakening to a fully aware consciousness. Moreover, he is soon to be exposed to the full rigors of adult responsibility. Before he can assume those responsibilities he must find out who he is. This is a turbulent time of personal exploration in regard to himself, his fellows, his society, and the cosmos. During this time he will, if his development is normal, form a significant view of himself in all these dimensions.

He must find out about his own real motivations, his desires and ideals. He must come to some terms with his past, and project some kind of satisfactory future. He will define his role in society and his faith concerning the powers of destiny.

Erikson wisely suggests that college life can be conceived of as a kind of moratorium during which these necessary explorations can be undertaken. The student is released for a time from the close supervision of his family, and he has not yet assumed the responsibilities for a family of his own; nor has he yet undertaken the responsibilities of full self-support and citizenship. For this reason, ideally, he should be granted an environment in which experimentation, with its inevitable turbulence and mistakes, can go on without too great penalties. Later the stakes are too high for too much experimentation. Earlier he was unaware of the issues involved. It is a wise college community that understands and provides satisfactorily for this crucial age by offering that balance of freedom and responsibility and that atmosphere of significant ideals and wisdom about life in which the issues of this period can be resolved most satisfactorily. Of course, since we are dealing here with free human beings who must make their own experimentation and choose for themselves, there is no environment that can guarantee success in every case. One of the justifications for the study of religion in the university is that it may provide some of the wisdom that is sorely needed at this juncture.

*The Concept of Maturity.* Maturity represents the final term in Erikson's persistent life concerns. It is my contention that mature religion and mature personality are interrelated and interpenetrating. Maturity is, of course, a normative rather than a descriptive term. That is, it is a standard for judging persons and religion rather than a purely descriptive account of the facts. Normative concepts are hard to justify in science, but this one seems to be a logical requirement for a coherent psychology of religion. It is simply impossible to understand human beings, or their religion, without assuming some ultimate criterion like maturity. The reason for this is that personality and religion alike are dynamic—they move with reference to goals, and betray a constant struggle with standards not yet actualized into practice. The goals themselves are partially hidden and move upward as soon as they are perceived or partially achieved. Neither personality nor religion can rest short of maturity—and maturity itself, instead of being a fixed point, seems to be a dynamic state of growth.

## Mature Religion

Gordon Allport defines mature religion from a psychological point of view as follows: "The maturely productive religious sentiment . . . is an interest-system within the structure of the individual's personality basically like any other well-developed interest-system. Like other mature sentiments, it is well differentiated, which means that the individual at various times can view its sub-parts and their relation to one another; it is dynamic in its own right, that is, it plays an important autonomous part in the motivational life of the individual regardless of its own origins; it is productive of conduct consistent with the nature of the sentiment, and engenders a conscience appropriate to the values involved.

"Because of its special nature, however, the religious sentiment in some respects does differ in degree if not in kind from other mature sentiments. It is certainly more comprehensive, since it aims to join all experience into a single meaningful system. It is likewise a uniquely integral system in that it aims to give one leading directive to the life as a whole.

"Finally, because of the limited certainties that plague any religious belief, there is a heuristic quality to this sentiment; it is held with loyalty for the very purpose of discovering all the good and all the truth that may issue from it."[21]

This is a good beginning. Following Allport's lead, let us characterize a religion of maturity in the following terms:

*Comprehensive.* In being comprehensive, mature religion will, as Allport says, "join all experience into a single meaningful system." Another way of putting this is to say that mature religion grasps the whole man without leaving out any part of him—thought, feeling, or action. It is to be distinguished from a segmental kind of religion that can be contained in watertight compartments. Men who believe themselves to be religious and yet say that their faith in God has nothing to do with economics or politics do not understand this comprehensive kind of religion.

*Really Ultimate.* In mature religion, the ultimate that dominates the whole man in this comprehensive way must be truly ultimate. That is, it must be a reality which stands for the very best he can know or think. If he is dominated by a lesser value than he knows, however dimly—such a value as, say, the party or race or nation—then he is bound to a religion less than mature. In religious terms, he falls into idolatry. When, for example, the great Japanese Christian, Toyohiko Kagawa, was on trial for denying the supremacy of the Emperor, he asked the judge whether the Emperor had created the earth and all living beings in it. Despite his patriotism, the judge had no answer to this question. Obviously the Emperor was not the ultimate.

*Heuristic.* This term is taken from science and merely means "helping to discover or learn." In this context it means that a mature faith will be a means of discovering more and learning more, a faith that teaches men how to transcend it while remaining the same. What is involved in this characteristic is clearer when we consider those that follow:

✗*Growing.* Mature religion is never finished. Its realities are never exhausted and never fully actualized into situations. As St. Paul wrote to the Philippian church, "Not that I . . . am already perfect; but I press on. . . ."[22] Mature religion presses on. The mature man never says, I am a finished product. The mature faith can never be perfectly defined and finished. That is God's prerogative, not man's.

*Tested and Reliable.* A mature faith changes, to be sure, but not with the wind. It grows, but not with the weather. It has a quality of fixity that yields deep security coupled with maximum elasticity. Its changelessness amid change arises from the fact that, like science, it produces its own standard for growth. As it outgrows itself, it becomes more essentially the same. It is a pity that these words seem so paradoxical, but they describe mature religion quite literally. The man who knows God does not outgrow God, but God leads him to outgrow his immature views of God. Thus God remains God while changing in the mind of the growing person. A parallel can be seen in science, where growth and stability are commonly seen together.

The danger in pointing out the need for security in faith is that it will become rigid and fixed, cocksure and authoritarian. But the true security of faith lies in its infinite flexibility and growing power. The next characteristic is akin to this one:

*Includes Doubts About Itself.*[23] A mature faith continuously criticizes itself. This is the meaning of the prophetic tradition. The doubts about divinity itself, when taken with high seriousness, are a mark of the religious spirit. The religious reason for this is that the ultimate transcends man, and man must be continuously reforming in the light of the new quality of being as it is revealed to him. The doubts are thus means of clarification. Doubts without faith are a pathway to cynicism and personal degeneration. Combined with the faith that inspires them, they expose false securities and idolatrous views. They foster growth.

*Informs Conscience and Provides Moral Guidance.* Mature religion inspires continuously evolving ideals, but it goes beyond this. It demands a harmony between what men believe and what they do. This harmony is in striking contrast to the common run of men who pretentiously announce high ideals and then behave according to passion and self-interest.

*Gives Power to Actualize Human Possibilities.* Mature faith does more than inform the conscience or provide moral guidance. It is deeper than the moral consciousness in that it gives life itself and the power to actualize the possibilities that conscience can envisage. Moralism is an immature religion. By itself, it produces pride and self-concern instead of humility and openness to values beyond the self. This is more apparent in the next concept:

*Provides Love and Courage.* Mature religion is opposed to the self-enclosure that is apparent in limited sympathies or hate. It engenders, at its best, a universal openness and charity. A conventional religion, confining sympathies to one's own group, or a timid agreement with society as it actually exists, is a manifestation of deficient faith. Such openness—inviting as it does threats from both within and without—is impossible without a quality that Tillich calls "the courage to be."

The career of St. Paul manifested this quality of courage to a high degree. "We are afflicted in every way," he wrote to the Corinthian church, "but not crushed; perplexed, but not driven to despair; persecuted, but not forsaken; struck down, but not destroyed; . . ."[24]

*Experienced Immediacy.* Mature religion transcends theory and system. At its best, it becomes a direct personal experience whereby faith is verified in feeling and willing, as well as in thought. Mature religion opens out into dialogue with the life-world in its fullness, leading to wonder, awe, and glad receptivity. It is this quality of immediacy, somewhat akin to the experience of beauty, that gives religion an ecstatic character and fills its adherents with joy under the most varied circumstances. Joy, in fact, seems to be the most characteristic mark of mature religion at its best.

In the light of this list, it is possible to indicate briefly the characteristics of an *immature* religion: (1) Immature religion is segmental rather than comprehensive. (2) It is characterized by devotion to lesser rather than the highest values. (3) It tends to fixate its believers in a rigid and ungrowing state, favoring regressive and inverted tendencies of personality rather than growth. (4) On the score of reliability, it tends to produce anxieties and uncertainties, on one hand, and dogmatic fanaticism and rigidity on the other. The fanatic makes up for his lack of real confidence by a show of bigotry and intolerance, which allow no room for any questions or doubts. Immature religion makes no clear connection between beliefs and conduct, often remaining in the sphere of sentimental idealism or thoughtless approval of social conventions. (6) In place of the power to actualize human possibilities, it often substitutes mere moralism or petty conscientiousness that impoverishes personality by both pride and guilt. (7) Lacking a quality of immediacy, it lives entirely in the abstract and conventional or seeks false ecstasies in unusual experiences, excessive emotionalism, or even in drugs. (8) Because immaturity in religion is always some form of self-worship, it is especially prone to all the deficiencies of attempted self-salvation: Paul Tillich summarizes these as (a) Legalism—the attempt to save oneself through obedience to moral regulations; (b) Asceticism—the attempt to save oneself through heroic self-denial, usually in the form of physical deprivation; (c) Sacramentalism—identification with a sacramental system of worship; and (d) Emotionalism—the search for exotic experiences through mystical practices or in some other way.

## THE MATURE PERSON

Turning now from religion to the field of personality, let us look briefly at the efforts of psychologists to define the mature person. There is perhaps no area where religion and psychology have so wide a common interest. True to the nature of psychological investigation, I must point out that these criteria of maturity are tentative and subject to continuous redefinition in the light of fresh evidence. With that proviso, let us examine some of these criteria.

The mature person is aware, first of all, of the difference between his authentic or true self and his conventional or unessential selves. This distinction has been variously described. P. A. Sorokin indicates four levels of selfhood: (1) The level of unconscious drives and needs. (2) The level of bioconscious egos: the system of conscious drives and wants based upon bodily needs. (3) Sociocultural egos: the whole system of values and commands derived from the culture in which a person lives, especially from the groups in which he is a participating member. (4) The superconscious egoless self. This last level, he says, is the region of true selfhood. It is the center from which spring all the truly creative powers of personal being.[25]

Paul Tournier, the Swiss psychiatrist, distinguishes between the *person* and the *personage*. The personage is the mask which a person wears in his various roles in society. It is the man as he appears to be. Behind this personage is the real man. But the real man is often lost in the personage as he becomes more and more involved in the social game in which, as Tournier says, each seeks "to disemble his own real thoughts, his secret intentions, while trying to unmask those of his neighbor."[26] Since there is no community, however intimate, where this game is not played, at least in part—keeping countenance, eyeing one other, calculating—the person suffers the fate of near-eclipse. To quote Tournier again, "Our personage clings to our person by dint of long schooling which has made us what we are."[27]

Karen Horney[28] and Fritz Kunkel,[29] following another Swiss psychiatrist Carl Jung,[30] distinguish the true self from the image of the self that has been built through a lifetime, artfully avoiding the creative center of one's being. This ego-image, which is not the real self, is filled with false values and distorted concepts, leading to a lifetime of painful struggle to live by them.

However the case might be put, it seems that a coherent account of personality must make some such distinction, as these writers have suggested, between a real and unmanifested self, and an unreal, manifested self. The mature man knows this difference. He does not identify himself with his bodily urges, his cultural images, or his neurotic illusions—even when he realizes how powerfully they are at work in and through him. He continually seeks to unveil and manifest a self that is more fundamental than these, a self more expressive of his true and authentic nature.

Another way of putting this, which extends our concept significantly, is Maslow's way of referring to the mature person as self-actualizing. The self-actualizing person acts out of his real nature rather than out of personal deficiencies, such as biological need, a lack of being loved, or a deprived social status. The "fully growing and self-fulfilling human being," writes Maslow, "[is] the one in whom all his potentialities are coming to full development, the one whose inner nature expresses itself freely, rather than being warped, suppressed, or denied."[31] This inner nature is not, like our biological instincts, "strong and overpowering."[32] It is rather, he writes, "based upon the unconscious and preconscious perception of our own nature, of our own destiny, or our own capacities, or our own 'call' in life."[33]

Maslow believes that such an assumption is required for any reasonable explanation of the differences between sick and healthy, or uncreative and creative people. It is the only way to account, he believes, for the strikingly different styles of "love." Some people "love" in order to make up for something lacking in themselves; they reach out to possess. Others joyfully affirm other people in their own uniqueness. The first kind of love stifles and destroys both parties, the second kind enriches both.

A third dimension of maturity is insight. The mature person knows himself, both the authentic and inauthentic selves, the true and the sham. He knows his drives and needs, the deficiencies stemming from his inheritance and upbringing, his failures, and his pretensions. He knows these along with his vacillation between the real and the pretentious, and at the same time he *accepts himself*. Self-rejection is the error of the person who identifies himself with a false self-image. Lacking insight into his authentic self, he is bound to serve a false one. Self-acceptance is not self-justification; it is simple realism. He knows the person he is, and he moves on from that point toward his maturity. This process can be seen dramatically in psychotherapy when the patient suddenly perceives himself as he is and takes responsibility for himself. From this moment, growth toward a different self can begin.

Another dimension of maturity is integration. The mature person has found a meaning for his life which gives it full orientation. He knows who he is, what he is living for. He is prepared to take risks, to suffer, and to be someone unique. He is all of one piece. Cut into him at any point and you find the same quality of being.

Up to this point the characteristics we have noted are focused in the self. But the mature man is marked by a power to love and be loved, to relate freely and responsibly to the world in which he lives. Without such love there isn't any depth of personal insight or self-knowledge. Human existence is essentially relational, or, in the biblical sense, dialogical. The isolated person cannot be a full person. But love must be distinguished from an amiable agreeableness. True love does not spring from conventional conformity. Conformity is a sham love motivated by fear of the creative powers within, and a deep fear that going out to meet another human being fully would be personally destructive.

A seventh characteristic of the mature person is that he exhibits tension capacity. He is able to postpone satisfactions in the light of larger meanings and goals. He is not easily bribed by passing pleasures and privileges. Nor does he flee from suffering, but accepts it as an inevitable part of being human, and uses it as a means of growth. He knows that through adversity the flaws in his own life are more completely revealed than in prosperity, although, unlike the masochist, he does not need suffering to alleviate his hidden guilts.

Yet another characteristic of the mature person is freedom joined to a high sense of responsibility. His behavior is not other-directed, as Riesman says,[34] but inner-directed. He acts from his creative center, from his real self rather than from his ego-images. For this reason he knows that he is fully responsible for himself. Anton Boisen, in his incomparable account of a personal psychosis, has made this point very clear: The person who blames himself and accepts responsibility for his condition has a good prognosis; the psychotic who excuses himself continually and never reaches the point of self-blame has a poor chance of recovery.[35] Jean-Paul Sartre's illuminating chapters on self-deception in *Being and Nothingness*[36] make the same point. Man *is* his freedom, and the mechanism of self-excuse is a pure delusion.

Recent studies at the University of California[37] emphasize the finding that the mature person possesses inward and outward creativity. Inwardly he has the power of self-renewal; he springs back from depression and defeat. Outwardly, in his vocation and group living, he is a source of refreshing novelty. Unlike his immature counterpart, who lives by dependence upon external supports, he knows the power of a deeper life stirring within him, and he follows that light.

Because of this power of self-renewal and creativity, the mature person is always growing. He is not stuck somewhere in the process of growing up. He is not bound to self-concepts that are fixed in his personage, or his ego-image, but realizes a continuous evolution of the mysterious selfhood that can never be rounded out and finished.

# THE RELATIONSHIP OF MATURE RELIGION
## TO PERSONAL MATURITY

This recital of characteristics should already have made plain how closely allied are the concepts of maturity in religion and personality. The converse is also true: Immature religion and immature personality are mutually supporting. However, there is one thing that is not clear in many psychological accounts of maturity: What is the relationship between insight and outlook? What is the relationship between a person's world view and his personal adequacy? Is it possible to regard the world as indifferent or hostile to human existence and yet live by the standards of personal maturity? Can outlook contradict insight without destroying it? Is it possible, on one hand, to picture the world as mechanically determined, indifferent or hostile to human values, utterly meaningless, devoid of living responsiveness, and, on the other hand, to cultivate inner freedom, passionate commitment to human values, order one's life in a meaningful way, and live in open responsiveness to existence—all at the same time?

I do not think so. Outlook and insight are too interdependent to allow such splitting of the subjective and objective sides of existence. The following passage from Kierkegaard's *Fear and Trembling* expresses this view: "If there were no eternal consciousness in man, if at the foundation of all there lay only a wildly seething power which, writhing with obscure passions, produces everything that is great and everything that is insignificant, if a bottomless void never satiated lay hidden beneath all—what then would life be but despair? If such were the case, if there were no sacred bond which united mankind, if one generation arose after another, like the leafage in the forest, if the one generally replaced the other like the song of birds in the forest, if the human race passed through the world as the ship goes through the sea, like the wind through the desert, a thoughtless and fruitless activity, if an eternal oblivion were always lurking hungrily for its prey and there were no power strong enough to wrest it from its maw—how empty, then, and comfortless life would be!"[38]

It is my thesis that a mature personality assumes faith in a deeply supporting reality beyond the self—whether that faith is acknowledged or not. This thesis finds its sharpest challenge in those remarkable men whom we can call altruistic naturalists; I mean such men as Bertrand Russell or Albert Camus. These men unequivocally deny that there is any sign of support from the nonhuman world beyond themselves. Yet we cannot deny that their lives are marked by many signs of maturity well beyond that of the average human being. In a celebrated passage from his "Free Man's Worship," Russell describes his world view: "Brief and powerless is man's life; on him and all his race the slow, sure doom falls, pitiless and dark. Blind to good and evil, reckless of destruction, omnipotent matter rolls on its relentless way; for Man, condemned today to lose his dearest, tomorrow himself to pass through the gate of darkness, it remains only to cherish, ere yet the blow falls, the lofty thoughts that ennoble his little day; disdaining the coward terrors of the slave of Fate, to worship at the shrine that his own hands have built undismayed by the empire of chance, to preserve a mind free from wanton tyranny that rules his outward life; proudly defiant of the irresistible forces that tolerate, for a moment, his knowledge and his condemnation, to sustain alone, a weary but unyielding Atlas, the world that his own ideals have fashioned despite the trampling march of unconscious power."[39]

In another passage from the same essay Russell writes: "Man is the product of causes which had no prevision of the end they were achieving; that his origin, his growth, his hopes and fears, his loves and beliefs, are but the outcome of accidental collocations of atoms . . . and that the whole temple of Man's achievement must inevitably be buried beneath the debris of a universe in ruins. . . . Only within the scaffolding of these truths, only on the firm foundation of unyielding despair, can the soul's habitation be henceforth safely built."[40]

The question that arises is whether these instances of mature personality, coupled with so bleak a world view, strike down our thesis of a unity of insight and outlook. The answer cannot be simple and, in view of the stature of the men we are discussing, it will no doubt seem presumptuous. But the question must be faced.

An answer may take two directions. The first is that these men have proved by their lives that their verbalized beliefs do not correspond to their vital faith. Bertrand Russell's heroic struggle to prevent a nuclear holocaust, for example, betrays a passion for peace and civilization that vastly transcends his alleged belief that values and moral laws are purely personal and subjective. He speaks and acts like a prophet—while his theory would condemn him to passively emoting that the world is not as he would wish it to be. It is psychologically possible, I hold, to believe in the bottom of the heart what you cannot express off the top of your head.

This situation arises due to our ambiguous social inheritance—the mixture of modernity and premodernity that has been the patrimony of contemporary man. The modern mind excluded meaning and value from its premises, but men nevertheless lived by convictions that were retained from an older tradition, when the world was believed to be basically meaningful and life-value-producing. I am saying that Russell, and men like him, hold modern conceptions in the forefront of their consciousness, but still retain substantial remnants of a premodern consciousness. They live on borrowed moral and spiritual capital. They believe that because no consistent picture of the world can be devised that incorporates both modern and premodern concepts, integrity requires them to reject one or the other—and the prestige of science makes their choice clear. I am going to insist later that this choice need no longer be made; that it is, in fact, a contradictory position. Its contradictoriness is existentially manifest in the lives of the altruistic naturalists.

A second line of thought is more psychological. Every dimension of maturity involves a trustful interplay between self and nonself. It would be tedious to demonstrate this in every case. Let us consider a crucial instance. Immaturity is a form of self-enclosure marked by pride, fear, and hostility. It is informed by the conviction that the surrounding world stands against the self and will destroy it unless every measure of defense is artfully exploited. This is the logical position if the outer world is hostile, as Russell has indicated. In fact, we have examples of human beings who have built their lives on Russell's "foundation of unyielding despair," but instead of living as great scientists, philosophers, and social prophets, they lie curled up in the foetal posture in our mental hospitals. These catatonics "know" that every venture into the outer world is at best fraught with futility or danger. They believe in their hearts the creed of meaninglessness and hopelessness.

In the long run, I am saying, the conviction of meaninglessness cannot produce maturity. The creative man without hope is a contradiction; the loving man without faith is an impossibility. Occasional lapses, and they are rare, from this principle are the result of the cultural ambiguity which I have noted.

To repeat: Personal maturity and the outlook of faith are coherently related to one another; maturity is ultimately a matter of truth and is dependent upon an adequate world view. The Judaeo-Christian faith, which we have examined in the biblical section, supplies that kind of world view. How?

It provides, first, a view of the ultimate nature of things that supports at every point the possibilities of maturity—an ultimate that is best characterized as creative, holy, sovereign love. Second, it provides an adequate view of man: his freedom and his ambiguous use of it for good and ill; his social nature, made for the common life; his individual uniqueness; his ultimate responsibility to God, his fellows, and himself; his destiny as a mature "son of God"; and his concreteness as a creature of the earth. And, finally, it provides the necessary ingredients for growth into maturity: a security consistent with the utmost elasticity; a critique of all finite values and loyalties; a hope beyond the tragedies of human existence that saves from despair; a faith that banishes fear—even of death; a love that opens man to his fellows in a total and unconditional way; a motivation for the labor of being human, with all the difficulties involved in that enterprise.

This discussion of maturity has been set forth with simple directness, but we must now acknowledge that the concept of maturity in both psychology and religion is a relatively new and unexplored one. We are not at the end but at the beginning of a new era of investigation. Tentativeness is the only proper attitude. But this tentativeness will be informed by the excitement of a new orientation which promises to relate psychology more intimately to authentic human behavior, and to makre religion more responsive to psychological investigations.

### Is There Such a Class of Human Beings?[41]

Before closing this account of mature religion and mature personality, let us ask whether there is such a recognizable class of human beings—men marked by such self-knowledge, integration, devotion to an ultimate beyond the parochial limits of their culture, incorruptibility, humility and openness, charity and courage, as we have described?

The answer is that there is. This answer has to be qualified by the very standard we are employing. These men would deny that they are end-products. They would insist that they are still "on the way," that the ultimate lies beyond them, infinitely. The greatest among them when addressed as "Good Master" replied, "Why do you call me good? No one is good but God alone."[42] Yet the glory of the human race is that such men have lived and, fortunately, are still among us.

Let us be satisfied with one example taken from an age whose formal religion has long since perished—Socrates. His maturity was so impressive that the Christian theologians of Alexandria, hundreds of years after his death, believed that he had walked with the Logos before he became flesh in Jesus Christ. In every age his example inspires men who learn of him through his gifted disciple Plato.

Socrates taught that the true life involved a continuous examination into self and a progressive insight into the highest realities and values. These things he practiced continually. He preached against human domination by lesser passions and interests, yet he was capable of deep enjoyment in the social life of his time. Alcibiades, one of his students, said that Socrates alone seemed always to enjoy himself, whether banqueting or fasting. In the face of threats and bribery—and even more in the presence of subtle temptations— he proved incorruptible.

The philosopher C. E. M. Joad says of Socrates: "He is himself, and wholly in control of himself. He is, again, a man released; released, that is to say, from the solicitation of the desires and ambitions of the world. He cares nothing for the goods that appeal to most of us; for wealth, for fame, for comfort and popularity. Continuously he exhibits that nonattachment to earthly things that comes to most of us only in rare moments of aesthetic and perhaps moral experience. With the energy made available by his persistent refusal to dissipate his faculties in trivial pursuits or on behalf of unworthy ends, he pursues the good life and seeks the knowledge of reality. And with some measure of success. At first intermittently and then, as he grows older, more continuously, he pursues goodness and enjoys beauty."[43]

To the end, Socrates remains faithful to his religious calling to serve the nation by his criticism of its foolishness and partial wisdom. Despite his rational powers, he does not at any time despise the intuitive promptings of the "voice" that he believes guides him at crucial times. At the end, when he has been condemned to death by his fellow citizens, he reminds his followers to be of good cheer, for there is nothing to fear in dying; he warns them to avoid "unrighteousness" for it "runs faster than death."

In his death cell he calmly discusses the fate of the soul after death, refusing constantly to escape to the dishonor of safety. And, when the poisoned cup is offered, he drinks it off as though he were drinking a toast to a friend. It is no wonder that his follower Plato later wrote of that hour: "Such was the end . . . of our friend; concerning whom I may truly say, that of all the men of his time whom I have known, he was the wisest and justest and best."[44]

I trust that the value of a scientific study of religion in society and personality has become evident in these last two chapters. Despite its dangers, and despite the fact that it cannot give a complete account of religion, it is, nonetheless, one of the valid ways of approaching religion. Its values lie in two directions: It links the study of religion with the scientific temper that is one of the great achievements of our culture, and which will no doubt remain in high regard for an indefinite future. And, second, it forces students of religion to attend closely to observed facts, keeping theology relevant to the details of concrete human existence.

Authentic religion has nothing to lose and much to gain by a knowledgeable employment of science in its investigations, if, of course, faith is really grounded in the Real. In the long run only illusions will be damaged by such faithfulness to truth as we can know it, by any means whatever.

## SUGGESTIONS FOR FURTHER READING

Gordon Allport's *Becoming* (Yale University Press, 1955) and his *Individual and His Religion* (Macmillan, 1950) are books that show the close relationship between psychology and religion. Hadley Cantril and Charles H. Bumstead, eds., *Reflections on the Human Venture* (New York University Press, 1960) try to enlarge the sphere of psychological interest beyond the limits of academic psychology. Erik Erikson's *Childhood and Society*, rev. ed. (Norton, 1950) and his *Young Man Luther* (Norton, 1962) are extremely important for an understanding of personality that makes a fundamental place for religious faith.

New explorations in personality by the following writers are important for this field: Rollo May, ed., *Existence* (Basic Books, 1958); Carl Rogers, *On Becoming a Person* (Houghton Mifflin, 1961); David E. Roberts, *Psychotherapy and a Christian View of Man* (Scribner, 1950); Ian Suttie, *Origins of Love and Hate* (Julian Press, 1952); Abraham Maslow, *Toward a Psychology of Being* (Van Nostrand, 1962); and Paul Tournier, *The Meaning of Persons* (Harper & Row, 1957).

George Brantl, ed., *The Religious Experience*, 2 vols. (Braziller, 1964) shows the great variety of what is called "religious experience." Brantl classifies these varieties as a "way of being," "a way of seeing," and "a way of living."

For an approach to the psychology of religion through Eastern modes of thought, see two very interesting books: Alan W. Watts, *Psychotherapy East and West* (Pantheon, Random House, 1961) and D. T. Suzuki, Erich Fromm, and Richard De Martino, *Zen Buddhism and Psychoanalysis* (Harper & Row, 1960).

## NOTES

1. Gordon Allport, *The Individual and His Religion* (Macmillan, 1950), p. vii.

2. B. H. Streeter, *Reality* (Macmillan, 1934), p. 271.

3. Hadley Cantril and Charles H. Bumstead, *Reflections on the Human Venture* (New York University Press, 1960), p. xi.

4. Carl R. Rogers and B. F. Skinner, *Some Issues Concerning the Control of Human Behavior*, reprinted from *Science*, Vol. 124, No. 3231 (November 30, 1956, pp. 1057–1066. See p. 1 of the reprint.

5. *Ibid.*, p. 8.

6. Rollo May, ed., *Existential Psychology* (Random House, 1961), p. 40.

7. Carl Rogers, "Two Divergent Trends," in *ibid.*, p. 86.

8. Gordon Allport, *Becoming* (Yale University Press, 1955), p. 37.

9. Andras Angyal, *Foundations for a Science of Personality* (Oxford University Press, 1941), p. 72.

10. *Ibid.*, p. 165.

11. Gardner Murphy, *Personality* (Harper & Row, 1947), p. 270.

12. See my Chapter 2.

13. Angyal, *op. cit.*, p. 52.

14. In J. McV. Hunt, ed., *Personality and the Behavior Disorders* (Ronald, 1944), p. 69.

15. Tillich treats this whole subject of ambiguity at length in his *Systematic Theology*, III, 30–110.

16. In Abraham Maslow, ed., *New Knowledge in Human Values* (Harper & Row, 1959), p. 195.

17. She treats this topic in her *Philosophy in a New Key* (Harvard University Press, 1957), and in her work on art, *Feeling and Form* (Routledge, 1953).

18. A good source for this point of view is Franklin P. Kilpatrick, ed., *Explorations in Transactional Psychology* (New York University Press, 1961).

19. Erik H. Erikson, *Childhood and Society*, rev. ed. (Norton, 1950), pp. 272–273.

20. *Ibid.*, p. 250.

21. Allport, *op. cit.*, p. 124.

22. Philippians 3:12.

23. See M. Holmes Hartshorne, *The Faith to Doubt* (Spectrum, Prentice-Hall, 1963).

24. II Corinthians 4:8–9.

25. P. A. Sorokin, *The Ways and Power of Love* (Beacon Press, 1954), chap. 5, "Mental Structure and Energies of Man."

26. Paul Tournier, *The Meaning of Persons* (Harper & Row, 1957), p. 28.

27. *Ibid.*, p. 33.

28. Karen Horney, *Neurosis and Human Growth* (Norton, 1950).

29. Fritz Kunkel, *In Search of Maturity* (Scribner, 1943).

30. Carl Jung, *The Undiscovered Self* (New American Library, 1959).

31. Abraham Maslow, *Toward a Psychology of Being* (Van Nostrand, 1962), p. 4.

32. *Ibid.*, p. 3.

33. *Ibid.*, p. 6.

34. This is his chief analytic tool in *The Lonely Crowd*.

35. This is Anton Boisen's diagnosis in *The Explorations of the Inner World* (Harper & Row, 1936; Harper Torchbook, 1952).

36. Jean-Paul Sartre, *Being and Nothingness* (Philosophical Library, 1956), Pt. I, chap. 2.

37. For this study of 600 creative persons, see Frank Barron, *Creativity and Psychological Health* (Van Nostrand, 1963).

38. Sören Kierkegaard, *Fear and Trembling* (Doubleday, 1955), p. 30.

39. Bertrand Russell, "A Free Man's Worship" in *Mysticism and Logic* (Norton, 1929), pp. 46–47.

40. *Ibid.*, p. 46.

41. See C. E. M. Joad's answer to this question in *God and Evil* (Harper & Row, 1943), p. 275 ff.

42. Luke 18:19.

43. Joad, *op. cit.*, p. 275.

44. These are the concluding words of Plato's *Phaedo* (Jowett trans.).

# 17

# The Ethics of
# Divine-Human Dialogue

❖❘❖❘❖❘❖❘❖❘❖❘❖❘❖❘❖❘❖❘❖❘❖❘❖❘❖❘❖❘❖❘❖❘❖❘❖❘❖❘❖❘❖❘❖❘❖❘❖

No age has ever stood in greater need of moral wisdom than our own. Never before has mankind faced at one time so many and such novel problems. These problems are not, I believe, so much a sign of increasing wickedness as perplexities arising from human bafflement in the face of the powerful forces that are thrusting men and nations forward toward their destiny as citizens of a single world. But rapid forward motion can lead to a fall, and the failure to solve any one of a dozen major problems could postpone human hopes indefinitely. I mean such problems as the population explosion and hunger; economic development adequate to the rising expectations of the peoples in the have-not nations; political immaturity of both the new and old nations, whose peoples are still unaware of the requirements of the twentieth century; industrialization; nuclear weaponry; and conflicts between races, nations, and classes with uncompromising ideologies. We have a long way to go to make the world a safe and humane habitation for man, and ethics is, in the words of theologian Paul Lehmann, the "disciplined account of what it takes to make and keep human life human."[1]

Our need of moral wisdom paradoxically coincides with the fact that the present generation is heir to the wisdom of every culture of the past and present. It is in part this very richness of technical means and cultural ends— the variety of conflicting proposals and claims—that paralyzes us. We are like Peer Gynt, in Ibsen's play, who set out to master the world and returned from his adventures harrowed and broken, longing for a sign pointing, "Here lies they path!"

## BIBLICAL TRADITION IN ETHICS

We need a center to which to refer the varieties of wisdom to which we have fallen heir, a principle of relevance that will enable us to discover a feasible course of action, fixed enough to be a true guide, and flexible enough to deal with the prolific variety of life in the historic cultures.

It is my conviction that the biblical life of dialogue, initiated by God and turned toward every neighbor as a brother, could serve as such a center. That is why I propose to discuss for the next three chapters the ethical life in biblical perspective.

This may appear to be a somewhat parochial choice of subject matter. In part, no doubt it is. But it is indisputable that, in the main, the large social problems we are going to discuss have arisen out of the forces generated in the growth of Western civilization. And, further, the ethical consciousness of most Western students is bound, whether knowingly or not, to the ethical feelings and principles that have their origins in the Judaeo-Christian tradition. We discussed briefly, in Part Two, the ethics of Hinduism, Buddhism, and Taoism, but an extended discussion of Eastern ethics here would, I suspect, be largely academic. To be sure, we must at the proper time consider the challenge of Eastern thought—along with its ethical views—but this can be done more satisfactorily when we attempt to evolve a reasonable policy of dialogue among the world religions.

Another reason for choosing to discuss this biblical tradition in ethics is the relative absence of any satisfactory account of it in college textbooks. The classroom tradition in philosophical ethics makes it appear as if Judaeo-Christian religious conceptions were philosophically irrelevant to any serious ethical theory. Textbooks tend to relegate religious ethics to a simple-minded form of authoritarianism or traditionalism. This circumstance is doubly curious. In the first place, most of the ethical philosophies of the West are heavily indebted to Judaeo-Christian backgrounds, even when explicitly rejecting them. The utilitarian ethic of John Stuart Mill is a good example. What is his principle of "the greatest happiness of the greatest number" but a fragmentary restatement of biblical principles of justice and love, unfortunately leaving out several elements crucial to an adequate theory? Or, what is Kant's categorical imperative (act on the maxim that you can will to be universal) but a sophisticated formulation of the golden rule, minus the religious faith that would make it personally compelling?

In the second place, the ethical ideals to which most Americans appeal when verbalizing their ethical choices are nearly always explicitly religious. This is not surprising, since most of them received their earliest and most lasting ethical training in the family, and the majority of these families—

especially those who send their youth to college—regard themselves as loyal to the traditional Western faiths.

## Ethics and World Views

All ethical systems presuppose a world view. They are integrally related to some estimate as to the nature of things. Attempts to separate ethics from ontology—some view of the nature of being itself—can produce only superficial results. For value judgments and moral claims emerge coordinately with the way men see the world in which they live. What could be more natural to a skeptical materialist than to exalt a life of physical pleasure? Since the senses are the best clue to reality itself, what could be more reasonable than to regard their fulfillment as most apt? Sensate ethics and materialism in its various forms logically and practically belong together.

Or, what could be more reasonable to a Hindu than a lifetime of disciplined ascetic effort aimed at liberation into a realm beyond space and time through ecstatic meditation, believing as he does that the material world is maya—illusion?

These remarks are required in the face of widespread belief that ethics can be considered separately from world views. This belief leads to another mistaken view that a satisfactory ethic might evolve from sorting out wise sayings from various sources and compiling them into a system of moral guidance. Unfortunately, similar sayings from diverse world views often have very different meanings—meanings that cannot be fathomed without relating them to their religious or philosophical origins. Again, let me repeat, our problem is to discover a coherent center for those inescapable values and valid claims to which civilized men in their best moments find themselves consenting. That center, I believe, can be found in a careful reconsideration of the life-world of the Bible, with its concept of responsible dialogue in both the cosmic and human dimensions. In order to understand this life of dialogue, we must look first to its historic backgrounds.

## The Old Testament Background

Dialogic ethics is rooted in the life experience of the ancient Hebrews. The previous discussion of biblical religion (in Part Three) should make brief references to these background materials readily comprehensible. Old Testament ethics grows out of the dialogic relationship between God and the Hebrew people at Sinai. God speaks; the people hear and obey. The content of God's Word is spelled out in the covenant to which the people agree.

According to Genesis, man's dialogue with God began long before Sinai when God brought him forth from the dust of the ground by his creative Word. But the specifically Hebrew experience of dialogue began in the second millennium before Christ; it began with Abraham, who "obeyed

~~God"~~ ~~and left Haran for~~ a land he did not know. Sinai is the historic moment when the meaning of this long relationship is at last made clear. This covenant became the basis for what in Hebrew thought is called the "Law and the Prophets."

*The Law.* The demands of the Decalogue—the Ten Commandments—were set out in the most general terms. In order for them to serve as guides to practical social conduct it was necessary to translate them into detailed rules dealing with concrete situations. Thus the historic period following Sinai was a progressive translation of the ethical demands of the Commandments into concrete, positive law. The law forbidding killing, for example, required clarification. Taking the life of a legally convicted murderer, or an enemy of Israel, could not properly be regarded as killing in the prohibited sense of the word.

What came to be known as the Law of Moses, or the Mosaic law, was thus a multitude of regulations believed by the elders of Israel to be consistent with the original covenant, much as American law is regarded as constitutional when it is consistent with the spirit of the founding document.

Though this application to concrete cases is necessary if the primary ethical principles are to become effective in the life of a people, it has dangers. The chief danger is that the law may become so fixed and rigid that its contrived application to new situations may contradict the intention of the original covenant.

*The Prophets.* To counteract the legalism of the law, a freer and more critical spirit emerged in the great prophets, such as Amos and Isaiah, who leaped, as it were, back over the centuries of commentary to the original covenant itself. In a deeper sense they appealed to the life behind the covenant, to the living dialogue with God, who had delivered the law to Moses in the first place. They did not quote. They spoke with shocking directness: "Thus speaks the Lord, the God of Israel!" They were not commentators, but spokesmen. "The Lord hath spoken," cried Amos. "Who can but prophesy!"

The burden of the prophetic message was not in the strictest sense "new." The prophets believed that it was the true meaning of the original law. Like Jesus, they spoke "not to destroy but to fulfill" the Law, to make it freshly contemporary to men who had lost contact with their spiritual origins. But going back to sources is often revolutionary. The prophets extended the concept of Mosaic justice to universal proportions and laid the foundation for any defensible modern uses of the term. Unequivocally, they called for the practice of justice within and among all nations. If their messages often seem cast in dark and threatening terms, it is because of the calloused indifference of the people to their preachment. The prophets were utterly confident that men could not continue to practice injustice in God's world and get away with it indefinitely. In his own time God would bring down to dust all the proud and selfish institutions of powerful men.

The prophets also recast the ancient notion of a "chosen people." Israel, they said, must become the servant of all nations; God's intention was to gather all nations into a just society under the holiness of his sovereign rule, and Israel was his instrument to this end.

This development made the transition from the Kingdom of Israel to the Kingdom of God a natural one. This radical monotheism of God as the single universal sovereign, holy and merciful in his nature, became the central prophetic message.

However, the bitter historic experiences of the Hebrew people led to another change of emphasis in the idea of God's intention. The repeated disappointments that led from corrupt governments to disastrous defeats, produced the apocalyptic consciousness. This consciousness arose out of the apparent futility of the human effort to establish a kingdom obedient to the Holy Will. Since the ideal would not die, seeing that God is God, the seers prophesied that in his own time, God would establish his Kingdom by his own mighty acts. To accomplish this end he would work through a Messiah, a new servant, appointed by him and serving as his vice-regent on the earth.

It was in this form that the covenant ideal was transmitted to the time of the New Testament.

### The New Testament Background

If the central ideal of the Old Testament is God's kingdom of universal justice, the controlling spirit of the New is God's kingdom of universal agape, love. Jesus taught that justice—the Law—finds its fulfillment in love, that the Sovereign Ruler of the Universe is himself fatherly love, and that to choose obedience to his will is to choose to live under the spirit of love.

The Sermon on the Mount (Matthew, chaps. 5, 6, and 7) spells out many aspects of this fulfillment. The Law said, "You shall not kill," but Jesus says, "Everyone who is angry with his brother shall be liable to judgment. . . ." The Law said, "You shall not commit adultery," but Jesus teaches, "Don't admit lust into your heart." The Law said, "Tell the truth under oath," but Jesus says, "Let your 'yes' be 'yes,' and your 'no' be 'no.'" The Law said, "Love your neighbor and hate your enemy," but Jesus says, "Love your enemies and pray for those who persecute you, so that you may be sons of your Father who is in heaven."

In each of these cases the point is that God's intention in the original covenant was for men to increase their mutuality without limit. Wherever the Law worked against such mutuality—as in the burdensome Sabbath laws—Jesus plainly repudiated it.

Jesus taught that his ministry marked a special moment in human history—the drawing near of the Kingdom of God, which had been so long in coming. When he cried, "The Kingdom of God is at hand," he meant not only that it was imminent—coming at any moment—but that it had in some sense already come, that it was already being manifested with power in the fellowship which had grown up around his ministry. He taught that the power of sin and pride in human life was being broken and that men were freely able to press into the kingdom of agape. The choice was up to them. The intention of creation was approaching its consummation.

*The Ethics of Paul.* A popular misconception is that St. Paul subtly changed Jesus' teaching of a universal kingdom of love into a religion of personal salvation. This problem is much too complex to discuss here, but this view is mistaken. Over and over again Paul shows that he understands the new ethic of love, and his teaching adds depth to our comprehension of it. Consider, for example, his famous "hymn to agape," in the thirteenth chapter of his first Corinthian letter, where he urges his readers to follow the highest path of all:

> *I may speak with the tongues of men and of angels*
> > *but if I have no love, I am a noisy gong or a clanging cymbal;*
> *I may prophesy, fathom all mysteries and secert lore,*
> *I may have such absolute faith that I can move*
> > *hills from their place, but if I have no love, I*
> > > *count for nothing!*
> *I may distribute all I possess in charity,*
> *I may give up my body to be burnt,*
> > *but if I have no love, I make nothing of it.*
> *Love is very patient, very kind.*
> *Love knows no jealousy;*
> > *Love makes no parade, gives itself no airs, is never*
> > > *rude, never selfish, never irritated, never resentful;*
> *Love is never glad when others go wrong,*
> > *Love is gladdened by goodness, always slow to expose,*
> > > *eager to believe the best, always hopeful, always patient.*
> *Love never disappears.*
> > *As for prophesying, it will be superseded;*
> > *As for "tongues," they will cease;*
> > *As for knowledge, it will be superseded.*
> *For we know only bit by bit;*
> > *but when the perfect comes, the imperfect will be superseded.*
> *When I was a child, I thought like a child,*
> > *I argued like a child;*
> > *Now that I am a man, I am done with childish ways.*
> *At present we only see the baffling reflections in a mirror*
> *But then it will be face to face;*
> *At present I am learning bit by bit,*
> > *but then I shall understand, as all along I have*
> > > *myself been understood.*
> *Thus "faith and hope and love last on, these three"*
> > *but the greatest of all is love.*[2]

At his best—and we may admit that there were moments when he faltered in his exposition—the great Apostle clearly shows the difference between a legalistic religion of rules and a religion of freedom. His references to the sacrifice of Christ must be interpreted as the deepest symbol of God's unlimited love for man. His teachings have to be culled from informal letters to churches on practical matters. But time after time, if the central message is set in relief, it betrays the spirit of Jesus. His great formulation is "faith working through love," and that faith is an utter trust in God, who revealed in Jesus' life and death a love from which nothing in the whole creation can ever separate us. The revelation is that of a father "from whom every family in heaven and on earth is named" and whose intention is that all should be "filled with all the fullness of God."[3] It is only by picking some of Paul's lesser utterances on practical matters, or some passages where he molds Hellenic materials to his purpose, or where he falls into the old habits of rabbinic argumentation, that he can be interpreted as turning aside from the message that came from Jesus.

Besides, in Paul's writings we see revealed for the first time the inner struggles of a man seeking to realize personally and practically, in its fullness, what the new Kingdom of Love means. It is for this reason that some scholars have called Paul the "first Christian."


## AN ETHIC OF RESPONSIBLE DIALOGUE

In order to provide a focus for our understanding of the biblical ethic let us call it, following Richard Niebuhr, an ethic of responsible dialogue. We should be prepared for this notion after our frequent references to the dialogue of God and man which lay back of the Mosaic law, and which manifested itself so vividly in the prophets and again so fully in Jesus. The full human life, I am saying, is a life of response to the dialogue initiated by God; all our privileges and duties in existence can be best understood in this light.

H. Richard Niebuhr, in *The Responsible Self*, says that Western ethical thought can be viewed under two dominant images: (1) the image of man as a political being; and (2) the image of man as the maker and pursuer of goods. The first picture gives rise to all the legalistic theories of man's ethical existence. Law is the key word, leading to such concepts as contract, agreement, obligation. Here the search for a proper ethic is the pursuit of a primary law from which all lesser legal obligations would follow. The ethic of the philosopher Kant is the purest example of this kind of ethic.

The second picture—man as a maker and pursuer of goods—gives rise to all the ethical systems that interpret the right and the good in terms of some system of goods in which man's welfare lies. Aristotle and Mill, for example, agree that the highest good is happiness.

In contrast to these two images, the biblical metaphor is of man the answerer. God walked in the garden and called the first man, "Adam, where art thou?"[4] Adam should have responded as did Isaiah the prophet, "Lord, here am I!"[5] Instead, in shame, Adam hid himself—the first refusal to participate in the eternal dialogue which God set going in the creation of man. The story of mankind is the story of one or the other of those two reactions. The great saints of the Bible invariably say "Here am I." The rest conceal themselves from the voice that calls them and set their life course by some other principle.

The founder of modern philosophy, René Descartes, said that he existed in his own thought: "*Cogito, ergo sum*" ("I think, therefore I am"). But the result of such a conception is, as I have pointed out, a barren view of human existence. For of Descartes's "*cogito*" we may substitute this maxim: "*Repondeo, ergo sum*" ("I respond, therefore I am"). The fully existing man is the responding man—the responsible man.

Richard Neibuhr says that the fundamental maxim for such a man is this: "God is acting in all actions upon you. So respond to all actions upon you as to respond to his action."[6] Let us examine this maxim. It can be contrasted to religious idealism, which says, "Remember God's plan for your life," and to religious legalism, which says, "Obey God's law in all your obediences to finite rules."[7] The first contrast makes the individual the center of ethical concern—his development and destiny. The second makes rules and law the focus of concern. The frequent result of religious idealism is a kind of enlightened selfishness; the equally common result of religious legalism is a life burdened by restricting rules and regulations. Neither fully expresses the meaning of Christ's kingdom of sovereign love.

The biblical picture is of man set with his fellow man in creation by a God who from the beginning remains in intimate personal relationship with each of them. In his love he calls them into fellowship with him and with one another. As sovereign and holy Creator, he initiates and sustains the dialogue; as creature and sinner, man must hear and answer.

The whole story of the covenants—both old and new—is one of God's call and man's response. The new covenant offers to renew the dialogue in grace—that is, in freedom and forgiveness. Its spirit is the outpouring of costly and unlimited loving kindness from the Initiator of the dialogue himself.

### Dialogue as a Center of Reference

We have seen earlier that modern man, surrounded by all the various claims and goods of modern civilization, needs a center of reference by means of which he can set the rest in order. A biblical ethic of dialogue can serve that purpose. Perhaps this can be illustrated by pointing out the direction in which certain problems in the ethical life can be resolved.

*Rules.* The good life seems inevitably involved with rules. But an ethic of rules runs into several difficulties: The attempt to find a way of systematically relating rules so that they do not contradict one another always fails. Moreover, different societies and different men seem to find different rules suitable to their various styles of life. In any case, a life lived by rules is invariably cramped and rigid; this is especially true the more it is pursued conscientiously. And, worst of all, a legalistic ethic encourages self-centeredness.

These difficulties have led many thoughtful men into skepticism. If we think of life in terms of dialogue we can admit that there is no final system of fixed rules to which an ethical man owes allegiance. Man's allegiance is not to rules, but to the holy, living God who speaks through every event calling him to a fresh response. Rules he will have and use, since they are useful within limited contexts, but he knows that they are not ultimate. Some rules are so nearly universal that a breach if them would be rare indeed, but it is not to such rules that life really points. As Paul Lehmann says, "The Christian is not governed by moral rules and regulations." Rather he aims at freely cooperating with "what God is doing" here and now "to make life human life truly human."[8] At heart, the man of dialogue is free; living in the spirit of responsive love, he goes his way responsibly, fulfilling, out of his faithfulness, more of the rules than the rule-bound man can manage. This is what Paul means when he says that in the Spirit the Law is fulfilled. The call of God is, of course, not opposed to good law, but it is above the law in the sense that it is the source of the law itself, and in its fullness it fulfills that law.

*Values.* The good life seems equally to involve a pursuit of values and to require some kind of systematical ordering of these values. But this also falls into grave difficulties. Even good men have never been able to agree on what the highest value might be. When they have defined such a high value they cannot agree as to its meaning in actual situations. Moreover, values, like rules, as a clue to life have a way of focusing too much attention on the self and its value struggle, leading to a kind of self-enclosure that is fatal to the struggle itself.

Again, from the perspective of dialogue, we can admit that life will be filled with value choices, but they will be in the context of responsiveness and sharing. The good life will not be a collection of high values, but a continuous give-and-take among men who are responding in full to one another and to the Initiator of the dialogue. In this context the highest values find their full meaning, not as possessions of individuals, but as a quality which ebbs and flows in the living community. In short, in love.

What has been said of rules and values could be said of duties and virtues. The good life will be concerned also with these. But without this saving context of dialogic responsibility the dutiful man is still too legalistic, and the virtuous man is too self-centered and proud.

In thus making dialogue the center of reference it is not claimed that all difficulties about rules, values, duties, and virtues can be quickly resolved. What is claimed is that since the dialogue is their natural root, a return to that root will help overcome the contradictions that follow from taking the fruit by itself. If we begin with man responding in everything as to the call of God, who set him with his fellows in a community of love, the way is paved for the richest life of goodness and virtue. "The fruits of the Spirit," as St. Paul says, "are love, joy, and peace . . . against such there is no law."[9]

Moreover, such an ethic allows full play for the creativity, rationality, and all the varied wisdom that men have accumulated about the concrete good of life. The divine-human dialogue is fully contextual. It does not set down rules or ideals or values from an abstract realm above life itself; it accepts life in its fullness and responds in, with, and under that fullness to the God who created it.

Before leaving this discussion one further point needs making, especially in the light of some current discussions of what is now called situational ethics. The function of rules, standards of value, and concepts of virtue can perhaps best be understood as rigorously tested summaries of the long experience of the best men in their dialogic response to what God is doing in life to make it more human.

God, of course, knows every situation perfectly, and he always acts out of his holy love. He needs no rules or standards. His agapic nature is the standard. But because our knowledge is finite, and because our will is not always loving, we need to take these standards seriously as a protection against our ignorance and selfishness. The dialogic life is not one of casual disregard of the wisdom embodied in these useful summaries.

## THE STRUCTURE OF DIALOGUE

Though there are no set rules for dialogue, since it is a total responsiveness to the life-world in which man lives, there are nonetheless some elements that always appear in it, and that can for this reason be thought of, metaphorically, as its fundamental structure. This structure can be divided into these dimensions: the "spiritual" dimension; the creaturely dimension; and the dimension of sin and grace. (The word "spiritual" is set in quotes because the spiritual, in the full sense of the word, includes life in its wholeness and depth, not excluding its creaturely aspects.)

### The "Spiritual" Dimension

The elements of the "spiritual" dimension can be set down as follows:

*Justice.* The first element is justice. Justice is the recognition that each person belongs to the human dialogue by virtue of his mere existence. It is his claim to participate to the maximum of his capacity in the dialogue without any artificial liability, such as race. It is also a claim to equal access to the means of dialogue within the resources of the community. In Rashdall's phrase, it is "equality of consideration," or with Urban, "moral symmetry." But it should be clear that moral symmetry imposes duties upon each man as well as granting him rights.

Justice is not a specific arrangement of society that can be detailed in advance of the concrete situation to which it is applied. What is just in a given society cannot be judged until some knowledge is available concerning the detailed functioning of its institutions in particular situations. That is why we refer to justice as an element in the form or structure of dialogue, no matter where it takes place.

*Love.* Love, the second element, is not a law, but a spirit that goes out toward one's fellows, a spirit of openness, respect, and good will. Kant saw that this kind of good will was the one thing in the whole universe that was "good without qualification."[10] The New Testament gives us Christ as the model of that love. "Love one another as Christ has loved us," admonishes Paul. This brings the golden rule up to the level of full agape, to the level of the sacrificial love of Christ. This love encompasses, I believe, what Albert Schweitzer meant by "reverence for life."

*Faith.* By faith, the third element, we mean here an open trustfulness toward the ultimate quality of goodness that underlies all existence. It is a continuous affirmation of that goodness in the ongoingness of life. It is faith that sees a greater dialogue beckoning, leading us out from our provincial limitations to a greater mutuality and communion. When faith grows cold, men lose the nerve to love. They withdraw within their defensible perimeters and peer at life from that self-enclosure. Men learn very early that dialogue is risky and painful. For this reason, they need a power that liberates them from their fears and hostilities if they are to enter into human mutuality. Faith is thus an essential dimension of full dialogue.

*Freedom.* The fourth element is freedom. Dialogue operates in freedom; it acknowledges that we can refuse to answer. Our responding to God is our own response, though evoked by his love. Freedom means to live life from within outward rather than from the outside inward. It knows that life is more than the means of life, however sacred these latter may seem to be. Even "the Sabbath is made for man, not man for the Sabbath."[11]

*Creativity.* The fifth element of the "spiritual" dimension of dialogue is creativity. The ground of the divine-human dialogue is continuous creation. We must reject the fixity of the older traditional and legal concepts that arise quite naturally in static societies, under which the good life is thought of as adjustment to an established order. The order of the Kingdom of God is continuously coming into existence, and the ethical man is in tune with this universal birth process. Creativity is an act in which freedom, love, and faith are fused in a single hopeful leap into the future which is yet to be fully shaped. The dialogic man is the creative man, sensitive to the unlimited possibilities of life which have yet to be manifested.

This is not the place to marshal the evidence for this fact, but it should be noted that creativity is the product of a mysterious kind of communion with the being that surrounds men. The great artists, inventors, and productive men in all kinds of enterprises testify overwhelmingly to this fact. It is part of the dialogue, and when dialogue breaks down, creativity fails.

*Thought.* The sixth element is thought. Reflection, the ability to think about existence, is one of the supreme marks of man's dignity as man. It is also an indispensable feature of the dialogic man of our time. Thought is not essential to the masses of men in a traditional or authoritarian society, but a dynamic society of mutuality and freedom would be impossible without it. I do not think it an accident that Jesus included the word mind in his celebrated summary of the First Commandment. To enter this dialogue means to respond with one's mind as well as with the rest of one's powers.

*Joy and Peace.* Joy and peace make up the seventh element. A life lived by conscientious rules or the pursuit of values alone is a restless and troubled one. At its best—since the best men know well their limitations—it abounds in failure and disapppointment. But a life of responsiveness to the living Spirit is filled with immediate accomplishment despite failure. Even in failure, the end is at hand—in the One with whom one has to do at every moment of existence. The sting of continuous defeat is removed without removing the incentive to set oneself to try again and again. As T. S. Eliot says, "For us there is only the trying, the rest is not our business."[12] That is because dialogue is lived in a Presence whose very immediacy transmutes suffering and failure into victory.

## The Creaturely Dimension

Man is a creature. He exists bodily in space and time, in nature and culture. Dialogue is not a matter of pure spirit—even though it moves in the "spiritual" dimension we have just outlined. The fact of man's creatureliness conditions the divine-human dialogue in recognizable ways.

*Human Needs.* The circumstances of man's appearance and continuance in existence make him dependent on certain need fulfillments if he is to become a human being in any meaningful sense. Our universal human needs give rise to the basic institutions of all historical societies: (1) *The family:* Born a helpless infant, man needs the family for his physical and emotional sustenance. Moreover, he is born sexed, and full expression of his humanity takes note of this fact. (2) *Government:* No significant human life can be lived apart from the social order and collective action that government alone makes possible. (3) *The economy:* All societies must evolve the means of producing and distributing the goods needed for human existence. Below a certain level of economic achievement, human life degenerates into a subhuman condition where it would be fatuous to talk about dialogue at all. (4) *Culture:* Culture is the web of consensus that makes possible the innumerable acts of cooperation without which a society—and, in turn, man—cannot exist. It includes all the means of symbolic interaction, such as language, the arts, and custom. (5) *Education:* Man is born ignorant. He must learn from his predecessors all that he needs to become human. The fact that in modern societies the educational function is becoming separately institutionalized, in a way not found in earlier societies, is itself very significant for any mature ethical view. Human beings in some sense have a "right" to education by virtue of their right to become human. (6) *The church:* The church is the institutionalization of ultimate concern, the collective expression of man's understanding of the meaning of his existence. From what we have pointed out in previous chapters, it should be apparent that this institution is essential to the structure of full human dialogue. Paul Lehmann teaches that ideally the church should be a "laboratory of maturity," in which the dialogue between man and God and man and man reaches its highest expression.[13]

The reason for pointing out this creaturely dimension is to avoid the impression that dialogue is somehow an idealized or abstract standard for ethics. Dialogue occurs to man in his full concreteness.

Other perspectives—naturalism, idealism, rationalism, and so on—are abstractions from this full context. The truths that they possess are but fragments of the fullness from which they have been torn. Dialogue, in this sense, of course, is not merely words; it is the whole of life lived in open responsiveness. It includes all our powers—bodily, mental, and spiritual—and all our relationships, natural, social, and religious.

### The Dimension of Sin and Grace

A final dimension of the divine-human dialogue has yet to be accounted for; namely, human resistance to it. Though man is made for mutuality and communion, he unaccountably turns against it. The evidence for this propensity to selfishness—what Robert Penn Warren calls the "immitigable ferocity of self"[14] and T. V. Smith, ironically, "the noble impartiality of self-interest"—emerges always and everywhere in human association. Reinhold Niebuhr argues that the neglect of this lesson in ethics has led to the tragic illusions of secular utopianism and religious perfectionism.

*Sin.* Sin is not easy to define. It does not mean merely individual bad choices, particular "sins." It stands rather for the propensity of men to look upon themselves as the center of existence. This propensity is not "natural" in the sense that eating is both natural and necessary. It does not reside in our physical nature. In fact, it is not a drive or an impulse. It resides rather in our freedom, and in our free rejection of the good we know and approve. As the Latin proverb has it, "I see the good and approve it; the wrong is what I pursue." Paul wrestles with the same agonizing difficulty in his Roman letter.[15]

From another perspective, sin is the human refusal to affirm what we really are, our essential character as human beings, the kind of being God intended at our creation. From this point of view, what we do is often less sinful than what we neglect to do—the neglect of the whole region of our true potentialities as human beings. "An anti-moral act," writes Paul Tillich, "is not the transgression of one or several precisely circumscribed commands, but an act that contradicts the self-realization of the person as a person. . . ."[16]

Though sin is not a necessity of man's nature, its universality suggests that certain aspects of human existence tempt men to it. Three of them are fairly obvious. Precarious bodily existence makes men vulnerable. They become afraid and defensive. Their fears turn easily into haunting anxieties and their defensiveness into bitter hostility. The fact of their spatial and temporal location attracts men to values that are accessible and at hand. They resist the efforts of imagination that would lead them to postpone satisfaction now in order to have greater satisfactions later, or to seek values that are distant when lesser values can be had now for the taking. Most important of all, human beings grow up among selfish human beings and imbibe self-centeredness with their mother's milk.

An ethic that failed to take note of sin in human life could be properly charged with naïveté. It is for this reason that the Christian version of dialogue is commended here. The biblical faith recognizes the fact of sin and proposes a remedy for it—the grace of God. What is meant by this?

*Grace.* Men need help in their ambiguous efforts to escape from self-centeredness. Self-effort alone wraps the coils of self tighter. The self must be lured out of its anxieties and hostilities into the life of dialogues. Only an infinite love, working at the deepest levels of human nature, can perform this task. The Christian message is that such infinite love has manifested itself in Jesus, calling men back to their true selves in the communion with God and their fellows. The cross is the symbol of the utter selflessness and self-giving character of the divine love. It is the offer of grace to heal man's broken nature.

Humanly speaking, we can see why this answer makes sense. Only love can evoke love. Dialogue can be born only where someone enters openly and persistently into it, disregarding the costs. The persistent love of good parents or patient friends for the wayward is a dim reflection of the meaning of grace.

Jesus teaches that the Divine Love is like a shepherd who leaves the sheep that are safe in the fold, and goes into the wilderness to find the one that is lost. It is like the waiting father of the boy who has willfully left home and wasted his substance in riotous living. And, after his death, his followers said that it was like Jesus himself, who went to the cross forgiving those who killed him.

Whatever the image, the fact is that there is in human experience an immense testimony—so often neglected in discussions of ethics—to a love that sweeps through the narrow confines of the selfish human soul and carries it out into the sea of grace—the graciousness of God. In grace all human efforts at dialogue are transmuted into healing effectiveness.

In this chapter I have tried to outline an ethic that would do justice to the full range of human existence, one which could serve as a center of reference for the many puzzles and ambiguities which afflict our struggle with the right and the good. We have considered a possible answer in an ethic of responsible dialogue, the dialogue in which God speaks through the manifold conditions of human existence and man responds, first to God's importunities and then to his fellows. If we seek a summary of this point of view it can be found in Jesus' summary of the Law and the Prophets, with his own life as commentary: "You shall love the Lord your God with all your heart, with all your soul, with all your strength and with all your mind . . . and you shall love your neighbor as yourself."[17]

It remains now for us to apply this ethic to the particular problems of personal and social existence. This is the task of our next two chapters.

## SUGGESTIONS FOR FURTHER READING

For an over-all view of the relationship between Christian ethics and philosophy, see George F. Thomas, *Christian Ethics and Moral Philosophy* (Scribner, 1955). For a few of the most important books on Christian ethics by leading theologians, see the following: Paul Ramsey, *Basic Christian Ethics* (Scribner, 1950); H. Reinhold Niebuhr, *An Interpretation of Christian Ethics* (Meridian, World Publishing, 1956); H. Richard Niebuhr, *The Responsible Self* (Harper & Row, 1963); Paul Lehmann, *Ethics in a Christian Context* (Harper & Row, 1963); Paul Tillich's *Beyond Morality* (Harper & Row, 1963).

For the best account of dialogue, see again Martin Buber's *I and Thou* (Macmillan, 1958), and *Between Man and Man* (Beacon Press, 1955).

## NOTES

1. Paul L. Lehmann, *Ethics in a Christian Context* (Harper & Row, 1963), p. 251.
2. I Corinthians 13 (Moffatt trans.).
3. Ephesians 3:14, 19.
4. Genesis 3:9.
5. Isaiah 6:8.
6. H. Richard Niebuhr, *The Responsible Self* (Harper & Row, 1963), p. 126.
7. *Ibid.*
8. Lehmann, *op. cit.*, p. 305.
9. Galatians 5:22.
10. Immanuel Kant, *Fundamental Principles of the Metaphysics of Morals* (Liberal Arts, Bobbs-Merrill, 1949), p. 11.
11. Mark 1:27.
12. T. S. Eliot, *Four Quartets* (Harcourt, Brace & World, 1943), p. 17.
13. Lehmann, *op. cit.*, p. 101.
14. Robert Penn Warren, *Brother to Dragons* (Random House, 1953).
15. See especially Romans 7.
16. Paul Tillich, *Morality and Beyond* (Harper & Row, 1963), p. 20.
17. Matthew 22:37, 39.

# 18

# *The Responsible Person*

❖❖❖❖❖❖❖❖❖❖❖❖❖❖❖❖❖❖❖❖❖❖❖❖❖❖❖❖❖❖❖❖

The responsible person is one whose maturity has so ripened that he turns effortlessly from self-preoccupation to respond freely, in depth, to the entire life-world which God created out of love and for love. The responsible person, that is to say, is one who enters fully into the divine-human dialogue.

This conception follows from our previous discussions of psychology and ethics (chapters 16 and 17). It points to a more inclusive ethical ideal, the responsible society, which is the collective action of responsible persons. Here I want to delineate some of the dimensions of the responsible person, leaving an account of the responsible society to the next chapter.

What is meant by saying that a person is responsible? In the basic sense of the word we may say, first of all, that such a person responds, he answers, he presents himself to view; rather than withholding or reserving himself, he willingly interacts. He knows that his true life is in meeting. Moreover, this response is an act of freedom, not merely a reaction to his environment. But a dialogue of freedom in a world of free beings who are destined to grow together toward maturity in love has its conterpart in responsibility for both one's self and others.

## Responsibility for Self

No one has more drastically urged man's responsibility for himself than the philosopher Jean-Paul Sartre.[1] He makes this the prime mark of the authentic man. Human beings, he points out, are prone to blame their existence on forces other than themselves: their training, their heredity, social conditions, fate, and so on. The degree to which they succeed in believing these excuses determines the degree of their bad faith and self-deception. But, writes Sartre, human beings exist in their freedom. They are their freedom. For man there is no prexistent personal pattern, so standard way of existing as a human being. To be human means to live with the anxieties of choosing, in the knowledge that every choice is a choice of one's own being, a determination of the kind of person one is to be. In choice one creates his own essence.

Sartre contrasts his own plays and novels with those of the great realists, such as the novelist Émile Zola.[2] Zola, he says, excused his characters by tracing their behavior back to the social conditions which produced them. Sartre will not tolerate such excuses. All his characters are what they themselves have chosen to be. When they deny this, they simply fall into bad faith. The worst human being, he says, is the one who denies that he has chosen himself, and tries to place the burden of his existence elsewhere.

Sartre does not deny, of course, that men awake to life in the midst of all sorts of preconditioning circumstances: one is born male or female, for example; born in one nation or another, inheriting a given culture; and so on. But, says Sartre, man is still free to affirm or deny that heritage in a thousand ways. The born male may choose to be a homosexual, or a celibate, or a faithful married man, or a libertine. His sexuality may be given, but what he does with it is his own responsibility, and he deceives himself if he thinks otherwise.

Because of his doctrine of absolute responsibility, Sartre rejects religion. Religion, he holds, is just one more way for men to act in bad faith; blaming their existence on a power outside themselves. We must agree with him to a degree. Insofar as he rejects the idea of God as a separate entity, interfering with or determining human beings' lives in a mechanical way, his criticism is sound theology.

The dialogic view of God's relationship to human existence is of a different order. God creates man in freedom and for freedom. Every relationship which God initiates, ensures and promotes man's own responsibility and freedom. He waits with infinite patience for man freely to respond to his loving importunities. The paradox of human existence is that man is not self-created, but dependent; yet because of God's own nature as holy, creative love, he creates and sustains man in his responsible freedom. If Sartre had had the slightest inkling of this kind of divine-human relationship, he might not have made so total a judgment against religious faith. In essence, then, his major proposition is right: Man is born free and responsible for his own being. And whatever we may say about God's relationships with man must not compromise that fact.

### Responsibility for Others

Beyond being responsible for himself the responsible person is also responsible to and for others. This in several ways: First, he is open to them in the deepest possible manner. He seeks to be present to them whether they are present to him or not. In this openness he tries, so far as he is able, to respond in love, to concern himself with their need. Jesus illustrated this ideal in his story of the good Samaritan. The Samaritan who at great personal risk helped a Jewish traveler from Jerusalem to Jericho who had been robbed and beaten was regarded by Jesus' Jewish auditors as an alien beneath contempt. Yet the traveler's own Jewish countrymen, religious officials at that, had passed him by. The real neighbor is thus anyone who assists another in need.

The responsible person is last of all responsible to God. This means that he is continually open to the divine dimension of the dialogue. He looks upon all that happens to him as a meaningful communication from the source and ground of his existence. He is continually asking, at least implicitly: "What does this event mean? What is God's intention for the situation in which I find myself?" Insofar as he reads that meaning, he responds freely to it in faithful obedience. He knows that such obedience is no abridgment of his own nature, for he realizes that he is made for love, made for union with God and with his fellows.

## THE RESPONSIBLE PERSON IN DECISION

The responsible life is one of continuous decision. There are no preexisting patterns laid down whereby man may roll on effortlessly to a full existence. Life ceaselessly presents us with alternatives, and which of them will be actualized is up to us. Our decision has a real effect in the world, and is therefore of utmost importance.

But it would appear that in placing the context of the ethical life in the free flow of dialogue, we have made decision an impossibly difficult matter. The legalist—an advocate of the rule-type ethic—can readily make up his mind by comparing cases and applying the appropriate rules to the situation before him. But if, as I have said, there are no absolutely valid rules and laws, how does the responsible person operate?

Decision is a complex matter which involves the whole person in his whole situation. This complexity is the cost of living humanly. It is very like the processes in a court of equity, where there are no fixed laws or precedents to guide the court. The final judgment has to be made in broad terms of what is equitable, or just. Witnesses are heard, arguments and counterarguments are marshaled, examples are considered, and at last a verdict is arrived at and a decision is rendered that, in a sense, adds new dimensions to the human understanding of justice. In an analogous way the responsible man decides.

### The Context of Moral Decision

We are called upon to decide morally when the habitual pattern of moral choices has proved inadequate, as, for example, in the tensions now arising in the field of race relations. In lesser problems, where habitual patterns are satisfactory, decision is relatively easy—we see the right and we choose it. But when these patterns break down, deliberation thickens. We are neither sure of how to define the problem nor of what principles and values to call upon. In such a case the responsible man must throw himself unreservedly into the variegated context of life and work with fear and trembling toward an authentic decision. In doing this he engages in the most personal act possible, for essentially he is asking how to respond in depth as a human being to the confusing summons that life is directing to him.

### The Deliberation of Listening

Deliberation in this kind of problem is a complex act of listening. The responsible person knows that he must strain to be alert in every dimension of his being so that he will not shut off the dialogue with others that the situation is demanding.

He enters the moral situation equiped with a knowledge of some facts, rules, character habits, attitudes, and values. I mean such rules as "Always keep your promises," such moral habits as honesty or kindness, and such attitudes and values as arise, say, out of living in a democracy. But it is this stock of moral equipment that we are saying is inadequate. How, then, can he proceed?

He proceeds by faith, knowing that he may well be required to change in fundamental ways as he meets the situation before him. His received body of factual knowledge may be insufficient or filled with error. He reopens the quest for relevant information. In the race issue, for example, he cannot respond intelligently if he has faulty knowledge in biology or the social sciences. Much of what he thinks is knowledge may be ideological mythology that has grown up unconsciously over the years. He accepts this possibility, and painfully begins a reassessment.

The standard rules by which he has heretofore determined matters of racial justice may be inconsistent or irrelevant. He will begin the difficult process of going back to first principles, back even to what we have called the "structure of dialogue" in order to revise them upward.

His moral habits and attitudes may also appear, upon close examination, to be infected with prejudice, or prove to be mere peculiarities of a given class or historical period. He may, for example, as a good middle-class citizen, find it difficult to think of a lawbreaker as the moral hero he well may be. His values may also prove to be the product of limited experience, or of too constricted an imagination. He may never have considered, for instance, the lifelong sense of outrage that a nonwhite person must feel, living in a society that continually denigrates him by refusing to eat with or even near him or to allow him the personal services that are assumed to be the natural rights of everyone else.

What is called into question here is the reliability of our entire moral equipment for adequately judging such a problem as the racial situation and authentically responding to it. The greater and more novel the problem, the greater the personal overhauling that is required.

We may call this kind of deliberation "listening" because there is no conceivable presiding rule that can guide a person through such a thicket of questioning. He must literally feel his way, like a man making a scientific discovery or creating a new work of art. His posture in this situation is one of alert listening, the highest form of attentiveness for the slightest clues as to the direction in which a responsible solution may lie.

The complex elements of the situation—facts, values, attitudes, and so on—are not separate and unrelated items. They are elements in the single act of asking what God intends in the matter of race relations. They are a code to be deciphered, a language to be translated. In such situations God is calling the human race to a more human and just response than it has ever made before. The responsible man is the growing edge of that response.

Such listening is, of course, a prepared listening, a listening with all one's powers alert and inclined toward obedience to whatever leadings and insights might come; not despising traditional moral teaching, but using it as a vehicle of deepening awareness.

Paul Lehmann's concept of Christian ethics is relevant at this point. According to him, there is one prime principle that a responsible person will follow, and that is to cultivate an "imaginative and behavioral sensitivity to what God is doing in the world to make and keep human life human, to achieve the maturity of men, that is, the new humanity."[3] Of course, it is necessary to understand who we mean by God. Lehmann is referring to the God of the Judaeo-Christian Bible. If we were Hegelians we might ask what the Absolute was doing, or if we were Marxists we would ask what the material dialectic is doing. Nationalists often judge their own actions by asking what the nation is doing. But the dialogue that is at the center of this present discussion is focused on what God is doing. From the New Testament we know that this question could be rephrased What is love doing? But love also must be interpreted in the Christian sense, not in some other.

Part of our knowledge of what God is doing can be thus discerned from a careful study of the Bible. But to make this "rule" apply to the present moment it is necessary to invoke the guidance of the Spirit which illuminates

God's demands here and now. Listening, in this sense, becomes meditation and prayer, both alone and with others who share the faith that God speaks to man directly in this way.

### The Final Phase: Decision and Action

The conclusion of moral deliberation is not like a logical conclusion in mathematics, nor a factual conclusion in science, nor an abstract acceptance of some principle or value, but a conclusion that involves a blend of all of these in a peculiarly personal way. A moral decision is not merely a making up of one's mind; it is a risky making up of one's person. It requires what William James called the "dead heave of the will."

The reason for putting it this way is that by his decisions in moral matters a man decides what kind of man he is and is to be, and what kind of total relationships he will have with existence. His decision is thus a personal judgment about what reality in its depths is, what the world is fundamentally like, and to what destiny it is voyaging.

Because moral decision is so personally total it invariably involves faith. It cannot avoid encounter with one's ultimate concern. Faith here means much more than one's philosophy, for philosophies themselves have varying relevance to concrete situations. It means one's vital contact with the concrete forms of existence here and now.

In short, the responsible man chooses and acts concretely with his whole being, and this is what is called wisdom as distinct from knowledge. In the present terminology, he *responds*.

## MAN AND HIS SEXUALITY

Let us see how these suggestions apply to the problem of human sexuality. No one can evade this question, and few can doubt that it is of fundamental importance, for it is a prime issue in choosing to be authentically human. What a man does with his sexual powers has enormous potential for good or ill. Any discussion of this matter is set today in a context of widespread questioning of the traditional restraints and restrictions that religious teachings have placed upon sexual life.

### The Erotic Climate of Our Times

The first fact to be recognized is that we live in an erotic age, what Wilhelm Reich called "a sex affirming culture."[4] For better or for worse, the "lid is off the Id." P. A. Sorokin believes that our preoccupation with sex deserves to be called "the American Sex Revolution."[5] How revolutionary it is remains to be seen. But there seems to be no doubt that if we take as indicators current literature, mass entertainment, and social behavior as described in the "statistical naturalism" of such research scholars as Kinsey, sexual interest in our culture is very high indeed. The strident interest in sex is, no doubt, in part a rebellion against the sex mores of the past, and indicates a search for more significant standards. But the climate of erotic preoccupation does make any dispassionate discussion of the matter extremely difficult. The inevitable choosing of sides in a revolutionary period makes rational discussion appear to be an evasion.

## The Biblical View of Sex

Since we are oriented to biblical perspectives, we may profitably start with the biblical view of human sexuality. This may at first seem to be a side issue, but the fact is that the partisans in the present discussion appear to be largely ignorant of the biblical account, whether they argue for or against it. For the sake of brevity, let me summarize this point of view. Sex is the intention of the Creator. It is he who made humanity sexed. For this reason we may suppose that it has some important place in the divine-human dialogue. It cannot be ignored on the authority of the Bible. Moreover, upon his creation of man and woman, Genesis says, God looked and said, "It is very good." Sex is thus marked from the first with divine approbation. All views that regard sex as evil or to be denied or suppressed are unbiblical. One of the first divine commands is, "Be fruitful and multiply."[6]

To be sure, some venerable figures in classical theology, like Augustine, have argued that sex became tainted by the original sin of Adam and is therefore no longer "good" in the Edenic sense. But there seems to be no reason to suppose that sex is any more questionable on these grounds than any other creaturely power. In fact, it is man's egocentricity that perverts his sexuality, not the other way around. Pride perverts everything, and lust is the egocentric perversion of an originally innocent sensuality. Sin lives not in the body but in the will, with the resultant misuse of bodily powers. Sex, then, in itself bears the stamp of divine approval. As John Calvin wrote, the sexual act is "undefiled, honorable and holy, because it is a pure institution of God."[7]

Sex is a spiritual matter. That is, it is intimately connected with man in his wholeness or holiness. It cannot be thought of as a power segmented from the rest of his existence. What a man does with his sexuality is part of what determines the kind of being that he is and will be. Sex is, furthermore, a social concern. What men do with their sexuality affects not only themselves but their partners, their children, and ultimately even their community's share in historical destiny.

These biblical principles stand in contradiction, on the one hand, to puritan and medieval views in which sex is despised or feared, and, on the other, to neo-Freudian views that exalt sex as an all-determining force in human existence, or as a purely personal affair.

### The Human Meaning of Sexuality

We can broaden our inquiry by asking the meaning of human sexuality. Without some clue to this question, we cannot arrive at any wisdom about concrete sexual choices. Sex is the prime biological sign that man is made for dialogue. Sexually he is incomplete alone; he can neither fulfill himself nor perpetuate his kind without intimate relations with another human being of the opposite sex. Sex seems to have appeared very early in the evolutionary process. Biologists now believe that they detect signs of sexuality even at the level of the single cell: one-celled creatures appear, at least occasionally, to exchange nuclear substances prior to cell division, thus producing a more viable organism.

Psychologically, the joy of sexual union seems to be a mark of its "rightness," like the ecstasy of discovery or the contemplation of beauty. This joy is not the same thing as simple pleasure. It seems rather to spring from deeper sources. It carries with it the implication of fulfillment deeper than a mere pleasurable sensation can account for. This has given rise to the myths about an original race of men who possessed in a single organism the complementary qualities of both sexes. Plato recounts one version of this myth in the *Symposium,* his dialogue on ideal love. This original race, he says, was punished by the gods—perhaps out of envy—and was divided into separate halves, male and female. From that moment each of the separated halves was haunted by its memory of the primordial unity in which it had once existed, only finding for brief moments, in sexual union, the perfect joy of that original state.

This myth suggests grounds for the serious reflection that the joy of sexual union is not a mere passing pleasure, but an all too brief recovery of the ecstatic state of some original human unity.

Religions reflect this idea in their widespread use of sexual imagery. Indian temples, to the shocked astonishment of Western tourists, frequently show the supreme divine being in sexual union with his consort—indicating the unity of Brahman and maya. The Christian Church early employed the image of marriage to symbolize the relationship between Christ and his Bride, the Church. And mystics, such as the great St. John of the Cross, wrote their mystical commentaries around the poetry of spiritual marriage.[8]

Moreover, the Christian Church embodied in its sacramental marriage vows a clear statement of the divine agape as the proper relationship between man and wife. In these vows a man and woman promise to take each other "for better for worse, for richer for poorer, in sickness and in health, to love and to cherish. . . ." And they are questioned as to whether they intend, "forsaking all others," to keep themselves only unto each other, "so long as ye both shall live."[9] In essence, this is a joint promise of unconditional responsibility for the other person, no matter what may occur. It is an image of the divine love of God for man. Though it remains merely an ideal in human marriage, the fact that it commended itself to the Church as the only standard for sexual union is significant for a satisfactory view of human sexuality.

This view has substantial support from psychology. Harry Stack Sullivan points out that it is during adolescence that the prototype of all succeeding relationships is experienced. If that experience is a painful one, self-degrading and anxiety-provoking, the chances that the individual will advance in establishing satisfactory interpersonal relationships will be greatly reduced. Or, consider Erik Erickson's summary of what the sexual experience should include if it is to be of lasting social and personal significance: "Mutuality of orgasm—with a loved partner—of the other sex—with whom one is able and willing to share a mutual trust—and with whom one is able and willing to regulate the cycles of work, procreation, and recreation—so as to secure to the offspring, too, all the stages of a satisfactory development."[10] This, from Erickson's point of view, is the human meaning of sexuality in its largest context.

## RESPONSIBILITY AND SEX LIFE

Why cannot the pleasures of sex be innocently enjoyed without the responsibilities of dialogue? This is the question that is at least implicitly asked in the modern questioning about sex. It appears to many of the younger generation that rules and regulations restricting sexual freedom are arbitrary and old-fashioned, that they are hangovers from puritanical or Victorian notions that modern civilization has outgrown. They may even appear as a sign of envy on the part of the older generation for the sexual vitality of the young, and a resentment of pleasures that the older generation has somehow missed.

The question has more poignancy now that venereal diseases are rarer and more easily cured, and contraceptives seem really to contracept. Unwanted children or disease seem less likely than ever before to result from sex enjoyed outside of marriage. While there are still dangers of disease, and the prevention of pregnancy is not as certain as many believe, we must concede that these two possibilities are no sound foundation for answering the question we are asking. The answer lies in considering the sexual life in the light of an ethic of dialogue.

The case for a disciplined (i.e., responsible) sex life can be put as follows: In sexual matters, as in so many other things, existence confronts man with a forked path. "Life," writes Leon Blum, "does not give itself to one who tries to keep all its advantages at once. I have often thought that morality may perhaps consist solely in the courage of making a choice."[11] In the words of Robert Frost's celebrated poem,

> Two roads diverged in a yellow wood,
> And sorry I could not travel both
> And be one traveler. . . .[12]

### *Two Roads of Sex*

In sexual matters these two roads can be labeled "personalized sex" and "segmental sex."

Personalized sex is sex in the context of integral personal existence. It abides by the rule that sex is a matter of total personal expression—which is another name for love. Love in this sense is not merely high feelings accompanying an anticipated sexual relationship. It is the will to affirm the partner as a person, to assume responsibility for him (or her), to enter into a full—not a segmental—union. It recognizes that only a life disciplined enough to remain whole and personally significant in all its expressions can arrive at a truly human happiness.

Segmental sex looks upon sexual powers as an opportunity for passing enjoyment. It wants to "gather rosebuds" while it may. Sexual expression is not an act of "union," but a tasting, a sampling, a mere experiencing.

These diverse roads do not seem at the outset much different. It is at later stages that the differences become starkly apparent. One of the advantages of our age is that human experimentation with segmental sex has had wide publicity. This may appear to those concerned about the morality of youth to be merely intensifying the erotic climate of our time—and no doubt it does—but it also shows with appalling clarity just where this road ends, without each person having to find out—too late—for himself.

The journey of segmental sex begins in seemingly innocent enjoyment; it ends in cynical disillusionment and personal fragmentation. It begins with an exciting affair; it ends with a pathetic search for new partners. It begins with a desire to escape loneliness and separation; it ends with both these conditions aggravated to the point of despair.

In William Golding's *Free Fall*,[13] Samuel Mountjoy is possessed by a fervent desire to realize himself through the one he loves. He tries to probe the secret of Beatrice's being, hidden beneath her chastity. He asks, "What are you, where are you, how far do you extend? I want to be with you, around you, on you and in you, I want fusion and identity."[14] But in his quest for satisfaction he only finds failure. "Once a human being has lost freedom," he sadly realizes, "there is no end to the coils of cruelty. We are forced here and now to torture each other."[15] Once he has satisfied his physical passion and found that there was no union, and no identity for himself, he concludes: "It only reinforced the reality of physical life and destroyed the possibility of anything else, and made physical life not only three times more real, but contemptible."[16] In this state he leaves Beatrice and starts on a new search. For, after all, he thinks, "In this bounded universe where nothing is certain but my own existence, what is to be cared for is the quiet and pleasure of this sultan."[17] He ends with separation and complete enclosure within his own ego.

This story is told over and over again—*ad nauseam*—in modern literature.

Sex, which promises at the outside such high reward, becomes the ultimate weapon of exploitation and disillusionment. As meaninglessness increases, loneliness increases, and the wild search goes on to its inevitable fragmentation. And the story is not told by puritanical moralists, but by the "liberated" artists and writers—the Hemingways and Sartres—who describe human life as they have found it.

The road of segmental sex leads to this end. But it would be sentimental to assume that the other fork of the road leads easily to personal fulfillment. It takes a whole lifetime of the most watchful effort to bring all one's separate powers into a single expression of responsible dialogue. Marriage is a formal expression of sex in the context of responsibility. As such, it is the natural setting for human sexuality. But it does not for this reason supply a sovereign remedy for all the problems of the sex life. Formal marriage—whether civil or sacramental—is only a beginning in the long growth toward wholeness. And within it there are temptations to selfishness and cruelty that are all too familiar.

### Sex and Unmarried Youth

Nor do these remarks settle the difficult problems of the unmarried to discover some code for the relationship of the sexes. At best, it sets a framework of ethical ideals in terms of which such a code may be worked out. A code is needed, despite what we have said about legalism, for in the immediacy of social life, human beings need a rule of thumb to help them make their decisions. A code for permissible forms of affection, which can enhance the participant's possibilities of going on to personalized sex rather than segmental sex, is one of the needs of our time. Such a code can be worked out only by a trustful and frank examination by the young and old alike of the meanings of sex in the context of modern premarital social life. The code should arise out of the disciplined "listening" described earlier, not out of a simple and arbitrary moralizing by elders.

The time between sexual maturity and marriage is likely to be unnaturally long in any highly developed society that requires prolonged education of the young. Dealing with the tensions of such a prolonged period cannot be other than difficult and marked with failures. This is the more true because youth is also the period in life when one is learning to relate to members of the opposite sex, while at the same time engaging in a natural search for intimacy. In terms of personalized sex, the ideal would be to find the right person at the right time and be able to consummate this discovery in marriage.

This is not to suggest that early marriage is a solution for all problems. The fact is that young people who fall into the quagmire of early sexual intimacy are apt to be swallowed up before either has understood himself or his partner as human beings. The natural tensions of the premarriage period can be mitigated and made meaningful by the encouragement of real friendships with persons of the opposite sex. These friendships will tend to foster greater self-knowledge and understanding of human sexual relations than an early plunge into sexual intimacy. For in the long run human marriage is much more a matter of fruitful, lifelong companionship than of biological sexuality. A responsible society will search out ways of encouraging this kind of life among its unmarried youth.

Suggestions to make the interval before marriage a time of trial marriage, on the grounds that it would release sexual tensions and make for a more realistic marital preparation, are, from this point of view, sentimental proposals. They are sentimental because they assume that successful marriage is the result of feeling and overlook the indispensable element of commitment, which makes all the difference between a "trial" and the real thing. The trial marriage, or any other experimentation in premarital sexual intimacy, tends to educate a human being to segmental rather than personalized sex. This inevitably makes more difficult the emergence of a mature sexual relationship.

### Ethical Failure and Renewal

The raising up of an ideal of completely personalized sex, coupled with a recognition of the realities of our own natural desires and the erotic society in which we live, immediately suggests the high likelihood of failure in some degree or another. In every range of the divine-human dialogue the authentic man painfully realizes the depth of his own failures. This recognition of failure may be admirable, but it does threaten the ethical man with despair. To try and fail so frequently inevitably tends to weaken moral resolve.

Where, on the other hand, failure is not acknowledged, a person is led to use clever devices by which he persuades himself that he has indeed not failed at all. He may rationalize, excuse himself, or simply forget (repress, as the psychologists would say). He will probably also be tempted to lower his ethical standard to a level nearer his own performance.

The problem of ethical living can be stated as follows: How can a person maintain a growing ethical ideal, freely acknowledge his failures, and return to the struggle with unimpaired or renewed spirit? The answer to this does not lie in the realm of ethics. It leads directly to the religious ground in which the ethical life is rooted. Moral failure is an estrangement in the divine-human dialogue. The key to renewal is restoration through repentance and forgiveness.

Why cannot a person restore and renew himself by his own powers? The answer can be seen in the sphere of human relationships. If someone has been responsible for a breach of faith in his relationship with someone else, he cannot restore himself to the relationship; only the other person can do that. The faulty partner can initiate the restoration by freely acknowledging his fault, but he must wait upon the other to forgive and restore. In a much larger, though analogous sense, all the failures of men to live up to their highest ideals must be seen against the background of the divine-human dialogue. A man cannot forgive himself, for by his own choice he has proved himself to be unacceptable. The most he can do is repent of his failure and wait for the acceptance from the divine side.

The divine side of this dialogue is, as has been pointed out, a Being of infinite goodness, power, and love. He is not concerned to keep books on failure, but to renew and restore men continually to the communion of dialogue which he himself initiated and sustains.

This is the reason why the divine Agape and ethical living belong intrinsically together. They make a single tissue of life. The economy of the dialogue is thus not punitive, nor is it a legal arrangement for the payment of debts. It is a realistic account of humanity within the circle of moral and religious experience.

The trouble with sexual morality is that from the first awakening of sexual interest, human beings become involved in guilty behavior and find it hard—the higher their ideals, the harder—to believe that they can be forgiven. From this they turn to self-deception in its various forms, convincing themselves that they have not failed at all. But the accumulated sense of failure builds up a damning reservoir of guilt which breaks out in unexpected ways, postponing indefinitely the possibility of mature sexual responsiveness.

The same results occur in other areas of ethical struggle. For example, in the subject just ahead—the realm of vocation—how many persons have a profound sense of having taken a wrong turn and wasted their lives, but have no inkling of a way out of this moral wasteland? The creative divine forgiveness is such a way, and there is no moral failure that is beyond the healing power inherent in it.

## MAN AND HIS WORK

Another crucial area for the individual who would adopt a policy of responsibility is work. Unfortunately the contemporary ethos for work is that of a job chiefly associated with income and status. The young person asks, "What can I do that will yield the largest income, the greatest security, and the highest social status?" This kind of question invariably distorts the meaning of work from its true significance.

The true significance of work can be seen in the creation story of Genesis. The Creator worked for six days creating the world. Each day following his labors, and on the seventh for a whole "day," he "rested" to contemplate his work—and found that it was "good."[18] Jesus implied that God was not through working with his creation. He said, "My Father is working still. . . ."[19]

When man follows this pattern, he finds the meaning of his work. As a creature he shares his labors with the Creator, who still has work to do. The creation is not yet finished.

Incidentally, a curse of many otherwise venerable cultures—including that of the ancient Greeks—is the relegation of work to the "lower classes" on the assumption that work denigrates a man and that the "upper classes" are above such a necessity. Such cultures have no hope of meeting the rising expectations of humanity, unless these attitudes are radically changed. The fostering of such a change could be one of the greatest contributions of Western religion to the future well-being of the world.

The true meaning of work is not in the term "job," but in "vocation." Vocation (same root as "vocal") means a "calling." The word was used during early Christian history to mark a specifically religious life, but the Protestant Reformation broadened the meaning of the word to include work in the world. All work, the great reformers said, was a sacred response to the divine will. Worldly work, being a necessity for man's existence, was as divinely ordained as the work of the priesthood. The artificial limitation of vocation to "religious" callings, they said, had arisen from the false notion that man could make himself more holy by religious acts associated with the monastery. When salvation was seen as a gift freely given by God to men, it was no longer reasonable to seek God away from the world. What was required, according to this theology, was to obey God's call in whatever state a man found himself.[20] Work on this basis is rooted in the divine-human dialogue and can best be understood as an act of gratitude to God and a work of love toward one's fellows.

Without sentimentally ignoring the fact that the conditions of human existence at the present time make a choice of work impossible for many, we can point out that where such choice exists—and it exists to a remarkable degree for young Americans in institutions of higher education—the ideal of work choice would be something like the following.

First, find work that is fundamentally meaningful beyond income and status. Without intrinsic meaning, work is fundamentally destructive. "I have sometimes thought," writes Dostoevsky in his *House of the Dead*, "that the way to crush and annihilate a human being completely would be to set him to do an absolutely senseless and useless thing. If he were condemned to pour water from one tub to another and back again, or to pound sand in a mortar, or to carry a heap of earth backward and forward, I am convinced that he would either commit suicide within a few days or murder some of his fellow-sufferers in order to suffer death at once and be delivered from his moral torture, shame and degradation."[21] This is, of course, exactly what the technique of the Nazi concentration camp consisted in. Many prisoners found this situation so intolerable that they ran against the high-voltage wires around the enclosure and electrocuted themselves. Others simply became walking corpses.

Modern men have tried to escape meaninglessness by seeking high wages and the social status that followed reaching a high place in the work hierarchy. But this activity is merely a postponement of the question of meaning, and it is likely that the high incidence of illness and unhappiness, even among the well-paid, finds its source in an unconscious sense of the worthlessness of what they do for a livelihood. There seems no escape for a human being from the problem of meaning.

A second rule is to work at something that demands the whole man, with all his talents and energies. Segmental work, like segmental sex, tends to winnow the person until he is no longer human. Enlarging this rule, we may say: Work at something that creatively enlarges the human dialogue. The meaning of human life is in this enlarging dialogue, and daily work takes on meaning to the degree that it contributes to it.

A rough rule for enlarging the dialogue is to find work that speaks to human needs. Human need in our growing world population is infinite. Even within a wealthy nation like the United States there are pockets of extreme poverty. The so-called service professions are in continuous short supply because of the relative low status attached to some of them and the competition of higher pay in other work areas.

We can agree wholeheartedly with the Buddhist wisdom that makes "right livelihood" (also translated "complete vocation") one of the elements of the Eightfold Path to salvation. Happy is the man who finds his lifework in line with the highest meanings that he knows.


## MAN AND HIS AVOCATION


Two technological revolutions are changing the face of man's work-world: (1) the substitution of chemical, electric, and nuclear energy for muscle power, and (2) the substitution of so-called thinking machines for many of man's mental labors. We are still in the beginnings of these revolutions and have yet to dream of their full impact on human existence. But one thing is becoming clear: The individual's share of socially necessary labor to meet the needs of human survival will decline dramatically, enormously increasing the margins of human leisure. This, in turn, will pose a new problem for the responsible individual: How will he make this enlarged leisure humanly meaningful?

It is obvious that this released time and energy cannot all be spent in recreation, even in the basic sense of that word as re-creation. The so-called avocation will have to become a second vocation. There is no other way to keep modern life from losing much of its meaning.

What is meant here is that the responsible person will ask as profoundly as he is able, "What new labor am I called upon to do outside the calling in which I earn my living?" Once this question is seriously asked, a wide range of possibilities emerges. They lie in the regions of human relationship that are not covered by the fields of paid vocation. The following is a meager sampling of these areas: *Peace education:* The labor of creating a social and political climate in which the will to peace is generated and workable options to compulsion are demonstrated. The Peace Corps and the voluntary work-camp programs of churches are examples of such work. *Education:* There are many services a volunteer can render the educational program in his community, such as working with undermotived children, who cannot at present benefit from the official formal programs of the schools, or assisting in adult education. *Racial amity:* The creation of more opportunities for the races to know and respect one another, and the championing of the rights of citizens who, because of their color, have not yet attained first-class citizenship. *Church work:* The work of the churches depend primarily upon volunteer services for the implementation of its educational program and social services. *Social service:* And finally there is the rewarding field of volunteer work in hospitals and agencies such as the Red Cross. With the expanding efforts of government in the fight against poverty there are programs such as VISTA, the domestic counterpart of the Peace Corps. For those willing to train for it there is also the field of volunteer counseling which can greatly extend the benefits of our overburdened corps of professional psychologists and psychiatrists.

The unfinished tasks related to the growth of human beings toward their full participation in a truly responsible society are endless, and the progressive lowering of the requirements of the workaday world through automation will not abolish them; it may, in fact, increase them sharply. The man who is truly *responding* will be sensitive to these facts and find an avocation that can add significance to his own life and that of his fellows.[22]

The coming leisure may be considered a providential opportunity for the responsible populations of highly developed societies. It may offer to millions the opportunities for a lifelong education that the burdens of work formerly prevented or made difficult. They can break through the limitations of the years of formal education to take a generous look at the great cultural treasures, which they did not have time to do when they were young. In thus expanding their sympathies and knowledge they can qualify for citizenship in the entire human race at all times and places. They can also avail themselves of the classical and modern means of insight and spiritual enrichment that could vastly accelerate their own personal maturity.

I have tried to show what is meant by the responsible person by indicating his relation to three major areas of personal life: sex, work, and leisure. But the responsible person does not exist alone. He lives and works in society. This is his natural setting. For this reason, in order to complete the picture of an ethic of the divine-human dialogue, we must turn now to a consideration of the responsible society.

### SUGGESTIONS FOR FURTHER READING

Each of the major works suggested in the previous chapter has sections on both vocation and sex. For the latter subject, see also P. A. Sorokin, *The American Sex Revolution* (Porter Sargent, 1956). For a religious interpretation of work, see

Alexander Miller's *The Christian Faith and My Job* (Association Press, 1946), and Robert L. Calhoun, *God and the Common Life* (Scribner, 1935). David E. Trueblood's *Your Other Vocation* (Harper & Row, 1952) deals with avocations.

## NOTES

1. This is a fundamental theme in all his writings. It is especially clear in the chapter "Bad Faith" in *Being and Nothingness*; in *Existentialism* (Philosophical Library, 1947); and in his plays, *No Exit and Three Other Plays* (Vintage, Random House, 1955).
2. Sartre, *Existentialism*, p. 27.
3. Paul Lehmann, *Ethics in a Christian Context* (Harper & Row, 1963), p. 117.
4. Quoted in Donald B. Clapp, "The Sex Scramble on Campus," *Motive*, Orientation Issue (1962).
5. P. A. Sorokin, *The American Sex Revolution* (Sargent, 1956).
6. Genesis 1:28.
7. Quoted in Lehmann, *op. cit.*, p. 135.
8. See, for instance, St. John of the Cross, *Ascent of Mount Carmel* (Image, Doubleday, 1958).
9. From the Episcopal and Methodist marriage service.
10. Erik H. Erickson, *Childhood and Society*, rev. ed. (Norton, 1950), p. 266.
11. In Hadley Cantril and Charles H. Bumstead, *Reflections on the Human Venture* (New York University Press, 1960), p. 149.
12. Robert Frost, "The Road Not Taken," in *Modern American Poetry*, Louis Untermeyer, ed. (Harcourt, Brace & World, 1936), p. 231.
13. William Golding, *Free Fall* (Harbinger, Harcourt, Brace & World, 1962).
14. *Ibid.*, p. 105.
15. *Ibid.*, p. 113.
16. *Ibid.*, p. 123.
17. *Ibid.*, p. 128.
18. Genesis 1.
19. John 5:17.
20. See the basic works of Luther and Calvin for this point of view.
21. Quoted in Douglas Steere, *Work and Contemplation* (Harper & Row, 1957), p. 20.
22. Charles Wells' *Between the Lines*, a biweekly newsletter, contains a column, "What Can I Do?" that reports the stories of people who have discovered a way to express their second vocation creatively. Address: *Between the Lines*, Newtown, Pennsylvania.

# 19

# *The Responsible Society*

❖❘❖❖❘❖❖❘❖❖❘❖❖❘❖❖❘❖❖❘❖❖❘❖❖❘❖❖❘❖❖❘❖❖❘❖❖❘❖❖❘❖❖❘❖❖❘❖❖❘❖❖❘❖❖❘❖❖❘❖❖❘❖❖❘❖❖❘❖❖❘❖

There is no one authoritative pattern of a truly ethical society. Human history is a stream of changes that sometimes broadens into a torrent, as in our own time, and alters with those changes the ethical requirements. The definition of a responsible society, then, becomes a discussion of what seem to be the requirements of the divine-human dialogue under the conditions of modern life, conditions which in some respects are altogether new to human history. Never before, to mention only one prominent feature of the modern world, has history been truly world history. For this reason, the ethics of the medieval or early modern world will not suffice for us.

From the perspective of faith we must ask what the divine author of the dialogue is demanding of man in our time, what holy creative love is seeking as the composition of life in the latter half of the twentieth century. To answer this question we must combine two sets of facts: (1) the basic ethical substance of the Judaeo-Christian faith; (2) our vision of the direction of events in current history, which is another way, Paul Lehmann would say, of asking, What is God presently doing in the world?

The first set of facts I have already set forth in my account of the divine-human dialogue looking forward to the fullness of the Kingdom of God, where God will be everything to everyone. The second set of facts I must now briefly outline, running the risks that are obvious in such a sweeping summary of the times. The reason I must run this risk is that faith is not a superhistorical utopian pattern, but God's Will as it unfolds within the special times and circumstances that God in his sovereign governance of history has brought to pass. The New Testament word for this view of time is *kairos*. It means the "fullness of time" or the "proper time," when it is propitious for certain aspects of God's Will to unfold in events.[1] Thus, for example, Moses' appearance and leadership were peculiarly appropriate to his *kairos*, and Jesus also came in the "fullness of time." How shall we read our own *kairos*? There follow some of its major features. Others will see more deeply and more truly, but each man must essay his own description.

## CHARACTERISTIC ASPECTS OF OUR TIME

Perhaps the most salient aspect of our time is, as has been said, the fact that history is now world history. Events in even the most remote country reverberate through the entire world. Decisions in large countries send shock waves around the globe. The unit of human consciousness is rapidly becoming humanity-as-a-whole rather than classes, races, religions, nations, or even civilizations. This is not to say that men will cease to live and think within their special groupings, but that what they do and say there will have an increasing bearing on the rest of mankind. The web of human intelligence has become global. Every major dimension of culture shares in this global consciousness—science, religion, art, politics, economics. There is no turning back to more provincial understandings.

Certain aspects of modern culture have become so important in themselves that they have fostered the second salient feature of our time, namely, its dynamic character. The tempo of history is rising. Most of the cultures of the past have been what social scientists call "traditional" cultures, slow-moving, glacially slow. The ways of the fathers were the ways of the sons, unto the fourth generation. Models of boats unearthed in tombs 5000 years old are exact replicas of boats still used in the traditional cultures of the Middle East. But the historical tempo has so quickened that several major changes now take place within the lifetime of one generation.

Allied with this fast tempo is the third feature of modern existence: industrialization, the application of scientific technology to human affairs. It is the very nature of science and technology to change rapidly through research, altering with cold indifference old familiar ways. This, in turn, has led to the creation of huge institutions, public and private, for the profitable expansion and control of the industrial machine. It has made of the modern world an age of mammoth social structures that threaten to dwarf the men who created them. The most painful fact of all is the presence of weapons of global destructiveness. Under the umbrella of these weapons, human consciousness cannot return to the provincial securities of the past.

A fourth feature of modern history is the rising demand of the common people of every continent for significant participation in determining the events that affect their lives. They have become increasingly unwilling to trust their existence to the social elites who dominated the traditional cultures. When this tendency reaches political consciousness it takes on the forms of the various democratic and pseudodemocratic ideologies. It leads to a radical politicization of the world. Everything tends to become an affair of social negotiation, involving the arts of politics throughout every dimension of human existence, from trade unions to education and religion.

### Threats and Problems

This democratic thrust has expressed itself in the appearance of new and independent nations which are demanding a dignified and equal place in the sun. It has also raised a cry that the indignity of crushing poverty and preventable illness be removed as swiftly as possible. And, by one of those strange turns of destiny, it has produced a burgeoning world population that threatens to wipe out every advance toward these aspirations. For with food and medicine the number of human beings increases geometrically, outstripping the slower-paced economic development which alone could support them. This can only lead, unless the population problem is solved, to a series of desperate remedies that will wipe out all gains, and even force mankind back into a state inferior to that which preceded modern times.

We may regard these events as marks of God's intention without at the same time knowing exactly what they portend. We must accept them as the raw materials for the responsible man of our time. They are the facts that must be faced by any society that can call itself responsible. In themselves they seem to carry implicitly the call to a human dialogue on a world scale, a dialogue in which humanity can rise to a new level of historical existence as different from the recent past as that past differed from the times that preceded it.

### Effect of World Changes on Modern Man

Changes of such magnitude naturally arouse deep fears in human beings. It is equally natural that men should be tempted to believe that the disruption of the traditional order of things is the work of evil forces. Religious faith may unfortunately contribute to that interpretation wherever it lacks a clear prophetic understanding of the movement of history, and wherever it has become too closely identified with the prevailing social structure. It may for this reason ally itself with nostalgic reaction to change, thus making the transition to the inexorable future more painful. At the same time it is depriving that future of much-needed religious guidance and inspiration which would make it wiser and more humane. It may also, in this identification with the past, suffer the fate of all groups that worship passing social institutions as though they were divine.

This is not to say that modern man can live abstractly in a global way without attending faithfully to his citizenship in the local culture in which he lives. The concrete ethics of dialogue insists that individuals and families, communities and nations, are irreducible realities in the total dialogue. An abstract world unity is not the answer to the perplexities of global culture. We cannot simply jump clear of local history to participate in universal history. For this reason we must work our way through the problems of local justice and the construction of workable economic institutions, knowing all the while that local decisions have inevitable universal bearing.

### Need for a Sense of Destiny

Nor does a period of rapid change require that we despise the past. A wise conservativism that recognizes the values of true community in old institutions is as essential as an eagerness to get on with the future that is before us. Perhaps the most important thing of all is to infuse into our time, with all its changes and complex structures, a sense of significant destiny for humanity, a meaning in which human beings can participate and thus find significance for their own existence. The greatest danger of all is that the individual human being may become lost in the magnitude of events and that the whole drama may end in utter emptiness. This was less likely when events occurred on a smaller scale and the influence of individuals was more evident. An ethic for our day must provide for a great increase in the purposiveness of human life to match the magitude of global history.

We turn now to some elements of ethical thought that are essential in facing such a challenge. We will start with the basic issue of the essential nature of society.

## THREE CONCEPTS OF SOCIETY

The concept of a *responsible* society can best be understood by contrasting it with alternatives at two extremes: the concept of an *atomistic* society, and the concept of a *collectivistic* society. These contrasts show up in both secular social thought and theology. Let us consider secular thought first.

### Social Atomism

Social atomism holds that society is an artificial arrangement by which individuals who are concerned only for their own development and welfare associate with one another for the advancement of their selfish interests. The philosopher Thomas Hobbes (1588–1679), under the twin influence of the new physics and the chaos of English society of his day, was the first modern philosopher to systematically expound this theory.[2] He held that man is a social atom who is concerned only with himself and that his hand is, by nature, raised against every other man. He built his theory of society on the assumption that these social atoms would live brief, solitary, and brutish existences if they had no allies in their struggle for existence. For this reason, he wrote, men will form governments to act as policemen in the competitive struggle.

John Locke (1632–1704), a young contemporary of Hobbes, took a somewhat similar view and proposed a theory of social contract by which men form governments as the guarantor of their property and personal freedom.[3] A nineteenth-century English philosopher, John Stuart Mill (1806–1873), developed further the ethics of atomistic individualism.[4] He tried to show that in the individual's pursuit of his own good he must inevitably seek the good of his fellows. His point was: I defend your right because only in my so doing will you be persuaded to defend my right. According to this view, an individual has no intrinsic interest in the rights of others—they are merely instrumental to retaining his own rights. He seeks the "greatest happiness of the greatest number" only because in this way he will find support for his own pursuit of personal happiness.

The point of this atomistic view is that the individual is the sole locus of value, and society as such is merely an artificial instrument for the enhancement of that value. The individual has no other reasons for social participation than those that arise from his own personal interests.

### Social Collectivism

A collectivistic view of society is at the opposite pole from atomism. This view holds that society alone is real and the individual is only a means to its existence. Modern philosophies of collectivism stem mainly from the thought of the early-nineteenth-century philosopher Georg Friedrich Hegel (1770–1831). Hegel viewed history and society organically; all its institutions and enactments are expressions of the Absolute Idea, which alone is genuinely real.[5] Karl Marx (1818–1883) and his successors transposed Hegel's ideas onto a radical materialism in which human beings were viewed exclusively as material organisms engaged in material production, deriving their significance solely from the class positions that reflect the economic arrangements of society.[6] In communist theory, society is the unit of reality; the individual is an abstraction whose value is entirely dependent on his place in the productive scheme. In this scheme the individual has no intrinsic rights. Wherever such rights exist, they are temporary grants from the society itself. Modern fascism, whch is in many ways a middle-class reaction to communism, adopted the same collectivistic view of life and swallowed up the individual in the national state.

### The Responsible Society

Based on the divine-human dialogue, the responsible society contrasts sharply with both of these social philosophies. It recognizes that society, as the joint activity of human beings, has a value that cannot be looked upon as an artificial contrivance of self-centered individuals. Such social values as love, justice, social purpose, and so on, are themselves genuine human values, and no human being can be fully human who does not share in them as fully as he shares in his purely private struggle for self-development. On the other hand, the individual is himself a center of infinite value, which he possesses not by a grant from society but by virtue of his creation as a living being by God himself.

This concept of life and society holds that personal and social values are inextricably private and public at the same time. This stems from the very nature of human dialogue. The *I* cannot be affirmed without the *Thou*. Man is made for fellowship; his very inward existence is unthinkable without it. But that fellowship is not a mechanical togetherness; it is a living flow from person to person that has no meaning apart from the persons who join in it. Social existence, and the necessary institutions that make that form of human existence possible, are not artificial contrivances for personal gain. They arise out of the inherently social nature of man himself. Yet, on the other side, they derive their full life from the individuals who comprise them, having no life independent of those individuals.

It should be evident that this dialogic view is more complex than either of the others, and it is easy to slip unconsciously either to the side of atomism or that of collectivism. But it nevertheless represents an entirely different—and I believe truer—view of man than either of the others. Its implications for a philosophy of social ethics are tremendous. Some of these implications will be spelled out a bit further on. Before we do this, let us look briefly at the theological side of the matter.

## THEOLOGICAL VIEWS OF SOCIETY

The Old Testament background of religious thought is primarily focused upon society. A holy people characterized by justice was the chief concern of the Law and the Prophets. The social values of the community are in the foreground.

The New Testament—despite its primary social message of the Kingdom of God—brings the individual more into focus. For many reasons, the net impact of the New Testament was to exalt the infinite value of the individual in the eyes of God. This stemmed not only from the teaching of Jesus about God's concern for the individual and from St. Paul's interpretation of the death of Christ for each man, but it also arose naturally from the fact that the early Church was without a homeland. Having no access to political power or influential social institutions, it spread through the Roman Empire in the form of small, socially deprived groups.

Medieval social thought changed the focus again to society as a whole. Theologians like Augustine, at the beginning of the medieval period, and Thomas Aquinas, at the end of it, had a vision of a City of God[7] in which the whole society would reflect the divine order on earth. With the breakup of the medieval world, the individual component in theology came again to the fore in the independent thought of the Reformation. From that time forward, Protestant churches tended more and more to limit ethics to the sphere of the individual, leaving social concerns almost entirely to one side. The net effect of this neglect was to leave the social sphere open to nonreligious philosophies of the kind we have discussed above.

Throughout Christian history there has been a strong tension between the ethics of the individual and the ethics of society. This stems in part from the New Testament ethic of personal perfection in love, which seemed realistically inapplicable to the conduct of states. Jesus' words about turning the other cheek, for example, are not easy to assimilate to the social necessities of police action or national defense, without which few civil societies could exist under historic conditions. Medieval thought accommodated such teachings to its over-all social philosophy by looking on them as counsels of perfection for the few who were called to sanctity, and Protestant thinkers regarded them as only applicable to individuals in their relationship to other persons.

Such views are understandable, but they weaken the whole structure of religious ethics by splitting the living whole into two irreconcilable parts, personal and social. Recasting the whole ethic in terms of dialogue is an effort to bring back into organic unity these two aspects of religious thought—the social part, which emphasizes justice, and the personal part, which emphasizes love. The truth is that love which does not seek justice is sentimental, and justice without love is not truly just.

We must now interpret this dialogic ethic in its bearing on the conduct of the major institutions of society. First, let us consider the political order.

## RESPONSIBLE POLITICAL ORDER

The term "the responsible society" emerged into religious social thought from the First Assembly of the World Council of Churches in 1948. It was adopted during an attempt of these church leaders to define a truly ethical society against the background of tension between the totalitarian East and the capitalistic West. The members of the Assembly recognized that what we have called the alternative between an atomistic society, on one side, and a collectivistic society, on the other, was unthinkable. They therefore proposed the concept of the responsible society as a third path for man in his search for a humane social order.

The Assembly's manifesto set forth the concept of the responsible society: "A responsible society is one where freedom is the freedom of men who acknowledge responsibility to justice and public order, and where those who hold political authority or economic power are responsible for its exercise to God and the people whose welfare is affected by it."[8]

The meaning of this definition is clearer when the following commentary from the same source is added: "Man must never be made a mere means for political or economic ends. Man is not made for the State but the State for man. Man is not made for production, but production for man. For a society to be responsible under modern conditions it is required that the people have freedom to control, to criticize and to change their governments, that power be made responsible by law and tradition, and be distributed as widely as possible through the whole community. It is required that economic justice and provision of equality of opportunity be established for all the members of society."[9]

This definition is clearly opposed, on the one hand, to the atomistic irresponsibility of laissez-faire capitalism, which assumes that a just social order will follow automatically if everyone diligently pursues his own private profit, and, on the other hand, it is also opposed to communistic collectivism, which makes man the servant of the state. It underwrites the view that, at least under modern conditions, a responsible society is some form of social democracy. The "social" side of this will be examined under the ethics of economic institutions. At this point, let us see why democracy commends itself to thinkers who are committed to Judaeo-Christian ethical principles.

### The Ethical Case for Democracy

In the first place, the nature of man requires the democratic distribution of political power which is the essence of democratic government. Reinhold Niebuhr has expressed the complex character of this requirement: "Man's capacity for justice makes democracy possible; but his inclination to injustice makes democracy necessary."[10] If man were totally selfish he would be unable to conduct any government at all. If he were totally unselfish he would not need to distribute power so carefully among the governed. It is the mixed, or ambiguous, nature of man that calls for democratic structures in the distribution of social power. According to this view, no man can be trusted with unchecked power over other men; but when such power is checked, it is possible, with sufficient care, to manage a balance of forces from which an approximate social justice may emerge. Democracy, on these terms, is not an idealistic or utopian kind of government; it is government suited to men as we know them.

A second argument on behalf of democracy is that men need to participate in decisions that affect their own lives if they are to achieve the dignity of free and responsible men. This means that even if a select group of gifted leaders could produce "better" government than a democracy, it would still lack the educative ingredient by which men grow into maturity through self-government. Only men who govern themselves can emerge into full humanity. Good government is, then, not external to men; it is part of their functioning as men. Goodness cannot be imposed upon men; it must be freely chosen by them as their own good. Paternalism, however good, is ruled out by this consideration.

A third reason for favoring democracy is expressed in the following way by the theologian Walter Meulder in his important work *Foundations of the Responsible Society:* "Because man is by nature social and hence in need of his fellows who have an equal claim in spiritual worth with all others, because in their fallibility and proneness to self-centered decisions each must be corrected by all, and because they have personalities to actualize"[11] they must all participate in the public dialogue that precedes political decisions. Only a society of free discussion and thought can allow for the total wisdom of the community to be made available for the society as a whole. This means that free speech is not only a right but also a duty—the right and the duty are the same thing differently considered.

This is very different from the social theory that free speech is merely a private right that ends only at the point where it interferes with someone else's liberty. Mill went beyond his own atomistic premises when he eloquently defended free speech in these words: "The peculiar evil of silencing the expression of opinion is that it is robbing the human race; posterity as well as the existing generation; those who dissent from the opinion still more than those who hold it."[12] And this, of course, is true whether the opinion is true or false.

What has been said here of speech could be said of the other freedoms— the freedom to create new economic goods, to invent new social institutions, and so on. A responsible society is one that depends on each individual to contribute as deeply and as creatively as possible to the total complex of society.

A fourth consideration leads us to see that democracy is required by a humanity which is in the dynamic process of discovering the endless variety of good that can emerge in the divine-human dialogue. If the good were already fully known and crystalized into fixed patterns of living, democracy might not be needed. It would only remain to impose those patterns on succeeding generations of human beings. But the supreme good in life is in the dialogue itself as it creatively continues in its mysterious and unexpected way under the sovereignty of God. This point is especially important, for it is a proper reply to whose who believe that all religious ethics are authoritarian and nondemocratic. A dialogic ethic holds that men have not yet dreamed of the good that can come to man as he matures into his true heritage as a son of God. Therefore, to impose some traditional and rigid order upon man would be in utter contradiction to the dialogic freedom that is essential to every good that man can enjoy.

The foregoing considerations must not lead us to think that democracy is always and everywhere the best government for human beings. It is not to be equated with the will of God for all time. Moreover, democracy itself is not a finished fact, but an evolving possibility, depending in high degree upon historic circumstances.

Nor must we think that because the case for democracy in modern industrial states is strong, democratic societies cannot take a wrong turn and destroy both themselves and others. The voice of the people is not the voice of God. In political life there are no certainties, no way of guaranteeing that foolishness may not prevail. For this reason, those who believe that a democratically responsible society should prosper will be especially concerned to work for the social conditions that undergird it and make its success more probable. There is not space to indicate all these conditions, but a few may be mentioned: the continuous education of the citizenry in the meaning of their collective life; the wise structuring of political institutions so that democratic processes do not become bogged down in frustrating conflicts that prevent decisive policies; the continuous inspiration of society by a living continuity of artists, thinkers, and religious seers; and the solution of major economic and social problems as they arise, so that no significant part of the populace becomes too desperate to wait upon the democratic processes. If any of these are conspicuously lacking for any period of time, men will inevitably turn to other forms of social organization which appear to promise relief.

## RESPONSIBLE ECONOMIC ORDER

It is an accepted commonplace of social thought that the political and economic orders are intimately related to one another. The means of economic production and distribution interact continuously with governmental policy decisions. One of the conditions of democratic existence is a relatively prosperous and just economic system. Where chronic poverty is too widespread, or plutocracies of wealth are arranged alongside the dispossessed, the practice of political democracy will soon prove impossible. This fact has become apparent in the course of Western economic history, and it has led governments to ever greater participation in economic matters, leading in some places to outright socialism, where the means of production are taken over by the state.

The difficulty with the socialist solution to the search for a responsible social democracy is that it concentrates both political and economic power in the hands of the same people. We have already seen that one of the basic reasons for preferring the democratic organization of political power is that no person or group is incorruptible enough to be trusted with excessive power over his fellows. This same principle now warns against the socialist organization of economic life. Wisdom requires that the leaders of the economic system not be the same persons as those wielding political power. Where such a separation of powers exists there is a far greater chance that both economic and political injustices will be redressed in time.

This principle should not be carried so far, however, as to maintain that the political and economic realms should be completely unrelated. Economic history has all but destroyed the theory that economic well-being will automatically result from the pursuit of profit on the part of individuals. The Divine "Unseen Hand," that on early economic theory was supposed to keep such order, is now believed by modern economists to be mere wishful superstition or ideological rationalization. The rise of the so-called welfare state is a nonsocialist response to this state of affairs. The state, according to this view, is held responsible for mitigating fluctuations in economic cycles and relieving the human suffering that results from them, through retirement funds, unemployment insurance, and other political intervention in the economic order.

While there is room for debate over just what the wisest arrangements are, the indications are quite clear that strong democratic societies in this century will require some such relationship between the two spheres. It is even clearer that a responsible economic order will welcome such political intervention as the only way to achieve a reasonable economic justice and social peace.

This is not to say that the only way the economic order can be made responsible is through political action. The managers of the largest institutions of economic power—both business and labor—have in their hands enormous possibilities for human good. Fortunately, there is growing among such leaders the realization that they are in business not merely for profit but also for the public good; that, in short, they have a responsibility beyond the return of a reasonable profit to the owners of property, or high wages to workers.

We must ask what an economic system is for. The most obvious answer, in the light of modern industrial conditions, is that its purpose is to produce goods in such abundance that economic concerns may eventually recede from the foreground of human consciousness, allowing other values to take their place. This is rapidly becoming possible, at least in the centers of high economic activity in the West. The productive side of the equation is near solution, but we still have the problem of finding ways of distributing this productiveness in a manner that will not undermine productivity itself. It is this latter kind of problem that has required political action in concert with economic organization.

## GOALS OF ECONOMIC LIFE

For nearly half a century the churches have been increasingly concerned about the need to clarify the proper goals of economic life. One of the recent works in this field, *The Goals of Economic Life*,[13] a symposium undertaken at the request of the National Council of Churches and edited by A. Dudley Ward, will be worth paraphrasing here. Ward lists the proper goals under 11 headings:

(1) The production of goods for the survival and physical well-being of all members of society. (2) The right ordering of economic life so that participation in production, distribution, and consumption does not divide the commonwealth into warring factions, but produces instead a strong sense of participation and even of fellowship on the part of each member of the economy. (3) Each person in the productive system should have a position

which does not deprive him of human dignity; and, where men are clothed with power, they should wear it with humility as a public trust.

(4) All work should contribute to, or at least be consistent with, moral and social enlightenment so that men may participate intelligently in responsible economic decisions. (5) Production and consumption should contribute not only to abundance of goods but also to the aesthetic enhancement of life. The by-products of much industrial activity—slums, pollution of the water, air, and land, and the destruction of natural environments—are at odds with a truly humane economic order.

(6) Despite the uniformity of much mass production, a just economic order will provide ever-widening opportunities for creative imagination. Freedom is, of course, the primary condition for this, but the means by which freedom can live and breathe creatively are also a requirement. (7) Industrialism has produced widespread boredom, but a just economic order will regard variety and novelty, and other dimensions of human existence as important goals of its activity.

(8) An economic system should provide for the physical and psychological security of its members as far as its resources will permit. Economically this means social insurance of various kinds. Politically it means the balancing of economic powers so that differences can be settled by reasonable negotiation. Security also has another dimension: Modern economic exchange would be impossible without the moral ingredient which sustains at least a minimum degree of mutual trust among the participants. This moral ingredient, which contributes to the faithful keeping of contracts, maintains quality in goods, and allows for a vast extension of the credit system, correspondingly makes the economic system increasingly reliable for everyone concerned.

(9) Freedom should be another goal of the economy; the progressive removal of undue external restraints. Under modern conditions, we have already observed, such freedom will not appear automatically; it will occur only as the product of conscious cooperation between the various spheres of society. (10) The economy should move toward the day when all men will be treated with equal consideration and given the same opportunities regardless of their race, political and religious creeds, or cultural memberships.

(11) The climactic goal of an economic system is service to the personal growth of its members. The final test of every economic social institution is the kind of person it tends to produce, the quality of the community life it fosters, and the level of ultimate values and meanings it encourages. In this sense all economic activity points beyond itself toward noneconomic goals and purposes, and must be judged in the light of its contribution toward these goals.

This statement of economic goals is not merely the work of a few scholars; it also represents a summary of the growing consensus among the Christian churches of the world concerning norms for the evaluation of economic practices and processes. Statements by the World Council of Churches, for instance, in its publication (1954), of Section 11 of the "Responsible Society in a World Perspective" touches on all of the same themes: justice, order, and freedom. The old concept of limiting Christian ethics to personal matters is fading away. Equally instructive is the *Declaration of Freedom of Religion for all Men,* passed by the Ecumenical Council (Nov. 19, 1965), and the social encyclicals of the Roman Catholic Church, such as Pius XII's *Human's Genesis,* John XXIII's *Pacem in Terris,* and Paul VI's celebrated "No More War" speech before the United Nations in October, 1965.

Many years ago, William Temple, Archbishop of Canterbury, made the point that "the real crisis of our time is . . . not primarily a moral, but a cultural crisis."[14] It is not enough, he said, to insist on ideals or simply to intensify the will to pursue them. He understood the power of social institutions to form the lives of men. "Christians," he wrote, "must free their minds from illusions and become aware of the impotence of moral advice and instruction when it is divorced from the social structures which by their perpetual suggestion form the soul."[15]

## RESPONSIBLE CULTURAL ORDER

Modern society is so concerned with politics and economics that, in discussions of this kind, the intermediate cultural groupings, in which human beings associate more closely and intimately with one another, are often overlooked. A responsible society will be rich in responsible private associations—families, clubs, community organizations, professional associations, schools, churches, and so on. In fact, the larger the ultimate sphere of political and economic activity, the greater the need for intimate forms of human interaction which nourish human values at their best. If these associations—clubs and fraternities, for example—foster values that are at odds with the needs of a responsible society, they will impoverish both themselves and the culture in which they thrive. There is not space here to deal separately with such associations, but the principles of a dialogic ethic applied to them should be relatively plain by now. Each of them should enhance the status of its members as free and creative participants in the common life of their fellows, and receive such enrichment from these contacts that they all are strengthened in the task of growing into authentic human beings in their own right.

Since this book is a study of religion, we must consider more closely the religious side of the matter. Let us look at the relationship between religion and society from this ethical perspective.

## RESPONSIBLE RELIGIOUS ORDER

Responsibility in the religious order is complex because it seems to imply responsibility to two irreconcilable dimensions: the demands of faith, and the demands of the secular culture in which the man of faith lives. H. Richard Niebuhr, in a celebrated work, *Christ and Culture*,[16] outlined five distinct answers to this problem, answers that have appealed to one or another segment of the Christian community throughout its history. Understanding these classical solutions can help us answer the question before us.

*Christ Against Culture.* Those who follow this first solution see faith as continually and naturally at odds with culture—"What has Athens to do with Jerusalem!" In this response, men are called to an either-or decision, for one side or the other: Either embrace the world or leave it for God. This was the view of early monasticism, which provided a refuge where the pure soul could live away from the temptations of the world. In Protestantism, which abandoned the monastic solution, this view expressed itself in small perfectionist sects, such as the Mennonites, who renounce participation in politics and military life, and follow their own distinctive customs in communities closed off from excessive commerce with the world beyond.

*The Christ of Culture.* This second solution is at the opposite pole from the first. To adherents of this group Jesus appears, in the words of Niebuhr, as "a great hero of human culture history; his life and teachings are regarded as the greatest human achievement; in him, it is believed, the aspirations of men toward their values are brought to a point of culmination; he confirms what is best in the past, and guides the process of civilization to its proper goal."[17] This line of thought naturalizes faith, and in time identifies it with the form of society in which its advocates are living. One version of this solution appears in what might be called culture-Protestantism, which sees little tension between social life and faith. This movement of identification, Niebuhr says, reached its climax in the latter half of the nineteenth century. We have already discussed this era in the chapter on religion and society. In the twentieth century it expresses itself in thought that identifies the essence of the faith with those great values esteemed by democratic culture: "the freedom and intrinsic worth of individuals, social cooperation, and universal peace."[18]

A strong case can be made for both these options, but they tend to neutralize each other. On the one hand, the first group recognizes an undoubted truth, that the high perfection of faith can never be perfectly manifested in any particular social order, and that to imagine otherwise is to invite a primary disloyalty to the faith itself. On the other hand, the second group recognizes that God's sovereignty over the whole of social life cannot be expressed by withdrawal of any kind and that the full life of faith must express itself in the entire range of social and cultural institutions. An attempt to synthesize these viewpoints appears in the third option.

*Christ Above Culture.* This view holds that Christ is, in Niebuhr's words, "the fulfillment of cultural aspirations and the restorer of the institutions of true society. Yet there is in him something that neither arises out of culture nor contributes directly to it. He is discontinuous as well as continuous with social life and its culture."[19] This synthesis was most clearly set forth by

Thomas Aquinas in the thirteenth century as a rationale for late medieval culture. The life of faith, he taught, fulfilled the natural life of culture, climaxing the life of natural virtues with a crown of supernatural sanctity.

*Christ and Culture in Paradox.* With the destruction of the medieval synthesis, the Lutheran theologians of the Reformation proposed a fourth position, which holds that both faith and secular culture have authority from God, but that they remain in this sinful world in continuous opposition. Christian existence is a continuous tension in a life of obedience to "two authorities who do not agree yet must both be obeyed."[20] The man of faith is thus a citizen of two worlds at the same time.

*Christ the Transformer of Culture.* A fifth option holds with the first and fourth group that human nature is sinful and resistant to God's goodness and that culture promotes and transmits such sin. Yet those who embrace this view—such men as John Calvin or Augustine—hold that Christ is the converter of man in his culture and society. In the words of Frederick Denison Maurice (1805–1872), English theologian and chief founder of Christian Socialism, "The kingdom of God begins within, but it is to make itself manifest without. . . . It is to penetrate the feelings, habits, thoughts, words, acts, of him who is subject of it. At last it is to penetrate our whole social existence."[21] Niebuhr says of Maurice that "his attitude toward culture is affirmative throughout, because he takes most seriously the conviction that nothing exists without the Word."[22] In Niebuhr's own words: "Christ . . . is not only the head of the church (that is, the supreme authority within the sphere of faith), but the redeemer of the world (that is, also the supreme authority within the world of culture)."[23] He closes his study with these words: "The world of culture—man's achievement—exists within the world of grace—God's kingdom."[24]

How shall we choose among these five options? In this sphere each man stands where he must stand, and, no doubt, this is determined partly by the age and circumstances in which he views the claims of faith. There is no abstract right answer to this problem. On the whole, in this chapter I have been guided more by the concept of Christ as the transformer of culture than by the others, but we cannot deny the other perspectives totally. And it is a point of wisdom to realize the complexity of the problem which faithful men must face when they try to work out the details of their response to God's initiations in the course of the divine-human dialogue. And above all it behooves us to be charitable with those who take their stand on different ground.

## Separation of Church and State

Before leaving this subject it will be well to remark further on the church-state problem in American life.

First of all, the doctrine of separation of church and state has become widely accepted in American life, even among such groups as the Roman Catholics, who traditionally opposed it. Separation is accepted in the sense that the church must not become an arm of the state, nor must the power of the state be used either to control religion or coerce loyalty to it. Almost all parties to this question recognize that the history of church-state identification has been marred by persecutions and denials of freedom that are harmful both to civil society and pure religion.

But this must not mean the separation of religious influence from the state. If our premises are sound, a purely secular state, uninspired by faith, is doomed to pursue policies of irresponsibility that can only serve to bring it into disrepute with its people and, in turn, doom it to destruction. The state needs a healthy critic and an inspiring guide if it is to undertake its proper work on behalf of its citizens, and if it is to discharge its duties to the world as a whole.

### Education and the Church-State Problem

These general propositions do not, of course, give easy answers to the perplexing problems that face American citizens today. These problems arise chiefly out of the fact that the state has undertaken the major responsibility for education, and education without reference to ultimate concern is at best fragmentary and at worst blinding. The major church-state problem in American life today is how to seriously engage the young minds of each generation with matters of ultimate concern without abridging the institutional separation of church and state, which is part of our prized heritage. The answer cannot be found in simply reading parts of the Bible or praying short nondenominational prayers before class. It must get much more directly to the problem of confronting the student with the exacting claims of faith in personal and social life. And it must do this without allowing the public educational system to become an arm of denominationalism of any variety whatsoever.

A problem with analogous difficulties suggests that the issue is not completely insoluble; namely, the problem of instilling a wise patriotism and political wisdom in the student. This cannot be done without discussing political questions that divide the American public as seriously as its religious divisions. Such political education is being undertaken in the schools, though not as thoroughly as is needed for the health of the Republic. We demand of teachers in this field that they have wide enough sympathies to allow their students freedom of choice within the options that are open to American citizens. A solution to this problem might conceivably give clues to the way in which the analogous difficulty of religious instruction could be approached. Unfortunately, at the present time, hardly a start has been made on the matter. Informal approaches to this question out of school hours do not reach the numbers of citizens required nor do they educate the student in the range of claims that are integral to our religious culture.

### Role of the Church in Society

Another important aspect of the church-society problem is rooted in a fact noted earlier in our discussion of religion and society, that the churches of America tend to be identified with somewhat distinct social groups. For example, in another of H. Richard Niebuhr's works, *The Social Sources of Denominationalism*,[25] he points out that our religious divisions stem in large part from ethnic, regional, or sociocultural divisions that exist in the secular society and that condition religious institutions. If faith is to have a proper role in criticizing the ultimate concern of American life, and in offering needed guidance in personal and social policies, it must be rescued from too close an identification with such limited social interests.

In the light of our studies thus far, the Church's proper role in society can be summarized as follows: It should first of all keep clearly before itself the nature of its own ultimate commitments—the faith which alone justifies its existence in history. This it must do throughout the whole range of thought, worship, and life itself. It must first of all be the Church, not merely some minor aspect of the culture in which it thrives. Beyond this it should itself be a model of open human dialogue—a true fellowship of human beings under the sovereign love of God. In this role it would serve as an example of the kind of brotherhood and perfect justice that ought to prevail throughout the secular society in which it lives.

But the Church cannot live only to itself. It must foster in its members such a degree of courageous creativity in social matters that they can serve as reconcilers within the larger culture, proposing genuine solutions to vexing social problems as they arise. In so doing the Churches would qualify as the kind of "creative minority" which the historian Arnold Toynbee says built the basic institutions of every great culture.[26] They would be the "salt" and "light" that could keep a great society alive, growing, and ever renewing its energies.

In performing this function, the Church must not forget its prophetic mission as the conscience and critic of society. When it becomes too engrossed in its limited cultural interests it becomes an enemy of its own true existence and of the true interests of the rest of humanity.

## RESPONSIBLE WORLD COMMUNITY

It is impossible to define a responsible society in the modern world without recognizing that humanity has emerged into a global era. The unit of human thought can no longer be the community or nation, but the great globe itself.

This is implicit in all the great universal religions, which speak not to men of a given race or culture, but to man as man. But it is the twentieth century which has been given, for the first time in man's history, the task of evolving institutions—political, economic, and cultural—that can channel the evolving world-consciousness into fruitful expression.

On the political and economic side this means the kind of institution that already exists in the United Nations Organization. It is still too soon to predict into what kind of political order this should evolve. However, it is becoming clearer that there must be one universal law supporting universal human rights. Irresponsible nationalism and irresponsible wealth must be considered threats to the future of mankind. This is true not merely because world conflict with modern weapons would degenerate into world destruction, but because it is now clearly immoral that some of the human family should be deprived of the goods of life that are possible to them under conditions of modern knowledge.

The Universal Declaration of Human Rights promulgated by the United Nations represents a kind of world conscience on the matter of human rights and dignity. "It is," writes Horace Kallen, "a profession of faith . . . stating the substance of what mankind hope for in all human relations. . . ."[27] Though it was written without reference to any specific religious or humanistic tradition, we can consider it here as a charter of particulars for interpreting those rights that a responsible society would seek both for its own citizens and those of its neighbors.

*The Problem of War.* One of the unresolved ethical problems in religious thought is the problem of war. The amount of physical force available to potential combatants today is great enough to obliterate all humanity. The United States' atomic arsenal, for example, contains the equivalent of several thousand tons of TNT per person in the entire world. But the problem for faith is not new. It became acute for the Christian conscience as early as when Roman soldiers began to turn in large numbers to the Christian faith. Present-day theologians are divided as to the ultimate solution. Despite uncertainties, they are in agreement on some aspects of the problem. The nature of modern war, they agree, is so violent that it becomes indiscriminate, unjust, and suicidal. Once let loose, they hold, it soon outruns all moral bounds that rational men seek to set for it. They also agree, in the words of the Oxford Conference, that "war is always a demonstration of the power of sin in the world and a defiance of the righteousness of God as revealed in Jesus Christ. . . ."[28] As Paul Lehmann has said, "It is plain that the love of neighbor as a principle of action derived from the love of God excludes acts which initiate war or lead to war."[29] However, Christians are now agreed that the Christian response to war cannot in the nature of the case be simple. War is ethically ambiguous.

"War," writes Lehmann, "both contradicts what God is doing in the world to bring about a new humanity and is instrumental in this activity."[30] For this reason it is plain that for some Christians participation in war would be impossible. They feel required to witness against its inherently destructive and sinful character. Others may feel called by the same Christian conscience to participate in war on the grounds that the absence of supernational peace-keeping institutions requires military action on the part of national powers committed to a just international order. But even such participation must be informed by the realization that to engage in the acts of modern total war can only mean the destruction of civilized life for an indefinite time, and perhaps the destruction of mankind itself.

The main point is that in a situation as complex and ethically ambiguous as this, there may be, to be sure, one right intention and goal—the love of neighbor leading to the maturing of humanity as the family of God—but there is never one right action. To quote Lehmann again: "There are always acts to be done, the rightness of which consists in the fact that the actions bear the risk of obedience and as such are potentially instrumental to the divine activity in the world."[31] But ethical decision in a dialogical sense is contextual and vocational. As Christians, men may even oppose one another in practical affairs in the faith that God has the creative resourcefulness and power to make use of this opposition.

From another perspective, the problem is one of the place of power in human affairs. In the broadest sense all living beings manifest power merely by existing and acting. In this sense, therefore, power cannot be abolished except by doing away with all existence. Such thinkers as Tillich and Schweitzer have said that since power cannot be dispensed with, the essential problem is its proper use, not its abolition. At every level, from the rearing of children to the control of wayward nations, the real issue, according to them is to make power serve love and justice. This cannot be done except by a continuing universal work of reconciliation among human beings, from the most intimate personal relationship to the most impersonal affairs of state. In this light, the role of the responsible citizen is to work incessantly for those forms of social life that promote justice and that will progressively—if not permanently—diminish the most destructive expressions of power and replace them with creative and constructive ones. This is, to be sure, a rather abstract generalization, but it is a useful guide to the kind of labors that must be undertaken in any society that deserves to call itself responsible.

This principle constitutes a call to men in every walk of life to discover ways and means of interacting with their fellows in such a way that the power they exert in personal and institutional affairs will lead toward a creative peace. One of the largest areas for such reconciling labors is in the region of the conflicting ideologies by which men in different cultures live.

One of the major areas of such ideological difference is in the sphere of religion itself. Religious differences constitute one of the gravest challenges to the hope of achieving a creative peace among the great cultures of the world. It is in search of a policy of world understanding that we turn now to the question of the world religions in dialogue.

## SUGGESTIONS FOR FURTHER READING

Refer again to the general works on ethics suggested in Chapter 17. Walter Muelder's *Foundations of the Responsible Society* (Abingdon, 1959) is a comprehensive account of the social responsibilities of men from the perspective of faith. On the subject of war, I suggest Paul Ramsey, *War and the Christian Conscience* (Duke University Press, 1961). H. Reinhold Niebuhr's *The Children of Light and the Children of Darkness* (Scribner, 1944) is a defense of democratic concepts from a nonliberal theological point of view.

For documents on the social philosophy of Roman Catholicism, see *The Social Teachings of the Church*, Anne Fremantle, ed. (New American Library, 1960).

## NOTES

1. On this concept, see Paul Tillich, *The Protestant Era* (University of Chicago Press, 1948), chap. 3.
2. Thomas Hobbes, *Leviathan* (1561), available in Library of Liberal Arts (Bobbs-Merrill, 1961).
3. John Locke, *Two Treatises on Government* (1569). His *Letter Concerning Toleration* and the *Second Treatise of Government* are available in the Library of Liberal Arts (Bobbs-Merrill, 1963).
4. John Stuart Mill, *Utilitarianism* (1863), is available in Library of Liberal Arts (Bobbs-Merrill, 1957).
5. The *Introduction* to the *Philosophy of History*, published shortly after Hegel's death in 1831, sets forth this thesis. The *Introduction* has been reprinted by Library of Liberal Arts under the title *Reason in History* (Bobbs-Merrill, 1964).
6. For the crucial Marxist documents in which these concepts are set forth, see Sidney Hook, ed., *Marx and the Marxists* (Anvil, Van Nostrand, 1955).
7. *The City of God* (*De Civitate Dei*) is Augustine's great work on the philosophy of history, giving his view of Christian society, actual and ideal.
8. Quoted in Walter Muelder, *Foundations of the Responsible Society* (Abingdon, 1959), p. 19.
9. *Ibid.*
10. H. Reinhold Niebuhr, *The Children of Light and the Children of Darkness* (Scribner, 1944), chap. 2.
11. Muelder, *op. cit.*, p. 117.
12. Gregory Vlastos, *The Responsibilities of the College for Human Rights and Dignities* (Proceedings of the Pacific Northwest Hazen Conference, 1950), p. 16.
13. A. Dudley Ward, ed., *The Goals of Economic Life* (Harper & Row, 1953).

14. William Temple, *What Christians Stand For* (reprint of a supplement to *The Christian News Letter*, n.d.), p. 14.
15. *Ibid.*, p. 15.
16. H. Richard Niebuhr, *Christ and Culture* (Harper Torchbooks, Harper & Row, 1956).
17. *Ibid.*, p. 41.
18. *Ibid.*, p. 99.
19. *Ibid.*, p. 42.
20. *Ibid.*
21. *Ibid.*, p. 228.
22. *Ibid.*, p. 229.
23. *Ibid.*, p. 256.
24. *Ibid.*
25. H. Richard Niebuhr, *The Social Sources of Denominationalism* (Holt, Rinehart and Winston, 1929).
26. For the work of the "creative minority," see Arnold Toynbee, *A Study of History*, D. C. Somervell abridgment (Oxford University Press, 1947), Vol. I, Pt. 2.
27. Horace Kallen, "Secularism," *Journal for the Scientific Study of Religion* (Spring, 1965), pp. 145–146.
28. Muelder, *op. cit.*, p. 260.
29. Lehmann, *op. cit.*, p. 143.
30. *Ibid.*
31. *Ibid.*, p. 144.

# 20

# *The World Religions in Dialogue*

✧⟨✧⟨✧⟨✧⟨✧⟨✧⟨✧⟨✧⟨✧⟨✧⟨✧⟨✧⟨✧⟨✧⟨✧⟨✧⟨✧⟨✧⟨✧⟨✧⟨✧⟨✧⟨✧⟨✧⟨✧⟨✧⟨✧⟨✧⟨✧

Why, among all the pressing problems facing the twentieth century, should we concern ourselves with a dialogue among world religions? The reasons are impressive.

First of all, the interrelationship of the faiths of mankind in the twentieth century is of profound importance to the future of humanity on this planet. It is far more than a question of the feelings of religious partisans or the fate of venerable institutions. It has to do with an emerging world civilization. We are accustomed to think that the search for a world order is chiefly a political matter with some attendant economic considerations. But when we recall the way in which ultimate concern is the substance of all cultural forms, we realize that an authentic world culture cannot emerge without attending to the infusion of spiritual substance that can give it heart and meaning. The Dutch historian of religion, Johan Huizinga (1872–1945) acknowledges that world culture is being enriched and empowered by a host of fresh elements in modern life, but he says, "it lacks confidence in its own validity." "It has," he points out, "no standard of truth, no harmony, no real dignity and divine serenity."[1] The search for a wise policy of dialogue among the world religions is, then, a search for an authentic principle of humane world culture. This is made doubly difficult by a fact which Hendrik Kraemer has pointed out so clearly: "All religions *without exception* are functioning in coalescence with forms of social structure which are frameworks of a society of the past, or at any rate, of a type of society which is passing away. . . . Therefore all religions face the same huge proposition of achieving a break with their own social past."[2] (Author's italics.)

This observation is in harmony with a perception of the modern world as dynamically changing and needing directional principles to guide it in the course of such change. Culture-bound religious concepts may impede rather than help humanity at this particular juncture of human history. For this reason we need a policy of dialogue about the ultimate concerns of humanity, in which men can be faithful both to the truth and to the social necessities of the time. Unfortunately, truth and social necessity are not always compatible. There are powerful temptations to suppress truth in the interest of social peace, but this would surely be a shortsighted policy, and doomed to fail in the long run.

### Resurgent Classical Faiths

A second reason why dialogue is urgent is to be sought in another salient feature of our century: the astonishing resurgence of the classical religious faiths of mankind. After a long dormant period, during which they appeared to be easy pickings for Western missionaries or the emissaries of secular Westernization, they have experienced little short of a resurrection. They must now be counted as serious factors in any plan of relating cultures of the world to one another. Hinduism, Buddhism, and Islam, in their various forms, are bidding for the attention and loyalty of mankind, as they once did in their periods of initial growth. Islam is winning converts in Africa at an estimated rate of 3 to 1 over Christianity. Vendantic Hinduism proclaims itself unabashedly throughout the world as the natural homeland of the religious spirit and as superior to any religion of Semitic origin. The Theravada Buddhists, in their recent Sixth World Council (1954–1965), celebrating the 2500th anniversary of the death of its founder, Gautama Buddha, predicted a Buddhist world by the turn of the century. Zen Buddhism (Zen), as the most universally appealing form of Mahayana Buddhism, has shown unexpected ability to invade intellectual circles in the Christian West.

### The Quasi Religions

A third reason for the urgent need for dialogue is the rise of what Paul Tillich calls the "quasi religions." He refers to the secular philosophies which serve their advocates as life-orienting ultimate concerns, and which therefore function as religions. The most impressive of these quasi religions is communism, which has successfully overrun two vast regions once dominated by the great religions: Russia, once under the control of Christianity, and China, long identified with a complex of Buddhism, Confucianism, and Taoism. It presently challenges such traditionally Catholic areas as Latin and South America.

Another quasi religion is nationalism. In varying degrees it has undermined traditional religious loyalties in the West. It has also shown a capacity to unite with the reviving religions of the Near and Far East in an alliance against Western domination, both religious and secular. Islam and Arabian or Pakistani nationalism are all but indistinguishable. The same is true of Buddhism in such places as Ceylon and Viet Nam. In short, these religious revivals are associated with deep cultural stirrings and national aspirations. It should be obvious that conversations along these cultural and religious lines are urgent before impenetrable walls are allowed to rise.

Another quasi religion is worth noting: secular humanism. This faith, nourished largely by the rise of science in the West, has also found fertile seed-ground in almost all the strongholds of traditional religion. No world dialogue of faiths can ignore this fact.

One final consideration: The quasi religions constitute a much greater threat to each of the traditional religions than any one of the latter does to any of the others. There are those who believe that when the typically modern forces of technology and urbanization have done their work, the spirit of world culture will be essentially secular. An awareness of this common danger might lend strength to the present weak impulses toward interfaith dialogue.

### Dialogue Is Already Under Way

In a sense, argument is unnecessary, for the dialogue of religions and cultures has been going on for a long time. In the most general sense it has been going on informally from the most ancient times through what anthropologists call cultural diffusion. It was by this process that Buddhism spread from India to a new home in China and Japan, and by which Christianity spread from the Near East into Europe and the New World. We are all, whether we realize it or not, the products of this process. Ralph Linton, in a celebrated passage from his *Study of Man*, describes what I mean:

Our solid American citizen awakens in a bed built on a pattern which originated in the Near East. . . . He throws back covers made from cotton domesticated in India . . . or wool from sheep, domesticated in the Near East. . . . He takes off his pajamas, a garment invented in India, and washes with soap invented by the ancient Gauls. He then shaves, a masochistic rite which seems to have been derived from either Sumer or ancient Egypt.

Returning to his bedroom, he removes his clothes from a chair of southern European type and proceeds to dress. He puts on garments whose form originally derived from the skin clothing of the nomads of the Asiatic steppes, puts on shoes made from skins tanned by a process invented in ancient Egypt and cut to a pattern derived from the classical civilization of the Mediterranean, and ties around his neck a strip of bright-colored cloth which is a vestigial survival of the shoulder shawls worn by the seventeenth-century Croatians. Before going out for breakfast glances through the window, made of glass invented in Egypt, and if it is raining puts on overshoes made of rubber discovered by the Central American Indians and takes an umbrella, invented in southeastern Asia. Upon his head he puts a hat made of felt, a material invented in the Asiatic steppes.

On his way to breakfast he stops to buy a paper, paying for it with coins, an ancient Lydian invention. At the restaurant a whole new series of borrowed elements confronts him. His plate is made of a form of pottery invented in China. His knife is of steel, an alloy first made in southern India, his fork a medieval Italian invention, and his spoon a derivative of a Roman original. He begins breakfast with an orange, from the eastern Mediterranean, a cantaloupe from Persia, or perhaps a piece of African watermelon. With this he has coffee, an Abyssinian plant, with cream and sugar. Both the domestication of cows and the idea of milking them originated in the Near East, while sugar was first made in India. After his fruit and first coffee he goes on to waffles, cakes made by a Scandinavian technique from wheat domesticated in Asia Minor. Over these he pours maple syrup, invented by the Indians of the Eastern woodlands. As a side dish he may have the egg of a species of bird domesticated in Indo-China, or thin strips of the flesh of an animal domesticated in Eastern Asia which have been salted and smoked by a process developed in northern Europe.

When our friend has finished eating he settles back to smoke, an American Indian habit, consuming a plant domesticated in Brazil in either a pipe, derived from the Indians of Virginia, or a cigarette, derived from Mexico. . . . While smoking he reads the news of the day, imprinted in characters invented by the ancient Semites upon a material invented in China by a process invented in Germany. As he absorbs the accounts of foreign troubles, he will, if he is a good conservative citizen, thank a Hebrew deity in an Indo-European language that he is 100 per cent American.[3]

This same process of cultural diffusion is going on today at a much accelerated pace. In the field of religion it is a highly conscious affair. Scholars of all the major religions are reexamining their creeds and practices under the stimulus of heightened contacts with formerly remote regions of the earth. Consider two notable examples.

Khalifa Abdul Hakim, Director of the Institute of Islamic Culture in Lahore, Pakistan, claims that religion in the form derived from the sacred Koran "is a universal truth and can form the basis of a universal humanity, free to develop its infinite potentialities, unhampered by artificial restrictions and barriers. . . ."[4] But in setting forth this ideal he recognizes that it is "not the Islam of Muslim orthodoxies, but the fundamental attitude of Mohammed toward God and Man: One God, One World, One Humanity."[5]

Sir Sarvepalli Radhakrishnan, in a volume entitled *East and West, the End of Their Separation*,[6] has reinterpreted the basic concepts of Hinduism in a system, it is claimed, integrates all the aspirations of religions everywhere. "Rites, ceremonies, systems and dogmas," he writes, "lead beyond themselves to a region of utter clarity and so have only relative truth."[7] The region of "utter clarity" is the insight that the Hindu teaches is attained at the pinnacle of the ancient yoga discipline, when the trained disciple reaches his crowning ecstasy. This unity, writes Radhakrishnan, is the goal of mankind's spiritual quest, and the center in which the quarrel of religions can come to an end.

## THE DIALOGUE AND CHRISTIANITY

To a considerable extent both the preceding statements reflect the effects of Christianity upon Islam and Hinduism. The reason for this lies not only in the nature of the Christian faith and its natural effect upon those who are confronted by it, but also by the fact that historically it has been associated with Western culture, whose dynamic character since the fourteenth century has sent it into every culture of the globe.

The spread of the Christian faith has had a visibly pulsating character. In the first three centuries of its existence it spread from the confines of its origins in the Near East to the Roman Empire, becoming the official religion of the Roman Empire under Theodosius in 392 A.D. From this stronghold, missionaries ventured north as far as Scandinavia and northeast as far as Russia, making converts of the peoples in those lands.

After this initial burst of missionary activity it lay quiescent, partially stunned by the assaults of missionary Islam on the bastions of Christendom. The Palestinian cradle of the faith passed into the hands of non-Christian powers.

With the voyages of discovery which began in the fourteenth century, missionary activity began again, reaching west to the New World, east as far as Japan, and south into Africa. The traditional faiths of the Far East were in a moribund state and found it hard to resist the vigorous intruder. By the middle of the nineteenth century the native faiths began to bestir themselves and to answer back. With the powerful movements of men and nations in the twentieth century we have reached a stage where the non-Christian faiths are insisting upon treatment as equals or even as superiors.

But the impact of Christianity nevertheless remains, and to this extent determines the character of the future dialogue. Han Suyin, a non-Christian critic of Christian missionary activity, underscores this fact in her book, *A Many-Splendoured Thing*, where she describes her impressions of the many missionaries pouring through the Church Guest House in Hong Kong after their expulsion from China by the Communist government:

In this room were the remains of a hundred years of missionary work in China. A hundred years of devotion, sacrifice, and good works. For the glory of their God, in unselfish zeal; men and women of 29 denominations had gone to baptize the heathen, teach their variety of the Only Truth, heal the sick, feed the hungry, fulfill themselves and the will of their God. . . . In this room were the people who had worn down our traditions, broken our selfishness, awakened our social conscience, armed us with ideals, dragged our scholars from their poetic torpor and our peasants' superfluous babies from the cesspits, built our universities, our hospitals and our puritanism. They also had made New China. Although now we cast them out as instruments of foreign aggression, they have also made us. We were part of each other.[8]

Whatever one may think of the missionary activity of Christianity, he cannot deny that among its social consequences is the arousing of the local faiths of the cultures in which it worked. It is a workable policy for dialogue with these aroused faiths that we now seek. Before looking at policies that command the greatest logical plausibility, let us examine three that seem inadequate, despite the fact that they are widely thought to be enlightened.

### Three Inadequate Policies

The three are: (1) indifferentism and tolerance, (2) syncretism, and (3) neutralism. The policy of tolerance based upon indifferentism holds that the religion a person or group embraces is of minor importance. There is therefore no reason why an attitude of wide tolerance should not prevail in the future relationship among the religions. Syncretism is a policy of melding together appealing elements from various religions into a working complex that will have a richness greater than any one of the historic faiths. The syncretist sees the future religion of mankind as a great treasurehouse of all the most precious elements in all the religions. Neutralism holds that one should remain uncommitted to any faith whatsoever so that he can understand and appreciate them all. This seems especially appropriate to the scholar or cultural historian who aspires to deal impartially with manifestations of religion of whatever kind.

Why are these seemingly humane and tolerant policies inadequate? The chief reason is that they fail to recognize the true meaning of religion as ultimate concern. If religion is indeed ultimate concern, it is impossible to take the attitudes toward it which these policies enjoin. One may assume an attitude of indifference or neutrality or the attitude of a connoisseur toward almost anything, but not toward one's real ultimate concern. When anyone takes these attitudes toward a given group of religions you may be sure that his ultimate concern lies somewhere else.

Will Herberg, for example, contends that the present large hearted tolerance of religious groups toward one another in America today is due simply to the fact that none of them really stands at the focus of ultimate concern. Americanism, he says, is the real concern, and therefore a policy of social peace and religious harmony naturally seems wise. But ask these same citizens to tolerate communism and you will see how intolerant they can become. The reason, says Herberg, is that communism is perceived as a real threat to their ultimate concern, which is American nationalism. Or challenge the scholar (who studies religions with a benign indifference) with the view that scientific investigation is a false approach to life, and you will discover how intolerant he can be when faced with an attack on an ultimate that grips him.

As the sociologist William L. Kolb points out: "It is not a question of the possibility or the impossibility of a nonreligious person studying religion, but rather the question of what is the ultimate concern commitment of the person who is studying the ultimate commitment of other people."[9]

The point is that in searching for a way to dialogue among religious faiths we are involved in a sticky question: how to conduct ourselves creatively in the presence of those who do not share our ultimate concern, or who may regard it as a mark of darkness and even wickedness. These three policies miss that point. There is no one who is neutral in all things. Everyone has some ultimate concern. There is no privileged position above all human faith commitments.

Another important fact should be made clear: Not all faiths are good. Hitler's return to primitive German paganism led to an orgy of mass murder. Such quasi religions as nationalism are quite capable in a nuclear age of sacrificing the whole human race to the pride of a few. Only a madman could take an indifferent attitude toward all religions.

Let us turn now to some other alternatives, which, whatever their defects, at least reveal some understanding of the meaning of religion in the life of man.

### Radical Displacement

The policy of radical displacement[10] holds that one religion is true and the others are false, and that the "true" religion should replace the "false" ones. This is somewhat of an oversimplification, as we shall see, but it will do for a start. Early Islam held this view and was willing to enforce it by the sword. But it was not long in making some exceptions: those who, along with Islam, belonged to the parent tree of the Semitic faiths—Judaism and Christianity. These two religions were tolerated because, like Islam, they taught the worship of the One God.

Radical displacement was also the policy of the early Christian missionary movement. It regarded the non-Christian faiths as sinful error and sought to convert as many adherents as possible. Missionaries did not show the slightest regret at the possible extinction of the native religions which their converts had formerly practiced.

The modern mind is quick to reject this policy as a mark of an unenlightened mind. But, unfortunately, this rejection is rarely well-informed. It is often merely sentimental and covertly relies upon the policies which we have just rejected as inadequate.

Let us look at the case for radical displacement as far as possible through the eyes of some Christian thinkers who hold it with some degree of sophistication. Briefly, the three chief arguments against this policy can be stated in this way. First of all, it does not stand to reason that in the vast enterprise of religious questing known to the human race, only one group of people should have come upon the truth, all the rest having ended up in darkness. Toynbee, for example, quotes sympathetically the Roman orator and statesman Symmachus in a fourth-century debate with Ambrose, Christian bishop of Milan, over the removal of a pagan shrine from the Senate building: "It is impossible that so great a mystery should be approached by one road only."[11] Second, a study of the major religions shows that they are quite alike in many significant ways. Total displacement, therefore, seems unsuited to the religious situation. The third argument against displacement is that the attitude of superiority fostered by this policy is a rather ugly and dogmatic one, which automatically detracts from whatever plausibility it might have.

Hendrik Kraemer, a scholar of deep sophistication in cultural history, but who nevertheless believes that in some sense the policy of radical displacement is correct, might answer these charges in this way: In the first place, there are many beneficial truths that have been discovered by one group of men and enjoyed by the rest only after they have been spread abroad by cultural diffusion. The wheel, for example, remained absent from the New World until brought over from the Old. Science with its many potential benefits is cheifly the product of Western society. Other cultures are wise to adopt these benefits even when it means abandoning their less successful investigations into nature.

Moreover, the first criticism assumes that religious truth is the result of human searching. The biblical view, Kraemer would say, is not that religious truth comes from human investigations or searching, but from God's self-revelation to man when and where he will, not because the recipients of that revelation arc worthy, but simply because God in his sovereignty has chosen to do so for reasons we cannot presume to say we know.

The futility of human searching for God, this view holds, stems from the fact of sin. Though man was originally created with a natural witness to God in his heart, sin has destroyed it, so that no true knowledge of God can now be had save by those who have received the Christian revelation. Religion, which is claimed by some to be man's honest search for the divine, is, in the theology of Karl Barth, the realm of man's attempt to justify and to sanctify himself before a capricious conception of God, arbitrarily invented in the vain imaginings of man's own mind.

Regarding alleged similarities among religions, Kraemer insists that despite their apparent similarity they have distinctly different meanings, because they are related to a different center of ultimate commitment. Forgiving one's enemy, for example, may mean many things. It may mean that he who forgives is simply following an expedient policy of social peace, or that he is afraid, or that he doesn't wish to ruffle his spirits with a life of contention, or that he is merely indifferent to the one forgiven. It may mean, as in Christianity, that God has commanded such forgiveness in emulction of his own gracious mercifulness. This remark applies to every example of alleged similarity, for the issue at stake is not whether there are marginal similarities, but what these things mean when they are related to their natural center. This is important for anyone who would understand the teachings of a religion. Taken separately, the teachings may appear to mean something quite different from what they mean to those who see them in the light of an entirely different ultimate concern.

So far as the attitude of dogmatism is concerned, Kraemer could reply that the man who lives his life under the revelation of the true God has nothing to be proud or arrogant about. What has been revealed does not belong to him, it is not the product of his spiritual powers. He is merely the servant of the truth that has been entrusted to him. Moreover, it is surely not fair to accuse a man of dogmatism just because he is convinced that he has truth to share. The modern medical man is not being dogmatic when he insists that penicillin is a better treatment for yaws than magical potions. The reason we do not accuse him of that, I suspect, is that we know he is right. The reason we do accuse the missionary of dogmatism is that we think he is wrong. But that is merely our own judgment concerning ultimate truth; it is not necessarily a fair account of the man being accused.

Nevertheless, with all that has been said, it is the opinion of most American Christian scholars that the policy of radical displacement is inadequate. We would be wise, however, to remain in respectful dialogue with such able protagonists of this view as Hendrik Kraemer in order not to fall into errors in other directions.

One further variation of this view needs to be stated before considering some other alternatives. Karl Barth, as we learned in our definition of religion, holds that all religion is merely man's way of hiding from God. And this, he would say, is true of Christianity as a religion, as well as all other faiths. Barth believes that God revealed himself in Jesus Christ to put an end to religion. This view has given rise in recent times to the expression "religionless Christianity,"[12] a concept we have already encountered in the thought of Dietrich Bonhoeffer. This seemingly contradictory phrase means simply that what the Christian has to recommend is not Christianity as a religion, but Christ as God's word to man. Christianity as a religion is simply a cultural product and comes as much under God's judgment as any other religion. The missionary, in this sense, is wrong if he tries to displace, say, Buddhism with Christianity, one religion with another. What he must do is present Christ divested of all the trappings of Western culture in which he has been concealed.

We need not pretend that this is an easy conception. Presenting Christ may seem as much like a religion as any other. There is not space to deal with this complex issue here, but Christians must consider it seriously in any policy which they would devise for dialogue with other faiths. For it is precisely the cultural elements in religions that seem to make them unsuited to universality. Universal religious truth, in this sense, must be transcultural. The question worth pondering is: How shall we know that we are possessed of such a truth? Fascinating as this question is, we must postpone an attempted answer until a later section.

## Dialogue on the Basis of the Hindu Vedanta

Several thinkers of the highest caliber have proposed that a key to the dialogue among religions can be found in the Hindu philosophy of the Vedanta. We have already briefly noted two modern exponents of this view:

Sir Sarvepalli Radhakrishnan and Sri Aurobindo. The Vedanta is likewise the basis of the Hindu mission to the West inspired by the life and thought of their sainted wise man, Sri Ramakrishna (1834–1869), and his greatest apostle, Swami Vivekananda. It is this conception which animates Aldous Huxley's *Perennial Philosophy.*[13]

According to this doctrine, the religions of man may be viewed as stages in religious development or growth. Some, like animism and idolatry, are still at the child's level. As men grow in their understanding, they see that the real meaning of these religions lies far beyond them in the ultimate Oneness of all reality in Brahman. Just as the adult can appreciate the stages of growth through which the child is passing, just so the mature religious man can appreciate the earlier stages of religious development.

The Vedanta, then, appears as the highest common factor in all the faiths of mankind. Given time and experience, mankind is bound to move toward its essential goal of final realization of Oneness. The practical strategy, in the meantime, is twofold: First, curb the more turbulent actions of the immature so that they do as little as possible to impede the growth of others or themselves, and then teach the highest wisdom as broadly as possible so that men will recognize it and come more swiftly to their maturity.

This policy is expansive in its tolerance. For example, Ramakrishna taught that, when speaking of the Ultimate, which "some call God, others the Self, the Whole, Being or Nothingness," it makes no difference whether one addresses reality as "Him, or It, or Thou, or whether one thinks: 'I am He (It).' "[14] India is a good example of the policy in practice. The religions of that subcontinent range all the way from the most primitive religions to the enlightenment of the sages. The sage sees no inconsistency in this motley collection of religious practices; he patiently waits for the children to grow up.

An important question to be asked is: What attitude does this policy prescribe toward Western religions? The answer: Western theistic religions such as Judaism, Christianity, and Islam are in the next to last stages of maturity. The reason for this judgment is that so long as God is regarded as separate from the worshipper or from the world, the full truth of the unqualified Oneness of reality has not yet been realized. In the Vedanta, God is seen as a mere appearance of Brahman, who alone is real and who (which) embraces everything in a total way. Adherents to the Vedanta philosophy hold that the final disappearance of this dualism in Western religion is foreshadowed by some Western mystics whom they regard as the highest representatives of religion in the West.

Mysticism does indeed seem to have common properties in East and West. As Hocking says, "Mystics recognize mystics across all boundaries."[15] But it is also true that mystics have been looked upon with suspicion in the Semitic faiths. Some of them, like the Christian mystic Eckhart, have been condemned for heretical teaching, and others, like the Moslem mystic Al-Hallaj, have been put to death.

This is not the place to examine mystical experience with the care which it deserves. However, the central issue at stake can be made clear: Which theology is the proper interpretation of mystical experience?

The Vedantist says that the Vedanta is the proper meaning of that experience, and that this meaning is self-evident to the person who reaches the state of ecstatic samadhi or nirvana. But according to Christian, Moslem, and Jewish theology, it is blasphemy to claim that, through mystical experience, man, the creature, becomes identical with the Creator God. Each of these Western faiths has its own interpretations of the mystical experience— and it is not one of merging into identity with the Divine. It is this quarrel over interpretation that must be recognized as a decisive difference between Hindu versions of religion and those of the Semitic faiths.

If my observations have been correct, we are prepared for the conclusion that while the Vedanta may be a policy for the Hindu in his dialogue with the Western faiths, it cannot be the policy of dialogue for the latter, for they reject the Vedantic interpretation of religious experience as alien to the essential character of their own religions. For all his urbanity and tolerance, Radhakrishnan has been unable to appreciate this difficulty, and he criticizes Christianity for claiming to be the "highest manifestation of the religious spirit."[16] But it should be plain from his own writing that he regards Vedantic Hinduism as the highest manifestation of the religious spirit. Of course, he may be right, but he can hardly blame adherents of other faiths if they refuse to agree with him.

The Christian, for example, would insist that man's unity with God is not a manifestation of the religious spirit at all, but is God's own work of grace through his revelation in Christ and the Holy Spirit. According to this view, religious experience cannot of itself come anywhere near the transcendent reality of God himself. From yet another point of view, the Jewish thinker Martin Buber, who for a time was a practitioner of ecstatic mysticism, says that the experience of ecstatic oneness serves only to separate man from the world, and that it is therefore not the achievement of Unity and Oneness which Oriental thinkers claim it to be.

## Dialogue on the Basis of Christian Logos Theology

The dilemma of the Christian, in dialogue with other faiths, is how to remain faithful to the truth received through the Christian revelation, and, at the same time, to acknowledge the wisdom that is so evident in the non-Christian faiths. Viewing the history of dialogue, he can see that too great an openness, with too little sense of distinctive Christian truth, leads to the vacuous syncretisms that I criticized above. Some such fate seems to have overtaken an early form of Christianity, Nestorianism, which traveled all the way to ancient China before it disappeared in the sands of alien cultures. On the other hand, the attitude of radical displacement seems too restricted and narrow, for both secular and religious reasons. The secular reasons are fairly obvious: The policy of radical displacement arouses the deepest resentment and resistance among non-Christians, and leads to a situation of bitterness that is hardly conducive to social peace or human understanding. The religious reasons will become apparent in the following explanation of the doctrine of the Logos, to which we now turn in the search for a workable policy of interfaith dialogue.

The key biblical passage upon which the doctrine of the Logos is based is the first chapter of St. John's Gospel, where the author gives the cosmic background for the coming of Jesus Christ:

In the beginning was the Word [Logos], and the Word [Logos] was with God, and the Word [Logos] was God. He was in the beginning with God; all things were made through him, and without him was not anything made that was made. In him was life, and the life was the light of men. . . .

The true light that enlightens every man was coming into the world; he was in the world, and the world was made through him, yet the world knew him not; he came to his own home, and his own people received him not. . . .

And the Word [Logos] became flesh and dwelt among us, full of grace and truth; we have beheld his glory, glory as of the only Son from the Father.[17]

Logos is the Greek word which in the English text is translated Word. This word made its appearance in Greek thought around 500 B.C. in the works of the Greek metaphysician Heraclitus of Ephesus (the probable place, incidentally, where St. John's Gospel was composed hundreds of years later). It is hard to be certain of its exact meaning. But some things seem fairly clear. It was used in Greek thought to indicate the intelligent cause of the world and the world changes which occur according to natural law. It is thus, in some sense, a cosmic principle in the process of self-expression. St. John says that it was God's means of creating the world. He also says that this Logos became a human being in Jesus Christ so that men could behold his glory directly—even handle and touch it.

The word changes to Nous (Mind or Reason) in the philosophy of Plato, but the meaning is roughly the same. It appears later in the writings of the Stoics as well. In short, it is a key term in the Greek understanding of life.

It is reasonable to suppose that St. John used the term in order to make the Christian revelation understandable to people not familiar with Hebrew modes of thought. It is, in short, the product of the first major dialogue of the Christian faith with the non-Christian world.

Around the year A.D. 100 there was born in Syria a Greek named Justin, who was to become known as Justin the Philosopher. This man made his pilgrimage to the various philosophers of the time in search of spiritual wisdom. Later he himself taught the doctrines of Plato. In due time he became a Christian. But he did not reject the wisdom he had found in philosophy. He claimed rather that the Logos he saw in Christ had also taught the Greek philosophers, insofar as they lived "according to the Logos." He even called the noble Socrates and Plato "Christians before Christ," who was himself the supreme manifestation of the Logos.[18]

The historian of religion A. C. Bouquet, who believes that the Logos doctrine is the best instrument for shaping a Christian theology of dialogue with the non-Christian faiths, writes as follows: "The logical implications of this teaching are so important that they deserve careful examination, since it has been affirmed that the statement about 'Christians before Christ' is capable of being extended so as to embrace most of the sages of Asia, and to include, for instance, Sankara, Lao-Tzu and Mo-ti and even perhaps, paradoxically as it may seem, the Jew Karl Marx, as among those who have lived and talked 'according to the Logos.' "[19]

Paul Tillich, thinking along these same lines, writes that "Eastern wisdom, like every other wisdom, certainly belongs to the self-manifestations of the Logos and must be included in the interpretation of Jesus as the Christ, if he is rightly to be called the incarnaton of the Logos."[20] He further mentions what we have already noted, that "the encounter with the world religions puts a task before Christian theology which is very similar to that of the early church in its encounter with Hellenistic culture."[21]

Bouquet says that as the incarnate Logos, Christ is both fulfiller and judge of all the manifestations of God's wisdom in history. He is fulfiller in that what is given dimly or fragmentarily elsewhere is given clearly and wholly in him. He is the judge in that whatever contradicts him is not divine wisdom but human error. Thus the Logos doctrine enjoys an expansive relationship with the traditions of wisdom both East and West, but it retains a central principle of discrimination in Jesus Christ. Augustine could say that "the true religion had existed always and was called Christian only after the appearance of Christ."[22] He regarded the pre-Christian eras as in a real sense preparatory to Christ's appearance, in exactly the same way in which the Old Testament era of Hebrew history was preparatory to his coming.

Tillich writes that "early Christianity did not consider itself as a radical exclusive, but as the all-inclusive religion in the sense of saying, 'All that is true anywhere in the world belongs to us, the Christians.' "[23] But he adds the proviso which makes this Logos doctrine different from syncretism: "This astonishing universalism, however, was always balanced by a criterion which was never questioned: the image of Jesus as the Christ, as documented in the New and prepared for in the Old Testament."[24] This principle of judgment, or discrimination, means that in the dialogue of Christian with non-Christian forms of wisdom, some things will be discarded as incompatible with the truth. For example, it is unlikely that the Vedantic goal of reabsorption into the Absolute is compatible with the eventual victory of the Kingdom of God. Both cannot be true. This view does not, therefore, take the position that all religions are equally true.

It should be clear that, though this Logos theology holds out a hand of fellowship to non-Christians, it is a distinctly Christian philosophy of interfaith dialogue, one not suited to non-Christian. It is a Christian version of the highest-common-factor philosophy of dialogue.

Is there a policy of dialogue not drawn from one of the religions? This is a natural question, when we review the results of our quest so far. The answer is that there is not. The policy of dialogue that anyone, or any group, can live with is one that is derived from his or their own ultimate concern; that is, from his or their own faith. The challenge of our age is for each faith (religious or quasi-religious) to discover in its own tradition the basis for a policy which can at least keep the interfaith dialogue open, understanding, and charitable. For some faiths this may prove impossible. Take an unimportant but instructive example: In seventeenth-century England, one Ludowicke Muggleton and his cousin, John Reeve, claimed to be God's chosen prophets. Muggleton composed the *Third and Last Testament of Our Lord Jesus Christ.* The creed of the faithful who gathered around these two men as Muggletonians was: "I do believe in God alone, likewise in Reeve and Muggleton." And this little band and its successors went on to sing for more than two hundred years:

> *This is the Muggletonians' faith,*
> *This is the God which we believe;*
> *None salvation knowledge hath,*
> *But those of Muggleton and Reeve;*
> *Christ is the Muggletonians' king,*
> *With whom eternally they'll sing.*[25]

## How To Carry on the Dialogue

From this brief survey of principles it is possible to suggest how the dialogue among religions should be carried on. First of all, we must keep the dialogue going; we must keep the various faiths of mankind talking to one another, however contrary their views.

A second suggestion follows from this. Each faith is under the obligation to examine itself closely, using both internal and external criticism of its views. By internal criticism I mean the examination of a faith to see whether it is consistent with itself. By external criticism I mean studying a faith to see whether it is adequate to deal with the totality of life facts as a religion should. If religion is the ultimate concern which directs the life of individuals and groups it cannot be really ultimate if it is not adequate to the whole range of life facts. An example of this would be to ask how a given faith deals with, say, science or the aspirations of the twentieth century for a decent world order. Under the spur of such criticism—internal and external—a given faith would be compelled to present itself in its most logical and adequate form.

Third, let men study not only their own faiths, but sincerely learn about others, not to refute or criticize or deny them, but to understand them so far as possible from their own point of view. This means letting each faith be itself, with all its uniqueness. Nothing is to be gained by blurring differences that actually exist among the religions of man. Such a study will no doubt also reveal common values that are presently obscured in the heat of partisanship.

A fourth suggestion is this: Let members of the various faiths learn to listen with an open spirit to one another. They need not agree to agree, they need only listen. Listening, of course, means more than keeping silent while others speak; it means attending to and sympathetically considering what is being said. This implies the possibility of using insights from other religions whenever possible, trying them out in relation to one's own faith. A couple of works by Roman Catholic scholars illustrate this: Dom Aelfred Graham's *Zen Catholicism*,[26] and Jean-Marie Deschenet's *Christian Yoga*.[27] And going well beyond this, it means being prepared, at least in principle, to change commitments. St. Paul suggested a good rule for this depth of sharing: speak the truth in love.[28]

Last of all, let the various faiths prove their worth by practical labors on behalf of mankind. Most of the great faiths—including the quasi religions—claim to teach benevolence. Let them demonstrate in fact the quality of that benevolence on the needy body of mankind. They can best prove themselves as they work meaningfully for the dignity of man, the peace of the world, and for the mitigation of its poverty and ignorance.

This inquiry began with the conviction that a policy of interreligious dialogue in a global and nuclear age is of supreme importance. It can be concluded by saying that if any one faith, or combination of faiths, possesses the final truth for man, a free and open dialogue which includes a deep sharing of life and substance among men and peoples, is the most likely climate in which that truth may make its fairest claims and be acknowledged in the course of history. As Paul Tillich says, "The way is to penetrate into the depth of one's own religion, in devotion, thought, and action. In the depth of every living religion there is a point at which the religion loses its importance, and that to which it points breaks through its particularity, elevating it to spiritual freedom and with it to a vision of the spiritual presence in other expressions of the ultimate meaning of man's existence."[29]

Such intimate give-and-take cannot but raise many difficult questions about the logic of faith and the nature of religious knowledge. It is to such questions that we turn in our next section.

## SUGGESTIONS FOR FURTHER READING

For the specific problem of the dialogue between religions I have found A. C. Bouquet's *The Christian Faith and the Non-Christian Religions* (Harper & Row, 1958) the most suggestive of creative solutions. The most serious challenge to Bouquet's view is the well-documented work of Henrik Karemer, *Religion and the Christian Faith* (Westminster, 1956). Another work from the Christian perspective is Edward J. Jurji's *The Christian Interpretation of Religion* (Macmillan, 1952). Its subtitle suggests its content: *Christianity in Its Human and Creative Relationship with the World's Cultures and Faiths*. Joachim Wach's approach is more sociological in his writings edited by Joseph M. Kitagawa: *The Comparative Study of Religions* (Columbia University Press, 1958). Arnold

Toynbee's approach is, of course, historical in *Christianity Among the Religions of the World* (Scribner, 1957). See also his Gifford Lectures on the dawn of the higher religions and the search for a Being worthy of man's worship: *An Historian's Approach to Religion* (Oxford University Press, 1956).

Paul Tillich's work is always interesting, and his *Christianity and the Encounter of the World Religions* (Columbia University Press, 1963) is no exception. An earlier book by Kenneth Saunders is a sympathetic account of both Eastern and Western religion: *The Ideals of East and West* (Macmillan, 1934). F. S. C. Northrop approaches the problem from a philosophical point of view, with the philosophy of science especially in mind, in *The Meeting of the East and West* (Macmillan, 1947). An important work by another philosopher also concerned with world understanding is W. E. Hocking's *The Coming World Civilization* (Harper & Row, 1956). Kraemer's sophisticated rebuttal to works of this kind is contained in his *World Cultures and World Religions* (Westminster Press, 1960). Radhakrishnan's *East and West, the End of Their Separation* (Harper & Row, 1954) is profoundly Eastern in perspective.

## NOTES

1. Quoted in Hendrik Kraemer, *World Cultures and World Religions* (Westminster, 1960), p. 346.

2. *Ibid.*, p. 349.

3. Ralph Linton, *The Study of Man* (Appleton-Century-Crofts, 1936), pp. 326–327.

4. Khalifa Abdul Hakim, "One God, One World, One Humanity" in Ruth Nanda Anshen, ed., *Moral Principles of Action* (Harper & Row, 1952), p. 597.

5. *Ibid.*

6. Sarvepalli Radhakrishnan, *East and West, the End of Their Separation* (Harper & Row, 1954).

7. Quoted in *Time*, October 15, 1956, p. 89.

8. Quoted in Kraemer, *op. cit.*, p. 289.

9. William L. Kolb, in *Proceedings of the Hazen International Conference of the Sociology of Religion*, Washington, D.C., September, 1962, p. 20.

10. "Radical displacement" is a term coined by William Ernest Hocking in *Rethinking Missions, A Laymen's Inquiry After One Hundred Years* (Harper & Row, 1932).

11. Arnold Toynbee, *Christianity Among the Religions of the World* (Scribner, 1957), p. 112.

12. For an exposition of "religionless Christianity," see Alexander Miller, *The Renewal of Man* (Doubleday, 1955) and Daniel Jenkins, *Beyond Religion* (Westminster, 1963).

13. Aldous Huxley, *Perennial Philosophy* (Harper & Row, 1945).

14. Quoted in Kraemer, *op. cit.*, p. 373.

15. *Ibid.*, p. 358.

16. *Ibid.*, p. 363.

17. John 1:1–4, 9–11, 14.

18. A. C. Bouquet, *The Christian Faith and the Non-Christian Religions* (Harper & Row, 1958), pp. 137 ff.

19. *Ibid.*, p. 138. See chapter 6 for

the history of the word Logos.

20. Paul Tillich, "On the Boundary Line," *The Christian Century*, December 7, 1960, p. 1436.

21. *Ibid.*

22. Quoted in Paul Tillich, *Christianity and the Encounter of the World Religions* (Columbia University Press, 1963), p. 34.

23. *Ibid.*, p. 36.

24. *Ibid.*

25. Quoted in C. E. M. Joad, *God and Evil* (Harper & Row, 1953), p. 23.

26. Dom Aelfred Graham, *Zen Catholicism* (Harcourt, Brace & World, 1963).

27. Jean-Marie Deschenet, *Christian Yoga*, Roland Hindmarsh, trans. (Harper & Row, 1960).

28. Ephesians 4:15.

29. Tillich, *Christianity and the Encounter*, p. 97.

## PART SIX

# LOGIC, SCIENCE, AND GOD

# 21

# *The Logic of*
# *Religious Language*

❖❖❖❖❖❖❖❖❖❖❖❖❖❖❖❖❖❖❖❖❖❖❖❖❖❖❖❖❖❖❖❖❖❖❖

One of the fruits of modern thought has been an unprecedented refinement of the instruments of logical thought. The investigation of religion cannot fail to take these achievements into account, even if only a glimpse of their riches can be afforded in a general introduction such as this. In the next two chapters we will examine the new approach to the logic of religious language and the present status of the dialogue between science and religion. After this brief introduction we will then apply some of the lessons of this study to the perennial question: How do we know God? The section will conclude with an essay on another recurring problem, the aspect of human experience which seems most to challenge faith—the mystery of evil.

## UNDERSTANDING THE LOGIC OF
## RELIGIOUS LANGUAGE

Why study Religious language? This is a natural question, since the topic may give the impression of being quite artificial. The fact is that language is a vehicle in which we carry on our dialogue with the reality around us. It is also the chief medium for communion with our fellows. Without being aware of it, many of our difficulties in carrying on that dialogue arise out of ignorance of the way language works. Many intellectual difficulties in religion arise from misunderstanding the logic of religious language, for, as we shall see, it does have a logic of its own, quite distinct from the object-language of science and practical affairs.

## *The Rise of Linguistic Analysis: The Vienna Circle (1924–1936)*

Logical Analysis, one of the two most influential movements in modern philosophy,[1] grew out of the efforts of philosophers to resolve some recurring problems in science. Though its major positions were nearly all anticipated by David Hume in the eighteenth century, this school of thought owes its modern beginnings to a group of philosophers known as the Vienna Circle, founded by Morris Schlick in 1924. These men were scientists by profession or avocation, and were eager to bring philosophy into harmony with their scientific studies. Planck, Carnap, Frank, and Schlick were theoretical physicists; Hahn, Mengers, and Gödel were mathematicians; and Neurath was an economist and sociologist. Wittgenstein, who was highly influential in the circle, though he never attended its meetings, was an engineer.

The views of this group can be summarized as follows:[2] Science alone can give us any facts. It alone is competent to tell us "what is the case." Philosophy's role is not to tell us about the world. That is up to science. Philosophy's business is to analyse the way language is used—especially the way it is used in the sciences. Any statement that purports to tell us about the world must be related in special ways to our sense perceptions. They alone can yield information about existence.

In addition to referential or fact statements (which are always part of some science), there are two other kinds of language. One of these is tautologies. A tautology is a statement that tells us nothing about the world. It only tells us how we intend to use certain words. For example, the statement "All triangles are three-sided" does not tell us about certain shapes in the world; it merely tells us that when we use the word triangle we will always mean a "three-sided" figure. A tautology is, therefore, an absolutely certain statement, whereas statements about facts always carry with them a degree of probability that they may be mistaken.

In addition to factual statements and tautologies, there is a third kind of language which Carnap called "expressive language." Expressive language does not tell us anything about the world, nor about how we will use words. It merely expresses the feelings and attitudes of the speaker.

When we ask where religious language fits into this scheme, we are told that it is entirely expressive. This is also true of ethical and aesthetic language. Religious language may appear to refer to "what is the case," as, for instance, when someone says, "Jesus is the Son of God." But this statement does not qualify as a statement of fact, since there are not sense perceptions to which the crucial words refer. It must, therefore, be an expression of some kind of feeling on the part of the speaker. The Viennese philosophers would say that such words are therefore factually meaningless.

The most famous teaching of this school was the so-called verification theory of meaning: The meaning of an assertion is the way in which it is verified. We have already explained the meaning of this definition above, but to repeat: A statement is factually meaningful only where the major terms in the statement refer to some sensory experience to which the speaker can point, either directly or indirectly. For example: *This is a table* or *There is life on Mars.* All other statements are pseudo propositions and are factually meaningless. For example: *Angels hover around the earth* or *God is good.*

Thus, according to this doctrine, most, if not all, religious and theological language is factually meaningless. Its real significance is emotive, that is, as expressions of subjective feeling. For example: *Hurrah* or *Alas!*[3] It shouldn't be hard to see why this classification was a critical challenge to religious thinkers. They could hardly stand still for the claim that all their writings were merely subjective emotion.

But as the doctrines of the analytic schools came under further critical study, the logical empiricists developed serious trouble of their own. The question they found hard to answer was this: Is the verification theory of meaning itself meaningful? On their own premises they had three options, none of which were very satisfactory: First, it is a tautology, in which case it doesn't give us any information at all, except about how analysts intend to use words.

Second, it is an empirical statement. In this case it must be based upon an adequate sampling of all allegedly meaningful statements. It would, then, like all empirical statements, be not a firm rule for linguistic usage. But this would also contradict the position that philosophy isn't an empirical study and doesn't tell us about matters of fact.

A third possibility remained: that it is an expressive statement. In this case it would merely tell us about the feelings of the positivists who framed it. The final option—the one most often accepted—is that the verification theory of meaning is simply a definition of the method which analytical philosophers propose to use. But in this case, of course, there should be no objection if other thinkers choose to use other ways of doing philosophy.

Analysts could hardly accept any of these options without giving up the whole case. The complicated efforts of the logical empiricists to refine their position in such a way as to meet these objections are too detailed to engage us here.[4] However, let me conclude with this observation, which the interested student can verify for himself: The whole enterprise gives the clear impression of men whose faith had been placed wholeheartedly in what I have called, in previous chapters, the premises of modernity. What it comes to is this: They were wholeheartedly convinced of the truth of these premises and defended them like men whose ultimate concern has been assaulted. They were simply convinced that the universe contained nothing but sense contents—though they were prevented by their own principles from making such a clear statement of their views. That would itself have been an unverifiable statement, and therefore meaningless.

## The Change to Functional Analysis

These logical difficulties, coupled with a rising interest in the role of symbols in human life, gradually shifted the direction of analytic philosophy. The early studies were concerned with the meaning of meaning. The new studies sought to answer the question: What function does a given set of symbols perform? Instead of asking what the statement "God exists" means (if anything), they now ask, What does the speaker hope to accomplish, or what function does the statement perform?

Wittgenstein, one of the major figures in early positivism, was convinced by his own research that his earlier work had been a great oversimplification, and that the program of building a perfect language for reporting facts could not be carried out successfully. He departed from Bertrand Russell's dictum: "The essential business of language is to assert or deny facts."[5] He decided that language has many functions that are obscured by such a narrow perspective. In preparing his posthumously published work *Philosophical Investigations*,[6] he painstakingly worked at the analysis of these many functions, most of which involved different uses than that of reporting or denying facts. He noted that we are also often giving orders or obeying them, making up stories, telling jokes, asking, thanking, cursing, greeting, praying.[7] The meaning of these linguistic expressions would escape us if we insisted on treating them as either asserting or denying facts. Instead, it is important to discover how an expression is used. As Wittgenstein once said, "An expression has meaning only in the stream of life."[8]

Functional analysis made it increasingly plain that these various "language-games" are so different in their logical structure that it would be a great error to judge them exclusively by the standards which are uniquely suited to scientific reporting. Analysts became less dogmatic and more attentive to the way in which language is actually used in human communication. As a result of these studies, it has become increasingly apparent that in the total body of human language, invented for the many purposes of human sociality, there are many different "languages"; different, that is, in the logic that controls their various functions.

In the following examples, consider the differences among several important categories of language by noting how they behave in practice.

*Scientific language:* Example: "This liquid is $H_2O$." If you were to contradict it by saying, "No, it is HCl," the dispute could be settled by following the rules of scientific investigation.

*Personal Preference Language:* Example: "This coffee tastes good." If someone were to say, "It tastes terrible," the original statement would not be contradicted. Personal preferences can be changed, but they cannot be contradicted. What tastes "good" to one person may taste "bad" to another.

*Practical language:* Example: "Wear a coat if you don't want to catch cold." Such language is partly governed by scientific rules and partly not. A person who said "I never wear a coat, but I never catch cold" would not be contradicting the intention of the original statement.

*Moral or ethical language:* Example: "It is wrong to steal." This statement is partly empirical; that is, it refers to acts that can be observed—someone taking property legally in the possession of another. Is this kind of language reducible to the rules of personal preference? "Would that man did not steal!" If someone said, "I like stealing," would he have contradicted the original statement? Or is it merely practical language? If someone said, "I have learned to take other people's property without anyone knowing about it," would we reply, "Well, then, it is not wrong for you to steal"?

It is my judgment that something is left over after moral language has been analyzed in this way. What is left over is not easy to say. Linguistic philosophers have made two interesting suggestions. The first, a proposal by R. M. Hare, is that moral language is exhortation or command language, like "Please shut the door."[9] As Carnap says, "Actually a value statement is nothing else than a command in a misleading grammatical form."[10] Moral statements differ from this example only because they are concerned with more important preferences and habits of life than door-shutting. According to this rule, "It is wrong to steal" can be translated "Don't steal." And this means, among other things, that the speaker intends to follow his own directive.

The second proposal, by the philosopher J. O. Urmson, is that moral language is used for grading activities, comparable to sorting apples. When you say "Stealing is wrong" you are putting a label on theft just as when you label an apple as of "medium quality."

These suggestions illuminate moral language to some degree, but they do not exhaust its meaning. If we ask the person using moral language to justify his rules for commanding or grading, what answer may we expect? Hare answers this question in a very important passage from his work *The Language of Morals:* "If pressed to justify a decision completely, we have to give a complete specification of the way of life of which it is a part. This complete specification is impossible in practice to give; the nearest attempts are those given by the great religions, especially those which can point to historical persons who carried out the way of life in practice."[11]

Hare presses further and says: "If the inquirer still goes on asking, 'But why should I live like that?' then there is no further answer to give him, because we have already . . . said everything that could be included in this further answer. We can only ask him to make up his own mind which way he ought to live: for in the end everything rests upon such a decision of principle."[12]

This, it should be noted, is a case of referring moral language finally to the religious dimension; that is, to one's ultimate concern. The final meaning of moral language then becomes, somehow, religious.

*Aesthetic language:* Example: "Isn't the mountain beautiful!" Would the response "I think it is ugly" be a contradiction? Not if aesthetic statements are personal-preference statements. If they are mere preferences, then they merely give vent to the feelings of a person or group, and these cannot be contradicted. But if aesthetic language is used to specify some nonpersonal element in the situation—a quality of a painting or a landscape, for example —then the function of aesthetic language must be considered in a different way. How? We are back again to our remarks about moral language. Beauty is a complex good that men use in making judgments about situations that are not merely matters of personal preference. It is perfectly reasonable to say, "I believe it is beautiful, but I don't yet like it." Such a statement implies that I *ought* to like it, however—which is different from saying, "I don't like cream in my coffee, but I ought to like it that way."

What I am saying is that in aesthetic judgments, as in moral judgments, there is more involved than personal or group taste. If we carried out this analysis of function completely, I suspect we would arrive at the same point Hare arrived at in his analysis of moral language; that is, that this particular good which we have called "beauty" belongs somehow to the way in which we ultimately perceive the world in which we live. Its final justification will turn out to be whatever justification can be given for religious statements.

### The Nature of Religious Language

> *The Lord is my shepherd, I shall not want;*
> *he makes me lie down in green pastures.*
> *He leads me beside still waters;*
> *he restores my soul.*[13]

That is religious language. Note what it might look like translated entirely into scientific language:

> *The Lord is my external-internal integrative mechanism,*
> *I shall not be deprived of gratification for my*
> *viscerogenic hungers or my need-dispositions*
> *He motivates me to orient myself toward a*
> *non-social object with affective significance,*
> *He positions me in a nondecisional situation,*
> *He maximizes my adjustment.*[14]

The reason why this is amusing is that it completely misses the point of the original. It makes what is known in linguistic philosophy as a "category mistake," that is, misapplying rules that are proper to one kind of language to another that is distinctly different, like saying, "Saturday is in bed" or "The equator is late."[15]

Another category mistake makes the following remark amusing: Whistler came home one day and saw his mother standing by the window. In surprise he said, "Mother, you're off your rocker!"

An example of this in the religious sphere would be to suppose that the Roman Catholic expression for Mary, "the Mother of God," is linguistically on the same level as "mother of Whistler." By the biological rules governing the latter expression "Mother of God" is an absurdity. But to the devout Catholic saying his prayers the expression is by no means absurd.

The reason for this is that religious language performs different functions than does biological or practical language—or in fact than does any other kind of language. It is time to spell out these complex functions.

## The Functions of Religious Language

Religious language is the language of ultimate concern and total life orientation. It therefore has the function of expressing the complex depth-dimensions of human existence. In its complexity it is like a cord woven out of many interrelated strands. Some of these can be sorted out as follows:

First, the man who sincerely prays, "Our Father who art in heaven, Thy kingdom come, Thy will be done . . ." is expressing his deepest emotions and his most inclusive attitudes. More than that, he is also indicating his life policy, his intention to behave in certain ways in the total range of life situations.

Second, this language does more than express attitudes and life policies; it refers beyond the speaker to a Being which is both beyond and yet inclusive of himself—God. Religious language is thus reference language; to be sure, not like scientific language, yet nonetheless referential. The attempt to save the meaningfulness of religious language by dropping its referential character is a defense that is false to an essential element in its meaning.

And yet this referring function of religious language is different from the referring function of thing-language. Perhaps the difference can be seen in the fact that in its most characteristic forms religious language is an address to the Self-Existent, to the Eternal Thou to whom the words refer. We do not address a table when we speak of it; that is, we do not speak to it, but about it. Conversely, we never properly speak about God, but only to God. It is as though when we say, "God is omniscient," we intended "O Thou who knowest all!" To speak about something is in some way to treat it as a thing. God cannot be a thing. He is always subject, never merely object. Therefore there is always some element of awed address in genuine religious talk.[16]

There is a fourth function of religious language yet to be noted. In praying the Lord's Prayer the speaker is doing more than referring—he is relating, by his words, to that Being in a special way. His language is itself a religious act. A secular analogy will make this clear. A governor who concludes a ceremony by saying "I declare this bridge open" is not merely referring to something apart from his speech; he is doing something with his words. The words don't represent the act of opening the bridge; they are the act. In the same way, the words "Thy will be done" are already an instance of God's will being done in the man who sincerely prays to him in this way.

A fifth function of religious language is commitment. In prayer a man is expressing, and at the same time making a total commitment. As Ian Ramsey says, "It is commitment suited to the whole job of living—not one just suited to building houses, or studying interplanetary motion, or even one suited to our own families, and no more."[17] Religious talk constitutes a personal pledge. If we observe a man behaving in some way inconsistent with this pledge, we do not generally say he is mistaken; we call him a hypocrite. He will himself feel that such a breach is sinful. If a man were to say, for example, "I believe that the highest commandments are to love God with all my heart, soul, mind, and strength, and my neighbor as myself," and then turn harshly on someone near him, we should have to conclude that he did not understand or intend what he had just said. Thus, a disparity between religious language and existence is a breach in the life of the speaker of the deepest sort. Contrast this with a factual assertion like "This is water." If it turns out to be a clear liquid that merely appears to be water, we should say that the speaker was simply mistaken, not that he was a hypocrite. In literal talk we compare words with things. But in religious talk we consider the quality of a whole life. "To speak this language is not so much to speak the truth," writes Robert Jordan, "as to be in the truth, or, in the language of the gospels, to do the truth."[18]

A sixth function of religious language is to create. In praying "Our Father" the speaker is creating, at the same time that he is expressing, the deepest communion of the human family with itself and with its Sustainer and Source. In the light of standards of religious faith drawn from biblical sources, such words function to deepen man's relation to man and man's relation to God; that is, they are part of the divine-human dialogue which is the very heart of the human enterprise.

To sum up: Religious language (1) expresses emotions and attitudes, (2) indicates life policy and intentions to behave in certain ways, (3) refers to the character of Ultimate Being, chiefly in the form of address, (4) relates the speaker to that Being in a special way, (5) makes a total personal commitment, and (6) creates human and divine-human fellowship.

## BIBLICAL LANGUAGE

In the foregoing material I have used the Lord's Prayer, an example of religious language from the West. The analysis would have been somewhat different had we looked instead at a famous Hindu formula used in uncounted thousands of meditations by devotees of the Vedanta: "Thou art That." Perhaps enough has been said to indicate how an inquiry into that language might proceed. But in order to succeed in such an analysis it would be necessary to understand Vedantic Hinduism as its own practitioners understand it.

Similarly, in order to understand biblical language it is necessary to study the Bible with care and to know how it is used by those for whom it is the standard of religious usage. We may note one major difference between biblical language and the mystical language of the East, namely, its historical character. To pray, for example, for God's Kingdom to come on earth as it is in heaven is to become a citizen of that Kingdom as it was announced by Jesus. This, in turn, means to join oneself to the whole history of salvation as it is described in the Old and New Testaments. What this means cannot be repeated here, since we have in any case looked at it in some detail in previous chapters. But to summarize briefly: To use biblical language is to become a member of the family of faith which began with Abraham and extends to the present day. This means that it is Church language, the language of a historical community which has endured throughout time and which still lives. By analogy, to use the English tongue is to place oneself in the inheritance of the English-speaking peoples everywhere. If one cannot feel such a membership, he is unlikely to really understand many of the basic expressions in that language. This is why translation is often so difficult.

The current Roman Catholic effort to translate the Mass into the local tongues of the people has run into precisely such difficulties. Some of them are amusing, at least to those who are not faced with the responsibilities of the situation. In Italy, for example, the phrase "body of Christ" cannot be translated into Italian because in that language it is a common local curse. In Tuscany, reports *Time* magazine, "the clerics find it embarrassing to end the Mass with *Andate in pace* (Go in peace)," because locally it is "the most common way to shoo away a beggar."[19] Among some of the islanders of the South Seas a literal translation of the name for God would be "Big fellow master too much who bosses heaven and ground." It would be very awkward indeed to insert that phrase into every prayer which pronounces the divine name.

Linguistic understanding is an old piece of business for the student of the Bible. As Paul Lehmann says, "Christian theology has from the beginning been . . . a theology of language."[20] In the myth of Babel, for instance, the fate of men who defied God was the confusion of their language and therefore of their understanding of one another. In the imagery of Pentecost the divine fire came upon the Apostles as "tongues of fire," and they preached to men of all nations with a miraculous new understanding. In the St. John's Gospel, it is the Word which becomes flesh in Christ, and when the Reformation broke out its major concern was for the "Word of God." In the chapter on biblical scholarship I have already described the current interest in language (hermeneutics) among contemporary scholars.


## VARIETIES OF LOGIC IN LANGUAGE

We have seen that religious language performs a rich and complex function. This function, in turn, calls for a correspondingly appropriate logic. This can be seen by a brief comparison of the logic appropriate to different kinds of language.

The logic of tautologies, for example, is essentially one of noncontradiction. If I intend to use language in a certain way (e.g., to define a triangle as an enclosed plane with three straight sides), then I must make certain not to forget how I have defined my terms. Errors would consist in contradicting the original definition.

The logic of empirical or factual statements is essentially the set of working rules that controls successful scientific investigations. By contrast, the logic of ethical language is fundamentally existential and dialogic. It is controlled by what I have called the dialogic human situation. It is essentially a logic of existence and action, not of speculative thinking, though it does have metaphysical aspects. Examples of this use of language appear in the chapters on ethics (17, 18, and 19) and need not be repeated here. Nor have we the space to discuss the logic of aesthetic language, which follows yet different rules.

### The Logic of Religious Language

The logic of religious language is like ethical language in being existential and dialogic, but its metaphysical overtones are more decisive.

"Argument in religious matters," writes Ramsey, "has a very odd function; its purpose being to tell such a tale as evokes the 'insight,' the 'discernment' from which commitment follows as a response."[21] If, for example, I say, "God exists," you might reply, "What evidence have you for your state-

But in fundamental ways the religious statement is different from the ment?" But this reply indicates that you have not understood my statement. Since the statement "God exists" has the same grammatical form as "A planet exists between the Sun and Venus," you have mistakenly thought that the former was an empirical statement, like the latter.

scientific one. Suppose we translate the brief statement "God exists" into its existential equivalents. They might go something like this: "I, the speaker, am utterly gripped, possessed, judged, and convicted by the unlimited goodness of Ultimate Reality"; or, "My whole being—body, mind, and spirit—stands or falls by my relationship to the unconditioned loving kindness and holy awesomeness of Ultimate Being"; or, "My whole being exists only in, through, and for the utterly irresistible sublimity of the ground of all existence." To invite the speaker to say more in this case is to open one's self to the deepest personal encounter, leading not to an argument or to a display of factual data, but to possible conversion. But how does one convince another person of such a life orientation? Certainly not by a display of facts. The logic of God's power to grip a man unconditionally is not the logic of factual reference.

It is much more like the logic of a *presence* (for instance, the presence of another person to whom we say "Thou"), for which no scientific evidence is appropriate. Gabriel Marcel points out that the peculiar logic of presence has been completely ignored or misunderstood by those who would reduce all our knowledge to knowledge verified in a scientific or quasi-scientific manner. He writes that the kind of philosophy that "stresses the activity of verification . . . ends by ignoring *presence*—that inward realization of presence through love which infinitely transcends all possible verification because it exists in an immediacy beyond all conceivable mediation."[22]

We cannot, at this point, go into this more deeply, but it should be apparent that the logic of religious argument is much more than an intellectual affair. The truth-claim of such a commitment could only be convincing to another person who himself discerned somehow the ultimate value of existence in an entirely different mode, and could not finally grasp the truth of such a way of life without embracing it himself. As the old hymn puts it: "The love of God, what it is only his loved ones know."

If someone were to say (following Bertrand Russell's own testimony of faith), "I exist in and through an accidental collocation of material atoms— this and nothing more," a Christian would be faced with an alternative life orientation. He might reply, "How regrettable! Your life is so meaningless." The options here would be between the Christian faith and scientific skepticism, and the choice between these two cannot be settled by appeals to matters of physical fact. For what is at stake is, on one side, the validity of a philosophy that limits itself to matters of scientific fact and, on the other, another philosophy that claims that the world of experience is permeated by significance which is vastly richer than mere sense contents.

## THE SYMBOLIC CHARACTER OF RELIGIOUS LANGUAGE

The vocabulary of thing-language is sensory. If we wish to refer to things, we appeal to the data of our senses. The bulk of daily language is oriented to this fact-referring task.

When we wish to speak of realities that are not things, we must have recourse to linguistic devices that elicit spiritual insight on the part of our hearers. Let us take a secular example. Suppose we wished to speak of love to one who has gone away. We could write prosaically, "I love and miss you." But this would scarcely convey our full meaning. We might, however, had we the skill of Conrad Aiken, write these words:

> Music I heard with you was more than music
> And bread I broke with you was more than bread,
> Now that I am without you all is desolate,
> All that was once so beautiful is dead.[23]

Or suppose we wished to express a longing to escape the pain of a wasting illness. We could borrow the words of the poet Keats, as he listened to the song of the nightingale:

> I have been half in love with easeful Death,
> Called him soft names in many a mused rime,
> To take into the air my quiet breath;

> *Now more than ever it seems rich to die,*
> *To cease upon the midnight with no pain,*
> *While Thou art pouring forth thy soul abroad*
> *In such an ecstasy!*[24]

Or, if we desired to note the mysterious power of beauty over man's transient existence, we might again find expression in Keats' lines from the same ode:

> *Thou wast not born for death, immortal Bird!*
> *No hungry generations tread thee down;*
> *The voice I hear this passing night was heard*
> *In ancient days by emperor and clown:*
> *Perhaps the self-same song that found a path*
> *Through the sad heart of Ruth, when, sick for home,*
> *She stood in tears amid the alien corn;*
> *The same that oftimes hath*
> *Charmed magic casements, opening on the foam*
> *Of perilous seas, in faery lands forlorn.*[25]

Symbolism is the natural language of the spirit, as literal prose is the natural language of practical affairs. It is no more possible to understand religious language with a literal mind than it would be to carry on a conversation in a foreign tongue that one has not studied.

The meanings conveyed by religion are not abstract systems of theological ideas or equally abstract truths, nor are they maps of heaven or hell. Such language would be nonreligious through and through. It would have nothing to do with the realities of the life of faith.

Religious language intends to speak in the fullest and most concrete way of the situation in which man finds himself existing. And to speak of this requires more than literal prose. Some religious people believe that "not literally" means "not really." This is the fear of religious literalists, who struggle against sophisticated interpretations of religious language as a betrayal of faith. The Catholic philosopher Austin Farrer makes it clear why such a fear is misplaced. "There is a current and exceedingly stupid doctrine that symbol evokes emotion and exact prose states reality. Nothing could be further from the truth: exact prose abstracts from reality, symbol represents it. And for that very reason, symbols have some of the many-sidedness of wild nature."[26]

"Symbolic" does not mean "not really," "inconceivable," or "abstract"; it means not being capable of being expressed in a literal model. We cannot for instance make a literal model of a person who is present to us as a person. But we can certainly conceive it and represent it to ourselves symbolically.

Language becomes symbolic when the realities to which it witnesses are not capable of being literally pointed out. Its essence lies in its use of form and symbol to convey more than the literal words themselves will bear. It does not have to be in so-called verse form. Consider the symbolic richness of these words of St. Paul: "O the depth of the riches and wisdom and knowledge of God! How unsearchable are his judgments and how inscrutable his ways! . . . For from him and through him and to him are all things. To him be glory forever. Amen."[27]

### Some Forms of Religious Symbolism

Let us take a brief look at some of the most significant elements in religious symbolism. *Narrative:* Ian Ramsey says that religious communication is largely dependent on stories that awaken insight. The Bible is filled with narratives, historical and fictional. The meaning of the Scriptures can only be grasped as the significance of these narratives breaks through. The great writers of Hebrew history recounted the events of the past to make clear the meaning and destiny of the Hebrew people. Jesus told parables for those who had ears to hear. His followers told the story of his life, death, and resurrection. Part of the great literature of Buddhism consists of tales of the Buddha's many lives, each illustrating the meaning of the more abstract teachings.

Of course, not all narrative is religiously significant. "On the third day he rose from the dead" is grammatically similar to "On the third day he rose from his bed,"[28] but the second does not have the symbolic richness of the first. The second is literal while the first possesses such significance that it cannot be translated satisfactorily into literal prose equivalents.

*Dialogues.* Where truth is subtle and requires participation in order to be grasped, dialogue (instead of plain exposition) seems to be an indispensable medium. Religious literature East and West is filled with such dialogues. No one understood more clearly the reasons for using this form of communication than that great master of dialogue Plato. He refused to write summaries of his views because, he said, no summary could do justice to the Truth that he was seeking. That truth, he claimed, would flash out in conversation among men of good will, and sustain itself like a flame illuminating every issue.[29]

*Metaphor, Paradox, and Analogy.* A *metaphor* is a figure of speech in which one thing is likened to another, different thing, thereby adding depth of meaning to the original reference. For example, Shakespeare says, "All the world's a stage, and all the people in it merely players." In a flash, a new dimension has been added to our understanding of human existence. Where literal talk falters, metaphor is eloquent. The gifted poet is able to inflame this insight again and again.

Some great metaphors for God are Father, Love, Creator, Sovereign, Judge, Saviour, Truth, Self-Existent, Ultimate Concern. We cannot speak literally of God, but through such figures of speech we can communicate meaningfully with and about him. "Him" is itself a metaphor, and so are "Person" and "One," the former drawn from human personality, the latter from mathematics. The "Trinity" is another metaphor used to denote the unity of God in view of the varying ways in which he is partially apprehended in Christian experience. When these great metaphors degenerate into literalism, they lose their depth-dimension and cease to communicate religious meaning.

*Paradox* is like metaphor in that it employs two apparently incompatible elements of thought to give a new dimension of depth to understanding. It is a paradox, for example, to say that God is both stern and gentle, that he is at once judgment and mercy. Such a statement, like all true paradoxes, is not a simple contradiction, like "round-square." In a fruitful paradox, the apparently opposite meanings have a way of forcing the mind to drop conventional ideas and stir itself to grasp some new dimension of significance. The highly paradoxical Chinese Tao Tê Ching begins with this stanza:

> *The Tao that can be told of*
> *Is not the Absolute Tao;*
> *The Names that can be given*
> *Are not Absolute names.*[30]

And then the author goes on, paradoxically, to tell of the Tao (the Way) in seventy more stanzas. The enduring spiritual appeal of his book testifies to the fact that he has successfully spoken of what "cannot" be spoken of.

*Analogy* is a favorite symbolic device of theologians. It is simply a special kind of metaphor. By taking elements in our finite understanding—like goodness, or perfection, or cause—and refining away their finite limitation, the theologian hopes to speak significantly about the qualities of the Infinite, namely, God. "Analogy is a relation between objects," says Austin Farrer, "capable of being classed as a species of 'likeness.' "[31] This means, comments Frederick Ferré, that "man is 'good' in a way literally appropriate to man's finite nature. Thus, the classical doctrine concludes, 'God's goodness' is neither something unrelated to 'man's goodness' nor merely identical to human virtue."[32]

The technical problems of the use of analogy in theology are beyond our province here. However, it should be clear that it is another linguistic method for talking about a subject matter that cannot be managed literally. The devotees of sense-oriented semantics are not likely to find it very illuminating, for they reject the premises upon which it proceeds.

The word *myth* has come to stand, in ordinary speech, for a falsehood. This is unfortunate, for myth is one of the most powerful and pervasive forms of religious symbolism. Plato resorted to myth when he found that he could not express his meaning, even in the depth-language of dialogue. An example of this is his celebrated Myth of the Cave in the *Republic*. But most myth is not the creation of individuals—or at least their inventors have been lost in the dimness of antiquity. Joseph Campbell, in his fine work on myth, *The Hero with a Thousand Faces,* says that "the symbols of mythology are not manufactured; they cannot be ordered, invented, or permanently suppressed. They are spontaneous productions of the psyche, and each bears within it, undamaged, the germ power of its source."[33]

In this theory of myth Campbell joins other famous names in the study of symbolism: Freud, Jung, Eliade, Tillich, Cassirer, Bevan. They all confirm the judgment that myth is a basic symbolic form that shapes itself in the human spirit, bearing a freight of meaning that cannot be grasped in any other way. To quote Campbell again: "It would not be too much to say that myth is the secret opening through which the inexhaustible energies of the cosmos pour into human cultural manifestation."[34] This is quite a claim, but the great archetypal myths which recur over and over again in dreams and in the folklore of all peoples seem to support it. Philip Wheelwright underscores the same view: "The essence of myth is that haunting awareness of transcendental forces peering through the cracks of the visible universe."[35]

Our difficulty with myth is that we live in a largely unmythical world. Does that mean that we have outgrown mythology, as children outgrow toys? This is, of course, the claim of those who insist that we must accept a literal scientific world of bare fact. But another view is that we have been misled by our achievements in manipulating facts, and that our fascination with things has allowed our inner life to become cold and impoverished. This impoverishment, it is said, with good reason, is part of the reason for modern man's anxiety and fear. It is one more symptom of his rootlessness in the cosmos, his alienation from the ground of his existence.

Modern man's penalty for neglecting the great myths that spring from the depths of his being is to invent outrageous myths, which we call "ideologies," without realizing their mythic character: myths of national origins, racial superiority, fantastic historical destinies. Because modern man is literal-minded he imagines that these are accurate accounts of verifiable facts.

Great myths present profound visions of the world and its meaning. Each religion is controlled by a dominant myth, or cosmic story, at the heart of its view of the world. The karmic myth of the "eternal return," the myth of cyclical time, lies at the base of Hinduism. The myth of the divine Son come down from Heaven for the salvation of man, crucified, resurrected, and returned to Heaven, lies at the heart of Christianity. Is the word myth disturbing when applied in this way to Christianity? It is not in any way intended to imply that the story of redemption is untrue, only to say that it is not a part of profane, or secular, history. It is a cosmic story; conveying a great meaning, it becomes the basis for a total way of life.

Again we should be warned against the attempt to treat such symbols literally. The Apostles' Creed, for example, says of Jesus that "He ascended into heaven and sitteth at the right hand of God the Father." Surely it impoverishes these words to imagine God seated on a throne somewhere in "heaven" with Jesus beside him! And yet the meaning is clear to the man of faith who finds in Jesus the central key to the meaning of life and death. "Myth," writes Martin Buber, "is not the subsequent clothing of a truth of faith; it is the unarbitrary testimony of the image-making vision and the image-making memory, and the conceptual cannot be refined out of it."[36]

This discussion cannot but remind us of Rudolf Bultmann's program of demythologizing, which we discussed earlier. At first glance this program may seem to contradict the above claims on behalf of symbolism. But the contradiction is, I believe, only apparent. Bultmann is asking us to do two things: First, refuse to take myth literally. Second, don't rely upon myths that have lost their symbolic power, or which suggest meanings contrary to a contemporary understanding of the world or to the existential meanings of the Gospel.

*Sacrament* is faith's most characteristic symbolic form, for it is a symbol of total action. In sacramental action the participant not only means something (as in telling a story), he *is* something. The man, the symbol, and the religious reality represented by the sacrament are joined together in a unifying action. When, for example, a devout Christian eats the bread of the Holy Communion, he not only recalls the historic meaning of the first such meal in the upper room and the sacrifice which followed, but he also participates in that meal here and now in fellowship with his Lord.

A sacrament is thus not intellectual or aesthetic, but existential in the sense that the participant enters into the meaning of the symbol with his whole existence.

### The Inescapable Difficulty

Is there a neutral language for discussing religion? This is a natural question, for if there were we could perhaps understand one another better across the barriers of our religious differences. Moreover, words like "God," "divine," "religious," "supernatural," and even "good," "bad," "right," and "wrong," are words with unpleasant connotations in American academic circles. If we could dispense with them perhaps the study of religion might proceed with less opposition in colleges and universities.

Unfortunately, there is no such language. The logic of the human situation precludes it. In the academic community, for instance, another set of words has a highly favorable ring: "humanity," "nature," "science," "welfare," and so on. These are rhetorical keys to the ultimate concern of scholars who have become wary of traditional religion, but they are nonetheless far from "neutral" language.

In a charming essay on the Platonic dialogue *Phaedrus*, Richard Weaver discusses Socrates' ironic argument for a neutral language for use in affairs of the heart. With a logic that appeals to our objective scientific consciousness he proves that the lover ought really to prefer the neutral language of the nonlover. "People are in the habit of preferring their lovers," he writes, "but it much more intelligent, as the argument of Lysias runs, to prefer a nonlover."[37] This is so because the nonlover will be more objective and prudent.

The absurdity of this conclusion arises from the fact that the communion of lovers cannot be carried on in neutral language; it simply does not conform to the realities of the situation. Religious language is similar in this sense to the language of love, and all attempts to provide a nonlover's neutral language cannot but fail dismally.

## THE FINAL TEST OF MEANINGFUL
## LANGUAGE

Language—and here I mean all the symbolic forms that adorn human culture—arose as an instrument of communication. It sprang out of man's communion with life about him. As such it is immensely rich and complex.

As culture became more specialized, specialized languages were invented for particular purposes: the language, for example, of mathematics, technology, or science. Today mathematicians work to invent new artificial languages with which to "talk" to computers. Some of these languages are highly efficient for their purposes, and it is tempting to use them as models for all language. This was the mistake of the positivists. Because scientific language was so successful in scientific inquiry it was easy to believe that the key had been found to language in general. But all specialized languages lack richness. Their success lies in their clarity in dealing with a specific subject matter. But outside that province they are inept and even crippling. Imagine, for example, a biologist wooing his sweetheart in scientific language.

The plain fact is that specialized languages simply avoid the basic meanings that human beings need to communicate in order to be human. As the existentialist F. H. Heinemann has said, "The abusive and much abused term 'senseless' shamefully covers the death of living issues."[38]

The final test of meaningful language is the enhancement of human communication in depth; that is, communion in the profoundest sense of the word. True language creates community, because it communicates meanings that ennoble and unites human beings and open them to one another. If this is so, then it should not be presumptuous to claim that religious language is language that is meaningful in the highest sense of the word. The philosopher Philip Phenix has put it this way: "Perhaps the goal of unified knowledge—of that Truth which unites all partial truths—is not to be reached by restrictive definitions and reductive procedures, but by the progressive enlargement and interweaving of the various communities of intelligible discourse [language]. The ultimate unity would then consist not in a single set of facts, but in one community of persons who in all the manifoldness of their experience would be able to understand one another."[39] Religious language would then have its justification as part of that deep communion of such an understanding community.

### *SUGGESTIONS FOR FURTHER READING*

There are several excellent books that deal directly with religious language: Ian Ramsay, *Religious Language* (Macmillan, 1963); Frederick Ferré, *Language,*

*Logic, and God* (Harper & Row, 1961); and John Hutchison, *Language and Faith* (Westminster Press, 1963).

For a close reexamination of theological arguments from a linguistic point of view, see especially Anthony Flew and Alasdair MacIntrye, eds., *New Essays in Philosophical Theology* (Student Christian Movement, 1955) and Basil Mitchel, ed., *Faith and Logic* (G. Allen, 1957).

Three books on the history of linguistic analysis are recommended: The simplest is G. J. Warnock, *English Philosophy Since 1900* (Oxford University Press, 1958). J. O. Urmson's *Philosophical Analysis* (Oxford University Press, 1956) is the best for the development of this philosophy between World War I and II. For a critical history of the movement, see Brand Blanshard, *Reason and Analysis* (Open Court, 1962). The advanced student will want to attempt the most celebrated classic of the later phases of this movement: Ludwig Wittgenstein's *Philosophical Investigations* (Macmillan, 1953). For a classic of the earlier period, see A. J. Ayer, *Language Truth and Logic* (first published 1935 by Victor Gollancz; reprinted by Dover, n.d.).

Good books on symbols used in religious language are numerous. From among these I suggest the following: Edwin Bevan's now famous *Symbolism and Belief* (G. Allen, 1938) and the equally noted work of Ernst Cassirer, *Language and Myth* (Harper & Row, 1946); Joseph Cambell, *The Hero with a Thousand Faces* (Meridian, World Publishing, 1956); Philip Wheelwright, *Metaphor and Reality* (Indiana University Press, 1962); Mircea Eliade, *Myth and Reality* (Harper & Row, 1963); and F. W. Dillistone, *Christianity and Symbolism* (Collins, 1955).

## NOTES

1. The other is existentialism.

2. For historical and critical treatments of analytic philosophy, see Suggestions for Further Reading at the end of this chapter.

3. A. J. Ayer's *Language, Truth, and Logic* (Oxford University Press, 1936; reprinted by Dover Publications, n.d.) is a typical account of emotivism; see especially chapter 7.

4. See Brand Blanshard's *Reason and Analysis* (Open Court, 1962) for the changes sustained by the theory to meet continued criticism.

5. Quoted in Frederick Ferré, *Language, Logic and God* (Harper & Row, 1961), p. 11.

6. Ludwig Wittgenstein, *Philosophical Investigations* (Macmillan, 1953).

7. *Ibid.*, pp. 11–12.

8. In Norman Malcolm, *Ludwig Wittgenstein, A Memoir* (Oxford University Press, 1958; paperback, 1962), p. 93.

9. R. M. Hare, *The Language of Morals* (Oxford University Press, 1964).

10. Rudolph Carnap, "The Rejection of Metaphysics" in Morton White, ed., *The Age of Analysis* (New American Library, 1955), p. 217.

11. Hare, *op. cit.*, p. 69.

12. *Ibid.*

13. Psalm 23.

14. Alan Simpson, R. A. Baker, and Lester del Rey, "The Twenty-Third Psalm–Modern Versions"

in R. A. Baker, ed., *A Stress Analysis of a Strapless Evening Gown* (Prentice-Hall, 1963), pp. 71–72.

15. Blanshard, *op. cit.*, p. 345.
16. This is Buber's view in *I and Thou* (T. Clark, 1937; Scribner, 1958).
17. Ian Ramsay, *Religious Language* (Macmillan, 1963), p. 39.
18. Robert Jordan, "To Tell the Truth," *Christian Scholar* (Winter, 1964), p. 310.
19. *Time*, July 30, 1965, p. 53.
20. Paul L. Lehmann, *Ethics in a Christian Context* (Harper & Row, 1963), p. 237.
21. Ramsay, *op. cit.*, p. 41.
22. Gabriel Marcel, *The Philosophy of Existence* (Philosophical Library, n.d.), p. 6.
23. Conrad Aiken, "Discordants," in *Collected Poems* (Oxford University Press, 1953), p. 18.
24. From John Keats' "Ode to a Nightingale."
25. *Ibid.*
26. Austin Farrer, *The Rebirth of Images* (Beacon Press, 1963), p. 21.
27. Romans 11:33, 36.
28. Ramsay, *op. cit.*, p. 130.
29. See Plato's Seventh Letter in

30. Plato, *Epistles* (Liberal Arts, Bobbs-Merrill, 1962), pp. 236–237, 241.
31. Lin Yutang, ed., *The Wisdom of China and India* (Random House, 1942; Modern Library, 1955), p. 583.
32. Quoted in Frederick Ferré, *Language, Logic and God* (Harper & Row, 1961), p. 69.
33. *Ibid.*, p. 71.
34. Joseph Campbell, *The Hero with a Thousand Faces* (Meridian, World Publishing, 1956), p. 4.
35. *Ibid.*, p. 3.
36. In Henry A. Murray, *Myth and Mythmaking* (Braziller, 1960), p. 355.
37. Martin Buber, *Hasidism and Modern Man* (Philosophical Library, 1948), p. 41.
38. Richard Weaver, *The Ethics of Rhetoric* (Henry Regnery Co., 1965), p. 4.
39. F. H. Heinemann, *Existentialism and the Modern Predicament* (Harper Torchbooks, Harper & Row, 1958), p. 24.
40. Philip Phenix, *Philosophy of Education* (Holt, Rinehart and Winston, 1958), p. 320.

# 22

# *Science and Religion*

❧❧❧❧❧❧❧❧❧❧❧❧❧❧❧❧❧❧❧❧❧❧❧❧❧❧❧❧❧❧

The domestic peace of Western civilization has often been disrupted by
fraternal quarrels between science and religion that obscure the deep ties
binding them to a common ancestry and destiny. A careful reading of the
history of science would show that the real story has far more often been one
of cooperation and mutual support than of antagonism. Nearly all the great
men, for example, who figured in the formation of classical physics and
chemistry were devoutly religious and looked upon their science as a way of
serving God.

As science developed and Western culture, for diverse reasons, moved away
from religious to secular views of life, philosophies of science were proposed
that raised serious questions about the inherited faith of Western man.
Under their influence, our happy contemplation of the flood tide of physical
knowledge and power became plagued with anxieties over an equal ebb tide
of spiritual wisdom. The situation is without parallel in history, for, thanks to
science, the species is now able to destroy itself and even to make the planet
uninhabitable. Man's inherent quarrelsomeness, unchecked by a civilizing
religious faith, may drive him to choose this dreadful option. It is this distress-
ing prospect that we considered at length in Part IV of this study.

## The Point of View

It should be evident by now that the point of view of this book is not antiscience. It is, however, critical of science wherever scientific pretensions become inflated to idolatrous proportions. Modern man needs a world view in which he may live fully and richly, a world view that has room not only for science but also for the humanities, the arts, and faith as well. Science is not fundamentally at odds with religion nor religion with science; it is misconceived interpretations of science and religion that breed conflict.

From the outset of our study I have urged the use of science in nearly every problem that we have examined, and I restate here my conviction that a faith that is not refreshed by scientific perspectives and purified by scientific criticism is unable to serve as an adequate religion for modern man. And, conversely, a science that is not nourished by faith and guided by its wisdom is likely to bring the human species to ignoble self-destruction.

The thesis, then, is that science and religion urgently need one another, and that when each is properly understood, the areas of conflict between them can be substantially reduced to proportions no greater than the normal conflicts of interpretation and practice that exist within science and religion themselves. As Tennyson wrote:

> Let knowledge grow from more to more,
> But more of reverence in us dwell;
> That mind and soul, according well,
> May make one music as before,
> But vaster. . . .[1]

## WESTERN ORIGINS OF THE FAITH-SCIENCE PROBLEM

I have referred to this conflict as a "fraternal quarrel." Science in its modern sense arose in the West, and it is in Western history that the major problems posed by science have arisen. It is the religion of the West, Christianity, which first had to grapple with the challenge to faith posed by this vigorous offspring of Western culture. Christianity had already made a beginning with the fundamental questions in its earliest encounters with the protoscience of ancient Greece, and from the outset of its career of expansion beyond Hebrew culture it had sought some kind of harmony with the rational categories of Hellas.

Eastern religions have only recently been exposed to the problems that have a long history among us. This explains why our chief concern is with Western religious categories. An essay on the relationship between science and an Oriental faith, such as Buddhism, would be substantially different. One of the major questions in such an essay would be whether science can thrive when grafted onto the Buddhist apprehension of existence. Japan may answer that question in time, though there are strong indicators that point to a profound crisis of the ancestral faith of that country, where science and its offspring, modern technology, are strong. All cultures will in time experience the impact of the scientific revolution. The resulting exotic compounds of faith and technology are impossible to predict.

## CONFLICTS IN THE FAITH-SCIENCE RELATIONSHIP

In this complex faith-science relationship conflicts have arisen in five relatively distinct areas:

1   Conflict over the respective rights of science or religion to pronounce authoritatively on the factual structures of the world.

2   Conflict over the best methods of getting and authenticating knowledge.

3   Conflict over world views presumed to follow from, or to be required by, either science or religion.

4   Conflict between religious and scientific styles of life.

5   Struggles between religious and scientific communities.

### Conflict ( 1 ): Authority Over Knowledge

From the beginnings of modern science, with the laying of the cornerstone of physics in the seventeenth century, science came into conflict with religion when it claimed the right to describe the structures of the physical world in accordance with its own methods, without interference from religion.

The reasons for this are historical. In the year of Columbus' voyage to the New World almost all intelligent Europeans believed in a world-picture that was a composite of Aristotelian philosophy, Christian theology, and common sense. The earth was the center of the universe; below were the infernal regions where the punitive fires of hell burned darkly, above were the heavens rising in concentric circles, each purer than the last, until they reached the realm and dwelling place of God and his angels and the final haven of the blessed saved.

With the publication of Galileo's *Dialogue* (1632), in which the Ptolemaic system, which held that the sun moved around the earth, was discredited in favor of the Copernican system, which maintained that the earth moved around the sun, this world-picture was rudely challenged. But it was not merely science that was at stake in the *Dialogue*. The guardians of the social order saw in the new science a challenge to the rationale of the entire social system that would bring down the whole superstructure of church and state.

In the Church's harsh treatment of Galileo, forcing him to kneel and deny his science, we see a scientist whose right to free investigation had been infringed; the Medieval Church authorities saw an incipient social revolution nipped in the bud.

Within half a century, however, with new discoveries following hard upon Galileo's work, culminating in the work of Sir Isaac Newton, it became impossible for an intelligent person to deny the truth which had been plain to Galileo. The Church backed off from the practice of silencing physicists and embraced the new cosmology of Newtonian physics. Galileo's vindication was for the Church an ignominious retreat which the world cannot easily forget. The relationship of science and religion still bears the scar of that first celebrated encounter. Unfortunately, the full range of issues and the details of the encounter are not generally known. The whole episode is wrapped in mythical clouds that research has only recently begun to dispel.[2]

Nor was the Church allowed to remain at rest. Science continued to develop in realms other than physics, producing further challenges to what remained of the medieval world-picture. Geologists greatly enlarged the timespan of the earth's duration and soon threatened the enshrined belief that creation had taken place only a few thousand years before Christ. Literal belief in the universal Noahic flood became impossible for those acquainted with the fossil evidence. Biologists suggested even more disturbing theories about the evolution of living organisms, including man himself. And, finally, the social sciences began proposing hypotheses about personal and social behavior which clashed at many points with cherished religious beliefs.

This whole struggle is understandable, but misconceived. Science has legitimate sovereignty in the realm of describing the factual structures of human existence. In fact, science could be defined as the disciplined method for authoritatively determining those structures. Movements of the sun and earth, the age of heavenly bodies, the mechanisms of inheritance, detailed accounts of the past, and the correlation of psychological and social events, all of these are scientific matters which religious faith has no special ability to determine. If biological evolution, for example, is to be refuted, it must be refuted by biologists using the tools of biological research. It is not the function of religious faith to authoritatively determine these things.

Consider a familiar example: the story of creation in the first two chapters of Genesis. This story has often been placed in opposition to biology and geology, and the faithful have been told that if they accept the Bible they cannot accept the conclusions of the sciences, and vice versa. This needless confrontation is the product of a misunderstanding of both religious faith and science. The scriptural account of creation is not a factual account in the scientific sense of the word. Rather, it is a narrative that illuminates the meaning of nature. The religious claim in Scripture is not that the species were created all at once in unchanging form, that light came before the making of the sun, or that sea creatures preceded land animals, and so on.

The Scriptures tell us something different and far more important. They tell us that the realm we call "nature" is not self-sufficient, that it is dependent for its existence upon God. The story teaches that nature is fundamentally good in the intention of its great Source, and that it is not in itself a barrier to spirit. It says that man's existence is intended and purposeful, that he is not the product of blind forces, but of a Being who is sovereign, holy, creative love, and that every moment of human existence should be filled with awe and thanksgiving to Him for the inestimable gift of life and existence.

The quarrel with science over the physical origins of the earth and its living species had the terrible effect of obscuring the biblical message and forcing a false and bitter option between faith and intellectual integrity. On the other hand, the accounts of astronomy, geology, and biology neither refute nor establish this scriptural meaning, though, for the man of faith, emancipated from these wrongheaded quarrels, they may greatly enlarge the sense of wonder, gratitude, and awe which faith itself teaches.

Instead of opposing scientific investigations, religious faith should have encouraged them. The fact that the Judaeo-Christian religion sees man as a physical creature living his life in this created world means that he has the strongest reasons to learn how the world is organized, what properties its various substances have, and how they bear on man's earthly welfare. The Bible, moreover, as a historical work, invites the illumination of its social and cultural background through the application of scientific, historical investigations.

These remarks are not intended to imply that no problems for faith will arise in connection with the factual deliverances of the sciences. That is saying too much. It is merely to affirm that at this level of factual description there is no natural enmity between the two, and that the bitter quarrels in these spheres have been misconceived.

### Conflict (2): Methods of Testing Knowledge

This debate over method parallels in principle the debate over the factual content of knowledge: The methods of science are appropriate to its special genius for describing the factual structures of the world, whereas the methods of faith are appropriate to discerning and responding to the dimensions of meaning in and beyond those structures.

*Scientific Method.* Present-day scientific authorities are very chary of designating *the* scientific method, and with good reason. Hundreds of substantial books have been written on the subject without the hoped-for decisive definition. Max Black, a modern logician, has said, "In spite of renewed efforts at clarification . . . on the part of distinguished scientists and philosophers, universal agreement concerning the nature of scientific method is still lacking."[3] The well-known scientist and educator James Conant has recently criticized the idea that one can speak of *the* scientific method in any meaningful sense at all. And the philosopher of science P. W.

Bridgeman, after a lifetime of trying to define it, concluded that the "scientific method is nothing more than doing one's damnedest with one's mind, no holds barred."[4] This, of course, defines not only science, but every kind of free human inquiry, whether scientific, humane, artistic, or religious.

Despite these weighty objections—yet keeping their warnings in mind—we can say that some common traits do seem to characterize the scientific attitude toward inquiry.[5] The first is that science places heavy reliance on the data of sense experience, especially those sense experiences that seem to report the objective aspects of the world. Pain, for example, is less important scientifically than sight.

Second, science aims at objectivity in the sense that it seeks a description of things as they are in themselves, independent of human desires, hopes, and expectations. Third, science holds up the ideal of eliminating bias through the practice of public verification.

Fourth, science, as Max Black says, searches for "abstract structures." That is, it seeks theories that place its detailed sense observations in a generalized theoretical structure. But, unlike unbridled rationalistic speculation, it insists that all such theories be subject to constant testing through observation and experiment. Good scientific theory must be ultimately testable in terms of sensory data of some kind.

In sum then, we can say that science seeks understanding of the natural world through coherently relating the world of objects to one another in space and time, using such categories as cause and effect. As a method it purposely ignores purpose or meaning in the objects it examines. In this sense it is a highly specialized and successful method designed for a special task.

*The Method of Faith.* Religion has no quarrel with the methods of science as such. The quarrel arises only when these methods are declared to be the only methods of human understanding. I have already recounted what I believe to be the disastrous consequences of such a view, in the chapters on the crisis of modernity. Consider one more example. P. W. Bridgeman, holding that science was man's only tool of knowledge, concluded quite logically that "an enduring society is not possible . . ."[6] among a community of men composed exclusively of persons gifted with the intelligence to attain full scientific enlightenment. What he meant was that scientific intelligence, which dealt strictly with factual structures, would empty all moral and spiritual significance out of human existence, and that a human society which realized that these values were purely subjective emotions without any status in the real world would fall apart. This reveals the bankruptcy of scientific method taken as a sole way of understanding.

The way in which men learn about authentic values, moral claims, and religious meanings—the method of faith—is even more complex than the methods of science. It is therefore even more rash to attempt to characterize it. Even to talk about faith in terms of "method" seems to suggest a caricature from which we naturally shrink. I will nonetheless hazard it for purposes of contrast.

In the first place, faith, like science, is responsive to experience, but it does not interpret "experience" so narrowly. For religion, experience is not only sense experience, but the whole range of human experience, including value and meaning and their characteristic frustrations in suffering and sin. The primary experience with which faith is concerned is man's struggle to orient himself to the totality of what he believes to be reality. Sense experiences are a part of this struggle, but they are not the decisive part. It is not as a sensory reporter that the religious man interprets his experience, but as a struggling self in the midst of a struggling community of other selves.

For these reasons, in the second place, the method of religion is not "objective" in the scientific sense. A misunderstanding might arise at this point. Religious inquiry is not *subjective* in contrast to *objective* science. Faith is as interested as science in the truth which has authority over all knowledgeable men. But, in the pursuit of this truth, faith attends to those experiences which characterize man as a meaningful, seeking being, not as a mere reporter of physical facts. This means that he is not objective in the sense that he is detached from his own experiences. Rather, it is those very experiences from which he cannot detach himself that bear the universal significance of faith. He cannot separate himself from them in the way he can from his experiences of sensory observation. He is himself part of the data he must evaluate.

Objectivity is therefore not a proper characterization of the method of religious inquiry. We cannot, for example, know patriotism without being a citizen, or love without being in love; nor can we know God without a deep relationship of faithfulness to him.

The scientific method systematically turns the world into objects. The dogmatic philosopher of science may then naively assume that the world is therefore nothing but a collection of objects. This is but the consequence of uncritically employing a single method, like wearing dark glasses and complaining that the world is badly illuminated. The main point is this: Since faith is a life of total response to the claims of ultimate concern, these concerns can only be known existentially, not objectively. To repeat, this is because religious knowledge is not about objects. It is about ourselves in relationship to the whole of reality insofar as we can respond to it. This kind of global, or over-all understanding cannot be surmised by the analytic and objective methods of science; nor, for that matter, can the understanding involved in ethical and esthetic knowledge.

Some philosophers would have us restrict the term knowledge to the kind of understanding that emerges through the sciences. This would be an agreeable semantic rule, unless it implied that religion is merely personal and subjective and that science alone talks about the structures of reality. Faith judgments are not restricted to personal and subjective levels however much they involve them. They are understandings about the real world and about the duty and destiny of human beings in that world—though they do not compete with science in describing its space-time structure.

While discussing the question of method, it must be observed that one of the great needs of our time is for a greater clarity on just what criteria religious men should use to settle the varieties of truth claims that religious experience begets. Nothing discredits religious claims to knowledge so much as bitter and indecisive quarrels among men of faith, even when they belong to the same religious tradition. By contrast, scientists are more or less forced to supply, along with their various fact claims, the methods by which these claims can be verified by others. The success of science in the adjudication of rival claims has made religion appear, by contrast, like a jungle of private or group prejudices. This contrast is exaggerated by the way in which scientific and religious history has been written, but the contrast is nonetheless there.

*Recent Efforts at Dialogue over Method.*   Our time is favored with many profound discussions of faith and science. It is not unreasonable to say that never before have the issues been so carefully delineated. One such work is Harold K. Schilling's *Science and Religion, An Interpretation of Two Communities.* Its chief merit lies in the fact that the author turns aside from the oversimplified caricatures of both fields, and tries to describe how science and religion function in actual practice. "We are told," he writes, "that the authority of religion stems fundamentally from so-called 'revelation,' a mysterious process by which God is said to have transmitted historical, scientific and religious knowledge, contained in an inerrant Bible, that is unattainable by ordinary rational means, while that of science is based on evidence and reason, without appeal to anything as meaningless as 'revelation.' "[7]

This false contrast, he says, leads to the misleading conclusion that "in religion one must take things by unquestioning faith in spite of the absence of proof; whereas in science one rejects everything not based on logical demonstration and experimental verification."[8]

Schilling maintains that these false notions can be corrected by observing the actual work of science and faith rather than by naively accepting the "balcony views" of them that are common in textbooks. Viewed from the "road" rather than from the "balcony" many of the differences disappear and the remaining contrasts prove to be complementary rather than contradictory.

Schilling contends that there is a "continuous spectrum of cognition and knowledge, extending from the physical sciences, through biological and social sciences, through the arts to religion."[9] "Some characteristics of knowledge and the cognitive process," he says, "vary continuously within the spectrum from one end to the other, but others remain constant," and that we can therefore "speak of 'knowledge' in all these fields and assert that in an important sense the way it is attained is the same for all of them."[10] Here are some elements of Schilling's analysis: Science and religion both need and use creedal statements of faith. Religious faith is faith in God, whereas scientific faith is faith in nature. The difference between the two is not the faith element but the object and level of faith. The level of faith in science is what Schilling calls "preliminary concern." "In the one case man has attained insight about nature," he writes, "in the other God has disclosed Himself to man."[11]

Alfred North Whitehead, in *Science and the Modern World*, made the point several decades ago that "science is an enterprise in which reason is based upon faith" which cannot justify itself by its own methods, for it is faith which guides and gives coherence to the conclusions of scientific practice. . . . This faith springs from direct inspection of the nature of things so disclosed in our own immediate present experience . . . [that it is] impervious to the demand for a consistent rationality."[12] By this he meant that when logic contradicts experience, experience takes precedence over logic.

This scientific faith, like religion, expresses itself in creeds, which Schilling calls "I-believe statements." Some elements in these creeds, he suggests, are the following: (1) The principle of cause and effect, which "expresses the great insight that nature is orderly, and to a large extent predictable. . . ."[13] (2) The principle of conservatism of matter-energy, which declares that "nature is permanent, that its fundamental physical entity, unlike many of its forms, is not transient or subject to elimination or destruction."[14] (3) The "dogma of Evolution," which "also sees system, order, cause, and effect in the 'natural history' of the world."[15]

Creedal statements in both science and religion are not arbitrary dogmatism, but are based upon long encounters with experience. These creeds have emerged slowly and painfully in man's effort to understand the flux of experience. They are different from a simple noting of the experiences themselves, each taken separately. As Schilling says, these creeds "stand [not] for specific information, but over-all understanding."[16]

Critics of religion often argue that creeds are restrictions on experience, and no doubt they have often been perverted to this end. But their chief purpose is to clarify lines along which further experiences will be rewarding rather than illusory or frustrating. In this sense they function precisely as scientific creeds do. Wherever this is not the case, Whitehead's warning is perfectly in order: "Religion will not regain its old power until it can face change in the same spirit as does science. Its principles may be eternal, but the expression of those principles requires continual development. . . ."[17]

As a matter of fact, a careful reading of the history of religious beliefs will show development as well as stability. The formal creedal statements of Christianity, for example, took thousands of years to achieve their current form. An authoritative work such as Philip Schaff's *Creeds of Christendom* makes this abundantly plain. The more informal—but often nonetheless important—creeds of faith also change with time. Consider Schilling's list of religious ideas that have been abandoned in the course of time:

(a) The Bible is historically and scientifically inerrant. (b) The worship of God requires sacrifices of flesh and blood. (c) It is God's will that the enemies of God's people be annihilated in time of war. (d) There is a real place in space called hell. (e) Sinners who do not make their peace with God are after death consigned to "eternal hell fire." (f) There is a real place in space called heaven where God sits on a throne. (g) there are personal beings called angels with spiritual bodies and with the power to intervene in nature and men's lives. (h) There are, similarly, personal evil beings called demons. (i) God created the world several thousand years ago. (j) After the world had been created for some time God destroyed virtually all life on it by a deluge that covered the whole planet, and only those human beings and animals were saved that were in a ship called Noah's Ark.[18]

A similar list could be made of scientific ideas that have been abandoned with time. It would include such items as absolute space and time, ether, vortexes, epicycles, and so on.[19]

On the other hand, writes Schilling, there are elements of religious faith that have stood the long test of critical examination and can be regarded as religious insights that are "permanent and certain":

(a) God has created and now upholds the world. (b) He has created man in His own image. (c) God is good, loving, just, and merciful. (d) God came among men in Jesus Christ to save them from sin. (e) God forgives. (f) God makes known His will. (g) God reveals His love for all men. (h) God demands that men love and serve one another. (i) God calls upon men to resist evil. (j) God bestows upon men His Holy Spirit. (k) God provides the necessities and blessings of life. (l) God has conquered, removed the sting of death. (m) God bestows on men eternal life. (n) God "called" Abraham and covenanted with him. (o) In the Exodus experience God delivered "His people" from bondage in a "miraculous" way. (p) At Mount Sinai God gave "His people" "the law." (q) Through the prophets God called men to social justice.[20]

Both scientific and religious creeds, then, change with a growing understanding of scientific and religious experience. But this experience is not isolated and personal. Christian creedal statements, for example, testify, as Schilling says, "not only to what they have experienced individually and privately, but to what they know others have experienced also, and they know this by having cross-checked with others."[21] In this sense, religious faith is vindicated, if not verified, by experience in much the same way as scientific faith is vindicated by experience. To be sure, the scientist, dealing with more restricted and manageable data, can make his claims more precise and even measurable, but the principle of cross-checking is not different.

The third point in Schilling's analysis is that both religious and scientific thought involve their members in a deeply personal way.[22] Science is not as detached as a simpler account might suggest. A faithful account of scientific discovery discloses that scientists do their work against a rich background of value judgments and intuitive understandings that involve much more than the scientist's sensory and logical equipment. Their commitment to their specific project, their devotion to science, their strong fellow-feeling for others engaged in the same inquiry, their intuitive hunches and guesses highlighted by occasional brilliant flashes of inspiration—all these are more existentially involving than the mechanical procedures that are often set forth as "scientific method." The following words of the celebrated physicist Philip Frank make this point: "The main activity of science . . . consists in the invention of symbols from which our experience can be logically derived. This system is the work of the creative imagination which acts on the basis of our experience. The work of the scientist is probably not fundamentally different from the work of the poet."[23]

The philosopher-scientist Michael Polanyi has contributed substantially to an understanding of these issues. He distinguishes two kinds of knowing: tacit knowing and explicit knowing.[24] Tacit knowledge is the whole body of convictions about reality which men build up over the whole range of their experience and thought. Such tacit knowledge can never be fully written out and made precisely clear. Whenever we attempt such precision—as in science or technology—we have what Polanyi calls explicit knowledge. A map is a good example. It states explicitly certain relationships that are presumed to be true of the territory mapped. However, the map maker and the map reader tacitly understand a multitude of things that are not included in the map. If they did not, they could not understand the map. Nor can a map ever include everything in the territory—only the territory itself can do that.

Tacit knowledge is the realm of insight or wisdom about life, and it precedes all successful attempts to make some part of it explicit. Polanyi cites Plato's argument in the *Meno* where Socrates points out that the search for a solution to a problem appears to be an absurdity. "For," writes Polanyi, "either you know what you are looking for, and then there is no problem; or you do not know what you are looking for, and then you are not looking for anything and cannot expect to find anything."[25]

In answer to this puzzle, Polanyi replies that in all inquiry there is always a preliminary tacit understanding of the reality being investigated, an understanding which, though vague, nonetheless guides the search into clarity. Inquiry in this way always involves faith of some kind based upon the whole of experience as comprehensively understood by the inquirer himself. If he did not have such an understanding (as distinct from knowledge) he would not know how to frame his question or how to sort his evidence. From this perspective, says Polanyi, scientific inquiry is not different from what the Christian Church Fathers described as *fides quaerens intellectum,* believing in order to know, or, faith seeking understanding.[26]

In the light of this we can distinguish two different phases in the so-called steps of the scientific method: the primary steps of discovery, and the secondary steps of verification. It is the latter that have been popularized, much to the distortion of our understanding. The primary steps, involving primarily tacit knowledge, are comparatively vague, and are the common property of all kinds of creative thought. They involved, as Graham Wallas once pointed out: preparation, incubation, illumination, and—only then—verification. The unwarranted identification of science with the last step only has separated science artificially from the whole body of human inquiry.

Lastly, Schilling holds that both religion and science are community enterprises. They are not the product of individuals working alone. This is generally recognized in religion, but it is equally true in science. The scientific community, like the religious community, lives by a shared faith, its traditional values, its interests, rules, and customs. It enlarges its understanding by sharing discoveries and eliminates freakish or offbeat notions by consulting the consensus of the scientific community.

In conclusion, we can say that the quarrel between science and religion over method can be turned into a fruitful dialogue if we will only attend carefully to what each is doing. The methods are different but not absolutely different; in their difference they do not contradict but rather complement one another, and in their similarity they underscore the general human process by which understanding grows.

### Conflict (3): Over World Views

Both science and religion tend to create world-pictures as a by-product of their specialized perspectives on existence. More often than not it is these world-pictures, or cosmologies, that conflict rather than science or religion as such.

I have already described the three-storied universe which Galileo's science made untenable. Religious thinkers soon had to dissociate their faith from this world-picture. The scientists then took their turn at picture-painting. By the late nineteenth century they had designed an infinite world-machine, without mind, meaning, or direction. As late as the eighteenth century the poet Pope was able to write with easy assurance, "A mighty maze! but not without a plan."[27] But by Tennyson's time, a century later, the mechanical world view had triumphed, and he sadly wrote, " 'The stars,' she whispers, 'blindly run.' "[28] The word "blind," in fact, became the favorite adjective for the working of the natural scheme.

But this world-picture was as hopelessly specialized as was its medieval predecessor. Instead of being drawn from the widest range of human experience, it was formed from a highly specialized body of data useful to scientists. Galileo's genius had turned human attention to the aspects of the world that could be studied quantitatively—its mass, extension, and motion. He asked *how* the world moved, not *why* it moved. Every event that he studied could be described in all its essentials in terms of matter in motion. These events, moreover, followed causal laws, and could be completely explained in terms of those laws without any reference to purpose or ends. All the qualitative differences of the world—its colors, tastes, sights, and smells—he thought could be accounted for in strictly quantitative terms.

Two comments are called for. First, this world-picture provided a mortal challenge to the Christian faith. So long as this was held to be the essence of science, bitter conflict was inevitable. Second, this world-picture was not science; it was a philosophical speculation based upon the data of classical physics while ignoring other reaches of human experience.[29] But so long as scientists believed that their speculations were authentic science, and so long as they ignored the data that make up the heart of faith-understanding—such data as value, purpose, persons, and meaning—the conflict was bound to be perpetuated. By the late nineteenth century the respective roles of science and religion had been reversed. In the sixteenth century it was religion which refused to take into account new experiences and new data; in the nineteenth century it was science which had become narrowly dogmatic about the data of human experience, limiting itself to the quantitative sensory data that were grist for its own mills. It took the revolution of twentieth-century science to raise fundamental doubts about its own dogmas.

*Philosophy in the Role of Mediator.* What is the remedy for this state of affairs? The answer seems to lie in the revival of the kind of philosophy that would serve as a critic of such partial world views, making clear that they are schemes generated from specialized ways of looking at the world. Such a philosophical program would serve to relate these varying world-pictures to one another in the world of common experience and truth. It would illuminate the Logos which underlies the logic of each separate field of human thought and experience. Such a philosophy might, of course, be tempted to vault itself into the place of authority and arrogate to itself an absolute status. This has happened in the past. At the time of Thomas Aquinas (13th century) Aristotle had become *the philosopher* and was quoted with the same assurance as Scripture itself. To perform its proper task, philosophy must remain reconstructive, redoing its work in each generation as fresh insights become available from the whole range of human experience. If this were done humbly and well, there is no reason why faith and science should suffer the conflict of lopsided and partial perspectives.

This mediative role for philosophy has been severely challenged by both secular and religious thinkers. There is, unfortunately, not space to do justice to this rebuttal. But in essence it is as follows: Many modern philosophers have been persuaded that philosophy lacks the ability to adjudicate truth claims. This, they hold, is the prerogative of science alone. Philosophy must limit itself to the task of analyzing the function of language in its various spheres. We were employing this technique in the preceding chapter on the logic of religious language. They go further, holding that science itself is completely nonmetaphysical—that is, it cannot reveal to us what the world is in itself. On this view, science is limited to finding correlations among possible sense experiences. It has no word whatsoever on what lies beyond those experiences; indeed, the whole issue of what lies beyond is regarded as a meaningless question. Furthermore, neither science nor philosophy can give any authoritative guidance on the questions of morality and esthetics except what can be said about possible sense experiences. The "meanings" of morality and esthetics—right and wrong, good and bad, beautiful and ugly— which philosophy claimed to deal with in the past, are held at best to be purely private feelings and at worst to be strictly nonsense.

There are modern theologians who agree with this account of philosophy and science. They believe that it supports their own view of faith in two ways. First, it removes the possibility that either science or philosophy could claim to perform the functions of faith—orienting man to Ultimate Reality. Second, it harmonizes with their view of Christianity, which holds that only with the revelation of God in Christ does Reality break through the circle of experience and show itself to man.

This viewpoint deserves more attention than we can give it here. In my opinion, it purchases a harmony between science and religion at the cost of cutting the ground of reality from under every human enterprise in order to preserve the exclusive authority of the Christian revelation. The persistent and immemorial intuitions of faith which claim to hear the Real speaking through the natural world—in reason, in art, in conscience, and in all human affairs— are summarily dismissed as sinful and idolatrous presumptuousness, or at least as innocent illusions of the human heart. But one might ask whether a revelation of God in such a world of phantoms would be recognized, much less understood and responded to. When Jesus said to his disciples, "You believe in God, believe also in me," he seemed to imply a prior knowledge of God from history and nature, in terms of which alone His own appearance becomes luminously comprehensible. The question, in short, is whether this doctrine of discounting our natural knowledge abilities is not too harsh a way to preserve the realm of faith from pretenders. It is also moot to ask whether any of the humane disciplines, including science, could thrive on a diet so deficient in the vitamins of reality.

It was for just such a reason that Einstein, a short time before his death, rejected such a view, saying, "I am not a logical-positivist." When asked by Hans Reichenbach on another occasion how he came to discover the laws of relativity, he replied to his astonished questioner (who held the view of science just described), that "he found it because he was so strongly convinced of the harmony of the universe."[30] Reichenbach then confessed that "the critical attitude may make a man incapable of discovery; and, as long as he is successful, the creative physicist may very well prefer his *creed* [!] to the logic of the analytic philosopher."[31]

Einstein's remark, I note, was a faith statement, expressing his implicit confidence in the inherent rationality of a Reality which human minds can grasp only because, as he said, it graciously "manifests itself in sublime wisdom and radiant beauty." There is good reason to suppose that science depends upon some such faith. In the West this faith has been largely supplied and maintained by Judaism and Christianity. It is a moot question whether science could survive the death of such a faith.

H. G. Wells describes the disillusionment that settled upon him when he gave up the faith that science somehow unveiled the mysteries of nature: "There was a time when my little soul shone and was uplifted at the starry enigma of the sky. That has gone absolutely. Now I can go out and look at the stars as I look at the pattern of wallpaper on a railway station waiting room." Is it not reasonable to predict that if this were to become the prevailing view of any generation of astronomers they would be the last of their clan? And what is said here about stars could equally well be said of atoms, organisms, societies, and indeed all the objects that lure scientists to their studies. When every thing is stripped of meaning and value, what reason would then remain for the painstaking expenditure of human energy which we call scientific inquiry? The death of faith would be the death of science as well.

### Conflict (4): Between Styles of Life

The practice of science and religion has given rise to differing styles of life. By style of life I mean a set of attitudes, evaluations, typical habits, and approaches to problems which characterize a particular way of living. The differences give rise to misunderstandings between science and religion that are not logical but personal and psychological in character.

The religious man considers the world as personal and valuable, whereas the scientist tends to consider it as the realm of impersonal law. Faith is concerned primarily about spiritual welfare, inner moral worth, growth in love, joy in the immediacy of a relationship to God, and a loyalty to Jesus Christ and his way. Science is interested in the world of nature as observed through the senses, and with the growth of scientific knowledge which offers man control over nature.

The man of faith has grave doubts that human existence can be infinitely improved by changing the environment or improving techniques of human manipulation. This is in part based upon a deep concern for man's spiritual nature and also on anxiety over the selfishness and sinfulness of man. His optimism is focused on God rather than on man and his works. The scientist, on the other hand, is enthusiastic about extending knowledge and control over nature to man himself. He has a strong optimism about what changes could be made in man through expanded scientific knowledge.

Finally, religious faith holds that man's salvation is from God through faith, whereas science tends to see man's salvation as coming from man's own activities through science.

If it be acknowledged that religious faith is ultimate concern, whereas scientific faith is, as Schilling says, "preliminary concern," these contrasts need not become logical contradictions. The issue is simply this: Can a man live his life out in the awareness that the world is God's creation and that God is prior in all things, and at the same time cultivate all the characteristic attitudes and skills that make for great science? My answer is Yes, and this answer has the support of many of the very greatest names in the history of science, the great Newton himself being one of the foremost.

But we must go further than a mere possibility. My view is that unless something like this occurs, science will destroy itself, and mankind along with it. For science, like any other segmental activity of man, must be set in an over-all, controlling world view that keeps it humbled to its proper place in the divine-human order. We could have made these same contrasts, using politics instead of science, and come to exactly the same conclusions. How can a man be active in the affairs of his nation, exhibiting the salutary emotions of patriotism and public concern, and yet find his fundamental orientation at a deeper level in his relationship to God, who has priority in all things?

The practical answer to this question lies in learning the art of alternation between one's "preliminary" and "ultimate" concerns, between work and contemplation, means and ends. There is no logical reason why a man of faith should not embrace a high enthusiasm for science, and alternate quite naturally between work and worship. This is really quite normal. Let us hope, for example, that scientists alternate between impersonal science and personal passion in their family relationships. Why not between scientific and religious faith? Would this make a less efficient scientist? Far from it. If the line of thought in this chapter is correct, this may be the only way to save science for itself.

## Conflict (5): Struggles Between the Two Communities

Schilling's well-made point about the communal nature of both science and religion has sociological implications. Organized communities of interest tend to become centers of selfish power. In the hands of persistently wayward human beings this power is often used to dominate others. This has nothing to do with science or religion as such. It applies to any and all human communities. The history of the conflict between religion and science can in part be interpreted as the desire of these two communities to entrench and enlarge their own spheres of influence. When this happens, we find scientists fighting theologians and theologians fighting scientists, not because of some bone of contention between the subject matters but because of the natural human inclination to power and the equally natural human failure to understand by sympathetic imagination what other people regard as valuable and true—as their ultimate concerns.

The remedy for this difficulty is not a logical but a human one. Understanding can come only as the two communities engage in genuine and humble dialogue with one another.

The natural human power struggle has implications that go beyond the science-religion controversy. In the modern world, science is not so much threatened by the religious community as by the political community. Science never has had complete autonomy in the societies where it flourishes. After having won freedom from religious interference, it moved under the dominance of the prevailing secular cultures of the modern world. At the present time, it is all but completely captive to the sovereign national state. In Russia, China, and the nations seeking to develop economically this is dramatically clear. But it is also true in England and America, where national security dominates the flow of research funds and controls what discoveries may be publicly shared in scientific journals. This in turn shapes the whole contour of the world of science. As a "preliminary" concern, science will always be prey to those who would control it for something more ultimate. For this reason the future of science as a free exercise of the human spirit requires, in my opinion, that it make firm alliance with the most humanely and spiritually enlightened members of society. In this way faith may save not only men's souls but science as well, so that science may fulfill its promise as a servant of man rather than his potential destroyer.

The relationship of science and religion is, as we have seen, a complex one. But it need not be, for that reason, a hostile or unfriendly one. In fact, I believe that only if religion comes to terms with science in all its richness, and only if science comes to terms with faith's deep meanings, can a genuinely humane world culture emerge from the present fragmentation of interests and powers. Only a dialogue carried on in the deepest good will and integrity can achieve this goal.

This chapter will serve as a preface to the task we are presently to undertake, a direct examination of the knowledge that religious faith claims to have—a knowledge of God.

### SUGGESTIONS FOR FURTHER READING

A good first book on this subject is H. K. Schilling's *Science and Religion* (Scribner, 1962). Arthur Stanley Eddington's *Science and the Unseen World* (Macmillan, 1929) is an older classic not to be forgotten. Two other books directly to the subject are C. A. Coulson, *Science and Christian Belief* (University of North Carolina Press, 1955) and A. F. Smethurst, *Modern Science and Christian Belief* (Abingdon, 1957). For a reexamination of the world-picture of science leading to a view more congenial to faith, see Alfred North Whitehead's *Science and the Modern World* (New American Library, 1948); Karl Heim's *Christian Faith and Natural Science* (Harper & Row, 1957), and my *Reality and Prayer*, Chapter 2 (Harper & Row, 1957). In somewhat the same vein, though approached through biological evolution rather than physics, the famous Jesuit philosopher Pierre Teilhard de Chardin has two books that have excited wide interest: *The Phenomenon of Man* (Harper Torchbooks, Harper & Row, 1961) and *The Divine Milieu* (Harper & Row, 1960). Henri Bergson's classic *Two Sources of Morality and Religion* (Holt, Rinehart and Winston, 1936; Anchor, Doubleday, 1954) should be read as a companion to Teilhard de Chardin.

For historical surveys, see again Alfred North Whitehead's *Science and the Modern World*; E. A. Burtt's *Metaphysical Foundations of Modern Science* (Anchor Book; Doubleday & Co., 1954) and *Types of Religious Philosophy*, rev. ed. (Harper & Row, 1951); and the historian Herbert Butterfield's *Origins of Modern Science* (Macmillan, 1951). Arthur Koestler's new history of science, revealing the more unscientific aspects of the beliefs of the noted scientists should be examined: *The Sleep Walkers* (Hutchison, 1959).

Michael Polanyi is one of the most astute scientist-philosophers pointing out the personal, nonscientific elements in the scientific enterprise. His major work is *Personal Knowledge* (University of Chicago Press, 1962; Harper Torchbook, Harper & Row, 1964). Two small paperbacks on the same theme are *The Study of*

Man (University of Chicago Press, 1963) and *Science, Faith, and Society* (University of Chicago Press, 1964). I would also suggest two other small books: J. Sullivan, *The Limitations of Science* (New American Library, 1954) and John Day, *Science Change and the Christian* (Abingdon, 1965).

# NOTES

1. From his *In Memoriam.*
2. See de Santillana, *Crime of Galileo,* and Arthur Koestler, *The Sleep Walkers* (Hutchinson, 1959).
3. Max Black, *Critical Thinking* (Prentice-Hall, 1946), pp. 334–335.
4. P. W. Bridgeman, *Reflections of a Physicist* (Philosophical Library, 1950), p. 351.
5. Black, *op. cit.,* chap. 17.
6. P. W. Bridgeman, *The Intelligent Individual and Society* (Macmillan, 1938), p. 200.
7. Harold K. Schilling, *Science and Religion, An Interpretation of Two Communities* (Scribner, 1962), pp. 4–5.
8. *Ibid.,* p. 5.
9. *Ibid.,* p. 12.
10. *Ibid.*
11. *Ibid.,* p. 130.
12. Alfred North Whitehead, *Science and the Modern World* (New American Library, 1948), pp. 24–25.
13. Schilling, *op. cit.,* p. 130.
14. *Ibid.*
15. *Ibid.*
16. *Ibid.,* p. 131.
17. Whitehead, *op. cit.,* p. 168.
18. Schilling, *op. cit.,* p. 111.
19. Arthur Koestler discusses these ideas in his history of science, *The Sleep Walkers.*
20. From Schilling, *op. cit.* (slightly modified), p. 110.
21. *Ibid.,* p. 62.
22. This point has been made with great thoroughness by Michael Polanyi, *Personal Knowledge* (University of Chicago Press, 1958; Harper Torchbooks, Harper & Row, 1964).
23. In Schilling, *op. cit.,* p. 42.
24. Polanyi, *op. cit.* This thesis is less technically explained in his *The Study of Man* (University of Chicago Press, 1963).
25. Michael Polanyi, *Science, Faith, and Society* (University of Chicago Press, 1964), p. 14.
26. *Ibid.,* p. 15.
27. Quoted in Whitehead, *op. cit.,* p. 77.
28. *Ibid.,* p. 74.
29. Of course, the whole picture has changed radically with the coming of contemporary physics.
30. Hans Reichenbach, "The Philosophical Significance of the Theory of Relativity," in Herbert Feigl and May Brodbeck, eds., *Readings in the Philosophy of Science* (Appleton-Century-Crofts, 1953), p. 197.
31. *Ibid.*

# 23

# *The Nature of*
# *Religious Knowledge*

❖❖❖❖❖❖❖❖❖❖❖❖❖❖❖❖❖❖❖❖❖❖❖❖❖❖❖❖❖

With the discussion of our two previous chapters on religious language and science, we are now prepared to assault directly the question of religious knowledge. The claim that there is such a thing as authentic religious knowledge stands today in an embattled condition. Not only do its critics assail it but faith is a problem even to its own adherents, who on their part seek with anxious longing for an account of their religion that can stand respectably alongside of the towering eminences of scientific knowledge. It is the purpose of this chapter to elucidate the nature of religious knowledge in such a way that its rightful place among the valid knowledge claims of modern man may be recognized. To do this we must begin with a consideration of the general nature of human knowledge.

## THE NATURE OF KNOWLEDGE

In the broadest sense, human knowledge is the fruit of reflection on experience that has proved to be reliable in subsequent reflection on experience. Experience contains a mixture of subjective and objective elements—that is, some parts of our experience are the product of something beyond us, and other parts of our experience are the product of our own activities as experiencing selves.

Knowledge is, furthermore, a transaction that involves four aspects: a knower, the knowable, the act of knowing, and the encompassing field that includes all of them. There is always someone who knows, or thinks he knows, the subject matter of his knowledge, the experience-reflecting process by which he knows, and the encompassing reality in which such processes are possible. Unfortunately, it is not always self-evident just which elements in knowledge are supplied by the reality we are seeking to understand and which are supplied by us as knowers.

Hadley Cantril and his associates at Princeton University have experimented with these problems. He constructed two identical rooms which are viewed through lenses that permit one eye to see one room and the other eye to see the other. The two images are melded by the viewer into a single perception. Cantril then placed his wife in one room and the carpenter who built the rooms in the other. When he looked through the glasses he saw only one person. This person, he knew, was unquestionably his wife, but she was bald and had a mustache like the carpenter. His problem was to explain this odd perception. He reasoned that he saw his wife as the primary person because she was more important to him than the carpenter. But his senses could not reject the carpenter totally, so some of his physical characteristics were fused with the figure of his wife. Cantril's perception, then, was explainable only in terms of some kind of transaction between the data supplied by his senses and his psychological equipment as a perceiver.[1]

It is the function of reflective thought to sort out these elements to determine which are objective, which subjective, and which are intimations of the bond that hold the two together. In this matter, natural science gained a very early advantage. The scientists of the sixteenth century hit upon a workable rule for determining just which experiences were relevant to the natural world they were investigating. As scientists they were not concerned with the whole range of human experience, not even with the total spectrum of sense experience, but only with those sense data that were needed to make measurements of the mass, extension, and motion of physical objects. For their purposes at least, they were prepared to relegate all other experiences to the realm of purely subjective interest.

It is this view of knowledge that has played such a heavy role in modern thought. In thus settling upon certain narrow features of our sense experiences as the sole clues to objectivity, these early thinkers bequeathed to us a deep suspicion about the validity of all nonscientific claims to knowledge. This situation is abnormal and needs correction. It came about due to a historical accident—the particular setting in which modern science originated and flowered.

To correct this abnormality, we must go back to more general notions of knowledge. Knowledge is not limited to verified perceptions drawn from reflection upon a particular slice of sense data alone, but upon the whole range of human experience. The hypnotic narrowing of reality-giving experience to the particular slice of experience useful to scientists must be viewed as a provincialism that can be broken only by exploring other forms of knowledge rooted in other human experiences.

I am not contending that selecting a segment of experience for special study is bad. In fact, it is inevitable and, wisely conducted, it is the foundation of the vast edifice of scientific thought. The process is methodologically correct. "It fixes attention," writes Alfred North Whitehead, "on a definite group of abstractions, neglects everything else, and elicits every scrap of information and theory which is relevant to what it has retained."[2]

Its success, however, depends upon the judicious choice of abstractions. We now realize how judicious our scientific forebears were in their choice. We have the body of modern science as evidence. However, as Whitehead has warned, "the triump is within limits. . . . The neglect of these limits leads to disastrous oversights."[3] One of these disastrous oversights is the neglect of knowledge in the realm of values and spirit, in the dogmatic assurance that nothing worth knowing lies outside the sense data by which thinkers in this field have become hypnotically fascinated—what Whitehead calls "an arbitrary halt at a particular set of abstractions."[4]

In a celebrated passage, Whitehead comments on the paradoxical outcome of the scientific philosophy which was interested only in sense experiences useful for measuring mass, extension, and motion in the physical world, while relegating the source of all other experiences to the subjective workings of the perceiver: "Thus the bodies are perceived as with qualities which in reality do not belong to them, qualities which in fact are purely the offspring of the mind. Thus nature gets credit which should in truth be reserved for ourselves: the rose for its scent: the nightingale for his song: and the sun for his radiance. The poets are entirely mistaken. They should address their lyrics to themselves, and should turn them into odes of self-congratulations on the excellency of the human mind. Nature is a dull affair, soundless, scentless, colourless; merely the hurrying of material, endlessly, meaninglessly."[5]

To summarize: Reflection upon human experience yields differing bodies of knowledge depending upon the particular segment of experience that is analyzed. Sense data of a particular sort yields the knowledge we term physics. Another kind of data lies at the base of the social sciences, and still another kind at the foundation of reliable knowledge in ethics or aesthetics, and yet another at the base of our religious knowledge.

Especially important is the distinction between those kinds of knowledge that deal with the world as a collection of objects and those that read the meaning of existence in terms of personal participation and value. These two different perspectives are not rivals, though they have often been so misconceived. In truth they supplement one another. Donald Mackay, an authority on physics and cybernetics, gives an illuminating analogy: "To treat a description in the language of the observer," he writes, "as if it were a rival of a description in the language of an actor is rather as if someone who did not understand algebra were to try to 'debunk' a printed algebra problem by proving that there was 'nothing but ink' on the page." He goes on to say: "Of course he would be telling the truth. There is nothing but ink there. But the algebra problem is not a ghost inhabiting one of the ink patches. He will never find it as something left over after making an inventory of all the ink on the page. He will find it only by a different approach to the very same data."[6]

The present crisis in human affairs, which clamors for guidance in terms that "objective" science cannot supply, has made men more eager to examine the possibilities of some authentic knowledge touching on meaning and value which can be known only by participation.

A parable from natural history suggested by Gerald Heard illustrates modern man's plight. The sand martin is driven by instinct to bore some three feet into sandstone in order to lay her eggs. When she chooses to make her nest in sandstone fences built by man, the hapless creature bores clear through the wall before she exhausts her instinctive impulse to drill. Finding no suitable nesting place for her eggs, the unhappy martin bores hole after hole, never finding a place to raise her brood and fulfill her life impulse.

Such is modern man, equipped with analytic capacities sharpened to rapier point by preoccupation with material knowledge. "He digs with his keen intellect," writes Heard, "sufficiently deep into the meaning of things so that at that depth he might then go on to master those exercises whereby he might become an actual experient and manifestation of the Good, the True and the Beautiful."[7] "But," he concludes, "the critical boring faculty cannot be stopped, and the constructive, creative, integral power is never let come into play."[8]

A classical example of this temper of mind appears in the concluding chapter of David Hume's *Enquiry Concerning Human Understanding* (1748), words which have become the motto of the school of thought which I am here criticizing: "If we take in our hand any volume . . . let us ask, does it contain any abstract reasoning concerning quantity or number? No. Does it contain any experimental reasoning concerning matter of fact and existence? No. Commit it them to the flames, for it can contain nothing but sophistry and illusion."[9]

In the beginning this theory of knowledge was launched as a protest against the restriction of inquiry by theology. But like many revolutions which age turns into reaction, it has become in our day a dogmatic and arbitrary restriction against looking at the possible meaning in wider reaches of experience. It is, in short, too much *a priori* and too little empirical.

## THE RANGE OF KNOWLEDGE

Consider the following list of knowledge claims:

Water is two parts hydrogen and one part oxygen.

All organisms alive today have evolved from simpler organic forms.

If all *As* are *Bs* and all *Bs* are *Cs*, then all *As* are *Cs*.

$6 \times 7 = 42$.

I am a free, responsible agent who cannot be explained by mechanical principles.

I am not alone; the world exists; other people exist.

Other people are conscious, free, responsible agents who ought not to be treated as mechanical objects.

Murder is wrong.

Mozart's music is more than pleasant; it is beautiful.

Some people are my friends.

Democracy is better than totalitarian dictatorship.

A scientific career is a worthy human vocation.

My life is meaningful.

Love is better than hate; personal integrity is better than corruption, charity than selfishness, heroism than cowardice.

The whole of life tends toward a high purpose.

The power and meaning of existence is creative, holy love.

Nearly every one of these claims, so far as they can be validated, requires a method of investigation that is different from that needed for the others, and it would be easy to expand the list. Only the first two claims are strictly scientific concerns, and even they require different approaches. Yet all of them are plausible, and, if they are sufficiently qualified, probably true. This is not a work on theories of knowledge, so we cannot stay to expand these ideas. But the point should be clear that human beings live by many kinds of knowledge that cannot fall within the restrictions of scientific method.

One thing these claims do have in common, however, is that they are the fruit of experience that has been sifted by the process of reflection. Science is the fruit of thinking about the data of our senses. Morality is the fruit of thinking about our experiences of obligation and value. Esthetic knowledge is the fruit of thinking about our experience of beauty. Religious knowledge is the fruit of thinking about our spiritual experiences. In each case the activity of "thinking" is somewhat different, and follows, as we have said earlier, a logic appropriate to its subject matter.[10] The scientist expresses his vision of the world in formulas or laws. The artist expresses his by producing a concrete thing of beauty which is itself a part of the thing to which he points—for it is always symbolic of more, and that is why it excites the perceiver so profoundly and so enhances his feeling of being alive. The moral man expresses his vision in responsible deeds, through participating in the dialogue, by saying Thou to his fellows. The religious man uses all these ways, and more. He longs to participate fully in the life-world of God in all its richness. He desires to hallow the world as the place of the divine-human meeting, where God speaks of all he wishes to say to man and to do for and with him.

## THE NATURE OF RELIGIOUS KNOWLEDGE

Religious knowledge is, first of all, a dim comprehension of the characteristics of the encompassing Reality which enable that Reality to arouse in human beings an ultimate concern. Some account must be given of the reason why Reality grips us in this way. This quality cannot be found in the world of mere objects as described by science; or, to put it another way, that aspect of the world that enters into scientific accounts is already shorn of all value properties and cannot, therefore, become an object of concern. On this level one fact is as good as another.

Nor can this quality be located entirely within the subjective realm of the thinker, for then it is not possible to understand why he is gripped and summoned by his religious perception. Were a man to discover that his faith was merely a psychological matter, it would evaporate in the light of that knowledge.

Another way of saying this, is that religious knowledge is existential rather than either subjective or objective. These words are used in a special way. Objective knowledge is appropriate for the world of objects, including those objects that psychologists study, such as attitudes and interests. Subjective thought, if there is any such thing, would be confined entirely to the subjective feelings of the thinker himself. Existential thought is concerned with the orientation of the thinker in the world, not his immediate orientation, but his ultimate orientation, the direction that determines the meaning of his existence as a man.

The goal of such thinking is not to know objects in their relationship to one another, but to comprehend somehow the meaning of one's self and one's relationship to Reality as a whole. Truth in this case would emerge not as some correspondence between theory and fact but as a kind of communion between the thinker and reality. Insofar as such knowledge comes to be expressed in symbols, it is subject to the logical restrictions which we noted in the previous chapter as belonging to religious utterance.

Such an utterance would take the form of a conviction, which is different from a mere statement of fact. We would not say, for instance, that we had a conviction that water is two parts hydrogen and one part oxygen. But we would say this about a claim that, for example, courage is better than cowardice or that God is the proper name for Reality. This calls attention to the fact that in faith the knower is laid under the power of a convictor—a kind of truth that puts him under an inescapable claim.

Both Augustine and the philosopher Epicurus believed in supernatural beings, but the latter could not be said to have religious knowledge in the sense in which we are using the term here. Epicurus insisted that the existence or nonexistence of the gods made no difference to human beings in any case, since events were already determined exclusively by the motion of the primordial atoms that constituted the world. Augustine, on the other hand, could not think of God without realizing the demand for a response which that thought laid upon him. "Thou awakest us to delight in thy praise," he wrote in his *Confessions*. The point is that religious knowledge, when it is authentic, awakens response and conviction, not merely recognition and assent.

This illustration suggests another characteristic of religious thought: The convictor whom one knows in religious knowledge is more active than the passive facts discovered in science. It is as though the investigator discovers that *he* has been found rather than that he has made a conquest of knowledge. The truth known as a body of convictions cannot be merely my own discovery; it also has the quality of revelation—something given me, or laid upon me.

It is this characteristic of religious knowledge which may have led the philosopher Wittgenstein to distinguish fact statements from all value judgments. Values do not arise out of facts; rather, he wrote, "They make themselves manifest."[11] Another statement seems to express the same thought: "It is not how things are in the world that is the mystical, but that it exists."[12] Religious knowledge arises when the supreme value of life—Reality —unveils itself to us and illuminates us. We need not accept Wittgenstein's restriction that such illumination cannot be put into words. The poets belie him. But we must realize that verbalizing this kind of knowledge calls for a different language than the one used for communicating facts. We will also have to accept the fact that no decisive argument can be formulated to force another person to see what has been given in our own vision. Religious proofs function rather in the way in which literary or art criticism functions, to persuade the listener to take another look at what he has misvalued in the hope that he will see what the artist has himself seen. It functions to evoke vision, not to present decisive logical conclusions. Proof is in this sense not a demonstration but a showing. But it is a showing that depends upon humble waiting until that which shows itself does in fact show itself.

There is a lovely statement by Simone Weil to this same effect. "In the last resort," she says, "certainty is always of the nature of immediate and self-evident knowledge in which reality itself is present, and, as it were, declares itself to us; and this is precisely what we mean by 'experience.'"[13]

Another characteristic of religious knowledge is that it is communal; it takes place in a historical community of shared faith. This follows from the demands for existential involvement which we have just discussed—the thinker must be deeply engaged in the living community of which he is a part. Such thought cannot be performed by an impersonal calculating machine.

It is important to make this point clear, because in our scientific tradition we have accorded the highest place to the detached—that is, "unprejudiced"—thinker, and have regarded membership in a religious community as a prejudicial factor, a liability that distorts rather than clarifies thought. The point is that religious thought, above all others, sees truth through the total experience of persons and groups, not in abstraction from them. Reality as a whole includes the thinker and his living community, and, in fact, the whole of history as well as nature. For this reason, whatever the risks of prejudicing the case, we have no alternative in religious inquiry but to work through living communities of faith toward the truth we seek.

The final characteristic of religious knowledge is the paradoxical fact that it deals with an impenetrable mystery which nevertheless manifests itself to us. A comprehensive and coherent grasp of reality as a whole could be known only to God alone—to a Being which embraces directly the whole of reality— spirit and matter, ideal and fact, past and future.

The magnitude of the infinite mystery tempts us to agnosticism. But such a position is not strictly possible, because this kind of world estimate is not optional. We cannot but choose to react to existence in terms of our own understanding of it, however limited that understanding may be. And this applies with as much force to the atheist as to the theist. But the one thing that should be closed to religious reflection is dogmatic finality in any literal sense. We know some things and know them very well, but we do not know everything, and even what we know is shrouded (perhaps we should say brightened) with infinite mystery. The symbols of faith represent a mixture of knowing and not knowing, of certainty and mystery. As St. Paul says, "Now we see through a glass darkly."[14] Such mystery surrounds all our knowledge, of any kind whatsoever. Richard Hofstadter, Physics Nobel Laureate, is reported by Loren Eiseley as saying wistfully, "Man will never find the end of the trail." Sören Kierkegaard somewhere expressed the central issue when he said that in religious faith there comes a point where it is important to understand that one cannot understand further.

This view is required not only by the fact that integral truth is infinite, but also because our knowledge of that truth, involving as it does the total thinker and the total human community of which he is a part can be consummated only in the complete organic unity of all men with the truth about Reality. This would be the transformation of man into the Kingdom of God. "Man," in Nietzsche's phrase, would be "overcome" and a new race of beings joined totally to reality would have superseded him.

The purpose of this brief summary of the characteristics of religious knowledge has been twofold: First, to show the sense in which religious knowledge has characteristics peculiar to itself—though shared in part by all other knowledge, and second, to prepare for the special methods and unique claims that religious knowledge must take to itself.

Broadly speaking, my proposal has been that human experience has many facets and that the business of knowledge proceeds by reflection on all of them, not merely on that segment which we call sense experience. Further-more, proceeding in this way, we discover a wide variety of different kinds of knowledge claims—scientific, ethical, esthetic, and religious.

## A Note on Method

If religious truth is truth of a special kind, then it follows that it demands a method that is suitable to searching out that kind of truth. In the first chapter I began making suggestions about the methods proper to religious inquiry, and I shall continue to do this. It would be too repetitious and space-consuming to develop at this point a complete essay on the subject. However, a few summary remarks may be useful.

Religious knowledge is given dimly in our present experience to the degree that we willingly participate in existence. We must begin with this knowl-edge, dim as it is, and turn away from suggestions that we begin somewhere else. Religious knowledge can only come from religious data, but this does not mean that these data are separate from our ordinary experience. It means only that religious experience is a particular dimension of that experience—namely, the dimension of depth, where a man finds his life grounded, or established.

By a continuous alternation between experience and reflection—somewhat like Plato's dialectic, only more existential—we can clarify what our experi-ence actually means. It can unfold the order implicit in that experience.

In such a dialectic we must naturally relate what we claim to know to counterclaims and criticism. Doubt is not alien to a growing understanding of faith; in fact, it is required by it. But in our doubts we take up the role that can best be called that of a participant-observer.

As doubts are resolved realistically in a growing faithfulness, there emerges a growing religious coherence. But this is not merely a personal matter. The whole process involves practicing and testing faith in the living community of others who are faithful in the same way.

An illustration of how this method works in an area of knowledge closely analogous to religion will perhaps clarify what these suggestions mean. This analogous area is the realm of interpersonal knowledge.

When we seek knowledge of another human being as a person rather than as an organism or a physical object, we must be prepared to abandon our posture as an "objective observer" and enter into full personal relationship as participant-observer. In such a relationship the other person emerges as something quite other than a collection of objective facts; he becomes an agent like ourselves, equal in dignity to us and requiring a corresponding attitude of respect.

As our knowledge of the other person grows, we find that we cannot talk about him with the language of neutral fact. We use the language of convic-tion and evaluation. Such a deepening of personal knowledge, moreover, involves us in personal risks, commitments of loyalty, and shared intimacies that have little place in factual inquiries. Shared intimacies, moreover, have the quality of revelation rather than discovery, for they can be known only as the friend unveils them himself.

Furthermore, this kind of knowledge can come into its fullness only in the context of mutual love. As Simone Weil wrote, "Among human beings, only the existence of those we love is fully recognized."[15] Such love, which Weil also says is "the only organ of contact with existence," also entails the willingness to share in mutual suffering. Lacking that willingness, the holy of holies, which is the inner reality of another human being, is forever excluded from view.

As this metaphor suggests, personal knowledge entails mystery. The deeper our knowledge, the more we love, suffer, and share the being of another, the more wonderful becomes the mystery of his being.

All this is by way of analogy—a very close analogy—to the kind of knowledge that faith has of the spiritual reality called "God." It is not a rival to other ways of knowing; rather, it is a more total or intimate *knowing*, a reading of the meaning of all the facts that come to us through other channels of reflection and experience.

With a general outline of the kind of knowledge we are concerned with before us, we are prepared to turn to the more specific question: How do we know the God who is the ultimate concern of the major faith of Western man, Christianity?

### SUGGESTIONS FOR FURTHER READING

For the claim that there are other kinds of knowledge besides that which conforms to scientific standards, see T. M. Greene, *Moral, Aesthetic, and Religious Insight* (Rutgers University Press, 1957). Philip Wheelwright in *The Burning Fountain* (Indiana University Press, 1954) also makes this claim. Erich Frank's *Philosophical Understanding and Religious Truth* (Oxford University Press, 1945) is an excellent account of the limits of reason in matters of religious truth. Most of the books already recommended in this section (Part Four) are also relevant to this subject. I would suggest two more: William T. Blackstone, *The Problem of Religious Knowledge* (Spectrum, Prentice-Hall, 1963), which discusses the impact of contemporary philosophical analysis on the question of religious knowledge. From a nonanalytic point of view, H. J. Paton's Gifford Lectures, *The Modern Predicament* (Macmillan, 1955) is an excellent account of the crisis of religious knowledge precipitated by science.

In a more epigrammatic way, the inimitable Simone Weil has illuminated the nature of religious knowledge in *Waiting for God*, Emma Craufurd, trans. (Capricorn, Putnam, 1951). For a nontheistic point of view, see Henry Bugbee, Jr., *The Inward Morning*, Intro. by Gabriel Marcel (Collier, Crowell-Collier, 1961). William Barrett's selection of the writings of D. T. Suzuki will give a good idea of the Oriental concept of religious knowledge: *Zen Buddhism, Selected Writings of D. T. Suzuki* (Anchor, Doubleday, 1956).

## NOTES

1. For a study of transactional theory of knowledge, see F. P. Kilpatrick, ed., *Explorations in Transactional Psychology* (New York University Press, 1961), and Hadley Cantril and Charles H. Bumstead, *Reflections on the Human Venture* (New York University Press, 1960).

2. Alfred North Whitehead, *Science and the Modern World* (New American Library), p. 200.

3. *Ibid.*

4. *Ibid.*, p. 201.

5. *Ibid.*, p. 55.

6. Quoted in John Baillie, *The Sense of the Presence of God* (Yale University Press, 1912; Charles Scribner's Sons, 1962), p. 216.

7. Gerald Heard, *Is God Evident?* (Harper & Row, 1948), p. 139.

8. *Ibid.*

9. David Hume, *An Enquiry Concerning Human Understanding* (Open Court, 1912), p. 176.

10. This is the thesis of a fine book by a Kantian scholar: Theodore M. Greene, *Moral, Aesthetic, and Religious Insight* (Rutgers University Press, 1957).

11. Ludwig Wittgenstein, *Tractatus Logico-Philosophicus*, D. F. Pears and B. F. McGuinness, trans. (Routledge, 1961), 6.522.

12. *Ibid.*, 6.44.

13. In E. W. F. Tomlin, *Simone Weil* (Yale University Press, 1954), pp. 44–45.

14. I Corinthians 13:12. (KJV).

15. Simone Weil, *Gravity and Grace* (Putnam, 1952), p. 113.

# 24

# *The Knowledge of God*

"How do you know there is a God?" This is the way the question is usually put, and the expected answer is usually some kind of "argument for the existence of God." By now we should see that this way of phrasing the question distorts the whole inquiry. When the question as to the existence of God is asked, the proper reply should be, "Everyone has a god of some kind; which god are you referring to?" Martin Luther asked, "What does it mean to have a god, or what is god?" And he answered his own question as follows: "Trust and faith of the heart alone make both God and idol. . . . For the two, faith and God, hold close together. Whatever then thy heart clings to . . . and relies upon, that is properly thy God."[1]

No one asks whether Zeus really exists or existed. Zeus is no longer the name for anyone's ultimate concern. When gods are left behind, the question of their "existence" fades away. And conversely, when they are in full sway their "existence" is fully evident. The believer does not ask whether his god exists; he worships him. The philosopher Wittgenstein, upon hearing a remark of Kierkegaard's to the effect "How can it be that Christ does not exist, since I know that He saved me?" remarked, "You see! It isn't a question of proving anything!"[2]

If we agree that it is God of the Judaeo-Christian Bible—the God of sovereign, holy, creative love—that we are asking about, then, we must rephrase the question as follows: "How do we know that Reality is so

399

gracious?" Richard Niebuhr would say that this is still too theoretical, as though the question of God were abstract rather than existential. How, he might have asked, can we be theoretical or detached when we are thinking about the concern "our heart clings to"?

If we were to inquire, "What reasons would convince a speculative, detached mind of the existence of God?" there are many difficulties, not the least of which is that there are no such speculative, detached minds where faith is concerned. Everyone is moving in, away from, or toward some faith. Such is the nature of human nature. Detachment is possible only in matters that have little bearing on the existence of the thinker himself.

Niebuhr suggests that the real question is "How is faith in God possible for me?" This question cannot be answered in general. It must, and could only be, asked by an existing individual, and his answer will be tested with his life.

Unfortunately, if we were limited to this form of the question we would have to refrain from discussing it, unless the author were to undertake a personal confession of faith, which is clearly out of place here. The next best thing that we can do is to keep Niebuhr's warning in mind, and phrase the question somewhat more generally, while keeping its existential overtones: "How have men come to have faith in God?" or "What considerations have led men to faith in God?" It is the reader alone who can translate the answers to these questions into the existential mood.

## THE CASE OF ARTHUR KOESTLER

When we ask What considerations have led men to faith in God? we are asking what would persuade a man to become in effect a different person, to radically shift his basic assumptions about existence, and to live in a drastically different way. This is not the logic of ordinary argument, which leads one to accept the conclusions of a syllogism. It is, to give it another name, the "rhetoric of conversion." Rhetoric in the dictionary sense means the art of using words so as to persuade or influence, nor merely to conclude an argument successfully. Conversion means changing one's life, not merely changing one's mind. This kind of rhetoric depends heavily on the total context of the argument, and often includes the quality of person who is responsible for it. Alcibiades, for example, confessed that when he was in the presence of his teacher Socrates he felt ashamed to be the kind of person he was. The rhetoric of conversion is for this reason a kind of "argument" that goes on in an interpersonal context and involves the listener to the very depths of his being.

Arthur Koestler, a modern novelist and essayist, makes a useful study for our purposes, because he has written extensively about the circumstances that led to his two conversions: one to Communism, the other away from it. "I went to Communism," he wrote in his autobiography *The Secret Writing,* "as one goes to a spring of fresh water, and I left Communism as one clambers out of a poisoned river strewn with the wreckage of flooded cities and the corpses of the drowned. . . ."[3]

This change was not without antecedents. Koestler's pre-Communist days were filled with a mounting rebellion and frustration induced by the disintegrating German social order that followed the defeat of World War I. The conventional middle-class perspective in which he had grown up offered scant hope of solution. Every way he turned, the confusion became more confounded as his bitterness and despair deepened. Then he fell under the spell of Communism. As he studied Marxism new ways of viewing the social facts appeared. The more he looked at things in this new way, the more sense they made. He describes the final shift in these words: "By the time I had finished with Engel's *Feurerbach* and Lenin's *State and Revolutions*, something had clicked in my brain and I was shaken by a mental explosion. To say that one had 'seen the light' is a poor description of the intellectual rapture which only the convert knows (regardless to what faith he has been converted). The new light seems to pour in from all directions across the skull; the whole universe falls into pattern like the stray pieces in a jigsaw puzzle assembled by magic at one stroke. There is now an answer to every question; doubts and conflicts are a matter of the tortured past. . . ."[4]

The new faith was the fruit of combining reason and experience in a special way. The logical elements in this conversion are apparent. But the change was more than logical. Existential elements—anxieties, hopes, fears—played the greater part. When Koestler had shifted onto these new premises, his whole outlook changed. From the new perspective he could live again; he had found a meaningful life orientation.

He repeated this pattern as he moved toward his second conversion—away from Communism. As he lived and worked within the Communist framework, incoherencies appeared, and along with them came new doubts and anxieties. For seven years he remained loyal to his new faith, even risking death on its behalf. And then a new loosening of the personal foundations took place. Three times he narrowly escaped death by torture and execution. Instead, he was reprieved by imprisonment in solitary confinement. In prison he experienced some mystical "hours by the window," which absolutely assured him that beyond the rational and sensory world was another reality which alone made sense of the other two. Already he had moved beyond the pale of his Communist faith.

Logical elements played a role in this change, too. He became increasingly aware of the contradictions within Communist theory and between theory and practice. This increasing incoherence led him to seek something beyond Communism. When the shocking circumstances of his arrest had disturbed his own personal life sufficiently to make him ready for a change, he moved into yet another circle of faith.

These examples show both the limits and role of reason in the rhetoric of conversion. Rational argument cannot lead a man logically from one world perspective to another, but it can do two things: First, it can show the coherence of the new world view, just as the writings of Lenin showed the logic of Communism to the young Koestler. And, second, it can become a useful critic of such discrepancies in the axioms of life as are unfolded in the process of living. It can thus prepare for personal shifts to different ultimates even though it cannot consummate the shift. Reason in this sense functions, as Socrates said, as a midwife. But the vital process is existential rather than purely logical, involving, that is, the whole man.

## THE DIVISION OF THE ARGUMENT

In the remaining part of this chapter I want to do two things. First, I want to answer the question, How have men come to faith in a God of Holy Love? In answering this question I want to stay as close as possible to the factors which actually work in faith-making, rather than deal with theoretical issues. Second, I want to examine the theoretical issues by attempting an answer to the further question, How do we know that Reality is Holy Love? I know how closely this second question is tied to the existential elements in the first queston, but there are some things that cannot be easily said except in terms of the second. For example, we must examine briefly the classical "arguments for the existence of God." These arguments scarcely arise in answering the first question since they have not played much of a role in faith-making. These things will be clearer as we deal with them. So to our first question.

### How Have Men Come to Faith in a God of Holy Love?

We must note at the outset that not all of the following will apply equally to all men of faith. But most of them are common enough to be considered in this broad context.

*Through Discovering the Limits of Human Thought and Power.* When human thought and will exult in a sense of limitless power, the human spirit is furthest away from the experience of life which gives rise to religious faith. Faith arises concurrently with an awareness of a limiting power which confronts human existence inexorably with insurpassable boundaries and which is nonetheless known to be the source of life itself. This seems to be characteristic of primitive religion, which always expresses its most intense passions in those areas of life that are fraught with risk and danger. It corresponds to the consciousness of dependence which Schleiermacher regarded as the central feature of religion. At the opposite pole is the secular attitude of complete human self-sufficiency and self-determination, the attitude exemplified by the planners of the biblical Tower of Babel which was to reach to the very heavens. The Bible sees this ambition as sinful and vaulting pride, which the limiting Power inexorably blights with confusion and disintegration. The sacred Ultimate is first known, then, as the limiting or encompassing Reality which cannot be penetrated by unaided human thought or action. This is the primordial sense of the Mysterious Other which stands over against human life. It has received many names—Fate, Destiny, Providence—but its limiting presence is the first stage of religious consciousness.

*Through Seeking and Finding.* Despite the omnipresence of the encompassing power which limits man, his own relationship to it is ambiguous and mysterious. From earliest times he has felt it to be full of some tremendous import that escapes his grasp. It is this that has made religion a quest and a seeking. And it is because men have believed that this quest has been rewarded that they have grown in faith. In one degree or another they have confirmed the Gospel promise: "Seek and you shall find. . . ."[5]

It was the prophet Jeremiah who first fully grasped the paradoxical truth of faith-seeking: "You shall seek me and you shall find me; for when you seek me with all your heart, I will let myself be found by you."[6] The mysterious encompassing Other cannot be found by human power alone, but if the seeking is seriously undertaken by the whole man, the divine graciousness lets Himself be known. The "object" of faith is strictly beyond human grasp, but nonetheless is known by those who fulfill the conditions. The knowing or finding is itself also paradoxical. For the man of faith is more likely to speak of "being known" or "being found" than of "knowing" or "finding." As the Psalmist says: "O Lord, thou has searched me and known me!"[7]

This, after all, follows from the nature of the God who is being sought. If He is Holy Love, then He initiated the search and will consummate the finding. This is the meaning of Jesus' parable of the good shepherd who leaves the flock to rescue the one sheep which has gone astray. One writer suggests that to speak of the human search for God is like saying that a mouse seeks and finds the cat. "Whither shall I go from thy Spirit? Or whither shall I flee from thy presence? If I ascend to heaven, thou art there! If I make my bed in Sheol, thou art there! If I take the wings of the morning and dwell in the uttermost parts of the sea, even there thy hand shall lead me, and thy right hand shall hold me."[8]

"Being found" stands in contrast to the kind of "finding" that men experience, say, in mathematics, when the correct answer becomes apparent. Being found means to be grasped by a Power which sets man in entirely new relationships to himself, his fellows, and his world. It is an existential finding. Its "proof," if one dares use this word for it, is the self-verifying quality of the new claims, their irresistible power over life and thought.

At this point a question naturally arises: Why is God so hard to find? Why doesn't everyone successfully conclude this inquiry? Why isn't God more evident? This is not at all easy to answer. The philosopher Immanuel Kant said that the main reason is that if God were completely self-evident to every man, faith would have no moral quality. Such self-evidence would take away man's freedom to withhold or give his consent to the divine-human dialogue. Communion with God is the highest level to which human growth can attain. As such it logically requires the effort of inquiry, decision, and risk.

Kierkegaard is concerned with the same question when he considers God's problem as a teacher of mankind. To appear before man as an omnipotent and omniscient teacher would be to overawe the creaturely student. He must therefore, said Kierkegaard, appear in disguise. Jesus, he said, was a supreme example. In him, God appeared as a carpenter and a prophet from a despised region of a despised country. Only in this way could the process of religious growth be accommodated to man's condition as a finite creature.

Another answer can be found along another line of thought. Man is free, but he mysteriously misuses his freedom. This turning back upon himself blinds him to the way in which God is continually showing himself—in nature, in history, and in the soul of man. Sin seems to make man impervious to God's showing of himself in the usual ways. The way of God to man becomes more devious, and requires of man that fundamental turning around which is the meaning of repentance. Once this turning around has taken place, then, as if in a state of fresh innocence, all creation speaks again of the divine Presence.

*Through Membership in a Community of Faith.* Human knowing never takes place in isolation. Men think and live in communities. Nor do men undertake the divine search alone. The God of Holy Love is known through participation in a community with a history. That God's actions are a part of history is the whole burden of the Bible. This means that the search for God does not begin with each individual without important antecedents. He hears of God from his fellows; he participates in the meanings which God has given to their common history; he worships God with his community. In this sense, he may not recall a time when he did not know God, just as he may not remember a time when he did not know the language of his culture.

To be sure, he must sometime undertake the search for himself. He cannot come to meaningful faith as a piece of driftwood in the stream of tradition. He cannot passively inherit his tradition. He must seek with his whole heart, just as his ancestors did, and recapitulate the history of faith himself, but he does not do it without the support that comes from the faithful community.

Again, it is the God of Holy Love who has taken the initiative, God himself who has guided this process and who has cultivated human fellowship with Him in this living history. Only in a life of love and holiness could such a God be known, and these can only be experienced in a community which more or less exemplifies them.

*Through Moments of Illumination.* The poet T. S. Eliot writes of

> *the unattended*
> *Moment, the moment in and out of time,*
> *The distraction fit, lost in a shaft of sunlight,*
> *The wild thyme unseen, or the winter lightning*
> *Or the waterfall, or music heard so deeply*
> *That it is not heard at all, but you are the music*
> *While the music lasts.*[9]

We have considered Koestler's mystical "hours by the window." Such moments are reported in the religious traditions of all peoples and are recurring experiences of men in every age. The nineteenth-century Hindu saint Ramakrishna was only ten years old when he fell into ecstasy as he watched a flight of crane while passing through a paddy. Later, as a grown man, he reported an even more profound experience while meditating in a temple at Dashineswar: "The buildings . . . vanished from my sight, leaving no trace whatsoever, and in their stead I saw a limitless, infinite, effulgent Ocean of Consciousness. . . . What was happening in the outside world I do not know; but within me there was a steady flow of undiluted bliss, altogether new, and I felt the presence of the Divine Mother [Kali]."[10]

Such experiences have persuaded men that Reality vastly transcends the limits of the sensory or rational world of ordinary experience. Skeptics may write them off as disorders of the human psyche, but to those who enjoy them, even when induced by drugs, they have constituted irrefragible evidence of a More beyond. William James cites the experience of a friend who wrote as follows: "There was not a mere consciousness of something there, but fused in the central happiness of it, a startling awareness of some ineffable good . . . and after it went, the memory—persisted as the one perception of reality. Everything else might be a dream, but not that."[11]

James also makes a very important point in connection with this witness: "My friend, as it oddly happens, does not interpret these experiences theistically, as signifying the presence of God."[12] Mystical moments, in short, may witness to a mysterious Beyond which is Within, but they do not necessarily witness to a God of Holy Love. What shall we make of this fact?

Illuminative and mystical moments, despite many common properties, are capable of diverse interpretations. They almost always grant to their subjects an invincible sense of a portentous and glorious "reality" beyond ordinary experience, and the language in which these experiences are described shows remarkable similarities across widely ranging cultural differences. So striking are the similarities that some have been led to believe that mysticism could serve as an empirical basis for a universal theology. But unfortunately the differences are as important as the similarities. In fact, the great rifts in interpretation which afflict religion cut right through the mystical literature itself. Hindus, for example, see in mystical ecstasies the verification of their views of life, and Christians return the compliment. The Vedantic Hindu feels himself immersed in the ocean of undifferentiated Being whereas the Christian feels himself drawn into union with the God of Holy Love. The interpretations of mysticism are, in fact, almost as numerous as the cultures of mankind.

We need not be concerned here with any final interpretation of such illuminative moments. It is enough to point out that experiences of this kind have supported man's movement toward faith. If mysticism does not speak with absolute clarity about a God of holy love, this is because these experiences are (in Eliot's words) only "hints and guesses," which must be understood in the larger context of historical faith. Thus, for example, Lady Juliana of Norwich speaks confidently of her mystical elevations as "revelations of divine love," while Ramakrishna felt the "presence of the Divine Mother." This latter case is interesting, because Hinduism commonly claims that ecstatic experiences are self-interpreting. During his most ecstatic period, Ramakrishna was thought by his colleagues to be mad. A convocation of Brahmin pundits examined him and pronounced him sane, much to his own relief. They reached their verdict by comparing Ramakrishna's experiences with the orthodox Hindu scriptures and finding them in substantial agreement, thus relieving him of the belief that his own experiences were mere personal vagaries. I cite this case to show how mystical experiences depend for their interpretation upon a wider cultural context.

The fact that these experiences are inevitably colored by the cultural setting in which they occur does not diminish their importance as arousers of faith. But it does strongly suggest that they do not carry their full interpretation with them. In mystical experience something seems to transcend the sensual world—this much is given; but what that Something or Someone is, is not clear from the experience alone.

*Through Dialogue.* In mystical experience subject and object tend to be merged into an ecstatic all-embracing Oneness. The person is dissolved in a blissful ocean of undifferentiated feeling. He loses himself in the aesthetic joy—"you are the music while the music lasts." But many men have known the divine not so much through ecstasy as through being addressed by God in a divine-human dialogue. This is the characteristic experience of the Bible. God addresses man, and he responds. I used this concept of dialogue earlier to indicate what a biblically inspired life would be like.

Moses turns aside to see a burning bush, and hears God speak to him. He asks the divine Presence for his name. The King James version of the Bible translates the response in impersonal terms: "I Am That I Am," as though God were declaring himself to be Pure Being. Martin Buber says that a better translation of the Hebrew is "I will be Present as I will be Present," which is not a declaration of some eternal essence of being, but a promise of continued dialogue, as though God were saying to Moses, "Call on me, and I will answer."

Moses then is commanded to return to Egypt and lead the Israelites out of slavery, for, as the Lord says, "I am the God of Abraham, of Isaac, and of Jacob"—that is, the God of Moses' ancestors, the great patriarchs of the Israelites. In this historical context, Moses' comprehension increases. He remembers the promise of God to Abraham. Reluctantly, but without delay, he obeys the command. The Bible is full of such colloquies. The Psalms, for example, are rich in prayers of direct address and in testimonies of God's replies, in fulfillment of the prophetic promise, "You shall call me and I will answer you; you shall pray to me, and I will listen to you."[13]

Martin Buber has built his entire theology around the concept of dialogue.[14] Man, he says, only comes to himself in saying *Thou* to another. *I-Thou* is the primary word of man's existence in the world. The moral claim of another person is a kind of address, his demand to be addressed in return, to be treated as a "thou" rather than an "it." Buber holds that man cannot "experience" other people or God; he can only respond to their address. In authentic response to the Other man knows both himself and the Other.

*Through Faith.* When Einstein expressed an awed certainty of the Reality which though "impenetrable to us" nonetheless manifested itself "as the highest wisdom and the most radiant beauty," he witnessed to the paradox of possession-nonpossession which characterizes man's relationship to the Ultimate. How, we might ask, could he know logically that which was "impenetrable" to him? How could he be sure that the "radiant beauty" which he enjoyed was an expression of an even greater beauty beyond his perception?

Socrates discusses the same mysterious state of affairs in the *Meno* where he is discussing with Menon the faith that animates his philosophy. "You argue," he says to Menon, "that a man cannot enquire either about that which he knows, or about that which he does not know; for if he knows, he has no need to enquire; and if not, he cannot; for he does not know the very subject about which he is to enquire."[15] Socrates' answer to this problem is not very satisfactory, since he appeals to a dubious belief in reincarnation. But his positive faith in inquiry is very important. In spite of the fact that he says that he knows nothing, he nonetheless expresses a faith in inquiry which is in itself a kind of faith knowledge of the first order: "Some things I have said of which I am not altogether confident. But that we shall be better and braver and less helpless if we think that we ought to inquire, than we should have been if we indulged in the idle fancy that there was no knowing and no use in seeking to know what we do not know;—that is a theme upon which I am ready to fight, in word and deed, to the utmost of my power."[16]

This paradoxical relationship of participation—nonparticipation is the life of faith.[17] In faith, men believe that they know more than they know, that they are destined for more than they have achieved. "Faith," according to the writer to the Hebrews, "is the assurance of things hoped for, the conviction of things not seen."[18]

Logically, this whole claim could be written off as groundless. But existentially this odd language seems to express most accurately man's experienced relationship to the highest truth and goodness. It is the truth that man does not yet possess that lures him on; it is the goodness he has not yet embraced that makes his life meaningful. Faith thus refers to Reality beyond that known in the experience of either mystical possession or direct dialogue. Or perhaps it would be better to say that both mystical experience and dialogue presuppose faith as their ground. Reality does not disclose itself completely to the mystic, nor does the dialogue unveil the mystery of God's being. There is always the transcendent Beyond which lures the mystic or prophet yet further.

If we were concerned with knowledge of determinate facts, faith might be written off as belief without sufficient grounds. But in the realm of existence, faith seems to be a distinguishing mark of humanity at its growing best. For faith is man's unfailing contact with Reality even when his own powers fail. It is the experience of meaning when every evidence testifies to meaninglessness, the rising hope that even in failure a new life awaits one in the coming hour. Faith is the power to sense the awe in things when they have become dull and commonplace, the light that shines in events when our eyes have become tired with watching. Faith awakens the warmth of forgiveness when we have grown cold with bitterness and hurt, and arouses love for someone whom all observations have disclosed as unlovable. Faith can transfigure human sorrow and irreplaceable loss with the certainty of joy and hope. It can assure of Reality's acceptance and healing when one is sick with moral failure and seemingly impregnable self-concern. This same faith can cast a man into despair about himself when he is proud and self-sufficient, and bring him out of his despair into humble self-acceptance. Faith can illuminate the way one must take when the light of experience and thought has grown dim. Faith is the absolute assurance that nothing, absolutely nothing in all creation, can separate us from the Holy Love which we but dimly see and but haltingly grope after. Faith, thus understood, is God's grip on man, the power of the Hand that cannot be loosed, the Life that is everlasting.

This catalogue is not a panegyric in praise of faith. It is a sober account of the experience of multitudes who say that this is why they cannot turn away from the God of Holy Love.

St. Paul was tempted, when defending his religious authority, to appeal to mystical experiences, ecstasies, and ascents to heavenly regions, but when he spoke about the fundamental ground of his own assurance he appealed not to his experience but to the graciousness of God he saw coming toward him in Jesus Christ. It was this graciousness which he said claimed him, healed him, and kept him at his arduous tasks. His confidence, he tells us, was not in his ecstatic abilities or claims of wisdom but in the Holy God who knew him.

Faith, then, appears to be the fundamental clue to man's relationship to the ground of his own existence—a relationship that includes partial participation in that ground and partial exclusion from it. This seems to be an accurate account of men who are led on from what they are to continuously higher levels of personal achievement and maturity. It is God who is faithful in this relationship, and man who is the receiver of His benefaction. It is ultimate Reality which is faithful in this relationship and man who is ambiguously faithful-unfaithful. This leads us to our next point.

*Through Growing Coherence of Life and Thought.* Erich Frank's words seem to be quite true: "Man's whole life is a struggle to gain true existence, an effort to achieve substantiality so that he may not have lived in vain and vanish like a shadow. Whether he is a believer or a skeptic . . . this idea of existential truth is the driving force of all his thought and action."[19] The reason men have believed in a God of Holy Love is that they have discovered in faith a growing coherence in their life and thought, an increase of undoubted meaningfulness. They have realized that this has come to them as a gift in the midst of their own betrayals and failures, so long as they have continued to seek again. They have found themselves growing into a deeper integrity and a more invincible courage despite their flaws and fears. And perhaps most important of all, they have found themselves knit up to their fellows in a love that surpasses any temperamental kinship they may feel. They have found in looking to God a universally expanding concern for all life springing up within them, tearing them away from their selfish pre-occupations.

This love, which surpasses any rational extension of self-interest, becomes the medium in which the "knowing" becomes most strong. As St. John writes, "We know that we have passed out of death into life, because we love the brethren."[20]

The growing coherence is more than that of thought—it is the knitting up of life itself, within and without, the sense of unity healing all the alienations that torment the human spirit. But, and this is our transition to our topic, it is also grasped as a coherence of thought, a sense of the largest truth the human mind can grasp. It is this emergence of the life of faith as the truth about existence that permits us to pursue our inquiry into another realm.

### How Do We Know that Reality Is Holy Love?

In this section we have considered those elements in human experience that have influenced men toward faith. I have tried to answer why men have believed in a God of Holy Love. But in thus emphasizing the existential character of the case, we have been led to consider the conviction that animates the man of faith; namely, that the whole universe of nature, history, and human experience speaks to him of God, who himself is Reality.

Recall that our first question was, How have men come to faith in a God of Holy Love? This, we saw, was an existential way of putting the question—and the right way. Now we are asking a more theoretical question about the nature of Ultimate Reality. The reason we are asking this question is that faith comes to see its view of the world as the truth about that world. What I am going to do here is to translate that view of the world into the form of a rational hypothesis about the world. Before doing so, however, certain presuppositions must be made clear.

*Presuppositions of Rational Argument About the Nature of the World.* First, all rational arguments about reality as a whole proceed from some finite perspective. There are no cosmic philosophers, no universal minds. Human beings live and think concretely in time and space. The choice of perspective is decisive in determining the way the world looks. The view of the world as the creation of Holy Love is the result of seeing it from a perspective that has been radically impregnated by the Christian revelation. The biblical story, culminating in the coming of Jesus Christ, is the key which opens the door onto such a landscape.

If it be objected that this is mere provincialism, I reply that every thinker is in exactly the same position. He must fasten on some event or experience that in his clue to the meaning or meaninglessness of the world. Some will find it in the realities of industrial conflict (Marxism), or in the experience of ecstatic contemplation (Buddhism), or in the revelation of the Archangel to the Prophet Mohammed (Islam), or in the arrival of Man on the biological scene after the eons of biological evolution (Humanism).

The rational test of each perspective is its power to make a coherent and comprehensive account of the wide ranges of human experience. If the believer in a God of Holy Love claims truth for his view, it is because he believes that his chosen perspective offers the widest sweep and the most coherent account of the enigmatic human story.

Other views, he must concede, offer partial understanding—as, for example, Marxism did for the young Koestler. No view that has commended itself to intelligent men is likely to be devoid of some plausibility. No view—even our own, we must also concede—can be totally coherent. But it is integral to the view we are exploring that man is incapable of grasping the world as a rational unity, for the world is unfinished and its transcendent purposes have yet to be made clear. As Marcel says, we know God in a "broken world." In this sense, even its incoherencies and limits are predicted from within the theistic perspective.

A second presupposition of all rational arguments about Ultimate Reality is that without some experience of depth the argument will seem meaningless. As the British Jesuit Father Turner says, "Traditional theistic argument no longer cuts any ice." The reason, he argues, is that we are "suffering not from too much logic, but from too little contemplation. . . . Aristotle thought that philosophizing started out from wonder. . . . I suspect that [modern] logical theories take the direction that they do because . . . wonder . . . is no longer there."[21]

If the world is taken for granted as having no significance beyond its mere appearances, metaphysical arguments of all kinds will appear vain. Jacques Maritain writes of a "primordial intuition of being" which precedes all logical argument about the structure of the world. This primoridal intuition, he says, "is both the intuition of my existence and of the existence of things." The existence of things, he continues, is felt to be independent of me and limiting me in a "totally self-assertive and . . . implacable" way. "At the same time I realize that I exist," he says, "[I am] thrown back into my loneliness and frailty by this other existence by which things assert themselves and in which I have positively no part, to which I am exactly as naught." He sums up his point in these words: "Thus the primordial intuition of being is the intuition of the solidity and inexorability of existence; and, second, of the death and nothingness to which my existence is liable. And third, in the same flash of intuition . . . I realize that this solid and inexorable existence, perceived in anything whatsoever, implies—I do not yet know in what form—some absolute, irrefragable existence, completely free from nothingness and death."[22]

What Maritain is saying, if I understand him, is that the intelligibility and value of being must be grasped intuitively before any arguments about existence can get under way. But, of course, in modern thought, say in the case of Sartre, it is just this intelligibility and value of being which is at stake. Maritain would no doubt reply that Sartre is blind about the nature of being, and I am inclined to agree; but arguments cannot dislodge him. This is what we mean by saying that the argument presupposes some experience of significant depth.

These remarks lead directly into our next point: that rational argument is simply faith taking a logical form. Anselm long ago said that rational argument is "faith seeking understanding," in contrast to the idea that faith can be generated or established by reason. I have already expressed doubts about this later possibility, though it might be useful in a longer discussion to distinguish degrees of faith. How much faith, we might ask, is needed before argument can have the effect of clarifying and strengthening faith? I suspect that for some—Koestler seems an example of this type—the exposure of logical structure may generate growth in a faith that is present only in very small degree.

Another consideration seems to be relevant to the ambiguity-ridden modern student. He may actually half embrace a number of conflicting faiths. He may be part humanist, part nationalist, part materialist, and part Judaeo-Christian. In this case, spelling out the logic (or illogic) of these faiths may have the effect of winnowing unlikely faiths from more solid possibilities.

In the light of these remarks let us turn to the classical arguments for the existence of God to see how they exemplify our presuppositions.

## CLASSICAL ARGUMENTS FOR GOD [23]

### The Cosmological Argument

This argument, the cosmological, can be summarized as follows: Something exists, therefore God exists. The world, so the argument goes, plainly exists, but its nature is such that it could not possibly be the source of its own existence; therefore it must derive from some Being whose existence is in itself, some Self-existent. Look at any item in the world—say, a tree. That tree does not exist by its own power, it came from some previous existent. And this existent came from some previous existent, and so on. But each of these existents is "contingent"; that is, each of them is a dependent existent. But this means that no matter how far back you trace any given thing's existence you will never find an adequate explanation until you come to an existent that doesn't depend, in turn, upon a previous existent. When you come to this point you have reached God, who in this argument is defined as a Being who exists in his own right, or "necessarily."

What is the force of this argument, and what are its limitations? There are many interesting ramifications in the large literature of the subject, but, briefly, the force of the argument seems to be that if the world is rational things do not spring unaccountably from nothing. Everything must have a sufficient cause. An infinite regress (tracing contingent causes backwards without end) is profoundly unsatisfactory because it never arrives at a true explanation. Therefore some adequate Final Cause is required. But note that the argument begs the question: It assumes that the world is rational. But that is the proposition we set out to prove. We could, with Hume, or with Sartre, sadly confess that the world is absurd and that contingent things are simply there, that they have no explanation at all. In the face of such a confession the argument is powerless.

What this argument does, then, is to give logical form to the primordial conviction of faith that the world is rational, that things do not happen without a sufficient cause. It says that God is the creator and sustainer of being who exists in his own right and that the world is dependent upon him. Of course, this argument is highly abstract. The rationality of being which simply affirms that no contingent existent exists by itself leads us only to a bare "Self-existent." It doesn't speak of God's holiness or love. In this sense the argument is religiously defective, for the worship of the living God is not limited to a Self-existent.

### The Teleological Argument

Other classical arguments fill in some of these deficiences. The famous teleological argument points out that the world appears to be ordered toward goals or ends; that the inorganic supports the organic, and the organic supports the human and spiritual. This purposeful order seems to require a Purposer, a world architect. To a man of faith, who sees in every corner of the world the signs of God's purposes at work, this argument is persuasive. But it too begs the question: It assumes what it proves. How?

First, it repeats the assumption of the cosmological argument that all things have a sufficient cause, that the world is rational at heart. And second, it assumes that there is a difference between "higher" and "lower"—that the life of a man is more valuable than the life of a worm. This means that the value distinctions that men make are not subjective, but are somehow characteristics of things themselves. That is, it assumes that such things as beauty, moral goodness, and holiness are the fair fruits of life at its best, and that, conversely, ugliness, moral corruption, and sinful pride are bad.

Without these two assumptions the argument doesn't make any sense. But these are the things the argument set out to prove, and they are rejected by many skeptics. With the failure of the assumptions the argument doesn't move.

What, then, is the force of this argument? It lies in the clarity with which it spells out the rationality of the world as faith grasps it. The more evidence showing the marvelous interdependence of things conspiring to produce life and value, the more clearly the man of faith, or the man searching for faith, sees what faith really means. In the hands of able thinkers like Tennant or Bertocci the argument is very persuasive indeed.[24]

The teleological argument has, I believe, an additional force not generally noticed. I put it forward somewhat diffidently, despite a conviction that it is logically sound, because it may appear to claim too much. However, for what it is worth, the argument seems to force thought toward the extremes of belief or skepticism, excluding any middle ground as untenable. It makes clear that the skeptic must somehow believe that all the intricate ordering of the world, with its power to produce life, mind, and value is a colossal accident, or at best the product of mindless "Nature" which blindly produces its offspring, and as blindly destroys them. All the coherencies between scientific thought and the order of nature, all the interpenetration of values in personal character, all the fair beauty of this world, all these must be regarded as mere randomness. Sartre would appear to have drawn the only correct conclusion—at the end of his *Being and Nothingness*—existence is nauseatingly absurd and "man is a useless passion."

The late Albert Camus is an interesting case in point. He held that there is a vast discrepancy between the meaninglessness of nature and the dignity of man at his best with all his ideals of humane civilization. But he failed to ask how such altruistic men can be produced by such a meaningless nature. We should recall Darwin's doubt whether the human mind could be trusted, since it was fundamentally the "mind of a monkey."

Camus also failed to ask how his ideals could have validity if man, who is a part of absurd nature, is the source of them. My point is that if this issue were pressed, it would be necessary to give up the notion of absurdity in nature or extend it to the whole of man's existence. In that case, we would be back at total faith or total skepticism.

### The Ontological Argument

The third classical argument for the existence of God is the ontological. In substance it contends: (1) God is the name of the being than whom no greater can be thought, and (2) the greatest being that I can think of must have *existence* as one of his attributes, because otherwise I could think of another being greater than this nonexistent God—namely, a God who existed. Therefore, God must exist. In short, a contingently existing perfect being is a contradiction in terms.

The chief objection to this argument since the time of Kant has been that "existence" is not a predicate. Norman Malcolm points out that "a king might desire that his next chancellor should have knowledge, wit, and resolution; but it is ludicrous to add that the king's desire is to have a chancellor who exists."[25] Existence would not then appear in a list of desirable characteristics or predicates of the new chancellor. If existence is not a predicate, however, you cannot make an argument about God using it in this way.

Charles Hartshorne replies to this objection as follows: It is true that existence is not a necessary qualification for the description of, say, a cat or an island, because such things may or may not exist. But to say that the ultimate basis of all being (whatever it is) may or may not exist doesn't make sense. Therefore, necessary existence seems to be an element in the description of what ultimately is. Ultimate being is in fact the only entity of which such a predicate is required. And this is the main logical force of the argument.

Another objection to the ontological argument is that the concept "necessary" applies only to propositions, not to things. Given the proper definitions, it is necessary that $2 + 2 = 4$, but the expression "God necessarily exists" does not refer to propositions but to some kind of fact or other.

To elucidate these matters adequately it would be necessary to introduce the large literature of modern philosophy on this point, and that is clearly not feasible here. However, a remark or two is in order. Father D'Arcy says that the concept of necessity as applying to existence arises out of our common human experience that certain things have to happen if other things happen. For instance, if a man falls from a great height onto cement he is bound to be hurt. D'Arcy then goes on to say that the concept of God's necesary existence belongs to this species of experience.

In the spirit of David Hume, we may reply that we do not actually experience the necessity of being hurt in a fall from a height; it is only that these things have occurred so regularly that we imagine that they are necessarily connected. From the strictly logical point of view no doubt Hume is correct. Perhaps the universe is merely a random affair that has accidentally exhibited sufficient order during our lifetime to impress us with the thought that it is necessarily so ordered. There is no way logically to persuade a skeptic to the contrary.

However, this line of thought does open up what is at stake in the argument: the issue of whether the universe is as a matter of fact a random affair or not. The theist takes his common experience in faith as a starting point, then goes on to show that God is the basis of all connections between events that make them rational. He can do this, moreover, only if He is himself the Being who exists in his own right and by his own power and not at the pleasure of some other force beyond himself. But if the premise that ordinary experience is a partial mirror of reality is rejected, the argument cannot move.

It is thus not as a rational construction that the ontological argument interests us most. It is rather because this argument is a rational way of stating the theistic vision of life. As a matter of fact, this argument arose in the context of religious faith, and I believe that it could not have arisen in any other. I say this because the chief religious significance of the argument lies in the contention of faith that to be God, God must be more perfect than all our thoughts of God, and that he could not be such a God unless he were the foundation of all existence. This is another instance of what Erich Frank calls transposing "the act of faith into the medium of rational thinking."[26] In a sense, the ontological argument states in a nutshell that the thrust of religious history is toward a "being than whom no greater can be thought" and a recognition that none other than such a God could serve as God for man.

The argument does one other thing, however. It seems that a denial of the ontological argument, like the denial of the other two, forces its critics to the conclusion that nothing really "necessary" exists; that the ultimate connections of existence are therefore purely arbitrary; that at base, reality is quite possibly a wildly gyrating and absurd concatenation of forces that may or may not produce anything at all, like the monkey at the typewriter who eventually produces a novel by random typing. In short, its denial seems to force the critic toward the extreme of skepticism in just the same way as does the rejection of the other two arguments (which, philosophers have pointed out, really presuppose this argument anyway). The ontological argument, then, does not prove the conclusions of faith, but it does make all intermediate or middling skepticism untenable—it forces the critic to the extreme position. It makes clear what the human options are.

It may be objected that this still leaves some form of naturalism or pantheism as an option. This is doubtful for the following reasons: Nature, to qualify as an option to absurdity, would have to have the qualities the arguments ascribed to the Ultimate Existent, namely (1) self-sufficiency, or the power of self-generation; (2) adequacy for the creation of the highest values; and, *perhaps* (3) be the highest ultimate which men could conceive.

On all three counts Nature seems inadequate, since all its elements appear to be contingent, that is, dependent upon antecedent causes. Moreover, nature could not be an adequate account of, say, reason or persons, unless nature were itself at least as rational as human reason or as personal as human persons. But to attribute such qualities to nature would surely be to transcend what naturalists mean by nature. Finally, men can conceive something higher than nature, namely, the creator of nature, who is Holy Love.

### Note on the Confrontation of Theism and Absurdity

Before trying to state the case of theism in more modern terms, let us examine something which the foregoing discussion has brought to the fore: If rational argument leaves us undecided between theism on one side and a philosophy of absurdity on the other, how shall one side persuade the other? How shall we decide between them?

Professor John Hick compounds this difficulty by saying that theism and atheism can make an equally good account of all the data of human experience. Let us suppose for the argument that he is right. He appeals to an example from the writing of R. M. Hare to explain what he means. Suppose that "a lunatic is convinced that all the professors in a certain college are intent upon murdering him. It will be vain to try to allay his suspicions by introducing him to a series of kindly and inoffensive professors, for he will only see a particularly devious cunning in their apparently friendly manner."[27] All the evidence will be quite capable of reasonable interpretation in terms of the paranoid obsession of the lunatic.

How shall we persuade such a person? Surely not with logical argument, for, as we have seen, the data can be as well accounted for on the paranoid's hypothesis as upon the contrary view that he has nothing to fear. The answer is that though he cannot be persuaded by argument he can be persuaded by life itself. If the paranoid counsels with a skilled physician, for example, he will in time come to see that his fears were not really grounded in fact. He will overcome his doubts enough to venture back into trustful human association. It is as though reality had somehow presented itself to him and won him over where argument failed.

This unveiling of Reality itself is the final resort in all matters of faith. The man who believes in a God of Holy Love contends that Reality will in time persuade those with whom arguments are of no avail. Presumably the converse is also possible: that with time all men will discover the emetic absurdity of existence. We are then back again at faith. What remains is to test life to the full, to live it without blinkers, and to let the truth decide the issue.

## The Argument from Value

The argument can be stated in this way: Man's total value experience—moral, aesthetic, social, and religious—represents facts of human existence. As such they require an adequate explanation. That explanation must be nothing less than God.

Hastings Rashdall states the moral argument in this way. "Metaphysical presuppositions . . . are necessary to the very existence of an ethical system which can be regarded as representing and justifying the deliverances of the moral consciousness."[28] He admits that the terms "right" and "good" do not contain explicit reference to any theological or metaphysical theory of the universe. But he contends that the meaning of these terms cannot be made explicit without "necessitating the adoption of certain views concerning the ultimate nature of things and the rejection of other views."[29] Materialism or skepticism, for instance, must have the effect of reducing these experiences to less than their evident experienced significance. But if the character of Reality is essentially a holy will, these experiences can be understood as the reasonable product of that Reality. "We may be able," writes Rashdall, "perhaps, to give some meaning to morality without the postulate of God, but not its true or full meaning." The full meaning of moral obligation is moral objectivity; namely, that the claim of morality stands over against all human awareness or contrivance.

But this last remark reveals the way in which this argument, like all the others, begs the question, presupposes what it intends to prove. How? It presupposes that the moral consciousness is the awareness of an objective standard apart from the personal or social interests of human beings. But this is just what the argument intends to prove. Skeptics invariably regard morality as a species of human interest not involving any absolute claim. It is the absolute character of the moral claim that is itself in doubt.

The same line of thought applies to the other value experiences—beauty or religious experience, for instance—which theists have claimed as evidence for God. In order that these experiences may serve as evidence in the argument, they must have a status at the outset that is debatable from a skeptical point of view. Aesthetic experience can easily be looked upon as simply a special kind of pleasure, having no more intrinsic metaphysical significance than the satisfaction of eating a good meal.

Father D'Arcy summarizes the argument from the religious experience of awe in these words: "As there are inanimate and animate objects which we come to distinguish and react to differently; and as there are right and wrong actions, which incite us to admiration or indignation; and as there are lovely things and persons, in whose presence we feel a special kind of emotion; so, as man has always felt a special emotion [awe], which is distinct from any of the others and is incapable of being produced by them, it must have been produced by an adequate object; and this object, as a being to whom we pay homage in awe and prostration and sacrifice, must of itself be adorable or worshipful. . . . Otherwise this attitude of ours would be unintelligible and our apprehension vain."[30]

We may comment on this argument in the same vein as our remarks concerning the moral argument. What is at stake is the characteristic of the experience of awe itself—whether it is what the theist says it is or what the skeptic says it is. As the philosopher Hobbes once remarked, "The man who says that God spoke to him in a dream says no more than that he dreamed that God spoke to him." The experience may have had overtones of blessedness for the man who enjoyed it, but the skeptic can regard such experiences as the product of special biochemical conditions. The fact that many of these experiences can be stimulated under drugs suggests just this conclusion to the skeptic.

Is this argument, then, without any force at all? This would be going too far. It has the same force as the other arguments: It is a rational way of stating the faith of the man who knows God in and through his own value experiences. John Baillie, for instance, does not argue from moral experience to God. He points out that in the absolute claims of his moral life he experiences the presence of God.[31] In morality, he says, he knows that he does not belong to himself, but to another. The same thing may be said of the experience of sublime beauty, wisdom, love, or so-called mystical experience through ecstatic prayer or contemplation.

In all these cases it is impossible to assume that the experiences are given data that the skeptic must first accept, and then use logic to force a theistic conclusion. The experiences simply don't have the same characteristics for the skeptic and the man of faith. To the man of faith God is immediately given in his experiences of values, though, of course, with varying degrees of awareness. God, so to speak, shows himself in them. If the skeptic is to be convinced he must be shown, not by argument, but by life itself.

The arguments are not useless, for they may be said to constitute the clearest formulation of the experience itself as known to men of faith. They fail, however, to force a theistic conclusion upon those who do not share the vision of faith itself.

It is this line of thought which led the philosopher John Wisdom to remark in his celebrated essay "Gods" that "the existence of God is not an experimental issue the way it was."[32] The existence of God is not "a chain of demonstrative reasoning" from given facts. It is a special way of seeing those facts. For instance, in a court trial the facts may all be accepted as given, but whether or not it proves to be an instance of negligence is the result of a particular way of viewing those facts. And this conclusion, if it may be called such, is not a simple line of reasoning, but "a matter of the cumulative effect of several premises, not of the repeated transformation of one or two."[33] "Things are revealed to us," writes Wisdom, "not only by the scientists with microscopes, but also by the poets, the prophets, and the painters. What is so isn't merely a matter of 'the facts.' "[34] It is a matter of seeing the facts in a new light. For instance, he writes, "A difference as to whether a thing is beautiful is not a factual difference. . . ." How is such a question settled? The procedure, says Wisdom, "consists not only in reasoning and redescription as in the legal case, but also in a more literal re-setting before with re-looking or re-listening,"[35] until the new perspective reveals itself. The differences between men as to whether God exists, Wisdom concludes, is not so much like a scientific debate; it "is more like a difference as to whether there is beauty in a thing."[36]

It is in the setting of these considerations that I want to turn now to a brief statement of the case for theism, not as an argument, but as a way of reviewing the dimensions of the world which evoke the theistic vision of reality.

## A BRIEF STATEMENT OF THE CASE FOR THEISM

The statement that follows is a formal expression of the coherence that life appears to have from the point of view of faith in a God of Holy Love. It is presented in the spirit of Voltaire's comment: "In the opinion that there is a God, there are difficulties; but in the contrary opinion there are absurdities."[37]

### Theism Makes the Most Sense of Religion

A God of Holy Love makes the most sense of religion as a persistent human phenomenon. Religion, as we have pointed out earlier, has been a persistent accompaniment of humanity from the dimmest past to the immediate present. Even pre-man seems to have intuited his experience religiously. I find untenable the skeptical view that the all-but-universal perception of Spirit shining through and underlying existence is a colossal illusion imposed somehow upon man by mindless forces. This is not a simple appeal to universal consensus—after all, there have been near-universal prejudices now known to be false. But religion is not an unexamined opinion. It has withstood the rigorous critique of multitudes of mankind's most acute thinkers, East and West. Skepticism has been popular only in brief periods of human thought and represents a small minority dissent.[38] The count would be even more decisive if we were to sort out the genuine skeptics from those who were merely anticlerical, not anti-God, in their thought. Voltaire was such a person. He opposed the Church, but not faith in God. And many critics of religion are not opposed to some kind of transcendental faith, but are motivated chiefly by distaste for the pretentions of churchmen whom they think threaten human dignity and freedom. In fact, they are often clearer spokesmen for faith than their more anxious clerical opponents.

The development of religion makes sense on our hypothesis. Its course, as I pointed out in Chapter 3, has been toward an object of faith that could withstand the demands of true ultimacy. Thus the religious leadership of mankind has progressively rejected polytheism and magic and the worship of natural forces or ethnic groupings; it has sought out an Ultimate which stands above all this. This dialectical process is far from over, but its direction seems clear enough. And all attempts to hearken back to more primitive notions prove to be untenable.

A skeptical hypothesis can make nothing of this progressive development, since all religion, even that of the saints, must be interpreted, on these grounds, as having the same rootage in mere illusion.

Perhaps the most persistent alternative to our view of religion is not that of the total skeptics but of the altruistic humanists. My doubts on this point are as follows: First of all, mankind is not a proper focus of absolute religious commitment. Man is a proper object of loving concern but a poor symbol of Ultimate Reality. This should be clear to an age which has seen mass slaughter and torture on the largest scale in history—often in the name of humanity. Second, if it be objected that the humanist only devotes himself to man at his ideal best, some solid account must be given of the notion of "ideal best," which is not merely human opinion. Ideals, to be standards of human aspiration must, in short, be established in something above man, in some ideal order that "man at his best" discovers and submits to. But if we amend humanism in this way—as I believe all the most impressive humanists—like Julian Huxley, John Herman Randall, Melvin Rader, John Dewey, and others—really do—then humanism gives way to a belief in the trans-human, and is on its way to at least partial agreement with the theistic hypothesis.

Humanism is a plausible view only in the context of opposition to some religious tradition that has fallen into need of reform. It operates well in such a context. But in the context of total skepticism, most of its ideal content falls into question along with the rest of religious faith. I have already suggested that the idealism of an Albert Camus is an untenable middle ground between faith and skepticism. The same can be said even of Sartre who puts his skeptical existentialism forward as a "humanism."[39] Sartre's attempts to defend the ideal ethic of responsible freedom accord very poorly with his view of man as a "useless passion" and as a "hole" in being. I suspect that the ethical vigor of his defense of freedom and rationality is a hangover from faith in an order of ideal values which he has formally rejected. The criminal degenerate Genêt seems to be a more logical fruit of Sartre's own premises, and there is little in Genêt's own writing of the noble defense of responsible freedom which Sartre has made his chief theme.

### Theism Gives the Most Coherent Account of Man's Noetic Experiences

We have discussed some of these noetic experiences in the chapter on psychology and religion. I refer to the following: the experience of responsible freedom, moral obligation, and love; the experience of reason; the experience of beauty; the struggle against alienation of all kinds—guilt, loneliness, and selfishness; and the experience of creativity.

Theism says that man in his experience of responsible freedom is in dialogue with the freedom-giving eternal Spirit. "For freedom," writes St. Paul, "Christ has set us free."[40] Only in the experience of freedom can man rise to his true humanity. Moral obligation is not a bond but a claim which man learns throughout his life and responds to freely when he is at his best. It is not a prison, but a form of freedom itself, the freedom to become fully human in fellowship with other human beings. Morality at its best merges into a universal good will, into a concrete expression of love for one's fellow human beings.

It is hard to see how any coherent account of these qualities of man at his best can be given apart from theistic premises. As mere wishes of man, moral claims lose their characteristic quality and fall into a class with all the other wishes of mankind, good and bad. For Bertrand Russell to say that the moral demand not to kill means merely his own wish, "Would that men did not kill!" is to reduce its authority to the same level as Hitler's wish that all the Jews were dead.

These same objections obtain against the ideal of reason. Unless reason somehow appeals to a "truth" which is above man and his desires, individual or collective, the workings of the human mind become mere rationalizations, and truth itself is lost sight of. From a theistic point of view, reason is human participation in the universal Logos, which expresses itself through all things. It is a partial grasp of the order that lies at the base of existence. The search for truth in all its forms becomes one with the noblest pursuits of man. And this search, we believe, alike animates science, art, and the quest for social justice.

Beauty is in the same case. Skeptical views can only regard beauty as a kind of pleasure no different in value than, say, the grossest sensual enjoyments. The theistic view that beauty is part of the divine nature best accounts for its ineluctable lure to men in all ages. It makes the most sense of the high value men have rightly placed on the search for, and appreciation of, beauty in all its manifestations.

If theism is true, man's long struggle against all forms of alienation—guilt, loneliness, selfishness, and so on—makes good sense. The struggle against alienation is the converse of the struggle for true communion. Man's dissatisfaction with himself as separate or hostile, his longing to become united substantially to himself, his fellows, with nature, and with all the ideal powers that he glimpses in his moments of illumination, is all meaningful if his source is God and if his destiny is Holy Love.

On skeptical grounds this struggle makes no sense. Man should be satisfied with himself or, at the very least, should employ drugs or some other purely material means of quieting his unpleasant feelings of guilt or failure. True skepticism should logically express itself in a colossal self-satisfaction and disregard of all typically human problems. The fact that skeptics do not assume this posture suggests that despite themselves they witness to the claims of an ultimacy beyond themselves.

Creativity is an essential element in human life at its best. But this is because we sense intuitively the wonder and nobility of the creative quest grounded in the Creator himself. On skeptical grounds creativity can be nothing more than mere change. It should have no more value than a venture into the novel and unexpected. Unless creativity in science and art, for example, is a discovery of new truth and beauty, wherein does its value lie, or from whence would its power over the human spirit derive?

If space permitted, this analysis could be made more detailed, but the point is always the same: The typically human doesn't make sense except on transcendental grounds.

### Theism Makes the Most Sense of Man

All we have just written applies to this point as well, that theism makes the most sense of man. However, we want to appeal here to the appearance on the human scene of man at his best—the great saints, sages, and wise men—and of man at his worst—the degenerates, criminals, and fools. It is the ambiguity of man that theism notes: his capacity for rising to the heights of sublimity and his power to drift into the depths of degeneration. Theism recognizes all the nobility of man sensed by the humanists and all the evil of man noted by his critics. It sees man standing between unthinking nature and God, made for communion with his Creator but free to choose a more degrading fate. Theism says that man, both in his successes and his failures, is himself the witness to something more than himself.

### Theism Makes the Most Sense of Nature

Nature is the seedbed of man and history. On theistic grounds it is the creation from which springs all life and which supports with its potencies every human aspiration toward divinity. As the great Jesuit paleontologist Pierre Teilhard de Chardin says, "By his respect for the spiritual powers still latent in matter, the Christian may often bear a striking resemblance to the worshippers of the earth."[41] Teilhard's own vision of the earth, seen from the perspective of his Catholic faith, revealed nature as "bathed inwardly in light."[42] Such, says theism, would be man's normal perception of nature if men were not blinded by their skepticism or false worship of nature herself, or, perhaps, by some wrong religion. It may be that a misinterpretation of theism as an enemy of nature, a viewpoint found in many theologians who should have known better, has favored atheistic naturalism's rise in Christian civilization.

Evolution is a case in point. From a theistic perspective, informed by science and aware of its biblical origins, nature is unfinished, "groaning," as St. Paul says, in its pregnancy with the future "sons of God." Creation is unfinished and in a state of "yet to be."

To Teilhard, this all seemed so clear that he distinguished men of no faith from men of faith, not by their formal protests of belief but by observing whether they feared or welcomed the developing future of nature and history. In this, I believe, he stands firmly on the solid premises of faith in a God of Holy Love.

Turning to a nontheistic view of nature, one finds it difficult not to be amazed at the contradictions between the descriptions of nature and attitudes toward nature. I cannot catalogue all the possibilities, but in general the discrepancies lie in the fact that nature is most often described in scientific terms as wholly mindless and purposeless, and then is praised for giving rise by "emergence" (a name for sheer miracle!) to all the forms of life and mind, and somehow supporting all the highest ideals of altruistic humanism. Again I must sadly note that those who look upon nature as vain and even nauseating seem more logical than those who turn away from God to the earth in hope of finding a better deity.

### Theism Makes the Most Sense of History

Theism says that the Creator is also Lord of History. For this reason, the rich texture of historical reality makes, from His view, a growing pattern: Each culture and epoch, in its unique relationship to eternity, conspires toward even greater possibilities to come. Faith sees in the twentieth century with all its agonizing struggles and terrifying powers the movement of men and nations toward a God-inspired future. This is not a humanistic faith in automatic progress, for men possess, as we have seen, an essential freedom to reject the meaning of their lives. However, the Eternal is still Lord and governs history in his own way. The Apostle Paul expressed the goals in the symbolism of the Gospel: "He destined us in love to be his sons" and "He has made known to us . . . the mystery of his will . . . to unite all things in him, things in heaven and things on earth."[43]

There is not space to consider alternative, nontheistic philosophies of history. But in general they must necessarily fail to find in the forces of nature sufficient grounds for their view, or, alternatively, they must take such a dim view of man's historical possibilities that they deliver man to complete cynicism about the future. Moreover, under the guidance of such views, the nature of the forces governing history is misconstrued, and men are constrained by absurd philosophies to commit atrocities.

## Theism Makes the Most Sense of the Struggles of Men Who Resist Theism

Theism understands the struggles of men who reject God for whatever reason. It makes clear why such rejection is bound to result in personal agony and social suffering. It also illuminates the true significance of the critic of faith who speaks more clearly for God than the churches when the latter have become calloused defenders of privilege or ignorance. Thus, certainly, in many countries, the atheistic communist is best understood as an unwitting servant of justice and right wherever the Church has been content to silence free thought and to ignore the cries of the oppressed.

In the case of Marxism, surely, such idealism fades as soon as its adherents become doctrinaire materialists and believers in unlimited violence against their fellow human beings. This is only to say that the idealism of social revolution springs not from atheistic sources but from the inner voice of conscience, which often speaks most eloquently among the disinherited. Its true meaning is the transcendent Truth which cannot be stifled, either by limited philosophies or by the obtuseness of official religion.

In this chapter I have tried to state the case for theism, first existentially, then objectively. It is obvious that the issues raised deserve a much more extended treatment. But I believe that the main lines of the discussion are sound. The principal argument is simply that theistic faith makes the most sense of human life, and of all the partial coherencies that have been noted in alternative views.

One large question still remains to be discussed: the problem of evil. It is my belief that theism makes the most sense of evil, but because in the history of skeptical thought evil has been looked upon as the chief argument against faith, I have set aside the next chapter in which to consider it more fully.

## SUGGESTIONS FOR FURTHER READING

Many works appropriate to this part of the study have already been suggested in previous parts of this section. Peter Bertocci's *Introduction to the Philosophy of Religion* (Prentice-Hall, 1951) is an excellent introduction from a liberal and nonanalytic point of view. Willem Zuurdeeg's *An Analytical Philosophy of Religion* (Abingdon, 1958) is a postliberal, analytical, and valuable contribution.

Roger Hazelton's *On Proving God* (Harper & Row, 1952) is a balanced account of the problems of theistic logic. John Hick's *Faith and Knowledge* (Cornell University Press, 1957) examines the same subject from the perspective of analytical philosophy. William Ernest Hocking's *Meaning of God in Human Experience* (Yale University Press, 1912) is a classic not to be neglected, especially since many of his arguments have a markedly modern tone. The late John Baillie's Gifford Lectures, *The Sense of the Presence of God* (Yale University Press, 1912; Scribner, 1962) is a fitting conclusion to his distinguished scholarship in the field of religious knowledge.

Three excellent books of readings, among others, are John Hick's *The Existence of God* (Collier, Crowell-Collier, 1964); Hicks, ed., *Classical and Contemporary Readings in the Philosophy of Religion* (Prentice-Hall, 1964); and Geddes MacGregor and John Wesley Robb's *Readings in Religious Philosophy* (Houghton Mifflin, 1962).

For the classical arguments, see Jacques Maritain, *Approaches to God* (Harper & Row, 1954). On the more empirical side, Peter Bertocci's *Empirical Arguments for the Existence of God in Late British Thought* (Harvard University Press, 1938) is an excellent summary. Lawrence J. Henderson's *Fitness of the Environment* (Macmillan, 1913) is an extended treatment of the teleological argument. Gerald Heard's *Is God Evident?* (Harper & Row, 1948) gives this argument a more modern turn. In this form it is very persuasive.

Hocking's *The Meaning of God in Human Experience* is oriented almost completely toward the ontological argument, as is the work of Charles Hartshorne. W. Reese and Hartshorne have treated this historically in a large work *Philosophers Speak of God* (University of Chicago Press, 1953; Phoenix Book, 1963). I think that John Baillie is best on the moral argument in *The Sense of the Presence of God*. His argument also bears on the significance of religious experience as well. See W. T. Stace, *The Teachings of the Mystics* (New American Library, 1960) and W. R. Inge, *Christian Mysticism* (Meridian, World Publishing, 1956) for the meaning of mystical experience. Rudolf Otto's *The Idea of the Holy* (Oxford University Press, 1943) must be mentioned here again.

On the logic of metaphysical systems, see S. W. Pepper's *World Hypotheses* (University of California Press, 1961) for a positive appraisal; John Hick's *Philosophy of Religion* (Prentice-Hall, 1963) for a negative one.

The skeptical arguments have never been better put than in David Hume's *Dialogues Concerning Natural Religion* (Hafner, 1953) and J. S. Mill's three essays on religion: *Nature* and *Utility of Religion* (Liberal Arts, Bobbs-Merrill, 1958) and *Theism* (Liberal Arts, Bobbs-Merrill, 1957), though these have enjoyed some logical refinements at the hands of contemporary analytical philosophers. See Hick's *The Existence of God* for some of these.

A new journal of philosophical theology shows promise of importance: *Religious Studies*, edited by Professor H. D. Lewis (Cambridge University Press); the first number appeared in October, 1965.

## NOTES

1. Quoted in H. Richard Niebuhr, *Radical Monotheism and Western* *Culture* (Harper & Row, 1961), p. 119.

2. In Norman Malcolm, *Ludwig Wittgenstein, A Memoir*, (Oxford University Press, 1958; paperback, 1962), p. 71.

3. Arthur Koestler, *The Invisible Writing* (Macmillan, 1954), p. 15.

4. Arthur Koestler, *Arrow in the Blue* (Collins with Hamish Hamilton, 1952), p. 230.

5. Matthew 7:7.

6. Jeremiah 29:13–14 (Goodspeed-Smith, trans.).

7. Psalm 139:1.

8. Psalm 139:7–10.

9. T. S. Eliot, *Four Quartets* (Harcourt, Brace & World, 1943), p. 27.

10. Nikhilananda, trans. and ed., *The Gospel of Sri Ramakrishna* (Ramakrishna-Vivekananda Center, 1942), p. 14.

11. William James, *Varieties of Religious Experience* (Longmans, 1928), pp. 60–61.

12. *Ibid.*, p. 61.

13. Jeremiah 29:12.

14. In *I and Thou* (T. Clark, 1937; Scribner, 1958).

15. Plato, *Meno*, 80.

16. *Ibid.*, 86.

17. This is Paul Tillich's analysis in *The Courage to Be* (Yale University Press, 1952), chap. 6.

18. Hebrews 11:1.

19. Erich Frank, *Philosophical Understanding and Religious Truth* (Oxford University Press, 1945), p. 116.

20. I John 3:14.

21. *Time*, July 30, 1951.

22. Jacques Maritain, *Approaches to God* (Harper & Row, 1954), pp. 4–5.

23. For a brief account of these classical arguments, see *ibid*.

24. F. R. Tennant, *Philosophical Theology* (Macmillan, 1928–1930), 2 vols., and Peter A. Bertocci, *Introduction to the Philosophy of Religion* (Prentice-Hall, 1951).

25. Norman Malcolm, "Anselm's Ontological Argument," in John Hick, ed., *The Existence of God* (Collier, Crowell-Collier, 1964), p. 50.

26. Quoted in John Hutchison, *Faith, Reason, and Existence* (Oxford University Press, 1956), p. 150.

27. John Hick, *Philosophy of Religion* (Prentice-Hall, 1963), p. 98.

28. Hastings Rashdall, "The Moral Argument for the Existence of God" in John Hick, ed., *Classical and Contemporary Readings in the Philosophy of Religion* (Prentice-Hall, 1964), p. 268.

29. *Ibid.*, p. 269.

30. M. C. D'Arcy, *No Silent God* (Harper & Row, 1962), pp. 44–45.

31. This is the substance of his argument in John Baillie, *The Sense of the Presence of God* (Yale University Press, 1912; Scribner's, 1962).

32. John Wisdom, "Gods" in Hick, ed., *Classical and Contemporary Readings* p. 413.

33. *Ibid.*

34. *Ibid.*, p. 417.

35. *Ibid.*, p. 421.

36. *Ibid.*

37. Quoted in John Herman Randall, Jr., *Making of the Modern Mind*, rev. ed. (Houghton-Mifflin, 1940), p. 296.

38. For study of the sociological

periods in which various philosophies have been popular, see P. A.
Sorokin, *Crisis of Our Age* (Dutton, 1945), chaps. 3 and 4.

39.  Jean-Paul Sartre, *Existentialism*
(Philosophical Library, 1947).

40.  Galatians 5:1.

41.  Pierre Teilhard de Chardin; *Le
Milieu Divin* (Fontana, Collins,
1964), pp. 118–119.

42.  *Ibid.*, p. 118.

43.  Ephesians 1:9–10.

# 25

# The Problem of Evil

❖❖❖❖❖❖❖❖❖❖❖❖❖❖❖❖❖❖❖❖❖❖❖❖❖❖❖❖❖❖❖❖

Despite the fact that the presence of evil in the world has been regarded as the chief evidence against theism, we are going to examine in this chapter the thesis that (1) the presence of evil is consistent with the existence of a God of Holy Love, and, beyond that, it is (2) one of the chief grounds of religious faith.

The problem has nowhere been more clearly stated than in the words of the Greek philosopher Epicurus (342?–270 B.C.) quoted by the modern skeptic David Hume: "Is he [God] willing to prevent evil, but not able? then is he impotent. Is he able, but not willing? then is he malevolent. Is he both able and willing? whence then is evil?"[1]

The attempt to solve this problem, to "justify," as Milton says, "the ways of God to man," has been called "theodicy" since the philosopher Leibniz gave it the name early in the eighteenth century (in his work *Theódicí,* 1710). But despite profound discussions of the problem since ancient times, there has arisen an uneasiness in modern thought about the way in which the question has been posed. It parallels the modern concern over the question of the so-called existence of God which I discussed in the last chapter, and it may be disposed of in much the same way. To begin, let us consider a distinction which Gabriel Marcel introduced several decades ago in his essay "On the Ontological Mystery,"[2] the distinction between "problem" and "mystery."

## THE DIFFERENCE BETWEEN "PROBLEM" AND "MYSTERY"

"Problems" arise in the context of a world of mere functions, a world in which every part is clearly demarked as a "thing" or "object" in relation to other things, much as the parts of a machine are related to one another. When the machine goes wrong a problem arises which, given the proper technique, can be tracked down and solved. Evil as a problem is thus the question, Why does the machine run so badly? Which of its parts are out of order?

A "mystery," Marcel tells us, "is a problem which encroaches upon its own data, invading them, as it were, and thereby transcending itself as a simple problem."[3] His meaning becomes clear when he applies the concept of mystery to the question of evil. "In reflecting upon evil," he writes, "I tend, almost inevitably, to regard it as a disorder which I view from the outside and of which I seek to discover the causes or secret aims. Why is it that the mechanism functions so defectively?" It finally comes to this: "The evil which is only stated or observed is no longer evil which is suffered: in fact, it ceases to be evil."[4]

This is a subtle point and perhaps needs to be restated: Looked upon with detachment evil is simply a puzzle, and as such is not evil but only a technical disorder. But the evil that is truly evil is that which I experience through personal involvement, something I suffer, even when it apparently touches only others. This is evil as a mystery. As mystery it is no longer merely problem, because I cannot any longer "solve" it by technical or rational means. I can only somehow respond to it with either hope or despair, faith or cynicism, love or indifference. And this response, involving as it does my entire being, remains to the very end as mysterious as my whole existence and the ground of being from which it springs. For now I must somehow take into account the Power that thrusts me forward despite my suffering into hope, or (if I react faithlessly) that seems to leave me forlorn and abandoned in my despair.

If these distinctions are valid, then we must distinguish between dealing with evil as a problem and as a mystery. The existential treatment of evil as mystery is the more fundamental and puts the question in the right way. But there is also some secondary value in dealing with the question in objective terms as a problem. This secondary value springs in part from the fact that even when stated objectively the inquiry may have existential results—affecting, that is, the living stance of the person who considers it. Also, we may defend this secondary inquiry not because the case for theism stands or falls on these technical grounds, but on the grounds that theism (or any other world view) has some obligation to put itself forward as a reasonable hypothesis about human existence.

## Evil as a "Problem"

The poet MacLeish, in his play *J.B.*, states the problem cryptically:

> *If God is God He is not good,*
> *If God is good He is not God.*[5]

We may as well accept at the outset the fact that this problem cannot be solved. It can, however, be clarified in such a way that its negative force is mitigated. This must not be done by hedging the problem, or by appealing at the outset to paradoxes. If the question is easily answered, it was too lightly asked. And, as Professor Aiken has reminded us, "If you make up a self-contradictory sentence, it won't miraculously become sense just because you have put the word 'God' as its subject."[6] And he points out quite correctly "that obscurity and obfuscation do not suddenly become edifying when transposed into a theological key."[7]

## The Biblical Drama of Job

The book of Job was written in response to the problem and mystery of evil. Job, a righteous man, suddenly finds himself bereft of all his worldly goods, his many children, and, at last, his health and reputation. Lying on an ash heap scraping his sores with a broken potsherd, he cried, "Man wastes away like a rotten thing, like a garment that is moth-eaten."[8] He fills the air with his complaint: "Man that is born of woman is of few days, and full of trouble."[9] He calls upon God to appear and justify himself, to show why he, an innocent man, should suffer such pangs.

Three friends visit him in his adversity and some are eloquent with explanations of his difficulties. They mouth the prevailing theology of the time: Job must have secretly sinned, and these disasters are God's righteous retribution.

> *Think now, who that was innocent ever perished?*
> *Or where were the upright cut off?*
> *As I have seen, those who plow iniquity*
> *and sow trouble reap the same.*[10]

But the author of the book insists that Job had not sinned, either openly or secretly. The fact is that the innocent do suffer. MacLeish, in his modern drama of Job, puts it this way:

> *Millions and millions of mankind*
> *Burned, crushed, broken, mutilated,*
> *Slaughtered, and for what? For thinking!*
> *For walking round the world in the wrong*
> *Skin, the wrong-shaped noses, eyelids:*

> *Sleeping the wrong night in the wrong city—*
> *London, Dresden, Hiroshima.*[11]

He sums it up saying:

> *Job is everywhere we go,*
> *His children dead, his work for nothing,*
> *Counting his losses, scraping his boils,*
> *Discussing himself with his friends and physicians,*
> *Questioning everything—the times, the stars*
> *His own soul, God's providence.*[12]

The optimism of the nineteenth century misled our predecessors into understating the problem. They thought of evil as a brief disorder of the cosmic machine that progress would soon make right. Our time is more disposed to recognize the deep tragedy of existence, and the universal panorama of suffering. The catastrophes of the twentieth century came as abrupt awakenings to the believers in easy solutions. Our time is an age of deep anguish over the appalling disintegration of human life. It is this fact that animates much of our best contemporary literature.

If we cannot, then, dispense with this problem lightly, can we nonetheless reach a "clarified cosmic optimism," as Hartshorne says, by putting it in a perspective that makes it less incoherent, while at the same time retaining a deep sensitivity to its anguish? It is this task which I wish to undertake.

## WHAT ARE THE CONDITIONS FOR
## A GOOD WORLD?

If we can answer this question in such a way as to show that evil is a likely if not necessary ingredient in a good world, we will have in some small measure mitigated or at least delimited the region of the problem. What are the conditions for a good world which, taken together, seem to involve at least the possibility of evil? I believe that any reasonable list would include the following: finitude, order, freedom, growth, suffering and real danger, sensitivity, human solidarity, and a world capable of improvement.

*Finitude.* A world, any world, by definition must be finite in contrast to the infinity of God. This means that the things and creatures in it are limited in a variety of ways. But such limits mean that things are bounded by other things, and people are bounded by other people and things together. These limits, inherent in finitude, may lead to conflicts. Ignorance, a form of man's limitation, for example, may lead to illness or death. Cities may be built on geological faults and collapse in an earthquake, or unknown viruses may sweep away whole populations, as in the case of the Black Plague. Conditioned existence thus opens up the possibility of an indefinite number of ills to which flesh is heir. Even God's omnipotent goodness could not alter this fact.

*Order.* A good world must also possess some impersonal structure. In our world reliable structure is involved with almost all the good we can experience. By it we develop rational powers in the study of nature, and by cooperating with it we attain all the benefits of science and technology. Order is likewise necessary to the moral life. Moral existence requires that acts have consistent consequences.

But of course this very order will at the same time lead to some suffering. As F. R. Tennant says in his *Philosophical Theology*, if water is to play its beneficent role in nature, we cannot be rid of its power to drown us. And this goes for all the other aspects of the physical order as well. To be sure, the order of the world might be different; but any world, to be a good world, would have to possess the properties of predictable structure.

*Freedom.* Order and finitude would not necessarily lead to suffering if there were not also the admixture of freedom. Men could be so designed that they automatically avoided conflict with things and other people—but they would then be automatons, mere machines, not persons. The possibility of personality, love, creativity, truth, and the divine-human dialogue itself depends upon freedom. Thomas Henry Huxley once wrote: "If some great Power would agreed to make me think always what is true and do what is right on condition of being turned into a sort of clock, I should instantly close with the bargain."[13] But surely he is wrong to think that either thought or conduct would possess the quality of truth or moral merit under such conditions. Mere human machines would lack all the properties that men have come to regard as spiritual. Truth as a human value requires the struggle with error, and morality implies a struggle with the possibilities of doing evil.

Freedom implies also the possibility of a profound turning in upon one's self in egoistic preoccupation, a turn which compounds all our human problems. In fact, it is the Christian claim that this inversion of human interest is the meaning of sin, with all its terrifying consequences. The Buddha, treating the same problem, saw it as the source of the illusions that foster all the deepest suffering that befalls the human race. But all these consequences are worth the risk of the goodness that can follow upon a right use of freedom. Viktor Frankl, who suffered the horrors of Auschwitz and Buchenwald, once said he would rather live in a world that can produce a Hitler or an Ann Frank than in a world or nation of pure conformity.

*Growth.* Free finite beings must grow from ignorance to knowledge, and from unawareness of themselves and their responsibilities into moral beings. In the process of that growth there lie the possibilities of many failures. Full-fledged wholeness of personality cannot be created without antecedents, even by an omnipotent God. When we are moved by pity to spare a creature the struggles involved in growth, we often act cruelly rather than wisely. The child must learn some things for himself. A grade-school class watching a butterfly struggling to free itself from the cocoon discovered this truth when they snipped the last strands which bound it. As a result of their intended kindness the creature never flew, for the desperate struggle if completed would have served to unfold its beautiful wings.

*Suffering and Real Danger.* A world in which life enjoyed unbroken pleasure without risks would not produce the highest forms of human existence. In this sense suffering and real danger seem to be requirements of the best possible world. Aldous Huxley's *Brave New World* is an imaginative account of a world in which no appetite remained unsatisfied for long, and where every necessary human action was conditioned to take place without pain or forethought. As his story unfolds it becomes clear to the reader that this is not paradise, as we are wont to think of it, but hell; not a hell of suffering, but of the complete absence of all the higher qualities of human existence. The savage who blunders into this paradise of pleasure at last rebels: "I don't want comfort, comfort. I want God, I want poetry, I want real danger, I want freedom, I want goodness, I want sin." "In fact," said Mustapha Mond (the "Controller" of the society), "you're claiming the right to be unhappy." "All right, then," said the savage defiantly, "I'm claiming the right to be unhappy."[14]

*Sensitivity.* A great deal of suffering stems from the extraordinary sensitivity of the human organism and spirit. But the sensitivity that sustains an exquisite enjoyment of beauty and depth of response to the whole environment is also a sensitivity that can yield an anguish of torment. The hand by which we can enjoy the texture of ivory will also produce unbearable pangs if it is crushed in a machine. The spirit that can respond to the widest ranges of human experience is likewise liable to suffer with the whole reality to which it responds. If men were duller they would suffer less, but they would also feel less, and consequently be less.

*Human Solidarity.* If love is the ultimate meaning of human existence, then the indissoluble connections between human beings will invariably broadcast throughout the whole web of life messages of pain and suffering as well as joy and well-being. If God had made each human atom separate and isolated from his fellows, men would have been spared much suffering, but they would also have been deprived of the depths of fellowship in which lie the ultimate meaning of human blessedness. Even Omnipotence cannot spare the innocent from suffering with the guilty if love is an ultimate goal. If sons quarrel, the father may spare them personal injury by permanently separating them, but he will also thus prevent their knowing one another as brothers.

*A World Capable of Improvement.* The theist claim is that the world exists in order that free moral beings may grow toward their fullness in free response to the environment. A good world must thus be capable of improvement. If the critic discovers evils in existence, this is just what the theist would expect. A finished world would not be a good world. A far higher level of goodness is attainable only through an open world, in which development through choice and suffering is possible.

If these eight conditions for a good world are considered together, a great deal of the suffering of humanity can be understood as necessary to a Holy God's creation of the world. But a further fact needs to be added: God's own participation in it. Holy Love cannot be passive to the world's need, and the world, to be truly good, needs the presence of its Creator, not as a spectator letting mankind suffer what is needful to fulfill His purposes, but as a co-sufferer, a full participant.

## THE MEANING OF GOD'S GOODNESS AND POWER

The problem of evil can be further mitigated by examining what could be meant by God's "goodness" and "omnipotence." Both these concepts are ambiguous in Epicurus' statement of the problem of evil with which the chapter began.

The concept of an omnipotence which can do anything whatsoever is meaningless. Omnipotence means possessing all the power there is, not some abstract ability to do anything at all. Can God make a weight so heavy that he cannot lift it? Can Holy Love act with rashness or ill will? Can an unlimited power create a finite world that lacks all the characteristics of finitude? As Thomas Aquinas says, "Nothing which implies contradiction falls under the omnipotence of God." Such questions are merely verbal.

Moreover, the meaning of God's omnipotence must be considered in the light of God's nature. Such power is a concrete idea, not an abstraction. The power of Holy Love is not an external or mechanical power such as we obtain by abstraction from the concepts of physics. The omnipotence of Holy Love lies in the fact that this love works supremely within all the elements of creation under the conditions of God's own being as Holy Love. This is the meaning of asking, as we have done, the conditions of a truly good world.

The same analysis applies to the concept of perfect goodness. The meaning of perfection is Holy Love. The happiness which God wills for the world is not a hedonistic paradise like the animal bliss of Huxley's *Brave New World*, but a holy happiness, a blessedness of human fulfillment. We are tempted to think that God's goodness would put an end to earthquakes or wars, but this, I have tried to point out, would be not true goodness but mere senti-mentality.

*Weatherhead's Suggestions.* During the Second World War, when men were naturally asking about the evils that were so tragically apparent, the English clergyman Leslie Weatherhead spoke to their concerns in his little book entitled *The Will of God.*[15] We can use his suggestions as a summary of what we have been saying. God's will, he said, can be considered under three headings: (1) the *intentional* will of God, (2) the *circumstantial* will of God, and (3) the *ultimate* will of God.

The crucifixion of Jesus is a prime example. It was not God's intention that

Jesus be crucified. God's intention was that men should follow Jesus, not crucify him. God's intention in each situation is for the good. Why, then, such crucifixions? The answer is that the cross was the will of God *under those circumstances*. The circumstances were the fruit of evil, but a refusal to allow the crucifixion would have been an even greater evil. But God's will reaches beyond what he can accomplish in a given circumstance. He wills that ultimately his holy will shall be done. We don't know how he will accomplish this end, we only know that he will do it through his Sovereign Holy Love.

We can thus say that God always intends goodness, but that under certain circumstances he permits a limited evil in order that his ultimate will may be done.

### Other Mitigating Considerations

*Animal Suffering.* There are other considerations that further mitigate the problem of evil. The first concerns the problem of so-called "natural evil." Moral evil, we can see, might be needful at least as a possibility for a good world. But how about the pain and suffering of the subhuman creation? Biological evolution, for example, has vastly extended the panorama of wastefulness and suffering in the animal world. In its early stages, evolutionary theory painted nature "red in tooth and claw," clearly inconsistent with Sovereign Holy Love.

Several remarks need to be made in reply. First of all, this picture of nature as filled with violence and rapine is no longer an accurate picture of nature. It came about through preoccupation with a crude notion of "survival of the fittest." But the fittest, it now turns out, were not necessarily the most violent.[16] Sensitivity, intelligence, and social cooperation are more important. Indeed, the most violent species have long since perished. Modern tigers, for example, are far less capable of violence than their saber-toothed ancestors. The mastodons and their massive contemporaries are known only through their skeletal remains. The winners in the evolutionary "struggle" are the descendants of a small, unarmed creature whose curiosity exceeded its craftiness.

Second, the image of a massive totality of world-pain in the animal creation is the product of human sentimentality. Pain is always suffered by an individual organism, not by a species. It is not cumulative. It never exceeds the limits of what can be suffered by one individual.

Moreover, we must not project the sensibilities of man onto the subhuman world. There is reason to believe that pain varies with the degree of awareness. If this is so, the insects, for example, must be thought of as operating in a kind of somnambulism, not much different from condition of a human being under anesthetic. Wasps, for example, have been observed quietly feeding after their abdomens have been removed.

As the conditions for healthy existence diminish with shortage of food or excessive cold, there is an apparent decrease of sensibility that makes the result much less painful than we should imagine were we ourselves in the same situation.

Most animals are healthy; they could not survive otherwise. They respond to their instinctual drives quite freely within a supportive environment. They must therefore be counted as "happy" within the meaning of that term which is applicable to them. Death usually comes swiftly as soon as they are weakened through disease or age. And in this contest with their natural enemies we must not suppose the kind of awareness that anticipates suffering or death and thus increases its significance.

These considerations must not be misused to diminish human respect for the feelings of the animal world. Nor do I wish to imply that suffering is wholly absent. Sensibility brings suffering, and the higher the species, no doubt the more it is capable of pain. But these facts need to be considered in the context that we have suggested, not romanticized, as though every creature experienced the world as we do.

A third element needs to be introduced even though it is more speculative; namely, the probability that freedom and its necessary counterpart, feeling, are never wholly absent in the world, even at the level of so-called nonliving matter. Alfred North Whitehead, in opposition to the mechanistic world view of classical physics, proposed a view of the world as alive and responsive.[17] "Dead facts" are, in his opinion, abstractions. If this is so, God's governance of the natural world contests with the mystery of freedom and the consequences of choice, even among the atoms. If this is true—and Whitehead has made an impressive case for it—it would certainly be consistent with the nature of a living God of holy love, and would explain in part some of the disorder that manifests itself even in the framework of nonliving nature.

*The Ontological Priority of Goodness.* In both the natural and moral world another fact prevails that tends to mitigate the problem of evil: the parasitic nature of evil. It is said that a good test of whether a man is a pessimist or an optimist is to ask whether a black-and-white checkerboard is "black on white" or "white on black." Theism says that this world is black on white. The good is prior to the bad.

Evil cannot exist without the good. Sickness depends upon health; amputation or blindness is deprivation of a good; theft and dishonesty depend upon honest acquisition; even crimes cannot be planned without cooperation and rational thought; and lies are not believed unless they are thought to be true. Murder, rape, and destruction all presuppose a good world to be plundered or destroyed. Even the cynic cannot propose his views without presupposing the power of reason, a faithful medium of communication, and an audience to take it seriously.

Pure evil is without power to exist by itself. The nearest one comes to pure evil is what Kant called the "radical evil" of an ill will. But the power of such a will is itself an affirmation of existence: it depends upon being for its own being. All this is not to say that evil is not evil, but only that its presence is dependent, that it feeds upon the good.

*Sovereign Love Has Time To Deal with Evil.*  Our estimate of the cosmic situation is necessarily affected by our limited view from this particular moment in time. Theism holds that the problem of evil is easier to bear when we reflect that Sovereign Love has both the time and the power to transmute evil into good. Many a pain of childhood becomes meaningful with maturity. The present pangs of creation, like the pangs of childbirth, become more than bearable when we consider that the future is in the hands of Holy Love, who, as Whitehead declared, can best be conceived under the image of a "tender care that nothing be lost."

Immortality and the Kingdom of God are two symbols of the theist's faith in a future in which the sufferings of the past and present will be understood and accepted because they will have been transmuted into the goodness which God intends. In the words of St. Paul, "I consider that the sufferings of this present time are not worth comparing with the glory that is to be revealed to us."[18] With this hope even the sting of death is removed.

## CONCLUSIONS ON EVIL AS A PROBLEM

In the light of these considerations, may we say that the problem has been solved? That would be saying too much. The most we can say for a rational hypothesis is that it may be true. The idea of Holy Love is not inherently incompatible with the evils of existence. But whether the world is really the work of Holy Love cannot be proved from an inspection of the world around us. John Hick has stated the case correctly: "We cannot tell from within the world, during the brief period of observation afforded by a man's life on this earth, or indeed by scrutinizing the entire scroll of recorded history, whether this earthly scene is a 'vale of soul making' or a 'fortuitous concourse of atoms.' All that we can say is that in spite of the antitheistic evidence [the presence of evil] the religious claim may nevertheless be true."[19]

But the very tentativeness of this conclusion is consistent with theistic faith, for it still leaves the tension between evil and goodness which is necessary for the highest human life—the life of courageous suffering and overcoming love. It prevents that easy judgment on human ills that might cut the nerve of our struggle against them as God wills that struggle.

### Evil as a "Mystery"

We have considered evil in a somewhat detached way as a problem. But we began by seeing that this way of treating the matter inherently distorts it, for the evil that does not touch us is not really evil. To come to real grips with evil we must examine it existentially—that is, as something that involves us.

This requires that we restate the whole question. Let us consider three ways of doing this.

*Three Ways of Putting the Question Existentially.* In Dostoevsky's *Brothers Karamazov*, Ivan tells the following story to his brother Aloysha. An arrogant general who owned hundreds of hunting dogs, one day heard that a serf boy, a little child of eight, had thrown a stone in play and hurt the paw of the general's favorite hound. The boy was immediately taken from his parents and locked up all night. Dostoevsky continues the story as follows: "Early that morning the general comes out on horseback, with the hounds, his dependents, dog-boys, and huntsmen, all mounted around him in full hunting parade. The servants are summoned for their edification, and in front of them all stands the mother of the child. The child is brought from the lock-up. It's a gloomy, cold, foggy autumn day, a capital day for hunting. The general orders the child to be undressed; the child is stripped naked. He shivers, numb with terror, not daring to cry. . . . 'Make him run,' commands the general. 'Run! run!' shout the dog-boys. The boy runs. . . . 'At him!' yells the general, and he sets the whole pack of hounds on the child. The hounds catch him, and tear him to pieces before his mother's eyes!"[20]

Ivan then says to his brother, "Imagine that you are creating a fabric of human destiny with the object of making men happy in the end . . . but that it was essential to torture to death one tiny creature [as this boy was tortured] . . . would you consent to be the architect on these conditions?"

The saintly Aloysha's reply was, "No, I wouldn't consent."[21]

In the face of tragedy—when we are personally responsive to it—most of our rational explanations pale into insignificance.

A second way of asking the question is suggested by Job. On the existential level he asked not why the world contained so much evil, but why he was born to suffer?

> *Let the day perish wherein I was born,*
>  *and the night which said,*
>   *'a man-child is conceived.'*
> *Let that day be darkness!*
>  *May God above not seek it,*
>   *nor light shine upon it.*
>
> *Why did I not die at birth,*
>  *come forth from the womb and expire?*[22]

The question of evil may be put this way: What degree of suffering would make me choose never to have been born? At what point would I curse my own existence and the natural powers that brought me forth?

A third way of asking the question is suggested by a parable of the Oxford philosopher Basil Mitchell: "A member of the resistance movement in an occupied country meets a stranger who deeply impresses him as being truthful and trustworthy, and who claims to be the resistance leader. He urges the partisan to have faith in him whatever may happen. Sometimes the stranger is seen apparently aiding the resistance and sometimes apparently collaborating with the enemy. But the partisan continues in trust. He admits that on the face of it some of the stranger's actions conflict with this trust. However, he has faith, even though at times his faith is sorely tried, that there is a satisfactory explanation of the stranger's ambiguous behavior."[23]

The question now takes this form: At what point in your experience of the evils of existence are you prepared to abandon faith and take on an attitude of cynical rejection?

These three ways of stating the existential question of evil are of course interrelated, but they have the merit of appealing to personal decision and faith rather than intellectual probabilities. Intellectual probabilities may help at times to lighten the burden of faith, but ultimately the issue becomes personal, and each man has then to decide whether it is "black on white" or "white on black," whether the goodness of a Holy Love is at the heart of things or not. And this calls not for intellectual conclusions so much as life-orientation.

### Faith's Answer to These Three Questions

Would you have made the world with its suffering? Aloysha says that he would not. But God has done so; therefore the only conceivable response of the faithful man is that he must remain faithful before the mystery of a goodness which must be vastly greater than any good or evil that he knows.

I may feel like cursing my existence, as Job felt at the outset of his suffering, but since God has brought me into being and providentially allowed me to come to this pass, therefore I must accept my existence and drink the cup of anguish to the full.

I may be tempted to lose faith in God's governance of the world when I see the evil in it, but the saints remind me that I am inclined to give up too soon. When Julia de Beausobre was tortured for six months in Lubianka prison she kept recollecting that Love was coming to her in the unlikely form of her tormentors. At what point could she say, I have passed the point at which I can any longer understand these experiences as permitted by Holy Love, and will therefore turn from loving to hating? Her persistence beyond all reasonable limits of anguish permitted her final glimpses of the Presence of God, even in such a demonic place.[24]

In each of these answers the challenge of incomprehensible evil leads to greater faith. And in each case the faith that does not weaken in the face of evil is the kind we admire most, because, since it has been stripped of all self-interest, it strikes us as the most authentic. Any man can through his own strength remain confident in the face of reasonable rebuffs, but when that strength has been far surpassed, only faith can sustain him.

## The Answer of Job

Job called upon God to appear and give an account of his governance of the world; to explain—in our terms—the problem of evil. The cosmos of his pain seemed to bear no mark of God's Presence:

> Behold, I go forward, but he is not there;
>     and backward, but I cannot perceive him;
> On the left hand I seek him, but I
>     cannot behold him;
> I turn to the right hand, but I
>     cannot see him.
>
> I am hemmed in by darkness,
>     and thick darkness covers my face.[25]

When God finally speaks out of the whirlwind, he offers no such explanation as Job demands. Job is confronted first by the impenetrable mystery of things—the vastness, opaqueness, and majesty of the creation. He realizes that they are indeed beyond his comprehension—even if some explanation were offered for them. But MacLeish is wrong when he says that God merely overawes Job: "Throwing the whole creation at him! Throwing the Glory and the Power."[26] In the face of this confrontation Job confesses that he has asked for an explanation which he could not have grasped. The mystery of existence is in its nature only fathomable to the Eternal Spirit from which it springs. Human reason, admirable as it is for so many tasks, is here completely beyond its depth.

But God does not leave Job with the mystery of things; he offers the mystery of his own Presence in, with, and through them. Nature in herself is immeasurably fascinating, wonderful enough to embrace with all her enigmatic pains; but with God himself now evident, Job can cry: "I had heard of thee by the hearing of the ear, but now my eye sees thee; . . . I know that . . . no purpose of thine can be thwarted."[27]

This conclusion, however, depends upon Job's faithfulness in affliction. During the darkness he must love the God who is absent, remaining faithful though deprived of light. Existentially, suffering is thus a test, not a problem. Not that God sends evils to test us—that, we know, is not God's way. But when the evils come, they provide the test in which life is purified and brought to its noblest form of being. Simone Weil explains: "Affliction makes God appear to be absent for a time, more absent than a dead man, more absent than light in the utter darkness of a cell. A kind of horror submerges the whole soul. During this absence there is nothing to love. What is terrible is that if, in this darkness where there is nothing to love, the soul ceases to love, God's absence becomes final. The soul has to go on loving in the emptiness, or at least to go on wanting to love, though it may only be with an infinitesi-

mal part of itself. Then, one day, God will come to show himself to this soul
and reveal the beauty of the world to it, as in the case of Job. But if the soul
stops loving it falls, even in this life, into something almost equivalent to
hell."[28]

### The Answer of the Cross

In the cross of Christ the story of Job is renewed in greater depth. There is
the affliction, the darkness, and the sense of separation; but there is the
Presence again—not as a vast brooding mystery, but as a participant in the affliction. This is the crucifixion as men of faith see it; not the martyrdom of a
good man, but God's own sharing in the pangs of his creation. It is the symbol
of God himself passing through the depths of suffering in his own world,
assuring men that "All shall be well, and all manner of thing shall be
well."[29] Or, as Weil says, "This infinite distance between God and God, this
supreme tearing apart, this agony beyond all others, this marvel of love, is the
crucifixion."[30]

When evil is thus perceived as a mystery—an evil in which one participates—when it is persevered in with love, a man will, as Simone Weil says,
"hear this note from the lowest depths into which affliction has thrust
him."[31]

### Wrong Answers

Sometimes these responses of faith are confused with wrong answers. Job's
comforters thought that the answer was simple: All suffering is the consequence of sin. This enabled them to assume the intolerable position of
standing in judgment on their fellow man, pointing out his sins in the midst
of his anguish. In so doing they merely compounded the evil. When God
appears to Job these false comforters are condemned for their false vision.

In Albert Camus's novel *The Plague*, Father Paneloux enters the pulpit and
explains to the suffering population that the plague has come upon Oran as a
judgment for its sins. "Calamity has come upon you, my brethren, and, my
brethren, you deserve it. . . ."[32] "For plague," he goes on, "is the flail of God
and the world His threshing-floor, and implacably He will thresh out His
harvest until the wheat is separated from the chaff."[33]

As the plague continues and many more perish indiscriminately, Paneloux
is confronted with the death of an innocent child. In a second sermon, a
noteworthy change becomes evident. Detached meditation on the problem of
suffering has given away to personal participation. "Instead of saying 'you' he
now said 'we.' "[34] Mindful of the innocent child's sufferings, he abandons all
rational explanations, and, like Aloysha, cries, . . . "who would dare to assert that eternal happiness can compensate for a single moment's human
suffering?"[35] Paneloux points out that this plague is a time of testing beyond

rational human powers, in which men are forced either to cynicism or faith: "We must believe everything or deny everything."[36] But ultimately, as Paneloux sees, believing is not the real issue. The issue is between remaining or fleeing. To believe really means to remain. "My brothers," he says, "each one of us must be the one who stays!"[37]

If the law of divine retribution is a false answer, so is the widely held view that suffering and evil are somehow illusory. The trouble with this view is that it demands that we abandon the only light we have in affliction: that something is dreadfully wrong, which must somehow be set right. The salutary thing about suffering is that it gives a very solid sense of reality, beside which the world of comfortable pleasure is very nearly illusion. A man in comfort may dream, but a man in anguish knows with his whole being the terrible certainty of his own existence and the reality of the world that oppresses him. "I suffer, therefore I am" is much more convincing than Descartes's "I think. . . ." Illusion is an answer that takes away the good with the evil, and leaves man with mere emptiness.

## HOW SUFFERING REVEALS GOD

Suffering reveals the inadequacy of the world. One might think from reading the literature of theodicy that religion springs from the satisfactoriness of experience. Nothing could be further from the case. All the historic faiths, and all deep personal faith, spring from a realization of the inadequacy of the world.

Camus is right when he has Dr. Rieux, the humanist who has led the fight against the plague in Oran, say, "Until my dying day I shall refuse to love a scheme of things in which children are put to torture."[38] He is right in realizing that one cannot worship the order of nature. But he is wrong in assuming that this precludes faith in God. For the religious consciousness springs from the realization that it is just this unfinished and unsatisfactory nature of the world that gives man his clearest sense of God. Suffering and evil purify man of self-love and illusion, destroying all finite idols that would present themselves for his worship. It makes atheists of us in the sense that it destroys all our idols, all our images of God as a factor in nature, or as the world of nature itself. But for true faith such atheism is salutary. For God is not the "scheme of things" at all. As Simone Weil writes, "Religion, insofar as it is a source of consolation, is a hindrance to true faith: in this sense atheism is a purification."[39]

To be sure, God may be thought of as the Creator, or Gound of this world, but the world is not the measure of God; rather, He is the world's measure. Faith arises as the affirmation of this fact. In the phrases of the ontological argument, "God is the being than which no greater can be thought." Certainly we can "conceive" of a being greater than the world—Rieux's outcry is proof of that.

Camus's mistake, then, is to turn from faith in a "scheme of things" to faith in man, in sympathy for fellow sufferers, and in the courage that fights plagues without hope of ever finally overcoming them. This is also MacLeish's recourse in *J.B.* "Blow on the coal of the heart," whispers Sarah, J.B.'s wife, as she returns to him in his suffering,

> *Blow on the coal of the heart.*
> *The candles in churches are out.*
> *The lights have gone out in the sky.*
> *Blow on the coal of the heart*
> *And we'll see by and by. . . .*[40]

But this is merely to return to one of those discredited features of the world—the presumption of human constancy. If the light of existence has really gone out—if evil has done its terrible and salutary work of disillusionment—how can one turn sentimentally to the fragmentary and inconstant human love that we know is so infected by selfishness and fear?

Camus thinks that somehow, in an absurd world, this little piece of it which we call humanity can be trusted. But this is a forlorn and incoherent faith. Or perhaps we should say that it is a spark of the fire of true faith that Camus was great enough to hold on to. His celebrated remark, that in the midst of winter he found in his heart an eternal spring, suggests that this might have been the case, even though he did not recognize it as part of any official religion.

Russell, Freud, and Marx give another version of this humanism when they say that religious faith is merely a form of compensation for the failures of life: "pie in the sky" to make up for the humble pie that is human fare here. While this may be true of much childish religion—which, incidentally, suffering purges away—it is not true of the faith of the saints. "Let me suffer or die" is their bench mark. The faith of the saints is a response to a constant and holy love that steadies them in their suffering and makes them realize the "faith that overcomes the world"; that is, a response to a sovereign and holy love that burns more brightly in adversity and brings a true standard for judging man and the world.

Suffering reveals God in another way: Only through faith do we properly see and judge the evil of the world. To know that the world contains evil is to hold on to a standard that can judge the world. We could, to be sure, know that pain is unpleasant without such a standard. But we could not pass the judgment on existence which Camus's Dr. Rieux does without implying a truth about goodness that surpasses humanism.

What we mean is simply this: The question of evil cannot be raised without having a standard of goodness by which to judge existence. To say that Hitler was evil in torturing and murdering six million Jews is already an affirmation of judgment on the world. Such a standard cannot be simply a protest against personal pain. It must imply a rule that is beyond personal and social subjectivism in all its forms, a rule that says, not Would that I did not suffer, but Evil ought not to be! If there is no such standard, then all the wailing of the human race against suffering is merely a scientific fact of no particular importance. It certainly cannot be employed to stand in judgment upon existence, as Camus does. What it comes to is this: The very recognition of evil as evil requires a transcendental standard to make it a valid recognition. The whole force of naturalism has been to diminish the meaning of the ethical to "pleasure" or "self-interest" in one of its many forms. But when one has embraced such naturalistic views, the very standard by which evil is known as evil is broken.

It is the saints who perceive the great tragedy of evil in the world, because they have retained hold of the one valid measure of that evil—the violation of Holy Love in all its forms. This is the paradox of remaining faithful amidst suffering—that if one abandons faith because of evil, evil no longer can be perceived as evil. We can say that Russell, Freud, Marx, and all others who abandon theism on account of evil must always fail to understand the true meaning of evil, because they must understand it somehow in the wrong context.

Another paradox of evil is that it reveals the God who is with us in the suffering. The world of comfortable men does not see God, nor do they want to see him—the only God there is, a God of holy, suffering love. They dread the loss of their comforts, but they pay the price for them—illusion. Jesus says that those who will see Reality will be those who mourn, who are humble in heart, who know their need, whose hearts have been purified of all double-seeing and who look singlemindedly toward God.[41] Such are men purged by suffering. But the Gospel says more than that. It says that in suffering men become aware of the Presence who suffers with them, a divine Companion who is, as Mauriac says, "our brother covered with wounds." Faith, in this deep sense, springs out of the cleansing fire of personal failure—not out of success. And yet——

As in our discussion of the knowledge of God, we have come not to a reasonable hypothesis, but to an existential faith, a faith that makes betrayal or unfaithfulness to God on account of suffering an unthinkable alternative. It is thus that life claims those who understand their life orientation, their ultimate concern, as directed toward a sovereign, creative, and holy love. This is the life of faith, hope, and love, to which we shall turn in our next section.

## SUGGESTIONS FOR FURTHER READING

One of the clearest statements of the problem of evil occurs in C. E. M. Joad, *God and Evil* (Harper & Row, 1943), written during the horrors of World War II. It is interesting because he finally concludes that none of the proposed solutions is logically workable; he nonetheless comes to a positive theistic conclusion, a fact that supports my contention that a profound consideration of the problem of evil may lead to faith. In his classic work *The Meaning of God in Human Experience* (Yale University Press, 1912), William Ernest Hocking, in his own unique way, also argues that a proper understanding of the evil in the world leads to a theistic conclusion. A fine little book from the point of view of faith is Nels F. S. Ferré's *Evil and the Christian Faith* (Harper & Row, 1947). Another is Nelson Pike's *God and Evil* (Prentice-Hall, 1965).

Julia de Beausobre's *Woman that Could Not Die* (Gollancz, n.d.) is a personal view of evil by one who suffered it with faith. The writings of Simone Weil (recommended in Chapter 24) show this same profound grasp of the meaning of suffering.

Literature is full of questions about the evil in existence. See especially, Dostoevsky's *Brothers Karamazov* (Modern Library, 1937); Archibald MacLeish's play *J. B.* (Houghton Mifflin, 1958); Albert Camus' *The Fall* (Vintage, Random House, 1956); and many of Kafka's stories—see *Selected Short Stories of Franz Kafka* (Modern Library, 1952).

## NOTES

1. David Hume, *Dialogues Concerning Natural Religion* (Hafner, 1953), p. 66.

2. Gabriel Marcel, "On the Ontological Mystery" in *The Philosophy of Existence* (Philosophical Library, 1949), chap. 1.

3. *Ibid.*, p. 8.

4. *Ibid.*, p. 9.

5. Archibald Macleish, *J. B.* (Houghton Mifflin, 1958), p. 11.

6. Henry David Aiken, *Reason and Conduct* (Knopf, 1962), p. 172.

7. *Ibid.*

8. Job 13:28.

9. Job 14:1.

10. Job 4:7–8.

11. MacLeish, *op. cit.*, p. 12.

12. *Ibid.*, p. 13.

13. Quoted in Harris Franklin Rall, *Christianity* (Scribner, 1940), p. 329.

14. *Ibid.*, p. 323.

15. Leslie Weatherhead, *The Will of God* (Abingdon, 1944), chap. 1.

16. See Gerald Heard, *Is God Evident?* (Harper & Row, 1948), chaps. 3 and 4.

17. In his *Science and the Modern World* and *Modes of Thought.*

18. Romans 8:18.

19. John Hick, *Faith and Knowledge* (Cornell University Press, 1957), p. 18.

20. Dostoevsky, *The Brothers Karamazov* (Modern Library, 1937), p. 288.

21. *Ibid.*, p. 291.

22. Job 3:3, 4, 11.

23. As related in John Hick, *Philosophy of Religion* (Prentice-Hall, 1963), p. 99.

24. For her remarkable story, see Julia de Beausobre, *The Woman that Could Not Die* (Gollancz, n.d.).

25. Job 23:8–9, 17.

26. MacLeish, *op. cit.*, p. 136.

27. Job 42:5, 2.

28. Simone Weil, *Waiting for God*

(Capricorn, Putnam, 1951), p. 121.

29. The words of Lady Juliana of Norwich, a late medieval English mystic.

30. Weil, *op. cit.*, pp. 123–124.

31. *Ibid.*, p. 124.

32. Albert Camus, *The Plague* (Modern Library, 1948), pp. 86–87.

33. *Ibid.*, p. 87.

34. *Ibid.*, p. 200.

35. *Ibid.*, p. 202.

36. *Ibid.*

37. *Ibid.*, p. 205.

38. *Ibid.*, p. 197.

39. Simone Weil, *Gravity and Grace,* Arthur Wills, trans. (Putnam, 1952), p. 168.

40. MacLeish, *op. cit.*, p. 153.

41. Matthew 5:3–8.

## PART SEVEN

# THE
# RELIGIOUS MEANING
# OF BEING HUMAN

# 26

# *The Need for Roots*

We have traveled a long and devious route in this study of religion, despite the fact that the treatment of many subjects has been necessarily sketchy and that many others have been ignored altogether. One thing should be clear by now: religion is a human concern which extends vertically and horizontally into every dimension of human existence. This leads to the thesis that I want to develop in this section: The religious life, in the best sense, is a way of being fully human. By this I mean that to be religious is not some special way of existing reserved for certain people, but the way to essential human existence as such. It arises out of the character of our being human and speaks to that condition.

It does this by answering to three fundamental human needs[1]: the need for roots, the need for hope, and the need for communion. Man cannot live well on the surface of life, in a purely horizontal dimension. He has need for roots, a sense of drawing his power of being from some depth that cannot be exhausted by the demands of living. As a time-bound being he also cannot help but live his life toward the future—a time containing all the possibilities of pain and promise. A future without a profound basis in hope immeasurably diminishes human existence to mere prudent calculations, and excludes the zest of creative adventure without which a man does not fulfill himself.

But the most fundamental human need is for communion. If he cannot say *Thou* to the universe which surrounds him, if he finds himself limited in a selfish preoccupation with his own needs, he is of all men the most to be pitied. Man is made for communion—a kinship with all being, which he senses in the beauty of the world and in companionship with everything that lives. It is my contention that the fulfillment of these needs—for roots, for hope, and for communion—is to be found in religion at its best. In this chapter we will be concerned with the first. In the West the concept that has been most directly related to the need for roots is faith. Faith suggests in all our enterprises of thought and action the haunting sense of some background or depth beyond our immediate attention and beyond the power of our logic to clarify perfectly.

## SOME MEANINGS OF FAITH

Unfortunately, faith does not always invoke the sense of depth. In academic circles it is often a "snarl" word, evoking the image of a person opposed to reason, evidence, and free inquiry, a closed-minded dogmatist who sits in constant judgment upon "unbelievers." I want to rescue this word, if possible, from such unfortunate connotations. Let us start by examining this word and its synonyms in ordinary usage.

*Examples of Usage.* (1) I believe that this liquid is acid. (2) I believe that we could increase production by buying new machines. (3) I have faith that men can reach the moon. (4) I have faith that democracy is better than fascism. (4) I trust you. (5) I trust my doctor's treatment of my case. (6) I place my faith in medicine. (7) I place my faith in mankind. (8) Jesus said, "You believe in God, believe also in me." (9) Jesus said, "Have faith, with God all things are possible."

It should be obvious that the meanings of "believe" and "trust" or "faith" vary considerably in these examples. Keeping them in mind let us see if we can sort out some of these meanings.

*Faith as Rational Hypothesis Guiding Inquiry.* In both scientific and practical rational action, faith often means simply an educated guess that is used to guide experimentation. Such a guess outruns present evidence, but it is kept responsible to what is already known and functions as a means for extending knowledge.

*Faith as a Value Judgment.* When we say, "Democracy is better than totalitarianism," we are expressing a confidence in the values which we believe inhere in the democratic way of life. We could not prove this point decisively, but we may believe it nevertheless. And we would insist that it is not an unreasonable conviction.

*Faith as Confidence in a Right Course of Action.* This usage combines the two foregoing uses. "Right course" in this case means both a judgment about the probable course of future events, and about the value of those events. Again we cannot prove this future, but we may count on it, and act in the light of our estimate of it.

*Faith as Trust.* Here we begin to verge on a more religious use of the word. If we trust a person we have faith in him beyond any provable limit. Our faith is an estimate of another person which leads us into a particular kind of relationship to him. This is close to our meaning when we say, "In God we trust." Trust, though it contains rational elements, is predominantly intuitive and volitional, and involves risk.

The difference between trust in a human person and trust in God is that the latter involves a total or full personal response. This response is not appropriate toward fallible human beings—one of the reasons, incidentally, why humanism is an inadequate faith. It is also doubtful that religious trust can be placed in an impersonal principle. "A principle, " writes Marcel, "in so far as it is a mere abstract affirmation, can make no demands upon me because it owes the whole of its reality to the act whereby I sanction or proclaim it."[2] In fact, he goes on to say, "It might be a sacred duty for me to deny a principle from which life has withdrawn and which I know that I no longer accept, for by continuing to conform my actions to it, it is myself— myself as presence—that I betray."[3] Marcel's meaning here seems to be that faith is only appropriate toward a reality that is concrete and thus not an abstraction, toward a being which is more "present"—that is, more "personal"—than I am. This leaves open the question of whether Ultimate Reality is personal, but it closes the door to faith in the merely impersonal.

*Faith as a Dialectic of Commitment and Possession by Reality.* This point defies simple statement, for to express it we must say two things at the same time: First, that faith is the completely personal act of courageous commitment; and, second, that faith is a state of being gripped by the Reality which evokes the commitment. Since the commitment we are talking about is religious—that is, total—commitment, it could be properly evoked only by a reality to which commitment can be freely and fittingly given. Commitment or faith in this sense was expressed by the humanist who answered the question, "Why do you work for human freedom?" with the reply, "I do what I *must* do!" In this case, an alternative way of living is unthinkable.

*Faith as Total Life Orientation.* Using a phrase of Heidegger's, we may say that faith is one's way of "being-in-the-world." But men are in the world in a way that is radically different from the way things are in the world. Things are simply there. Man must choose his way of being there. This choice is his life orientation, and it is also his way of being human in a particular way.

Man is not born human, nor is his humanity fixed in his genes. He does not have a given nature such as, say, a dog or bird. His nature is in the process of coming to him through his choices, loyalties, and commitments. It is thus through faith that man's being is communicated to him. The Apostle Paul believed that his being was coming to him in its fullness as he committed himself to the Holy Love which carried him forward to an end he could not fully foresee. In the dialectical sense indicated above, faith is man's participation in his own making as man.

Henri Bergson seems to be saying something of this sort when he distinguishes between two kinds of religion.[4] One kind of religion is rigid and fixed. The other kind is an extension of the evolutionary process—a movement toward unseen, though felt, goals. Religion in this latter sense has a prophetic quality about it. The prophets felt the inner tide of events, the movement of history, the will of God. They felt borne along on the deepest current of being—in a phrase of the poet Edward Field, "Knowing, if not the place, the way there."

William James put this another way when he announced his faith in the hidden and insignificant things, much as St. Paul lived by "seeing the invisible." "I am done with great things and big things, great institutions and big successes," James wrote. "I am for those tiny invisible molecular moral forces that work from individual to individual: creeping in through the crannies of the world like so many soft rootlets or like the capillary oozing of water, but which, given the time, will rend the hardest monuments of man's pride."

Faith in this sense is a life hypothesis confirmed only in living. But it is more than that: It is a deep awareness of the fitness of that hypothesis beyond any collection of evidence one could marshal.

The question is sometimes asked, Why cannot men fabricate faiths in accordance with their own tastes? The answer is that unfortunately they do—and are led on to illusions of all kinds. But if faith is a genuine response to Reality, then the content of faith will not be an arbitrary invention of men, but a reflection of some profound dimension of Reality itself.

In a celebrated phrase, Paul Tillich describes faith as the "courage to be."[5] This courage means standing forth as oneself with the deep sense that in so doing one is authentically expressing the ground of being which is working in and through him. It means the affirmation of authentic human existence amid all the temptations to get lost in mere triviality or distraction. "Courage" is a good word, for it conveys the element of total risk which faith involves, and from which no human being can be absolved.

## SOME QUESTIONS ABOUT FAITH

Misuses of the word faith have given it a bad reputation. Russell thinks that faith is merely "believing upon insufficient evidence." But he has only the logic of the sciences in mind, as though man could live his whole life scientifically. To him, belief in God is like believing in Zeus, a wholly unprovable and unlikely story, and therefore to be eschewed by reasonable men. By now, we should be able to see that this is a complete misunderstanding of the issues of faith.

Believing things that are unsubstantiated by evidence can be personally unfortunate, and if we combine passion with such belief we get fanaticism. Fanaticism has been so often regarded as the meaning of faith—or at least its natural consequence—that it will be worth while to contrast faith and fanaticism.

## Faith and Fanaticism

This can be fairly brief, for to treat this item at length would be to re-traverse all that I have said so far. Faith and fanaticism are as far apart as Gandhi and the Hindu partisan who assassinated him; Abraham Lincoln and John Wilkes Booth; Voltaire and Robespierre; Martin Luther King, Jr. and Birmingham's Bull Conner.

The man of faith and the fanatic look alike superficially. Each has a certain assurance, high purposiveness, a powerful sense of direction, a disdain of opposition, and a willingness to suffer for the cause. But there are deep differences. The fanatic refuses all criticism or dialogue. He cannot stand doubt of any kind. He feels he has the truth—all of it—and is in need of no new data or new growth. He is satisfied with himself. His ears are shut, and his mouth is open. The man of mature faith welcomes critical examination and frank dialogue with his critics. He carries his doubts along with his faith. He seeks new truth, new data. He is open, wondering, waiting for the fullness he seeks. He is ready to witness to his faith, but he is also ready to listen.

The fanatic's chief tools are hate and destruction. He is willing to lie or destroy for the cause with slight provocation. His strategy is to divide and conquer his enemies, whom he sees all about him in a corrupt world. The man of faith employs chiefly the tools of love and truth. This calls to mind two phrases used by St. Paul when he advised new Christians: "Speaking the truth through love" and "faith working through love." Faith seeks wholeness and a completed fellowship, everything united in God.

Fanaticism seeks quick solutions, is easily impatient and exasperated. Faith is able to endure tension, to wait, to let the field grow to the harvest. The fanatic is fixed in some distorted image of the past. He hates the present and wants to turn back the clock. The man of faith is confident of the future; he accepts change; he moves into the future, which he feels has a deep continuity with the best of the past.

Perhaps the greatest difference is this: The fanatic is a broken man, an unsure man, who hates himself. Basically, he is afraid to stand alone. He has no real sense of personal worth. He is forced therefore to pretend a confidence he doesn't have. In this pretense he acts out of deep compulsions that he does not understand and cannot control. He projects onto the world all the unhappiness and pain he feels within himself. The man of faith is also a broken man in the sense that he does not put his trust in himself. But he knows a Reality which can be trusted and which can make something of him and of his world. He has a source of reliance unknown to the fanatic, which if known to him would transform him into a man of faith. As Karl Barth says, "Faith is the possibility which belongs to men in God, in God Himself, and only in God, when all human possibilities have been exhausted."[6] The man of faith knows the meaning of guilt and anxiety, but he has transcended them in a larger life. The fanatic is too threatened to acknowledge his guilt and anxiety; he must therefore compulsively deny them and project his hostility upon the world in a passion of hate.

### Faith and Reason

A final question about faith is its relationship to reason. Fundamentally they are not opposed to one another, though superficially they may appear so. Paul Tillich distinguishes between "technical reason," which deals with the problems of science and practicality, and "reason in depth" or "ontological reason," which is reason in depth. Ontological reason acknowledges, in the words of Viktor Frankl, that "Logos is greater than logic," that there is a kind of coherence that runs through the realms of value and of life choices, and which, like the iceberg, is seven eighths submerged. The part that appears above the surface is usually thought to be the whole of reason. And this false identification is the source of all our difficulties with these subjects. The psychiatric patient who recovers uses reason, but not technical reason. The lover of beauty does likewise. He senses the fitness of his response to the loveliness that appears in his life.

Faith in this sense is a kind of reason—the reason of total personal involvement, the reason of participation. To be sure, as we have pointed out, the language of Logos is not the language of formal logic or of literal statements. It is the language of symbol and myth. However, it is not therefore merely subjective or personal. It reflects in its devious and metaphoric way the truth that cannot be caught in a formula. In the words of the poet:

> *Reason has moons,*
> > *But moons not hers*
> *Lie mirrored in her sea,*
> > *Confounding her astronomers*
> *But, oh, delighting me.*[7]

If we understand faith in this sense we can see the indissoluble link between faith and the knowledge of God. Faith as total, free, personal, and responsible participation in existence is the only way in which the encompassing Reality can become "known" to man. It is the fitting response to the continuing self-revelation of God through humble repentance and obedient trust.

## FAITH AND "THE FAITH"

Throughout this discussion we have been alternating between faith in the basic sense of the word and the particularity of a given faith—"the faith." Because faith is not an abstract affair it always eventuates in some concrete religion. As Martin Buber says in his definition of religion, it is the "covenant of the Absolute with the particular,—revelation in the 'lived concrete.'"[8]

This is, of course, the glory and power of religion—as distinct from, say, philosophy—and also the source of its many difficulties and scandals.

Sometimes the question is asked, Do we need an organized church? The answer is that ultimate concern is incomplete unless it is embodied concretely, and this entails an institution with all its limitations. Of course, no embodiment of a profound religion can be fully adequate, and the faithful must be forever searching for more adequate expressions of their deepest convictions. In the present age there is a great floating population that has never come to harbor in any given religion. They cruise about, freighted with a cargo of doubts, uncertainties, and half-formed beliefs. This is no doubt the penalty for the dynamic changes that are characteristic of modernity. But this free-floating state is not normative for religion. Such people, in spite of their sincerity and intellectual honesty, have almost all the disadvantages of faith with few of its advantages.

But to return to the concreteness of lived religion. It was pointed out earlier that this concreteness takes the form of organization (churches), specific forms of worship (cults), historical statements of belief (creeds), and particularized ways of living (codes). Let us briefly examine these as they manifest themselves in the major faith of Christendom.

## THE CHURCH

What is "the Church"? The answer seems simple enough to the layman, who will point perhaps to the building in which he and his neighbors worship. But the answer is much harder to come by. It is obvious to sensitive men of faith that institutional churches are not the Church; their relationship to the true Christian Church is oblique. Consider the following definitions, each one more concrete than the last: (1) The Church is the fellowship in time and eternity of all those who have turned toward the Reality which is the source and ground of all existence. (2) The Church is the fellowship through out history of those who have acknowledged the God of Holy Love as seen in Jesus Christ and witnessed to by the Holy Spirit. (3) The Church is the aggregate of those who are members or constituents of one of the historic Christian churches. The Church in the first two definitions is the invisible Church, known only to God. It is the Church as last defined that men ordinarily think of as "the Church."

But the Church in this third sense draws its religious meaning from the Church in the first two senses. Otherwise, it is merely one more human institution with all the ambiguities of human institutions. It is this that makes any single definition impossible. Ideally, the concrete Church should be a fellowship of faith rooted and grounded in God and turned out from itself in total love toward the whole world, as God himself is turned toward that world in love. This would be a grounded community, expressing itself concretely in its creative acts toward men and society. Fortunately, some such understanding of the Church is becoming more and more widely accepted among theologians of many denominations. As this becomes more widely accepted, churchmen are becoming more critical of the merely human features of their denominations, not the least of which is their tendency to divisiveness.

### The Problem of Church Unity

The most sensitive spirits in the Christian churches have long felt that divisiveness is its greatest scandal, for it betrays that compromise with human selfishness and preoccupation with local interests from which faith and love should liberate human beings. In the chapter on religion and society (15) we discussed the sociological forces that lead to division, and there is no reason to say more than to mention their relevance here. What we did not discuss there, however, is the great new movement toward unity in Christendom.

In the centuries since the sixteenth-century Protestant revolt, the churches have been splitting into very small splinter groups. Dr. Truman Douglass calls this the "denominational presupposition—the uncritical assumption that the denomination and its enterprises are the proper objects of ultimate loyalty."[9]

The twentieth century has seen a great reversal of this withdrawal into separateness. The "denominational presupposition" is everywhere under criticism. The ecumenical movement is the fruit of this criticism. "Ecumenical" is derived from the Greek word which means "of or from the whole inhabited world." Specifically it refers to the unity of the entire Christian Church. The following chart[10] shows the number of ecumenical events—church unions, joint conferences, and so on—that have taken place during twenty-year periods since the beginning of the nineteenth century. The increase is dramatic.

| Number of Events | Twenty-Year Periods |
| --- | --- |
| 8 | 1801–1820 |
| 9 | 1821–1840 |
| 21 | 1841–1860 |
| 31 | 1861–1880 |
| 34 | 1881–1900 |
| 124 | 1901–1920 |
| 142 | 1921–1940 |
| 174 | 1941–1960 |

The following list indicates the major mergers of denominations in recent times: 1925—United Church of Canada, formed by union of Methodists, Congregationalists, and Presbyterians; 1927—Church of Christ in China, formed by union of Presbyterians, Congregationalists, English Baptists, Methodists, Reformed, United Brethren, and the United Church of Canada; 1929—United Evangelical Church of the Philippines, formed from United Brethren, Congregational, and Presbyterian Churches; 1931—Congregational

Christian Churches merge; 1934—Evangelical and Reformed Church, formed from Evangelical Synod of North America and the Reformed Church of the United States; 1938—United Church of North India; the Reformed Church of France, formed from a union of the Free Evangelical Churches, the Methodist Church, the Reformed Evangelical Church, and the Reformed Church; 1939—The Methodist Church, formed by the union of the Methodist Episcopal Church, the Methodist Episcopal Church South, and the Methodist Protestant Church; 1946—The decision to continue the Church of Christ in Japan, which had been formed from all the Protestant groups which united under wartime pressure from the Japanese government; 1947—The Church of South India, organized by merger of the South India United Church, the Methodist Church, and four dioceses of the Church of India, Burma, and Ceylon; 1957—The United Church of Christ, formed by the Congregational–Christian Churches and the Evangelical and Reformed groups; 1961—the American Lutheran merger of several synods (which added four more synods in 1962). This listing will give some idea of how the old tendency toward schism has been reversed, and indicate that momentum is being gathered for a unified Church more representative of the spirit of Jesus.

On the world scene, the ecumenical spirit has expressed itself in interchurch gatherings on faith, order, and works. These conferences, beginning with the Edinburgh Conference in 1910, were consummated in 1948 with the formation of the World Council of Churches, which included the Protestant Episcopal and Eastern Orthodox branches of Christendom. The third assembly of this body met in New Delhi, India, in 1961; at that time the great body of Russian Orthodoxy was formally included.

### The Blake-Pike Proposals

In late 1960, in San Francisco, Eugene Carson Blake, then stated clerk of the General Assembly of the United Presbyterian Church in the U.S.A., spoke from the cathedral pulpit of the Right Reverend James Pike, Protestant Episcopal Bishop of California. With the Bishop's approval, Blake set forth certain proposals for union among Presbyterians, Episcopalians, Methodists, and the United Church of Christ. These proposals strike so close to the heart of Church unity problems on a wider scale that they are a good example of the kind of dialogue which may lead to unity.

The Blake-Pike proposals are based on the belief that the two most significant principles concerning the nature of the Christian Church today are, first, the Protestant principle of reform, and, second, the Catholic principle of the continuity of the historic Church. The reform principle emphasizes faith, Scripture, continuous leadership of the spirit, and freedom; catholicity holds to the solidarity and continuity of the church, the integrity of the historic clerical ordination, and the care of the sacraments.

Blake made proposals which he hoped would satisfy these two dimensions of the Christian Church. To satisfy the Catholic side he proposed the following: (1) Reestablishment of the historic connection of the clergy with the past by a great meeting of mutual reconsecration of the clergy. (2) A reaffirmation of the traditional creeds of Christendom. (3) A reaffirmation of the importance of the sacraments as more than simply symbols or memorials.

To satisfy the reform tradition he proposed the following: (1) A continuing reformation under the biblical Word of God through the guidance of the Holy Spirit. This means that Scripture and Spirit would stand in judgment on all historic tradition. The new emphasis would be Word and Sacrament. (2) A democratic church government. The historic episcopacy would be acknowledged, but the laity would be likewise recognized as ministers. Bishops would be simply pastors to pastors, not a special order of their own. The church would not be controlled hierarchically from the top down. (3) A church in which "the fellowship of all in the service of each" would be the rule. There would be no distinctions in the fellowship, no higher or lower. (4) Room would be made for a wide diversity of theological thought and worship. The "United Church" would not be a church of conformity, but of freedom. There would be room for both liturgy and evangelical witness.

It would misrepresent the situation to claim that these proposals were everywhere met with loud cheers, or that they will actually be used for concrete action by the Christian churches. The problem is too complex to expect a single set of proposals to dispel once and for all differences that took centuries to emerge and crystallize into institutional forms. But the Blake proposals have the merit of a wide imaginative vision, and they do treat most of the major problems that prevent a union of churches belonging to widely diverse traditions.

### Vatican II

Of utmost importance among the recent events of significance for the unity of Christian churches is the Second Vatican Ecumenical Council of the Roman Catholic Church, known as Vatican II.[11] For three years more than 2000 bishops from all over the Catholic world labored in Rome to bring substance to Pope John XXIII's hope for *aggiornamento* (updating) and spiritual renewal of the Catholic Church. John's purpose in calling the Council, according to one commentator, was "to make the ancient message of the Roman Church intelligible to the modern mind, to affect a reconciliation with all other Christian bodies, and to build bridges of mutual respect and cooperation with other groups of believers—Jews, Moslems, and the religions of the Far East."[12]

Though there is continuing debate as to the success of Vatican II, there is no question but that it represents the beginning of a new era in Roman Catholic life and thought. Doubts about the effect of the Council's work are chiefly related to the possibility of implementing its Declarations, most of which were adopted by an overwhelming majority of the bishops and cardinals in session. On the theoretical side, the achievements are impressive, if one considers the background against which they were worked out. Some of them were as follows: A decree of ecumenism which called for interfaith understanding and good will. Another of the same order held out a hand of fellowship to the Jews by absolving them of their traditional sole responsi- bility for the crucifixion of Christ. And a third established a commission on relationship with the non-Christian religions.

Other actions tended to support this movement toward some kind of unity with non-Catholics of all kinds. One of them was the declaration on freedom of religion. For the first time in its history, the Roman Catholic Church declared the right of all men to religious liberty and the iniquity of using state power to infringe the right of private conscience in religious matters. Free- dom was also declared for theologians and biblical scholars to work at the business of interpreting the ancient symbols of the Christian faith in modern terms and to use historical critical methods of biblical interpretation without prejudicing scholarly matters by dogmatic limitations.

But more important than any specific actions of the Council was the new spirit which Pope John engendered when he called it. This new spirit has turned the Roman Catholic Church outward toward the world in which it lives and works and invited fellowship with men of other faiths. When we remember that the Roman Catholic Church is by far the largest segment of the Christian family, such changes suggest a brighter future for the eventual unity of faith. This is not to say that such unity will take place within any foreseeable future, but it is a fact that the spirit of unity has been given a fresh new impetus at a time when it had already achieved considerable momentum outside Roman Catholic circles.

Another effect of the Council which does not directly bear upon the question of Church unity has been to make the world aware of the profound theological work and intense humanitarian interest that prevails in certain sectors of the Roman Catholic Church. This was made possible in part by the prominent place which was given for the first time to Protestant observers at the Council. At last non-Catholics heard of such men as Hans Kung, Karl Rahner, E. H. Schillebeeckx, and Augustin Cardinal Bea. Protestants were also stirred by the realization that the Roman Catholic Church was girding itself to speak to the major social problems of the age. Pope Paul VI's address to the United Nations (October, 1965) made clear that from the Christian perspective the whole human race and its welfare must be considered, that faith cannot be contained within the confines of ecclesiastical considerations.

Whether the promise of all these stirrings in the ancient Church of Rome will be fulfilled, only the long future can tell. It is certain, however, that the Roman Catholic Church has passed out of what could be called its post- Reformation phase into the modern era.

## THE MEANING AND WORTH OF WORSHIP

In the foregoing account we have seen how faith becomes "the faith" as it expresses itself in a concrete social institution, the church. A second way in which faith becomes "the faith" is its expression in a cultus, a way of worship. Men do not worship in general; they worship concretely in some particular way. The way of worship in Christendom is the accumulated heritage of three thousand years. Complete Christian worship consists of two interrelated parts: that part which was inherited from the Hebrew tradition of the Old Testament, and that which grew out of the New Testament community's experience of Jesus Christ and his gift of the Holy Spirit.

Lifelong members of the Christian churches often do not understand why they worship as they do. They do not understand that the standard Protestant service is a pattern that grew out of the Hebrew synagogue* service of the Old Testament community. The Jerusalem Temple service left little influence because of its final destruction in A.D. 70, and because the Jews of the Diaspora (those scattered through Europe after the Exile from the Holy Land) were both unfamiliar with it, and forbidden by their faith to duplicate its rites outside of Jerusalem.

The Protestant service, like its synagogue counterpart, is primarily a form of worship centered in the read and preached scriptural Word in a setting of praise and prayer. The final form of this worship evolved from a logic of its own. This service has four main movements. First, the invocation and praise of God, reminding the worshippers in whose Presence they are. Second, prayer, beginning with confession, appropriate to men who are aware of the holiness of God, and moving on to thanksgiving, petition, and intercession in response to His love. Third, the proclamation of the message of the Scriptures through readings from the Old and New Testaments and the sermon. Fourth, the humble, self-offering of the worshippers to God. These acts are interspersed with appropriate declarations of faith and songs of praise by either the congregation or choir or both. Nearly all Protestant services are variations on these themes.

Though this form of worship betrays its Christian character through the reading and preaching of the Gospel, the distinctively Christian contribution to liturgy appears most decisively in the Eucharist ("showing thanks"), which Roman and Anglican Catholics call the Mass, the Eastern Orthodox call the Divine Liturgy, and which Protestants refer to as the Lord's Supper, Holy Communion, or the Communion service. In the early Christian Church this service was added to the synagogue-based service in commemoration of the sacrifice of Christ. In the beginning, the sharing of the bread and wine, in emulation of Jesus' last supper with his disciples, was no doubt rather simple.

---

* Derived from the Greek word *synagoge*, meaning "assembly," or "a bringing together."

The basic elements of this service were: (1) The prayer of consecration, which normally contained the following elements: thanksgiving for creation, providence, and redemption; a memorial of the Lord's words and acts of institution; and a humble confession of faults and total self-offering of the worshiper preparatory to approaching the consecrated elements. (2) The breaking of the bread and pouring of the wine. (3) The communion—in which the worshipers and celebrants partake of the consecrated elements. (4) The dismissal with prayer. With the passage of time these features were elaborated and crystallized into the highly ritualized forms which we know today.

The fully developed Christian form of worship, then, is a Christianized synagogue service to which has been added a memorial of the sacrifice of Christ. Instead of the arbitrary collection of activities which laymen often think it to be, the Christian service of worship is thus a product of slow historical development based upon the Judaeo-Christian experience of God.

There is one more feature of Christian worship that is harder to define, the so-called free worship that characterized the history of spontaneous revivals and that is practiced today by many small sects. This form of worship is unstructured and often ecstatic in nature, sometimes expressing itself in the so-called speaking in tongues. Its Christian roots lie in the ecstatic communities of the early Church, such as the church at Corinth. If the Christianized synagogue service celebrates God the Father, and the Eucharist, God the Son, these free services celebrate God the Holy Spirit. We must keep in mind that these distinctions are for the purpose of analysis, and that all authentic Christian worship is trinitarian in nature; but it is interesting to see how historical differences can be traced to emphases upon different aspects of the Christian understanding of God.

### The Meaning of Worship

In its most generic sense, worship is the celebration of ultimate concern. It is a spontaneous and natural response to deity. In this sense worship is like a holiday or birthday party, in which a community or personal event is celebrated. Even these secular celebrations become stylized with feasting, dancing, singing, fireworks, or speech-making. Thus the institutional worship that we find in the churches is a stylized form of celebration.

But with religious as with secular celebrations, the meaning of the event determines what acts are appropriate. The worship of the God of sovereign, holy, creative love, revealed through the history of the Jews and culminating in Jesus Christ, will naturally draw many of its features from that sacred history. As in patriotic celebrations where tales of national glory are related, so in Christian worship, the stories of the past are retold and commented on. The very retelling runs the risk of boredom, but it has the advantage of the accumulated significance of the ages about it. It has an authority of its own.

Worship, not unnaturally, thus becomes celebration with specific prescribed elements.

But the telling of tales and the singing of songs is complemented by actions that are called sacraments. Sacraments are holy acts in which the worshiper and deity interact. The sacred food is not contemplated; it is eaten. The worshiper partakes of these sacred materials, praying that something of the life of God will become part of his own life. This is a natural extension of the acts of celebration in which meanings are danced or sung out until the worshiper feels them throughout his whole being. To take a quasi-secular example, Harold Taylor describes the end of a summer-long educational experiment with students of many different loyalties from many foreign countries. In a closing seminar, visiting American Negroes who had been working for civil rights invited them to sing "We Shall Overcome." Taylor comments on the effect as follows: "As the wide circle of young people from everywhere in the world, white and black, Asian and African, Western and Eastern, stood side by side with their teachers and their new American friends, singing 'We shall make a new world,' in a world's variety of voices and accents, all trace of cynicism, skepticism, and even self-consciousness vanished. At that moment each knew in his bones that to make a new world was possible."[13] Such is the effect of worship when it is fully enjoyed by its participants.

Worship thus makes vivid again the focus of commitment, makes the ideal seem within range of the possible, and unifies all dissonant personal and group elements around a central loyalty.

### The Meaning of Prayer

Prayer, like worship, is another form of religious concreteness. In the Judaeo-Christian tradition, prayer is primarily a colloquy of spirit to Spirit, in which the whole life of the creature is poured out before the Creator in humble openness and need. Because the God before whose face such prayer takes place is a God of Holy Love, mature prayer is readily transformed into intercession on behalf of the world's need. This may appear to the uninitiated as a kind of begging, but this is a gross misunderstanding. God already knows the needs of man, but man needs to express them in the presence of God. This is necessary for two reasons: First, man needs to see himself as he really is in the Presence of the final truth, and he can do this only by being fully there with all his specific human frailties. Second, God waits upon man's consent to pour out upon him the goodness that he intends. The relationship between God and man is not automatic; like gravity, it is a living interrelationship, and prayer is the most intimate expression of that fact.

Prayer takes many forms that we cannot discuss here. It may begin in words and pass on to meditation. From meditation it may become a wordless "being there" in the Presence. The mystics are our best guide to this last kind of prayer, which, unfortunately, is scarcely glimpsed by those who are totally preoccupied with words and forms. The saints are our best guide to the radical transformation into authentic humanity that takes place in men to whom God is a continuous Presence. Their power of expressing love vastly exceeds what seems "reasonable" to human beings still enclosed within their own calculating egocentricity.

## Creeds

We have yet to discuss one further way in which faith becomes concretely "the faith," namely, in creeds. At first glance, a creed seems to be a fixation of faith, a limitation that is almost contrary to the spirit of faith itself. If the function of creeds is misunderstood, this can, and often has been, the case. We have already discussed the flexible and experiential character of creeds in our treatment of some of the similarities between beliefs in science and in religion. It is not necessary to repeat those observations here.

One thing is worth noting, however, and that is that authentic faith eventually expresses itself concretely in symbolic form. The embodied character of human thought and existence makes this inevitable. Faith does not grow in the air; it feeds upon historical and communal roots, and climbs upon frail trellises of socially conditioned symbols. The Christian faith has from the beginning sought to express itself with varying degrees of adequacy in creeds. But with the changing circumstances of history these creeds have required restatement. Each restatement bears the marks of the time in which it was issued—the language, the current social and religious concerns, and the prevailing challenges to faith. But the restatements, insofar as they have been successful symbols of the substance of the faith, have served to lay its essential meaning bare. The early Christian community was satisfied with the affirmation "Jesus is Lord." But, without denying this, the Church had to go on to show in what way this Jesus was related to the God of creation and history, and to the continued presence of the Eternal in the worshiping community. The result was the so-called Apostles' Creed of a much later time. With the rise of new varieties of religious thought, the clarification had to continue, and in the fourth century (A.D. 325) the famous Nicene Creed was issued.

In our own day each time a union of two churches from different traditions is contemplated, the leaders of those communions search for a new way of stating the faith that will do justice to the meanings that have become precious to each of them. The challenge to Christendom today is to find a way of expressing the meaning of the Christian faith in such a way that it is adequate to the nearly a billion believers of all varieties of cultural and ecclesiastical experience—not some lowest common denominator, but the highest symbol around which they may all rally in loyalty to God. This multitude includes Catholics and Protestants; Orthodox, neo-orthodox, liberal, neo-liberal, and conservative; liturgical and nonliturgical; hierarchical and democratic; citizens of many cultures—East and West, rich and poor, civilized and primitive. Needless to say, an expression of their common faith cannot be discovered in an afternoon's committee work. Fortunately, there is a common substance that has become clearer with the passing centuries—a Center focused in God, Christ, and the Holy Spirit—but what these primordial symbols mean here and now is another matter. The search for adequate symbols is itself a work of faith making the highest demands upon the life and thought of men. It is likewise an expression of man's longing for a fuller and more human future, which belongs to the second great human need, hope. This is the topic of our next inquiry.

## SUGGESTIONS FOR FURTHER READING

Paul Tillich's *Dynamics of Faith* (Harper Torchbooks; Harper & Row, 1957) and his *Courage To Be* (Yale University Press, 1952) are fine accounts of the meaning of faith in the generic sense. See also the Rudolf Bultmann collection, already recommended, *Existence and Faith*, Schubert M. Ogden, trans. (Meridian, World Publishing). Henri Bergson, *Two Sources of Morality and Religion* (Holt, Rinehart and Winston, 1935; Anchor, Doubleday, 1954); Simone Weil, *Gravity and Grace*, Arthur Wills, trans. (Putnam, 1952); and Martin Buber, *I and Thou* (T. Clark, 1937; Scribner, 1958) also illuminate this basic conception.

For more traditional types of theological statements from various points of view, see these: For liberal Protestantism—Harold L. DeWolf, *A Theology of the Living Church* (Harper & Row, 1960). For Roman Catholicism—Karl Adam *The Spirit of Catholicism* (Harper Torchbooks, Harper & Row, 1964). For neo-orthodox Protestantism—Frederick Gogarten, *The Reality of Faith* (Westminster, 1959), and Emil Brunner, *Our Faith* (Scribner, 1960).

Three books from the neo-orthodox, liberal, and conservative points of view are good short introductions to the contrast of perspective within the Protestant community: Hordern, *The Case for a New Reformation Theology*; DeWolf, *The Case for Theology in Liberal Perspective*; and Edward John Carnell, *The Case for Orthodox Theology*. (All three published by Westminster, 1959.)

For the present debate within Protestant circles known as the "God is dead" movement, see John Robinson's *Honest to God* (Westminster, 1963) and David L. Edwards' *The Honest to God Debate* (Student Christian Movement, 1963). A valuable report on this movement can be found in Ved Metha, "The New Theologian," a series of three long articles in *The New Yorker*, November 6, 13, and 20, 1965.

The best single work interpreting the worship of the Christian churches is Evelyn Underhill, *Worship* (Harper & Row, 1937). Geoffrey Parrinder's *Worship in the World's Religions* (Association Press, 1961) is a good study in contrast and supplements the more theoretical approaches to other religions. My own *Reality and Prayer* (Harper & Row, 1957), is based upon the Protestant and Catholic traditions of the West.

For ecumenism, see the following: Walter Marshall Horton, *Christian Theology, An Ecumenical Approach* (Harper & Row, 1955); Augustin Cardinal Bea, *Unity in Freedom, Reflections on the Human Family* (Harper & Row, 1964); Robert McAfee Brown, *Observer in Rome, A Protestant Report on the Vatican Council* (Doubleday, 1964); and John A. O'Brien, ed., *Steps to Christian Unity* (Doubleday, 1964). This last book is a collection of statements by both Protestants and Roman Catholics.

An excellent statement on the meaning of the Church is contained in H. Richard Niebuhr, *The Purpose of the Church and Its Ministry* (Harper & Row, 1956).

## NOTES

1. A celebrated work on these three is Harry Emerson Fosdick's *The Meaning of Being a Christian* (Association Press, 1964), originally published separately as *The Meaning of Faith, The Meaning of Prayer, The Meaning of Service.*

2. Gabriel Marcel, *Homo Viator* (Harper Torchbooks, Harper & Row, 1951), p. 22.

3. *Ibid.*

4. Henri Bergson, *Two Sources of Morality and Religion* (Holt, Rinehart and Winston, 1935; Anchor Book, Doubleday & Co., 1954).

5. Paul Tillich, *The Courage to Be* (Yale University Press, 1952).

6. Karl Barth, *The Epistle to the Romans* (Oxford University Press, 1933), p. 22.

7. I have been unable to find the source for this poem.

8. This is Buber's concept of faith throughtout all his works: the quotation is from *I and Thou* (T. Clark, 1937; Scribner, 1958).

9. Quoted in H. P. Van Dusen, *One Great Ground of Hope* (Westminister, 1961), p. 128.

10. *Ibid.*, pp. 159 ff.

11. Vatican I, the first ecumenical council, was held in 1869–1870. Vatican II met in four sessions, the first opening on October 11, 1962, the last in October, 1965. Attending were 2540 bishops and cardinals, representing 550 million Catholic laymen.

12. F. E. Cartus, "The Vatican Council Ends," *Harper's Magazine*, September, 1965, p. 103.

13. Harold Taylor, "World University," *Saturday Review*, November 14, 1964, p. 64.

# 27

# The Need for Hope

❖❖❖❖❖❖❖❖❖❖❖❖❖❖❖❖❖❖❖❖❖❖❖❖❖❖❖❖❖❖❖❖❖❖

Hope has been a feature of human existence since man descended from the trees and risked a fateful new life on the ground. Socrates is one of the great prophets of hope in Western history. Opposing the cynicism that dominated the sophistic critics of his day, he worked unremittingly toward an ideal of integrity and justice, though he suffered martyrdom for his pains. In a conversation toward the end of Plato's *Republic*, Socrates suddenly asks Glaucon whether, since man's three score and ten years are but a little thing in comparison with eternity, an immortal being should think seriously of this little space rather than the whole. Glaucon, who represents cultivated Athenian youth at its best, makes a dutiful reply, then exclaims, ". . . what is this that you mean?" "Have you not perceived," rejoins Socrates, "that our soul is immoral and never dies?" At which Glaucon can only stare in astonishment, and reply, "No indeed, that I have not; have *you?* Dare *you* say that?"[1]

This is the first clear expression of Western man's intimation that the petty span of human existence might have an import that infinitely transcends ordinary thought. Hebrew literature expressed the matter differently, but this will concern us later on. Before we become involved in such matters, it will be well to examine the concept of hope more generally.

## SOME MEANINGS OF HOPE

"*I Hope*" . . . *versus* "*I Hope That.* . . ." Gabriel Marcel suggests that hope has two forms that must be distinguished from each other—hope as

a rational calculation, suitable for dealing with problematic matters that are
predictable, and hope as a mysterious vitality arising from the deep springs of
man's metaphysical origins.[2] When I say, for instance, "I hope that I'll
recover from this serious illness," I may be merely calculating my chances
medically. But even if the medical prognosis is bad, I may still hope. My hope
may not presume to take the specific form of an expected recovery, but I may
nevertheless not lose heart. And this hope, as opposed to despair, may well be
a factor in recovery, should it occur. It is this kind of hope that religion is
primarily concerned with—hope in the generic sense, not a rational "hope
that. . . ." The rational kind of hope is calculated; the other is unconditioned and absolute, and arises from deeper encounters with existence. It is
the hope of Job when everything, including rational hope, has been swept
away. Religious hope is thus a mystery, not a problem.

*Hope as Affirmation in Life Orientation.* Hope that is not mere calculation is, like faith, a kind of life orientation. It is, in fact, an attitude toward
life that is informed by faith. The man of faith does not despair, because he
knows, despite hard facts and inauspicious appearances, that his life is rooted
in an inexhaustible source of goodness. Hope in this sense carries a man
toward his destiny with the power to express his life in creative works of
love.

Hope is thus the sense of a "tide in the affairs of men which . . . leads on
to fortune." It is a presentiment of the future impregnating the present.
Marcel writes, "A woman who is expecting a baby, for instance, is literally
inhabited by hope."[3] This holds whether she wants the child or not. The
future is in her as a life which she shares but which is not her own. St. Paul
uses the same figure of speech in writing about the hopes of humanity: . . .
"the creation waits with eager longing for the revealing of the sons of
God. . . . We know that the whole creation has been groaning in travail
together until now. . . . For in this hope we were saved. Now hope that is
seen is not hope. . . . But if we hope for what we do not see, we wait for it
with patience."[4]

*Hope Is a Way of Being Fully Human.* A man cannot despair with his
whole being any more than he can hate or will evil with his whole being.
Why? Because the act of despair is already an expression of human vitality
and is partially informed by hope. If Descartes could find his own existence
established even in his doubts (for if he doubted, he must exist), he could
likewise have found it in despair. But despair is the minimization of human
existence; it is life at its lowest point, on the verge of passing over into
nothingness. Its best instances can be found in mental hospitals.

Hope, in contradistinction from this, is life affirmation. It is a way of being
open to the whole of things, persons, and events. It is full engagement with
existence in its most profound depths.

*Hope Is a Kind of Fidelity and Courage.* If we think of hope as a kind of
self-deception that believes that things will happen that are quite unlikely to
happen, hope is merely foolishness. But at the level we are thinking of it,
hope is a kind of fidelity and courage in living. Cynical despair, in this sense,

is a kind of infidelity, a failure of nerve, a lack of fundamental courage. It is a species of selfish rationalization for withdrawing from life. The stoic lives halfway between hope and despair. He stands fast amidst events that are evil, but he cannot radiate affirmation to his fellows. He has withdrawn into his impregnable inner citadel. At best, he can express pity for the human race. But love requires something more, for love is a fuller affirmation than pity; it re-creates those whom it touches, lifting them to their highest possibilities. It is no surprise that stoics rarely write poetry or produce art of high merit. For art and poetry are essentially expressions of hope, even when their subject matter is negative. Consider, for instance, the affirmation of life in Van Gogh's final paintings, when he was battling with a mental illness which he knew would destroy him personally.

In a straightforward religious sense, then, hope is the affirmation of God and his being. To fall into despair is to confess that one has abandoned God—or to believe that God has abandoned him. It is a confession of personal dereliction.

Viktor Frankl, who suffered unspeakable things as a Jewish inmate of German concentration camps, says that all prisoners came eventually to a fork in the road—either to lose hope and die, or to hope against hope. Some tried to postpone this decision by believing every rumor of early release. Some even set dates to live toward. But when the day of hoped-for release had passed, they lost heart and died miserably. Those who survived as human beings continued to hope, and found that it was a solid rock upon which human existence could be sustained despite the most inauspicious circumstances.[5]

*Hope and Modern Man.*   Modern society is full of calculated expectations, but it is also starved for real hope. Marcel writes: "Life in this world has become more and more widely looked upon as a sort of worthless phenomenon, devoid of any intrinsic justification. . . ."[6] From the viewpoint of despair, life is just such a "useless passion." But hope sees the ordeal of modern man as related to events that are part of his making as man. The primary fact of social existence today is that man, who has for millennia lived in settled and traditional societies, is now uprooted and mobile. He is becoming, despite himself, modern. Change is painful, for it requires that man himself change. And this is the most painful of all. Hope sees this required change as man becoming what he essentially is, a movement toward his true destiny.

The stripping away of traditional supports for calculated, rational hope—the systems and organizations by which men have lived—is painful but salutary. It lays bare the only real ground on which man may stand in hope and on which he may build his unforeseeable future.

*Hope is Directed Toward "Last Things."*   Hope, as we have been describing it, is concerned with man's destiny, with his final state beyond calculated events. In this context, death is the final challenge. The theological term for reflection on "last things" is "eschatology," from the Greek word *eschaton* meaning "last" or "end." But men have a choice of beliefs; "end" can mean "finish," or it can mean "goal." Let us consider this concept in more detail.

### Symbols of Hope

The major symbols of hope in the Judaeo-Christian faith are these: (1) the Kingdom of God, (2) the coming of the Messiah (either the first coming expected by the Jews, or the Second Coming expected by the Christians), (3) resurrection from the dead, (4) immortality, (5) heaven and hell, and (6) eternal life.

*Warning Against Literalism.* We have already laid the foundation for the kind of betrayal that occurs in religion when its symbols are taken literally. Religious hope is not *hoping that,* it is more fundamental affirmation. It expresses itself in symbols that should be understood as means of widening, not narrowing, hope. To refuse the literal meaning does not mean to reject the substance of a symbol. A literal statement puts limits on hope, a symbolic expression leaves it unconditional and absolute. If, for instance, we set a date for the Second Coming of Christ, we set a limit that leads later to cynicism and loss of faith. This has happened many times in history. Ancient Jews— like Nehemiah, who limited hope to the literal reconstruction of Jerusalem— led their people into eventual disappointment, even if they temporarily succeeded. Or again, those who took the prophetic message to promise a universal kingdom ruled by a Jewish king from Jerusalem, were led into desperate measures that served only to burn away the substance of real hope.

Consider one more example of what happens when eschatological symbols are taken literally. Jesus was challenged by his critics with a rabbinical puzzle: If a woman successively marries seven brothers, as each in turn dies, whose wife will she be in the resurrection? Jesus replied that his questioners knew "neither the Scriptures nor the power of God."[7] He said that the conditions of human marriage do not obtain in the resurrection—indicating by this remark that men must not think about symbols of hope in this literal way. The Sadducees who raised this point were like modern men who, having taken the language of religion literally, find it impossible to believe in it any longer. But if we can purge ourselves of literalism, we may be ready to grasp the substance which this language expresses.

## SOME MEANINGS OF ESCHATOLOGICAL SYMBOLS

The "Kingdom of God" is a metaphor based upon human government. At the height of ancient Judaism's prophetic movement, this ideal kingdom was conceived as a reign of universal justice in which wars would cease and every man would sit peacefully under his own shade tree. As God's kingdom, this is no mere human ideal; it is the ultimate meaning of all human community and the true end toward which it properly strives. All societies come under the judgment of this standard and are measured by the degree to which they manifest universal justice and human inclusiveness. Also, as God's kingdom, it is not merely the work of human effort. It is the good that God himself brings about in, through, and beyond all human striving. This transcendental —or vertical—relationship of God to human history cannot be spoken of literally. He is not simply some "external" or "internal" force at work. His relationship to human community is a mystery, and in this sense the Kingdom of God must remain, even for faith, the mystery of God's Presence in the human community.

"The Coming of the Messiah" is a metaphor related to the larger symbol of the Kingdom. It underscores the fact that it is God's power that will bring it to pass. In Christianity it also symbolizes the centrality of Jesus Christ's role and his significance in the scheme of things. What preceded him was preface; since his coming the Kingdom is being ushered in, and he will dominate its final consummation. The literal symbols here are the personal appearance, final judgment, and so on. Again, the substance of this symbolism lies beyond the images. To say that Christ ushers in and presides over the Kingdom's final phrases, is to say that the power and goodness that were present in Jesus is the meaning and end of all historical communities. To say that he judges men at some universal and final accounting, is to say that the deeds of all men are measured by the life which he taught and lived. Of course, these translations of this symbolism are not adequate; they omit the unforeseeable glory of God's own way of accomplishing his ends. Nor are they proposed as substitutes for the poetry of the Bible. That poetry has more to say than we can translate into prose, and by now men of faith should know it. But once we understand that we must reach for the substance beyond the symbols we are on the way to grasping that substance in some fundamental way.

The notions of an "end time" make this clear. The concept of "a time when time will come to an end" is strictly unimaginable. No literal meaning can be attached to it any more than to a "time" before creation, when, as one wit put it, God was planning the punishment of fools who asked such questions. But though the concept of an "end time" is not capable of a literal construction, it nevertheless is pregnant with a meaning that can preserve mankind from gross misunderstandings of its own history, and direct human beings toward their true fulfillment.

"Resurrection" and "immortality" are two more symbols of the "end time." Immortality is not a Hebrew concept. The Bible rarely mentions it, the biblical word being "resurrection." Resurrection symbolism, if taken literally, carries with it all sorts of objectionable notions, such as graves opening, particles of long-decayed bodies coming together again, and so on. But purged of such literalism, this symbol reminds us of things that make the concept of "immortality" pale by comparison. It stands for the fullness of eternal life in contrast to the Homeric Greek nether limbo of a shadowy afterlife, so pale and ineffectual that Achilles, returning from that region, complained to Odysseus that he would rather be the slave of the lowest mortal than dwell there.[8]

Resurrection also stands in contrast to the abstract immortality of which Socrates spoke in the *Phaedo*. It emphasizes that the future of man is not less but more concrete than his existence in time and space. But we limit the usefulness of this symbol when we try to flesh out that existence with mundane details. This must be avoided if the symbol is to do its work. Strictly speaking, Martin Buber is correct in saying that upon death he expects to pass beyond anything that he could imagine, that he would not even speak of "going on in time." But this kind of reverent agnosticism is not skepticism, nor need it turn its back on the symbolism of resurrection, properly understood.

What is the place of the resurrection of Christ in this symbolism? In the first place, like the imagery of the Second Coming, it places him at the center of the whole process. He is the "first born" of the sons of God. What happened to him is the standard for what can happen to all others. But, it may be asked, is this merely a symbol? The word "merely" is already a cynical note. No symbol is "mere"; it stands for "more," not less. For the Christian faith the resurrection of Christ is not a concept, but a fact. But this fact is of so extraordinary a character that it cannot be discussed in the fact language in which we talk of mundane events. The resurrection "body" is no ordinary body; it behaves in a way transcending all the laws of ordinary existence, passing through locked doors, unaccountably appearing and disappearing. Hence, even here we must be prepared by a kind of understanding that transcends the literal consciousness. The acceptance of Christ's resurrection is a faith-understanding.

In a purely historical sense, Christ's resurrection lifted resurrection symbolism out of the care of a small Jewish sect and made of it a universal interest and possibility. Thus St. Paul could write to his disciple Timothy of "Jesus, who abolished death and brought life and immortality to light through the Gospel."[9]

What is the relationship between resurrection and immortality? Any adequate discussion about immortality must be conducted in the light of these considerations, for if "immortality" is to serve as an adequate symbol for the "end time," the concrete values of resurrection symbolism will have to be fused with it. Even this, however, would represent a considerable improverishment of the total biblical expectation of the Kingdom of God which, though including a tender care for the individual, is a symbol of the destiny not of individuals but of the whole human race.

"Heaven" and "hell" figure more popularly in this discussion than any other eschatological symbols. Even when they are not explicitly mentioned they remain in the background of religious discussions as though they were the real issue at stake. What is their true significance?

The first thing is to recognize the primary assumption that lies behind all such discussions in Judaeo-Christian contexts, namely, the character of God as sovereign, holy, creative love. Anything said about heaven and hell must be consistent with that major premise. If for the moment we accept a "going on" after death, the question becomes, What will such a going on be like? We agree with Buber that in the most fundamental sense we cannot imagine it. But this does not mean that we cannot discuss it meaningfully.

It is meaningful, for instance, to point out that the Christian religious heritage includes a concept of hell that contradicts the Christian understanding of God and the best human experience. James Joyce gives the following account of sermons he heard as a young Catholic student:

Now let us try for a moment to realize, as far as we can, the nature of that abode of the damned which the justice of an offended God has called into existence for the eternal punishment of sinners. Hell is a strait and dark and foul-smelling prison, an abode of demons and lost souls, filled with fire and smoke. . . . By reason of the great number of the damned, the prisoners are heaped together in their awful prison, the walls of which are said to be four thousand miles thick: and the damned are so utterly bound and helpless that, as the blessed saint, Saint Anselm, writes . . . they are not even able to remove from the eye a worm that gnaws. . . . The horror of this . . . prison is increased by its awful stench. All the filth of the world, all the offal and scum of the world, we are told, shall run there as to a vast reeking sewer . . . and the bodies of the damned themselves exhale such a pestilential odor that, as Saint Bonaventure says, one of them alone would suffice to infect the whole world.
But this stench is not horrible though it is, the greatest physical torment to which the damned are subjected . . . place your finger for a moment in the flame of a candle and you will feel the pain of fire . . . the sulphurous brimstone which burns in hell is a substance which is specially designed to burn forever and forever with unspeakable fury. . . . It is a fire which proceeds directly from the ire of God, working not of its own activity but as an instrument of divine vengeance.[10]

It was this description of a type of religious teaching that inspired Joyce to write:

> There was once a lounger named Stephen
> Whose youth was most odd and uneven.
> He throve on the smell
> Of a horrible hell
> That a Hottentot wouldn't believe in.[11]

Several questions arise. First, is such a portrait of God's vengeance consistent with either his justice or his love? The answer, surely, is that it is not. As Erasmus said, "They are not as impious who deny the existence of God as those who picture him as inexorable." Second, such a hell would not only violate God's justice and love, it would also defeat his sovereignty. For if his purpose in the creation of man was good, he would then be in a position of having been outmaneuvered by his own creation. To be sure, man is free, but that is the problem which Eternal Love set itself in the beginning. Someone has proposed a suggestive metaphor for these things: the metaphor of a master chess player who cannot be defeated. Man is free to make his moves, but the sovereign Creative Spirit can always outmaneuver him. God is never at a loss. His ultimate will cannot be defeated.

A third question is this: Does human nature need such teaching for disciplinary purposes? This is harder to answer, for it asks, in effect, not whether this doctrine is true, but whether it has had a good effect on the conduct of human beings. In general, most observers of human behavior would give a negative answer to this question. But even if a positive answer were given, would there not still remain the question of whether the good behavior engendered was admirable or not? Would it not merely add to our estimate of the sum total of craven fear in the human heart? A goodness that resulted from a fear of hell and the bribery of heaven would not be the kind of goodness that the saints taught and lived. It would even be inferior to ordinary human virtue unsupported by faith.

What, then, is the meaning of hell? Should the symbol be discarded? I think not, if it can be purged of its false connotations. Hell properly stands for the fact that at the time of death the human spirit carries with it the consequences of its own earthly existence. Life has consequences in a moral universe, and the decisions of a finite life have a kind of ultimate importance that must not be sentimentally minimized. The consequence of saying No to life is an arrested or regressive state of being that shuts man off from the blessing of Reality. No fires are needed. The light of truth is itself a sufficient flame. When Viktor Frankl, concentration camp victim, was asked "What would you do if Hitler came into your psychiatric office for counseling?" he replied, "I'd let him have his consciousness." Surely that would be retribution enough! "The mind is its own place," wrote the poet Milton, "and can of itself make a heaven of hell, a hell of heaven."

Sartre's play No Exit, which has been called "hell in a second-class hotel," illuminates our meaning. Three people die and find themselves in a hotel room which they cannot somehow decide to leave. For an eternity they must stare at one another malevolently and feel the inner torment of personal lives that are horrifying to contemplate. Dante's Inferno portrays hell in similarly appropriate terms. Those who spent their lives in anger, for instance, spend eternity locked in ice, biting and cursing one another. Those who could not decide either way, for or against the good life, are swept perpetually back and forth by the cold winds that issue from howling deserts. But even here we must see the work of love—letting men work out the issue of existence to the full, until they can come to themselves and turn to loving. Meanwhile, of course, God is not simply standing by allowing the results of a freedom with which he will not interfere. He is constantly seeking fresh means to rouse men from their heedless ways and even suffering with and for them in their plight. This in no way diminishes the seriousness of decisions in this life; it makes them more significant. And we need not wait until death to see what is involved. The steady deterioration of the alcoholic is already a manifestation of hell, but not so terrible as the historic refusal of man to live at peace. The horror of war has few rivals, and man's inhumanity to man has produced depths of torment equal to anything the theological imagination can invent.

When we turn to the meaning of heaven, we are less well equipped with satisfactory images. A heaven of comfort would soon pall and become a hell, a kind of reverse "no exit." The only heaven we can imagine is one that allows for unlimited personal and social growth under conditions we cannot possibly imagine.

"Eternal life" is the symbol for the "end" meaning of human existence used by St. John in the fourth Gospel. This late Gospel was faced no doubt with questions about the postponement of the Second Coming and with uncertainties about the prevailing eschatological imagery. Some scholars have even held that it was written as a counterexpression to the highly imaginative final book of the New Testament written by another author, *The Revelation of St. John.*

St. John reports Jesus as saying, . . . "he who hears my words and believes in him who sent me hath eternal life. . . ."[12] In this telling of the Gospel, eternal life is a quality of existence here and now—a way of living in the presence of eternal hope, beginning at the moment of faith's dawning. It stretches from that moment without end to Eternity, filled with the love of God as revealed in Jesus Christ. In one of his Epistles St. John makes this plainer: Those who love the brethren with a holy love have already passed from death to life.

### The Existential Character of Eschatological Symbols

St. John's symbolism provides a good transition to a concept that clarifies a great deal of our discussion: All eschatological symbols are existential. That is, they are a call to life here and now, not a set of speculations about the future. In this sense, even the gross imagery of hell is a call to a different life. Scholars have used the expression "realized eschatology" for St. John's treatment of eternal life. Realized eschatology means that the fullness of the end-time is here already, that the blessed life in, with, and for God begins with man's turning toward Him, with the death of selfish ego-preoccupation, not with the death of the body, which is then merely an incident in eternity.

With this in mind, we are ready to answer another important question, what is the best preparation for the "next life"? The answer: Live well now, concretely, in the fullest human sense, in trust, hope, openness, creativity, and love. "Salvation" can be understood in this light not as a ticket granting entrance into a place, but as emergence into a state of genuine coexistence with God and with one's fellows.

### The Negative End-Time Symbol: Death

The human experience that gives vitality to eschatological symbolism—removing the whole discussion from mere speculation—is the fact of death. This often makes men uneasy even when they seem to be affirming their faith. One wit reports a conversation in which his companion said, "Of course, if you press me, I believe I shall enter into eternal bliss; but I wish you would not talk about such disagreeable subjects."

### Facing the Prospect of Death

A Greek dramatist puts the basic issue squarely: "For death no man has found a cure." Death appears to be the zero which when multiplied by all human achievements produces zero. Meaning, Hocking reminds us, is not a spotty thing. This is so because no human event is merely what it is—it is always put in a larger setting, and this in turn is referred to a setting of yet more general proportions. Thus the meaning of an event spreads imperceptibly to the whole. It is not just a question of this pleasure or that, this particular good or that, but of the whole in which these goods appear. If this be so, then to assert the meaninglessness of the whole human enterprise will have a reflective effect on every particular meaning. It will, in fact, render the parts suspect. "A meaningless whole," writes Hocking, "implies a meaningless part."[13]

Hocking applies this principle to the enigma of death: "Draw your line around the man at his death, cut across all the lines of aspiration, snuff out all his major questions, quash all his claims, declare all his unfinishedness a zero to the cosmos, and the nerve of all this concern for justice is also cut. Humanism tries to borrow for its humanitarian zeals an inherent worth in the individual human being which its premises forbid him to have. Without this continuance, his present cannot hold its own meaning and worth."[14]

Pressing the point still further—to tie meaning to the self whose meaning a given act is—Hocking writes: "The true meaning of a deed is what it means to the self which performs it; without this self the deed has no meaning at all; it is the 'being' which sustains all 'doing,' that assigns to it whatever depth of meaning it may have. In this sense there is no meaning at all except in the being of this self. And if this self vanishes, and all like it, meaning vanishes out of the world. No achievement can keep the person alive, but the continuance of the person is a guaranty that such values as that shall not reduce to nothing."[15]

These reflections are not attempts at some philosophical doctrine. They are an analysis of the conditions under which meaning becomes available to human beings. What I am saying is that truly human meaningfulness requires an unlimited perspective, a general frame of reference to which there is no arbitrary boundary. It is this fact that integrates the meaning of hope with the natural human concern about the prospects of surmounting death.

Life lived in the prospect of death has universally induced a deep melancholy, even among brave men. Homer comments:

> Like a race of leaves the race of man is.
> The wind in autumn strows the earth with old leaves,
> Then the spring the woods with new endows.

Noting in this perpetual cycle the sadness of mortality, he speaks of the "tears in things." Walter Pater, commenting on this Homeric passage, writes,

"Leaves, little leaves—thy children, thy flatterers, thy enemies."[16] The optimism of "If winter come, can spring be far behind?" is subverted by the thought, If summer come, can winter be long approaching? Nature gives small comfort in the face of death, especially to a race which can anticipate its sad denouement.

### The Real Sting of Death

But even physical death must be taken symbolically. The sting of death is not physical; it is spiritual. Its poison is the death of hope, the destruction of the good life. Human consciousness is inevitably eschatological—that is, it is projected toward its "end" as a goal. If this goal is nothingness, the emptiness of that end effects with melancholy the entire enterprise. If in the long epochs of cosmic time our sun will swell up like Betelgeuse and consume the earth, if this heat death is the true destiny of humanity, if all is to be reduced to ashes—all the morning brightness of poetry, music, and art, all the noon-day understanding of science and philosophy, all the wisdom of the prophets and sages, all the labors of love by saints and servants of mankind—if all these are to be consumed like refuse thrown to the fire, what consolation can comfort man as he goes his mortal way?

In contemplation of such a finale, one can but feel a deep sympathy for the Greek poet Theognis, who, in the sixth century B.C., wrote despairingly,

> Not to be born, never to see the sun
> No worldly blessing is a greater one.
> And the next blest is speedily to die,
> And lapt beneath a load of earth to lie.[17]

The sting of death, then, is the poisoning of hope, the extinguishing of all possibility of a full human existence here and now.

### Death and Faith

Contrast the mood of naturalistic pessimism with the transformation that death undergoes at the hands of faith. "The last enemy to be conquered," wrote St. Paul, "is death," but he was firm in his belief that this is exactly what God has accomplished in the Gospel. For those who share that faith, the sting of death—not physical death—has been removed. The words of an unknown author who, in the period between the Old and New Testaments, wrote the book entitled the Wisdom of Solomon (in the Douay Version, the Book of Wisdom), express the faith of pre-Christian Judaism:

> God created man for immortality
>     and made him in the image of his own eternity.
> The souls of the righteous are in the hands of God,
>     and no torment will ever touch them.

*In the eyes of the foolish they seem to have died . . .*
   *but they are at peace.*
*For . . . their hope is full of immortality. . . .*
*Those who trust in him will understand truth,*
   *and the faithful will abide with him in love. . . .*[18]

Consider one more instance, the death of Francis of Assisi, greatest of the medieval saints: "Then the blessed St. Francis, lying on his bed, spread his hands out to the Lord with very great devotion and reverence and said with great joy of mind and body, 'Welcome, my Sister Death,' "[19]

Why, then, death at all? A full answer to this question lies beyond our vision. But some things seem fairly clear. First, physical death seems to have a place in the economy of our universe. It clears the world each generation, permitting the freshness of new cultures, new populations, and new adventures in living.

Second, death, by putting a final term to all activities in this space-time epoch, gives importance to each living moment and each decision. Life assumes an urgency that it might not have without such a limit. It serves in this case like a frame on the painter's canvas, limiting, but thereby giving specific value to this particular work.

Third, death may serve to release the individual from the local accidents of his finite life, allowing him to set aside physique, habits, and all the local elements of thought, language, and culture. It may serve as a purgation necessary for a proper "entrance into eternity."

## Death and Hope

Is not this hope for a life to come a false comfort for the weak? This question is parallcled by another: Would it not be nobler to live courageously without the crutch of such a belief? These questions cannot be answered decisively, but we may consider the following. There is first the question of truth. It is not noble to live by a lie just because the truth might be comforting. Nor is it noble to stagger through life crippled by denying oneself something that human nature needs for its fullness. On the physical level this is obvious. A man in need of vitamins who thought it nobler to live without them would be considered a fool, even though he showed great fortitude in bearing his deficiency diseases.

Moreover, as we have already pointed out, there is, second, a sense in which the denial of hope is not so much a kind of honesty as betrayal. What we have said on this above need not be repeated here. If hope is a kind of fidelity to oneself and to God, then the denial of hope is not a species of honest courage, but a kind of infidelity. This remark is not to be taken as a judgment on skeptics but as a comment on the framework in which hope is understood by those who live by it.

There is, third, a prevailing view in the West that belief in immortality is a wish-projection. This is a misunderstanding that could arise only in an optimistic society. In societies living on the verge of starvation, infested with all sorts of diseases, and threatened with all kinds of natural dangers, the desire is for release into oblivion, for a final extinction of the self. Reincarnation, for example, as understood in ancient India, was a horror to be avoided. The whole religious praxis of Hinduism and Buddhism was directed toward release from the wheel of existence. Or, if we need a Western example, consider Hamlet's longing to escape from his plight by suicide: "To die . . . to sleep!" It was the waking which disturbed him, not the prospect of extinction.

The modern theory of wish-projection was proposed by Marx and Freud in a culture that was basically optimistic, a society in which life was good and men could hope. Where hopelessness seizes human life, it does not occur to man that prolonging it might be good.

### The Ground for Hope

As faith sees it, there is only one ground for hope and that is the holy love of God. Man does not know, Hocking reminds us, "through self-consciousness what in himself might render him viable beyond death."[20] This, after all, is not so strange. "He does not so much know," Hocking comments, "what it is that keeps him alive in his present situation."[21] With a careful appraisal of his own nature, man sees at most the possibility of immortality, his "immortability," as Hocking calls it. But the power to actualize this possibility does not lie with man; it lies, if anywhere, in the Ground of his being, the Source from which he sprang and by which he remains alive.

When Martin Buber was asked about what lies on the other side of death, he replied, "I think death is the end of everything that we are able to imagine. Therefore, this means that we cannot, and we should not, imagine life after death merely as a going on in time. Time is just something that we know in this life here, just as we know space; and just as space, so time is omitted from eternity. I don't imagine a going on in time, but I am certain of entering eternity. And though I cannot imagine it, I know I shall enter it, and this means that one can be more certain of God's existence than of his own existence."[22]

Why should belief in a God of Holy Love entail immortality? Harry Emerson Fosdick has expressed the connection most clearly: "Let the interior fellowship of the soul with God be once conceived in terms of mutual care, so that as the soul adores and trusts the Most High, the Most High values and supports the soul, and the corollary is bound to be drawn that such a relationship predicts its own continuance."[23]

Buber's certainty of God's existence rather than confidence in his own being and Fosdick's grasp of God as love are the ground of any responsible assertion of immortality. But, it might be asked, suppose that God does not intend immortal existence for the human species? The answer of faith is simple: If not immortality, then something better, but we have absolutely no conception—nor even the slightest clue—of what would be better in the light of Holy Love than some kind of eternal communion under whatever conditions God might create. Moreover, all the great symbols of the Judaeo-Christian hope are social—the Kingdom of God being the most central of all—and the preciousness of human existence belongs to the essence of such symbols.

The Buddhists, to be sure, propose nirvana as a superior destiny, but it is hard to be clear as to just what nirvana means. The Buddha himself was silent on this score. Certainly if nirvana means "extinction," a "blowing out of the flame," then we must regard it as a symbol of resignation, not hope. But many commentators claim that it represents a state so high above analogies to ordinary human existence that it is misleading to speak of "existence" at all, and that nirvana is a symbol of the utmost richness. If this latter is an accurate interpretation, then what we have said of immortality goes also for nirvana. Perhaps, in this case, nirvana is an intimation of that egoless state of pure love analogous to what is meant by the Judaeo-Christian faith in immortality. In our present state of knowledge we cannot decide this point.

## INTIMATIONS OF IMMORTALITY

As a final consideration, let us look at those features of human existence that seem to tell in favor of man's immortality. Before plunging directly into this matter, let us attend briefly to the negative evidence. Two matters seem primary: First, there is the evidence we have of the dependence of human consciousness upon the states of the body. Illness, fatigue, material deficiences of air, food, or water, damage to the brain through chemical substances or accident—all these deeply affect personality. The conclusion would seem to follow that at death, with the disintegration of the body, personality would cease to exist. Of course, no one could witness the cessation of personality, since, by definition, no one would be there. But the thrust of the evidence seems to tend in this direction. This, however, is only one side of the story. The effects of attitudes and personal decisions upon bodily states is also impressive, both in common sense experience and in medicine. In the latter, the findings are indeed striking, some investigators going so far as to say that nearly every illness—including accidents—cannot be understood without noting the accompanying psychological factors.

We need not take an extreme position on this matter to see that the evidence of psychosomatic interaction favors the case we are considering: that there is a nonphysical component in the human person that operates on its own principles in interaction with the body and need not necessarily share its fate.

The second negative observation can be stated succinctly: The most telling evidence against the self's prospects of indefinite existence is that it had a beginning. As the Buddhists say, "All component things pass away." Everything that was contrived or created is marked with finitude.

The reply to this is that if God intends immortality for part of his creation, he is perfectly capable of accomplishing it. The argument does tell, however, against any claim that the soul is "naturally" immortal. Whatever the soul's prospects, they do not depend on its own resources.

Medieval philosophers argued that since the soul was "simple" it could not disintegrate. But these arguments about the soul's simplicity, based upon Aristotelian premises about personality, have become suspect under the attrition of modern psychological studies. These studies have revealed the enormous complexity of personality, and the unending struggle in every person between the forces of disintegration and integration. Whatever simplicity the soul may possess is the fruit of long effort and growth, not the result of some inborn characteristic.

The evidence we are now to consider is acknowledged to pose only probabilities. They are intimations of immortality, not proofs. Their essential meaning can be summarized this way: The human spirit shows a partial freedom from the conditions of space-time bodily existence which suggests that those conditions may not be final for its own expression, and that the death of the body need not be equated with the death of personality.

### The Nature of Thought

The laws of thought are not the laws of things. Things are affected by causes; thought is affected by reasons. Thought is free; it transcends the things that it considers. The life of thought which moves in the mind of the astronomer, for instance, obeys different laws than the objects he looks at through his telescope.[24] If this were not so, there would be no science. The mind that presents evidence for a theory cannot be understood as a mere effect of physical causes—or his claim would be rejected. If we know that the reason a person is talking in a certain way is due to some disorder of his brain, we do not consider what he says; we call a doctor. If a person making a supposed truth claim is under physical duress, his witness is impeachable. He is not free. Only a free mind can witness to truth. (This, incidentally, makes all behavioristic theories of truth suspect on their own grounds.)

Thought, then, witnesses to a component of human personality that does not conform to the causal laws of space-time events. And since death is just such a space-time event, the thinker may not be subject to it.

### Moral Responsibility

Like thinking, moral responsibility assumes an agent who can consider freely what his duty is and choose or not to obey it. A moral claim, like a truth claim, is a reason for behavior, not a cause of behavior. It is not a physical force. Moreover, as Kant pointed out, the moral claim itself originates beyond the agent himself, laying him under obligation. And this implies that the Reality from which the claim derived cannot be lightly regarded as an ill will, nor even as some kind of non-will. Furthermore, it would seem that the subject of an absolute moral law—the human person—cannot be justly treated as a mere thing by the very source of law which laid the command upon persons not to treat persons as mere things. Morality is a dialogue with goodness which does not come under the laws of cause and effect any more than does valid thought. Here again we have a component of human personality that lies outside the space-time continuum and so is not subject to its laws.

This same consideration applies to all of man's activities in the course of which, as an agent, he must operate freely and responsibly among values, persons, and things. All these represent a human transcendence of the actual. Artistic creation is another good example. But I need not repeat the pattern of the argument in each case.

### Memory and Purpose

Memory is a transcendence of the present moment which includes the past in its compass. When I remember anything I grasp my continuity through all the changes of time since that remembered event. I recall myself as a child or as a youth, yet I am now still myself as this grown man. Memory is thus a temporary immortality of identity through changes of the most radical sort.

Purpose, likewise, is a form of time-transcendence. Here and now I envisage a future toward which I shall bend all the space-time events that will come to pass throughout that future. If today I plan to give a lecture tomorrow, and tomorrow I actually deliver it, my purpose has functioned throughout this time-span, as in some small way superior to it. Not being omniscient or omnipotent, both my memory and purposing can fail; but this is only to say that I am not God, and that any final transcendence depends upon a Being beyond myself.

### Character

Human beings do not merely persist through time; they often grow more valuable. Moreover, human character increases in its coherence and significance even as bodily powers wane. Nothing suggests quite so dramatically the loose relationship between body and spirit as the spectacle of human courage in the face of bodily disintegration. Of course this courage is finally helpless against the tide of age or disease, but it suggests that relative freedom from mere physical circumstance to which we are calling attention.

### Extrasensory phenomena

Such phenomena as telepathy, psychokinesis, and the like, operating as they do outside any known physical laws, transcending all the familiar limitations of time and space, suggest again this free component of human personality.

To be sure, the very existence of such phenomena is debated. But it is interesting to note that the debate is now carried on largely aside from the evidence. Those who reject the very thesis we are presenting—that an aspect of the human mind transcends time and space—also reject the carefully documented experimental evidence for ESP. Their rejection is largely based upon incredulity rather than contrary evidence.[25] This is no place to debate the evidence itself, except to say that it has been accepted by some of the world's most eminent men of science and letters. Nor are they all religious theists. C. D. Broad, for example, for years president of the London Society of Psychical Research, was a distinguished analytic philosopher. Others of his caliber could easily be named, but it would be to no purpose.[26]

The point is that here again is evidence for a component of the human mind that might be a candidate for immortability.

### Love

Love, like all the primary activities of the human being at his best, carries with it intimations of immortality. Since we will be considering this topic in the next chapter, I need only mention it here.

### Self-transcendence

Self-transcendence has been a characteristic of all the evidence we have considered so far, but there is an aspect of it that needs special note. The following incident, recounted by William Ernest Hocking, will make clear what we mean. "We are," he wrote, "in the position of the patient who arrived near midnight at the door of the Berlin Psychopathic Institute, and having awakened the staff, demanded admission on the ground that he was out of his mind: '*Ich bin verrückt,*' he said. This was irregular, for patients out of their minds are not supposed to admit it, hence the rules required certificates of physicians. But since this patient was confessing his deficiency, the authorities in that emergency saw no reason why the routine should be insisted upon: he was admitted, and the subsequent examination showed that his diagnosis of his own condition was correct."[27]

This is a curious affair. It is no surprise that the court was later troubled by this patient who was both sane and insane at the same time. But it is a normal characteristic of human consciousness that it is able to transcend itself. The sane self which judges the disordered self is a common fact of human experience—in guilt, for instance. It runs through all psychotherapy. Anton Boison, who passed through deep psychosis, testified to an interior sanity that led him to struggle against his own illness. This power of self-transcendence also seems to point again to a component of personality that is not subject to the conditions of time and space, but orders itself according to a different dimension of reality.

*The Experience of Dying.* This power of transcendence has often been observed by those whose business places them at the bedside of the dying. To cite Hocking again, he holds that Tolstoy's remarkable story *The Death of Ivan Ilyitch* is based upon, and gives a vivid account of an actual experience, the experience which will be ours as we emerge—when, as the Sanskrit text puts it, "the grass core is drawn out from its sheath."[28]

*Religious Experience.* Religious experience is not likely to constitute evidence for those who reject religion, but both the exalted moments in contemplation and the quieter experiences of answered prayer, coupled with a growing sense of personal meaning come to those who enjoy them as irrefragable proofs of their participation in a Reality which transcends the visible space-time world.

As in the exposition of faith, I have here tried to clarify the generic meaning of hope and then interpreted the more specifically religious symbols of hope in the light of that meaning. We turn now to our final chapter, which, because it is the last, may arouse some hope in the reader, if not love. But it is love, the fulfillment of our need for communion, that crowns the whole enterprise, and without which our inquiry would be in vain.

## SUGGESTIONS FOR FURTHER READING

The best single analysis of hope is Gabriel Marcel's *Homo Viator* (Harper Torchbooks, Harper & Row, 1962). Both Bergson's *Two Sources* and Tillich's *Courage to Be*, recommended in Chapter 26, can also be interpreted as studies in hope.

For the theological symbols of hope, see Howard Clark Kee, *The Renewal of Hope* (Association Press, 1959). William Ernest Hocking's *The Meaning of Immortality in Human Experience* (Harper & Row, 1957) is the best single analysis of man's immortability. C. S. Lewis' *The Great Divorce* (Macmillan, 1950) is a delightful parable of the meaning of bodily resurrection. Oscar Cullman contrasts the notion of "immortality" with "resurrection" in *Immortality of the Soul or Resurrection of the Dead?* (Macmillan, 1958). See the new theological orientation to the resurrection of Jesus Christ in H. Richard Niebuhr, *Resurrection and Historical Reason* (Scribner, 1957).

## NOTES

1. Plato, *Republic*, Bk. X (608b), W. H. D. Rouse trans.

2. Marcel, *Homo Viator* (Harper Torchbooks, Harper & Row, 1962).

3. *Ibid.*, p. 31.

4. Romans 8:19, 22, 24–25.

5. Viktor Frankl, *Man's Search for Meaning* (Washington Square Press, 1963).

6. Gabriel Marcel, *Faith and Reality*, vol. 2 of *The Mystery of Being* (Gateway, Regnery, 1960), p. 166.

7. Mark 12:24.

8. *Odyssey*, Bk. XI.

9. II Timothy 1:10.

10. James Joyce, *Portrait of the Artist as a Young Man* (Viking, 1956), pp. 119–121.

11. In James Joyee, Letter to Ezra Pound, April 9, 1917, in Albert Stuart, ed., *Letters of James Joyce* (Viking, 1957), pp. 102, 143.

12. John 5:24.

13. William Ernest Hocking, *The Meaning of Immortality in Human Experience* (Harper & Row, 1957), p. 114.

14. *Ibid.*, p. 143.

15. *Ibid.*, p. 150.

16. The lines of Homer are quoted from an imagined speech of Emperor Marcus Aurelius in Walter Pater's novel *Marius the Epicurean*, chapter titled "The Divinity That Doth Hedge a King" (Modern Library, n.d.), pp. 166–167.

17. In Will Durant, *Life of Greece* (Simon and Schuster, 1939), p. 94.

18. Wisdom of Solomon, 2:23; 3:1–4, 9.

19. "The Mirror of Perfection," Chap. CXXII, *The Little Flowers*; *The Mirror of Perfection*; and *The Life of Saint Francis* (Dent, 1910).

20. Hocking, *op. cit.*, p. 74.

21. *Ibid.*

22. Interview in the BBC's *Listener*, January 18, 1962, p. 127.

23. Harry Emerson Fosdick, *Guide to the Understanding of the Bible* (Harper & Row, 1938), p. 291.

24. See an analysis of this point in Alburey Castell, *The Self in Philosophy* (Macmillan, 1965), chap. 2, "Two Modes of Behavior: Activity and Process."

25. See the debate on this question in *Science*, Vol. 123, No. 3184 (January 6, 1956).

26. See J. B. Rhine, *The Reach of the Mind* (Sloane, 1947) for the history of these investigations.

27. Hocking, *op. cit.*, pp. 114–115.

28. *Ibid.*, p. 251.

# 28

## *The Need for Communion*

The meaning of being fully human can now be affirmed as follows: to live with a sense of roots, to be drawn on by hope, and to dwell in deep communion with all that lives. Or, to put it more simply: to remain faithful, to radiate hope, and to express love. Only in this way does the significance of the human enterprise become manifest. All forms of infidelity, cynicism, and ill will are so many ways of denying authentic humanness. And the worst denial of all is ill will.

If we could understand love we would be in a fair way to understand the meaning of our entire inquiry, for love is not only the basic need of human beings, it is also the crown of the spiritual life.

### THE MANY FORMS AND MEANINGS OF LOVE

Unfortunately, love itself is an ambiguous concept. It is related that when the psychiatrist Alfred Adler heard that a very self-centered young Viennese woman had fallen in love, he asked, "Against whom?"[1] We use the word love to mean many things—"I love rare steak," "I love tennis," "I love my country," "I love my wife," "I love humanity," and so on. We need a semantic of love.

But this semantic, I am sure, would reveal not only the differences in our various uses, but also an underlying unity. For love is a single thing that spreads itself out in the creation under a multitude of guises—even the disguise of selfishness. The reasons for this assertion will become clearer as we proceed.

Love's expression ranges widely from the infant to the most mature human being. The infant's love is a response to the continued satisfaction of its organic needs. This is likewise true of the young child, but with the rise of self-awareness, it takes an egoistic turn. The romantic love of the young lover makes him feel deliciously lost in the world of his beloved; yet he is capable of the most savage reaction when his love is unrequited. The artist and scientist are urged onward by the tide of a great desire, a divine *eros*, by which the greatest inquiries and efforts of men have mounted toward sublime achievements. The religious lover begins, no doubt, in his own needs, but with maturity his love begins to reflect the egoless agape of God. In the saint—both religious and secular—turned outward toward the whole creation, we see love in its highest manifestation.

As different as these various loves may seem, they are all part of the same fundamental agapic energy by which the scattered leaves of the universe are, as Dante wrote, "bound by love in one volume."[2]

## THE HUMAN NEED OF LOVE

Love is mankind's greatest need. Biologically the human organism is the product of procreative love. In its infancy it can perish through lack of it. "To love and be loved," writes Ashley Montagu, anthropologist and social biologist, "is as necessary to the organism as the breathing of air."[3] The French psychologist René Spitz observed and filmed the death of thirty-four foundlings in a foundling home. These infants had all their needs cared for except that of motherly love. Lacking this, they sickened and died. After three months of separation from their parents, the infants lost sleep and became shrunken, whimpering, and trembling. After an additional two months, most of them began to look like idiots. Twenty-seven foundlings died in their first year of life; seven in the second. Twenty-one others lived longer, but they "were so altered that thereafter they could be classified only as 'idiots.' "[4] This need for love is recognized by baby doctors in the U.S. as TLC (tender, loving care) and is even prescribed for the nurses to carry out.

Sorokin and Hansen, describing the effects of lack of love on adults, wrote: "Modern psychosomatic medicine correctly views the strong emotional disturbances, especially of an aggressive, inimical, hateful, and antagonistic kind, as one of the basic factors of cardiovascular, respiratory, gastro-intestinal, eliminative, skin, endocrine, genito-urinary, and other disturbances."[5]

In researches comparing the longevity of aggressively egoistic and unaggressive, altrustic human beings, it has been shown that the latter have a much longer span of life. A life of love, says Sorokin, summarizing these researches, "seems to invigorate the health and prolong the life span of eminent and saintly altruists, in spite of their ascetic practices, lack of necessities, and other supposedly unhealthy conditions of their life and activity."[6]

We can summarize the biological significance of love in Montagu's words: "To inhibit or prevent the expression of love is to do violence to the needs, to the structure, and to the functioning of the organism."[7]

The human need of love is also strikingly manifest in psychology. The ability to give and receive love freely, without guilt, is perhaps the highest criterion of mature personality. The denial of love is the repression of the person's potential expansion into his world. The egoist, says the Russian philosopher Vladimir Soloviev, lives by the motto: "I am the center, while the whole world is only a circumference."[8] But in that self-enclosed ego-centered world the person suffers from paranoid fears and envies that eat away his prized self-sufficiency. Only generous love can cast out fear, hatred, envy, and greed, and lead a human being to a style of life that is conducive to peace of mind and happiness.

The egoist thinks that he truly loves himself, but this is only an illusion. If he cannot love others, he cannot love himself. As Erich Fromm says, "The affirmation of one's own life, happiness, growth, and freedom is rooted in one's capacity to love, i.e., in care, respect, responsibility, and knowledge."[9] The converse, he says, is likewise true: If an individual is able "to love only others, he cannot love at all."[10]

What is true in biology and psychology is, if anything, even more true in man's social relations. Human society has always depended on a minimum good will among its members. As I pointed out in our study of religion and society, some kind of basic agreement or consensus is the *sine qua non* of social existence. Good will becomes even more urgent when different societies are forced to find a way of getting along with one another. The ancient Chinese sage, Mo Ti (*ca.* 475–393 B.C.) stated the case quite clearly: "A thief loves his own family and does not love other families, hence he steals from other families in order to benefit his own family. Each grandee loves his own clan and does not love other clans, hence he causes disturbances to other clans to benefit his own clan. Each feudal lord loves his own state and does not love other states, so he attacks other states in order to benefit his own state. The causes of all disturbances . . . lie herein. . . . It is always from want of equal love to all."[11]

Mo Ti foreshadowed the essential human problem of our own time. It can be stated quite simply as follows: Unless human groups can surmount their tribal egoism and manifest a solid membership in the wider community of humanity itself, the future of the human race is very problematic. Unfortunately, human history has been a catalogue of man's inhumanity to man, most often perpetrated in the name of some lesser loyalty. Lack of broad human sympathy has bred wars between tribes, states, religions, cultures, classes, "chosen people" and "inferior people," and so on. As P. A. Sorokin says, "Mountains of corpses and seas of human blood have been sacrificed to the Moloch of warfare between exclusive tribal solidarities. In an endless rhythm of today's victors and tomorrow's victims, the groups have been succeeding one another in a process of mutual extermination."[12] With the advent of scientific methods of destruction, this cycle is bound to come to an end, either in total desolation or the rise of a new altruism.

But even if such an end is forestalled, modern man is threatened by other dangers. The very nature of modern life threatens the dehumanization of life, the reduction of man to his particular functions, producing a mere "punch-card" man. The growing size of nations, governments, business concerns, labor unions, and even of churches, threatens this reduction of human beings to the level of interchangeable parts.

Machines, for instance, promised man a new Eden in which bread would no longer be eaten "by the sweat of his brow." But, uncontrolled by love, machines have only tended to make man unimportant, robbing him of the very meaning of his labor and dooming him to a meaningless leisure. The way of love reminds us that the human being is the greatest of the world's "natu-ral" resources, and that no task is so important as bringing this resource to its fullest completeness. A mature love would allow for the individual in his uniqueness. It would prize all personal differences, and foster the unforseeable consequences of continued creativity. A society characterized by such love could flower into genuine humanness.

With the foregoing dimensions of human life as a foundation, we are now prepared to consider man's need of love from a religious perspective. Love, in its highest sense, is the meaning of the spiritual life. This is demonstrated not only in Christianity, but also in the other more developed faiths. Take Christianity first.

The unveiling of God as Holy Love is the end point of the Christian revelation. When the Gospel writer penned the words, "God is love," the true light had finally broken through.[13] The following are selected passages from St. John's Epistles: "Here we have a clear indication who are the children of God. . . . if we love one another God does actually live within us, and His love grows in us toward perfection. . . . Love contains no fear—indeed, fully developed love expels every particle of fear, for fear always contains some torture of feeling guilty. We know we have crossed the frontier from death to life because we do love our brothers. . . . [Thus] the man who does obey God's command [to love] lives in God and God lives in him, and the guarantee of his presence with us is the Spirit He has given us."[14]

If it be objected that the Christian Gospel has been most often promul-gated in the form of stories about Jesus, it must be replied that this part of the Gospel—what is now called the Gospel (*Kerygma*)—is distorted or meaningless without the Teaching (*Didaché*). The teaching is the clue to Christ's life and his life is the clue to his teachings. Christ cannot be under-stood except as an emblem of inexhaustible divine love. If he conveys a judgment on humanity, that judgment is on man's lack of love; it is not a sign of God's ill will toward man.

The non-Christian faiths likewise appear historically to have moved toward this same goal. E. A. Burtt traces, for instance, the movement of Buddhist thought from a doctrine of narrow self-salvation to the Mahayana doctrine of universal love. In the Mahayana, he says, "The essence of spiritual realization, in relation to the blindly craving and frustrated unhappiness that precedes it, is liberation. . . . its culminating—that is, its dependably peace- and bliss-producing—quality is love. And by love, here, Buddha meant no dependent attachment to a person or object through whom one hopes to find his longings satisfied, but an unlimited self-giving compassion flowing freely toward all creatures that live."[15] He illustrates his words with a quotation from the Sutta-Nipata:

> *May creatures all abound*
>
> *in weal and peace; may all*
> *be blessed with peace always;*
> *all creatures weak or strong,*
> *all creatures great and small;*
> *creatures unseen or seen,*
> *dwelling afar or near,*
> *born or awaiting birth,*
> *—may all be blessed with peace!*
>
> .   .   .
>
> *Just as with her own life*
> *a mother shields from hurt*
> *her own, her only, child,—*
> *let all-embracing thoughts*
> *for all that lives be thine.*
>
> *—an all-embracing love*
> *for all the universe*
> *in all its heights and depths*
> *and breadth, unstinted love,*
> *unmarred by hate within,*
> *not rousing enmity.*
>
> *So, as you stand or walk,*
> *or sit, or lie, reflect*
> *with all your might on this;*
> *—'tis deemed "a state divine."*[16]

This ideal also expresses itself in the Islamic faith. In the Moslem Koran Allah says:

> *Surely in trouble have we created man. . . .*
> *And who shall teach thee what the steep (path) is?*
> *It is to ransom the captive,*
> *Or to feed in the day of famine*

> The orphan who is near of kin, or the poor that
>   lieth in the dust;
> Besides this, to be of those who believe, and
>   enjoin steadfastness on each other,
>   and enjoin compassion on each other.
> These shall be the people of the right hand. . . .[17]

The Moslem comprehension of love reached its highest pitch in the Moslem mystics. For his order of Sufi dervishes, the great Persian mystic Rumi (1207–1273) wrote his famous "Song of the Reed Flute." A central passage celebrates the ecstatic love of God:

> Hail to thee, then, O LOVE, sweet madness!
> Thou who healest all our infirmities!
> Who art the physician of our pride and self-conceit!
> Who art our Plato and our Galen!
> Love exalts our earthly bodies to heaven,
> And makes the very hills to dance with joy!
> O lover, 'twas love that gave life to Mount Sinai,
> When "it quaked, and Moses fell down in a swoon."
>
> Did my Beloved only touch me with his lips,
> I, too, like the flute, would burst out in melody.[18]

Neo-Hinduism, under the inspiration of Ramakrishna and his greatest disciple, Vivekananda, has taught the same truth—that the proof of unity with the Divine is a life of loving service.

It has also been the end point of humanistic thought at its best: Camus, Russell, Julian Huxley, Fromm, and others have joined in praise of love as the central spire in the true habitation of man.

We need not accept the uncritical view that all of these expressions of love are identical in meaning. What they actually mean cannot be discerned without the dialogue among faiths which I urged in an earlier chapter. But the drift of thought seems fairly evident, and no understanding of these faiths can be looked upon as complete without coming to terms with love.

## SOME CONCLUSIONS ABOUT LOVE

We may now draw our conclusions about the meaning of love. In the first place, love is an *openness to the ontological depths of human existence*. It is a sense of the infinite power of Being by which life came into existence, by which it is sustained in its highest flights, and by which its destiny is determined. Self-enclosure is simply cutting one's self off from true Being. In religious terms, such self-enclosure is hell. "Nothing burns in hell," says the *Theologia Germanica*, "except self-will."

Love is thus inseparably tied to faith and hope. It is simply the affirmation of them both. It is the outward result of dwelling in that inexhaustible ocean of Cosmic Being which is the life of faith, and which sends up from its own depths the springs of hope. This is why St. Paul says that, though prophecy, ecstatic religious experience, and knowledge may fail—belonging as they do to the childhood of humanity—love will never fail.[19] It cannot fail, for it is of the nature of Ultimate Being itself.

It also appears to be true that *all the highest human energies converge in love.* The scientist and the artist, for instance, must be considered as lovers. They cannot forebear giving the closest attention to the world in which they live; their creativity is inspired by a passion for the world—its things or qualities, its forms or its truth. The statesman and the productive worker (both management and labor) are likewise enamored of goals which they cannot forget. The rewards of reputation or profit are small compared to the satisfaction of the work itself.

Love is also the power that *joins the universal and the individual* into one actuality. It issues in what Teilhard de Chardin calls the "granulated" character of the actual world—atoms, molecules, cells, and so on, up to human individuals. In religious terms, we could say that love is inherently "incarnational"—it seeks embodiment in things, persons, and institutions. It is not content to remain abstract.

We cannot say directly how love is the essence of creativity, justice, or truth. But when we explore the meaning of these terms we discover that they are incomplete without love. Truth without love is not the full truth, but merely an abstract of life. Justice without love is not true justice, but an insufferable legalism. Creativity without love is mere novelty or change without significance or direction. And, conversely, love without truth, justice, and creativity is a caricature of love—mere sentimentality.

And the same applies to holiness. Holiness without love soon degenerates into an ugly self-righteousness. But in its supreme manifestation sanctity becomes holy love—the words we have used to characterize the Supreme Being Himself.

## SOME PRACTICAL CONCLUSIONS

To merely talk about or contemplate love is to betray it. The truth of love is a call to existence. It demands of us a life of action. For surely the primary task of our generation is to discover a strategy for love, a practical way of making love manifest on the largest scale.

In education this would mean not only the liquidation of factual ignorance; it would also mean an attack on all forms of alienation, with the goal of liberating the truly human dimension in man. This would be "liberal education" in its most literal sense.

Our goal should be the creation of a true "remnant" community that would increasingly dedicate itself to humanity as the humble servant of all.

This "remnant" would be a true elite, not an elite of talent, wealth, or birth, but an elite to which any human being could aspire by merely being as human as possible.

Charles Raven has said that the true function of faith is the creation of community. That is our biggest task: the creation of a universal community that will not smother lesser groupings in a monolithic sameness, but will nourish them for the expression of their highest and most unique powers. If religion served this purpose it would indeed be the "salt" and "light" which the founder of Christianity intended it to be. There would be no need for great sophistication here: It would mean to begin to love, to learn from love, and to create the conditions of love.

In his poem "The Base of all Metaphysics," Walt Whitman imagines a professor addressing his class for the last time. It makes a fitting conclusion to our inquiry:

*And now, gentlemen,*
*A word I give to remain in your memories and minds,*
*As base and finale, too, for all metaphysics.*

*(So to the students the old professor,*
*At the close of his crowded course.)*

*Having studied the new and antique, the Greek and Germanic systems,*
*Kant having studied and stated, Fichte and Schelling and Hegel,*
*Stated the lore of Plato, and Socrates greater than Plato,*
*And greater than Socrates sought and stated, Christ divine having studied long,*
*I see reminiscent today those Greek and Germanic systems,*
*See the philosophies all, Christian churches and tenets see,*
*Yet underneath Socrates clearly see, and underneath Christ the divine I see,*
*The dear love of man for his comrade, the attraction of friend to friend,*
*Of the well-married husband and wife, of children and parents,*
*Of city for city and land for land.*[20]

## SUGGESTIONS FOR FURTHER READING

The most celebrated book on love is Anders Nygren's *Agape and Eros* (Westminster Press, 1953). M. C. D'Arcy's *Mind and Heart of Love* (Holt, Rinehart and Winston, 1947; Meridian, World Publishing, 1956) is a reply to this work from a Roman Catholic point of view. Another book by Paul Tillich is worth consulting: *Love, Power, and Justice* (Oxford University Press, 1960).

For the psychological material on man's need for love, see Ian Suttie, *Origins of Love and Hate* (Julian Press, 1952); Sorokin, *The Ways and Power of Love* (Beacon Press, 1954); Ashley Montagu, ed., *The Meaning of Love* (Julian Press, 1953); and Erich Fromm's *The Art of Loving* (Harper & Row, 1956).

Material for a study of the ideal of compassionate love in other religions has already been suggested in Chapters 4, 5, and 6.

## *NOTES*

1. Howard Whitman, "The American Way of Love," *Tacoma News Tribune,* November 8, 1964.
2. In the final Canto of the *Paradiso.*
3. Ashley Montagu, "The Origin and Meaning of Love" in Ashley Montagu, ed., *The Meaning of Love* (Julian, 1953), p. 19.
4. *The New York Times,* April 27, 1952.
5. P. A. Sorokin and Robert C. Hanson, "The Power of Creative Love" in Montagu, ed., *op. cit.,* p. 124.
6. Sorokin, *The Ways and Power of Love,* p. 475.
7. Montagu, *loc. cit.*
8. Sorokin, *op. cit.,* p. 10.
9. Erich Fromm, *The Art of Loving* (Harper & Row, 1956), p. 60.
10. *Ibid.*
11. Quoted in Sorokin, *op. cit.,* p. 459.
12. *Ibid.,* p. 461.
13. I John 4:8.
14. Selected from I John 3, 4. (Phillips trans.)
15. E. A. Burtt, ed., *The Teachings of the Compassionate Buddha,* (New American Library) p. 46.
16. *Ibid.,* pp. 46–47.
17. 90th Surah from the Koran, J. M. Rodwell, trans. (Everyman's Library, Dutton, n.d.).
18. In "Rumi," in *The Persian Poets,* N. H. Dole and Belle M. Walker, eds. (Crowell-Collier, 1901), pp. 208–209.
19. I Corinthians 13:8–13.
20. "The Base of All Metaphysics," in "Calamus," *Leaves of Grass.*

# EPILOGUE

# *The Need for Decision—*
# *a Faith of One's Own*

❖❘❖❘❖❘❖❘❖❘❖❘❖❘❖❘❖❘❖❘❖❘❖❘❖❘❖❘❖❘❖❘❖❘❖❘❖❘❖❘❖❘❖❘❖❘❖❘❖❘❖❘❖❘❖❘❖

A student began the concluding paragraph of his final examination in a religion course with these words: "Now that *religion* is over. . . ." If at this point "religion is over," our enterprise has failed. Properly speaking, when the instruction is finished, the student has just begun. And this is nowhere so clear as in religion. Questions? Of course; they will always be present—and rightly so.

A person writing to the author of the controversial book *Honest to God,* says, "I have never been able to go to a church service without having a wild desire in the middle of the sermon and sometimes in the lessons to stand up and start asking questions which I felt sure to the average churchgoer, priest, or layman, would sound utterly blasphemous."[1] This letter writer confessed that he felt "pangs of guilt" for having such desires.

But he need not have punished himself with such guilt feelings. In ultimate matters, all men, no matter how well informed, live by their faith. This is the essence of the matter. Questions that arise in this context are drawn from the urge for more light, more truth, and are the marks of faith itself.[2] But the questions that are occasioned by religion cannot be answered from without. Religious truth is not spectator truth; it is the truth won through full participation in life at the greatest depth. All this means that without personal decision none of our study can come to fruition.

We have traveled a long and what must seem to the reader a most devious

495

road in our inquiry. Unfortunately, the length of the road is proportional to the number of questions that men are prone to ask. The fact is, that with the growth of knowledge every area of life is being confronted with increasingly difficult questions. The only way to avoid them is to remain innocently ignorant. But that way is not open to anyone who has come this far in his education.

The only live option is to press forward to a faith in which a man can live with full integrity. But this can only be done by the man himself. A man's religion cannot be left to others. It is the most personal issue of life. We may be content to let someone else do our thinking in science, but in those regions that bear on the direction of our own life, we must take full responsibility for our thought, choices, and decisions. The issue is what kind of person we are choosing to be, and what kind of society we are willing into existence. Man comes into the world unfinished. His biological nature matures according to the genetic plan. But his human nature waits upon his decision. The choice is up to him. To be sure, he may—indeed, he must—learn from others, and we hope that this inquiry has not wholly failed those who are searching for direction. But maps and signs on the road do not make a pilgrimage. Only the traveler can decide his route, and make the journey.

To make an appeal for personal decision in the midst of such large-scale social problems as our world faces, may seem petty, but the solution of these problems waits upon a certain type of man. As Karl Jaspers has said: "The untruth of the present state of affairs . . . cannot be remedied by great political actions. No improvement is possible unless the individual is educated by educating himself, unless his hidden being is awakened to reality through an insight which is at the same time an inner action, a knowledge which is at the same time virtue. He who becomes a true man becomes a citizen."[3]

This is not to say that the message of faith is merely personal. It is only to say that it cannot be less than personal. Each person bears the responsibility for his own authentic response to the call to be fully human. When he responds to that call he is immediately drawn out into the whole world of social action. But his action becomes the outward manifestation of his spiritual vocation, the expression of his enlarging humanity.

The issue, then, is to find a faith of one's own, a place to stand where one can see the most, integrate the most, and live most deeply, remaining open and vulnerable, and discovering at last that this posture is the most invulnerable of all.

## NOTES

1. David L. Edwards, *The Honest to God Debate* (Westminster, 1963), pp. 57–58.

2. See Holmes Hartshorne, *The Faith to Doubt;* also Tillich's treatment of this theme in all his works, espe-

cially in *The Courage to Be* (Yale University Press, 1952).

3. Karl Jaspers, *The Great Philoso-phers* (Harcourt, Brace & World, 1962), p. 17.

# INDEX